OSBORN'S
CONCISE LAW DICTIONARY

AUSTRALIA
The Law Book Company Ltd.
Sydney: Melbourne: Brisbane: Perth

CANADA
The Carswell Company Ltd.
Toronto: Calgary: Vancouver: Ottawa

INDIA
N. M. Tripathi Private Ltd.
Bombay
and
Eastern Law House Private Ltd.
Calcutta

M.P.P. House
Bangalore

ISRAEL
Steimatzky's Agency Ltd.
Jerusalem: Tel Aviv: Haifa

PAKISTAN
Pakistan Law House
Karachi

OSBORN'S

CONCISE
LAW DICTIONARY

SEVENTH EDITION

BY

ROGER BIRD, LL.B.

Registrar, Yeovil & Weymouth County Courts

LONDON
SWEET & MAXWELL
1983

First Edition	1927
Second Edition	1937
Third Edition	1947
Fourth Edition	1954
Second Impression	1958
Third Impression	1960
Fourth Impression	1962
Fifth Impression	1963
Sixth Impression	1963
Fifth Edition	1964
Second Impression	1970
Third Impression	1974
Sixth Edition	1976
Seventh Edition	1983
Second Impression	1986
Third Impression	1987
Fourth Impression	1990
Fifth Impression	1990

Published by
Sweet & Maxwell Limited now of
South Quay Plaza
183 Marsh Wall, London.

Computerset by Promenade Graphics Ltd., Cheltenham
and printed in England by Clays Ltd, St Ives plc

British Library Cataloguing in Publication Data

Osborn, Percy George
   Osborn's concise law dictionary—7th ed.
   1. Law—England—Dictionaries
   I. Title   II. Bird, Roger
   344.208'6   KD313
   ISBN 0–421–29670–4
   ISBN 0–421–29680–1 Pbk

PREFACE

In preparing this new edition of Osborn, I have tried to bring its contents up to date for readers in 1982 while retaining as much as possible of the work of my predecessors. Thus some parts of the book are entirely my own work whereas others (*e.g.* Easements) are virtually unaltered. Most of the entries have been revised and amended to some extent.

Any author of a work of this size soon realises the need to make difficult choices between the claims of a desire to offer a comprehensive account of the law on the one hand and lack of space on the other. In this respect I have followed the pattern set by my predecessors and tried to provide a succinct guide to the most important points of law while recognising that this is not a complete legal encyclopedia. As always, changes in the law have overtaken some of the entries in the text. To take but one example, the Administration of Justice Act 1982 has brought about changes in the law relating to (*inter alia*) Fatal Accidents, Interest and Wills. At the time of writing, legislation is about to be passed bringing about changes in Employment Law, with particular reference to the Closed Shop. Lack of space prevents mention of many other changes.

I am grateful to Don Raistrick, Librarian of the Supreme Court Library, for the preparation of the list of Law Reports and their abbreviations, and to the staff of Sweet & Maxwell Ltd. for their help and encouragement to me during the writing of this book. I must also express my thanks to my wife for her extraordinary patience and fortitude in typing a near indecipherable manuscript.

The law is stated as at September 1, 1982.

ROGER BIRD

West Pennard
Somerset
December 21, 1982

CONTENTS

A

CONCISE
LAW DICTIONARY

A

A1 at Lloyd's. A ship entered in Lloyd's Register of Shipping as of the highest class.

A and B Lists. See CONTRIBUTORY.

a coelo usque ad centrum. [From heaven to the centre of the earth.] In principle, the extent of the right of the owner of property. See CUJUS EST SOLUM, etc.

a fortiori. [Much more; with stronger reason.]

a mensa et thoro. [From board and bed.]

a posteriori. [From the effect to the cause.] Inductive reasoning.

a priori. [From the cause to the effect.] Deductive reasoning.

A.R.(Anno Regni). [In the year of the reign.]

a tempore cujus contrarii memoria non existet. [From a time of which there is no memory to the contrary.] See MEMORY.

a verbis legis non est recedendum. [You must not vary the words of a statute.]

a vinculo matrimonii. [From the bond of matrimony.] See DIVORCE.

Ab.:Abr. Abridgment (*q.v.*).

ab antiquo. [From old times.]

ab initio. [From the beginning.] When an authority or licence is given to a person by the law, and he abuses it, he becomes a trespasser *ab initio*, and everything done by him in purported exercise of such authority or licence becomes wrongful. See *Six Carpenters' Case* (1611) 1 Smith L.C. See NULLITY; TRESPASS AB INITIO.

ab intestato. [From an intestate.]

abandonment. The relinquishment of an interest, claim or thing. In marine insurance when there is a constructive total loss (*q.v.*) the insured may abandon the subject matter insured to the insurer or underwriter by giving notice of abandonment to him within a reasonable time. Thereupon the insured is entitled to the insurance moneys and the insurer or underwriter to the subject matter insured.

An easement (*q.v.*) may be lost by abandonment, of which non-user for 20 years may be sufficient evidence. But customary rights cannot be lost by disuse or abandonment (*New Windsor Corporation* v. *Mellor* [1975] Ch. 380).

There is abandonment of an action when it is no longer proceeded with, or of an appeal when it is withdrawn. See DISCONTINUANCE.

Abandonment of a child means leaving it to its fate. This is an offence (Children and Young Persons Act 1933, s.1).

abatement. A reduction, allowance, or rebate. An abatement *pro rata* is a proportionate reduction of the amount of each of a number of debts or claims, as where a fund or estate is insufficient for payment of all in full.

abatement of action. A suspension or termination of proceedings in an action for want of proper parties or owing to a defect in the writ or service. Formerly almost every change of interest after the commencement and before the termination of proceedings caused an abatement. But now a cause or matter is not abated by the marriage, death or bankruptcy of any of the parties, if the cause of action survives; nor by changes in title during the pendency of the suit; nor by the death of either party between verdict and judgment (Ord. 15, r.7). Criminal proceedings are not terminated by the death either of the prosecutor or of the Sovereign, but on the death of the accused the proceedings drop. See PLEAS IN ABATEMENT.

abatement of freehold. The entry of a stranger upon land on the death of the owner, prior to the heir. (Obsolete.)

abatement of legacies. The receipt by legatees of none or part only of their legacies owing to insufficiency of assets. General legacies not given in payment of a debt due to the legatee or in consideration of the legatee abandoning any right or interest, abate proportionately between themselves, unless the intention is clear that any particular legacy shall be paid in full. Specific legacies take priority over general legacies, and are liable to abatement only if the assets are insufficient for the payment of debts. Demonstrative legacies are not subject to abatement unless the assets are insufficient for payment of debts, or until the fund out of which payment is directed becomes exhausted. See LEGACY.

abatement of nuisance. To remove or put an end to it, as an alternative to bringing an action. An occupier of land may terminate by his own act any nuisance by which that land is injuriously affected, *e.g.* by cutting off overhanging branches of trees. Notice may be necessary to the other party if it is necessary to enter on his land to abate the nuisance, except in case of emergency.

A public nuisance may be abated by anyone to whom it does a special injury, but only to the extent necessary to prevent such injury, *e.g.* to remove a fence unlawfully erected across a highway. See NUISANCE.

Local authorities have statutory powers to secure abatement notices in respect of statutory nuisances. See *e.g.* the Public Health Act 1936, ss.91–99; Public Health (Recurring Nuisances) Act 1969, s.3.

abatement of purchase-money. The reduction of the agreed purchase price by way of compensation, when a vendor has misdescribed property and is unable to convey it as described.

abator. One who abates, or terminates, a nuisance by his own act.

abbreviatio placitorum. A collection of cases decided in the superior courts from the reign of Richard I down to the commencement of the Year Books.

abdication. Renunciation, particularly of an office or responsibility. Royal Abdication, *i.e.* abdication of the throne can only be effected by Act of Parliament. See, *e.g.* His Majesty's Declaration of Abdication Act 1936.

abduction. The wrongful taking away of a person. Under the Sexual Offences Act 1956, it is an indictable offence (1) to take away or detain against her will any woman of any age with intent to marry her or have sexual intercourse with her or to cause her to be married to or have sexual intercourse with any other person either by force or for the sake of her property or expectations of property (s.17); (2) unlawfully to take out of the possession and against the will of any person having the lawful care of her, any unmarried girl being under the age of 16 (s.20), irrespective of whether the defendant believes her to be, or she appears to be, over that age; (3) to take any unmarried girl under 18 out of the possession and against the will of her lawful guardian with the intent that she will have illicit sexual intercourse with a man or men, unless the defendant has reasonable cause to believe she is over 18 (s.19); (4) to take a female defective out of the possession of her parent or guardian against his will with intent that she shall have unlawful sexual intercourse with men or a particular man. Reasonable belief that the woman was not a defective is a defence (s.21).

abearance. Behaviour.

abet. To aid in the commission of an offence. A person may be found guilty of aiding and abetting although the principal is acquitted (*R.* v. *Cogan* [1975] 3 W.L.R. 316). See ACCESSORY.

abeyance. The condition of an inheritance which has no present owner, *e.g.* a peerage.

abeyance of seisin. An interruption in the tenancy of a freehold. It was a rule of the common law that the seisin must always be "full," *e.g.* the tenancy of the freehold be uninterrupted, and any attempted disposition of land which would produce an abeyance of the seisin was void. This rule ceased to operate when the Law of Property Act 1925 came into effect.

abjuration. Forswearing or renouncing by oath: an oath to leave the realm for ever, taken by a person who had claimed sanctuary (*q.v.*).

abode. Habitation or place of residence; the place where a person ordinarily lives and sleeps at night. For purposes of immigration law a person has "the right of abode" in the United Kingdom in the circumstances set out in the Immigration Act 1971, s.2 (as amended by British Nationality Act 1981, s.39), *i.e.* either that he is a British citizen (*q.v.*) or that he was a Commonwealth citizen (*q.v.*) having the right of abode under s.2(1)(*d*) or s.2(2) of the Act of 1971 immediately before the commencement of the 1981 Act and has not ceased to be a Commonwealth citizen in the meantime.

abominable crime. The term used in the Offences against the Person Act 1861, s.61, to describe the felonies of sodomy and bestiality. See BUGGERY.

abortion. A miscarriage, or expulsion of a human foetus before gestation is completed. Until 1967 procuring or causing an abortion was an offence. Under the Abortion Act 1967 procuring an abortion is not an offence where the pregnancy is terminated by a registered medical practitioner and two registered medical practioners are of the bona fide opinion that continued pregnancy would involve risk to the mother's life, or injury to the physical or mental health of the mother or existing children of her family or that there is a substantial risk that if the child were born it would be seriously handicapped by physical or mental abnormalities.

abridgment. A digest of the laws of England, *e.g.* Viner's, 1741.

abrogate. To repeal, cancel, or annul.

abscond. To go away secretly, to evade the jurisdiction of the court. It can amount to an act of bankruptcy. See BANKRUPTCY. Absconding by a person released on bail is an offence. See BAIL.

absence. If a person has not been heard of for seven years, and the circumstances are such that, if alive, he would have been heard of, the presumption of death arises, but not as to the date of death (*Re Phene's Trusts* (1869) L.R. 5 Ch.App.139). The court may, however, order that death be presumed at any time if sufficient evidence is shown. See the Matrimonial Causes Act 1973, s.19; Domicile and Matrimonial Proceedings Act 1973, Sched.6. See also BIGAMY.

absence beyond the seas. Absence from the United Kingdom (*q.v.*).

absente reo. [The defendant being absent.]

absoluta sententia expositore non indiget. [When you have plain words capable of only one interpretation, no explanation of them is required.]

absolute. Complete and unconditional. (1) A rule or order which is complete and becomes of full effect at once, *e.g.* decree absolute, charging order (*q.v.*) absolute, garnishee order (*q.v.*) absolute. Contrast and see NISI. (2) An estate which is not defeasible before its natural expiration.

absolute assignment. An assignment of a whole debt (and not merely a portion of it), free from conditions but including an assignment by way of mortgage, or by way of trust. See ASSIGNMENT OF CHOSES IN ACTION.

absolute discharge. The court may grant a convicted person an absolute discharge (Powers of Criminal Courts Act 1973, s.7).

absolute interest. Full and complete ownership; a vested right of property which is liable to be determined only by the failure of appropriate successors in title.

absolute title. The registered proprietor of lands registered with an absolute title has a State guaranteed title that there is no other person who has a better right to the land (see Land Registration Act 1925, s.5).

absolve. To free from liability or guilt.

absque hoc. [Without this, that.] The commencing words of a traverse, or denial, in the old pleadings.

absque impetitione vasti. [Without impeachment of waste (*q.v.*).]

absque tali causa. [Without the alleged cause.] See DE INJURIA.

abstract of title. A chronological statement of the instruments and events under which a person is entitled to property, showing all incumbrances to which the property is subject. Specimens are given in Schedule 6 to the Law of Property Act 1925 (see s.206(2)). Over-reached interests are not to be included in an abstract (*ibid.* s.10).

An abstract must be supplied by the owner of land to a purchaser under a contract of sale: also it is usually required by an intending mortgagee. Such of the expenses of verifying the abstract as are to be borne by the purchaser are specified in *ibid.* s.45(4). See CURTAIN PROVISION; TITLE.

abundans cautela non nocet. [There is no harm done by great caution.] To remove doubts, there is often expressed what would otherwise be implied.

abuse. Vulgar abuse, insult, or vituperation afford in general no ground for an action for defamation.

abuse of distress. Where animals or chattels lawfully distrained are worked or used. It is a ground for an action of conversion.

abuse of process. Abuse of legal procedure. A frivolous or vexatious action as, *e.g.* setting up a case which has already been decided by a competent court (see *Stephenson* v. *Garnett* [1891] 1 Q.B. 677, and *Hunter* v. *Chief Constable of W. Midlands* [1981] 3 All E.R.727, H.L.). If a plaintiff induces the defendant by fraud to come within the jurisdiction so that he may be served with a writ the court will set aside the service as an abuse of the process of the court. See VEXATIOUS ACTIONS.

abuttals. The bounds of land; the parts at which it abuts on other lands.

ac etiam. [And also.]

accedas ad curiam. [Go to the court.] A writ by which a tenant could remove his case from the Court Baron into the Court of Common Pleas.

acceleration. Where an estate or interest in any property in remainder or expectancy falls into possession sooner than it otherwise would, by reason of the preceding interest being or becoming void or determined by surrender, merger, lapse, or extinguishment. No writ of acceleration may be issued in respect of a peerage which has been disclaimed (Peerage Act 1963, s.3(2)).

acceptance. (1) Tacit acquiescence or agreement imported by failure to reject a thing offered; thus acceptance of rent may create a tenancy or waive a notice to quit. (2) The act of assenting to an offer. Acceptance of an offer to create a contract must be made while the offer still subsists by the offeree who must know of the offer; it must conform with the offer and must either be communicated to the offeror or the requisite act must be done. (3) Acceptance of goods within the Sale of Goods Act 1979, s.35(1) is: (*a*) where the buyer intimates to the seller that he has accepted them; or (*b*) where the goods have been delivered to him and he does any act in relation to them which is inconsistent with the ownership of the seller; or (*c*) when, after the lapse of a reasonable time he retains the goods without intimating to the seller that he has rejected them. Note however the exception to (*b*) above contained in s.34(1), namely that where a buyer has not previously examined goods, he is not deemed to have accepted them until he has had a reasonable opportunity of examining them for the purpose of ascertaining whether they are in conformity with the contract.

acceptance of a bill of exchange. When the person on whom the bill is drawn writes his signature across the bill, with or without the word "accepted," he thereby engages to pay the bill when due (Bills of Exchange Act 1882, ss.17–19). Acceptance *supra protest* is where a bill of exchange has been protested for non-acceptance by the drawee; anyone may thereupon accept it for honour of the drawer or indorsers (*ibid.* ss.65–68).

acceptance of service. Where a solicitor writes on a writ of summons that he accepts service of the writ on behalf of the defendant, personal service is not required and the writ is deemed to have been served on the day the indorsement is made (Ord. 10, r.1(2)).

access. (1) The opportunity of sexual intercourse between husband and wife. It is a presumption of law that a child born during lawful wedlock or within the period of gestation after its termination is legitimate, but evidence that access by a husband to his wife at the necessary time was impossible or highly improbable will rebut the presumption. The evidence of a husband or wife is admissible in any proceedings to prove that marital intercouse did or did not take place between them during any period (Matrimonial Causes Act 1973, s.48). (2) Access to children, *i.e.* the right of a non-custodial parent or grandparent to see and share the company of children of the family, usually after divorce or separation proceedings. Access to children is a basic right of a parent and is only refused in the most unusual circumstances (*S. v. S.* [1962] 1 W.L.R. 445). (3) Approach or the means of approach, *e.g.* there is a right of access to a highway by the owner of adjoining land.

Accessio. The doctrine of Roman law, founded on the right of occupancy, that the additions to property by growth or increase belonged to the owner of that property.

accessio cedit principali. [An accessory thing when annexed to a principal thing becomes part of the principal thing.] The accessory thing becomes the property of the owner of the principal thing; as, *e.g.* in alluvion, dereliction, and the addition of buildings and plants to the soil, the birth of offspring of animals, etc.

There is also *accessio* in the combination of things belonging to different persons in a single article; *e.g.* the shoeing of A's horse with B's horseshoes. In principle, the ownership of chattels is not divested, but possession may be awarded at the discretion of the court to the person whose interest in the combined or new chattel is the more substantial, on the terms that he pays the value of the other's interest.

accession. (1)Succeeding to the Throne. "The King never dies," and the heir to the throne accedes immediately on the death of the reigning Sovereign. The new Sovereign makes a declaration as prescribed by the Accession Declaration Act 1910. See ACT OF SETTLEMENT.

(2) A mode by which original acquisition of territory may take place, without any formal act of taking possession (see *The Anna* (1807)5 C.Rob.373).

accessorium non ducit, sed sequitur suum principale. [The incident shall pass by the grant of the principal, but not the principal by the grant of the incident.]

accessorium non trahit principale. [An accessory thing does not carry with it the thing to which it is accessory.]

accessory. Before the abolition of the distinction between felony and misdemeanour (see FELONY), accessories were those concerned in the crime, otherwise than as principals, who actually committed the crime. An accessory before the fact was one who directly or indirectly procured by any means the commission of any felony but who was not actually or constructively present at the commission of the felony. If he was present, he was a principal in the second degree. An accessory after the fact was one who, with knowledge that a felony had been committed, received, relieved, comforted or assisted the felon, or in any way secured or attempted to secure the escape of the felon (Accessories and Abettors Act 1861, as amended by the Criminal Law Act 1977, Sched.12).

It follows from the assimilation of the law to that applicable to misdemeanour (*q.v.*) that accessories before the fact are to be treated as principal offenders and punishable as such (Accessories and Abettors Act 1861, s.8). The offence of being an accessory after the act has lapsed (*R. v. Charles Fisher* [1969] 1 W.L.R.8) but is replaced by a new and substantially similar, offence of assisting a person who has committed an arrestable offence. See ARREST.

In treason (*q.v.*) there are no accessories. All are deemed principals and punishable as such.

A person who aids, abets, counsels, or procures the commission of a summary offence is treated as a principal (Magistrates' Courts Act 1952, s.35).

accident. In the popular and ordinary sense, accident denotes an unlooked-for mishap or an untoward event which is not expected or designed (*Fenton* v. *Thorley* [1903] A.C. 443 at 448, 451). Inevitable accident means an accident the consequences of which were not intended and could not have been foreseen by the exercise of reasonable care and skill. It is, in general a ground of exemption from liability in tort. See ACT OF GOD.

In equity, accident means such an unforseen event, misfortune, loss, act, or omission as is not the result of any negligence or misconduct by the party applying for relief. If a deed or negotiable security were lost, equity would enforce the plaintiff's rights under the document on his giving, if necessary, a proper bond of indemnity to the defendant.

In criminal law, on a charge of murder, the defence of accident may be a complete defence, or may justify a conviction for manslaughter only.

accident cases. The fact that serious injuries have been incurred in accidents is not a "special circumstance" so as to lead to a trial by jury. The judges have evolved scales of damages with which juries would be unfamiliar (*Sims* v. *William Howard & Son Ltd.* [1964] 2 Q.B. 409, C.A.).

accommodation agencies. These are regulated by the Accommodation Agencies Act 1953 made permanent by the Expiring Laws Act 1969. See *Saunders* v. *Soper* [1975] A.C.239.

accommodation bill. A bill of exchange which a person has signed as drawer, acceptor, or indorser, without receiving value therefor and for the purpose of lending his name to some other person (Bills of Exchange Act 1882, s.28(1)).

accommodation land. Land occupied or used in conjunction with other land or premises, as a matter of convenience.

accommodation works. Gates, bridges, fences, etc., constructed and maintainable by a railway or canal concern or the Railways Board, for the accommodation of the owners or occupiers of adjoining lands.

accomplice. Any person who, either as a principal or as an accessory, has been associated with another person in the commission of any offence. The evidence of an accomplice is admissible, but the judge must warn the jury of the danger of convicting on such evidence unless corroborated, and if this warning is omitted a conviction may be quashed. See ACCESSORY; CORROBORATION.

accord and satisfaction. The purchase of a release from an obligation, whether arising under contract or tort, by means of any valuable consideration, not being the actual performance of the obligation itself. The accord is the agreement by which the obligation is discharged. The satisfaction is the consideration which makes the agreement operative (*British Russian Gazette Ltd.* v. *Associated Newspapers Ltd.* [1933] 2 K.B. 616 at 643–644). Thus there is accord and satisfaction where the parties to a contract agree that one of them shall give, and the other shall accept, something different in kind from what he was bound to give or accept under the contract. The general rule is that accord without satisfaction does not discharge a contract after breach, but the promise of something different will discharge the original cause of action, provided the intention was that the new promise itself should be taken in satisfaction and not the actual performance of it (*Morris* v. *Baron*[1918] A.C.1 at 35).

account, action of. At common law, an action lay for not rendering a proper account of profits, as *e.g.* between partners. It became obsolete and was replaced by the equitable remedy of an account. A plaintiff may endorse his writ, with a claim for an account. The taking of accounts is assigned to the Chancery Division.

Equity allows an account in aid of an equitable right, and in aid of a legal right in cases of principal against agent, mutual accounts, special complication, and as ancillary to an injunction.

account, current. A running account kept between parties with items on both sides; *e.g.* a banking account. See APPROPRIATION.

account duty. The duty imposed in 1881 upon personal property above the value of £100 passing at death but not subject to probate duty (*q.v.*). Replaced first by estate duty and, since 1975, by Capital Transfer Tax (*q.v.*).

account on the footing of wilful default. An account taken on the footing that the accountable party is liable not only for sums actually got in, but for all moneys which, without his wilful neglect or default, might have been possessed or received. Thus, where it is proved that a debt was due to a trust estate, the burden is thrown on the trustee or executor to show why he did not get it in. Similarly, a mortgagee in possession is liable to acount not only for the rents and profits he actually receives, but for those he would have received if he had used the greatest possible care.

account, settled. A settled account is a statement in writing of the account between two parties, one of whom is under a duty to account to the other, which both of them have agreed to and accepted as correct. The plea of a settled account is a good defence to an action for an account, but the plaintiff may in reply allege error or fraud. Leave may be given him to "surcharge and falsify," *i.e.* add items in his favour which were omitted, and strike out items against him which were wrongly inserted, or to show errors. If fraud be proved the account will be set aside.

account stated. (1) An admission of a sum of money being due from one person to another, who are under no duty to account to each other, from which a promise to pay is implied by law; *e.g.* an IOU. It is not necessarily binding: it may be shown to have been given in mistake, or for a debt for which the consideration has failed or was illegal. (2) An account which contains entries on both sides of it, and in which the parties have agreed that the items on one side should be set against the items on the other side, and the balance should be paid. The items on the smaller side are set off and deemed to be paid by the items on the larger side, from which arises a promise for good consideration to pay the balance.

accountable receipt. An acknowledgment of the receipt of money, or of any chattel, to be accounted for by the person receiving it.

accountant-general. The officer of the Supreme Court in whom funds paid into court are vested: the Clerk of the Crown (*q.v.*) (Judicature Act 1925, s.133; Administration of Justice Act 1965).

accountant to the Crown. Any person who has received money belonging to or for and on behalf of the Crown, and is accountable therefor. See CROWN DEBTS.

accounting, false. It is an offence for a person dishonestly or with a view to gain or with intent to cause loss to another (1) to destroy, deface, conceal or falsify any account or any record or document made or required for any accounting purpose; or (2) in furnishing information for any purpose to produce or make use of any account, or any such record or document which to his knowledge is or may be misleading, false or deceptive in a material particular (Theft Act 1968, s.17).

accounts and inquiries. The court may at any stage of the proceedings direct any necessary accounts and inquiries to be taken and made in chambers (Ord.43, r.2).

accounts, falsification of. Falsification of accounts is an indictable offence under the Theft Act 1968, ss.17–20.

accredit. To furnish a diplomatic agent with papers, called credentials or letters of credit, which certify his public character.

accretion. The act of growing on to a thing; usually applied to the gradual accumulation of land from out of the sea or a river. If the accretion to land is imperceptible, it belongs to the owner of the land, but if sudden and considerable it belongs to the Crown. Accretions from the sea are annexed to the relevant parish or community (Local Government Act 1972, s.72). See ACCESSIO; ALLUVION; DERELICTION.

accrual. A right is said to accrue when it vests in a person, especially when it does so gradually or without his active intervention, *e.g.* by lapse of time, or by the determination of a preceding right. When a fund or other property is increased by additions which take place in the ordinary course of nature or by operation of law, the additions are said to accrue either to the original fund or property, or to the person entitled to it.

accumulation. The continual increase of principal by the re-investment of interest. By the Law of Property Act 1925, replacing the Accumulations Act 1800, accumulation of income is restricted to: (a) the life of the settlor; (b) 21 years thereafter; (c) the duration of the minority of any person or persons living or *en ventre sa mère* at the death of the settlor; (d) the duration of the minority of any person or persons who would have been entitled to the income if of full age (s.164); and (in respect of instruments taking effect on or after July 16, 1964), (e) a term of 21 years from the date of the making of the disposition, and (f) the duration of the minority or respective minorities of any person or persons in being at the date of the disposition (Perpetuities and Accumulations Act 1964, ss.13, 15(5)). If the purpose is the purchase of land, then (d) is the only period admissible (Act of 1925, s.166). The restrictions do not apply to accumulations for the payment of debts of the settlor, for raising portions for children, and in respect of the produce of timber or wood (*ibid.* s.164). So far as the direction to accumulate is void for excess, the income belongs to those who would have been entitled thereto if such accumulation had not been directed.

A beneficiary may put an end to a trust for accumulation which is exclusively for his benefit and demand the property when he becomes *sui juris*. The exercise of this right is facilitated by s.14 of the Act of 1964. See PERPETUITY.

accumulative sentence. A sentence of imprisonment, which is to commence at the end of another sentence already imposed.

accusare nemo se debet; accusare nemo se debet nisi coram Deo. [No one is bound to accuse himself except to God.] A witness is not bound to answer any question which in the opinion of the court would incriminate him.

accusatorial procedure. It is a common law principle that the responsibility for collecting and presenting evidence lies with the party who seeks to introduce that evidence. Contrast and see INQUISITORIAL PROCEDURE.

accused. One charged with an offence.

acknowledgment of debt. An admission in writing signed by the debtor or his agent, that a debt is due, which revives a debt which is statute barred. By the Limitation Act 1939, s.24, where a right of action has accrued in respect of a debt and there is such an admission made, the right of action is deemed to have accrued on the date of the acknowledgment. See LIMITATION, STATUTES OF.

acknowledgment of deeds. Deeds purporting to dispose of the property of a woman married before January 1, 1883 had, in general, to be executed by her husband, as well as by her, and had to be acknowledged by her before a judge or a commissioner appointed for the purpose, who examined her separately as to her knowledge of, and consent to, the contents of the deed, and indorsed a memorandum as to the fact on the deed. Rendered unnecessary by the Law of Property Act 1925, s.167.

acknowledgment of right to production of documents. A writing given by a person who retains possession of title deeds which cannot be delivered over to a purchaser. The possessor is obliged to produce them for proving or supporting the title of any person entitled to the benefit of the acknowledgment, and to deliver to him true copies of or extracts from them (Law of Property Act 1925, s.64).

acknowledgment of service. (1) Service of a writ or originating summons issued in the High Court is now acknowledged by the defendant "Properly completing an acknowledgment of service . . . and handing it in at, or sending it by post to, the appropriate office . . ." (Ord.12, r.1(3)). "The substitution of Acknowledgment of Service for the Entry of Appearance . . . is perhaps the most important, far-reaching and radical reform in the integrated package of reforms which have recently [*i.e.* 1981] been introduced relating to the commencement of proceedings in the High Court" (notes to Ord.12, r.1).

(2) For many years an acknowledgment of service has been the document by which service of a Petition for divorce issued in the Divorce Registry (*q.v.*) or a divorce county court (*q.v.*) was acknowledged – see Matrimonial Causes Rules 1977, rr.14 and 15.

acknowledgment of wills. If a will is not signed in the presence of witnesses, the testator must acknowledge his signature in their presence (Wills Act 1837, s.9).

acquiescence. Assent to an infringement of rights, either expressed, or implied from conduct, by which the right to equitable relief is normally lost. See LACHES.

acquittal. Discharge from prosecution upon a verdict of not guilty, or on a successful plea of pardon or of *autrefois acquit* or *autrefois convict* (*q.v.*). Acquittal is a bar to any such subsequent prosecution.

acquittance. A written acknowledgment of the payment of a sum of money or debt due.

act in law. An act of a party or person having legal effect; *e.g.* the making of a contract or conveyance. See also ACT OF LAW.

act in pais. [Act in the country.] An act or transaction done or made otherwise than in the course of a record or deed.

act of attainder. See ATTAINDER.

act of bankruptcy. An act of a debtor upon which a bankruptcy petition may be grounded, if committed within three months before the presentation of the petition; something done or suffered by a debtor which may give the court jurisdiction to make a receiving order (see Bankruptcy Act 1914, s.1).

The acts of bankruptcy may be summarised as follows:

(1) If in England or elsewhere a debtor makes: (*a*) a conveyance or assignment of his property to a trustee or trustees for the benefit of his creditors generally; (*b*) a fraudulent conveyance, gift, delivery or transfer of his property, or of any part thereof; (*c*) any conveyance or transfer of his property or any part thereof, or creates any charge theron, which would be void as a fraudulent preference if he were adjudged bankrupt.

(2) If with intent to defeat or delay his creditors he: (*a*) departs out of England; or (*b*) being out of England remains out of England; or (*c*) departs from his dwelling-house; or (*d*) otherwise absents himself; or (*e*) begins to keep house.

(3) If execution levied against him by seizure of his goods and sale, or held by sheriff for 21 days.

(4) If he files in the court a declaration of his inability to pay his debts, or presents a bankruptcy petition against himself; or fails to comply with a bankruptcy notice; or gives notice to any of his creditors that he has suspended, or that he is about to suspend, payment of his debts.

Where there is failure to make any payment required by an Administration Order (*q.v.*) a court having bankruptcy jurisdiction may revoke the administration order and made a receiving order (*q.v.*) (see Insolvency Act 1976, s.11 (not yet in force)).

act of God. An accident or event which happens independently of human intervention and due to natural causes, such as storm, earthquake, etc., which no human foresight can provide against, and of which human prudence is not bound to recognise the possibility. It will relieve from absolute liability in tort.

act of grace. An Act of Parliament giving a general and free pardon.

act of indemnity. An Act passed to legalise transactions which, when they took place, were illegal, or to exempt particular persons from pecuniary penalties or punishments for acts done in the public service, as in time of war, which were breaches of the law. The Indemnity Act 1920 restricted the taking of legal proceedings in respect of such acts.

act of law. The effect of the operation of law, *e.g.* succession to property or intestacy. See also ACT IN LAW.

Act of Parliament. The legislative decree of the Queen in Parliament; a statute. There are the following kinds of Acts: Public, General, Local, Personal and Private. Acts are now given chapter numbers by reference to the calander year in which they are passed (Acts of Parliament Numbering and Citation Act 1962).

An Act comes into force on the day on which it receives the Royal Assent (*q.v.*) unless otherwise provided, with effect from the last moment of the previous day (Acts of Parliament (Commencement) Act 1793). See APPOINTED DAY; ROYAL ASSENT; STATUTE.

Act of Settlement 1701. The statute 12 & 13 Will. 3, c.2, which enacted:

(*a*) That after the death of William III and of the Princess Anne (afterwards Queen Anne) and in default of issue of either of them, the Crown should descend to Sophia, Electress of Hanover and the heirs of her body, being Protestants.

(*b*) That the Sovereign shall be a member of the Church of England as by law established and shall vacate the throne on becoming or marrying a Roman Catholic.

(*c*) That judges should hold office during good behaviour and be paid fixed salaries, but might be removed from office on the address of both Houses of Parliament. See now Judicature Act 1925, s.12.

(*d*) That no pardon under the Great Seal of England should be pleadable to an impeachment (*q.v.*).

act of state. An act of the Executive as a matter of policy performed in the course of its relations with another state, including its relations with the subjects of that state, unless they are temporarily within the allegiance of the Crown. It is an exercise of sovereign power which cannot be challenged, controlled or interfered with by municipal courts. Its sanction is not that of law but that of sovereign power, and whatever it be, municipal courts must accept it, as it is, without question (*Salaman* v. *Secretary of State for India* [1906] 1 K.B. 613 at p. 639; *Sobhuza II* v. *Miller* [1926] A.C. 518).

It includes an act done by an agent of the Crown whether previously authorised, or subsequently ratified (*Buron* v. *Denman* [1848] 2 Exch.Rep. 167).

Act of Supremacy. The statute 1 Eliz. 1, c.1, passed in 1558 to establish the supremacy of the Crown in ecclesiastical matters.

Act of uniformity. An Act of Parliament regulating Public Worship. See particularly the statute 14 Car.2, c.4 passed in 1662, which legalised the Book of Common Prayer and which was repealed (except for ss.10 and 15) by the Church of England (Worship and Doctrine) Measure 1974 which permits the General Synod (*q.v.*) to sanction alternative forms of service.

acta exteriora indicant interiora secreta. [External actions show internal secrets.] Intention may be inferred from a person's acts.

actio. [Roman law.] An action; the right of suing before a judge for what is due. Also proceedings or form of procedure for the enforcement of such right. The main forms of *actio* were as follows:

arbitraria: the formula directed the judge, if he found the plaintiff's claim valid, to make an order that the defendant should make amends to the plaintiff; *e.g.* to give up the thing claimed, and at the same time fixing the sum that the defendant ought to pay the plaintiff in case he should fail to make amends as ordered.

bona fidei: an equitable action. The formula required the judge to take into account considerations of what was fair and right as between the parties.

directa: an action based immediately on the very text of the law, or arising from an essential part of the execution of a contract.

hypothecaria or *quasi-Serviana:* allowed in all cases where an owner retained possession, but agreed that his property should be a security for a debt.

in personam: a personal action, in which the plaintiff claimed that the defendant ought to give, do or make good, something to or for him.

in rem: a real action, in which the plaintiff claimed that, as against all the world, the thing in dispute was his.

(in rem) confessoria: an action to try a right to a servitude, brought by the owner or the dominant land against the owner of the servient land.

(in rem) negativa: an action brought by the owner of the servient land, who alleged that his adversary was not entitled to a servitude which he claimed; or that he himself was entitled to his land free from the servitude claimed.

mixta: a mixed action; an action with a view both to the recovery of a thing and to the enforcement of a penalty that was both real and personal, or rather that was entirely personal but in one respect more or less similar to a real action; *e.g. familiae erci scundae,* which involved the adjudication of particular things to the parties. "Actions are mixed in which either party is plaintiff."

noxalis: an action brought against a master for delicts committed by his slave, or for damage done from wantonness, heat or savage nature, by his tame animals. The master could free himself from liability by delivering up the offending slave or animal to the person agrrieved.

praejudicialis: an action preliminary to proceedings with a view to ascertaining a fact which it was necessary to establish before going on with the case; as whether a man was free or a freedman, or was the son of his reputed father.

quod metus causa: open to a person who had alienated property or undertaken an obligation under the constraint of intimidation (*metus*) or violence (*vis*).

serviana: an action which gave the landlord of a farm a right to take possession of the stock of his tenant for rent due, when the tenant had agreed that the stock should be a security for the rent.

stricti juris: strict law; the formula limited the attention of the judge to the purely legal considerations involved.

utilis: an action granted by the Praetor, in the exercise of his judicial authority, by means of an extension of an existing action to persons or cases that did not come within its original scope.

actio personalis moritur cum persona. [A personal action dies with the person.] No executor or administrator could sue or be sued for any tort committed against, or by, the deceased in his lifetime (except injuries to property); the right of action in tort was destroyed by the death of the injured or injuring party, because an act of tort was regarded originally as purely punitive and only later as compensatory. The rule is now confined to causes of action for defamation (Law Reform (Miscellaneous Provisions) Act 1934, s.1(1), as amended). Exemplary damages are not recoverable (s.1(2), as amended).

action. A civil proceeding commenced by writ or in such other manner as may be prescribed by rules of court.

In early times actions were divided into criminal and civil, the former being proceedings in the name of the Crown, and the latter those in the name of a subject.

"Action" generally meant a proceeding in one of the common law courts, as opposed to suit in equity. Actions were divided into real, personal, and mixed: real (or feudal) actions being those for the specific recovery of lands or other realty; personal actions, those for the recovery of a debt, personal chattel, or damages; and mixed actions, those for the recovery of real property, together with damages for a wrong connected with it.

A plaintiff at common law had to sue by one or other of certain forms of actions or writs. They were: (1) on contract: (*a*) covenant, being on a deed alone; (*b*) assumpsit, being on a simple contract only; (*c*) debt, being either on a deed or on a simple contract; (*d*) *scire facias,* being on a judgment; (*e*) account; and (*f*) annuity; (2) in tort: (*g*) trespass *quare clausum fregit,* to real property, and trespass *de bonis asportatis,* to goods; (*h*) case; (*i*) trover; (*j*) detinue; and (*k*) replevin; (3) the mixed action of ejectment.

The Common Law Procedure Act 1852 provided that it should not be necessary to mention any form or cause of action in any writ of summons, and all forms of action are now abolished. See also ACTIONS, REAL; ACTIONS, SUCCESSIVE; EJECTMENT; PENAL ACTION.

action in rem. An action in the Admiralty Court commenced by the arrest of the *res,* the ship.

action on the case. The writ of trespass was issuable for wrongs done to person, land, or chattels, and also in a number of unclassified cases, when the writ was said to be issued *super casum* [on the case], because the particular circumstances of the case were set out in the writ. Later, the writs of trespass and trespass on the case separated out, and the action of trespass on the case was called "action on the case." From this action, "the fertile mother of actions" a number of actions were evolved not coming under specific heads. (See Plucknett's *History of the Common Law,* at pp. 372–373.) See IN CONSIMILI CASU.

actiones nominatae. The approved forms of writs. See ACTION ON THE CASE.

actions, real. Proceedings at common law by means of which a freeholder could recover his land: (1) actions commenced by the Writ of Right to decide the question of title to land. Actions were delayed by dilatory pleas (essoins), and trial by battle was possible; (2) Possessory Assizes, to decide questions of disseisin, or recent dispossession; (3) Writs of Entry. The real actions were displaced by the action of ejectment (*q.v.*) and were largely abolished by the Real Property Limitation Act 1833. See ACTION.

actions, successive. All damages from the same cause of action must be recovered in one action, except: (1) where there is unaccrued or unknown damage at the time the first action is brought; (2) where there is the violation by the same act of more than one distinct right; (3) where there are distinct wrongful acts; (4) where there are continuing injuries; in which cases further, or successive, actions may be brought.

active trust. A trust calling for actual duties by the trustee. See BARE TRUSTEE.

Acts of union. With (1) Wales: the statute (1536) 27 Hen.8, c.26; (2) Scotland: 1706, 1707; (3) Ireland: 1800.

actus curiae neminem gravabit. [An act of the court shall prejudice no one.]

actus Dei nemini facit injuriam. [The act of God prejudices no one.] See ACT OF GOD.

actus legis nemini facit injuriam. [The act of the law injures no one.]

actus non facit reum, nisi mens sit rea. See ACTUS REUS and MENS REA.

actus reus. The elements of an offence excluding those which concern the mind of the accused. The phrase "derives, I believe, from a mistranslation of the Latin aphorism Actus non facit reum nisi mens sit rea. Properly translated this means 'an act does not make a *man* guilty of a crime unless his mind be also guilty.' It is thus not the actus which is reus but the man and his mind respectively" (*Haughton* v. *Smith* [1973] 3 All E.R. 1109, *per* Lord Hailsham L.C.).

ad arbitrium. [At will.]

ad avizandum. [To be deliberated upon.]

ad colligenda bona. [To collect the goods.] A form of grant of administration where the estate is of a perishable or precarious nature, and where regular administration cannot be granted at once.

ad diem. [To the day appointed.].

ad eundem. [To the same class.]

ad hoc. [For this purpose.]

ad idem. [Of the same mind; agreed.] See CONSENSUS AD IDEM.

ad interim. [In the meanwhile.]

ad litem. [For the suit.] See GUARDIAN (6).

ad medium filum viae (or **aquae**). [To the middle line of the road (or stream).] The normal boundary of lands separated by a road or river.

ad quaestionem facti non respondent judices; ad quaestionem juris non respondent juratores. [The judge does not decide questions of fact and the jury do not decide questions of law.]

ad quod damnum. [To what damage.] A writ formerly issued to a sheriff: (*a*) before the Crown granted a right to hold a fair, market, etc., within the bailiwick or area, for which the sheriff acted: it directed the sheriff to inquire what damage might be done by such grant; (*b*) before a licence was given by the Crown to alienate lands in mortmain; the licence did not issue unless a return *ad damnum nullis* was made so as to show that no man would be injured; (*c*) before a licence to make or divert a road was given.

ad referendum. [For futher consideration.]

ad rem. [To the point.]

ad sectam. [At the suit of.]

ad summam. [In conclusion.]

ad terminum qui preterit. Writ of entry which lay for a lessor and his heirs when a lease had been made for a term of years or for a life or lives, and, after the expiration of the lease, the lands were witheld from the lessor or his heirs by the tenant or by some other person. Abolished by the Real Property Limitation Act 1833, s.36.

ad valorem. [According to the value.] Duties which are graduated according to the value of the subject-matter taxed.

ad ventrem inspiciendum. [To inspect the belly.] See DE VENTRE INSPICIENDO.

address for service. Address, within the jurisdiction, where writs, notices, summonses, orders, etc., may be served. An address for service as regards the plaintiff must be stated in the endorsement upon the writ (Ord. 6, r.5); and as regards the defendant, in the acknowledgment of service (Ord. 12, r.3).

ademption. The complete or partial extinction or withholding of a legacy (but not of a devise of real estate) by some act of the testator during his life other than revocation by a testamentary instrument; *e.g.* the sale of an object specifically bequeathed. Where a father or person *in loco parentis* provides a portion by his will by a legacy, and subsequently in his life makes or covenants to make another gift also amounting to a portion, the legacy is adeemed, either wholly or in part.

adherent. Being adherent to the Queen's enemies in the realm, giving them aid or comfort in the realm, or elsewhere, is treason (Treason Act 1351). See *R.* v. *Casement* [1917] 1 K.B. 98, at 137.

adjective law. So much of the law as relates to practice and procedure. (Bentham.)

adjourned summons. (1) A summons in the High Court before a master which is remitted to the judge. (2) A summons in any court which stands adjourned for further hearing.

adjournment. The suspension or putting off of the hearing of a case to a future time or day. See SINE DIE.

adjudication. (1) A judgment of decision of the court; *e.g.* the order which declares a debtor to be bankrupt. (2) The decision of the Commissioners of Inland Revenue as to the liability of a document to stamp duty.

adjunctio. [Roman law.] A form of *accessio*; the joining of materials belonging to one person with something belonging to another; *e.g.* when one weaved another's purple into his own vestment.

adjusters. Average adjusters are employed by marine insurers to compute the general average and particular average losses arising out of an insured marine loss.

adjustment. The operation of settling and ascertaining the amount which the assured, after allowances and deductions are made, is entitled to receive under a policy of marine insurance, and of fixing the proportion which each underwriter is liable to pay. See AVERAGE.

admeasurement of dower. The writ in an action formerly brought by an heir against the widow of an ancestor who was alleged to withhold more land for her dower than she was entitled to.

admeasurement of pasture. The writ in an action formerly brought by one commoner against another commoner alleged to have put more beasts on the common than was lawful.

14

administration action. An action assigned to the Chancery Division to secure the due administration of the estate of a deceased person by the court. Proceedings may be begun by a writ or an originating summons taken out by a creditor or any person interested in the estate as legatee, divisee, next-of-kin, etc., or by the personal representative himself (Ord.85).

The effect of an order of the court for the general administration of the estate is that the personal representatives cannot exercise their powers without the sanction of the court and the creditor cannot sue the personal representatives for a debt.

Formerly an administration bond was required in all cases. Under the Judicature Act 1925, s.167, as replaced by the Administration of Estates Act 1971, s.8, the court may require the administrator to produce sureties; no such guarantee is required from an executor.

administration of estates. The collection of the assets of a deceased person, payment of the debts, and distribution of the surplus to the persons beneficially entitled by the deceased's personal representatives (*q.v.*).

Small estates may be administered by the Public Trustee if he sees no reason to the contrary. If the estate is insolvent it may be administered in bankruptcy. See ADMINISTRATION ACTION.

The order in which the assets of the deceased are applied in payment of debts, where the estate is solvent, is (subject to directions in the will):

(1) Property undisposed of by will.
(2) Property not specifically devised or bequeathed, but included in a residuary gift.
(3) Property specifically appropriated or devised or bequeathed for the payment of debts.
(4) Property charged with the payment of debts.
(5) The fund retained to meet pecuniary legacies.
(6) Property specifically devised or bequeathed.
(7) Property appointed by will under a general power (Administration of Estates Act 1925, s.34, Sched. 1, Part II).

Where the assets are insufficient for the payment of debts, *i.e.* where the estate is insolvent, the debts are payable, in the following order:

(1) Funeral, testamentary and administration expenses.
(2) As in bankruptcy (Administration of Estates Act 1925, s.34, Sched.1, Part I).

administrative law. The law relating to the organisation, powers and duties of administative authorities (Dicey). The subordinate branch of constitutional law consisting of the body of rules which govern the detailed exercise of executive functions by the officers or public authorities to whom they are entrusted by the Constitution; for example, the law relating to town and country planning.

administration order. An order providing for the administration by the county court (*q.v.*) of a debtor's estate. The total debts must not exceed the limit of the current county court jurisdiction. See County Court Act 1959, s.148, as amended. See also ACT OF BANKRUPCY.

administrative tribunals. Tribunals concerned with administrative law or matters concerning large numbers of persons or concerns, where questions arise involving the conferring of rights, or the restriction or loss of rights of individuals.

The Council on Tribunals, created in 1958, is continued under the Tribunals and Inquiries Act 1971, to keep under review the constitution and workings of the tribunals listed in Schedule 1 to the Act (as amended).

The control of the courts over administrative tribunals is by judicial review (*q.v.*). Judicial or quasi-judicial functions can be reviewed by the courts, but not purely administrative acts.

administrator. A person appointed to manage the property of another, particularly the person to whom a grant of administration is made. See LETTERS OF ADMINISTRATION.

administratix. A female person to whom letters of administration are granted.

Admiral or **Lord High Admiral.** An officer entrusted by the Crown with the charge of the seas, with jurisdiction over naval and maritime matters and over wrongful acts committed on the high seas or in navigable rivers, excerised by means of the Court of the Admiral. The criminal jurisdiction of this court was ultimately transferred to the Central Criminal Court and the Judges of Assize. The civil jurisdiction of the court, which became the High Court of Admiralty, is vested in the Admiralty Court (*q.v.*). The naval functions of the Lord High Admiral have, since 1827, been exercised by the commissioners for executing the office, *i.e.* the Admiralty (*q.v.*).

Admiralty. The Lords Commissioners of the Admiralty who have succeeded to the administrative or naval functions, but not the judicial, of the Lord High Admiral. The Board of Admiralty consisted of the First Lord of the Admiralty, who was a member of the Government, the First, Second, Third and Fourth Sea Lords, who were naval officers, and a civilian, the Civil Lord of the Admiralty. They are now merged in the Ministry of Defence.

Admiralty Court. A court created by the Administration of Justice Act 1970, as part of the Queen's Bench Division of the High Court. Its jurisdiction comprises the Admiralty and prize business formerly the function of the Probate, Divorce and Admiralty Division of the High Court. (See Ord. 75). Certain county courts have Admiralty jurisdiction limited in amount (County Courts Act 1959, ss.56–61; S.I. 1949 No.2059).

Admiralty, droits of. When a state of war exists, enemy goods seized in English ports go to the Crown as *droits* of Admiralty. Formerly derelict ships and wreckage on the high seas were condemned as *droits* of Admiralty; they are now dealt with under the Merchant Shipping Acts.

admissions. Statements, oral, written, or inferred from conduct, made by or on behalf of a party to a suit, and admissible in evidence, if relevant, as against his interest. They are either formal or informal. (1) Formal admissions for the purpose of the trial may be made on pleadings, as *e.g.* where a contract and the breach are admitted (Ord.27). (2) Informal admissions may be made before or during the proceedings.

In criminal proceedings admissions may be by plea of guilty, by a statement of facts by the accused, or in the form of a confession (*q.v.*).

admittance. The lord of a manor was said to admit a person as tenant of copyhold lands forming part of the manor when he accepted him as tenant of those lands in place of the former tenant; *e.g.* on the surrender, devise, or death intestate of the former tenant. Copyholds were abolished by the Law of Property Act 1922 on January 1, 1926.

admittendo clerico. A writ directed to the bishop requiring him to admit a clerk.

adolscens. [Roman law.] A person between the ages of puberty (14 in boys, 12 in girls) and majority (25).

adopted child. A child in respect of which an adoption order has been made. See ADOPTION OF CHILDREN.

adoptio. [Roman law.] The transfer of a person from the *potestas* of one man to that of another: (1) by imperial rescript, under which a man may adopt men or women *sui juris* (*adrogatio* (*q.v.*)); (2) by the authority of a magistrate, under which a man may adopt men or women *alieni juris*.

adoption of children. Prior to the Adoption of Children Act 1926 the institution of adoption was unknown to English law. The law was consolidated by the

Adoption Act 1958 extended by the Adoption Acts 1964 and 1968 amended by the Children Act 1975 and again consolidated by the Adoption Act 1976.

The court may make an adoption order on the application of a married couple where each has attained the age of 21, or on the application of one person where he has attained the age of 21 and (*a*) is not married or (*b*) is married but (*i*) his spouse cannot be found, or (*ii*) the spouses are permanently separated and living apart, or (*iii*) his spouse is by reason of ill-health, whether physical or mental, incapable of making the application. An adoption order is not to be made on the application of the mother or father of the child alone unless the other natural parent is dead or cannot be found or there is some other reason justifying his or her exclusion.

An adoption order vests the parental rights and duties relating to the child in the adoptor and extinguishes inconsistent rights. An adoption order may not be made in relation to a child who is or has been married. It may be made notwithstanding that the child is an adopted child. An adopted child is to be treated in law as if he had been born in wedlock and as if he were not the child of any person other than the adopter or adopters. It prevents the child from being illegitimate.

An adoption order requires the consent of each parent or guardian of the child unless such consent is dispensed with by the court. The welfare of the child is the first consideration and so far as practicable his wishes are to be given effect to. The child is to live with the adopters before an adoption order is made. The wishes of the parents or guardians as to religion are to be given effect too.

Local authorities are under a duty to establish an adoption service. Adoption societies require the approval of the Secretary of State. See AFFILIATION ORDER; LEGITIMACY.

For the purposes of the devolution or disposition of property, the adopted person ranks as a legitimate child of the adopter.

Adoption orders may be made by the Family Division of the High Court, a county court or a magistrates' court.

The Registrar General maintains an Adopted Children Register.

An adopted child is a "child" for the purposes of the Matrimonial Causes Act 1973; see s.52(1).

adoption of contract. The acceptance of it is binding, notwithstanding some defect which entitles the party to repudiate it.

adoptive act. An Act of Parliament which does not become operative until adopted by a public body or a particular number of voters in an area.

adrogatio. [Roman law.] The oldest form of adoption, applicable only in adoption of persons *sui juris*. Originally it took place under the sanction of the Pontifex, and in the *comitia curiata*, as an act of legislation; superseded under the Empire by the imperial rescript.

ads=ad sectam. [At the suit of.]

adscriptus glebae. [Attached to the soil.] See VILLEIN.

adult. See FULL AGE.

adulteration. The mixing with any substance intended to be sold of any ingredient which is dangerous to health or which makes the substance something other than that as which it is sold or intended to be sold. It is an offence under the Food and Drugs Acts and other Acts.

adultery. Voluntary sexual intercourse between persons of the opposite sex one of whom is married to a third party.

That the respondent has committed adultery and the petitioner finds it intolerable to live with the respondent may constitute proof that a marriage has broken down (Matrimonial Causes Act 1973, s.1). See DIVORCE.

17

The parties to any civil proceedings instituted in consequence of adultery and the husbands and wives of the parties are competent to give evidence in the proceedings and a witness whether a party to the proceedings or not is not excused from answering any question by reason that it tends to show that he or she has been guilty of adultery (Matrimonial Causes Act 1965, s.43(2); Civil Evidence Act 1968, s.16(5)). In any civil proceedings the fact that a person has been found guilty of adultery in any matrimonial proceedings is admissible in evidence (Civil Evidence Act 1968, s.12).

Adultery was formerly a tort actionable by writ of trespass in an action of criminal conversation (*q.v.*). The action was abolished but damages could be claimed against a co-respondent but this was abolished by the Law Reform (Miscellaneous Provisions) Act 1970, s.4.

advancement, equitable doctrine of. If a purchase or investment is made by a father, or person *in loco parentis*, in the name of a child or by any person under an equitable obligation to support or make provision for another, a rebuttable presumption arises that it was intended as an advancement (that is, for the benefit of the child), so as to rebut what would otherwise be the ordinary presumption in such cases of a resulting trust in favour of the person who paid the money. The doctrine also applies to a purchase made in the name of a wife (*Tinker* v. *Tinker* [1970] P.136).

advancement, power of. Trustees of trusts constituted after 1925 may apply capital moneys for the advancement or benefit, as they think fit, of any person entitled to the capital of the trust property; provided that the advancement does not exceed one-half of the presumptive or vested share or interest of the beneficiary in the trust property, and is brought into account as part of such share , if and when the beneficiary becomes entitled to a share of capital (Trustee Act 1925, s.32). Land may be advanced (*Re Collard's Will Trusts* [1961] Ch.293).

adventure. Formerly, the sending of goods abroad at owner's risk in a ship in the charge of a supercargo or agent who was to dispose of them to the best advantage.

An adventure in the nature of trade, is treated as a trade under Sched.D, Income and Corporation Taxes Act 1970, ss.109, 526(5).

adverse possession. An occupation of land inconsistent with the right of the true owner: the possession of those against whom a right of action has accrued to the true owner. It is actual possession in the absence of possession by the rightful owner, and without lawful title. Time does not begin to run under the Statutes of Limitation unless there is some person in adverse possession of the land (Limitation Act 1939, s.10).

If the adverse possession continues, the effect at the expiration of the prescribed period is that not only the remedy but the title of the former owner is extinguished (*ibid.* s.16). The person in adverse possession gains a new possessory title which cannot normally exceed in extent or duration the interest of the former owner. See LIMITATION, STATUTES OF.

adverse witness. A witness adverse to the party examining him: he may with leave of the court be cross-examined by the party calling him. See HOSTILE WITNESS.

adversus extraneos vitiosa possessio prodesse solet. [Prior possession is a good title of ownership against all who cannot show a better.]

advertisements offering a reward for the return of stolen property and promising that no questions will be asked, constitute an offence. The printer and publisher are also liable (Theft Act 1968, s.23).

An advertisement of goods for sale is an invitation to make offers, and is not itself an offer. The display of advertisements is subject to control under the Town and Country Planning legislation. See PLANNING.

Advertisements relating to hire-purchase must comply with the Consumer Credit Act 1974, ss.43–54. Insurance advertisements must conform with regulations made under the Insurance Companies Act 1974. Fraudulent inducements to invest on deposit are dealt with by the Protection of Depositors Act 1963, as amended. Advertisements for the treatment of venereal disease are subject to the Venereal Disease Act 1917, as amended by the Medicines Act 1968, Sched.5, para.1, Sched.6.

Advertisements relating to abortion and certain diseases are prohibited by the Pharmacy and Medicines Act 1941, ss.8,9. Anonymous advertisements offering to take care of children are prohibited by the Children Act 1958, s.37. Persons exhibiting indecent advertisements are punishable summarily under the Indecent Advertisements Act 1889; Criminal Justice Act 1967, Sched.3, Part I. Local and Public authorities are exempt (Indecent Advertisements (Amendment) Act 1970). Aerial advertising is regulated under the Civil Aviation (Licensing) Act 1960; Civil Aviation Act 1971, Sched. 11.

Discriminatory advertisements are unlawful under the Race Relations Act 1968, s.6 and the Sex Discrimination Act 1975, s.38.

advice, letter of. A letter from one merchant or banker to another concerning a business transaction in which both are engaged.

advice note. The document sent by a railway undertaking to the consignee intimating that his goods have arrived and informing him that if the goods are not fetched away the railway undertaking will only keep them as warehousemen and not as carriers, thereby reducing their liability to liability only for negligence.

advice on evidence. The opinion of junior counsel given after pleadings have closed as to the witnesses to be called and the documents to be put in evidence.

Advisory Conciliation and Arbitration Service (ACAS). A body set up under the Employment Protection Act 1975 whose function is to improve industrial relations and encourage the extension, development and reform of collective bargaining. It arbitrates and advises in industrial disputes and may issue codes of practice.

advocate. One who pleads the cause of another in a judicial tribunal; barristers or solicitors. Formerly, a member of the College of Advocates, with the exclusive right of practising in the Ecclesiastical and Admiralty Courts. The College of Advocates was abolished by the Court of Probate Act 1857.

advocate, Crown. Formerly the second law officer of the Crown in the Court of Admiralty.

Advocate General. An officer of the Court of Justice of the European Communities (EEC). The position has no exact parallel in common law jurisdictions save possibly *amicus curiae* (*q.v.*), since the advocate general is neither a judge nor an advocate for one of the parties. He advises the court, making reasoned submissions on matters referred to it. See COURT OF JUSTICE OF THE EUROPEAN COMMUNITIES.

advocate, King's. Formerly the principal law officer of the Crown in the Admiralty and Ecclesiastical Courts.

Advocate, Lord. See LORD ADVOCATE.

Advocates, Faculty of. The body which has the exclusive right of appointing advocates or members of the Scottish Bar.

advow, avow, or **avouch.** To vouch; to call on the feudal lord to defend his tenant's right.

advowson. The perpetual right of presentation to a church or benefice being a rectory or vicarage. It is the right of patronage and is real property. No transfer can be made within one year of an institution, it must transfer the whole interest of the conveying party, and every transfer must be registered. When two vacancies have occurred in a benefice after July 14, 1924, the right of patronage is incapable of sale (Benefices Act 1898 (Amendment) Measure 1923, s.1). This provision, however, has no application to sales of land to which rights of patronage are appendant (*ibid.*). See also the Benefices Measures of 1930 and 1933. See NEXT PRESENTATION.

advowson appendant. An advowson annexed to a manor or some corporeal hereditament.

advowson in gross. An advowson belonging to an individual, and not annexed to a corporeal hereditament.

aedificatum solo, solo cedit. [What is built on the land is to be regarded as having become part of the land.] See QUICQUID PLANTATUR SOLO, SOLO CEDIT.

aequitas. Equity (*q.v.*).

aequitas sequitur legem. [Equity follows the law.]

affidavit. A written statement in the name of a person, called the deponent, by whom it is voluntarily signed and sworn to or affirmed. It must be confined to such statements as the deponent is able of his own knowledge to prove, but in certain cases it may contain statements of information and belief with the sources of grounds thereof (Ord.38, r.3.) The parties to civil proceedings may agree that their case be tried upon affidavit (Ord.38, rr.25–30), and the court may order that any particular facts, or the evidence of any particular witness, shall be proved by affidavit (Ord.38, r.2). Affidavits are of infinite variety.

affidavit of documents. See DISCOVERY.

affiliation order. An order that a man adjudged by a court of summary jurisdiction to be the father of the bastard child of a single woman, or widow, or married woman living apart from her husband, shall pay a weekly sum without deduction of income tax for the maintenance and education of the child (Affiliation Proceedings Act 1957, as amended). An affiliation order may be enforced by distress or committal (Magistrates' Courts Act 1952, ss.64, 74, as amended). In any civil proceedings the fact that a person has been adjudged to be the father of a child in affiliation proceedings in the United Kingdom is admissible in evidence (Civil Evidence Act 1968, s.12). Where an illegitimate child is adopted the adoption order extinguishes any duty arising by virtue of an order of a court to make payments, so far as the payments are in respect of the child's maintenance for any period after the making of the order (Children Act 1975, s.8(3)(*b*)).

Affiliation proceedings may also be taken by a custodian to whom custody of the child has been given by a custodianship order (s.45). See also Domestic Proceedings and Magistrates Court Act 1978, ss.49–53.

affinity. Relationship by marriage; the relationship between a husband and his wife's kindred, and between the wife and her husband's kindred; but there is no affinity between a person and the relations by marriage of his or her spouse. The degrees of affinity within which a marriage is void are set out in the Marriage Act 1949, s.1, Sched. 1, as amended by the Marriage (Enabling) Act 1960, and the Children Act 1975, Sched.3, para.8 (effect of adoption).

affirm. (1)To elect to abide by a voidable contract; (2) to uphold a judgment; (3) to be allowed to give evidence without taking the oath, either on the ground that taking an oath is contrary to the person's religious belief, or that the person has no religious belief (Oaths Act 1878, s.5(1)). An affirmation may be made where it is not practicable to administer an oath as required by a person's religious belief.

affirmanti non neganti incumbit probatio. [The burden of proof is upon him who affirms, not upon him who denies.] See PROOF.

affray. Unlawful fighting or display of force to the terror of the Queen's subjects. It need not be in a public place (*Button* v. *D.P.P.* [1965] 3 All E.R. 587). One person acting alone may cause an affray (*Taylor* v. *D.P.P.*[1973] 2 All E.R. 1108).

affreightment. A contract made either by charterparty or by bill of lading, by which a shipowner agrees to carry goods in his ship for reward. See also FREIGHT.

age, full. See FULL AGE.

agent. A person employed to act on behalf of another. An act of an agent, done within the scope of his authority, binds his principal. If a person professes to contract as agent on behalf of another as principal, although without the latter's authority, the latter may subsequently ratify the contract. Otherwise if a person represents himself to have authority to act as agent when he has none, he is liable for breach of an implied warranty of authority (*Collen* v. *Wright* (1857) 7 E. & B. 301).

Once an agent has brought his principal into contractual relations with another, he drops out, and his principal sues or is sued on the contract. Agents are:

(1) Universal.—Appointed to act for the principal in all matters, *e.g.* where a party gives another a universal power of attorney.

(2) General.—Appointed to act in transactions of a class, *e.g.* a banker, solicitor. The scope of authority of such agent is the authority usually possessed by such agents, unless notice is given to third parties of some limitation.

(3) Special.—Appointed for one particular purpose. The agent's scope of authority is the actual authority given him.

See also DEL CREDERE AGENT; FACTOR; POWER OF ATTORNEY.

agent of necessity. A person who in urgent circumstances acts for the benefit of another, there being no opportunity of communicating with that other. Thus a person may be bound by a contract made by another on his behalf, but without his authority; *e.g.* the master of a ship, in an emergency, may contract and bind the owner. The implied authority of a deserted wife to pledge her husband's credit as agent of necessity was abrogated by the Matrimonial Proceedings and Property Act 1970, s.41.

agent provocateur. The admissible limits in the involvement of the police with informers for the purpose of obtaining evidence were considered in *R.* v. *Birtles* [1969] 1 W.L.R. 1047 at p.1049; *R.* v. *McCann* (1971) 56 Cr. App. R. 359; *R.* v. *McEvilly* (1975) 60 Cr. App. R. 150; and *R.* v. *Sang* [1979] 3 W.L.R. 263.

aggravated assault. An assault upon a boy under 14 or any female of an "aggravated nature"; *i.e.* by its violence (s.43 of the Offences against the Person Act 1861, as amended by Criminal Justices Act 1925, s.39 and the Criminal Justice Act 1967, Sched.3, Part I). A matrimonial order may be made on the ground of aggravated assault (Matrimonial Proceedings (Magistrates' Courts) Act 1960, s.1(1)).

aggravated burglary. See BURGLARY.

aggravation, matter of. Matter in pleadings which only tends to increase the amount of damages and does not itself constitute a ground for action.

agistment. Where a person takes in and feeds or depastures horses, cattle or similar animals upon his land for reward. An agister is, therefore, a bailee for reward, and is liable for damage to the cattle if he uses less than ordinary diligence.

agnates. Kinsmen related through males. In Roman law *agnati* were persons so related to a common ancestor that, if they had been alive together with him, they would have been under his *potestas*. See COGNATI.

agreement. The concurrence of two or more persons in affecting or altering their rights and duties. An agreement is an act in the law whereby two or more persons declare their consent as to any act or thing to be done or forborne by some or one of those persons for the benefit of the others or other of them. Such declaration may take place by (*a*) the concurrence of the parties in a spoken or written form of words as expressing their common intention, (*b*) an offer made by some one of them and accepted by the others or other of them (Pollock). The requisites of an agreement are: two or more persons, a distinct intention common to both, known to both, referring to legal relations and affecting the parties (Anson). See CONTRACT.

agricultural holding. The aggregate of the agricultural land comprised in a contract of tenancy, not being a contract under which the said land is let to the tenant during his continuance in any office, appointment or employment held under the landlord (Agricultural Holdings Act 1948, s.1). An agricultural tenant must have 12 months' notice to quit at the end of a year of the tenancy.

agriculture. Includes horticulture, fruit growing, seed growing, dairy farming and livestock breeding and keeping (Agricultural Holdings Act 1948, s.94). See also Rent (Agriculture) Act 1976 which provides security of tenure in some cases for workers employed in agriculture.

aid by verdict. Defects in the old common law pleadings, if not demurred, could not be objected to after verdict, unless of a very serious kind. They were said to be aided or cured by the verdict.

aids. Payments from feudal tenants by military or socage tenures to their lords for: (1) Ransoming the lord's body. (2) Knighting the lord's eldest son. (3) Marrying the lord's eldest daughter. Abolished by 12 Car.2, c.24.

aiel. A grandfather.

air. The enjoyment of air is a natural right. There is no absolute right in the owner of land to the enjoyment of an uninterrupted passage of air over the land of another, but the right to a defined current of air can be acquired as an easement (*q.v.*). Pollution of air by another may be restrained, unless an easement has been acquired by such other. A general duty is imposed on persons to avoid polluting the air (Health and Safety at Work, etc. Act 1974, s.5), and see the Control of Pollution Act 1974, ss.75–81.

The owner of land is entitled to the ownership and possession of the column of space above the surface *ad infinitum*. See AIR NAVIGATION.

Air Force. The Air Force was constituted by the Air Force (Constitution) Act 1917. The enlistment discipline of the R.A.F. was provided for in the Air Force Act 1955 which is continued in force by order made under s.222(4).

The Air Council which controlled the Air Force is merged in the Ministry of Defence.

air navigation. This is controlled under the Civil Aviation Acts 1949 to 1978. No action lies in respect of trespass or nuisance by reason only of the flight of aircraft over any property at a reasonable height, but the owner of aircraft is laible for all actual damage done while in flight, whether to person or property, without proof of negligence. Such liability, however, is subject to certain limitations of amount, and third party risks must be insured against (Civil Aviation Act 1949, s.40).

The Carriage by Air Act 1932 gave effect to the Warsaw Convention of 1929, and provided for the liability of carriers for death or injury to passengers and damage to goods. The Carriage by Air Act 1961 gave effect to the Hague protocol amending the Warsaw Convention, and the Carriage by Air (Supplementary Provisions) Act 1962 gave effect to the supplementary convention signed in Mexico. The Civil Aviation (Eurocontrol) Act 1962 gives effect to the Eurocontrol Convention of 1960 relating to European co-operation for safety of air navigation. As to aviation security see Aviation Security Act 1982.

alba firma. White rents: quit-rents payable in silver or white money in contradistinction to "black rents," *i.e.* reserved in work, grain, etc.

alderman (originally Ealdorman (*q.v.*)). An alderman is now either an alderman of the City of London or an honorary alderman of a county, Greater London, a district or a London borough appointed under the Local Government Act 1972, s.249.

aleatory contract. A wagering contract.

alia enormia. [Other wrongs.] The concluding allegation in declarations in the action of trespass, consisting of the general words "and other wrongs to the plaintiff then did."

alias (alias dictus) [Otherwise called.] A false name.

alias writ. A second writ, issued after a former one had proved ineffectual.

alibi. [Elsewhere.] A defence where an accused alleges that at the time when the offence with which he is charged was committed, he was elsewhere. Notice of intention to raise an alibi must be given (Criminal Justice Act 1967, s.11). See *R.* v. *Lewis* [1969] 2 Q.B. 1.

alien. At common law an alien is a subject of a foreign state who was not born within the allegiance of the Crown. "Alien" now means a person who is neither a Commonwealth citizen (*q.v.*) nor a British Protected Person (*q.v.*) nor a citizen of the Republic of Ireland (British Nationality Act 1981, s.50(1)). An alien has full proprietary capacity except he may not own a British ship nor may he exercise the franchise. See DEPORTATION; IMMIGRATION; NATURALISATION.

alien ami or **friend.** The subject of a foreign state with which this country is at peace.

alien enemy. The subject of a foreign state with which this country is at war, or one who is voluntarily resident or carries on business in enemy territory including enemy-occupied territory (*Sooracht's Case* [1943] A.C. 203). A company is an alien enemy if it is controlled by persons who are alien enemies (*Daimler Co. Ltd.* v. *Continental Tyre and Rubber Co. Ltd.* [1916] 2 A.C. 307).

Enemy aliens resident in the enemy country cannot sue in the English Courts (*Porter* v. *Freudenberg* [1915] 1 K.B. 857), but enemy alien civilians resident in this country with licence of the Queen may sue (*Schaffenius* v. *Goldberg* [1916] 1 K.B. 184). An alien enemy has no right to a writ of habeas corpus.

Trading with the enemy was a common law misdemeanour, but the provisions of the Trading with the Enemy Act 1939 now apply. See also Distribution of German Enemy Property Act 1949.

alienato rei prefertur juri accrescendi. [The law favours the alienation rather than the accumulation of property.]

alienation. The power of the owner or tenant to dispose of his interest in real or personal property. Alienation may be voluntary, *e.g.* by conveyance or will; or involuntary, *e.g.* seizure under a judgment order for debt.

alieni juris. [Roman law.] A person under *potestas, manus* or *mancipium* as opposed to *sui juris* (*q.v.*).

alimentary trust. A protective trust (*q.v.*).

alimony. Alimony was the term used to describe the allowance to a married woman when she was under the necessity of living apart from her husband. The term is no longer used in matrimonial causes and is replaced by maintenance pending suit and permanent financial provision thereafter. See MAINTENANCE.

alio intuitu. With a motive other than the ostensible and proper one.

aliquis non debet esse judex in propria causa quia non potest esse judex et pars. [No man ought to be a judge in his own cause, because he cannot act as a judge and at the same time be a party.]

aliter. [Otherwise.]

aliud est celare, aliud tacere. [Silence is not the same thing as concealment.] But active concealment is equivalent to a positive statement that the fact does not exist, and is a deceit.

aliunde. [From elsewhere.] From another place or person.

all fours, on. Strictly analogous.

allegans contraria non est audiendus. [He who makes statements mutually inconsistent is not to be listened to.] See *e.g.* ESTOPPEL.

allegans suam turpitudinem non est audiendus. [A person alleging his own infamy is not to be heard.]

allegation. A statement or assertion of fact made in any proceeding, as for instance, in a pleading; particularly a statement or charge which is, as yet, unproved.

allegiance. The tie which binds the subject to the Queen in return for that protection which the Queen affords the subject; the natural and legal obedience which every subject owes to his Sovereign. Breach of allegiance is the basis of the crime of treason (*q.v.*). Local allegiance is the allegiance owed by every alien while he continues within the dominions and the protection of the British Crown, and even after that protection is temporarily withdrawn, owing to the occupation of the British territory by the enemy in time of war (*De Jager* v. *Att.-Gen. of Natal* [1907] A.C. 326). Allegiance is also owed by an alien who receives and retains a passport from the Crown; and this is so even after the alien has left the realm (*Joyce* v. *D.P.P.* [1946] A.C. 347).

The oath of allegiance has to be taken on appointment by judges and justices of the peace, and by Members of Parliament on taking their seats, and clergymen before ordination.

allocation. Appropriation of a fund to particular persons or purposes. See APPROPRIATION.

allocatur. [It is allowed.] The certificate of the taxing master as to the amount of costs allowed.

allocutus. The demand of the court to a prisoner convicted of treason on indictment as to what he has to say why the court should not proceed to pass judgment upon him. It is an essential step in a trial.

allodium. Lands not held of any lord or superior, in which, therefore, the owner had an absolute property and not a mere estate.

allonge. A slip of paper annexed to a bill of exchange for endorsements when there is no room for them on the bill (Bills of Exchange Act 1882, s.32(1)).

allotment. (1) The allocation or appropriation of property to a specific person (or persons) called the "allottee," *e.g.* the partition of land held jointly among the several owners.

(2) The appropriation to an applicant by a resolution of the directors of a company of a certain number of shares in the company, in response to an application. This is generally done by sending to the applicant a letter of allotment, informing him of the number of shares allotted to him. A return of allotments has to be made to the Registrar of Companies (Companies Act 1948, ss.47–52).

Smallholdings allotted to the "labouring poor." See the Allotments Acts 1908 to 1950.

Alluvio. [Roman law.] Alluvion: an imperceptibly gradual deposit of soil from a river or the sea.

alteration. A material alteration of an instrument, *e.g.* an alteration of the date of a bill of exchange whereby payment would be accelerated, invalidates the instrument. Alterations in deeds are presumed to have been made before execution; in wills, after, and are ignored unless duly executed or proved to have been made in fact before execution of the will.

alternative averments. The statement in the same count of an indictment of an offence in an alternative form in conformity with the enactment constituting the offence (Indictment Rules 1971, r.7).

alternative counts. An indictment is divided into separate clauses, known as counts; and in each count a separate offence may be charged if the charges are founded on the same facts, or are part of a series of offences of the same or similar kind (Indictment Rules 1971, r.4).

alternative, pleading in the. Either party may include in his pleading two or more inconsistent sets of material facts and claim relief thereunder in the alternative.

amalgamation. The merger of two or more companies or their undertakings. See Companies Act 1948, ss.206, 208.

ambassadors. Diplomatic agents residing in a foreign country as representatives of the states by whom they are dispatched. See DIPLOMATIC PRIVILEGE; EXTERRITORALITY.

ambiguitas verborum latens verificatione suppletur, nam quod ex facto oritur ambiguum verificatione facti tollitur. [A latent ambiguity in the words of a written instrument may be explained by evidence; for it arose on evidence extrinsic to the instrument and it may therefore be removed by other similar evidence.] See AMBIGUITY.

ambiguitas verborum patens nulla verificatione excluditur. [A patent ambiguity in the words of a written instrument cannot be cleared up by evidence extrinsic to the instrument.]

ambiguity. A double meaning. A patent ambiguity is one which is apparent on the fact of the instrument, as where a blank is left. A latent ambiguity is one not apparent on the face of the instrument, as where a testator bequeaths property to his niece, Jane, and it is proved that he had two nieces so named. Parol evidence is admissible to explain a latent, but not (in general) a patent, ambiguity.

ambulatoria est voluntas defuncti usque ad vitae supremum exitum. [The will of a deceased person is ambulatory until the latest moment of life.]

ambulatory. Revocable for the time being; a provision whose operation is suspended until the happening of some event upon which the provision becomes operative and binding. A will is ambulatory until the death of the testator.

amendment. The correction of some error or omission, or the curing of some defect, in judicial proceedings. In criminal proceedings, the amendment of indictments is now governed by the Indictments Act 1915, s.5. The Crown Court may, in the course of hearing an appeal, correct any error or mistake in the order or judgment under appeal (Courts Act 1971, s.9). In civil proceedings in the High Court, the court may, at any stage of the proceedings, and on any terms as to costs or otherwise amend any defect or error in any proceedings, and all necessary amendments shall be made. A writ or statement of claim may be amended once without leave (Ord.20).

amends, tender of. An offer to pay a sum of money by way of satisfaction for a wrong alleged to have been committed.

amenity. That which is conducive to comfort or convenience. See, *e.g.* "Standard amenities" relating to a dwelling (Housing Act 1964, s.43), "loss of amenity" in connection with personal injury claims (*q.v.*).

amerciament or **amercement.** A pecuniary punishment for an offence in respect of which the offender stood in the court of his lord, whether the King or a subject, at the mercy (*a merci, in misericordia*) of the lord. Except where the courts were restrained by custom or legislation, an amerciament was entirely in the discretion of the court, while a fine was fixed and certain.

amicus curiae. [A friend of the court.] One who calls the attention of the court to some point of law or fact which would appear to have been overlooked; usually a member of the Bar. On occasion the law officers are requested or permitted to argue a case in which they are not instructed to appear.

amnesty. A pardon for offences granted by an Act of Parliament which is originated by the Crown.

amortisation. Provision for the payment off of a debt, or for the wasting of an asset (*e.g.* a lease), by means of a sinking fund.

amotion. Removal from office.

an, jour et waste. See YEAR, DAY AND WASTE.

ancestor. Any of those relatives from whom descent by blood may be traced, whether through the father, or mother; the person prior to 1926, to whose property an heir succeeded on intestacy. By the fifth rule of intestate succession to realty (based on the Inheritance Act 1833), on failure of lineal descendants or issue of a purchaser, the land "descended" to his nearest lineal ancestor.

ancient demesne. The manors which were in the actual possession of the Crown during the reigns of Edward the Confessor and William the Conqueror, and which in Domesday (*q.v.*) are styled *terrae regis* or *terrae regis Eduardi*. The tenants in ancient demesne originally could sue or be sued on questions affecting their lands only in the Court of Common Pleas or the Court of Ancient Demesne of the manor. Abolished by the Law of Property Act 1925, s.128.

ancient documents. Documents which are at least 20 years old and which, when produced from proper custody, and are otherwise free from suspicion, prove themselves, no evidence of their execution needing to be given. Prior to the Evidence Act 1938 the period was 30 years.

ancient lights. The right of access of light to any building, actually enjoyed for the full period of 20 years without interruption, when the right becomes absolute and indefeasible, unless enjoyed under some express grant (Prescription Act 1832, s.3). The acquisition of a prescriptive right to light may be prevented by the registration of a local land charge (Rights of Light Act 1959).

ancient monuments. Protection is afforded by the Ancient Monuments Consolidation and Amendment Act 1913, the Ancient Monuments Act 1931, the Historic Buildings and Ancient Monuments Act 1953, and the Field Monuments Act 1972. Building preservation orders and lists may be made under the Town and Country Planning Acts. See also HISTORIC BUILDINGS.

ancients. The former name of the older barristers of an Inn of Court. Certain of the senior barristers of the Middle Temple are still called ancients but only for dining purposes.

ancillary. Auxiliary or subordinate, *e.g.*

(1) Ancillary relief, *i.e.* subservient or incidental relief. Where a plaintiff seeks to recover damages and an injunction, the injunction is by way of ancillary relief.

(2) Ancillary relief in matrimonial causes (*q.v.*), *i.e.* where a party to proceedings for divorce, nullity or Judicial separation seeks an order for financial provision (*q.v.*)(see Matrimonial Causes Act 1973, s.23; FINANCIAL PROVISION).

(3) Ancillary credit business, *i.e.* business relating to credit brokerage, debt adjusting, debt counselling, debt collecting credit reference agency. See Consumer Credit Act 1974, s.145(1).

ancipitus usus. [Of doubtful use.]

angary, right of. The right of a belligerent state in time of war, and in case of necessity, of seizing the property of neutrals, subject to payment of compensation. See *The Zamora* [1916] 2 A.C.77.

animals. The common law rules with regard to strict liability in respect of animals *ferae naturae* were abolished by the Animals Act 1971. Where damage is caused by an animal of a dangerous species the keeper of the animal is generally liable. In the case of an animal not of a dangerous species the keeper is liable for damage which that particular animal is likely to cause (s.2). A trespasser cannot, as a rule, recover damages (s.5(3)). The keeper of a dog is, as a rule, liable for damage by killing or injuring livestock (ss.3,5). The owner or person in charge of a dog worrying livestock on agricultural land is guilty of an offence (Dogs (Protection of Livestock) Act 1953; Criminal Justice Act 1967, s.92, Sched.3, Pt. I).

Straying animals may be detained and the damage caused by them is recoverable with the expense of keeping them. The common law remedy of distress damage feasant is abolished (Animals Act 1971, ss.4–7).

The common law rule that the occupier of land adjoining a highway was under no obligation to prevent his animals straying on the highway is abolished and the owner may be liable for negligence. This does not apply to animal on common land or on a town or village green (s.8).

Power to protect livestock (including poultry) from worrying by dogs is given by s.9. This provision does not wholly supersede the common law rules laid down in *Cresswell* v. *Sirl* [1948] 1 K.B. 241. A person who kills a dog in protection of his sporting rights cannot justify his action as being in protection of his property (*Gott* v. *Measures* [1948] 1 K.B. 234).

It is an offence to allow horses, cattle, sheep, goats, or swine to stray or lie on or at the side of a highway. This does not apply to animals on common, waste or unenclosed ground (Highways Act 1959, s. 135; Criminal Justice Act 1967, s.92, Sched.3, Pt. I; Highways Act 1971, s.33).

An owner is not liable for the trespass of his dog or cat (*Buckle* v. *Holmes* [1926] 2 K.B. 125).

Wild creatures tamed or untamed are, in general, capable of being stolen (Theft Act 1968, ss. 1,4). See also DANGEROUS WILD ANIMALS.

animus cancellandi. [The intention of cancelling.]

animus dedicandi. [The intention of dedicating.] At common law the ownership of the soil of a highway is in the adjacent owners, they having dedicated it to the public.

animus deserendi. [The intention of deserting (a spouse).] See DESERTION.

animus et factum. [The combination of the intention with the act.]

animus furandi. [The intention of stealing.] See THEFT.

animus manendi. [The intention of remaining.] One of the necessary elements of domicile (*q.v.*).

animus quo. [The intention with which.]

animus revertendi. [The intention of returning.] Animals accustomed to go and return—*e.g.* pigeons in a dovecote—continue the property of their owner until they lose the *animus revertendi*.

animus revocandi. [The intention of revoking.] *e.g.* a will.

animus testandi. [The intention of making a will.]

annates. Synonymous with first fruits or *primitae*, the first year's whole profits of every spiritual preferment; originally payable to the Pope, then by the statute 26 Hen. 8, c.3, to the Crown, and from 1703 to the Commissioners of Queen Anne's Bounty (*q.v.*). By the First Fruits and Tenths Measure 1926, as from July 16, 1926, first fruits and tenths were either extinguished or provision was made for their redemption.

anni nubiles. The marriageable age of a woman. At common law 12 years of age. Now it is 16 years of age (Marriage Act 1949). Parental consent is required to the marriage of persons under 18 years old but a magistrates court may give such consent where parents refuse (Family Law Reform Act 1969). Application may also be made to a county court (Act of 1949, s.3; County Court Ord. 47, r.1).

annual return. A document which a limited company (*q.v.*) must file annually with the Register of Companies (*q.v.*). It must be filed within 42 days after the company's annual general meeting and must be accompanied by a copy of the auditor's report and balance sheet (Companies Act 1948, ss.124 and 126 and Sched. VI, Sched. to Companies (Annual Return) Regulations 1977).

annual value. The value placed on land or hereditaments for rating purposes. The gross value is the rack-rent; *i.e.* the rent for which the property is worth to be let by the year, the landlord paying for repairs, insurance and expenses, the tenant paying the rates. The net annual value, or rateable value, is the gross value less the statutory deductions. See the General Rate Act 1967, s.19; General Rate Act 1970, s.1.

annuity. A yearly payment of a certain sum of money. If charged ón real estate it is commonly called a rentcharge.

Annuities given by will are pecuniary legacies payable by instalments, and where the will directs the purchase of an annuity for A for life, A is entitled to take the purchase-money instead.

Only the interest portion of a purchased annuity is liable to income tax.

annul. To deprive a judicial proceeding of its operation, either retrospectively or only as to future transactions.

annulment. (1) Annulment of adjudication of bankruptcy (*q.v.*) (see Bankruptcy Act 1914, ss.29, 31).

(2) Annulment of marriage. See NULLITY OF MARRIAGE.

(3) Appeal for annulment (of an action of the EEC Council or Commission) (Treaty of Rome, Arts.173 and 174).

answer. (1)An answer to interrogatories (Ord. 26, r.1). (2)The defence of a party to a petition of divorce (Matrimonial Causes Rules 1977, r.18).

ante-date. To date back. See Bills of Exchange Act 1882, s.13.

ante litem motam. Before litigation was in contemplation. Declarations by deceased relatives made *ante litem motam* are admissible to prove matters of family pedigree or legitimacy.

antenatus. A child born before the marriage of its parents.

ante-nuptial. Before marriage.

anticipation. The act of assigning, charging or otherwise dealing with income before it becomes due. See RESTRAINT ON ANTICIPATION.

antiqua statuta or **vetera statuta.** Old statutes passed before the reign of Edward III.

Anton Piller. See PILLER, ANTON.

apices juris non sunt jura. [Legal principles must not be carried to their most extreme consequences, regardless of equity and good sense.]

apology. In actions for libel contained in newspapers, etc., it is a defence to publish an apology accompanied by payment of money into court by way of amends. An apology may be pleaded in mitigation of damages in any action for defamation (Libel Acts 1843, 1845).

In cases of unintentional defamation, an offer of amends may be made, consisting of the publication of a suitable correction of the words complained of and a sufficient apology to the party aggrieved by them (Defamation Act 1952, s.4(3)).

apostasy. The total renunciation of Christianity by one who has been educated in or professed that faith within this realm.

appeal. Any proceeding taken to rectify an erroneous decision of a court by bringing it before a higher court. There is no right of appeal against the order or judgment of a court of competent jurisdiction unless expressly provided for.

(1) Appeals from the county court lie to the Court of Appeal (*q.v.*). Leave may be required (Supreme Court Act 1981, s.108(1)–(5); County Court Appeals Order (S.I. 1981 No. 1749)). Appeals must be brought within four weeks.

(2) Appeals from a district registrar lie to judge in chambers (Ord.58 (4)); appeal from a master of Q.B.D. lies to judge in chambers or, in certain circumstances, to the Court of Appeal (Ord. 58, rr.1,2).

(3) Appeals from judge in chambers lie to the Court of Appeal (Ord. 58, r.7, but see Supreme Court Act 1981, s.18).

(4) Appeals from judgments or orders of the High Court lie to the Court of Appeal and are brought within four weeks (Supreme Court Act 1981, ss.16–18; R.S.C. Ord. 59).

(5) Appeals from the Court of Appeal are by Petition to the House of Lords (*q.v.*) with the leave of the Court of Appeal or of the House of Lords.

(6) Appeals from Courts of Summary jurisdiction lie to the Crown Court (*q.v.*) (Courts Act, s.56, Sched.9).

(7) Appeals from justices by way of case stated lie to a Divisional Court (*q.v.*) Queens Bench Division (Ord.56, r.5).

(8) Appeals from justices in domestic proceedings (*q.v.*) lie to a Divisional Court of the Family Division.

(9) Appeals from the Crown Court in indictable cases lie to the Criminal Division of the Court of Appeal. See CRIMINAL APPEAL.

(10) Appeals from tribunals (*q.v.*), *e.g.* industrial tribunals (*q.v.*) will depend on the machinery set up by the statute which created the tribunal. Appeal may lie to the High Court on a point of law. See also JUDICIAL REVIEW.

Appeal, Court of. See COURT OF APPEAL.

appeal of felony. An accusation of having committed a felony made by one person against another. The person charged had the right to trial by battle, which took place between him and the accuser, the combatants being each armed with a leather shield and a cudgel, and having to fight for a day, or until one of them gave in. Abolished by the statute 59 Geo.3, c.46. See BATTLE, TRIAL BY.

appearance. The formal step formerly taken by a defendant to a High Court action after he had been served with the Writ. Now replaced by acknowledgment of service. See ACKNOWLEDGMENT OF SERVICE.

appellant. One who appeals. See APPEAL.

appendant. Incorporeal hereditaments are appendant if they arose originally because the land over which they are enjoyed, and the land to which they are annexed, formed part of the same manor; *e.g.* a right of common, of pasture. See APPURTENANT.

appendix. The matter bound up with the parties' cases, in appeals to the House of Lords, or Privy Council, and consisting of the evidence, judgments, etc., given in the courts below. See *Practice Direction (H.L.)(House of Lords Documents)* [1964] 1 W.L.R. 424.

apply, liberty to. A direction by a judge or master enabling parties to come to the court again without taking out another summons.

appointed day. The day fixed for an Act of Parliament to come into operation.

appointee. One in whose favour a power of appointment is exercised.

appointment, power of. A power, given by deed or will, to appoint a person or persons to take an estate or interest in property, whether real or personal.

The person to whom the power is given is called a donee of the power, and when he exercises it he is called the appointor. The person in whose favour it can be exercised is the object of the power. A true power is discretionary: not imperative as is a trust. A general power of appointment is one where the donee may appoint to anyone including himself; a special power is one where the donee can only appoint in favour of specified objects. There is also a third class of power which is not special in the sense that there is a distinct class of objects specified among which a power to appoint is given, and yet is not general because some persons are excluded; *e.g.* a power to appoint to any person other than the donee of the power. Uncertainty as to the distinction between general and special powers for the purpose of the rule against perpetuities (see PERPETUITY) is removed by the Perpetuities and Accumulations Act 1964, s.7.

Powers must be exercised in the way indicated (if any); *e.g.* by deed or will, but equity may assist the defective execution of a power, *i.e.* where prescribed formalities for executing the power are not complied with. An excessive execution of a power is where the interests attempted to be created are either illegal or outside the scope of the power. A fraud on a power is where the power is exercised by the donee, not in accordance with the true purpose of the power, but to benefit himself, and may be set aside. An exclusive power is one enabling the appointor to select from amongst the specified objects of the power; a non-exclusive power is one which does not permit the entire exclusion of any one member; in the latter case a merely nominal or negligible appointment to one or more of the objects of the power was called an illusory appointment, and was invalid. Now, however, an appointment is not invalidated by the exclusion of any object, unless the power declares the amount of the share from which any object is not to be excluded (Law of Property Act 1925, s.158). See POWER.

apportionment. Division in proportion; the assignment of a share. At common law, where the owner of land died between two dates of payment of rent, the rent was not divisible and the executors of the decesed owner were not entiled to any rent for the broken period. The rent was either not payable, or went to the reversioner.

This rule was altered by the Apportionment Act 1870, which enacted that all rents, annuities, dividends, and other periodical payments in nature of income should, like interest on money lent, be considered as accruing from day to day, and should be apportionable accordingly.

The Act may, however, be excluded by the will.

apportionment of contract. The division of a contract into several distinct acts, or parts, the performance of one or more of which may give the right to enforce the contract to that extent against the other party. If some parts are lawful and some unlawful, the lawful parts can be enforced, while the unlawful are void, unless the consideration is illegal, when the whole contract is void.

appraisement. The valuation of goods or property, in particular of goods seized in execution, or by distraint, or under order of the court. Real property is usually valued by surveyors. Writs of appraisement of goods forfeited to the Crown were abolished by the Crown Proceedings Act 1947, Sched.1.

appraiser. A valuer; one who makes an appraisement.

apprentice. One who binds himself to serve and learn for a definite time from an employer, who on his part covenants to teach his trade or calling. A minor's contract of appreticeship, if substantially for his advantage, is binding on him.

appreticii ad legem. [Apprentices to the law.] Junior barristers.

approbate and reprobate. To blow hot and cold; a person is not allowed to take a benefit under an instrument and disclaim the liabilities imposed by the same instrument.

appropriation. Making a thing the property of a person. (1) The setting apart of goods or moneys out of a larger quantity as the property of a particular person; *e.g.* appropriating goods to a contract. (2) Appropriation by a personal representative is the application of the property of the deceased in its actual condition in satisfaction of a legacy (Administration of Estates Act 1925, s.41). (3) Appropriation of payments to debts. Where a debtor owes more than one debt to a creditor, any payment made can be applied in extinction of any of the debts at the option of the debtor, exercised at the time of payment; otherwise the creditor may appropriate up to the last moment. Where there is an account current between the parties the law presumes that they intended to apply the first item on the credit side to the first item on the debit side and so on. For example, in a banking account it is assumed that the sums first paid in are exhausted by the sums first paid out (*Clayton's Case* (1816) 1 Mer.572). As to appropriation of payments under a hire-purchase contract, see the Consumer Credit Act 1974, s.81(2). (4) Appropriation of supplies is the legalisation of the expenditure of public money by means of the annual Appropriation Act. (5) The attachment of an ecclesiastical benefice to the perpetual use of some religious house, or dean and chapter, or other spiritual person. (6) Theft Act 1968, s.3 defines appropriation as any assumption by a person of the rights of an owner. By section 1 of the Act any such dishonest appropriation of property belonging to another with the intention of permanently depriving the other of it is theft (*q.v.*).

approval, on. When goods are delivered to a buyer on approval the property in the goods passes to the buyer:

(*a*) when he signifies his approval or acceptance to the seller or does any other act adopting the transaction;

(*b*) if he does not signify his approval or acceptance to the seller but returns the goods without giving notice of rejection then, if a time has been fixed for the return of the goods, on the expiration of that time and, if no time has been fixed, on the expiration of a reasonable time (Sale of Goods Act 1979, s.18, r.4).

approved schools. These are being replaced by community homes (Children and Young Persons Act 1969, ss.35–59, Sched. 3, Sched.6).

approvement. The inclosure of part of a common by the lord of the manor, sufficient being left for the commoners. This can now only be done with the consent of the Secretary of State for the Environment.

approver. An accomplice who turns Queen's evidence (*q.v.*).

appurtenant. Such incorporeal interests as are not naturally and originally appendant to corporeal hereditaments, but have been annexed to them either by some express deed of grant, or by prescription; *e.g.* rights of common or of way. See APPENDANT.

aqua cedit solo. [Water passes with the soil.] As water is land covered with water, ownership of the water goes with ownership of the land covered by it.

aquae et ignis interdictio. [Roman law.] Forbidding the use of fire and water; an indirect mode of depriving of citizenship.

arbitration. The determination of disputes by the decision of one or more persons called arbitrators, *e.g.* in commercial matters. Differences between arbitrators are decided by an umpire. An agreement to refer a dispute to arbitration is called an arbitration agreement and if legal proceedings are instituted in contravention of the submission the defendant, but only before delivering pleadings or taking any other step in the proceedings, may apply to the court to stay them. The decision of an arbitrator is called an award. Arbitrtors have power to make and enforce interlocutory orders as if they were orders of the court. The High Court has power of judicial review of awards and may determine preliminary points of law. Appeal from the High Court only lies to the court of Appeal with leave of the High Court and where the High Court certifies a question of law of general public importance or some other special reason. See the Arbitration Acts 1950, 1975 and 1979. For "guidelines" as to judicial review and appeals see *Pioneer Shipping* v. *BTP Tioxede* (*The Nemo*) [1981] 3 W.L.R. 292, H.L. See also Supreme Court Act 1981, s.18(1)(9). For arbitration by County Court Registrars see COUNTY COURT.

Archbishop. The chief of the clergy within his province. The Archbishop of Canterbury is styled Primate of all England, and the Archbishop of York Primate of England. They are spiritual lords of Parliament.

31

Archdeacon. An ecclesiastical superior who is a visitor of the clergy in his district.

Arches, Court of. An ecclesiastical court the judge of which is the Dean of Arches. It entertains appeals from the Consistory Courts, and has taken over the jurisdiction of the Provincial Court of the Archbishop of Canterbury. See also the Ecclesiastical Jurisdiction Measure 1963, ss.3, 8, 13, 82.

arguendo. [In the course of his argument.]

argumentative affidavit. An affidavit which contains arguments as to the bearing of facts on the matter in dispute; prohibited by Ord.41, r.5.

argumentative plea. A pleading which states a material fact by inference only, and bad accordingly.

argumentum ab inconvenienti plurimum valet in lege. [An argument based on inconvenience is of great weight in the law.]

armed forces. The Army Act 1881, which required to be reviewed annually, recited that a standing army in time of peace was illegal without the consent of Parliament. It has been replaced by the Army Act 1955 which, with the Air Force Act 1955 and the Naval Discipline Act 1957, is amended and continued in force by the Armed Forces Act 1981.

armistice. A temporary but total suspension of hostilities by agreement between the Governments of the belligerents. A truce is a suspension of hostilities arranged by military commanders in the field.

arms length, at. The relationship which exists between parties who are strangers to each other, and who bear no special duty, obligation, or relation to each other; *e.g.* vendor and purchaser. *Cf.* UNDUE INFLUENCE.

Army Council. The body, created by letters patent in 1904, which administered the Army. It is merged in the Ministry of Defence.

arraign. To call a prisoner to the bar of the court by name, to read to him the substance of the indictment, and to ask him whether he pleads guilty or not guilty. See the Criminal Law Act 1967, s.6(1).

arrangement, deeds of. A man who is unable to pay his debts may arrange with his creditors, either privately or in the Bankruptcy Court, for discharge of his liabilities by partial payment of composition. If he arranges privately, he must conform with the Deeds of Arrangement Act 1914, as amended by the Administration of Justice Act 1925. See SCHEME OF ARRANGEMENT.

array, challenge to. See CHALLENGE OF JURORS.

array, commission of. Writs issued under the Assize of Arms 1181 to impress men for military service for defence of the realm.

arrears. Debts not paid at the due date.

arrest. To arrest a person is to deeprive him of his liberty by some lawful authority, for the purpose of compelling his appearance to answer a criminal charge, or as a method of execution. (1) Arrest on mesne process was to compel the defendant to appear in an action. (2) Arrest on final process was a mode of execution or enforcing judgment by means of the writ *a capias ad satisfaciendum.* (3) A ship or cargo may be arrested in Admiralty actions *in rem* by obtaining a warrant from the Admiralty Marshal. (4) A justices' warrant is the normal authority for the arrest of an offender. (5) Consequent upon the abolition of felony (*q.v.*) there has been created the "arrestable offence," *i.e.* an offence for which the sentence is fixed by law or for which a person (not previously convicted) may be sentenced to imprisonment for five years, or an attempt to commit such an offence (Criminal Law Act 1967, s.2(1)). Any person may arrest without warrant anyone with reasonable cause suspected of committing an arrestable offence (s.2(2)). Where an arrestable offence has been committed, any person may arrest without warrant anyone who with reasonable cause, is suspected of being guilty of the offence (s.2(3)). Where a constable, with reasonable cause, suspects that an arrestable offence has been committed, he may arrest without warrant anyone whom he, with reasonable cause, suspects to be guilty of the offence (s.2(4)). A constable may arrest without warrant any person who, with reasonable cause, is suspected to be about to commit an arrestable offence (s.2(5)). A constable may for the foregoing purposes enter (if need be by force) and search for suspects(s.2(6)). Any person may arrest any person taking part in an affray (*q.v.*). A person may use reasonable force to prevent any crime (whether an arrestable offence' or not) or in effecting or assisting in the lawful arrest of offenders or suspected offenders (s.3). Normally a police officer who arrests without a warrant must inform the person arrested of the ground of arrest (*Christie* v. *Leachinsky* [1974] A.C.573). An unlwful or wrongful arrest amounts to false imprisonment (*q.v.*). Arrest for minor offences is restricted by the Criminal Justice Act 1967, s.24. Powers of arrest are given by the Road Traffic Act 1972, s.164, in cases of dangerous or careless driving or cycling. See *Squires* v. *Botwright* [1972] R.T.R.462. Resisting a police constable in the execution of his duty may be dealt with under the Police Act 1964, s.51(3). A constable or ordinary citizen has a power of arrest without warrant where there is a reasonable apprehension of an imminent breach of the peace even though the person arrested has not at that stage committed any breach. (*R* v. *Howell* [1981] 3 All E.R.383. See also *Wills* v. *Bowley* [1982] 2 All E.R.654, H.L.)

arrest of judgment. In criminal cases the accused may at any time between conviction and sentence move that judgment be not pronounced because of some technical defect in the indictment.

arretted. Accused.

arson. The malicious firing of a house or other building. Now a statutory offence (Criminal Damage Act 1971, s.1(3)). Triable either summarily or on indictment (Criminal Law 1977, s.16(1)). It is not unlawful under Criminal Damage Act to set fire to one's own property, even as part of an attempt to commit fraud (*R.* v. *Denton* [1981] 1 W.L.R. 1446, C.A.).

articled clerk. A clerk under written articles of agreement to serve a practising solicitor in consideration of being initiated into the profession. See SOLICITOR.

articles. Clauses of a document; hence the word "articles" sometimes means the document itself, *e.g.* articles of agreement, articles of partnership, etc.

articles of association. See ASSOCIATION, ARTICLES OF.

articles of the peace. The complaint on oath of a person that he feared with reasonable cause that another person would do or cause to be done bodily harm to him or to his wife or child or burn his house; and the court, if satisfied that there were reasonable grounds of fear, was bound to require sureties for the peace. See now the Magistrates' Courts Act 1952, ss.91,92.

articles of war. The rules for the government of troops on active service issued under the prerogative of the Crown, prior to the Mutiny Act 1803. See MILITARY LAW.

articuli super chartas. The statute 1300, 28 Edw.1, confirming Magna Carta and Charta de Foresta.

artificial insemination. The conception of a child by artificial insemination of a wife from her husband, who is incapable of consummating the marriage, does not of itself debar the wife from obtaining a decree of nullity (*Slater* v. *Slater* [1953] P.235). Artificial insemination by donor means by semen obtained from a third person.
    With regard to cattle, see Agriculture (Artificial Insemination) Act 1946.

artificial person. An association which is invested by law with personality, *e.g.* a corporation or company.

asportation. The "carrying away" which was an essential ingredient of the common law offence of larceny. It included any removal of anything from the place which it occupied. The requirement of taking and carrying away does not form part of the definition of theft in the Theft Act 1968, s.1.

asportavit. [Did carry away.]

assault. The unlawful laying of hands on another person, or an attempt or offer to do a corporal hurt to another, coupled with an apparent present ability and intention to do the act. Assault is a crime punishable under the Offences against the Person Act 1861. Common assaults may be dealt with by courts of summary jurisdiction; the more serious forms of assault are indictable offences. Assaults on police constables may be dealt with under the Police Act 1964, s.51. Additional penalties for assault may be imposed under the Firearms Act 1968, Sched. 1, paras. 5, 9.

Assault is also a tort consisting of an act of the defendant which causes to the plaintiff reasonable fear of the infliction of battery (*q.v.*) on him by the defendant.

assay. The testing of the quality of an article, *e.g.* bread or silver, or the accuracy of weights and measures.

assembly, European. An institution of the EEC (*q.v.*) consisting of representatives of the Member States (Treaty of Rome, Art. 137). The Assembly has changed its name (in the English Language) to "European Parliament." It consists of delegates, some elected by universal suffrage and some nominated by the Parliaments of Member States. It has advisory and supervisory powers. Its most important power is its right, by Motion of Censure, to force the resignation of the Commission (*q.v.*) of the EEC (see Art. 144).

assembly, unlawful. See UNLAWFUL ASSEMBLY.

assent, of executor. The title of a legatee or devisee is not complete until the executor has assented to the legacy or devise. An assent to the vesting of a legal estate must be in writing, signed by the personal representative, and must name the person in whose favour it is given, and it operates to vest in that person the legal estate to which it relates (s.36(4) of the Administration of Estates Act 1925). It relates back to the date of the testator's death (unless a contrary intention appears) as, *e.g.* in the case of a specific legacy, but not in the case of residue, which does not come into existence until ascertained.

assent, royal. See ROYAL ASSENT.

assessed taxes. Taxes the amount or rate of which is assessed or fixed in each case, *e.g.* income tax.

assessment. (1) To quantify or fix the amount of damages, or the value of property. See INQUIRY, WRIT OF.

(2) The ascertainment of a person's liability to taxation or rates, etc.; the formal evidence of such ascertainment, *i.e.* the entry in the book of assessments duly signed and sealed; or the amount assessed.

assessor. (1) One who assists the court in trying a scientific or technical question (other than in criminal proceedings by the Crown) but who has no voice in the decision, *e.g.* Brethren of Trinity House may sit as assessors in the Admiralty Court and Court of Appeal, and the bishops in the Judicial Committee of the Privy Council in ecclesiastical appeals (Judicature Act 1925, ss.33(3), 98); (2) a person employed by an insurer to investigate and assess the amount of loss. In absence of the Parties' agreement the use of assessors in cases under the Race Relations Act 1976 is compulsory (see s.67(4)).

assets. Property available for the payment of debts. Real assets are real property, and personal assets are personal property. Legal assets comprise everything which an executor takes by virtue of his office, and with which he would have been charged in an action at law. Equitable assets are such as could only be reached in a court of equity:

From January 1, 1926, the rule is that real and personal estate, whether legal or equitable, of a deceased person, together with property over which a general power of appointment is exercised by will, are assets for payment of debts whether by simple contract or specialty (s.32 of the Administration of Estates Act 1925). See ADMINISTRATION OF ESTATES.

In commerce, assets are divided into fixed or capital assets, and current or circulating assets. The former are intended to be held and used in the business; the latter are intended to be realised in the course of trading.

assets by descent. Land which descended to an heir charged with the debts of his ancestor. The heir was liable for specialty debts in which he was bound, to the extent of the assets descending to him.

assets, marshalling of. See MARSHALLING.

assign. (1) To transfer property to. (2) An assignee (*q.v.*).

assignatus utitur jure auctoris. [An assignee is clothed with the right of his principal.]

assignee. A person to whom an assignment is made. A creditor's assignee was the equivalent of the modern trustee in bankruptcy.

assignment of choses in action. Choses in action were not assignable at common law, but choses in action, both legal and equitable, were assignable in equity. If the chose in action were legal, the assignee could only sue in the name of the assignor, but if equitable be could sue in his own name.

Negotiable instruments became assignable by the law merchant, and policies of insurance by statute. By the Judicature Act 1873, s.25, all legal choses in action were made assignable by law. Now by the Law of Property Act 1925, s.136(1) any absolute assignment by writing under the hand of the assignor (not purporting to be by way of charge only) of any debt or other legal thing in action, of which express notice in writing has been given to the debtor, or trustee is effectual in law (subject to equities having priority over the right of the assignee) to pass and transfer from the date of such notice: (*a*) the legal right to such debt or thing in action; (*b*) all legal and other remedies for the same; and (*c*) the power to give a good discharge for the same without the concurrence of the assignor. Assignments of equitable choses in action are untouched by that Act, and the assignee can still bring action in his own name. See ABSOLUTE ASSIGNMENT; CHOSES IN ACTION; EQUITABLE ASSIGNMENT; NOTICE.

assignment of contract. The general rule is that liabilities under a contract cannot be assigned. But they may be assigned with the consent of the other party to the contract (see NOVATION), and the parties may make them assignable, either expressly or impliedly. The original contracting party normally can procure the performance of the contract by someone else, but if his personal performance is essential under the contract, *e.g.* as in a contract to marry or to sing in opera, the liability to perform the contract cannot be assigned.

Rights or benefits under a contract may be assigned by legal assignment, equitable assignment, or by operation of law.

assignment of dower. Before a widow could take possession of any of her husband's land as tenant in dower, her part had to be assigned to her, either by agreement between her and the heir, or by the sheriff in execution of a judgment obtained by her.

assignor. One who assigns, or transfers.

assisa cadera. [A non-suit.]

assisa vertitur in juratam. [The assize turned into the jurata.] Anciently, the original writ commencing an action summoned an assize, but after the introduction of pleadings the jury were summoned after joinder of issue by writ of *venire facias*, and were known as the *jurata*.

assistance, writ of. Issued under Ord. 46, r. 1, for the purpose of putting a receiver or the sheriff into possession of specific chattels, such as securities or documents. See also POSSESSION, WRIT OF.

assisted persons. Persons receiving legal aid or advice (see LEGAL AID); persons receiving national or public assistance.

assize. [A sitting or session.] (1) A legislative enactment, *e.g.* the Assize of Clarendon, Novel Disseisin. (2) Assize Courts.

An assize passed in the reign of Henry II provided for the trial of questions of seisin and title to land by a recognition or inquiry of 16 men sworn to speak the truth, called the Grand Assize. Hence the proceedings, and the recognitors themselves, became known as the assizes.

Magna Carta provided that assizes of novel disseisin and mort d'ancestor should be taken only in the shire where the land lay, and for this purpose justices were sent into the country once a year; hence they were called justices of assize. Afterwards, the Statute of Nisi Prius (13 Edw. 1, c. 30) enacted that the justices of assize should try to issue in ordinary actions in the counties in which they arose and return the verdict to the court at Westminster.

All courts of assize have been abolished. The civil business of assizes is taken over by the High Court which may sit anywhere in England and Wales. The criminal jurisdiction of assizes is exercised by the Crown Court (*q.v.*) (Courts Act 1971, ss.1, 44, Sched. 8).

Assize of Clarendon (1166). Provided that 12 legal men of every 104 legal men from every township must present to the judges the crimes of which they knew. If the accused failed to clear themselves by ordeal, they were punished. This was virtually the origin of the Grand Jury.

assize of darrein presentment. [Last presentation.] A real action which lay where a man (or his ancestor under whom he claimed) had presented a clerk to a benefice, who was instituted, and afterwards, upon the next vacancy, a stranger presented a clerk, and thereby disturbed the real patron. It was a writ to have an assize to decide a disputed question of possession of an advowson pending a suit for ownership.

assize of mort d'ancestor. A real action which lay to recover land of which a person had been deprived on the death of his ancestor by the abatement or intrusion of a stranger. It extended the remedy introduced by novel disseisin to the case of persons claiming through the disseisee.

Assize of Northampton (1176). A re-enactment and enlargement of the Assize of Clarendon (*q.v.*).

assize of novel disseisin. A real action which lay to recover land which a person had recently disseised (*i.e.* dispossessed).

assize, petty. The assizes of darrein presentment, mort d'ancestor, novel disseisin, and utrum. Abolished by Real Property Limitation Act 1833.

assize rents. Fixed and certain rents.

assize utrum. A real action for trying the question whether land was a lay fee or held in frankalmoign.

associates. Officers of the common law courts, who were appointed by and held office at the pleasure of the Chief Justice or Chief Baron of each court, and whose duties were to keep the records of the court, to attend Nisi Prius sittings, make out the list of cases, conduct the jury ballot, note the judgment, make up the *postea* (or certificate of the result of trial) and deliver the record to the proper party.

Now, associates are officers of the Supreme Court, who superintend the entry of actions, and at the hearing sit below the judge and record the orders of the court, etc.

association, articles of. Regulations for the management and internal arrangement of a company (see the Companies Act 1948, ss.6–10). The First Schedule to that Act, Table A, consists of a specimen set of articles applicable to the case of a company, limited by shares. See also the Companies Act 1967, ss.14(8)(*c*), 130, Sched. 8, Part III.

association, memorandum of. Two or more persons may by subscribing their names to a memorandum of association and otherwise complying with the statutory requirements as to registration, form an incorporated company with or without limited liability (Companies Act 1948, s.1; Companies Act 1980, s.2). The memorandum must state (*a*) the company's name, (*b*) the situation of the registered office, (*c*) its objects. The memorandum of a company limited by shares or guarantee must also state that the liability of its members is limited, and if the company has a share capital, the memorandum must state its amount, and every subscriber must subscribe it with the number of shares he takes (*ibid*. s.2). The memorandum cannot be varied by the company itself (except in special circumstances) but only by application to the court. See also the Companies Act 1967, ss.46(5), 51(1); European Communities Act 1972, s.9(5), (6); Companies Act 1976, s.23; Companies Act 1980, Sched. B.

The memorandum of association delimits the powers of the company. See ULTRA VIRES.

assumpsit. [He promised or undertook.] The common law action which grew out of the action of trespass on the case. It was brought for the breach of an undertaking, a cause of action analogous of deceit. It gradually supplanted the action of debt and came into general use for the enforcement of an agreement not under seal (a simple contract), and for which an action of covenant would not therefore lie.

Actions of assumpsit were divided into *indebitatus* (common or money counts) and special counts. The former were brought to recover debts arising from contract; the latter for damages for breach of contract. They were abolished by the Judicature Acts 1873 to 1875.

assurance. (1) A surrender, conveyance, assignment or appointment under a power, of property. (2) Insurance (*q.v.*).

asylum. Originally a place in which there was safety from pursuit, then a place for the reception and treatment of the insane. By the Mental Treatment Act 1930, s.20, asylums are to be called "mental hospitals."

asylum, right of. (1) The right of vessels of a belligerent power to insist on admission of neutral ports when their vessels are in distress.

(2) The refusal of extradition, or to deliver up to the territorial sovereign, a person who has taken refuge in an embassy or place enjoying diplomatic immunity; popularly, to allow a fugitive from a foreign country to remain here.

ats. (*Ad sectam.*) [At the suit of.]

attachiamenta bonorum. Distress of a man's goods and chattels for debt.

attachment. (1) To attach a person is to arrest him under an order of committal (*q.v.*). It is employed in ordinary cases of disobedience to an order, judgment etc. or other contempt of court committed in the course of a suit or otherwise.

(2) Attachment of debts. See GARNISHEE PROCEEDINGS.

(3) Attachment of earnings. A county court may make an attachment of earnings order to secure payment of a sum due under a judgment or order of the High Court or a county court or payments under an Administration Order (*q.v.*). The order directs an employer to deduct specified sums from the debtor's earnings and pay them to the collecting officer of the county court. The order is

made on information which the debtor must supply regarding his income and liabilities and the employer may be asked to supply information as to earnings. The court must fix a protected earnings rate, *i.e.* the amount of earnings below which no deduction may be made. See Attachment of Earnings Act 1971, County Court, Ord. 27.

(4) See also MAREVA INJUNCTION.

attainder. That extinction of civil rights and capacities which formerly took place when judgment of death or outlawry was recorded against a person who had committed treason or felony. It involved the forfeiture and escheat of the land and goods belonging to the criminal, and the corruption of his blood, *i.e.* he became incapable of holding or inheriting land, or of transmitting a title by descent. It also produced by Acts of Parliament known as Bills of Attainder. Abolished by the Forefeiture Act 1870.

attaint. A person under attainder.

attaint, writ of. A summons to a grand jury of 24, to inquire whether a petty jury of 12 had given a false verdict. If so, the petty jury lost all civil rights. Abolished in 1825.

attempt. At Common Law.

An act done with intent to commit a crime and forming part of a series of acts which would constitute its actual commission if it were not interrupted. Attempt is now a statutory offence (see Criminal Attempts Act 1981).

If, with intent to commit an offence to which this section applies, a person does an act which is more than merely preparatory to the commission of an offence, he is guilty of attempting to commit the offence (s.1(1)). A person may be guilty of attempting to commit an offence to which this section applies even though the facts are such that the commission of the offence is impossible (s.1(2)).

In any case where

(*a*) apart from this subsection a person's intention would not be regarded as having amounted to an intent to commit an offence; but (*b*) if the facts of the case had been as he believed them to be, his intention would be so regarded, then, for the purpose of subsection (1) above, he shall be regarded as having had an intention to commit that offence (s.1(3)). Subject to certain limited exceptions (*e.g.* conspiracy, aiding and abetting) this section applies to any offence which, if it were completed, would be triable in England and Wales as an indictable offence (s.1(4)).

A person charged with attempt to commit an offence may be found guilty as charged, notwithstanding that he is shown to be guilty of the completed offence (Criminal Law Act 1967, s.6(3), (4)). A prison sentence on indictment is not to exceed the sentence for the completed offence (Powers of Criminal Courts Act 1973, s.18(2)). The same rule applies on summary conviction.

attendance allowance. Non-contributory benefit payable to those so disabled that they require constant attendance (Social Security Act 1975).

attendance centres. Courts of summary jurisdiction have powers to order offenders aged over 16 but under 21 to attend at attendance centres outside working or school hours for up to three hours at a time and for a total of 12–24 hours (Criminal Justice Act 1948, s.19 as amended).

attendant term. Where a long term of years created over a freehold for the purpose which later had become satisfied, was vested in trustees for the protection of the owner of the freehold it was said to be kept on foot "in trust to attend the inheritance." See SATISFIED TERM.

attest. To witness any act or event, such as, *e.g.* the signature or execution of a document, *e.g.* a will (*q.v.*).

attestation clause. The statement in a deed or will, etc., that it has been duly executed in the presence of witnesses.

attested copy. A copy of a document which is certified correct by a person who has examined it.

attorn. See ATTORNMENT.

attorney. (1) A person appointed by another to act in his place or represent him (see POWER OF ATTORNEY). (2) Formerly persons admitted to practise in the superior courts of common law; they represented suitors who did not appear in person. Since the Judicature Act 1873, they are entitled "Solicitors of the Supreme Court."

Attorney-General. The principal law officer of the Crown, and the head of the Bar. He is appointed by letters patent and holds at the pleasure of the Crown. He is usually a member of the House of Commons, but not normally of the Cabinet, and changes with the Ministry.

Civil proceedings by or against the Crown may be instituted by or against the Attorney-General in lieu of the appropriate Government Department. After proceedings have been instituted he may be substituted for the authorised Government Department, or *vice versa* (Crown Proceedings Act 1947, s.17). See RELATOR.

attornment. The agreement by the tenant of land to hold his land from the transferee of the owner of the fee, or reversion, which was formerly necessary to the validity of the grant of the reversion. He was said to attorn tenant to the new reversioner. By s.151 of the Law of Property Act 1925, the conveyance of a reversion is valid without attornment, and attornment without the lessor's consent is void.

auction, sales by. The Sale of Land by Auction Act 1867 makes it unlawful, where a sale is stated to be without reserve, for the vendor to employ a person to bid; but the vendor may, in the particulars or conditions of sale, reserve the right to bid and employ a person ("puffer") to bid accordingly. The Sale of Goods Act 1893, s.58 contains similar provisions. Agreements to abstain from bidding ("knock-out" agreements) are illegal, and give the vendor the right to treat the sale as fraudulent (Auctions (Bidding Agreements) Acts 1927 and 1969). In a "Dutch auction" the property is put up at an excessive price and is offered at deceasing prices until someone closes. See also MOCK AUCTIONS.

auctioneer. One who sells or offers for sale goods or land at any sale where persons become purchasers by competition, being the highest bidders. When a bid is accepted and the hammer falls, the contract comes into existence (see *Bristol Car Auctions* v. *Wright* [1972] 1 W.L.R. 1519), and the auctioneer then becomes the agent of both parties for the purpose of signing a memorandum to satisfy the Law of Property Act 1925, s.40. If the customer for whom the auctioneer sells goods has no title, the auctioneer is liable in tort for their value to the true owner.

auctoritas. [Roman law.] The authorisation of a tutor, the legal capacity in virtue of which the tutor completed the legal capacity of his pupil.

audi alteram partem. [Hear the other side.] That no one shall be condemned unheard is one of the principles of natural justice (*q.v.*).

audience, right of. The right to appear and conduct proceedings in court. Barristers have a right of audience in all judicial proceedings and an exclusive right in the High Court (save where solicitors have a concurrent right), Court of Appeal and House of Lords. Solicitors have right of audience in Magistrates courts, County courts, most Tribunals, some limited proceedings in the Crown court and in Bankruptcy matters in the High Court and Divisional Court.

audita querela. [Complaint having been heard.] A writ given in order to afford a remedy to the defendant in an action where matter of defence (such as a release) had arisen since the judgment, and on which the defendant applied to the court. The present practice is to apply for a stay of execution or other relief (Judicature Act 1925, s.41; Ord. 47, r. 1).

auditors. Originally officers of the Exchequer; examiners of accounts. Every company must appoint an auditor or auditors at each annual general meeting; in default, the Department of Trade appoints. The auditor must be a member of a recognised body of accountants. He must ascertain and state the true financial position of the company by an examination of the books. The auditor's report on the balance sheet and accounts has to be annexed to the balance sheet. (See Companies Act 1948, ss.147 *et seq.*)

The judge of the Chancery Court of York is styled Auditor.

aula regis. [The Hall of the King.] After the Conquest this was the King's Court or Curia Regis. From it all the courts of justice have emanated; likewise the High Court of Parliament and the Privy Council.

aulnager or **alnager.** An officer, first appointed in the reign of Edward III, whose duty it was to measure all woollen cloth made for sale in order to ascertain the duty payable to the Crown.

authority. (1) Delegated power; a right or rights invested in a person or body. An authority is a body charged with the power and duty of exercising prescribed functions, *e.g.* a local planning authority. A person vested with authority is usually termed an agent, and the person for whom he acts, the principal. A bare authority is an authority which exists only for the benefit of the principal, which the agent must execute in accordance with his directions. An authority coupled with an interest is where the person vested with the authority has a right to exercise it, partly or wholly, for his own benefit. A mere authority is revocable by the grantor at any time; one coupled with an interest is not. See AGENT.

(2) A decided case, judgment, textbook of repute or statutory enactment cited as an exposition or statement of the law. See PRECEDENT.

automatism. For the defence of automatism see *e.g. Bratty* v. *Att.-Gen. of Northern Ireland* [1963] A.C. 386; *Watmore* v. *Jenkins* [1962] 2 Q.B. 572 at p. 586.

autre droit, in. [In right of another.] *e.g.* an executor holds the deceased's property in right of the persons entitled to his estate.

autre vie. [The life of another.] See TENANT PUR AUTRE VIE.

autrefois acquit. [Formerly acquitted.] A special plea in bar to a criminal prosecution that the prisoner has been already tried for the same offence before a court of competent jurisdiction and has been acquitted. The plea can only succeed where the accused was in jeopardy on the first proceedings; that is, the merits of the prosecution's case have been gone into, so that the decision of the court was that the evidence was insufficient to support the prosecution. See also the Criminal Law Act 1967, s.6(5).

autrefois attaint. [Formerly attainted.] A plea in bar to a prosecution. See ATTAINDER.

autrefois convict. [Formerly convicted.] A special plea in bar to a criminal prosecution by which the prisoner alleges that he has been already tried and convicted for the same offence before a court of competent jurisdiction. For a full examination of the doctrine see *Connelly* v. *D.P.P.* [1964] A.C. 1254.

auxiliary jurisdiction of equity. Before the Judicature Act 1873, the jurisdiction of equity by which aid was lent to the plaintiff in a common law action, as by compelling discovery of documents.

auxilium. An aid. See AIDS.

aver. To allege, in pleading. See AVERMENT.

average. (1) The apportionment of loss incurred in mercantile transactions, such as contracts of affreightment or insurance, between the person suffering the loss and other persons concerned or interested; the contribution payable by such others to the person so suffering the loss (sometimes the term is applied to the loss or damage itself).

General average is any loss or damage voluntarily incurred for the general safety of the ship and cargo; *e.g.* where goods are thrown overboard in a storm for the purpose of saving the ship and the rest of the cargo. The several persons interested in the ship, freight and cargo must contribute rateably to indemnify the person whose goods have been sacrificed against all but his proportion of the general loss.

Particular average is loss or damage to the ship or cargo caused by a peril insured against (*e.g.* damage to goods due to sea-water), which loss falls on the owner of the ship or cargo concerned.

(2) Some petty charges, such as towage, beaconage, etc., which the owner or consignee of goods shipped on board a vessel is bound to reimburse the master or shipowner.

(3) A service of working with his beasts, which a tenant owed his lord.

averia. Cattle.

averium. Formerly, the best beast due as a heriot (*q.v.*).

averment. An allegation, in pleading.

avoid. To make void. A person is said to avoid a contract when he repudiates it and sets up, as a defence in a legal proceeding taken to enforce it, some defect which prevents it from being enforceable.

avoidance. Setting aside or avoiding or vacating. A bond is said to be conditioned for avoidance when it contains a condition providing that it shall be void on a certain event.

avow. To admit or confess.

avowtry. Adultery.

avulsion. The cutting off of land from the property to which it belongs, as may happen if a river changes its course. The ownership of the land remains unchanged. Compare ALLUVIO.

award. The finding or decision of an arbitrator. See ARBITRATION.

away-going crop. See WAY-GOING CROP.

B

back bond. A bond of indemnity given to a surety.

back-freight. Freight for the carriage of goods returned undischarged from the port to which consigned.

backing a warrant. Formerly the indorsement by a magistrate of a warrant issued by a magistrate of another district or jurisdiction, in order that it might be executed within the jurisdiction of the indorser. Now however, the Criminal Law Act 1977, s.38 (brought into operation on May 12, 1980) provides for the execution of unbacked warrants throughout the United Kingdom.

backwardation. A percentage paid by a seller of stock, deliverable upon a Stock Exchange account day, for the privilege of delaying delivery until the next account day. Compare CONTANGO.

bad. Wrong in law, ineffectual, inoperative, or void.

bail. An accused person is admitted to bail when he is released from the custody of officers of the Law on his giving security or accepting certain specified conditions. The grant of bail in criminal proceedings is governed by the Bail Act 1976. The Act establishes a general presumption in favour of bail (s.4). Bail may only be witheld in prescribed circumstances, *e.g.* that there are substantial grounds for believing that the defendant, if released, would fail to surrender to custody or commit an offence while on bail or interfere with witnesses (Sched.1). The person granted bail cannot be required to give any recognizance (s.3) but failure to surrender to custody is now a separate offence (s.6(2)). A person who absconds while on bail or fails to comply with any conditions imposed becomes liable to arrest (s.7). To agree to indemnify sureties constitutes an offence (s.9.). Bail may be granted by the police or by a magistrate. If bail is witheld by magistrates an accused person may apply to the Crown Court or High Court (s.5(6)) but the Lord Chancellor has no jurisdiction to entertain an application for bail (*R.* v. *Kray* [1965] Ch. 736). A person charged with treason may only be admitted to bail on the certificate of a secretary of state or by order of a High Court Judge (Magistrates Courts Act 1952, s.8).

In the event of an application for bail being renewed the duty of justices is only to hear any fresh matters on behalf of the defendants; matters which have been considered in earlier applications need not be re-examined (*R.* v. *Nottingham Justices, ex p. Davies* [1981] Q.B. 38).

The Crown Court's powers to grant bail are set out in the Supreme Court Act 1981, s.81.

As to whether bail should be granted in murder cases see *R.* v. *Vernege* [1982] 1 All E.R. 403 (note).

bail court. An auxiliary court of King's Bench, at Westminster, wherein points connected more particularly with pleading and practice were argued and determined; also known as the Practice Court.

bail-bond. A bond with sureties entered into by a defendant to a sheriff, on arrest upon a writ of *capias ad respondendum,* conditioned for the defendant's appearance within the required period; upon which he was entitled to discharge. See ARREST.

bailee. A person to whom the possession of goods is entrusted by the owner but not with the intention of transferring the ownership.

Any person is a bailee, who, otherwise than as an employee, either receives possession of a thing for another, or holds possession of a thing for another, upon an undertaking with that other, to keep and return or deliver to him the specific thing according to his directions.

A bailee has a special property or qualified ownership in the goods bailed, and may recover from a person who wrongly injures the goods the amount of the injury as damages, which (to the extent they exceed his own interest) are held by the bailee on account of the bailor.

The bailment is determined, and the right to possess the goods reverts to the bailor, if the bailee does an act entirely inconsistent with the terms of the bailment. Loss caused by an act not authorised by the terms of the bailment, though not otherwise negligent, will fall on the bailee, unless inevitable in any case. A bailee is bound to take care of the goods bailed and is liable for negligence, in general, as follows:

(1) Where the bailment is entirely for the benefit of the bailor, *e.g.* a gratuitous deposit, the bailee is only liable for gross negligence, *i.e.* culpable default, as in failing to take care to avoid a foreseen risk.

(2) Where the bailment is solely for the benefit of the bailee, *e.g.* a gratuitous loan of chattels, the bailee is liable even for slight negligence, *i.e.* the omission of the care of a vigilant person takes of his own goods.

(3) Where the bailment is for the common benefit of both bailor and bailee, *e.g.* pawn, or warehousing for hire, the bailee is bound to use ordinary care, and is liable for ordinary negligence, *i.e.* failure to take the care which an ordinary prudent man takes of his own goods.

A bailee whose original possession was innocent, could not be convicted of larceny at common law unless and until he committed a trespass by breaking bulk. Now, under the Theft Act 1968, a person is guilty of theft if he dishonestly appropriates property belonging to another with the intention of permanently depriving the other of it. Any assumption by a person of the rights of an owner amounts to appropriation (ss. 1, 3 (1)). See BAILMENTS.

bailiff. Formerly, an officer entrusted with the local administration of justice. Now a sheriff's officer or person employed by the sheriff to serve writs and make arrests and executions. The sheriff being responsible for their acts, his bailiffs are annually bound to him in a bond with sureties for the due execution of their office, and thence are called bound bailiffs (or popularly "bum-bailiffs").

Bailiffs of county courts are appointed by the Lord Chancellor. The office of High Bailiff of a county court is extinct.

bailiwick. The area under the jurisdiction of a bailiff or sheriff.

bailments. A delivery of goods on a condition, expressed or implied, that they shall be restored by the bailee to the bailor, or according to his directions, as soon as the purpose for which they are bailed shall be answered. Bailments were divided into six classes by Holt C.J. in his celebrated judgment in *Coggs* v. *Bernard* (1703) 2 Ld.Raym. 909; 1 Sm.L.C. 175, substantially as follows:

(1) *Depositum;* delivery of goods by one man to another to keep for the use of the bailor, gratuitously.

(2) *Commodatum;* a gratuitous loan of goods or chattels.

(3) *Locatio rei;* a loan of goods to the bailee to be used by him for hire.

(4) *Vadium, Pawn or Pledge;* delivery of goods or chattels to another as security for money borrowed of him by the bailor.

(5) *Locatio operis, faciendi;* delivering of goods or chattels to be carried, or for something to be done to them for reward.

(6) *Mandatum;* delivery of goods or chattels to be carried or for something to be done to them, gratis. See BAILEE; BAILOR.

bailor. One who entrusts goods to a bailee (*q.v.*). The bailor has the general property in, or general ownership of, the goods bailed.

bail-piece. Formerly, the undertaking of sureties, drawn up on parchment, to go bail.

balance order. The order enforcing payment of calls in the winding up, whether voluntary or compulsory, of a company. It is obtained on summons in chambers by the liquidator.

ballot. Any system of secret voting; introduced for the purpose of parliamentary elections by the Ballot Act 1872.

banc, or banco, sitting in. Sittings which, before the Judicature Acts came into force, were held at Westminster by the judges of the King's or Queen's Bench, the Common Pleas, and the Exchequer for the purpose of determining questions of law. These sittings were held not only during term but on certain appointed days after term. When sitting *in banc*, the judges dealt only with questions of law; when sitting at Nisi Prius or on circuit, they dealt only with questions of fact. Four judges usually sat together *in banc*, while at Nisi Prius or on circuit judges sat singly.

banishment. The compulsory quitting and forsaking of the realm; it might arise by abjuration (*q.v.*) or by authority of Parliament.

bank holidays. By the Banking and Financial Dealings Act 1971, s.1, Sched. 1, the bank holidays in England and Wales are Easter Monday, the last Monday in May, the last Monday in August, December 26, if it be not a Sunday, December 27 in a year in which December 25 or 26 is a Sunday and any other day appointed by Proclamation. January 1, has been so proclaimed. The popular meanings of bank holidays is a public holiday (*O'Neill* v. *George* (1969) 67 L.G.R. 358).

bank note. A promissory note, made by a banker, payable on demand, and intended to be used as money. By the Currency and Bank Notes Act 1954, s.1, the Bank of England was authorised to issue bank notes of such denominations as the Treasury might approve.

bank rate. See MINIMUM LENDING RATE.

banker. A person who receives the money of his customers on deposit, and pays it out again in a manner agreed upon. It includes a body of persons, whether incorporated or not, who carry on the business of banking (Bills of Exchange Act 1882, s.2). The number of persons in a banking partnership is restricted to 20 (Companies Act 1948, s.429; Companies Act 1967, s.119).

The relation between banker and customer is that of debtor and creditor (with a superadded obligation arising out of the custom of bankers to honour the drafts of customers), not of trustee and *cestui que trust* or of principal and agent.

bankers' books. The Bankers' Books Evidence Act 1879 makes a copy of any entry in a banker's book prima facie evidence of the contents of the entry and of the matters recorded therein, on the copy being proved to be correct (see Ord. 38, r. 13, notes).

The police may be granted permission to inspect an accused person's bank accounts (*Williams* v. *Summerfield* [1972] 2 Q.B. 513).

banker's drafts. A banker's draft is a draft payable on demand drawn by a banker on himself whether payable at the head office or some other office of his bank. In protection of a banker handling such drafts see the Cheques Act 1957, s.4. Such drafts are not bills of exchange or cheques but may be effectively crossed: Bills of Exchange Act (1882) Amendment Act 1932. See also Bankers Act 1979, s.47.

bankrupt. A debtor whose estate is vested in a trustee for division amongst his creditors, pursuant to an order of the court adjudicating him bankrupt.

bankruptcy. Proceedings in the High Court (or certain county courts) for the distribution of the property of an insolvent person among his creditors, and to relieve him of the unpaid balance of his liabilities. Only traders could be made bankrupt until the Bankruptcy Act 1861, s.69 made all debtors subject to bankruptcy proceedings. Married women could be adjudicated bankrupt only when trading, whether separately from their husbands or not (Bankruptcy Act 1914, s.125(1)). But by the Law Reform (Married Women and Tortfeasors) Act 1935, s.1, a married woman is subject to bankruptcy proceedings as if she were a feme sole.

Bankruptcy proceedings commence with the commission of an act of bankruptcy (*q.v.*), followed by a petition to the court for a receiving order for the protection of the estate. The property of the debtor then vests in an official receiver. A meeting of the creditors is held, and the debtor must submit a statement of affairs to the official receiver. The debtor is publicly examined before the Registrar, and if no composition or scheme of arrangement is approved, he is adjudged bankrupt, and his property vests in a trustee and becomes divisible among his creditors. Bankruptcy is annulled by an order of discharge (see the Bankruptcy Act 1914, s.26 and the Bankruptcy (Amendment) Act 1926). In the High Court, bankruptcy business is assigned to the Chancery Division. By the Insolvency Act 1976 the court may dispense with the public examination of a debtor (s.6) and may direct the automatic discharge of a debtor after five years (s.7). Where a person is convicted of an offence before the Crown Court and the loss or damage attributable to that offence (other than for personal injury) exceeds £15,000, the court may make a criminal bankruptcy order against him (but not if it makes a compensation order against him (Powers of Criminal Courts Act 1973, ss. 39–41)). See also TRUSTEE IN BANKRUPTCY.

bankruptcy notice. The notice served upon a debtor by a person who has obtained against him in any court a final judgment or order for an amount of £200 or more which judgment or order has not been stayed, and non-compliance with which within ten days of service constitutes an act of bankruptcy (*q.v.*) (see Bankruptcy Act 1914, s.1(1), (9) and s.2 as amended by Insolvency Act 1976, s.4.).

Once an act of bankruptcy has occurred by operation of law (*e.g.* the service of the bankruptcy notice) the court has no jurisdiction to extend beyond the prescribed ten days the time for filing an affidavit applying for leave to set aside a bankruptcy notice (*Re the Debtor* v. *Slater Walker Ltd.* [1981] 2 All E.R. 987).

banns of marriage. A proclamation in church of an intended marriage between the persons named. A marriage is invalid if there is no due publication of banns as required by the Marriage Act 1949, ss. 5–14, amended by the Pastoral Measure 1968, s.29(2), Sched. 3, para. 14.

bar. A partition across a court of justice. Only Queen's Counsel, solicitors (as officers of the court) and parties are allowed within the bar.

The Bar means the professional body of barristers.

In the Houses of Lords and Commons the bar forms the boundary of the House, and therefore all persons who have to address the House appear at the bar for that purpose.

To bar a right is to destroy or end it, *e.g.* bar an entail, or a debt under the Statutes of Limitation.

Bar Council. See SENATE OF THE INNS OF COURT AND THE BAR.

bare licensee. A mere licensee; a person who for his own purposes is permitted by the occupier of property to go or be upon that property, so as not to be a trespasser.

The occupier was only bound to warn the bare licensee of concealed dangers of which the occupier was aware, but by the Occupiers' Liability Act 1957 the occupier of premises owes the bare licensee the common duty of care. See also the Defective Premises Act 1972, ss. 4, 6(4).

bare trustee. One who merely holds property on trust with no interest in or duty as to the trust property, except to convey it when required according to the directions of the beneficial owner.

bargain and sale. A contract for the sale of any estate or interest in land, or of chattels, followed by payment of the agreed price, commonly applied only to land. The Court of Chancery held that as soon as a bargain and sale of land had been completed, the vendor held the land to the use or for the benefit of the purchaser. The Statute of Uses 1536 executed the use in favour of the purchaser, that is to say, gave him the same estate or interest in the land as the vendor had before the bargain and sale. The effect of this was that land might be conveyed secretly.

To prevent that result the Statute of Enrolments 1536 enacted that no bargain and sale of any freehold interest in lands should be effectual unless it were made by deed enrolled within six months. It was superseded by the lease and release (*q.v.*), and abolished by the Law of Property Act 1925, s.51.

barmote courts. Courts which administer the laws and customs relating to lead mining in the districts of Derbyshire.

baron. [Man.] "Baron and feme" meant husband and wife.

Before the Judicature Acts, judges of the Court of Exchequer were called barons and the chief judge of that court was styled the Lord Chief Baron of the Exchequer. See BARONY.

baronetcy. An hereditary dignity founded in 1611, taking precedence of knighthoods.

baronia. A land-holding, the tenant of which was a baron.

barony. The rank of a baron, the lowest rank in the peerage. A writ of summons to Parliament, followed by an actual sitting therein, formerly created a barony.

They are now created by letters patent. Baronies created by writ descend to the heirs of the original baron, and are consequently occasionally held by females. Baronies by letters patent descend in accordance with the patent.

barrator. One who commits barratry.

barratry. (1) The common law misdemeanour of habitually exciting or maintaining suits or quarrels. It was abolished by the Criminal Law Act 1967, s.13.

(2) Every wrongful act wilfully committed by the master or crew of a ship to the prejudice of the owner or charterer without his knowledge or connivance, *e.g.* sinking the ship or stealing the cargo.

Barratry is one of the perils of the sea generally insured against in policies of marine insurance, and a shipowner is commonly exempt under the bill of lading from liability in respect of any act of barratry (Marine Insurance Act 1906, Sched. 1).

barrister. A member of one of the four Inns of Court who has been called to the Bar by his Inn. Barristers have the exclusive right of audience in the High Court and superior courts. A barrister's professional conduct is under the control of the Senate of the Inns of Court and the Bar (*q.v.*) *Re S.* (*A barrister*) [1970] 1 Q.B. 160). A barrister intending to practise must spend 12 months as a pupil. His fees are an *honorarium,* and no action lies to recover them, nor is he liable for negligence in the performance of his professional duties (*Rondel* v. *Worsley* [1969] 1 A.C. 191). But a barrister's immunity from suit extends only to work which is so intimately connected with the conduct of the case in court that it could properly be said to be a preliminary decision on the course to be pursued at the hearing in court (*Saif Ali* v. *Sydney Mitchell & Co.* (*P. Third Party*) [1980] A.C. 198, H.L.).

base courts. Inferior courts, not of record, *e.g.* the Court Baron.

base fee. An estate which has some qualification, and which must cease or be determined whenever such qualification is at an end: a fee descendible to the heirs in general upon which subsists a remainder or reversion in fee simple, *e.g.* the estate of a tenant in tail in remainder who executed and enrolled a disentailing deed, but who did not get the consent of the tenant for life in possession (the protector of the settlement). Since 1925 base fees are equitable interests, and the disentailing deed need not be enrolled (Law of Property Act 1925, s.130).

base tenure. A tenure under which land was held by base services, *e.g.* villein tenure, the former equivalent of copyhold tenure.

bastard. A child born out of wedlock: an illegitimate child. At common law a bastard has no parents and cannot take property as an heir-at-law or next-of-kin through them. But he can found a family of his own. He can leave real property by will (Law of Property Act 1925, s.178). Upon the making of an affiliation order, the putative father becomes liable to contribute to the support of his bastard child, of which normally the mother has the custody with the liability to maintain the child. See AFFILIATION ORDER, LEGITIMACY.

bastard eigné. An elder son born before marriage.

bastardise. Formerly if the court made a decree of nullity of marriage, the effect was to make illegitimate any children of the marriage because the marriage was null and void *ab initio.* But by the Legitimacy Act 1959, s.2, the child of a void marriage is treated as the legitimate child of his parents if at all material times both or either of them reasonably believed that the marriage was valid.

bastardy order. An affiliation order (*q.v.*).

battery. The actual striking of another person or touching him in a rude, angry, revengeful or insolent manner. A common assault, whether or not including a battery, is a misdemeanour (see s.47 of the Offences against the Person Act 1861).

battle, trial by. The judicial combat: a method of trying the guilt of an accused person or a dispute as to the title to land, or a debt, by setting the two opposing parties to fight each other, the loser being punished, or failing in his claim, as the case might be. The combatants were each armed with a leather shield and a cudgel, and the fight lasted until the stars came out, or one of them gave in.

It was unknown to Anglo-Saxon law and was introduced from Normandy. Clerks, infants, and those over 60 years of age might employ champions, which right was later extended to all litigants in civil actions. It was abolished in 1819 by statute 59 Geo. 3, c. 46, after its invocation in the murder case of *Ashford* v. *Thornton* (1818) 1 B. & Ald. 405. (The challenge was there declined.)

bawdy house. A brothel.

beadle. A common law parish officer chosen by, and holding office at the pleasure of, the vestry.

bear. One who sells stocks or shares "short" on the Stock Exchange, *i.e.* without possessing what he sells, but intending to buy in later when the price has fallen and make a profit of the difference. See BULL.

bearer. The person in possession of a bill of exchange or promissory note payable to bearer (Bills of Exchange Act 1882, s.2). Payment of a bearer security may be claimed by anyone who presents it.

Bearer bonds pass by delivery and are negotiable securities. Coupons are annexed for detaching for the purpose of claiming interest or dividends. Bearer instruments are defined for stamp duty purposes by the Finance Act 1963, ss. 59–61.

Bedford Level. A district in the Eastern Counties, formerly known as the Great Level of the Fens, the draining of which was begun in 1634 by Francis, Earl of Bedford. A register was instituted for deeds relating to lands comprised in the Level. It was closed in 1920.

begin, right to. The right of the party to a suit on whom the main burden of proof rests to open his case first; which in criminal proceedings is always the prosecution.

behaviour. See UNREASONABLE BEHAVIOUR.

bench. The judges of a court of law.

bench warrant. A warrant issued by a court of record for the immediate arrest of a person against whom an indictment for treason or misdemeanour has been found. In cases where a bench warrant could issue it is now usual to issue an order for committal under Ord. 52. Power to compel appearance before a Crown Court is contained in the Courts Act 1971, s.13 as amended by the Bail Act 1976.

Benchers, or Masters of the Bench. The governing body of each of the four Inns of Court. Benchers have complete control of the property of their Inn. Subject only to an appeal to the Lord Chancellor and the judges of the High Court, sitting as a domestic tribunal and not as a court of justice, the Benchers have an absolute discretion as to the admission of students, as to calls to the Bar, as to disbarring, and also as to disbenching a member of their own bench. See further, SENATE OF THE INNS OF COURT AND THE BAR.

benefice. An ecclesiastical living, *i.e.* rectories, vicarages or perpetual curacies. As to the creation, alteration or dissolution of benefices, see the Pastoral Measure 1968 and the Incumbents (Vacation of Benefice) Measure 1977.

beneficial interest. The interest of a beneficial owner or beneficiary, as contrasted with the estate or intererst of a nominal or legal owner, *e.g.* a trustee.

beneficial owner. The person who enjoys or who is entitled to the benefit of property. In a conveyance for valuable consideration (other than a mortgage) by a person who conveys and is expressed to convey as beneficial owner there are

47

implied covenants (1) for right to convey; (2) for quiet enjoyment; (3) for freedom from incumbrances; (4) for further assurance (Law of Property Act 1925, s.76, Sched. 2).

beneficiaries. Persons for whose benefit property is held by trustees, executors, etc.; *cestuis que trustent.*

beneficium. [Roman law.] A privilege or benefit: (1) *competentiae:* the privilege of having the *condemnatio* limited to the extent of a person's means so that he should not be reduced to want; (2) *inventarii:* the full inventory made by the heir which, under Justinian, released him from all personal liability beyond the value of the estate; (3) *separationis:* the advantage of having a clear separation made between the property of testator and of heir.

benefit of clergy. Exemption of the persons of clergymen from criminal process. An accused clerk was handed over by the secular court to the bishop to be tried in the ecclesiastical courts. The privilege was extended to all able to read, but mere laymen could have the benefit only once, and were branded on the thumb to show they had had it. Many statutes were passed making felonies punishable without benefit of clergy. Women originally could not claim the benefit, but it was later extended to them. Benefit of clergy could not be claimed in treason nor in other cases provided for by particular statutes. It was abolished in 1827 by statute 7 & 8 Geo. 4, c. 28. See NECK VERSE.

benevolences. An early mode of raising money for the Crown. They purported to be voluntary loans, but were in fact forced contributions not intended to be repaid. They were afterwards levied as an anticipation of the lawful revenue. Prohibited by the Bill of Rights 1628.

benevolent society. A society formed for benevolent or charitable purposes and subject to the Friendly Societies Acts.

benignae faciendae sunt interpretationes et verba intentioni debent inservire. [Liberal interpretation should be the rule, and the words should be made to carry out the intention.]

bequeath. To give personal property by will, *e.g.* a legacy.

bequest. A gift of personal property by will. A residuary bequest is a gift of the residue of the testator's personal estate. A specific bequest is a bequest of property of a certain kind, *e.g.* a watch.

Berne Convention 1886. An international convention for the protection of literary and artistic copyright. It was modified at Berlin in 1908. The Copyright Act was passed in 1911 to give effect to the Convention in English law.

besaiel. (A great-grandfather.) A real action which lay for the recovery of lands of which the heir's great-grandfather had been seised at his death and abated by a stranger.

bestiality. The abominable crime of buggery committed with an animal, *i.e.* penetration *per anum* (Sexual Offences Act 1956, s.12).

betterment. Increasing the value of property by public improvements effected in its vicinity, and for which the owners may be required to contribute towards the cost.

betting. Risking one's money against another's on the result of a sporting or other event, the outcome of which is uncertain. A betting transaction is a bet with a bookmaker (Betting, Gaming and Lotteries Act 1963, s.55(1)). That Act, which is a consolidating Act, restricts the use of premises for betting transactions (s.1); bookmaking except under a bookmaker's permit (s.2); pool betting (s.4); betting on tracks (s.5); betting on dog racecourses (s.7). Agents of bookmakers, etc., must be authorised and registered (s.3). Street betting is prohibited (s.8). Special provisions apply to betting with young persons (ss. 21, 22). For minor amendments of the Act of 1963, see the Betting, Gaming and Lotteries (Amendment) Acts 1971 and 1980.

Pool betting is governed by the Act of 1963, ss. 1, 2, 4, 5, 9, 14, 16; the Act of 1971, s.1, the Betting and Gaming Duties Act 1972, the Finance (No. 2) Act 1975, s.2, and the Lotteries Act 1975, Sched. 3, para. 3. See LOTTERY.

Pool competitions may be promoted by charities and sporting clubs under the Pool Competitions Act 1971 (overruling *Singette* v. *Martin* [1971] A.C. 407).

betting house. Keeping a house, room, etc., used for the purpose of betting was an offence under the Betting Act 1853. See BETTING OFFICE.

betting levy. The Betting Levy Act 1961, replaced by the Betting Gaming and Lotteries Act 1963, established the Horserace Betting Levy Board (in place of the Racecourse Betting Control Board), and also the Horserace Totalisator Board, and provided for a levy on bookmakers. See also the Horserace Betting Levy Act 1969 and the Horserace Totalisator and Betting Levy Boards Act 1972.

betting office. Licensed betting offices may be established to which persons may resort for the purpose of betting with the holder of a betting office licence, who must be the holder of a bookmaker's permit, etc., or an accredited agent. Such agent must himself hold a betting agency permit before being granted a betting office licence (Betting, Gaming and Lotteries Act 1963, ss.9, 10). See also GAMING.

bid. An offer to buy at a given price a thing which is being sold by auction.

bigamy. The offence committed by any person who, being married, and while the marriage subsists, marries any other person during the life of the former wife or husband, whether the second marriage takes place in England or elsewhere. But it is a good defence that the former wife or husband has been absent for seven years at the date of such marriage, and has not been known to be living during that time (Offences against the Person Act 1861, s.57). Even if the seven years have not elapsed, bona fide belief of death on reasonable grounds is a good defence (*R.* v. *Tolson* (1889) 23 Q.B.D. 168). An honest belief on reasonable grounds of the invalidity of a previous marriage or of the death of the spouse (*R.* v. *King* [1964] 1 Q.B. 285) or that a decree absolute dissolved a previous marriage (*R.* v. *Gould* [1968] 2 Q.B. 65) is a defence.

bill. A letter or writing. (1) A parliamentary measure which, on receiving the Royal Assent, becomes an Act of Parliament; (2) a document by which proceedings were formerly commenced, *e.g.* a Bill in Chancery.

bill of attainder. Formerly a bill formulating an accusation against a peer, or other high personage, in a matter of public importance, declaring him to be attainted and his property forfeited.

bill of costs. A statement or account delivered to his client by a solicitor setting out in detail the work done on behalf of the client, and showing the amount charged for each item, including disbursements. The bill of costs to be enforceable must be signed by the solicitor, or one of the partners in a firm of solicitors, and must be delivered to the party to be charged, and no action to recover the costs can be brought until one month thereafter, save in cases of imminent bankruptcy, etc., of the client. See COSTS.

bill of entry. The account deposited at the Custom House giving particulars of goods imported or exported. See Customs and Excise Management Act 1979, ss. 37, 52, 53.

bill of exceptions. A statement of the objections of a party to a suit to the decisions of the judge on matters of law, which was then argued before a court of error. Abolished by the Common Law Procedure Act 1852, s.148. Now replaced by motion for a new trial.

bill of exchange. A form of negotiable instrument. "An unconditional order in writing, addressed by one person to another, signed by the person giving it, requiring the person to whom it is addressed to pay on demand, or at a fixed or determinable future time, a sum certain in money, to, or to the order of, a specified person, or to bearer" (Bills of Exchange Act 1882, s.3).

A bill is given by the drawer, and addressed to the drawee, who becomes the acceptor by writing his name across the face of the bill. The bill is payable to the payee, who must be named or indicated with reasonable certainty (*ibid.* s.7(1)). If the payee is a fictitious or non-existing person the bill may be treated as payable to bearer (*ibid.* s.7(3)).

bill of health. A document given to the master of a ship by the consul of the port from which he comes, describing the sanitary state of the place. It may be a clean, suspected, or foul bill.

bill of indictment. A written or printed accusation of crime made at the suit of the Queen against one or more persons.

Formerly, a bill of indictment was preferred to a grand jury, which, if of opinion that there was sufficient ground to put the accused on trial before the petty jury, endorsed "true bill" on the back of the bill, which then, upon presentment by the grand jury, became an indictment. Otherwise, the words "no true bill" were endorsed, and the bill was thrown out. By the Administration of Justice Act 1933, grand juries were abolished, and a bill of indictment is now preferred by being delivered to the proper officer of the court. When signed by him, it becomes an indictment. See GRAND JURY; INDICTMENT.

bill of lading. A document signed and delivered by the master of a ship to the shippers on goods being shipped. The "mate's receipt" is the acknowledgment of the actual taking on board ship of the goods. The bill of lading specifies the name of the master, the port and destination of the ship, the goods, the consignee, and the rate of freight. Copies are kept by the master, the shipper and the consignee. It is a document of title transferable by endorsement and delivery, giving the holder the right to sue thereon, but it is not a negotiable instrument, so that a transferee obtains no better title than the transferor has. See Carriage of Goods by Sea Act 1924.

Bill of Middlesex. The procedure whereby the Court of King's Bench acquired jurisdiction in civil cases between subject and subject.

The bill was issued to the sheriff of Middlesex commanding him to arrest the defendant for an imaginary trespass (in which the court had jurisdiction) and to bring him before the court. Then he was proceeded against for any cause of action. If the defendant was not to be found in Middlesex the sheriff made a return of *non est inventus* (*q.v.*); whereupon the court issued the process of *latitat* to the sheriff of the county in which he *latitat et discurrit* [lurks and runs about], reciting the Bill of Middlesex and the sheriff's return, and commanding the sheriff to arrest the defendant. Later process began immediately with the *latitat*. Abolished by the Uniformity of Process Act 1832.

Bill of pains and penalties. A Bill introduced, generally in the House of Lords but sometimes in the House of Commons, for the punishment of a particular person without trial in the ordinary way. Such person could defend himself by counsel and witness. The last such Bill was against Queen Caroline in 1820.

bill of particulars. A statement in writing of what a plaintiff sought to recover in an action, being an amplification of the plaintiff's claim as set out in the declaration or summons. See PARTICULARS.

bill of peace. A bill which could be filed in Chancery for the grant of a perpetual injunction to restrain all further proceedings at law by the litigants, or those claiming under them upon the same title.

Bill of Rights. The Declaration delivered by the Lords and Commons to the Prince and Princess of Orange and afterwards enacted as the statute 1 Will. & Mary, sess. 2, c. 2, which provided (*inter alia*) that:

(1) The suspending power, when exercised by the Crown without the assent of Parliament, is illegal;

(2) The dispensing power, as of late exercised, is illegal;

(3) Levying money by prerogative is prohibited;

(4) The subjects have a right to petition the Crown, and all commitments for so petitioning are illegal;

(5) Raising or maintaining a standing army within the Kingdom in time of peace is illegal, if done without the assent of Parliament;

(6) Speech in Parliament is to be free;

(7) Excessive bail, excessive fines, etc., ought not to be required or imposed; and

(8) The Protestant succesion to the throne of England to be ensured. See ACT OF SETTLEMENT.

bill of sale. A document intended to give effect to the grant of chattels where the possession remains unchanged. There are two classes of bills of sale: (1) absolute, purporting to be a complete transfer of the chattels by way of sale, gift or settlement; (2) by way of mortgage, where there is a transfer for the purpose of creating a security, subject to a proviso for redemption on repayment of the money secured.

The Bills of Sale Act 1878, s.4 defined bills of sale as including assignments, transfers, declarations of trust without transfer, inventories of goods with receipt thereto attached, or receipts for purchase money of goods, and other assurances of personal chattels, and also powers of attorney, authorities or licences to take possession of personal chattels as security for any debt, and also any agreement, whether intended or not to be followed by the execution of any other instrument by which a right in equity to any personal chattels, or to any charge or security thereon, is conferred. The Bills of Sale Act (1878) Amendment Act 1882 applies to bills of sale given by way of security for payment of money.

Every bill of sale to which the Bills of Sale Acts apply must be attested and registered at the central office of the Supreme Court within seven days of execution. The bill of sale must set forth the consideration for which it is given. If these provisions are not complied with a bill of sale within the 1878 Act is void only as against the trustee in bankruptcy, etc., or an execution creditor, in respect of the chattels comprised therein which are then in the apparent possession of the grantor, but as between the parties, it is valid: a bill within the 1882 Act is, however, absolutely void in respect of the personal chattels comprised therein. Bills of sale within the 1882 Act, if given or made in consideration of any sum under £30, are void; they must contain or have annexed an inventory specifically describing the personal chattels comprised therein, and are void unless made substantially in accordance with the form in the schedule to the Act.

bill of sight. The entry (*q.v.*) made by an importer of goods who is unable to make immediately a perfect entry of them (Customs and Excise Management Act 1979, s.38).

billeting. The quartering of soldiers and their horses in the house of a subject. The Petition of Right 1628 contained protests against the billeting of soldiers upon private persons, and it was declared illegal. Billeting of soldiers was subsequently legalised by the Mutiny Acts.

binding over. (1) Requiring a person to enter into a recognisance to perform some act, *e.g.* binding over a person to prosecute, or to give evidence. On committal for trial on an indictable offence, the accused person, if granted bail, is bound over to appear and stand his trial (Justices of the Peace Act 1361; Magistrates'

Courts Act 1952, s.7; Magistrates' Courts Rules 1968, r. 7; *R.* v. *Aubrey-Fletcher, ex p. Thomson* [1969] 1 W.L.R. 872).

(2) Magistrates have power on complaint to bind a person over to keep the peace or to be of good behaviour (Magistrates' Courts Act 1952, s.91).

(3) The Crown Court has a common law power, instead of imposing a punishment on a convicted person (other than a person convicted of murder), to require him to enter into recognisances with or without sureties to come up for judgment when called upon. He is usually also bound over to keep the peace and be of good behaviour.

(4) Any court of record having criminal jurisdiction has, as auxiliary to that jurisdiction, the power to bind over to be of good behaviour a person (including a witness) (*Sheldon* v. *Bromfield JJ.* [1964] 2 Q.B. 573) who or whose case is before the court, by requiring him to enter into his own recognisances or to find sureties on both, and committing him to prison if he does not comply (Justices of the Peace Act 1968, s.1(7)).

bingo. A duty of excise known as bingo duty is charged on the playing of bingo (Betting and Gaming Duties Act 1972, ss.17–20; Finance (No. 2) Act 1975, s.2).

birretum. The "black cap" or coif of the judges and serjeants-at-law.

birth. Notice of a child's birth must be given to the Area Health Authority within 36 hours of birth (National Health Service Act 1977, s.124). The birth of a child must also be registered (Births and Deaths Registration Act 1975). See also ABORTION; CHILD DESTRUCTION; CONCEALMENT OF BIRTH; WRONGFUL ENTRY INTO LIFE.

bishop. An ecclesiastical dignitary: one of the chief officers of the Church of England, and the chief of the clergy within his diocese.

On a vacancy occurring a *congé d'élire* is sent by the Crown to the dean and chapter bidding them elect a successor; the name of the successor is contained in the letters missive accompanying the *congé d'élire*. The permission to elect is a form only, and if the election is not made the Crown appoints by letters patent. After confirmation of the election by the vicar-general of the province, the bishop is consecrated and installed. The senior bishops are summoned to the House of Lords.

bishop, suffragan. An assistant to, or deputy for, a bishop.

black cap. A square cap worn over the wig by a judge of the High Court on solemn or State occasions.

black list. A stop list: a list of persons, firms, companies, etc., with whom no dealings are to be had: see *Thorne* v. *Motor Trade Association* [1937] A.C. 797.

Black Rod. The Gentleman Usher of the Black Rod is the official of the House of Lords analogous to the Serjeant-at-Arms of the House of Commons. He executes the orders of the House in taking offenders into custody, and assists in ceremonies.

blackleg. (1) One who wins money at cards or betting by dishonest practices; (2) one who continues to work during a strike.

blackmail. Originally, rent payable in cattle, labour or produce (*niger redditus*) as distinguished from rent payable in silver or white money. Subsequently it meant the toll levied by freebooters along the Scottish border.

A person is guilty of blackmail if with a view to gain for himself or another or with intent to cause loss to another, he makes any unwarranted demand with menaces (Theft Act 1968, s.21). See MENACES.

blank, acceptance in. An acceptance written before the bill is filled up. It is an authority to fill up the paper as a complete bill for any amount (Bills of Exchange Act 1882, s.20; Finance Act 1970, Sched. 8, Pt. V.). See INDORSEMENT.

blank transfer. A transfer of shares which is executed without the name of the transferee being filled in. Such a transfer, with the certificates of the shares, is frequently lodged as security for money, the intention being that the purchaser or mortgagee may later on fill in the blank and perfect his security by getting himself registered. If the articles of association require transfers to be by deed, the transferee cannot validly complete the transfer without a power of attorney under seal from the transferor. The circulation of blank transfers is prohibited by Finance Act 1963, s.67.

blasphemy. The public or criminal libel of speaking matter relating to God, Jesus Christ, the Bible or the Book of Common Prayer, intending to wound the feelings of mankind or to excite contempt and hatred against the Church by law established, or to promote immorality. It is a common law misdemeanour. In *R.* v. *Lemon* [1979] A.C. 617, H.L. it was held that the defendant's intention was irrelevant to a conviction for blasphemous libel.

blemishing the peace. There is no such offence as blemishing the peace, but a person found by a magistrate to have acted "in a manner whereby the peace is blemished" may be ordered to find a sufficient surety for his good behaviour (*R.* v. *London County Quarter Sessions* [1948] 1 K.B. 670).

blended fund. A mixed fund, derived from various sources, as, *e.g.* where a testator directs his real and personal estate to be sold, and disposes of the proceeds as forming one aggregate.

blockade. In international law, an act of war carried out by the warships of a belligerent detailed to prevent access to or departure from the enemy's coast or ports. The penalty for breach of blockade is confiscation, but it must be shown: (1) that the blockade was effective; (2) that the ship alleged to have violated the blockade had notice thereof; and (3) that she made ingress or egress in disregard of the blockade.

In the World Wars of 1914–18 and 1939–45, the "navicert" system (whereby only ships carrying papers issued by the Allied Powers could pass the contraband control) largely superseded the traditional form of blockade.

blockade, pacific. The temporary suspension of the commerce of an offending or recalcitrant State, by the closing of access to its coasts or of some particular part of its coasts, but without recourse to other hostile measures, save in so far as may be necessary to enforce this restriction. It is commonly resorted to in practice either by way of reprisals and as a method of redress short of war, or as a measure of international police.

blodwyte. A fine or composition for the shedding of blood. It was payable to the lord; while *wergild* (*q.v.*) or part thereof, went to the party injured or, in case of death, to his relatives.

blood. (1) That quality or relationship which enables a person to take by descent; (2) persons connected by blood relationship, that is, by being descended from one or more common ancestors.

One person is said to be of the whole blood to another when they are both descended from the same pair of ancestors, *e.g.* two brothers who have the same father and mother. Persons are said to be of the half blood to one another when they are descended from one common ancestor only, *e.g.* two brothers who have the same father but different mothers. Formerly, relations by the half blood were incapable of inheriting from one another, but this disability was removed by the Inheritance Act 1833. Since 1925 the half blood take on intestacy immediately after the whole blood of the same degree (Administration of Estates Act 1925, s.46; Intestates' Estates Act 1952, s.1, Sched. 1).

Where the paternity of a child is in question in any civil proceedings, a blood-test may be ordered by the court (Family Law Reform Act 1969, ss. 20–25). A blood sample may be ordered to be taken for comparison from a person held on suspicion of rape (*H.M. Advocate* v. *Milford* [1975] Crim L.R. 110).

A person who has been arrested for driving under the influence of drink or drugs may be required to supply for laboratory test a specimen of his blood or urine (see BREATH TEST).

blot on title. A defect in title.

Board of Control. The Commissioners appointed under the Mental Deficiency Act 1913, and who succeeded to the powers of the Commissioners in Lunacy. Their functions were transferred to the Minister of Health, and the Board of Control was dissolved pursuant to the Mental Health Act 1959, s.2.

Board of Green Cloth. The Counting House of the Queen's Household. It consists of the Lord Steward, the Treasurer, the Comptroller and the Master of the Household, with their clerical assistants.

Board of Trade. The Lords of the Committee of the Privy Council appointed for the consideration of matters relating to trade and foreign plantations (Interpretation Act 1889, s.12(8)). It consists of a Commission which never meets, its functions being discharged by the President of the Board. The office of the President of the Board of Trade is held by the Secretary of State for Trade. The Board of Trade is now the Department of Trade.

bocland; bookland. Before the Norman Conquest this meant land held by the King by book or charter, as opposed to folcland or laenland. At first such grants were made only to ecclesiastical bodies, but subsequently they were made to laymen.

bodily harm. Physical injury or pain, including illness due to nervous shock (*q.v.*). Grievous bodily harm means serious injury short of death. Intentionally to cause bodily harm is an indictable offence.

body of deed. The operative part of a deed as distinguished from the recitals.

bomb hoax. The sending or placing of any article or substance with the intention of inducing in some person a belief that it is likely to explode or ignite and cause personal damage or damage to property is an offence (Criminal Law Act 1977, s.51(1)). It is also an offence under s.51(2) of the Act to communicate information which is known to be false with a similar intention.

bona fide. In good faith, honestly, without fraud, collusion or participation in wrongdoing.

bona gestura. Good behaviour.

bona notabilia. Goods situated in another diocese to that in which a deceased had died.

bona vacantia. Goods without an apparent owner in which no one claims a property but the Crown, such as royal fish, shipwrecks, treasure trove. In default of any person taking an absolute interest in the property of an intestate, it belongs to the Crown, Duchy of Lancaster, or Duke of Cornwall, as the case may be, as *bona vacantia* and in lieu of any right to escheat (Administration of Estates Act 1925, s.36(1) (vi)). In practice, the Treasury may grant such property to the person who appears to have the most meritorious claim. In Roman law it was property left by a deceased person who had no successor. It generally went to the *fiscus*.

bona waviata. Waifs (*q.v.*).

bond. A single bond is a contract under seal to pay a sum of money (a common money bond), or a sealed writing acknowledging a debt, present or future. A double or conditional bond is where a condition is added that if the obligor does or forbears from doing some act the obligation shall be void. The person who binds himself is called the obligor, and the person in whose favour the bond is made is called the obligee. The bond usually consists of (i) the obligation or operative part, by which the obligor binds himself to pay the money; (ii) any recitals which may be necessary to explain the nature of the transaction; and (iii) the condition, which sets out the acts on the performance of which the bond or obligation is to cease to be of effect. Voluntary bonds are bonds given without valuable consideration.

A bond is also an instrument of indebtedness issued by companies and governments to secure the repayment of money borrowed by them.

bond washing. A type of transaction which seeks to avoid tax by the sale and re-purchase of securities. See the Income and Corporation Taxes Act 1970, s.469; Finance Act 1971, ss.37, 38, 69, Sched. 6, para. 70, Sched. 14, Pt. II; Finance Act 1973, s.25, Sched. 11.

bonded goods. Dutiable goods in respect of which a bond for the payment of the duty has been given to the Commissioners of Customs and Excise.

bonded warehouse. A secure place approved by the Commissioners of Customs and Excise for the deposit of dutiable goods upon which duty has not been paid.

bondsman. A surety, or person bound by a bond.

boni judicis est ampliare jurisdictionem. [It is the duty of a good judge to extend his jurisdiction.] (Not to be taken too literally.)

bonorum emptio or **venditio.** [Roman law.] The purchase or sale of an insolvent estate (the universal succession of a debtor), by or to one that offers to satisfy the largest proportion of the claims of the creditors; a praetorian mode of execution.

bonorum possessio. [Roman law.] (Possession of the property.) The praetorian situation corresponding to civil law *hereditas*; an inheritance to which a universal successor succeeded in virtue of the intervention of the Praetor.

bonorum possessor. [Roman law.] The praetorian heir. The universal successor of a deceased person in virtue of the intervention of the Praetor.

bonus shares. If a company declares a bonus out of undivided capitalised profits and allots to its shareholders in satisfaction of the bonus unissued shares in the company as fully paid up, the shares so allotted are capital and not income in the shareholders' hands (*Inland Revenue Commissioners* v. *Blott* [1921] 2 A.C. 171). Similarly unissued debentures may be issued as bonus debentures. Bonus shares or debentures can be paid for out of profits available for dividend if the articles of association so provide.

bookmaker. One who makes a business of taking bets. A person acting as bookmaker on his own account must hold a bookmaker's permit (Betting, Gaming and Lotteries Act 1963, s.2, Sched. 1). Bookmakers are subject to a levy by the Horserace Betting Levy Board (*ibid.* ss. 27–29; Horserace Betting Levy Act 1969, ss. 1–4). See also the Betting, Gaming and Lotteries (Amendment) Act 1971, s.1.

booty of war. Military arms, equipment and stores captured on land. It belongs to the Crown.

borough. A town incorporated by Royal Charter with a common seal, the right to hold lands and the right to contract, sue and be sued in the name of the *Mayor, Aldermen and Burgesses of——*.

As part of the reorganisation of local government all boroughs outside Greater London ceased to exist on April 1, 1974 (Local Government Act 1972, ss, 1, 20), but the Crown may on petition, confer by charter on a district the status of a borough together with the privileges, rights and dignities formerly belonging thereto (ss.245–248).

borough court. An inferior court of record for the trial of civil actions by charter, custom or otherwise, holden in a borough, *e.g.* the Mayor's and City of London Court; the Liverpool Court of Passage.

Borough courts were abolished on April 1, 1974 by the Local Government Act 1972, s.221, Sched. 28.

borough, English. A customary mode of descent, under which the youngest son inherited land to the exclusion of his elder brothers. It was abolished by the Law of Property Act 1922.

borstal institutions. Places in which offenders not less than 15 but under 21 may be detained and given such training and instruction as will conduce to their reformation and the prevention of crime (Criminal Justice Act 1948, s.48(1) (c)). A sentence of borstal training may be passed on young offenders in lieu of any other sentence (*ibid.* s.20; Criminal Justice Act 1961, s.1). In the case of an offender under 17 at conviction the court must be satisfied that no other method of dealing with him is appropriate. The period of borstal training is for not less than six months nor more than two years. Compulsory supervision following release runs for two years.

botes. Estovers or necessaries for husbandry. They include house-bote or fire-bote (wood to repair, or to burn in a house), plough-bote or cart-bote, hay-bote or hedge-bote. They may be claimed as rights of common. See COMMON.

bottomry bond. A bond entered into by the owner of a ship or his agent whereby, in consideration of a sum of money advanced for the purposes of the ship, the borrower undertakes to repay the same with interest if the ship terminate her voyage successfully, the debt being lost in case of the non-arrival of the ship. It binds or hypothecates the ship and freight, or the cargo.

bought and sold notes. Documents containing particulars of a transaction of sale or purchase delivered by a broker to his principals; as *e.g.* on the Stock Exchange.

bounds. Boundaries. The trespass committed by a person who excavates minerals underground beyond the boundary of his land is called working out of bounds. The person on whose land the trespass is committed may bring an action for damages or for an injunction, and an account of the minerals taken.

bounty. Moneys payable by the Crown, either as rewards, *e.g.* to the officers and crew of a Queen's ship, or as inducements to exporters, etc., or by way of charity.

Bovill's Act. The Petition of Right Act 1860 and also the statute 28 & 29 Vict. c. 86 relating to partnership (both now repealed).

boycotting. A concerted refusal to have any dealings with another person: so called after Captain Boycott in Ireland.

Bracton. The author of *De Legibus et Consuetudinibus Angliae* (The laws and customs of England), *temp.* Henry III.

brawling. The misdemeanour of creating a disturbance in a consecrated building or ground.

breach. The invasion of a right, or the violation of a duty.

breach of close. Trespass on land.

breach of contract. A breaking of the obligation which a contract imposes, which confers a right of action for damages on the injured party. It also entitles him to treat the contract as discharged if the other party renounces the contract, or makes its performance impossible, or totally or substantially fails to perform his promises. An anticipatory breach of contract is one which is made before the time for performance has arrived.

breach of privilege. Contempt of the High Court of Parliament, whether relating to the House of Lords or to the House of Commons, *e.g.* resistance to the officers of the House.

breach of promise. Breach of promise to marry gave rise to a right of action for damages at common law. This was abolished by the Law Reform (Miscellaneous

Provisions) Act 1970, s.1. The law relating to matrimonial property is applied to disputes between parties who have broken off an engagement (s.2). Gifts between engaged couples are returnable except the engagement ring (s.3).

breach of the peace. *i.e.* "breach of the Queen's peace"; apparently any crime or offence whatever. The preservation of the Queen's peace is the most ancient prerogative of the Crown. Every private citizen has the right to seize one who is about to commit a breach of the peace and detain him temporarily. Justices may take security from one whose behaviour leads them to believe that a breach of the peace will be caused, although no criminal charge is possible. The public performance of a play may amount to provocation of a breach of the peace (Theatres Act 1968, ss. 6–10). Insulting behaviour does not necessarily constitute a breach of the peace (*Bryan* v. *Robinson* [1960] 1 W.L.R. 506).This offence must now be tried summarily; maximum penalties £1,000 fine, six months' imprisonment or both (Criminal Law Act 1977, ss. 15, 30). See ARREST; BLEMISHING THE PEACE; PEACE; PUBLIC ORDER.

breach of trust. An improper act, neglect or default on the part of a trustee in regard to his trust, either in disregard of the terms of the trust, or the rules of equity. The measure of the trustee's liability is the loss caused thereby to the trust estate. Any profit accruing from a breach of trust, *e.g.* improper speculation or trading with the trust assets, belongs to the trust estate.

breath test. A constable in uniform may require a driver to provide a specimen of breath when he has reasonable cause to suspect that the driver is driving, attempting to drive or is in charge of a motor vehicle and either has alcohol in his body or has committed a moving traffic offence. A specimen may also be required from a person who has been driving, attempting to drive or is in charge of a motor vehicle and suspected either to have had alcohol in his body when driving and still to have alcohol in his body or to have committed a moving traffic offence (Road Traffic Act 1972, s.7 substituted and amended by Transport Act 1981, s.25 and Sched. 8). A breath test may lawfully be required when a police officer stops a car for a random crime check and then smells alcohol on the driver's breath (*Steel* v. *Goacher, The Times*, July 8, 1982). Failure to provide a specimen without reasonable excuse is an offence (s.7(4)). A person whose alcohol level is suspected to exceed the prescribed limit or who fails to provide a specimen may be arrested (s.7(5)). If so arrested and taken to a police station a person may then be required to provide either a specimen of breath or a specimen of blood or urine (s.8(1)). Failure to comply with the manufacturer of the breath test device's instructions is not in itself an offence and it is a question of fact and degree whether a defendant has failed to supply a specimen of breath within s.8 (*Corp* v. *Dalton, The Times*, July 30, 1982, Div. Ct.).

breve. [A short thing.] A writ.

brevia testata. Early forms of deeds of conveyance.

breviate. A memorandum of the contents of a Bill.

brewster sessions. The general annual meeting of the licensing justices. The Licensing Act 1964, consolidates the Acts relating to justices' licences for sale by retail of intoxicating liquor, etc.

bribery and corruption. Giving or offering any reward to any person to influence his conduct; or the receipt of such reward. See the Public Bodies Corrupt Practices Act 1889, the Sale of Offices Acts 1551 and 1809, the Honours (Prevention of Abuses) Act 1925, and the Representation of the People Act 1949, s.99. The bribery of public officers is a common law misdemeanour; the bribery of and by agents is a misdemeanour under the Prevention of Corruption Acts 1606 and 1916.

bridewell. A prison.

bridle-path. A highway along which there is a right of way on foot and a right of way on horseback or leading a horse, with or without a right to drive animals of any description along the highway (Highways Act 1959, s.295(1)).

Bicycles may be ridden on a bridleway (Countryside Act 1968, s.30; Road Traffic Act 1972, Scheds. 7, 9).

brief. A concise statement. The instructions furnished by a solicitor to a barrister to enable him to represent the client in legal proceedings. A brief consists, normally, of a narrative of the facts of the case and a reference to the relevant law. There are annexed counsel's opinion; a copy of material documents; formal pleadings; correspondence, and proofs of evidence of witnesses.

British citizen. A person may become a British citizen: (a) by being born in the United Kingdon to a parent who is either a British citizen or settled in the United Kingdom; (b) by being born in the United Kingdom to a parent who subsequently becomes settled here or himself becomes registered as a British citizen; (c) by being adopted by order of a court in the United Kingdom if the adopters or one of them is a British citizen; (d) by being born overseas to a parent who is a British citizen or is employed overseas in British Government Service or in the service of an EEC Institution (British Nationality Act 1981, ss.2 and 3). British citizenship may also be acquired by naturalisation (*q.v.*) or registration (*q.v.*).

British Commonwealth. See COMMONWEALTH.

British Dependent Territories Citizenship. A form of citizenship conferred on citizens of British Dependent Territories (see British Nationality Act 1981, ss. 23–25 and Sched. 6).

British Empire. The territories over which the King [Queen] exercised sovereignty, and the inhabitants of which owed allegiance to the British Crown; the British colonies together with the British Dominions of Canada, Australia, New Zealand, and the Indian Empire. The term fell into disuse and was replaced by British Commonwealth of Nations, or more simply, the Commonwealth (*q.v.*).

British Library. The British Museum library was transferred to the British Library together with the obligation under the Copyright Act 1911, s.15 to deliver a copy of every published book to the British Museum (British Library Act 1972).

British Museum. For constitution see the British Museum Act 1963. The Natural History Museum and the British Museum library (see BRITISH LIBRARY) have been separated from the British Museum. A copy of the script of any performance of a new play must be delivered to the British Museum (Theatres Act 1968, s.11).

British Overseas Citizenship. A person who was a citizen of the United Kingdom and Colonies immediately before commencement of the British Nationality Act 1981 and did not at commencement become either a British citizen (*q.v.*) or a British Dependant Territories Citizen (*q.v.*) became a British Overseas Citizen (Act of 1981, s.26). This category of citizenship is very much a residual one and carries no right of entry to the United Kingdom.

British protected persons. These are persons connected with places which were formerly protectorates (*q.v.*), protected states or United Kingdom trust territories and who become British protected persons by virtue of an order in Council made under section 38 of the British Nationality Act 1981 or earlier legislation.

British subject. Formerly a member, by citizenship, of the British state. By the British Nationality Act 1981 full citizenship is now conferred on British citizens (*q.v.*). The term "British subject" now has a lesser and transitional status and is similar to that of British Overseas Citizen (*q.v.*) except that a British subject cannot hold another citizenship at the same time (British Nationality Act 1981, ss. 30–35).

Britton. A law treatise *temp.* Edward I.

broadcasting. Publication for general reception by means of wireless telegraphy (Defamation Act 1952, s.16). It is publication in permanent form for purposes of libel and slander (*ibid.* s.1). Broadcasting without the permission of the performer is an offence (Dramatic and Musical Performers' Protection Act 1958, s.3 and the Performers' Protection Acts 1963 and 1972).

Broadmoor. A "special hospital," vested in the Secretary of State for Social Services, for those requiring treatment under conditions of special security, because of their dangerous, violent or criminal propensities (Mental Health Act 1959, ss. 97, 98).

brocage. A marriage brocage contract is one to procure a marriage for reward, and void (*Hermann* v. *Charlesworth* [1905] 2 K.B. 123).

broker. A mercantile agent for the purchase and sale of goods, stocks and shares, policies of insurance, etc. A broker cannot sue or be sued on a contract unless he signs a written memorandum with his own name.

brokerage. The commission on the price realised payable to a broker for his services.

brothel. A common bawdy house or a disorderly house: one used for purposes of fornication by both sexes, but not one so used by one woman only. Under the Sexual Offences Act 1956 it is an offence to keep a brothel, or to let premises for use as a brothel, or to permit them to be used as such (ss. 33–36). This is commonly a breach of covenant in a lease, which breach is incapable of remedy under s.146 of the Law of Property Act 1925.

Brothel includes premises resorted to for homosexual practices (Sexual Offences Act 1967, s.6).

brutum fulmen. A threat to which effect cannot be given.

bucket shop. The business of providing means for speculation in stock, shares, etc., carried on by an "outside broker", *i.e.,* a broker who is not a member of a recognised stock exchange, etc., and who is not therefore subject to the rules and regulations of such a body.

Budget. The annual statement made by the Chancellor of the Exchequer to the House of Commons soon after the commencement of the Government financial year which begins on April 1, containing the estimates of the national expenditure for the year, and proposals as to the taxes necessary to raise the amount required. It is followed by the Budget resolutions proposing the new taxation for the year, which are later embodied in the annual Finance Act.

buggery. Sodomy: the offence committed with mankind or with any animal, consisting of penetration *per anum*: punishable by the Sexual Offences Act 1956, s.12. An assault with intent to commit buggery is an offence under s.16. Homosexuality in private between two consenting persons who have attained the age of 21 years is not an offence (Sexual Offences Act 1967). There is no such offence as rape *per anum* (*R.* v. *Gaston* (1981) 73 Cr.App.R. 164, C.A.).

building lease. A lease, generally for a term of 99 years, at a rent known as a ground-rent, under which the lessee covenants to erect certain specified buildings on the land demised by the lease, and to insure and keep in repair such buildings during the term. At the expiration of the term the buildings become the property of the lessor subject to the right of a lessee to acquire the freehold (Leasehold Reform Act 1967, as amended). A mortgagee in possession may since 1925 lease for 999 years (Law of Property Act 1925, s.99(3)(ii)). See also Settled Land Act 1925, ss. 44, 46.

building society. One established for the purpose of raising, by the subscriptions of its members, a stock or fund for making advances to others of its members upon security of freehold or leasehold estate, by way of mortgate (Building Societies

Act 1962, s.1). A registered building society is a body corporate and must sue and be sued in its registered name.

bull. One who buys stocks or shares intending not to take delivery but to resell at a higher price.

Bullock order. In an action claiming relief against two defendants in the alternative, if the judge is satisfied that it was reasonable for both defendants to be joined, he will order the plaintiff to pay the costs of the successful defendant, and then add those costs to those which the unsuccessful defendant has to pay to the plaintiff (*Bullock* v. *L.G.O. Co.* [1907] 1 K.B. 264).

burden of a contract. The liability to perform a contract or discharge the obligations of a contract for the benefit of the other party to the contract.

burden of proof. See PROOF.

burgage tenure. A form of free land-holding, generally at a money rent, peculiar to boroughs, similar to the modern tenure in fee simple, but subject to local custom. It was abolished by the Law of Property Act 1922. See BOROUGH ENGLISH.

burgess. Formerly a Member of Parliament who sat for a city or borough. Now a person who is registered on the burgess roll of a borough, *i.e.* is entitled to vote at the borough elections.

burghmote. A borough court.

burglary. A person is guilty of burglary if (a) he enters any building or part of a building as a trespasser and with intent to commit any such offence as is mentioned below, or (b) having entered any building or part of a building as a trespasser he steals or attempts to steal anything therein or inflicts or attempts to inflict on any person therein any grievous bodily harm (Theft Act 1968, s.9(1)). The offences referred to above are offences of stealing, of inflicting grievous bodily harm or rape or doing unlawful damage (s.9(2)). Building includes an inhabited vehicle or vessel (s.9(3)). Burglary with firearms (including air guns) or imitation firearms or any offensive weapon or explosive is aggravated burglary (s.10). The offence of burglary at common law is abolished (s.32).

burial. At common law, every person may be buried in the churchyard of the parish where he dies, unless he was within certain ecclesiastical prohibitions (*e.g.* not having been baptised), and provided that the rites of the Church of England are observed. See Burial Acts 1852 to 1900; Cremation Acts 1902 and 1952.

business day. See the Bills of Exchange Act 1882, s.92; Banking and Financial Dealings Act 1971, ss. 3, 4.

business names. The Registry of Business Names has now been abolished (Companies Act 1981). Provision is now made for information which must be displayed or given by business trading under names other than the true names of their owners. Such businesses must display at their business premises and on their business stationery the names of the owners and an address at which documents may be served. This information must also be supplied to customers on request. Various other regulations are made concerning names of businesses (Companies Act 1981, ss. 22–30, 32, 34, 35, 109, 119(4),(5); Companies Act 1981 (Commencement No. 3) Order 1982).

by-laws or **bye-laws.** Rules made by some authority (subordinate to the Legislature) for the regulation, administration or management of a certain district, property, undertaking, etc., and binding on all persons who come within their scope.

By-laws are the means by which local authorities exercise their regulative functions, *e.g.* under the Public Health Acts. Such by-laws usually require confirmation by the Secretary of State, as the case may be. To be valid a by-law must be *intra vires,* reasonable in itself, certain in its terms and must not be retrospective or repugnant to the general law of the land. It must be published.

C

C.A.V. See CUR. ADV. VULT.

C.I.F. [Cost, insurance, freight.] A contract for the sale of goods where the seller's duties are (1) to ship at the port of shipment within the time named in the contract goods of the contract description; (2) to procure on shipment a contract of affreightment under which the goods will be delivered at the destination contemplated by the contract; (3) to insure the goods upon the terms current in the trade which will be available for the benefit of the buyer; (4) to make out an invoice of the goods; (5) to tender to the buyer the bill of lading, the invoice, and the policy of insurance. It is the duty of the buyer to take up these documents and pay for them.

ca. sa. See CAPIAS AD SATISFACIENDUM.

Cabinet. The committee or council of the Ministers of the Crown, presided over by the Prime Minister, and consisting of the political heads of the Government Departments and other officers, all of whom are members of the Privy Council. It is the supreme executive in the British Constitution, but its existence rests upon convention, not law, except that it has been recognised by the Ministers of the Crown Act 1937, which provided for salaries for Cabinet Ministers. It first emerged in the time of Charles II as a "meeting of His Majesty's Servants."

In theory the Cabinet is collectively responsible for the whole policy of the Government, but if the policy of a particular Minister is disowned, that Minister alone resigns.

cadit quaestio. [The matter admits of no further argument.]

caeteris paribus. [Other things being equal.]

calderbank letter. A "without prejudice" (*q.v.*) letter containing an offer to settle litigation may also state that it may be brought to the attention of the court on any issue as to costs at the conclusion of the matter (*Calderbank* v. *Calderbank* [1975] 3 All E.R. 333, C.A.).

calendar. The Calendar (New Style) Act 1750 and the Calendar Act 1751 substituted the Gregorian Calendar for the Julian Calendar, with the result that the 11 days between September 2 and 14, 1752, were cut out.

call. A demand upon the holder of partly paid-up shares in a company for payment of the balance, or an instalment of it, by the company itself; or, if the company is in liquidation, by the liquidator.

call to the Bar. The ceremony whereby a member of an Inn of Court is admitted as barrister (*q.v.*).

camera. [Chamber.] See IN CAMERA.

Camera Stellata. The Star Chamber (*q.v.*).

Campbell's Act, Lord. The Fatal Accidents Act 1846. See FATAL ACCIDENTS ACTS.

Campbell's Libel Acts, Lord. The Libel Acts 1843 and 1845. See APOLOGY.

Cancellaria Curia. The Court of Chancery.

cancellation. The drawing of lines across an instrument with the purpose of depriving it of effect.

Cancellation of a will does not revoke it, unless it is accompanied by a declaration executed by the testator in the manner in which wills are required to be executed (Wills Act 1837, s.20).

Candlemas. The Feast of the Purification; February 2.

cannabis. A controlled drug (Class B) under the Misuse of Drugs Act 1971. Defined by Criminal Law Act 1977, s.52.

canon. (1) A rule of the canon law, or ecclesiastical law. It is sometimes used as meaning a rule of the ordinary law, *e.g.* the canons of descent. (2) A minor ecclesiastical dignitary, member of the bishop's advisory council, who assists the dean.

canon law. A body of Roman ecclesiastical law, compiled from the opinions of the ancient Latin fathers, the decrees of general councils, and the decretal epistles and bulls of the Holy See. It was codified in the twelfth century by Gratianus, and added to by subsequent collections, and known as the *Corpus Juris Canonica*.

In this country, canon law means the law of the Church of England. Unless subsequently receiving the authorisation of Parliament or merely declaratory of ancient customs, such canons bind only the clergy and laymen holding ecclesiastical office, *e.g.* churchwardens.

Canute, Laws of. A code promulgated at Winchester, with the consent of the Witan (*q.v.*); apparently between 1028 and 1035, by King Canute.

cape. A writ used in the "real" actions. See ACTION.

capias. [That you take.] A writ for the arrest of the person named therein.

capias ad audiendum judicium. A writ to summon a defendant in a criminal prosecution to court to hear judgment pronounced against him.

capias ad respondendum. A writ issued for the arrest of a person against whom an indictment for a misdemeanour has been found, in order that he might be arraigned. Abolished by the Crown Proceedings Act 1947 (Sched.1).

capias ad satisfaciendum, or *ca. sa.*; a writ for the arrest of the defendant in a civil action when judgment had been recovered against him for a sum of money and had not been satisfied. Abolished by Supreme Court Act 1981, s.141.

capias extendi facias. A writ of execution issuable against a debtor to the Crown, which commanded the sheriff to "take" or arrest the body, and "cause to be extended" the lands and goods of the debtor. See EXTENT.

capias in withernam. A writ formerly used in cases where the defendant in an action of replevin had obtained judgment for the redelivery of the goods, and the sheriff had returned *elongata, i.e.* that the goods had been removed to unknown places. The writ commanded the sheriff to take other goods of the plaintiff to the value of the goods replevied, and deliver them to the defendant to be kept by him until the latter goods were returned.

capias pro fine. A writ issued for the arrest of one who had been fined for an offence against a statute. The writ authorised his imprisonment until the fine was paid.

capita. [Heads.] See PER CAPITA.

capital. The fund or *corpus*, the yield of which is profits or income. It bears the same relation to income as a tree does to its fruit. A tenant for life is entitled to income, and the remainderman to capital. The capital of a company is the amount of principal with which a company is formed to carry on business. The memorandum of a company having a share capital must state its amount and the division into shares of a fixed amount. The capital so stated and registered is the nominal capital: the issued capital is the total amount of capital issued in shares to members. Working capital is the amount of money necessary for the company actually to trade or cary on business (Companies Act 1948, Part II).

capital gains tax. Tax charged on capital gains (see Capital Gains Tax Act 1979).

capital offences: capital punishment. Capital murder as defined by the Homicide Act 1957, s.5, was a capital offence but that section has been repealed by the Murder (Abolition of Death Penalty) Act 1965. Now the only capital offences are treason (see below) and an act endangering life committed in connection with or furtherance of piracy (Piracy Act 1837, s.2). A sentence of life imprisonment is substituted for sentence of death or, in the case of a person under 18, a sentence of detention during Her Majesty's pleasure. The court may declare the period which it recommends should be served before release on licence (Murder (Abolition of Death Penalty) Act 1965, s.1).

The punishment for treason is hanging unless the Crown sees fit to alter the sentence to beheading (Treason Act 1814; Forfeiture Act 1870, s.3l.)

capital money. Sums paid to trustees under the Settled Land Acts as follows:
(1) Proceeds of sale of land or heirlooms, or reversions to leases;
(2) Fines for leases;
(3) Mining rents (three-quarters or one-quarter as the case might be);
(4) Proceeds of sale of timber (three-quarters where the tenant is impeachable for waste);
(5) Damages for breach of covenants by lessees.

Capital moneys may be applied principally in investments in trustee securities, loans on mortgage, purchase of land, and expenditure on improvements, *e.g.* under the Agricultural Holdings Act 1948 (Settled Land Act 1925, s.73).

capital punishment. See CAPITAL OFFENCES.

Under the Naval Discipline Act, the Army Act and the Air Force Act, sentence of death may be passed by courts martial on offenders serving in the Navy, Army and Air Force respectively for specified offences.

capital transfer tax. Capital transfer tax is a tax on the value transferred by chargeable transfers.The liability arises on lifetime gifts (made after March 26, 1974), on property owned at death and on settled property. It replaces estate duty as from March 13, 1975 (Finance Act 1975, ss.19–52). For exempt transfers see s.46, Sched. 6. See also National Heritage Act 1980, Pt. 11 (ss.8–15).

capitale crimen. [Roman law.] An accusation affecting the *caput* of the accused.

capitalisation. The conversion of profits or income into capital, as, *e.g.* by a resolution of a company. See *Blott's Case* [1921] 2 A.C. 171.

capite, tenure in. Tenure in chief. The holding of land direct from the King.

capitis deminutio. [Roman law.] A loss or diminution of *caput* (*q.v.*).

capitula. [Articles.]

capitulations. Agreements, concluded between Christian States on the one hand and non-Christian countries on the other hand, under which certain immunities and privileges were secured to subjects of the Christian State while in the territories of the non-Christian State. These subjects formed an extra-territorial community subject to the laws of their own country, and outside the jurisdiction of the local law.

caption. The formal heading of a legal document, stating before whom it was taken or made.

capture. (1) A mode of acquiring property, *e.g.* a *res nullius.* (2) The seizure of enemy property in war.

caput. [Roman law.] The three elements—freedom, citizenship and family rights.

car tax. A tax charged on vehicles made or registered in the United Kingdom at the rate of 10 per cent. of the wholesale value (Finance Act 1972, s.52; Finance (No.2) Act, ss.22–24).

carat. The metric carat is one-fifth of a gramme (Weights and Measures Act 1963, s.10). As to gold carats, see the Hallmarking Act 1973, Sched.1.

caravan sites must be licensed and are subject to planning control (Caravan Sites and Control of Development Act 1960 as amended). As to planning permission, see the Town and Country Planning Act 1971, ss.22, 23. As to protection from eviction, etc., see the Caravan Sites Act 1968. See also the Mobile Homes Act 1975; Rating (Caravan Sites) Act 1976.

care. A juvenile court (*q.v.*) may make a "care order" committing a juvenile to the care of a Local Authority (Children and Young Persons Act 1969, s.1; see also Children Act 1975, s.53).

care and control. The term used, usually in divorce or matrimonial proceedings, to describe the powers and responsibility of the parent or other person with whom a child lives. Contrast Custody (*q.v.*)—the two are not synonomous. Both parents may be granted joint custody but only one can have care and control. Orders under which one parent has sole custody and the other parent has care and control are rare and usually disapproved of (*Dipper* v.*Dipper* [1980] 2 All E.R. 722). See CUSTODY; JOINT CUSTODY.

careless and inconsiderate driving. A person who drives a motor vehicle on a road without due care and attention or without reasonable consideration for other road users commits an offence (Road Traffic Act 1972, s.3).

cargo. Goods shipped for carriage.

carnal knowledge. Penetration to the slightest degree by the male organ of generation. Proof of emission is not necessary (Sexual Offences Act 1956).

carriage by air. In the case of international carriage by air, the carrier is liable for damage sustained in the event of the death of a passenger, if the fatal accident took place on board the aircraft or in the course of embarking or disembarking. Where there is no special contract damages are limited to 250,000 francs per passenger (Carriage by Air Act 1961). The Fatal Accidents Acts (*q.v.*) apply to carriage by air.

carrier. One who has received goods for the purpose of carrying them from one place to another for hire, either under a special contract, *i.e.* as a bailee for reward, or as a common carrier.

carrier, common. One who, by profession to the public, undertakes for hire to transport from place to place, either by land or water, the goods of such persons as may choose to employ him. He is bound to convey the goods of any person who offers to pay his hire, and he is an insurer of goods entrusted to him; that is, he is liable for their loss or injury, in the absence of a special agreement or statutory exemption, unless the loss or injury was caused by an act of God or the Queen's enemies.

The Carriers Act 1830 provided (1) that no carrier by land is to be liable for loss of or injury to certain valuable descriptions of property (coin, jewellery, pictures, etc.) beyond the value of £10, unless their value was declared at the time of delivery; (2) that any carrier may require an increased rate of charge for such articles over the value of £10 by a notice affixed in his receiving house, and all persons delivering such articles are bound by the notice, without proof of its having come to their knowledge.

carry over. The postponement of the completion of a contract to buy or sell shares from one stock exchange account to another.

cartel. (1) An agreement between States as to the exchange of prisoners during war. (2) A manufacturers' union to keep up prices. See RESTRICTIVE TRADE PRACTICES.

cartel ship. A ship sailing during a state of war under a safe-conduct which protects her from molestation or capture when voyaging for the purpose of the exchange of prisoners under a cartel.

carucage. [*Caruca,* plough.] A tax anciently levied upon land.

case. See ACTION ON THE CASE; SPECIAL CASE.

case stated. The statement of the relevant facts in a case for the opinion or judgment of another court. May arise in the following instances;
(1) *By Magistrates.*
After the hearing and decision of a case by magistrates a party may require a case

to be stated for the opinion of the Divisional Court of the Queens Bench Division (Magistrates Courts Act 1952, s.87 and Criminal Law Act 1977, s.65, Sched.12).

(2) *By Arbitrator.*

Generally see ARBITRATION.

An appeal from an arbitrator to the High Court is now permitted solely on a point of law. The former provisions for statement of a case have been repealed (Arbitration Act 1979, ss.1(1), 1(2) and 8(3)).

(3) *Otherwise.*

Appeal to the Court of Appeal from the decision of the Lands Tribunal is by way of case stated.

The High Court may order any question or issue arising in proceedings already commenced to be tried (Ord. 33, r.3).

cassetur billa. [Let the bill be quashed.] An entry in the court records where an action commenced by a bill was discontinued.

cassetur breve. [Let the writ be quashed.] A method of discontinuing an action in the old common law practice.

casting vote. The deciding vote which a returning officer or chairman may have power to give when there is an equality of votes.

casual delegation. The principle whereby one who retains control of his chattel, *e.g.* a motor car, is held liable for injuries inflicted by a negligent borrower of it on a third person.

casual ejector. Down to 1852 the nominal defendant, Richard Roe, in an action of ejectment was called the casual ejector, because by a legal fiction he was supposed casually to come upon the land or permises and turn out the lawful possessors. See EJECTMENT.

casual pauper. A destitute wayfarer or wanderer who applied for relief.

casus belli. An act justifying war.

casus omissus. [An omitted case.] A matter which should have been, but has not been, provided for in a statute or in statutory rules.

catalla. [Cattle.] Chattels.

catching bargain. Originally a contract for a loan, made on oppressive terms, with an expectant heir (*q.v.*). Equity granted relief on the ground of constructive fraud, *i.e.* that the parties were not on equal terms, of which unfair advantage had been taken, and a hard bargain made. The onus was placed on the person seeking to enforce the contract to show that the transaction was fair and reasonable. The doctrine has been extended to all cases where parties do not meet on equal terms, or where one is under pressure without adequate protection, *e.g.* a contract between solicitor and client. But no purchase in good faith without fraud of any reversionary interest in real or personal property is liable to be set aside merely on the ground of undervalue (Law of Property Act 1925, s.174). See UNDUE INFLUENCE. (The county court may reopen extortionate credit bargains (Consumer Credit Act 1974, ss. 137–140).)

cathedrals. See the Cathedrals Measure 1963.

cattle-grid. A cattle-grid is a device designed to prevent the passage of animals, but to allow the passage of other traffic on the highway (Highways Act 1959, ss.87–97).

cattle trespass. See ANIMALS.

causa causans. The immediate cause: the last link in the chain of causation. It is to be distinguished from *causa sine qua non,* which means some preceding link but for which the *causa causans* could not have become operative.

causa falsa. [Roman law.] An untrue ground or motive; a cause or title wrongly thought to be just or legal.

causa justa. [Roman law.] A true or just cause, means, motive, or ground; a legal title; a fact in conclusive proof.

causa liberalis. [Roman law.] An *actio praejudicialis* brought to try whether a man was or was not free. Prior to Justinian an *assertor libertatis* [claimant for freedom] acted for the person whose freedom was in question, but Justinian gave the action directly to the person claiming his freedom.

causa lucrativa. [Roman law.] A ground that is purely gainful. A mode of acquisition without valuable consideration.

causa mortis. [Because of death.] See DONATIO MORTIS CAUSA.

causa proxima non remota spectatur. [The immediate, not the remote, cause is to be considered.] In marine insurance the loss must be a direct consequence of the peril insured against, so that if the proximate cause of the loss is not a peril insured against, there is no liability. Similarly, in contracts of carriage by sea, the shipowner is not liable for damage in case of "excepted perils" and the test is whether the excepted peril was in fact the direct or dominant cause of the loss or damage, though not necessarily the last cause in point of time. See *e.g. Hamilton* v. *Pandorf* (1887) 12 App.Cas. 518.

causa sine qua non. See CAUSA CAUSANS.

causation. The relation of cause and effect.

cause. An ordinary civil proceeding; an action.

cause lists. Lists of the actions and matters to be heard in the Supreme Court.

cause of action. The fact or combination of facts which give rise to a right of action.

cautio juratoria. [Roman law.] A guarantee by oath (under Justinian); a promise on oath made by a defendant sued in his own name that he will remain in the power of the court up to the end of the suit.

caution. (1) Under the Land Registration Act 1925 any person interested in land may lodge a caution with the Land Registrar, requiring him to notify any proposed dealings with the land.

(2) A warning to a person that his answers to questions may be used in evidence. Failure to caution may lead to the statement elicited being inadmissible in evidence against the person making it.

caveat. A warning. An entry made in the books of the offices of a registry or court to prevent a certain step being taken without previous notice to the person entering the caveat (who is called the caveator). Thus any person having, or claiming, an interest in the estate of a deceased person may enter a caveat at the Probate Registry and so prevent a grant of representation issuing in respect of that estate without reference to him.

caveat actor. [Let the doer beware.] A man is usually presumed to intend the probable causes of his acts. But see Criminal Justice Act 1967, s.8.

caveat emptor. [Let the buyer beware.] At common law, when a buyer of goods had required no warranty he took the risk of quality upon himself, and had no remedy if he had chosen to rely on the bare representation of the vendor, unless he could show that representation to have been fraudulent. By statute, however, a condition is implied that the goods are of merchantable quality and will be reasonably fit for the buyer's purpose, provided the buyer makes known to the seller the particular purpose for which he requires the goods, so as to show that he relies on the seller's skill or judgment, and the goods are of a description which the seller ordinarily supplies (Sale of Goods Act 1979, ss.12, 14; Supply of Goods (Implied Terms) Act 1973, s.3; Consumer Credit Act 1974, Sched. 4, para. 3, Sched. 5).

caveat venditor. [Roman law.] [Let the seller beware.]

census. The numbering of the inhabitants of the country. The Census Act 1920 provides that a census may be directed by Order in Council, provided five years have elapsed.

Central Criminal Court. (The Old Bailey.) A court having jurisdiction to try all offences committed in Greater London. The court is now a Crown Court (*q.v.*) but retains its title and the privileges of the Lord Mayor and aldermen of the City of London as judges of the court (Courts Act 1971, ss.4, 29, Sched. 2).

Central Office. The Central Office of the Supreme Court was established by the Judicature (Officers) Act 1879 to consolidate the offices of the masters and associates of the various divisions of the court. It has the following departments: 1 (1): Masters' Secretary's Department; (2): Queen's Remembrancer's Department; 2: Action Department; 3: Filing and Record Department; 4 (1): Crown Office and Associates' Department; (2): Criminal Appeal Office; 5: Supreme Court Taxing Office (see Ord. 63 and the Judicature Act 1925, ss.104, 105).

ceorl. A small freeholder or freeman. (Anglo-Saxon.)

cepi corpus. [I have taken the body.] When a writ of *capias* or attachment is directed to the sheriff for execution, when he has the defendant in custody, he returns the writ with an indorsement stating that he has taken him; called a return of *cepi corpus*.

certificate. A statement in writing by a person having a public or official status concerning some matter within his knowledge or authority.

certificate, land. A certificate under the seal of the Land Registry containing a copy of the registered particulars of a certain piece of land.

certificate of Master. When a question in an action or suit in the Chancery Division is referred to chambers, as where accounts or inquiries are directed, the result of the proceedings is stated in the Master's certificate, which is in the nature of a report to the court.

certificate of shares. A certificate under the common seal of a company specifying the shares held by a member of the company is prima facie evidence of his title (Companies Act 1948, s.81).

certificate, trial by. A mode of trial where the fact in issue was a matter of special knowledge, *e.g.* a custom of the City of London; now replaced by reference to arbitration.

certification officer. An officer appointed under Employment Protection Act 1975, s.7 to deal with the listing and certification of independent trade unions and functions relating to their funds.

certified copy. A copy of a public document, signed and certified as a true copy by the officer to whose custody the original is entrusted, and admissible as evidence when the original would be admissible. Also, it is provided by various statutes that certified copies of certain documents and entries shall be receivable in evidence if properly authenticated.

certiorari. A writ directed to an inferior court of record, commanding it to "certify" to the Queen in the High Court of Justice some matter of a judicial character. It was used to remove civil causes or indictments from inferior courts of record into the High Court, that they may be better tried, or if there has been abuse or error, re-tried. It has been replaced by Judicial Review (*q.v.*).

certum est quod certum reddi potest. [That which is capable of being made certain is to be treated as certain.]

cessante causa, cessat effectus. [When the cause ceases, the effect ceases.]

cessante ratione legis, cessat ipsa lex. [The reason of the law ceasing, the law itself ceases.] This maxim applies to the principles of the common law, but not to any considerable extent to statute law.

cessante statu primitivio cessat derivativus. [The original estate ceasing, that which is derived from it ceases.]

cessat executio. [Suspending execution.]

cesser. Ending or determination. A proviso for cesser was a provision in a settlement creating a long term of years to secure a sum of money, that the term should determine when the objects of the trust were fulfilled; rendered unnecessary by the Satisfied Terms Act 1845; replaced by the Law of Property Act 1925, s.5. A mortgage term, when the money secured by the mortgage has been discharged, becomes a satisfied term and ceases (Law of Property Act 1925, s.116).

cessio bonorum. [Roman law.] The surrender by a debtor of his property to his creditors in lieu of execution against his body. It did not release the debtor from his debts if he afterwards acquired property from which he could pay them without leaving himself in want.

cessio in jure. [Roman law.] A fictitious surrender in court by which a new title was conferred.

cession. A mode of acquisition of territory. The transfer of territory by one State to another, under pressure of war or by arrangement.

cestui que trust. A person for whom another is trustee: a beneficiary.

cestui que use. A person to whose use or benefit lands or other hereditaments were held by another person; *cf.* CESTUI QUE TRUST.

cestui que vie. Where a person is entitled to an estate or interest in property during the life of another, the latter is called the *cestui que vie.*

chain of representation. The executor of a sole or last surviving executor of a testator is himself the executor of that testator, and so long as the chain of such representation is unbroken, the last executor in the chain is the executor of every preceding testator.

challenge of jurors. An objection to persons returned to be jurors in a civil or criminal proceeding. Challenges are tried and determined by the court itself.

1. A challenge to the array is an exception to the whole jury on the ground that the person responsible for summoning the jurors in question is biased or has acted improperly. The right of challenge to the array is preserved by the Juries Act 1974, s.12(6).

2. Challenges to the polls (that is, to particular jurors) are made orally. A peremptory challenge may be made without showing any cause. The Treason Act 1695, allows peremptory challenges to 35 jurors but the right in all indictable offences is now restricted to seven (Criminal Law Act 1967, s.12(6)); Juries Act 1974, s.12). All or any of the jurors may be challenged for cause. Challenges for cause are (1) *propter honoris respectum,* as where a lord of Parliament is empanelled on a jury; (2) *propter defectum,* for some want or default in the individual juror; (3) *propter affectum,* for suspicion of partiality; (4) *propter delictum,* for some crime or misdemeanour. The fact that a person summoned to serve on a jury is not qualified to serve is a ground for challenge for cause (Juries Act 1974, s.12(4)). Any challenge must be made after the juror's name has been drawn by ballot and before he is sworn (s.12(3)). Any party to county court proceedings to be tried by a jury has the same right of challenge as in the High Court (s.12(2)).

challenge to fight. To challenge a person to fight, either orally or by letter, or to bear or provoke such a challenge, was a common law misdemeanour. The offence was abolished by the Criminal Law Act 1967, s.13.

Chamberlain, Lord. An officer of the Queen's Household, who changes with the Ministry of the day. He was formerly the censor of plays under the Theatres Act 1843 but that Act was repealed by the Theatres Act 1968.

Chamberlain, Lord Great. The officer in charge of the Houses of Parliament, with ceremonial duties.

chambers. (1) Rooms attached to the courts in which sit the judges, the masters and registrars for the transaction of legal business which does not require to be done in court. A judge sitting in chambers can exercise the full jurisdiction vested in the High Court (Judicature Act 1925, s.18). Masters (*q.v.*) sit in chambers. (2) Counsel's private offices, *e.g.* in the Temple or Lincoln's Inn.

champerty or **champarty.** That form of maintenance (*q.v.*) in which the person maintaining takes as his reward a portion of anything which may be gained as a result of the proceedings. The common law misdemeanour of champerty was abolished by the Criminal Law Act 1967, s.13. No person is liable in tort for champerty but it is contrary to public policy (s.14).

chancel. The liability of a landowner to repair the chancel of a church is enforceable in the county court (Chancel Repairs Act 1932).

chancellor. The judicial officer of a King, Queen, Bishop, or University, etc.

Chancellor, Lord High. The Lord Chancellor. The chief judicial officer in the British Constitution. Originally he was an ecclesiastic who acted as the King's secretary, and was keeper of the King's conscience. He is appointed by the delivery of the Great Seal, of which he is the keeper. He is a Privy Councillor and acts as Speaker of the House of Lords, where he sits on the Woolsack. He is the President of the Supreme Court (Supreme Court Act 1981, s.1(2)) and of the House of Lords sitting as the final Court of Appeal. He appoints the justices of the peace and the circuit judges, and nominates the judges of the High Court except the Lord Chief Justice. He is a Cabinet Minister. The Lord Chancellor is responsible generally for public records (Public Records Act 1958, s.1).

Chancellor of the Duchy of Lancaster. A member of the Cabinet with only nominal duties as such.

Chancellor of the Exchequer. An officer originally appointed to act as a check on the Lord Treasurer, and a judge of the Court of Exchequer sitting as a court of equity. Now he is nominally one of the Commissioners of the Treasury, but in practice is the Cabinet Minister at the head of the Treasury.

chance-medley. Casual affray. An assault in the course of a sudden brawl or quarrel, followed by the killing of the aggressor; now obsolete and to be considered as justifiable homicide, self-defence, or provocation.

Chancery Division. See COURT OF CHANCERY.

change of parties. (1) Where there is misjoinder or non-joinder; (2) where there is a change by death or some event after the action has commenced (see Ord.15).

chapel. In the Church of England, a chapel of ease is a detached place of prayers and preaching; a parochial chapel is one which has the privilege of administering the sacraments and the office of burial.

chaplain. A clergyman who conducts divine services in a chapel; clergymen with special appointments such as Chaplain to the Forces, as contrasted with the parochial clergy.

chapter. The canons or prebendaries forming the bishop's advisory council, the superior member of which is the dean.

character, evidence of. Evidence as to character of a party to judicial proceedings is not (in general) admissible, unless the nature of the proceedings puts his character in issue. A defendant in criminal proceedings may always adduce evidence of good character. He is not to be asked questions as to his bad character unless he has put forward his character as good or attacked the characters of the prosecutor or witnesses for the prosecution. The protection against cross-examination as to bad character is lost when the accused gives evidence against any other person charged in the same proceedings (Criminal Evidence Act 1979, s.1(1)).

At a trial for rape the complainant may not be asked questions about previous sexual experiences with a person other than the defendant except with leave of the judge (Sexual offences (Amendment) Act 1976; see also *R.* v. *Mills, The Times,* November 21, 1978, C.A.).

charge. In property law a charge is a form of security for the payment of a debt or performance of an obligation, consisting of the right of a creditor to receive payment out of some specific fund or out of the proceeds of the realisation of specific property. The fund or property is said to be charged with the debt thus payable out of it. The only property charges capable of subsisting at law are: (1) a rentcharge in possession charged on land, being either perpetual or for a term of years absolute; (2) a charge by way of legal mortgage; (3) tithe rentcharge annuities or similar charge on land not created by an instrument (Law of Property Act 1925, s.1 (2)). See FIXED CHARGE; FLOATING CHARGE.

In criminal law a charge is an accusation; a charge to a jury is the address of the presiding judge with regard to the duties of the jury.

charge by way of legal mortgage. A charge by deed expressed to be by way of legal mortgage was introduced by the Law of Property Act 1925, s.85(1). The legal effect of it is the same as if the mortgage had been made by means of a mortgage term created for three thousand years without impeachment of waste in favour of the mortgagee (*ibid.* s.87(1), and see Sched. 5, Form No. 1).

chargé d'affaires. A subordinate diplomatic agent, accredited to the Foreign Minister of the State where he resides.

charge sheet. A list of the particular charges, and of the persons charged, awaiting a hearing in a magistrates' court.

charge, statutory. The Law Society has a first charge for the benefit of the Legal Aid Fund on any property which is recovered or preserved for a person who is in receipt of, or has received, legal aid in respect of the proceedings in which the property is recovered or preserved (Legal Aid Act 1974, s.9(6). See also *Hanlon* v. *The Law Society* [1980] 2 All E.R. 199, H.L.).

charging order. A judgment creditor may apply to the court to enforce a judgment or order by imposing a charge by way of a charging order on any interest held by the judgment debtor beneficially in: (a) land; (b) securities; (c) funds in court; (d) under a trust (Charging Orders Act 1979, s.2). The application may be made to the High Court (see Ord. 50) or to a county court where the amount of the debt falls within the county court jurisdiction. A charging order may be made in favour of a solicitor for his Taxed costs on property recovered or preserved by him (Solicitors Act 1974, s.73). A separate judgment creditor of one partner in a firm may obtain an order charging that partner's interest in the partnership property (Partnership Act 1890, s.23). See also STOP ORDER.

charities. Charitable trusts are not subject to the rule against perpetuities, and do not fail for uncertainty. The public character of a charity is essential. The court leans in favour of charity, and will construe favourably gifts intended to be charitable. Charity in its legal sense comprises four principal divisions: trusts for the relief of poverty; trusts for the advancement of education; trusts for the advancement of religion; and trusts for other purposes beneficial to the community, not falling under any of the preceding heads. (*Per* Lord Macnaghten, *Income Tax Special Purposes Commissioners* v. *Pemsel* [1891] A.C. 531, at p.583.) The Charitable Trusts (Validation) Act 1954, and the Recreational Charities Act 1958, are of limited application. The Charities Act 1960 introduced beneficial changes in procedure and machinery for enforcement and supervision. See CY-PRES.

Charities are exempt from income tax (Income and Corporation Taxes Act 1970, s.360; Finance Act 1971, s.56, Sched.14, Part IV; Finance Act 1973, s.52).

Gifts to charity are exempt from capital gains tax (Finance Act 1972, s.119). Gifts to charity up to £50,000 are exempt from estate duty (s.121) and up to £100,000 from capital transfer tax (Finance Act 1975, Sched. 6, para. 10). Charity land is treated favourably under the Community Land Act 1975, s.25.

Charitable trustees have the powers of a tenant for life or settlement trustees.

Charity Commissioners. A body constituted by the Charitable Trusts Acts 1853 to 1939 to administer charities and charity property, and to settle schemes in relation thereto. These Acts were repealed by the Charities Act 1960, but the Charity Commissioners were continued (*ibid.* s.1, Sched. I).

charta. A charter. See MAGNA CARTA.

charter. Formerly any deed relating to hereditaments, especially deeds of feoffment; now a royal charter, which is a grant by the Crown, in the form of letters patent under the Great Seal, to persons therein designated, of specified rights and privileges.

charterparty. [*Carta partita,* a deed cut in two.] A written agreement by which a shipowner lets an entire ship, or a part of it, to the charterer for the conveyance of goods, binding himself to transport them to a particular place for a sum of money which the charterer undertakes to pay as freight for their carriage. The principal stipulations refer to the places of loading and delivery, the mode and time of paying the freight, the number of lay days (*q.v.*) and the rate of demurrage (*q.v.*). The charterparty may operate as a demise or lease of the ship itself with or without the services of the master and crew. The charterer then becomes for the time the owner of the vessel, and the master and crew become his agents or employees. The test is: has the owner parted for the time with the whole possession and control of the ship?

chase. A district of land privileged for wild beasts of chase, with the exclusive right of hunting therein. Franchises of free chase were abolished by the Wild Creatures and Forest Laws Act 1971.

chattels. (Latin, *Catalla,* Cattle.) Any property other than freehold land. Leasehold and other interests in land less than freehold are termed chattels real, as they savour of the reality. Chattels personal are movable, tangible articles of property.

cheat. The common law misdemeanour of fraudulently obtaining the property of another by any deceitful practice not amounting to felony, but of such a nature that it may directly affect the public at large. The common law offence of cheating was abolished by the Theft Act 1968, s.32(1), except as regards offences relating to the public revenue. Cheating at play is punishable under the Gaming Act 1845, s.17; Theft Act 1968, Sched. 2, Part III.

checkweigher. A person appointed to watch the weighing of coal in coal mines on behalf of the colliers (Coal Mines Regulation Act 1887, s.13; Mines and Quarries Act 1954, Sched.5).

cheque. A cheque is a bill of exchange (*q.v.*) drawn on a banker, payable on demand (Bills of Exchange Act 1882, s.73). The person making the cheque is called the drawer, and the person to whom it is payable is called the payee. When the cheque bears across its face the words "and Company", or any abbreviation thereof, between two parallel transverse lines, it is said to be crossed generally, and when it bears across its face the name of a banker, it is said to be crossed specially (*ibid.* s.76). A generally crossed cheque can be paid only through a bank, and a specially crossed cheque only through the bank specified. A holder of a cheque crossed "not negotiable" cannot give a transferee a better title than he himself has (*ibid.* s.81). Obtaining services by deception (*i.e.* using a worthless cheque in payment) is a specific offence (Theft Act 1978, s.1). Dishonestly obtaining goods by means of a worthless cheque also comes within the offence of obtaining property by a deception (Theft Act 1968, s.15).

71

Chief Baron of the Exchequer. The judge who presided in the Court of Exchequer (*q.v.*). His powers are now exercised by the Lord Chief Justice (Judicature Act 1925, s.35).

chief clerks. The old Masters in Chancery (*q.v.*). The Judicature Act 1873 transferred them to the Supreme Court and in 1897 they were entitled Masters of the Supreme Court.

Chief Justice of the Common Pleas. The judge who presided, before the Judicature Act 1873, in the Court of Common Pleas, and subsequently in the Common Pleas Division. His powers are now exercised by the Lord Chief Justice (Judicature Act 1925, s.35).

chief-rent. An annual or periodic sum issuing out of land. It now constitutes a Rentcharge (Rentcharges Act 1977, s.1). See RENTCHARGE.

child; children. For the purposes of the Children and Young Persons Act 1933, s.107 a child is a person under the age of 14 years. Under the Children Act 1975, s.107(1) and Adoption Act 1976, s.72(1) a child is a person under the age of 18 years. By s.52(1) of the Matrimonial Causes Act 1973 "child" in relation to one or both of the parties to a marriage includes an illegitimate or adopted child of that party and "child of the family" means both a child of both parties and any other child (except a foster child) who has been treated by both parties as a child of their family. A child under 10 years of age is exempt from responsibility for crimes committed by him. A child between 10 and 14 is presumed to be incapable of criminal intent but this presumption may be rebutted by proof to the contrary. A boy under 14 cannot commit rape.

The Protection of Children Act 1978 prohibits the taking of indecent photographs of children and related offences. It is an offence to incite a girl of under 16 to have sexual intercourse (Criminal Law Act 1977, s.45).

For the purpose of family inheritance 'child' includes both legitimate and illegitimate children and a child en ventre sa mere at the death of the deceased (Inheritance (Provision for Family Dependants) Act 1975, s.25 (1)). See also JUVENILE OFFENDERS.

child-bearing. There is no presumption in English law as to the time when a woman ceases to be capable of bearing children, although there may be such in practice. For the purposes of the rule against perpetuities it is presumed that a male cannot have a child under the age of 14 years and that a female cannot have a child under 12 years or over the age of 55 years (Perpetuities and Accumulations Act 1964, s.2).

child benefit. Payable weekly under the Child Benefit Act 1975 to the person responsible for one or more children. It supersedes family allowances (*q.v.*).

child destruction. The offence committed by any person who with intent to destroy the life of a child capable of being born alive, by any wilful act causes a child to die before it has an existence independent of its mother (Infant Life (Preservation) Act 1929, s.1). But see ABORTION.

child of the family. By section 52(1) of the Matrimonial Causes Act 1973 a child of the family is defined as a child of both the parties (to matrimonial proceedings brought under the Act) and any other child, not being a child who has been boarded out with those parties by a local authority or voluntary organisation, who has been treated by both those parties as a child of their family. The term is given the same definition by section 82(1) of the Domestic Proceedings and Magistrates Court Act 1978.

Chiltern Hundreds. The Hundreds of Stoke, Desborough and Burnham in Bucks. A Member of the House of Commons cannot resign his seat, but the acceptance of an office of profit under the Crown obliges him to vacate it, but may leave him eligible for re-election. The stewardship of the Chiltern Hundreds is considered such an office, and is granted to any Member who wishes to retire.

chirograph. Anciently a deed of two parts which were written on the same paper or parchment, with the word *chirographum* in capital letters between the two parts: the paper or parchment was then cut through the middle of the letters, and a part given to each party. If the cutting was indented, the deed was an indenture.

chirographum apud debitorum repertum praesumitur solutum. [A deed or bond found with the debtor is presumed to be paid.]

chivalry. Knight's service (*q.v.*). See COURT OF CHIVALRY.

chose. A thing; a chattel personal. A chose in possession is a movable chattel in the custody or under the control of the owner.

chose in action. A right of proceeding in a court of law to procure the payment of a sum of money (*e.g.* on a bill of exchange, policy of insurance), or to recover pecuniary damages for the infliction of a wrong or the non-performance of a contract. A legal chose in action is a right of action which could be enforced in a court of law; an equitable chose in action is a right which could only be enforced in the Court of Chancery, *e.g.* an interest in a trust fund or legacy. See ASSIGNMENT OF CHOSES IN ACTION.

Church Commissioners for England. The body formed by the merger of the Ecclesiastical Commissioners (*q.v.*) and Queen Anne's Bounty (*q.v.*) (Church Commissioners Measure 1947; Church Commissioners Measure 1964). The Church Estates Commissioners are members of the Church Commissioners.

Church of England. Since the Reformation, it has been a separate national church independent of the Pope. As an established church, its law is part of the law of England, *i.e.* ecclesiastical law. See CANON LAW; MEASURES.

churchwardens. Parochial officers of the Church. See the Church Wardens (Appointment and Resignation) Measure 1964; Synodical Government Measure 1969, Sched. 3, para. 11. The former duties of the church wardens relating to church property are now a function of the parochial church council (Parochial Church Council (Powers) Measure 1956, s.4).

Cinque Ports. The five harbours of Hastings, Romney, Hythe, Dover and Sandwich, and two other towns, Winchelsea and Rye, subsequently added to their number. Lying more immediately exposed to attacks from the French coast, they were placed under the special custody of a Lord Warden, who had a local jurisdiction in relation to civil suits and proceedings (Cinque Ports Act 1855).

Circuit judges. See CROWN COURT.

circuits. Divisions of the country for judicial business. Under the Courts Act 1971, ss.26–29, the country is divided into six circuits: Midland and Oxford; North-Eastern; Northern; South Eastern (including London); Wales and Chester; Western.

circuity of action was where two or more proceedings were taken to effect the same result as might be effected by one: abolished in practice by the right to raise a counterclaim at the trial of an action.

circumstantial evidence. A series of circumstances leading to the inference or conclusion of guilt when direct evidence is not available. Evidence which although not directly establishing the existence of the facts required to be proved, is admissible as making the facts in issue probable by reason of its connection with or relation to them. It is sometimes regarded as of higher probative value (*e.g.* finding a fish in the milk) than direct evidence, which may be perjured or mistaken.

citation. (1) The calling upon a person who is not a party to an action or proceeding to appear before the court. (2) The quotation of decided cases in legal argument as authorities.

citizenship. For the various classes of citizenship see BRITISH CITIZEN; BRITISH DEPENDENT TERRITORIES CITIZEN; BRITISH OVERSEAS CITIZEN; BRITISH SUBJECT; COMMONWEALTH CITIZEN.

city. A town corporate which has or has had a bishop, or which by letters patent has been created a city by prerogative of the Crown.

City of London Court. A court having a local jurisdiction within the City of London; practically a county court. See MAYOR'S AND CITY OF LONDON COURT.

civil, as opposed to (i) ecclesiastical; (ii) criminal; (iii) military.

civil action. Proceedings by way of action (*q.v.*) as contrasted with criminal proceedings.

civil death. Loss of legal personality, as on banishment or profession of religion, when the possessions of the person concerned devolved as on actual death, or were forfeited.

civil debt. Any sum of money recoverable on complaint, or declared by statute to be a civil debt, recoverable summarily. The proceedings commence by complaint and terminate by an order, which cannot be enforced by imprisonment unless the defaulter has, or has had since the date of the order, the means to pay and has failed to pay. Magistrate's Courts Act 1952, ss.50, 73.

civil law. Roman law; the *Corpus Juris Civilis.*

Civil List. Each sovereign since George II has at his or her accession surrendered to the nation the hereditary revenues (the profits of Crown lands etc.), and thereupon Parliament has made pecuniary provision for each sovereign for the period of his or her reign by an Act known as the Civil List, granting an annual sum for the support of the royal dignity and household. (The Civil List Act 1972 (as amended by S.I. 1975 No.133) fixed the Civil List at the yearly sum of £1,400,000.) See also the Civil List Act 1975.

Civil list pensions are small annual sums granted by the Crown to worthy recipients.

civil servant. A servant of the Crown, other than the holder of political or judicial office, who is employed in a civil capacity, and whose remuneration is paid wholly and directly out of moneys voted by Parliament. He is an officer employed in a department of the State with the approval of the Treasury. A civil servant is a person holding his appointment directly from the Crown, or one who has been admitted into the Civil Service with a certificate from the Civil Service Commissioners. He holds his office during the royal pleasure.

civiliter mortuus. [Civilly dead.] See CIVIL DEATH.

claim. The assertion of a right. A policy of assurance becomes a claim when the event insured against happens.

clam, vi, aut precario. [By stealth, violence or entreaty.] In order that the title of the owner of land may be barred under the Statutes of Limitation in favour of a person in possession of the land, the occupier must hold neither secretly, forcibly nor by leave of the owner.

Clarendon, Assize of. See ASSIZE OF CLARENDON.

Clarendon, Constitutions of (1164). Enactments passed to secure the jurisdiction of the King's Courts in certain matters of dispute between laymen and the Church.

clausulae inconsuetae semper inducunt suspicionem. [Unusual clauses always excite suspicion.]

clausum fregit. [He broke the close.] Trespass *quare clausum fregit* is the tort of trespass to land which consists in the act of entering upon land, or remaining upon land, or placing any material object on it, without lawful justification.

clean hands. A suitor or plaintiff who is free from any taint of fraud, sharp practice, etc. One who sues in good faith.

clear days. Complete days; exclusive of named first or last days. See Ord. 3, r.2.

clearance. A certificate by the Customs to the effect that a ship has complied with the Customs requirements and is at liberty to put to sea.

clergy. Persons in Holy Orders or ordained for religious service. The parish clergy are rectors, vicars, perpetual curates and curates.

clerk. Anciently, a priest or deacon, in Holy Orders or not.

clerk of arraigns. An assistant of the clerk of assize (*q.v.*). The office was abolished by the Judicature (Circuit Officers) Act 1946.

clerk of assize. The principal officer attached to the assizes. Courts of assize and, with them, clerks of assize have been abolished. See ASSIZE.

Clerk of the Crown, or Clerk of the Crown in Chancery. This officer performs the duties of the Clerk of the Hanaper (*q.v.*) and the Clerk of the Petty Bag (*q.v.*). He is Clerk of the court of the Lord High Steward, and Accountant-General (*q.v.*) of the Supreme Court (Judicature Act 1925, s.133).

Clerk of the Hanaper. (*Hanaperis,* a hamper.) Formerly an officer on the common law side of the Court of Chancery who registered the fines that were paid on every writ, and saw that the writs were sealed up in bags (or hampers), in order to be opened afterwards and issued. He also took account of all patents, commissions and grants that passed the Great Seal. See now CLERK OF THE CROWN.

Clerk of the House of Commons is appointed by the Crown as under clerk of the Parliaments to attend upon the Commons. He signs all orders of the House, indorses the bills sent or returned to the Lords, and reads whatever is required to be read in the House. He has the custody of all records and other documents.

Clerk of the Parliaments. One of the chief officers of the House of Lords. He is appointed by the Crown, by letters patent. On entering office he makes a declaration to make true entries and records of the things done and passed in the Parliaments, and to keep secret all such matters, as shall be treated therein. He indorses on every Act the date on which it receives the Royal Assent.

clerk of the peace. Formerly, an officer appointed by the Custos Rotulorum (*q.v.*) to keep the county records and to assist the justices of the peace in quarter sessions not only in drawing indictments, entering judgments, issuing process, etc., but also in administrative business. With the abolition of quarter sessions (Courts Act 1971, s.3) the offices of clerk of the peace and deputy clerk of the peace were abolished on January 1, 1972 (s.44).

Clerk of the Petty Bag. An officer of the Court of Chancery whose duty it was to record the return of all inquisitions out of every shire; to make out patents, summonses to Parliament, etc. See now CLERK OF THE CROWN.

clerk to the justices. Usually a barrister or solicitor of not less than five years standing who sits in court with lay magistrates and at their request advises them on questions of law, procedure and sentencing. See the Justices of the Peace Act 1979, s.28 for outline of clerk's duties. See also Lord Chief Justices' Practice Direction dated July 2, 1981.

Clerks of Records and Writs. Officers formerly attached to the Court of Chancery, whose duties consisted principally in sealing bills of complaint and writs of execution, filing affidavits, keeping a record of suits, and certifying office copies of pleadings and affidavits. By the Judicature (Officers) Act 1879 they were transferred to the Central Office of the Supreme Court, under the title of Masters of the Supreme Court.

clog on equity of redemption. The doctrine of equity that no mortgage deed may contain any stipulation or provision fettering or impeding the mortgagor's right to redeem, *e.g.* which unduly delays the time for redemption, or which is unfair or unconscionable or which is inconsistent with or repugnant to the right to redeem. Collateral stipulations or advantages were formerly void as an evasion of the usury laws, but they are now valid provided they do not clog the equity.

close. (Enclosed land.) A trespass on a man's land was formerly described as a breach of his close, or trespass *quare clausum fregit.*

close company. See the Income and Corporation Taxes Act 1970, ss.282–303; Finance Act 1971, s.25; Finance Act 1972 s.94, Scheds. 16, 17, 28, Pt. VI; Finance Act, 1973, ss.20, 21; Finance Act 1974, Sched. 7, para. 4; Finance Act 1975, s.39, Sched. 5, para. 24.

close rolls and close writs. Certain Royal letters sealed with the Great Seal and directed to particular persons, and not being proper for public inspection, were closed up and sealed on the outside. They were thence called writs close, and recorded in the close rolls.

close seasons. The varying periods of the year during which it is forbidden to kill or take game or fish.

closed shop. The term applied to the situation in which an employee may only obtain a particular job if he becomes and remains a member of a specified trade union, *i.e.* where the employer and trade union have a union membership agreement. Dismissal by reason of refusal to join or belong to a trade union may be fair (see Employment Protection (Consolidation) Act 1978, s.58(3)). In some cases, *e.g.* where the employee genuinely objects on grounds of conscience, it will be unfair (Act of 1978, s.58(3)(*a*)). See UNFAIR DISMISSAL.

closed shop agreement. An agreement whereby employers agree to employ only members of a trade union. Defined as a "union membership agreement" (see Trade Union and Labour Relations Act 1974, s.30(1) and Employment Protection (Consolidation) Act 1978, s.58(3)).

closing order. An order made by a local authority for closing a house which is unfit for habitation (Housing Act 1957, ss.17, 18).

closure. A device for bringing to an end a debate or speech. If the motion "that the question be now put" is carried, provided that not less than 100 members vote in its support, the debate must cease.

club. A voluntary association of persons for social or other purposes. It is not a partnership, and must sue or be sued in the names of the members of the committee, or the officers, on behalf of themselves and all other members of the club (see Ord. 15, r.12 n., Ord.81 r.1 n.). Members are liable only to the extent of their subscriptions. In a proprietary club the expenses are borne by a contractor, who receives the subscriptions of the members and makes his profit out of the difference.

A club is regulated by the rules agreed to by the members and for the time being in force. If a member is expelled from a club by a decision which has been arrived at without giving him an opportunity of being heard in his own defence, the court may grant an injunction, or give damages.

The sale or supply of intoxicating liquor in a club is regulated by the Licensing Act 1964. As to racial discrimination against non-members see Race Relations Act 1976, s.25.

coast. (1) The Coastguard is the force stationed on the coasts to prevent smuggling and invasion, and to assist navigation and ships in distress. By the Coastguard Act 1925 the force was transferred from the Admiralty to the Board (now the Department) of Trade. (2) The protection of the coast against erosion and encroachment by the sea is provided for by the Coast Protection Act 1949, amended by the Local Government Act 1972, Sched. 30.

cockfighting is illegal. The possession of cockfighting appliances is an offence (Cockfighting Act 1952). See also the Protection of Animals (Amendment) Act 1954, s.3.

code. The whole body of law; whether of a complete system of law, *e.g.* the Roman Law Code of Justinian; the Code Napoléon of France; or relating to a particular subject or branch of law, such as the Sale of Goods Act 1979, or Bills of Exchange Act 1882, which were statutes collecting and stating the whole of the law, as it stood at the time were passed.

codicil. A codicil is an instrument executed by a testator for adding to, altering, explaining or confirming a will previously made by him. It becomes part of the will, and must be executed with the same formalities as a will (Wills Act 1837, ss.1,9). The effect of a codicil is to bring the will down to the date of the codicil, and thereby to make the same disposition of the testator's estate as if the testator had at that date made a new will, with the original dispositions as altered by the codicil.

coercion. An act that is committed under physical coercion is not a criminal offence, but mere moral coercion is not a defence.

It was a common law presumption that a married woman who committed a felony other than homicide in the presence of her husband acted under his coercion and was not guilty of an offence, but this presumption was rebuttable. This doctrine was abolished by the Criminal Justice Act 1925, s.47, but it also provided that on a charge against a wife for any offence other than treason or murder, it is a good defence to prove that the offence was committed in the presence of and under the coercion of the husband.

cogitationis poenam nemo patitur. [The thoughts and intents of men are not punishable.] For the Devil himself knoweth not the mind of man (*per* Brian C.J.).

cognati. [Roman law.] Cognates. Persons related to each other by blood.

cognisance. Judicial notice or knowledge; jurisdiction.

cognitor. [Roman law.] An agent appointed to act for another in an action. He was appointed by a set form of words in the presence of the opposite party. He need not be present at the ceremony, but he did not become *cognitor* unless and until he consented to take up office. See PROCURATOR.

cognovit actionem. A written confession by a defendant in an action that he had no defence, on condition that he should be allowed a certain time for the payment of the debt or agreed damages. Now superseded by orders of the court made by consent for the entry of judgment or for the issue of execution at a future date.

cohabitation. Living together as husband and wife, even if not married. Cohabitation may affect a woman's right to supplementary benefit (see Supplementary Benefits Act 1976, Sched. 1, para.3(1)(b)). The criteria set out in the Supplementary Benefits Handbook and judicially approved in Commissioner's decision R(G) 3/81 and R(SB) 17/81 are: (a) common household; (b) stability of the relationship; (c) financial support; (d) sexual relationship; (e) children; (f) public acknowledgment of relationship. Absence of a sexual relationship does not preclude a finding of cohabitation.

cohaeredes sunt quasi unum corpus, propter unitatem juris quod habent. [Co-heirs are regarded as one person on account of the unity of title which they possess.] See *e.g.* COPARCENER.

coif. A white silk cap which serjeants-at-law wore in court.

collateral. [By the side of.] A collateral assurance, agreement, etc., which is independent of, but subordinate to, an assurance or agreement affecting the same subject-matter. A collateral security is one which is given in addition to the principal security. Thus a person who borrows money on the security of a mortgage may deposit shares with the lender as collateral security. See CONSANGUINITY.

collatio bonorum. [Roman law.] Bringing into hotchpot (*q.v.*).

collation. The admittance and institution of a clerk by a bishop to a benefice in the bishop's own gift.

college. A corporation created for the promotion of learning and the support of members who devote themselves to learning.

College of Arms. See HERALD'S COLLEGE.

colligenda bona. See AD COLLIGENDA BONA.

collision. Where ships are in collision caused by the negligence of both vessels, each is liable to make good the loss or damage in proportion to the degree in which she was in fault (Maritime Conventions Act 1911, s.1).

collusion. The arrangement of two persons, apparently in a hostile position or having conflicting interests, to do some act in order to injure a third person or deceive a court. In divorce, collusion was a bar to a decree but all the old bars to divorce, including collusion, were repealed by the Divorce Reform Act 1969. Collusion as a bar to a decree of nullity was abolished by the Nullity of Marriage Act 1971, s.6(1). See also the Matrimonial Causes Act 1973, s.19(6).

colony. A British colony is any part of Her Majesty's Dominions outside the British Islands except: (a) countries having fully responsible status within the Commonwealth; (b) territories for whose external relations a country other than the United Kingdom is responsible; or (c) associated states (Interpretation Act 1978, s.5, Sched. 1).

colour. Any appearance, pretext, or pretence, or fictitious allegation of a right; thus a person is said to have no colour of title when he has not even a prima facie title.

colourable. That which is in appearance only, and not in substance, what it purports to be.

comitatus. [A county.]

comitia calata. [Roman law.] Special meetings of the *Comitia Curiata,* summoned twice a year, and presided over by the Pontiff.

comity of nations. That body of rules which the States observe towards one another from courtesy or convenience, but which are not binding as rules of international law.

commendation. The act of an owner of land in placing himself and his land under the protection of a lord, so as to constitute himself a vassal or feudal tenant.

commercial cause. Causes arising out of the ordinary transactions of merchants and traders. See COMMERCIAL LAW.

Commercial Court. The Commercial Court was formally constituted by the Administration of Justice Act 1970, s.3 as part of the Queen's Bench Division of the High Court, thus giving statutory effect to the practice whereby, since 1895, commercial actions have been dealt with on a simplified procedure and expeditiously by a specialist judge. The practice is regulated by Ord. 72. The judge of the Commercial Court may act as arbitrator or umpire in disputes of a commercial character (s.4).

commercial law. The law of business contracts, bankruptcy, patents, trade-marks, designs, companies, partnership, export and import of merchandise, affreightment, insurance, banking, mercantile agency and usages.

commission. (1) An order or authority to do an act or exercise powers, *e.g.* an authority to an agent to enter into a contract; (2) the body charged with a commission, *e.g.* the Charity Commission; (3) an agent's renumeration.

commission, examination of witnesses on. The practice of taking the evidence of witnesses on commission has been superseded by the procedure under Ord. 39. See also the Evidence (Proceedings in Other Jurisdictions) Act 1975.

commission for racial equality. See RACE RELATIONS.

commission of assize. Formerly commissions issued to judges or Queen's Counsel, authorising them to sit at assizes for trial of civil actions. See ASSIZE.

commission of the peace. One by which the Crown appoints or "assigns" a number of persons to act as justices of the peace within a certain district. A separate commission of the peace is issued for each county (Local Government Act 1972, s.217). As to the form of a commission of the peace, see the Justices of the Peace Act 1979, ss.1, 5.

commissioners for oaths. Persons appointed by the Lord Chancellor to administer oaths (including affirmations and declarations) to persons coming before them (Commissioners for Oaths Act 1889, ss.1, 11). Every solicitor who holds a practising certificate has the powers of a commissioner for oaths (Solicitors Act 1974, s.81).

Commissioners of Crown Lands have been superseded by the Crown Estate Commissioners (Crown Estate Act 1961).

Commissioners of Customs and Excise. See Customs and Excise Management Act 1979, ss.6–18.

Commissioners of Inland Revenue. They are charged with the collection of income tax, corporation tax, capital gains tax, death duties, stamp duties and capital transfer tax (Inland Revenue Regulation Act 1890; Taxes Management Act 1970; Finance Act 1975, Sched.4).

Commissions for local administration. Bodies charged with dealing with complaints of maladministration by local authorities, police authorities and water authorities (Local Government Act 1974, ss. 23–34).

committal. The sending of a person to prison, generally for a short period, or temporary purpose, *e.g.* for contempt of court. It is effected in a summary way by the tipstaff to whom the order for committal is handed (Ord. 52 notes).

Committal for trial is the order made by the examining justices upon charges of indictable crime where they decide there is a strong enough case or sufficient evidence against the accused to warrant his being tried by jury. (See Magistrates' Courts Act 1952, ss.7–12; Criminal Justice Act 1972, Sched.5.)

committee. (1) A person to whom the custody of the person or the estate of a mental patient was formerly committed or granted by the Lord Chancellor. See COURT OF PROTECTION.

(2) Persons to whom any matter or business is committed or referred.

committee of inspection. A committe consisting of not more than five or less than three persons representing the creditors, for the purpose of superintending the administration of the bankrupt's property by the trustee (Bankruptcy Act 1914, s.20).

Committee of the Whole House. A parliamentary Committee consisting of the whole House of Commons, sitting without the Speaker in the Chair, to consider Bills which have been read a second time preparatory to reporting them to the House proper. The Committee of Ways and Means and the Committee of Supply are committees of the whole House for considering the raising of revenue and its allocation respectively.

commixtio. [Roman law.] The mixing together of materials belonging to different owners, the product being held in common or divided in proportion to the shares contributed.

commodatum. A kind of bailment (*q.v.*).

common. A right of common is the right of taking some part of any natural product of the land or water belonging to another. It may be created by grant or claimed by prescription or arise from the custom of the manor. It is an incorporeal hereditament and a species of *profit à prendre*. The four principal rights of common are (1) pasture, the right of feeding beasts upon the land of another; (2) piscary, the right of fishing in the waters of another; (3) estovers, the right of cutting wood, gorse or furze, etc., on the land of another; (4) turbary, the right of digging turves on the soil of another.

The Commons Registration Act 1965 provides for the maintenance of registers by local authorities containing particulars: (a) of common land; (b) town and village greens; (c) rights of common and rights of ownership of common land. A register is conclusive evidence of those matters (ss.1,10).

Any right of common originating in the forest law is freed from restrictions on its exercise (Wild Creatures and Forest Laws Act 1971).

A common is a piece of land subject to rights of common. The Secretary of State for the Environment has power to make rules to prevent further enclosures of commons or waste in urban areas, and to enable the public to have access for air and exercise (Law of Property Act 1925, ss.193, 194).

common assault. An assault not amounting to an aggravated assault.

common assurances. The legal evidence of the transfer of property by which a person's estate is assured to him: (1) under the old common law on the actual land to be conveyed by handing over a symbol of it; (2) by matter of court record; (3) by special local custom; (4) by a deed; (5) by will.

common bench. The Court of Common Pleas (*q.v.*).

common carrier. See CARRIER, COMMON.

common counts. Counts (*q.v.*) for money lent, for work done, etc.

common employment. The common law rule that a master was not liable to his servant for injuries resulting from the negligence of a fellow servant in the course of their common employment, unless there was on the part of the master want of care in selecting his servants, or personal negligence or omission to take reasonable precautions to ensure his servant's safety. Common employment meant work which necessarily and naturally in the normal course of events exposed servants engaged in that work to the risk of the negligence of the one affecting the other. The rule was modified by the Employers' Liability Act 1880, which placed a workman in certain cases in the same position as that of a stranger. It was abolished, and the Employers' Liability Act 1880, repealed, by the Law Reform (Personal Injuries) Act 1948.

common informer. A person who sued for a penalty under a statute which entitled any person to sue for it. Common Informer procedure was abolished by the Common Informers Act 1951.

common injunction. The injunction formerly granted in Chancery to prevent the institution or continuance of proceedings at common law which were inequitable, *e.g.* where an instrument sued on had been obtained by fraud. The injunction was addressed to the parties so proceeding, not to the common law court. It became obsolete after the Judicature Act 1873, when equitable defences could be pleaded in any court.

common jury. A jury consisting of ordinary jurymen, as opposed (formerly) to a Special Jury. See SPECIAL JURY.

common law. That part of the law of England formulated, developed and administered by the old common law courts, based originally on the common customs of the country, and unwritten. It is opposed to equity (the body of rules administered by the Court of Chancery); to statute law (the law laid down in Acts of Parliament); to special law (the law administered in special courts such as ecclesiastical law, and the law merchant); and to the civil law (the law of Rome).

It is "the commonsense of the community, crystallised and formulated by our forefathers." It is not local law, nor the result of legislation.

common law marriage and common law wife or husband. (a) Colloquial terms sometimes used to denote the relationship of a man and woman who live together as if man and wife without having gone through a legal ceremony of marriage. The term has no legal significance in its everyday sense as above, but see (b) below.

(b) A marriage which does not comply with the normal requirements (for which see MARRIAGE) can be validly contracted in any place abroad where the English common law prevails, and where either the local law is inapplicable, or cannot be complied with, or the local law does not invalidate such a marriage.

common lodging-house. A house in which poor persons are lodged by night for hire, they sleeping or eating in a common room (Public Health Act 1936, s.235).

Common Market. The popular name for the European Economic Community (see the European Communites Act 1972).

common pleas. Common law actions between subject and subject. See COURT OF COMMON PLEAS.

common recovery. See RECOVERY.

Common Serjeant. A judicial officer of the City of London, next below the Recorder, and a judge of the Central Criminal Court. The Common Serjeant is now a circuit judge (Courts Act 1971, Sched. 2, paras.(1), 2(2)).

common vouchee. The crier of the court vouched to warranty in the common recovery. See RECOVERY.

commonable. A thing over, by, or in respect of which a right of common may be exercised.

Commonwealth, The. (1) The English State during the period 1649–1660 when there was no actual King, although Charles II was deemed to have reigned from 1649 when Charles I died. (2) The association of the United Kingdom and the self-governing nations whose territories originally formed part of the British Empire (q.v.). The Commonwealth has not been recognised as an entity in international law. Each of the member States has separate membership of the United Nations. Those States are equal in status and not subordinate one to another. The Queen is the head of the Commonwealth.

States became members of the Commonwealth from time to time by statutes granting them representative self-government. Some are republics within the Commonwealth. Ireland, Pakistan and South Africa have left the Commonwealth. Burma is an independent State. Cyprus is an independent sovereign country, except for areas reserved to Her Majesty. The following are members of the Commonwealth: United Kingdom, Australia, Canada, New Zealand, Bangladesh, Bahamas, Barbados, Botswana, Ceylon (Sri Lanka), Gambia, Guyana, Ghana, India, Fiji, Jamaica, Kenya, Lesotho, Malawi, Malaysia, Malta, Mauritius, Nigeria, Sierra Leone, Singapore, Swaziland, Tanzania, Tonga, Trinidad and Tobago, Uganda, Zambia and Zimbabwe.

Commonwealth citizen. Every person who is a British citizen (q.v.), a British Dependent Territories citizen (q.v.), a British Overseas citizen (q.v.), a British subject (q.v.) or a citizen of a country listed in Sched. 3 to the British Nationality Act 1981 has the status of Commonwealth citizen (Act of 1981, s.37).

commorientes. Persons dying together on the same occasion where it cannot be ascertained by clear evidence which died first. By section 184 of the Law of Property Act 1925, death is presumed to have taken place in order of seniority. Where several persons died together in an air raid, the uncertainty which the section postulates existed, and the section applied (*Hickman* v. *Peacey* [1945] A.C. 304). For estate duty purposes, however, they are treated as having died at the same instant (Finance Act 1958, s.29; Finance Act 1969, Sched.17, Part III, para.17). The same rule applies in the case of capital transfer tax (Finance Act 1975, s.22(9)).

communis error facit jus. [Common mistake sometimes makes law.]

communities. Districts in Wales are divided into communities (Local Government Act 1972, ss.20, 27–36).

community homes. These will gradually supersede, *inter alia*, approved schools and detention centres (Children and Young Persons Act 1969, ss.35–50).

community land. See DEVELOPMENT LAND.

community of property. Where there is common ownership of property existing between spouses, as *e.g.* in California.

community service order. An order requiring an offender to do unpaid work (Powers of Criminal Courts Act 1973, ss.14–17).

commutation. The conversion of the right to receive a variable or periodical payment into the right to receive a fixed or gross payment.

companies court. There is no separate court which deals with matters arising from the operation of companies, *e.g.* winding up petitions. Such matters are dealt with by the Chancery Division (Group A) of the High Court (as to which see Ord. 102) or possibly, where the companies paid up capital does not exceed £120,000 by the County Court of the district in which the company's registered office is situated (see C.C.R., Ord. 46, r.16).

company. An association of persons formed for the purpose of some business or undertaking carried on in the name of the association, each member having the right of assigning his shares to any other person, subject to the regulations of the company. Companies are either incorporated or unincorporated.

An incorporated company is an entity distinct from its members. Companies are incorporated either (1) by charter; (2) by special Act of Parliament; or (3) by registration under one of the public general Acts relating to companies.

Companies are limited or unlimited, according as the liability of their shareholders is limited or not. In the case of an unlimited company each shareholder is liable to contribute to the debts of the company to the full extent of his property. For the liability of shareholders in a limited company see LIMITED COMPANY.

A limited company may be either a private company of a public company. All companies are private companies unless they satisfy the requirements of a public company. The distinction between private and public companies is shown in the name, *i.e.* a private company has the word "limited" as the last part of its name whereas the name of a public company must end with the words "Public Limited Company" or "PLC" A private company has to satisfy only one requirement, *viz.* that it shall not offer or allot any shares or debentures (*q.v.*) to the public (Companies Act 1980, s.15(1)). There is no limit on the number of shareholders. Both a private company and a public company must have at least two members (Companies Act 1980, Sched. 4). For the detailed requirements for a Public Company see the Companies Act 1980, ss.1(1), 2(2), 6(1)(*a*), 6(1)(*b*). For Transitional provisions for companies formed before 1981 see sections 8 *et seq.*

company secretary. By the Companies Act 1948, s. 177, every company must have a secretary, and a sole director may not also be secretary.

compass. Contriving or imagining, *e.g.* the death of the reigning monarch; a mental intention or design, which must be manifested by some overt (open) act.

compensatio. [Roman law.] Set-off; when the defendant brings up his claims against the plaintiff in order to have them reckoned in reduction of the plaintiff's demand.

compensation. A payment to make amends for loss or injury to person or property, or as recompense for some deprivation, *e.g.* compensation to the owner for the compulsory acquisition of his property. See *e.g.* the Land Compensation Act 1961; Land Compensation Act 1973.

compensation order. A court by or before whom a person is convicted of an offence may make an order requiring him to pay compensation for the injuries, loss or damage he has caused (Powers of Criminal Courts Act 1973, s.35). See *R.* v. *Miller* (1976) 68 Cr.App.R. 56, C.A.

As to compensation orders in respect of criminal damage to ancient monuments etc. see Ancient Monuments and Archaeological Areas Act 1979, s.29).

complainant. One who makes a complaint to the justices.

complaint. (1) A statement of the facts of a case made by the person aggrieved in commencing proceedings before justices of the peace to obtain an order for the payment of money (see Magistrates' Courts Act 1952, Pt. II). (2) A statement made to a third party by a female against whom a sexual offence has been committed. To be admissible in evidence in corroboration of the story of the prosecution, a complaint must have been voluntary and not elicited by leading questions, and it must have been made at the first reasonable opportunity.

completion. Completion of a contract for the sale of property consists on the part of the vendor in conveying with a good title the estate contracted for in the land sold and delivering up the actual possession or enjoyment thereof to the purchaser. On the purchaser's part, it lies in accepting such title, preparing and tendering a conveyance for the vendor's execution, and paying the purchase price.

compos mentis. [Of sound mind.]

composition. An arrangement between two or more persons for the payment by one to the other or others of a sum of money in satisfaction of an obligation to pay another sum differing either in amount or mode of payment; or the sum so agreed to be paid. A debtor, *e.g.* may propose to his creditors a composition in satisfaction of his liabilities (or a scheme of arrangement) as an alternative to bankruptcy.

compound. To agree to accept a composition.

compound settlement. A settlement constituted by a number of documents, deeds or wills, extending over a period of time.

compounding a felony. This offence has lapsed on the abolition of the distinction between felony (*q.v.*) and misdemeanour. But concealing an offence may be an offence under the Criminal Law Act 1967, s.5.

compromise. An agreement between parties to a dispute to settle it out of court.

comptroller. One who controls or checks the accounts of others; originally by keeping a counter-roll or register.

Comptroller and Auditor-General. The public officer who examines the accounts of Government Departments to see that public money is properly expended according to law and for the purposes for which it was voted. He reports to the Public Accounts Committee of the House of Commons, and draws attention to any financial extravagance or irregularities. His salary is charged on the Consolidated Fund and he holds office during good behaviour.

compulsory purchase. An order for the purchase of land made (possibly against the will of the vendor) under statutory authority. The legislation is consolidated in the Acquisition of Land Act 1981.

compurgation. Wager of law: a method by which the oaths of a number of persons as to the character of an accused person in a criminal case, or of a defendant in a civil case, were accepted as proof of his innocence in the one case or as proof in the other case that the claim made against him was not well founded. The persons who made such oaths were known as compurgators. It began to decline in the reign of Henry II, but continued available in the old actions of debt, detinue and account, until it was abolished by the Civil Procedure Act 1833.

concealment. Non-disclosure of a fact by a party to a contract. If active, and therefore fraudulent, it is a ground for rescission, but not otherwise, except in contracts *uberrimae fidei, e.g.* a policy of insurance.

concealment of birth. A person who by any secret disposition of the dead body of a child whether it died before, at, or after its birth, endeavours to conceal the birth is guilty of a misdemeanour (Offences against the Person Act 1861, s.60). On a trial of any person for the murder of any child, or for child destruction, or on the trial of a woman for infanticide, the jury, if they acquit of such charge, may find a verdict of concealment of birth (Infanticide Act 1938; Infant Life (Preservation) Act 1929).

conciliar. Pertaining to the Council.

conciliation. The bringing together of employers and employees in an endeavour to settle disputes. See ADVISORY CONCILIATION AND ARBITRATION SERVICE.

concilium magnum regni. The Great Council (*q.v.*).

concluded. Estopped.

concubinatus. [Roman law.] Concubinage; the permanent cohabitation of one man and one woman which did not give the father *potestas* over the children born to him by the concubine.

concurrent jurisdiction of the Court of Chancery. That part of equity which dealt with cases in which the common law courts recognised the right but granted no complete and adequate remedy, and where equity gave a better, *e.g.* specific performance and injunction.

concurrent sentences. Where the defendant is convicted of several offences at the same trial, the court has, in general, power to direct that the sentences shall be served concurrently (*i.e.* together or at the same time). Sentences run consecutively if they follow one upon the other.

concurrent writ. A copy of the original writ, including the date of the original, which remains in force for the same period as the original. One or more concurrent writs may be issued at the time of issuing the original, or within 12 months thereafter (see Ord. 6).

condemnation. The adjudication of a Prize Court on a captured vessel that it has been lawfully captured, which divests the owner of the vessel of his property and vests it in the captor.

condictio. [Roman law.] The general term for a personal action; an action where the plaintiff alleges against another that something ought to be given to or done for him. Originally a formal notice to be present on the 30th day to choose a *judex.*

condition. A provision which makes the existence of a right dependent on the happening of an event; the right is then conditional, as opposed to an absolute right. A true condition is where the event on which the existence of the right depends is future and uncertain.

An express condition is one set out as a term in a contract or deed. An implied condition is one founded by the law on the presumed intention of the parties, with the object of giving such efficacy to the transaction as the parties must have intended it should have.

A condition precedent is one which delays the vesting of a right until the happening of an event; a condition subsequent is one which destroys or divests the right upon the happening of an event.

A condition in a contract is a stipulation going to the root of the contract, the breach of which gives rise to a right to treat the contract as repudiated. See (and contrast) WARRANTY. See also CONDITIONS OF SALE.

conditional appearance. Before 1981 a defendant could enter an appearance in qualified terms reserving the right to apply to the court to set aside the writ or service thereof for an alleged informality or irregularity. This has now been abolished. An acknowledgement of service (*q.v.*) under the new procedure does not operate as submission to the jurisdiction nor waiver of irregularities. See Ord. 12, r.1.

conditional discharge. An order of conditional discharge may be made if the court does not think it expedient to impose a punishment and a probation order is inappropriate (Powers of Criminal Courts Act 1973, s.7).

conditional fee simple. A fee simple granted to a person with a condition that on the happening or non-happening of a specified event the grantor shall be entitled to re-enter; as, *e.g.* where the grantee is to take the name and arms of the grantor within a certain time. It is not a legal estate, not being a fee simple absolute.

conditional sale agreement. An agreement for the sale of goods or land under which the purchase price is payable by instalments and the property in the goods or land is to remain in the seller until the instalments are paid (Consumer Credit Act 1974, s.189(1)).

conditions of sale. The terms on which the purchaser is to take property to be sold by auction. Conditions of sale implied by law in the absence of any stipulation or intention to the contrary in the contract of sale are contained in Law of Property Act 1925, s.45. Under *ibid.* s.46, the Lord Chancellor issued the Statutory Form of Conditions of Sale, which apply also to contracts by correspondence.

In a contract for the sale of goods there is an implied condition that the seller has or will have the right to sell the goods. See Sale of Goods Act 1979, s.12.

condonation. Condonation of a matrimonial offence was formerly a bar to divorce but this is no longer the law (repealed by Divorce Reform Act 1969). Condonation remained a factor for consideration by magistrates exercising their matrimonial jurisdiction but this too has now been repealed (by the Domestic Proceedings and Magistrates Court Act 1978).

conduct money. Money given to a witness to defray his expenses of coming to, staying at, and returning from the place of trial.

conductio. [Roman law.] A hiring.

conference. In its legal usage, a meeting between counsel and solicitor to discuss a case. See also CONSULTATION.

confession. An admission of guilt made to another by a person charged with a crime. It is admissible only if free and voluntary; *i.e.* if it is not forthcoming because of any inducement, or threat, held out by a person in authority. It must not be made under hope of reward (other than spiritual) or fear of punishment in relation to the proceedings. The onus of proof that a confession was voluntary is on the Crown (*D.P.P.* v. *Ping Ling* [1975] 3 W.L.R. 419). Admissions may be obtained from a person by questions fairly and properly put to him by a police officer.

The Judges' Rules govern the practice in regard to police questioning a suspected person with a view to obtaining a confession.

confession and avoidance. A pleading which confesses (*i.e.* admits) the truth of an allegation of fact contained in the preceding pleading, but avoids it (*i.e.* deprives it of effect) by alleging some new matter by way of justification.

confidential communications. Communications between a party and his solicitor, or between the solicitor and counsel, made during and with reference to judicial proceedings, or in anticipation or for the purposes of such proceedings. If in writing, they are privileged from production or discovery; if oral, they are privileged communications. See *Waugh* v. *British Railways Board* [1979] 3 W.L.R. 150, H.L. See PRIVILEGE.

Confirmatio Cartarum. [Confirmation of Charters.] The statute 25 Edw. 1. See ARTICULI SUPER CHARTAS.

confirmation. A conveyance of an estate or right, whereby a voidable estate is made sure and unavoidable, or whereby a particular estate is increased.

confiscation. The seizure and appropriation of property as a punishment for breach of the law, whether municipal or international. Confiscatory or penal legislation of a foreign government, will not, in general, be enforced as regards property situated within the jurisdiction of the courts of this country. (See *e.g. Frankfurther* v. *W.L.Exner* [1947] Ch. 629.)

conflict of laws. An alternative name for Private International Law (*q.v.*).

confusio. [Roman law.] The mixing of liquids belonging to different owners. The product was held in common or divided in proportion to the shares contributed.

confusion of goods. The mixture of things of the same nature but belonging to different owners so that the identification of the things is no longer possible. The right to the ownership of the constituent parts is not in general lost by mixing, but possession of the mixture may be awarded to the party with the best right to it, subject, in a proper case, to compensating the owner of the other constituents.

congé d'elire. [Permission to elect.] A licence from the Crown to the dean and chapter of a bishopric to elect a bishop, accompanied by letters missive containing the name of the person to be elected.

congenital disability. A child may have a cause of action if born with some disability as a result of a tortious act done to one of its parents before birth or conception (Congenital Disabilities (Civil Liability) Act 1976); liability may extend to the child's mother if she was driving a motor vehicle at the time of the occurrence and the child was *in utero* (s.2).

conjugal rights. A married person is entitled to the society and the cohabitation of his or her spouse, unless they are judicially separated, or have agreed to live apart. But the husband is not entitled to exercise force to claim his rights. The suit for restitution of conjugal rights was abolished by the Matrimonial Proceedings and Property Act 1970, s.20.

conjuration. Conferring with evil spirits. It was an offence under section 4 of the Witchcraft Act 1735 for any person to pretend to exercise any form of witchcraft, conjuration, etc., but in this section conjuration was not limited to evil spirits only (*R.* v. *Duncan* [1944] K.B. 713): the gist of the offence was in the pretence. The Witchcraft Act 1735 was repealed by the Fraudulent Mediums Act 1951. See MEDIUMS.

connivance. The intentional active or passive acquiescence by the petitioner in the adultery of the respondent. Connivance is no longer a bar to the grant of a decree of divorce.

connubium. [Roman law.] The legal power of contracting marriage. The parties must (1) have citizenship; (2) not be within the prohibited degrees of relationship; (3) have the consent of their *paterfamilias*.

consanguinity. [Of the same blood.] Relationship by descent, either lineally, as in the case of father and son, or collaterally, by descent from a common ancestor; thus, cousins are related by collateral consanguinity, being descended from a common grandparent.

consensus ad idem. [Agreement as to the same thing.] The common consent necessary for a binding contract.

consensus facit legem. [Consent makes law.] Parties to a contract are legally bound to do what they have agreed to do.

consensus non concubitus facit matrimonium. [Consent and not cohabitation constitutes a valid marriage.] As to the consent of the court to the marriage of persons under 18 see the Marriage Act 1949, s.3; Family Reform Act 1969, s.2.

consensus tollit errorem. [Consent takes away error.] See ACQUIESCENCE.

consent. Acquiescence, agreement. It is inoperative if obtained by fraud. Consent is a defence to a charge of rape, but not in case of unlawful carnal knowledge, or indecent assault, except (in general) where the person against whom the act is directed is over 16, which is called the "age of consent." See VOLENTI NON FIT INJURIA.

conservation area. Areas of social or historic interest. See Town and Country Planning Act 1971, s.277 as amended by Town and Country Amenities Act 1974, s.1.(1)).

conservation (of plants and animals). The Wildlife and Countryside Act 1981 repeals and reenacts with amendments previous legislation relating to the protection of some wild animals, nature conservation, National Parks, Public rights of way and related topics.

conservators of peace. Officers appointed to maintain the public peace, *e.g.* the judges and sheriffs; justices of the peace (*q.v.*).

consideration. A valuable consideration in the sense of the law may consist either in some right, interest, profit or benefit accruing to one party, or some forbearance, detriment, loss or responsibility given, suffered or undertaken by the other (*Currie* v. *Misa* (1875) L.R. 10 Ex. 162, *per* Lush J.). The payment of a smaller sum is not consideration for the satisfaction of a larger (*Foakes* v. *Beer* (1884) 9 App. Cas. 605). An executed consideration is some value already given; executory consideration is value to be given in the future. Good consideration is not valuable, but based on natural love or relationship.

consignment. Goods delivered by a carrier to a consignee at the instance of a consignor.

consilium. [Roman law.] A public body that, *inter alia*, considered proposals for *manumission* under the *Lex Aelia Sentia.* It met on certain days at Rome and it held regular sessions in the provinces, on the last day of which *manumission* proposals were examined.

consistory court. The court of a diocese for enforcing discipline amongst the clergy. See the Ecclesiastical Jurisdiction Measure 1963.

Consolato del Mare. A code of the maritime law of the Mediterranean, *temp.* fourteenth century.

Consolidated Fund. The fund formed by the public revenue and income of the United Kingdom. The National Loans Fund set up by the National Loans Act 1968 operates in conjunction with the Consolidated Fund.

Consolidation Acts. Acts which sweep up and collect and re-enact in one statute the existing enactments on a certain subject. The Consolidation of Enactments (Procedure) Act 1949 laid down a procedure for consolidation where at the same time incidental corrections and minor improvements ought to be made; they must be approved by the appropriate parliamentary committee and the Lord Chancellor and the Speaker. In interpreting a consolidation Act it is proper to look at the earlier provisions which it consolidated (*I.R.C.* v. *Hinchy* [1960] A.C. 748, *per* Lord Reid). See also Interpretation Act 1978, s.17(2) (*a*), (*b*).

consolidation of actions. If several actions are pending in the same Division with reference to the same subject-matter, the court may order them to be tried together (see Ord.4, r.10).

consolidation of mortgages. The equitable doctrine that a mortgagee who held several mortgages by the same mortgagor on different properties could insist on the redemption of all, if the mortgagor sought to redeem any of them. The doctrine is now excluded by section 93 of the Law of Property Act 1925, unless a contrary intention is expressed in the deeds.

consortium. The association between husband and wife which embraces companionship, love, affection, comfort, mutual services and sexual intercourse. A husband has a right to the *consortium et servitium* of his wife, *i.e.* to her society and services. Any tortious act, therefore, committed against the wife is actionable at the suit of her husband if he was thereby deprived for any period of her society or services. *Consortium* normally implies cohabitation of the spouses, but it is not determined by the mere temporary absence of one spouse from another, as, *e.g.* on military service. A wife has the right to sue where an intentional or malicious act has resulted in total (and not merely partial) loss of consortium as she is entitled to enjoy the society, comfort, and protection of her husband and to be maintained by him (see *Best* v. *Samuel Fox & Co.* [1952] A.C. 716). Substantial damages may be recovered (*Lawrence* v. *Biddle* [1966] 2 Q.B. 504; *Cutts* v. *Chumley* [1967] 1 W.L.R. 742). See ENTICEMENT.

conspiracy. With some exceptions the common law criminal offence of conspiracy has been abolished by the Criminal Law Act 1977, s.5(1). The new statutory offence exists when any person agrees with any other person or persons that a course of conduct should be pursued which will necessarily amount to or involve the commission of any offence or offences by one or more of the parties to the agreement if the agreement is carried out in accordance with their intentions (s.1(1)). The consent of the D.P.P. is normally required for the bringing of proceedings (s.4). The common law remains unchanged in respect of conspiracy to defraud and also conspiracy to engage in conduct which tends to corrupt public morals or outrage public decency but which would not amount to an offence if carried out by a single person otherwise than in pursuance of an agreement (s.5).

Conspiracy is also a tort for which the injured person has an action for damages. A husband and wife are capable of conspiracy together (see *Midland Bank Trust* v. *Green* (*No.* 3) [1981] 1 All E.R. 744).

constables. Inferior officers of the peace. High constables were appointed at the courts leet of the franchise or hundred over which they presided. Their duty seems to have been to keep the peace within the hundred. Petty or parish constables were appointed by the justices in petty sessions for the preservation of the peace within their parish or township, and the service of the summonses and the execution of warrants of the justices of the peace. They have been superseded by the establishment of the modern police force. See ARREST.

constat. [It appears.] A copy or exemplification.

constituency. A geographical area for parliamentary and local government elections.

constituent. A person who appoints another by power of attorney to do some act for him. Also a voter in a constituency (*q.v.*).

constitution. Formerly a law or ordinance; now the form in which a State is organised. A constitution may be (a) unwritten, resting mainly on custom and convention; (b) written, drawn up in legal form; (c) flexible, capable of being altered by ordinary legislative act; (d) rigid, capable of being altered only by special procedure.

The British Constitution is unwritten and flexible; that of the United States is written and rigid.

constitutional law. All rules which directly or indirectly affect the distribution or exercise of the sovereign power (Dicey). So much of the law as relates to the designation and form of the legislature, the rights and functions of the several parts of the legislative body, the construction, office and jurisdiction of courts of justice (Paley). The rules which regulate the structure of the principal organs of government and their relationship to each other, and determine their principal functions. These rules consist both of legal rules in the strict sense and of usages, commonly called conventions, which, without being enacted, are accepted as binding by all who are concerned in government (Wade).

construction. The process of ascertaining the meaning of a written document. The judicial interpretation of statutes. "Construction of law" is a fixed or arbitrary rule by which a result follows from certain acts or words without reference to the intention of the parties.

constructive. Adjective to be used where the law infers or implies a right, liability or status without reference to the intention of the parties, *e.g.* the following TITLES.

constructive desertion. See DESERTION.

constructive dismissal. A dismissal to be inferred from the fact that the employer's conduct is such that the employee has no choice but to resign.

constructive fraud. Cases in which equity gives relief against acts and contracts, although untainted by any actual evil design, on the ground of general public policy or on some fixed policy of the law. They fall under three main heads; (1) Contracts which no man in his right senses would make. (2) Contracts which it is against conscience to enforce, as taking advantage of the weakness or necessities of another, *e.g.* a catching bargain (*q.v.*). (3) Underhand bargains tending to the prejudice of third parties, *e.g.* fraudulent preference, etc.

constructive malice. Where death resulted from an act of violence done in the course of, or in the furtherance of, a felony involving violence, *e.g.* rape (*Director of Public Prosecutions* v. *Beard* [1920] A.C. 479). Although there was no actual malice aforethought, it was held that there was constructive malice and the crime was murder. Constructive malice, however, was abolished by the Homicide Act 1957, s.1, which provided that where a person kills another in the course or furtherance of some other offence, the killing does not amount to murder unless done with malice aforethought.

constructive notice. See NOTICE.

constructive total loss. See TOTAL LOSS.

constructive treason. The doctrine that a conspiracy to do some act in regard to the King which might endanger his life was an overt act of compassing the King's death, and treason. It led to the passing of the Treason Act 1795. See TREASON.

constructive trust. A trust which is raised by construction of equity in order to satisfy the demands of justice and good conscience without reference to any presumed intention of the parties, as in the following cases: (1) vendor's lien for unpaid purchase-money; (2) purchaser's lien for prematurely paid purchase-money; (3) where a person makes a profit in a fiduciary position or out of trust property; (4) where a stranger intermeddles in a trust; (5) where a mortgagee sells under his power of sale, he is a trustee of any surplus realised.

constructive trustee. The person deemed to be a trustee in the case of a constructive trust (*q.v.*).

consuetudo est altera lex. [A custom has the force of law.]

consuetudo est optimus interpres legum. [Custom is the best interpreter of the laws.]

consuetudo et communis assuetudo vincit legem non scriptam, si sit specialis; et interpretatur legem scriptam, si lex sit generalis. [Custom and common usage overcome the unwritten law, if it be special; and interpret the written law, if it be general.] See CUSTOM.

consuls. Agents appointed to watch over the interests of the State or its nationals in foreign parts. The duties and privileges of consular officers are elaborately set out in the Consular Relations Act 1968 (as amended by the International Organisations Act 1968, s.12(2); Post Office Act 1969, Sched.11, Part II and the Diplomatic and Other Privileges Act, 1971, s.4, Sched.).

consultation. A conference with two or more counsel.

consumer. A person to or for whom goods or services are, or are sought to be, supplied in the course of a business carried on by the supplier and who does not receive them in the course of a business carried on by him (Consumer Credit Act 1974).

consumer credit. Governed by the Consumer Credit Act 1974 "Credit" includes a cash loan and any other form of financial accommodation. A "Personal Credit agreement" is defined as one in which the debtor is an individual, *i.e.* not a body corporate (s.8(2)). The Act provides for the regulation and licensing of those who carry on the business of granting consumer credit. By ss.137–140 the court has power to reopen a credit bargain which it considers extortionate and to do justice between the parties. See also FAIR TRADING.

consumer protection. Legislation which protects the interests of consumers (*q.v.*) (see Consumer Protection Act 1978).

consummated. Completed, *e.g.* a marriage is consummated when completed by ordinary and complete sexual intercourse. "Consummate" denotes coitus and not coitus which may result in conception. If either party is impotent or wilfully refuses to consummate the marriage such marriage is voidable by decree of nullity. See NULLITY OF MARRIAGE.

contango. A percentage paid by a buyer of stock, of which delivery is to be taken on a certain date, for being allowed to delay taking delivery until some other date. See BACKWARDATION.

contemporanea exposito est optima et fortissima in lege. [The best way to construe a document is to read it as it would have read when made.]

contempt of court. (1) Failure to comply with the order of a Superior Court, or an act of résistance or insult to the court or the judges.

(2) Conduct likely to prejudice the fair trial of an accused person, punishable by fine or commital to prison.

Before the Contempt of Court Act 1981 the "strict liability rule" applied to the Press *i.e.* conduct tending to interfere with the course of justice might be treated as contempt of court regardless of the contemnor's intent. Now this rule only applies to publications which create a substantial risk that the course of justice in the proceedings in question will be seriously impeded or prejudiced, where the proceedings are "active" (s.2). For a definition of "active" see Sched. 1. Section 5 provides that a publication of discussion in good faith of Public Affairs or other matters of public interest is not to be treated as contempt if the risk of impediment or prejudice to particular legal proceedings is merely incidental to the discussion (see also *Att.Gen.* v. *English* [1982] 2 All E.R. 903). Proceedings under the strict liability rule require the consent of the Attorney General or of a court having jurisdiction to deal with such proceedings (s.7).

It is contempt of court to obtain, disclose or solicit information in respect of a jury's deliberations in legal proceedings (s.8).

A court cannot require a person to disclose the source of information contained in a publication for which he is responsible unless it be established that disclosure is necessary in the interest of justice, national security or for the prevention of disorder and crime (s.10).

The Crown Court has the powers of the High Court in matters of contempt (Courts Act 1971, s.4(8)).

The County Court has the powers conferred by the County Courts Act 1959, ss.157–162 (see also *Whitter* v. *Peters* [1982] 1 W.L.R. 389, C.A.). Magistrates have no power to commit for contempt but provision is made in the Contempt of Court Act 1981 for punishing contempt in the face of Magistrates Courts. See also DISCOVERY.

contempt of Parliament. Whatever obstructs the due course of proceeding of either House of Parliament, or grossly reflects on the character of a Member of either House, is a breach of privilege, punishable by commitment.

contentious business. Probate proceedings in which there are contending parties, such as proving a will in solemn form, or revoking a grant of probate, as opposed to common form proceedings where there is no contest.

Continental Shelf. The seabed, and subsoil, outside territorial waters. See the Continental Shelf Act 1964, as amended.

contingent. That which awaits or depends on the happening of an event.

contingent remainder. A remainder limited so as to depend on an event or condition which may never happen or be performed, or which may not happen or be performed until some time after the determination of the preceding estate: *e.g.* to A for life, and then to B if he has attained 21. Every contingent remainder of an estate of freeholds had to vest either during the continuance of the prior particular estate, or at the very moment when that estate determined; or else fail. Thus, unless B was 21 when A died, B could never take the property. The Contingent Remainders Act 1877 however, saved from the operation of this rule every contingent remainder which would have been valid if originally created as a shifting use, or executory devise. By the Law of Property Act 1925, Sched. 1. Part I, all existing contingent remainders and all to be created subsequently are converted into equitable interests. See REMAINDER.

continuando. An allegation in the old action of trespass, of an injury, continuing from day to day.

continuation. If a buyer or seller of stock on the Stock Exchange is unable to complete the bargain on the next following Settlement Day, they may by agreement carry over or continue the bargain until the next account day.

continuous voyage. The doctrine that goods which would be contraband if carried to an enemy port can be dealt with as contraband even though they are being carried to a neutral port, provided that they are intended to be forwarded either by land or by sea from the neutral port to an enemy country.

contra bonos mores. [Against good morals.]

contra formam collationis (or **feoffamenti**). [Against the form of the gift (*or* feoffment).]

contra formam statuti. [Against the form of the statute.] Formerly a necessary ending to an indictment charging a statutory offence.

contra proferentum. The doctrine that the construction least favourable to the person putting forward an instrument should be adopted against him.

contraband of war. Such articles as may not be carried by a neutral to a belligerent, because they are calculated to be of direct service in carrying on war.

contract. An agreement enforceable at law. An essential feature of contract is a promise by one party to another to do or forbear from doing certain specified acts. The offer of a promise becomes a promise by acceptance. Contract is that species of agreement whereby a legal obligation is constituted and defined between the parties to it.

For a contract to be valid and legally enforceable there must be (1) capacity to contract; (2) intention to contract; (3) *consensus ad idem*; (4) valuable consideration; (5) legality of purpose; (6) sufficient certainty of terms. In some cases the contract or evidence of it must be in a prescribed form, *i.e.* in writing or by deed, and the rule that a contract must be supported by valuable consideration does not apply in the case of contracts of record or by deed.

There are the following kinds of contract: (1) of record, entered into through the machinery of a court of justice, *e.g.* a recognisance; (2) specialty, by deed; (3) simple or parol, *i.e.* in writing or oral; (4) implied, founded by law on the assumed intention of the parties; (5) quasi (*q.v.*), founded by law on the circumstances, irrespective of the wishes of the parties.

contract for sale of land. To be enforceable a contract for the sale of land or any interest in land must be evidenced by a written note or memorandum of the agreement signed by or on behalf of the party to be charged (Law of Property Act 1925, s.40(1)). See also EXCHANGE OF CONTRACTS; SUBJECT TO CONTRACT.

contract of employment. See EMPLOYER AND EMPLOYEE.

contracting out. Giving up the benefit of a statute in consideration of some alternative scheme or advantage. Statutes frequently restrict contracting out. See *e.g.* the Employment Protection Act 1975, s.118.

contracts re. [Roman law.] Real contracts arising from the delivery by one person to another of the subject-matter of the contract with intention of imposing obligations. There were: *Mutuum, Commodatum, Depositum* and *Pignus*, and sometimes *Indebiti solutio.*

contribution. The payment of a proportionate share of a liability which has been borne by one or some only of a number equally liable. See JOINT TORTFEASORS.

contributory. Every person liable to contribute to the assets of a company in the event of the company being wound up. The present and past members are liable in an amount sufficient for payment of the company's debts and liabilities and the costs of the winding up, and for the adjustment of the rights of the contributories amongst themselves. The list of contributories is made out in two parts, A and B. The A contributories are the existing members of the company and are primarily liable; the B contributories are the past members who have ceased to be members within the year preceding the winding up, and are only liable to contribute after the A contributories are exhausted. But a B contributory is not liable in respect of any debt of the company contracted after he ceased to be a member.

In the case of a company limited by shares, no contribution may exceed the amount of the unpaid liability on the shares. "Contributory" is nevertheless sometimes used to refer to persons holding fully-paid shares, and in the wider sense means a member of the company (see Companies Act 1948, ss.212–217).

contributory mortgage. A mortgage where the mortgage money is advanced by two or more persons separately. A trustee must not join in a contributory mortgage since by so doing he parts with his exclusive control of the trust property.

contributory negligence. The defence in an action at common law for damages for injuries arising from negligence, that the plaintiff's own negligence directly caused or contributed to his own injuries.

The original common law rule was if there was blame causing the accident on both sides, however small, the loss lay where it fell. This rule was mitigated by the doctrine of "last opportunity," *i.e.* that when both parties were negligent, the party which had the last opportunity of avoiding the result of the other's carelessness was alone liable.

The rule, however, that contributory negligence operated as a complete bar to the plaintiff's claim did not apply to collisions at sea, where by the fault of two or more vessels damage is caused to one or more of those vessels. The general rule of maritime law is that each vessel is liable for so much of the damage suffered by the other vessel as is proportional to its degree of fault, the remainder of the damage lying where it falls.

The law was altered by the Law Reform (Contributory Negligence) Act 1945, which provided that, where any person suffers damage as a result partly of his own fault and partly of the fault of others, a claim in respect of that damage is not to be defeated by reason of the fault of the person suffering the damage. The damages recoverable, however, are to be reduced to such extent as the court thinks just and equitable having regard to the plaintiff's share in the responsibility for the damage. But the court must first find and record the total damages which would have been recoverable if the plaintiff had not been at fault and the damages are apportioned according to the respective degrees of fault. See DANGER, ALTERNATIVE. In any circumstances in which proof of absence of negligence on the part of a banker would be a defence to proceedings by reason of the Cheques Act 1957, s.4 a defence of contributory negligence is available to a banker (Banking Act 1979, s.47).

controlled tenancy. A Protected or Statutory tenancy of a dwelling house whose rateable value does not exceed an amount stated in s.17(1)(a) of the Rent Act 1977 and which was created or whose previous contractual tenancy was created by a lease or agreement coming into operation before July 6, 1957 or is or was a tenancy to which subs. (3), (4) or (5) applies.

A controlled tenancy may, in certain circumstances, be converted into a regulated tenancy (Rent Act 1977, s.108). Limits on the rent are set by section 27. See PROTECTED TENANCY; STATUTORY TENANCY; REGULATED TENANCY.

contumacy. Refusal to obey the order of an ecclesiastical court. Such a refusal is now a matter of censure (Ecclesiastical Jurisdiction Measure 1963, ss.49, 54).

conusance. Acknowledgment; jurisdiction.

conversion. (1) In equity, conversion is the notional change of land into money, or money into land. The principle is that money directed to be employed in the purchase of land, and land directed to be sold and turned into money, are to be considered as that species of property into which they are directed to be converted. The effect of conversion is to turn realty into personalty, and personalty into realty, for all purposes. It occurs in four cases: (1) partnership land is treated as personalty; (2) under order of the court; (3) under a trust; (4) under a contract for sale or purchase of realty.

In the event of a total failure of the objects for which conversion was directed in a deed or will no conversion takes place. In the case of partial failure of the objects under a will, the property passes to the person entitled to it in its unconverted state, although he takes it in its converted form. In cases under deeds, the property reverts to the settlor in its converted form. See RECONVERSION.

(2) A tort, committed by a person who deals with chattels not belonging to him in a manner inconsistent with the rights of the owner. By section 1 of the Torts (Interference with Goods) Act 1977 conversion of goods, together with Trespass to goods, negligence resulting in damage to goods and any other Tort resulting in damage to goods is classed as "wrongful interference with goods" (q.v.). Detinue (q.v.) is abolished (s.2(1)).

An action lies in conversion for loss or destruction of goods which a bailee has allowed to happen in breach of his duty to his bailor (s.2(2)).

Although contributory negligence is not a defence to an action in conversion this rule is excluded from cases involving cheques. See CONTRIBUTORY NEGLIGENCE.

For a modern statement of the law relating to Trover (q.v.) see *Parker* v. *British Airways Board* [1982] Q.B. 1004, C.A.

conveyance. A mode of transfer of property; the deed or instrument other than a will whereby an interest in property is assured by one person to another. It includes a mortgage, charge, lease, assent, vesting declaration, vesting instrument, disclaimer, release and every other assurance of property, except a will

(Law of Property Act 1925, s.205 (1)(ii)). See FRAUDULENT CONVEYANCE; VOLUNTARY.

conveyancer. A barrister or solicitor who specialises in drawing conveyances.

Counsel experienced in conveyancing may be appointed conveyancing counsel to the court (Court of Chancery Act 1852; Judicature Act 1925, s.217; Administration of Justice Act 1956, s.14; Ord.31, rr. 5–8).

convict. Formerly, one sentenced to death or imprisonment for treason or felony. Now one found guilty of an offence and imprisoned.

conviction. The finding of a person guilty of an offence after trial. Summary conviction is conviction by a magistrates' court. Evidence of conviction is admissible in civil proceedings (Civil Evidence Act 1968, s.11). The evidence is conclusive for the purposes of defamation actions (s.13). See the Ecclesiastical Jurisdiction Measure 1963, ss.33–37; Church of England Convocations Act 1966; Synodical Government Measure 1969, s.1(4). See SYNOD. See also SPENT CONVICTION.

convoy. Ships of war protecting and escorting merchant ships.

coparcener; coparcenary. The descent of land on intestacy to several daughters as co-heirs; called coparceners or tenants in coparcenary. The tenure was abolished by the Law of Property Act 1925.

copyhold. Lands held by copyhold tenure; lands forming part of a manor, originally granted by the lord for tenancies at will merely, which by immemorial custom became converted into estates independent of the will of the lord in everything but name, and of various degrees of duration, according to the custom of the particular manor. Hence, copyhold was a customary tenure. Copyholds were so called because the evidence of the title to such lands consists of copies of the court roll of the manor, in which all dealings with the land were entered.

Copyhold tenure was abolished by the Law of Property Act 1922, and existing copyholds enfranchised.

copyright. The exclusive right of printing or otherwise multiplying copies of, *inter alia*, a published literary work; that is, the right of preventing all others from doing so. The infringement of this right is called piracy. Copyright extends to original, artistic, dramatic and musical works, and to recordings, films, and broadcasts. Copyright, in general, lasts during the lifetime of the author and for 50 years after his death. No assignment of copyright is valid unless in writing signed by or on behalf of the assignor. Licences may be granted in respect of copyright by the owner. See the Copyright Act 1956; Dramatic and Musical Performers' Protection Act 1958; Copyright Act 1956 (Amendment) Act 1982.

cor: coram. [In the presence of.]

coram judice. [In the presence of the judge.] Before a properly constituted or appropriate court.

coram non judice. [Before one who is not a judge.] The proceedings are a nullity.

co-respondent. A person called upon to answer a petition or proceeding jointly with another, *e.g.* in divorce.

corn rents. Additional sums payable in relation to land wholly or partly in lieu of tithes. The Corn Rents Act 1963 provides for the making of a scheme by the Commissioners of Inland Revenue for the apportionment, redemption and, in certain cases, the extinguishment of corn rent.

coroner. (Of the Crown.) A royal officer appointed from the ranks of barristers, solicitors and registered medical practitioners of at least five years standing. His duty is to inquire (hence the term "inquest") into the manner of death of any person who is slain or dies in suspicious circumstances or in prison. Originally his main function was to preserve the Pleas of the Crown, and in this sense the Lord

Chief Justice (*q.v.*) is the Principal Coroner of the Kingdom. A coroner is no longer bound to summon a jury save in a limited class of cases (Criminal Law Act 1977, s.56(1)) nor is he able to charge a person with murder, manslaughter or infanticide (s.56(2)). Where a body lies within the coroner's territorial jurisdiction and the coroner has reasonable cause to suspect a violent or unnatural death he is obliged to hold an inquest even though the deceased died overseas (*R. v. West Yorks Coroner, ex p. Smith, The Times*, July 31, 1982, H.L.). The coroner also has jurisdiction over Treasure Trove (*q.v.*).

corporation. A body of persons having in law an existence and rights and duties distinct from those of the individual persons who from time to time form it. It has perpetual succession, a name and a common seal. Service of writs or process is upon an officer of the corporation. A corporation sole consists of only one member at a time in succession, *e.g.* a bishop. A corporation aggregate consists of a number of persons, *e.g.* incorporated companies and municipal corporations.

Corporations were not originally liable for crime, but now a corporation can be indicted, and fines may be inflicted upon it, but it is not liable in respect of offences punishable only corporally. It cannot now be said that a corporation cannot have the necessary guilty mind or wrongful intention to commit a criminal act (*D.P.P. v. Kent and Sussex Contractors Ltd.* [1944] 1 K.B.146) and a limited company can be indicted for a conspiracy to defraud (*R. v. I.C.R. Haulage Ltd.* [1944] K.B.551). An act is done by a corporation if instigated or procured by those having control of it, and in purported exercise of the corporation's powers. A corporation is liable criminally for acts of omission, and for the acts of its employees committed in the course of their employment.

Companies and other corporations may enter into contracts through authorised persons with no more formality than an individual (Companies Act 1948, s.32; Corporate Bodies' Contracts Act 1960, ss.1,2).

corporation tax. A tax payable by companies on their dividends and other distributions under Schedule F of the Income and Corporation Taxes Act 1970 (s.232 as substituted by the Finance Act 1972, s.87).

corporeal property. Property which has a physical existence such as land or goods. See HEREDITAMENT.

corpus. [Body.] The capital of a fund, as contrasted with the income.

corpus delicti. The facts which constitute an offence.

corpus juris canonici. See CANON LAW.

corpus juris civilis. The body of Roman law contained in the Institutes, Digest, and Code compiled by order of Justinian, together with the Novellae, or constitutions promulgated after the compilation of the Code.

corroboration. Independent evidence which implicates a person accused of a crime by connecting him with it; evidence which confirms in some material particular not only that the crime has been committed, but also that the accused committed it. See ACCOMPLICE.

corrupt practices. Treating, undue influence, personation or the procuring thereof, bribery, or making a false declaration as to election expenses in connection with a parliamentary or other election. See the Representation of the People Act 1949.

corruption of blood. See ATTAINDER.

corsned. [The accursed morsel.] A piece of barley bread, weighing about one ounce, which an accused person, after certain quasi-religious invocations, was set to swallow. If he succeeded, he was held innocent: failure was proof of guilt.

cosinage. Consanguinity.

cost book mining company. A partnership formed for working a mine under local customs, *e.g.* in Derbyshire, Devon, and Cornwall.

costs in civil proceedings. The general rule is that a successful litigant in civil proceedings is entitled to his costs; costs abide the event. But they always are in the discretion of the court and there may be statutory or other restrictions on the award of costs (see below).

Costs may be payable on the following bases. (1) The party and party basis, that is all such costs as were necessary and proper for the attainment of justice or for enforcing or defending the rights of the party whose costs are being taxed (Ord.62, r.28(1); *Societe Anonyme Pecheries Ostendais* v. *Merchant Marine Insurance Co.* [1928] 1 K.B. 762).

(2) The common fund basis which is more generous than the Party and Party basis and includes the costs of all steps reasonably taken by a sensible solicitor in the interests of his clients (Ord.62, r.28(3)(4); *Francis* v. *Francis Dickerson* [1956] P.87).

(3) The trustee basis, *i.e.* where costs are payable out of a fund and no costs are disallowed unless they fall within certain exceptions.

(4) The solicitor and own client basis, where costs are allowed except in so far as they are of an unreasonable amount or unreasonably incurred.

(5) The indemnity basis, where all costs incurred are allowed except those unreasonably incurred or of an unreasonable amount, and in applying those exceptions the "receiving party" is given the benefit of the doubt (*E.M.I. Records Ltd.* v. *Ian Cameron Wallace Ltd.* [1982] 2 All E.R. 980, *per* Sir R. Megarry V.-C.). See generally TAXATION OF COSTS.

In some cases, *e.g.* where a judgment is taken in default the successful litigant is entitled only to fixed costs, *i.e.* costs prescribed by reference to a fixed scale. For costs in county court proceedings see COUNTY COURT.

A litigant in person is entitled to his costs incurred where costs would have been awarded if a solicitor had been instructed. Such costs are taxed or assessed under a special procedure (see Litigants in Person (Costs and Expenses) Act 1975 and R.S.C., Ord.62, r.28(*a*)).

costs in criminal proceedings. The court may order the costs of the prosecution or of the defence to be paid out of central funds or by the other side (see the Costs in Criminal Cases Act 1973 and Costs in Criminal Cases (Allowances) Regulations 1977). For the principles applicable to the award of costs to an acquitted defendant see Lord Chief Justices Practice Direction dated November 5, 1981.

couchant. Cattle lying down.

Council of Legal Education. The body charged with the examination of students of the Inns of Court for qualification for call to the Bar. See SENATE OF THE INNS OF COURT AND THE BAR.

Council of Ministers. The body of representatives of the Member States of the EEC (Treaty of Rome, 1957, Art.145).

counsel. A barrister (generally, practising barristers).

count. Paragraphs in an indictment, each containing and charging an offence.

counterclaim. A counterclaim may be made by a defendant who alleges that he has any claim, or is entitled to any relief or remedy against a plaintiff, instead of bringing a separate action. A counterclaim may also be made against any other person who is liable to him together with the plaintiff in respect of the counterclaim or the original subject-matter of the action (Ord.15, rr.2,3). A counterclaim must be separately pleaded. The plaintiff must serve his defence to the counterclaim within 14 days of service (Ord.18,r.3).

If a counterclaim for money exceeds the plaintiff's claim, judgment is given in favour of the defendant. If both claim and counterclaim succeed two separate judgments with costs are given.

counterfeit. Made in imitation. To falsely make or counterfeit any coin resembling any current coin is an indictable offence (Coinage Offences Act 1936, s.1). See also Counterfeit Currency (Convention) Act 1935.

counter-marque. Letters of counter-marque were formerly issued by one state as a reprisal for the issue of letters of marque by another state.

counterpart. A lease is generally prepared in two identical forms, called the lease and the counterpart respectively. The lease is executed by the lessor alone, and the counterpart is executed by the lessee alone, and then the lease and counterpart are exchanged.

county, trial by. Trial by jury. See IN PAIS; JURY.

county. Originally a shire, or portion of the country comprehending a great number of hundreds, under the sheriff. England is now divided into Greater London (see LONDON), five Metropolitan counties and 39 non-metropolitan counties. Wales is divided into eight counties. The Isles of Scilly constitute a separate local government unit (Local Government Act 1972, ss.1, 8, 265; London Government Act 1963, s.2).

county borough. Boroughs of not less than 50,000 inhabitants were created county boroughs and administrative counties under the Local Government Act 1888, s.31 and the Local Government Act 1933, s.1, Sched.1. They have now ceased to exist (Local Government Act 1972, s.1 (10)).

county corporate. A city or town which had by virtue of royal charters the privilege of being a county of itself, and not within any other county. This status has disappeared with the change in local government structure. See COUNTY.

county council. The elective bodies for the administration of the local government of the counties. See COUNTY.

county courts. The modern county courts, established by the County Courts Act 1846, are the busiest civil courts of this country. Each county court has jurisdiction over recovery of debts and civil actions arising within its district (which is not the same area as that covered by an administrative County) up to certain financial limits which are periodically increased by statutory instrument. The present limits of principal areas of jurisdiction are as follows;

(1) In contract and tort £5,000. (2) In actions for recovery of land net annual value for rating of £5,000. (3) In equity £30,000. There are also varied extensive jurisdictions under numerous Acts, some of which are mentioned in Sched.1 to the County Courts Act 1959 which is the principal Act governing county courts. The rules now applicable are the County Court Rules 1981. All Interlocutory applications and also actions for less than £500 are dealt with by the Registrar (*q.v.*). Actions and matters involving more than £500 are dealt with by the judge who is a Circuit Judge (Courts Act 1971, s.16, Sched.2). In respect of cases involving less than £500 special provisions as to Arbitration by the Registrar apply (C.C.R., Ord.19). Briefly this procedure is designed to assist the litigant in person and provides that there shall be no order as to costs (except for the fixed costs on the summons) save where the Registrar certifies that those costs have been incurred by reason of the unreasonable conduct of one party.

County court costs generally are on three scales depending on the amount of money involved. The county court also has extensive jurisdiction over enforcement of judgments by, *e.g.* execution (*q.v.*) attachment of earnings (*q.v.*), charging orders (*q.v.*), administration orders (*q.v.*) and garnishee orders (*q.v.*).

Any county court may be designated a divorce county court with jurisdiction to hear undefended matrimonial causes and ancillary matters whether defended or not (see DIVORCE). Most larger courts are so designated and also have jurisdiction in bankruptcy.

Appeals from the Registrar normally lie to the judge and from the judge to the Court of Appeal.

county palatine. A county the owner of which formerly had *jura regalia* (*q.v.*) or royal franchises and rights of jurisdiction similar to those possessed by the Crown in the rest of the kingdom; thus he had the power of pardoning crimes and appointing judges and officers within his county. The three counties palatine were Chester, Durham, and Lancaster, but they have long been united in the Crown. See PALANTINE COURT.

coupons. Detachable slips of paper annexed to a bond or debenture payable to bearer for the purpose of providing for the periodical payment of interest on the principal, usually half-yearly. The interest is payable only on presentation and delivery to the paying agent of the coupon referring thereto.

court. (1) A place where justice is administered; (2) the judge or judges who sit in a court; (3) an aggregate of separate courts or judges, as the Supreme Court of Judicature.

Court Baron. A civil court held in a manor, in which the free tenants or freeholders of the manor were the judges, and the steward of the manor was the Registrar. It entertained all suits concerning land held of the manor. The Customary Court Baron dealt with matters concerning the rights of copyholders. See COPYHOLD; COURT LEET.

court expert. An independent expert witness (*q.v.*) appointed by the court on an application by a party, in a non-jury case, to inquire into and report on any question of fact or opinion (Ord.40).

Court for Crown Cases Reserved. Created by the Crown Cases Act 1848 for the decision of questions of law arising on the trial of a person convicted of crime, and reserved by the judge or justices at the trial for the consideration of the court. For this purpose, the judge or justices stated and signed a case setting forth the question and the facts out of which it arose. The jurisdiction was transferred to the Court of Criminal Appeal by the Criminal Appeal Act 1907.

court leet. The court of criminal jurisdiction over the tenants resident within a manor in all matters in which the sheriff's tourn had jurisdiction; it also had the "view of frankpledge." It was a court of record; the steward of the manor was the judge, and the jury was formed from the suitors of the court. Abolished by Law of Property Act 1922.

court-martial. A court convened by or under the authority of the Crown to try an offence against military or naval discipline, or against the ordinary law, committed by a soldier or sailor in Her Majesty's service. There is an appeal to a Court-Martial Appeal Court under the Courts-Martial (Appeals) Act 1968 (as amended.)

Court of Ancient Demesne. The Court Baron (*q.v.*) of land in ancient demesne (*q.v.*).

Court of Appeal. The Court of Appeal was created by the Judicature Act 1873. Its constitution, practice and procedure are now governed by the Supreme Court Act 1981 (ss.2,3, 15–18, and 53–60). It consists of two divisions; the Criminal Division and the Civil Division. The Lord Chief Justice (*q.v.*) is the President of the Criminal Division and the Master of the Rolls (*q.v.*) is President of the Civil Division (s.3(2)).

The Civil Division has vested in it the former jurisdiction of the Lord Chancellor and Court of Appeal in Chancery and the Court of Exchequer Chamber. It hears appeals from the High Court, Judges in Chambers, the Divisional Court in civil matters and the County Courts.

The Court of Appeal consists of the following *ex officio* judges: (a) the Lord Chancellor; (b) any person who has been Lord Chancellor; (c) any Lord of Appeal in Ordinary who at the date of his appointment was, or was qualified for an appointment as an ordinary judge of the Court of Appeal or held an office within paragraphs (d) to (g); (d) the Lord Chief Justice; (e) the Master of the

Rolls; (f) the President of the Family Division; and (g) the Vice-Chancellor. However a person within (b) and (c) shall not sit unless at the Lord Chancellor's request he consents to do so. In addition there are not more than 18 ordinary judges known as "Lord Justices of Appeal".

For the Criminal Division see CRIMINAL APPEAL.

The Court of Appeal is bound to follow decisions of the House of Lords, its own previous decisions and those of the courts which it superseded. Where the previous decisions conflict the Court of Appeal must decide which to follow. See PRECEDENT PER INCURIAM.

For procedure see R.S.C., Ord 59. See also APPEAL.

Court of Arches. The Ecclesiastical Court of Appeal of the Archbishop of Canterbury. The judges of the Court of Arches are five in number including the Dean of the Arches (Ecclesiastical Jurisdiction Measure 1963, s.3).

Court of Chancery. This was the court of equity presided over by the Lord Chancellor, assisted by the Master of the Rolls, and judges of first instance, known as Vice-Chancellors. There was always a common law court and offices in Chancery which dealt with enrolments of deeds, the issue and sealing of writs and commissions, etc. Since the Judicature (Officers) Act 1879 they have formed part of the Central Office of the Supreme Court. The Court of Chancery was merged in the High Court of Justice by the Judicature Act 1873, and is now known as the Chancery Division (see Supreme Court Act 1981, s.5(*a*), Sched.1(1); R.S.C. (Amendment No. 2) 1982, rr.4–97).

Court of Chivalry. The court of the Lord High Constable and Earl Marshal in matters of honour and heraldry. The court was revived to deal with a complaint by the Manchester Corporation that their arms were being usurped ([1955] P.133).

Court of Common Pleas. One of the courts into which the *Curia Regis* was divided. It was originally the only superior court of record having jurisdiction in ordinary civil actions between subject and subject. It consisted of a Lord Chief Justice and five puisne justices. It was transferred to the High Court of Justice by the Judicature Act 1873, and is now represented by the Queen's Bench Division (see Judicature Act 1925, ss.18(1), 56(2)).

Court of Criminal Appeal. Created by the Criminal Appeal Act 1907, to replace the Court for Crown Cases Reserved (*q.v.*). The court was abolished by the Criminal Appeal Act 1966, and its jurisdiction transferred to the Criminal Division of the Court of Appeal. See CRIMINAL APPEAL.

Court of Error. A court of appeal.

Court of Exchequer. One of the courts into which the *Curia Regis* was divided. By the year 1200 it had a separate existence; but it continued to collect revenue in addition to trying cases, until the first Chief Baron was appointed in 1312. It was originally a court having jurisdiction only in matters concerning the public revenue, *e.g.* in suits by the Crown against its debtors; but it afterwards acquired, by the use of fictitious pleadings, jurisdiction in actions between subject and subject. It was formerly subdivided into a court of common law and a court of equity; but its equitable jurisdiction (except in revenue matters) was transferred to the Court of Chancery. Under the Judicature Act 1873, the jurisdiction of the Court of Exchequer was transferred to the High Court of Justice, Exchequer Division, until, in 1881, the three "common law" divisions of the High Court were merged into one. It is now represented by the Queen's Bench Division (Judicature Act 1925, ss.18(2), 56(2)). See QUO MINUS.

Court of Exchequer Chamber. A court of appeal from each of the three superior courts of common law, which consisted of the judges of the two courts other than those whose decision was being appealed against. By the Judicature Act 1873, the jurisdiction of the Exchequer Chamber was transferred to the Court of Appeal (see Judicature Act 1925, s.26(2)).

Court of Hustings. The oldest of the ancient City of London Courts.

court of inquiry. A court appointed by naval, military, air force authorities, etc., to ascertain the facts in some matter so that the propriety of instituting legal proceedings or taking disciplinary action may be considered. See also TRIBUNALS.

Court of Justice of the European Communities. Set up under the Treaty of Rome to give rulings on questions of law relating to the interpretation and application of the Treaty. It consists of one Judge from each Member State, assisted by Advocates General (*q.v.*).

For the circumstances when the English Courts may or must refer to the Court of Justice see the Treaty of Rome, Art.177; *H.P. Bulmer Ltd.* v. *J. Bollinger S.A.* [1974] 2 All E.R. 1226, C.A.; R.S.C., Ord.114; and C.C.R. Ord.19, r.11.

Court of King's [Queen's] Bench. The court originally held in the presence of the Sovereign. It was one of the superior courts of common law, having, ultimately, in ordinary civil actions concurrent jurisdiction with the Courts of Common Pleas and Exchequer. Its principal judge was styled the Lord Chief Justice of England. It also had special jurisdiction over inferior courts, magistrates and civil corporations by the prerogative writs of *mandamus, prohibition* and *certiorari,* and in proceedings by *quo warranto* and *habeas corpus.* It was also the principal court of criminal jurisdiction in England: informations might be filed and indictments preferred in it in the first instance. The King's [Queen's] Bench accordingly had two "sides." namely, the "plea side," for civil business, and the "Crown side," or "Crown Office," for the criminal and extraordinary jurisdiction. The court was merged in the Supreme Court by the Judicature Act 1873, of which it is now the Queen's Bench Division (see Judicature Act 1925, ss.18(2) 56(2)). See BILL OF MIDDLESEX.

court of last resort. A court from which there is no appeal.

Court of Passage. An inferior court of record with ancient jurisdiction over causes of action arising within the borough of Liverpool. The court was abolished by the Courts Act 1971, s.43 on January 1, 1972.

Court of Pie Poudre. The Court of the Dusty Feet, or of the Pedlars which anciently decided summarily and on the spot disputes which arose in fairs and markets. The court was abolished by the Courts Act 1971, s.43, on January 1, 1972.

Court of Policies of Assurance. A court of the City of London constituted by the statute 43 Eliz. I, c.12, for the summary decision, subject to appeal to the Court of Chancery, of all disputes as to policies of assurance. Obsolete.

Court of Probate. Formed by the Court of Probate Act 1857 to take over the jurisdiction of church and other courts in the matter of wills. Transferred by the Judicature Act 1873, to the Supreme Court of Judicature, where it is represented by the Family Division of the High Court (Judicature Act 1925, s.56(3); Administration of Justice Act 1970, s.1).

Court of Protection. The office of the Supreme Court for the protection and management of the property and affairs of persons under mental disability (Mental Health Act 1959, s.100). It has a Master, a deputy Master, and officers and clerks; all appointed by the Lord Chancellor (*ibid.* s.115). It was formerly called the Management and Administration Department.

court of record. A court whereof the acts and judicial proceedings are enrolled for a perpetual memory and testimony, and which has authority to fine and imprison for contempt of its authority. The Supreme Court is a superior court of record. The county court is an inferior court of record. Other inferior courts of record have been abolished by the Courts Act 1971, s.43.

Court of Requests. A minor court of equity, originally a committee of the King's Council, presided over by the Lord Privy Seal and two Masters of Requests. It heard poor men's causes and those of the King's servants. It fell into desuetude during the Protectorate.

Court of the Marshalsea. A court with jurisdiction within 12 miles of the King's Residence, where one at least of the parties was a member of his household.

Court of Wards and Liveries. Established in 1541 for the purpose of providing the King with an effectual means of asserting his rights with regard to the incidents of tenure by knight service, wardships, liveries, etc. Abolished 1660.

court roll. See COPYHOLD.

courts, inferior. See INFERIOR COURT.

courts of conscience. Courts for the recovery of small debts held by members of various corporations who, without the intervention of professional advocates, decided such cases as came before them.

courts of request. Inferior courts having local jurisdiction in claims for small debts. Abolished 1846.

covenant. An agreement creating an obligation contained in a deed. It may be positive, stipulating the performance of some act or the payment of money, or negative or restrictive, forbidding the commission of some act. Covenants may be used to serve the purpose of a bond (*q.v.*). A covenant is said to run with the land, or with the reversion, when either the liability to perform it, or the right to take advantage of it, passes to the assignee of the land, or the reversion, as the case may be. At common law covenants ran with the land, but not with the reversion; but the statute 32 Hen. 8, c.34 provided that both the burden and benefit of covenants should run with the reversion.

To run with the land covenants must "touch and concern" the thing demised, and must not be collateral or personal. An assignee of a lease is bound by negative covenants, and by positive covenants as to things actually in existence on the land, but not by covenants as to things not in existence, unless the original lessee covenanted for himself and his assigns. The Law of Property Act 1925, s.79, provided, however, that a covenantor shall be deemed to bind his successors.

In equity, negative or restrictive covenants run with the land, except against a bona fide purchaser for value without notice. Since 1925 restrictive covenants have to be registered as land charges. Positive covenants do not run with the land. The Lands Tribunal may discharge or modify restrictive covenants under section 84 of the Law of Property Act 1925.

covenant, action of. The action which down to the Judicature Acts 1873 and 1875 lay where a party claimed damages for breach of covenant.

covenant to stand seised. A covenant by a person seised of land in possession, reversion, or vested remainder in consideration of his natural love and affection, to stand seised of the land to the use of his wife, child or kinsman. By the Statute of Uses the use was converted into a legal estate, and the covenant operated as a conveyance. Obsolete.

covenant, writ of. A writ which lay for claiming damages for breach of covenant. Abolished by Real Property Limitation Act 1833.

covenants for title. The covenants entered into by a vendor in a conveyance of land on sale as to his title, giving the purchaser the right to an action for damages if the title subsequently proves to be bad. Formerly they were set out at length in conveyances, but by the Conveyancing Act 1881, s.7, they were implied by law by the use of the appropriate words. For example, if a person conveys, and is expressed to convey, "as beneficial owner," the following covenants are implied: (1) the right to convey; (2) quiet enjoyment for the purchaser; (3) freedom from incumbrances; (4) further assurance (*i.e.* to do all necessary acts to transfer the land to the buyer).

See now Law of Property Act, 1925, s.76, Sched.2.

covert-baron. A married woman.

coverture. The condition of being a married woman.

covin. A secret assent determined in the hearts of two or more to the defrauding and prejudice of another (Coke).

credit. (1) The time which a creditor will allow his debtor in which to pay, or the total amount which he will permit to borrow or to owe. See CONSUMER CREDIT.

An undischarged bankrupt commits an offence if he obtains credit to the extent of £50 without revealing that he is an undischarged bankrupt (Bankruptcy Act 1914, s.155, amended by Insolvency Act 1979, Sched.1. See also *R.* v. *Godwin* (1980) 124 S.J. 344, C.A.).

It is an offence under the Theft Act 1978 to obtain services by deception (s.1), to evade liability (for payment) by deception (s.2) or to make off without payment (s.3).

(2) Cross-examination as to credit means asking questions of a witness designed to test his credibility.

credit card. See the Consumer Credit Act 1974, ss.14, Sched.2. It is an offence to give a person a credit card if he has not asked for it (s.51). As to misuse see s.66. As to liability under a credit card, see ss.84, 171. The use of a credit card to obtain goods when the holders credit limit with the bank has been exceeded is just as much an offence of obtaining a pecuniary advantage by deception under the Theft Act 1968 as was the dishonest use of a cheque card, even though the victim was not induced to complete the transaction by a false representation (*R.* v. *Lambie* [1981] 2 All E.R. 776, H.L.).

credit-sale agreement. An agreement for the sale of goods under which the purchase price is payable by instalments but which is not a conditional sale agreement (*q.v.*) (Consumer Credit Act 1974, s.189, Sched.2). The property in such a transaction passes to the buyer immediately. Transactions under £5,000 come within s.8 of the Act unless exempt under s.16.

creditor. A person to whom a debt is owing. A secured creditor is a person who holds a mortgage, charge, or lien on the property of his debtor. In bankruptcy of the debtor, a secured creditor may either give up his security and prove for the whole debt, or realise it, or give credit for it, and prove for the balance (Bankruptcy Act 1914, Sched.2, paras 10–12).

cremation. The disposal of a dead body by burning in a crematorium (Cremation Act 1902; Cremation Act 1952).

crime. A crime may be described as an act, default or conduct prejudicial to the community, the commission of which by law renders the person responsible liable to punishment by fine or imprisonment in special proceedings, normally instituted by officers in the service of the Crown. Indictable offences (other than treason) were formerly divided into felonies and misdemeanours but the distinction between the two was abolished by the Criminal Law Act 1967, s.1.

crimen falsi. The common law offence of forgery (*q.v.*) and falsification.

crimen laesae majestatis. [The crime of injured majesty.] Treason and lesser offences against the Sovereign, *e.g.* insult.

criminal. A person found guilty of an indictable offence. See CONVICT; COURT OF CRIMINAL APPEAL; INFORMATION.

criminal appeal. A person convicted of an offence on indictment may appeal to the Criminal Division of the Court of Appeal against his conviction on any ground which involves a question of law alone, and, with the leave of the Court of Appeal on any ground which involves a question of fact or a question of mixed law and fact or on any other ground which appears to the Court of Appeal to be a sufficient ground of appeal. The leave of the Court of Appeal is unnecessary if the trial judge certifies that the case is fit for appeal (Criminal Appeal Act 1968, ss.1,45). The grounds for allowing an appeal against conviction are (a) that the verdict of the jury is unsafe or unsatisfactory; (b) that the judgment of the trial court was wrong in law; (c) that there was a material irregularity in the course of the trial. But the court may, notwithstanding that they are of the opinion that the point raised in the appeal might be decided in favour of the appellant, dismiss the appeal if they consider that no miscarriage of justice has actually occurred. If an appeal against conviction is allowed the conviction is quashed and, unless a new trial is ordered the trial court must enter a judgment and verdict of acquittal (Criminal Appeal Act 1968, s.2). The Court of Appeal has power to substitute for the conviction, a conviction for an alternative offence (s.3) and may substitute for the conviction a finding of insanity or unfitness to plead (s.6, Sched.1). The Court of Appeal may order a new trial (ss.7, 8; Courts Act 1971, Sched.11, Part IV).

With the leave of the Court of Appeal, a person convicted on indictment and in some other cases may appeal against sentence (other than a sentence fixed by law). The court may quash the sentence or substitute another sentence but the sentence may not be increased (ss.9–11 as amended).

Bail may be granted pending appeal (ss.19, 31, 45). Groundless appeals may be dismissed summarily (s.20). An appellant may usually be present at the appeal if he wishes it (s.22). The time during which an appellant is in custody pending appeal may be reckoned as part of the term of his sentence (s.29). Unless the court otherwise directs, a sentence takes effect from the beginning of the day on which it is passed (Criminal Justice Administration Act 1962, s.17; Criminal Appeal Act 1968, s.29(4)). The court is usually constituted of three judges (Administration of Justice Act 1970, s.9). The trial judge is not to be a member of the court (Criminal Appeal Act 1966, s.2(3)). The court may sit during vacation (s.2(5)).

An appeal lies from the Criminal Division of the Court of Appeal to the House of Lords on a point of general importance which ought to be considered by that House (Criminal Appeal Act 1968, ss.33–41; Courts Act 1971, Sched.8, para.57, Sched.11, Part IV).

An appeal from a Divisional Court in a criminal cause or matter lies to the House of Lords (Administration of Justice Act 1960, ss.1–4; Criminal Appeal Act 1968, Sched.7).

Where a person tried on indictment has been acquitted the Attorney General may refer a point of law arising in the case to the Court of Appeal for its opinion. The point may be further referred to the House of Lords (Criminal Justice Act 1972, s.36).

criminal bankruptcy. Where a person is convicted of an offence before the Crown Court (*q.v.*) and the loss or damage attributable to that offence (other than for personal injury) exceeds £15,000, the court may make a criminal bankruptcy order against him but not if it makes a compensation order (*q.v.*) against him (Powers of Criminal Courts Act 1973, ss.39–41).

criminal compensation. See COMPENSATION ORDER; CRIMINAL INJURIES COMPENSATION.

criminal conversation (crim. con.). The common law action which lay at the suit of a husband to recover damages against an adulterer. See ADULTERY.

criminal damage. A person who without lawful excuse destroys or damages any property belonging to another, intending to destroy or damage any such property or being reckless as to whether any such property would be destroyed or damaged is guilty of an indictable offence punishable with 10 years' imprisonment (Criminal Damage Act 1971, ss.1(1), 4). Criminal damage endangering life is punishable with life imprisonment (ss.1(2), 4). If committed with fire it may be charged as arson (ss.1(3), 11(1)). Threats of destruction are punishable with 10 years' imprisonment (ss.2, 4). Having custody of anything intended to cause criminal damage is punishable with 10 years' imprisonment (ss.3, 4).

criminal injuries compensation. A person who suffers personal injuries as a direct result of a criminal offence or of trying to arrest an offender or prevent a crime may apply to the Criminal Injuries Compensation Board for an *ex gratia* award of compensation. The scheme is now extended to crimes of violence within the family. Compensation is based on common law damages and may be reduced to take account of state benefits received by the claimant or the claimant's own behaviour. Application can be made by the dependants of a deceased victim.

criminal lunatic. An inmate of a criminal lunatic asylum: a "Broadmoor patient" (Criminal Justice Act 1948, s.62—repealed). See BROADMOOR.

cross-action. The bringing by a defendant in an action of another action against the plaintiff in respect of the same subject-matter. See COUNTERCLAIM.

cross-appeals. Where both parties to a case appeal.

cross-examination. When a witness has been intentionally called by either party (not merely to produce a document or be identified) the opposite party has a right, after examination-in-chief is closed or waived, to cross-examine him. It is not confined to matters proved in examination-in-chief, and leading questions may be put. Failure to cross-examine a witness generally amounts to an acceptance of his version of a transaction. See EXAMINATION.

cross-remainder. Where land is given in undivided shares to A and B for particular estates so that, upon the determination of the particular estates in A's share, the whole of the land goes to B, and vice versa.

Crown. The King in his public capacity as a body politic. "The King never dies": there is no interregnum. The Coronation is but an ornament or solemnity of power (*Calvin's Case* (1608) 7 Co.Rep. 1a). See ROYAL TITLE.

The Crown is the highest branch of the Legislature, the head of the executive power, and the fountain of justice and honour. As "the King can do no wrong," the Crown was not liable in tort, nor was it liable for the torts of Crown servants; they, however, are personally liable for their own torts. But a Petition of Right (*q.v.*) lay against the Crown. By the Crown Proceedings Act 1947, the Crown was put as nearly as possible in the same position as the subject in litigation. See CROWN PROCEEDINGS.

Crown Court. The Crown Court was established on January 1, 1972 by the Courts Act 1971 with exclusive jurisdiction in the trial of indictments and certain other jurisdiction previously exercised by Assize Courts and Courts of Quarter Sessions. The law relating to the jurisdiction and practice of the Crown Court is now set out in the Supreme Court Act 1981 (ss.8, 45–52 and 73–83). All proceedings on indictment must be brought before the Crown Court (s.45). The Crown Court also deals with appeals from magistrates and cases committed to the Crown Court for sentence. The jurisdiction of the Crown Court is exercisable by any judge of the High Court, or any Circuit Judge or Recorder (*q.v.*) (s.8(1)). When hearing appeals from or cases committed for sentence by Magistrates the Judge must sit with not less than two and not more than four Justices of the Peace (s.74(1)). When the Crown Court sits in London it is known as the Central Criminal Court (*q.v.*) (s.8(3)). Section 83 confers on the Lord Chancellor power to grant right of audience to solicitors.

Appeals from decisions on indictment are to the Court of Appeal Criminal Division. See CRIMINAL APPEAL.

Crown debts. Debts due to the Crown. See CROWN PROCEEDINGS.

Crown lands. The Crown Estate Acts 1956 and 1961, provide for the management of the Crown Estates by the Crown Estates Commissioners.

Crown Office. The office in which all the ministerial business of the Court of the King's [Queen's] Bench in respect of its prerogative and criminal jurisidiction was transacted. Now part of the Central Office of the Supreme Court. See CLERK OF THE CROWN.

Crown privilege. The right of the crown to object to producing a document in court on the ground that it would be against the public interest to do so. Privilege is claimed by affidavit made by the Minister or Permanent Secretary. See *Duncan* v. *Cammell Laird & Co.* [1942] A.C. 624; Crown Proceedings Act 1947, s.28. In *Conway* v. *Rimmer* 1968 A.C. 910, H.L. it was held that a Minister's claim to privilege was not necessarily conclusive and that the Judge might inspect the document in respect of which privilege was claimed. See also *Burmah Oil Co. Ltd.* v. *Bank of England* [1979]3 W.L.R. 722, H.L.

Crown proceedings. Legal proceedings instituted on behalf of the Crown to enforce the payment of sums or debts due to the Crown were formerly brought by way of Information on the Revenue side of the King's [Queen's] Bench Division, or by writ of summons in the High Court.

By the Crown Proceedings Act 1947, the Crown was, in general, made liable to be sued in contract or in tort, etc., as if it were a private person of full age and capacity, subject to the Crown's prerogative and statutory rights. Proceedings by or against the Crown are now brought by or against the appropriate Government Department, or the Attorney-General (*q.v.*). Judgment, however, cannot be enforced against the Crown; nor are injunctions or decrees of specific performance available against the Crown. In lieu, declaratory orders or judgments may be made against the Crown, and a certificate thereof given to the person in whose favour made (see Ord.77).

Crown Side. The prerogative and criminal jurisdiction of the Queen's Bench Division. It had an ancient jurisdiction of supervising inferior courts.

Crown Solicitor. The Director of Public Prosecutions (*q.v.*).

cruelty. Before the Divorce Reform Act 1969 cruelty was a Matrimonial offence and a ground for divorce. Since the 1969 Act behaviour which would previously have been classed as cruelty would be described as unreasonable behaviour which is one of the current grounds for divorce. See DIVORCE; UNREASONABLE BEHAVIOUR). Persistent cruelty continued to be a matrimonial offence justifying the making of a matrimonial order in the Magistrates Courts until the coming into force of the Domestic Proceedings and Magistrates Courts Act 1978 which also substituted the ground of behaviour. As between husband and wife therefore the term "cruelty" no longer has any legal meaning.

cui in vita. An action by which a widow could recover her lands if they had been aliened during the coverture of her husband.

cujus est dare ejus est disponere. [He who gives anything can also direct how the gift is to be used.]

cujus est instituere ejus est abrogare. [He that institutes may also abrogate.]

cujus est solum ejus est usque ad coelum. [Whose is the soil, his is also that which is above it.]

culpa. [Roman law.] Wrongful default. "*Magna negligentia culpa est*" (Paul).

culpa lata. [Roman law.] Incurred by extreme negligence; negligence so gross that it cannot but seem intentional. It amounts to *dolus* (fraud.).

culpa levis. [Roman law.] Incurred when a person falls short either of the care of a *bonus paterfamilias* (*in abstracto*) or the care that he ordinarily gives to his own affairs (*in concreto*).

cum liber erit. [Roman law.] The appointment of another man's slave as tutor is void, unless made with the condition "when he becomes free." Ulpian says that it is to be implied, if not inserted.

cum testamento annexo. [With the will annexed.] See LETTERS OF ADMINISTRATION.

cur. adv. vult. *Curia advisari vult* (*q.v.*).

cura; curatio. [Roman law.] The Office or function of the curator.

curator. [Roman law.] A guardian appointed to a person past the age of puberty to manage his affairs, when from any cause he is unfit to manage them himself.

curator bonorum distrahendorum. [Roman law.] A curator appointed for the purpose of selling a debtor's property and distributing among the creditors the amount realised.

curia advisari vult. [The court wishes to be advised.] In law reports contracted to c.a.v. It means that judgment was not delivered immediately, time being taken for consideration.

curia regis. The King's Court. See AULA REGIS.

cursitors (clerici de cursu). Clerks in the Chancery office whose duties consisted in drawing up those writs which were "of course."

curtain provisions. The provisions of the Property Acts of 1925 (so called because they placed naked equitable interests decently behind a legal curtain) which provided that, so far as possible, equities should not be abstracted or disclosed, and should be ignored by purchasers, even with notice of them, wherever the material interests of the beneficiaries were protected either by the Settled Land Act 1925, or by an express or statutory trust for sale vested in at least two trustees to whom all capital moneys are to be paid (Underhill).

A conveyance to a purchaser of a legal estate for money or money's worth will overreach any equitable interest or power affecting that estate, whether the purchaser has notice of it or not if the conveyance is made: (1) under the Settled Land Act 1925; or (2) by trustees for sale; or (3) by a mortgagee or personal representative in the exercise of his paramount powers; or (4) under an order of the court; provided that the equitable interest or power is capable of being overreached by the conveyance, and that any capital money arising from the transaction is paid in cases (1) and (2) to at least two trustees or a trust corporation, and in case (3) to the mortgagee or personal representative, and in case (4) into, or in accordance with the order of, the court (see Law of Property Act 1925, s.2).

curtesy of England, tenure by. See TENURE BY CURTESY OF ENGLAND.

curtilage. A courtyard, garden, yard, field, backside or piece of ground lying near and belonging to a dwelling house (*Pilbrow* v. *St. Leonard, Shoreditch Vestry* [1895] 1 Q.B. 433).

custode admittendo; custode removendo. Writs which anciently lay for the appointing or removing of a guardian.

custodes pacis. [Conservators or keepers of the peace.] They were called justices of the peace (*q.v.*) from 1368 onwards (42 Edw.3, c.6).

custodiam lease. Anciently, a grant by the King, under the Exchequer Seal, by which Crown lands were demised or granted to some person as custodian or lessee thereof.

custodian trustee. A trustee who has the custody and care of trust property, but not its management. See Public Trustee Act 1906. He is not a "bare trustee" (*q.v.*).

custodianship order. Order made under Children Act 1975, s.33 vesting legal custody of child in the applicant. The child's parents may not apply. Seen as alternative to adoption.

custody. (1) Confinement or imprisonment, *e.g.* remand (of accused person) in custody.

(2) Control and possession of some thing or person, *e.g.* to surrender oneself into the custody of the court (Bail Act 1976, s.2(2)).

custody of children. A person has actual custody of a child if he has actual possession of his person, whether or not that possession is shared with one or more other persons (Children Act 1975, s.87). Custody is also defined as "so much of the parental rights and duties as relate to the person of the child" (including the place and manner in which his time is spent) (Children Act 1975 s.86). The court has power, in proceedings for divorce nullity of marriage or judicial separation, to make orders for the custody and education of any child of the family under the age of 18 (Matrimonial Causes Act 1973, s.42). Custody may be awarded to one parent only or to both parents jointly. See JOINT CUSTODY.

The order normally provides for the non-custodial parent to have access to the child (see ACCESS TO CHILDREN). See also and contrast CARE AND CONTROL.

Orders made under Matrimonial Causes Act 1973, s.42 are made by a divorce County Court or by the Family Division of the High Court (Administration of Justice Act 1970, s.1, Sched.1). Custody orders may also be made by magistrates courts and where there are no matrimonial proceedings, the county court (Domestic Proceedings and Magistrates Court Act 1978, ss.8–15 and Guardianship of Minors Act 1971).

custom. A rule of conduct, obligatory on those within its scope, established by long usage. A valid custom has the force of law. Custom is to society what law is to the state (Salmond). A valid custom must be of immemorial antiquity, certain and reasonable, obligatory, not repugnant to statute law, though it may derogate from the common law.

General customs are those of the whole country, as, *e.g.* the general custom of merchants. Particular customs are the usage of particular trades. Local customs are customs of certain parts of the country.

customary freeholds. A superior kind of copyholds. The tenants hold by copy of court roll according to the custom of the manor, but not at the will of the lord. Abolished by the Law of Property Act 1922.

customary tenure. See COPYHOLD.

customs. The duties or tolls payable upon merchandise imported into the country. See Customs and Excise Act 1979.

custos brevium et recordorum. The keeper of the writs and records. Abolished by Superior Courts Officers Act 1837.

custos rotulorum. Keeper of the rolls or records. The first justice of the peace and first civil officer of the county for which he was appointed.

cy-près. The doctrine that where a settlor or testator has expressed a general intention, and also a particular way in which he wishes it carried out, but the intention cannot be carried out in that particular way, the court will direct the intention to be carried out *as nearly as possible* in the way desired. The doctrine is more particularly applied to charities. Thus, if a paramount charitable intention appears, a charitable gift will not be void simply because there is no such institution as is specified in the gift, but the property will be used for some similar purpose resembling as much as possible the specified object.

The Charities Act 1960, ss.13, 14, extends to some extent the scope of the doctrine: *e.g.* the application *cy-près* of surplus money, which would otherwise result abortively to unidentifiable donors is allowed.

D

D.P.P. The Director of Public Prosecutions (*q.v.*).

damage, criminal. See CRIMINAL DAMAGE.

damage-feasant. [Doing damage.] See DISTRESS DAMAGE-FEASANT.

damage, malicious. See CRIMINAL DAMAGE.

damages. Compensation or indemnity for loss suffered owing to a Tort or breach of contract or breach of some statutory duty committed by some other person. The principle is that the injured party should be put as nearly as possible in the same position, so far as money can do it, as if he had not been injured. Damages from the same cause must be recovered once and for all. The test by which the amount of the damages is ascertained is called the measure of damages and varies between different classes of action. Nominal damages are of trifling amount awarded contemptuously where breach of some legal right has been proved but the court considers that the plaintiff has suffered no real loss. In certain classes of case the court may award exemplary damages not only by way of compensation but as a punishment to the offender.

Industrial Tribunals may award damages in cases involving unfair dismissal (*q.v.*) and racial or sexual discrimination. See GENERAL DAMAGES; REMOTENESS OF DAMAGE; SPECIAL DAMAGE.

damnosa hereditas. [Roman law.] An inheritance which was insolvent.

damnum absque injuria. [Loss without wrong.] Loss or damage for which there is no legal remedy. For a modern example see *Smith* v. *Scott* [1973] Ch. 314.

damnum sentit dominus. [The lord suffers the damage.] The loss falls on him who is in law the owner.

damnum sine injuria esse potest. There may be damage or loss inflicted without any act being done which the law deems an injury. For instance, harm may be caused by a person exercising his own rights of property (*Mayor of Bradford* v. *Pickles* [1895] A.C. 587) or by trade competition (*Mogul Steamship Co.* v. *McGregor Gow & Co.* [1892] A.C. 25).

Danegeld. A tax on land levied to meet the expenses of the Danish invasions.

Danelage. The laws of the Danish part of the kingdom in the tenth century.

danger, alternative. The principle of law that where a person is suddenly put in a position of imminent danger by the wrongful act of another then what is done by that person in the agony of the moment cannot fairly be treated as negligence; *e.g.* jumping and sustaining injury from a runaway coach (*Jones* v. *Boyce* (1816) 1 Starkie 493; *The Bywell Castle* (1879) 4 P.D. 219). So a lady locked in a public lavatory is entitled to make reasonable efforts to escape (*Sayers* v. *Harlow U.D.C.* [1958] 1 W.L.R. 623).

dangerous chattels. See DANGEROUS THINGS.

dangerous premises. The liability to compensate persons injured on premises owing to their dangerous state is in general upon the occupier and not the owner. At common law the duty of an occupier differed according to whether the visitor was an invitee or licensee, but by the Occupiers' Liability Act 1957, the occupier owes the same "common duty of care " to all lawful visitors (s.2) except so far as his duty is modified by agreement.

As regards trespassers, the general principle is that he who enters wrongfully does so at his own risk and cannot complain if *e.g.* he breaks a leg by falling downstairs, or is bitten by the occupier's dog. The occupier owes no duty to the trespasser, except that he may not intentionally harm him by traps such as spring guns (*Bird* v. *Holbrook* (1828) 4 Bing 628). But the common law imposes a duty on occupiers to take such steps as common sense or common humanity would require to exclude trespassers or to warn them of, or reduce or avert a danger which may exist or arise on the premises, taking such steps as come within reasonable and practicable limits (*Herrington* v. *British Railways Board* [1972] A.C. 877, H.L.; *Pannett* v. *P. McGuiness & Co. Ltd.* [1972] 2 Q.B. 599, C.A.). See INVITEE; LICENSEE; TRESPASSER.

dangerous things. (1) The occupier of land who brings and keeps upon it anything likely to damage if it escapes, is bound at his peril to prevent its escape, and is liable for all the direct consequences of its escape even if he has been guilty of no negligence (*Rylands* v. *Fletcher* (1868) L.R. 3 H.L. 330). The exceptions to this rule are where there is consent or default of the plaintiff; act of a stranger; or act of God. As to dangerous animals see ANIMALS.

(2) Dangerous things are those which are specially likely to cause injury to those persons into whose possession they may come; *i.e.* ultimate transferees. The person putting dangerous things into circulation is responsible for damage caused by them to others if he misleads the recipient into thinking they are safe and they are not. He is also responsible if he is negligent. The case of dangerous things is a special instance of negligence where the law exacts a degree of diligence so stringent as to amount practically to a guarantee of safety (*per* Lord Macmillan, *Donoghue* v. *Stevenson* [1932] A.C. 562 at p.611–612). A manufacturer of products, which he sells in such a form as to show that he intends them to reach the ultimate consumer in the form in which they left him with no reasonable possibility of intermediate examination and with the knowledge that the absence of reasonable care in the preparation or putting up of the products will result in an injury to the consumer's life or property, owes a duty to the consumer to take that reasonable care (*per* Lord Atkin, *ibid.* at p.599).

dangerous wild animals. No person may keep any dangerous wild animal (as enumerated in Dangerous Wild Animals Act 1976) without a licence granted by the local authority (1976 Act, s.1).

Darrein Presentment. See ASSIZE OF DARREIN PRESENTMENT.

days of grace. Days allowed for making a payment or doing some other act after the time limited for that purpose has expired. Three days of grace were allowed for the payment of a bill of exchange but this was abolished by the Banking and Financial Dealings Act 1971, s.3.

de bene esse. To act provisionally or in anticipation of a future occasion; to take evidence for future use while it is available (Ord. 39, r. 1).

de bonis asportasis. [Of goods carried away.] See TRESPASS.

de bonis non. [Of goods not administered.] An administrator appointed to succeed a deceased administrator to complete the administration of an intestate's estate.

de die in diem. [From day to day.]

De Donis (Conditionalibus). The Statute of Westminster II. See ESTATE.

de ejectione firmae. The writ which originated the old action of ejectment (*q.v.*).

de executione facienda. Writs of execution.

de facto. [In fact.]

de homine replegiando. A writ which formerly lay to bail out one wrongfully imprisoned.

de ingressu. A writ of entry.

de injuria. An averment in pleading that the defendant of his own wrong and without the alleged cause had done the acts alleged as a defence.

de jure. [By right.]

de medietate linguae. A jury, on half of which consisted of aliens, before which aliens were formerly tried.

de minimis non curat lex. [The law does not concern itself with trifles.]

de non apparentibus, et non existentibus, eadem est ratio. [Of things which do not appear and things which do not exist, the rule in legal proceedings is the same.]

de novo. [Anew.]

de odio et atia. [Of malice and ill-will.] A writ which lay for a man committed to prison upon suspicion of murder, which commanded the sheriff to inquire whether the committal was upon just cause or suspicion or only upon malice and ill-will. If the latter then another writ issued commanding the sheriff to bail him.

de recte. A writ of right (*q.v.*).

de seisina habenda. [For having seisin.] The writ by which the King anciently enforced his right to year, day and waste (*q.v.*).

de son tort demesne. [Of his own wrong.] See EXECUTOR DE SON TORT.

De Tallagio non Concedendo. The statute 25 Edward I, which enacts that no tallage or aid shall be levied without the assent of the realm.

de ventre inspiciendo. Where the widow of an owner of land was suspected of feigning herself with child in order to produce a supposititious heir to the estate, the heir presumptive could have a writ *de ventre inspiciendo*, to examine whether she was with child or not; and if so, to keep her under proper restraint until delivered. Obsolete.

dead freight. Freight payable by a charterer in respect of cargo not shipped.

dead rent. The minimum rent payable under a mining lease, irrespective of whether minerals are won or not. A deficiency may be carried forward and set off against the rent in future years.

death, presumption of. See PRESUMPTION OF DEATH.

death duties, formerly death estate duty, succession duty and legacy duty, payable on property passing at death. Succession duty and legacy duty where abolished by the Finance Act 1949, s.27. Estate duty was superseded from March 13, 1975, by capital transfer tax (*q.v.*).

debenture. (1) A certificate of right to drawback (*q.v.*).

(2) An instrument usually under seal, issued by a company or public body as evidence of a debt or as a security for a loan of a fixed sum of money, at interest. It contains a promise to pay the amount mentioned in it, and is usually called a debenture on the face of it. "Debenture" includes debenture stock, bonds and any other securities of a company whether constituting a charge on the assets of the company or not (Companies Act 1948, s.455(1)). See *ibid*. ss.86–94. A debenture usually gives a charge over the company's assets or some form of security.

debenture stock. Stock representing money borrowed by a company or public body, and charged on the whole or part of its property. Borrowed capital consolidated into one mass for the sale of convenience (Lindley). It is almost invariably secured by a trust deed and the rights of the stockholders are primarily against the trustees.

debitor. [Roman law.] One against whom another possesses a personal right; one that can be compelled to perform an obligation.

debitor non praesumitur donare. [A debtor is not presumed to give.]

debitum connexum. A debt giving rise to a lien.

debitum in praesenti, solvendum in futuro. [Owed at the present time, payable (or to be performed) in the future.]

debt. A sum of money due from one person to another. Debts are (1) of record; *e.g.* recognisances and judgment debts; (2) specialty debts, created by deed; (3) simple contract debts; (4) Crown debts (*q.v.*); (5) secured debts, those for which security has been taken; (6) preferential debts (Bankruptcy Act 1914, s.33). See IMPRISONMENT FOR DEBT; PREFERENTIAL PAYMENTS.

debt-collecting. See the Consumer Credit Act 1974, ss.145–160.

debtor summons. The former equivalent of bankruptcy notice.

deceit. An action upon the case lay to recover damages caused by the fraud or false affirmance by the defendant of a thing within his knowledge. Now it is the tort consisting of the making of a wilfully false statement by words or conduct with intent that another shall act upon it, with the result that it is so acted upon and harm results. See FRAUD; MISREPRESENTATION.

deception. Obtaining property or a pecuniary advantage by deception is an indictable offence (Theft Act 1968, ss.15,16). It is also an offence to obtain services by a deception (Theft Act 1978, s.1(1)). "Obtaining services" means a situation where another person is induced to confer a benefit on the understanding that the benefit has been or will be paid for (1978 Act,s.1(2)).

declaration. (1) A formal statement intended to create, preserve, assert or testify to a right. (2) The decision of the court or judge on a question of law or rights. (3) A statement of claim in pleading.

Declarations consisting of statements made substantially contemporaneously with acts are admissible in evidence as forming part of such acts (or, *res gestae*).

Statements by deceased persons are admissible in evidence as follows: (1) against interest: declarations, oral or written, made by deceased persons against their pecuniary or proprietary interests; (2) in course of duty: declarations, oral or written, made by deceased persons in the ordinary course of duty, contemporaneously with the facts stated, and without motive to misrepresent; (3) as to public rights: declarations by deceased persons of competent knowledge, made *ante litem motam* as to ancient rights of a public or general nature; (4) as to pedigree: declarations made by deceased relations, *ante litem motam*; (5) dying declarations (*q.v.*); (6) as to contents, etc., of wills; (7) under the Inheritance (Provision for Family and Dependants) Act 1975, s.21. See DECLARATORY JUDGMENT.

Declaration of Paris 1856 concerned warfare on sea. It abolished privateering, recognised the principles that the neutral flag protects non-contraband enemy goods, and that non-contraband neutral goods under an enemy flag cannot be seized, and enacted the rule that a blockade, in order to be binding, must be effective.

declaration of solvency. The statutory declaration made by the directors of a company, and delivered to the Registrar of Companies, that they are of opinion that the company will be able to pay its debts in full within not exceeding twelve months from the commencement of the winding up. It is a condition precedent of a members' voluntary winding up (Companies Act 1948, s.283).

declaration of use or trust. A statement or admission that property is to be held to the use of or upon trust for a certain person. The ordinary mode of creating a trust when the trust property is already vested in the intended trustee.

declaratory judgment. A judgment which conclusively declares the pre-existing rights of the litigants without the appendage of any coercive decree (see Ord. 15, r. 16). The procedure under Ord. 15, r. 16 should not be used if criminal proceedings have been instituted in respect of the same matter (*Imperial Tobacco Ltd.* v. *Att.-Gen.* [1980] 2 W.L.R. 466, H.L.).

declaratory statute. One which declares or formally states what the existing law is on a given subject, so as to remove doubts.

declaration, statutory. See STATUTORY DECLARATION.

decree. An order of a court pronounced on the hearing of a suit.

decree absolute. A final and conclusive decree, which finally dissolves the marriage. See DECREE NISI.

decree nisi. Every decree of dissolution of marriage, whether for divorce or nullity, is in the first instance a decree nisi (nisi = unless) not to be made absolute until after six weeks unless the court orders a shorter time (Matrimonial Causes Act

1973, s.1(5); Matrimonial Causes (Decree Absolute) General Orders 1972 and 1973 rr.65, 66). The period of six weeks may be expedited by the court under certain circumstances (see Practice Direction 1977, 1 W.L.R. 759).

dedication. Granting a right of way to the public over private property. Ways over land are deemed to have been dedicated as a highway where used by the public for 20 years (Highways Act 1959, ss.34, 35).

dedititii. [Roman law.] Certain manumitted slaves who, in consequence of grave misconduct committed while they were slaves, were subjected to certain perpetual disabilities.

deed. A writing or instrument written on paper or parchment, signed, sealed and delivered, to prove and testify the agreement of the parties whose deed it is to the things contained in the deed. A deed generally consists of the following parts: the premises, the habendum, the tenendum, the reddendum, the conditions, and the covenants. See ACKNOWLEDGMENT OF DEEDS; ESCROW; RESERVATION.

deed of arrangement. See ARRANGEMENT, DEEDS OF.

deed of covenant. A covenant by a separate deed; *e.g.* to produce title deeds.

deed poll. A deed which is "polled" or smooth; *i.e.* not indented: a unilateral deed; *e.g.* for publishing a change of names.

deemed. To be treated as.

defamation. The tort consisting in the publication of a false and derogatory statement respecting another person without lawful justification. A defamatory statement is one exposing him to hatred, ridicule or contempt, or which causes him to be shunned or avoided, or which has a tendency to injure him in his office, profession or trade. It may constitute libel or slander (*q.v.*). It must be construed in its natural and ordinary meaning; if not defamatory in such meaning, it must be construed in the special meaning, if any, in which it was understood by the person by and to whom it was published.

It is for the judge to say whether the words are reasonably capable of a defamatory meaning, but for the jury to say whether under the circumstances of the case they in fact bear that meaning.

No action can be maintained for libel or slander unless there be a publication; *i.e.* a communication by the defendant of the defamatory statement to some person other than the plaintiff.

The Defamation Act 1952 makes a number of detailed amendments; *e.g.* to the defence of justification and fair comment. See APOLOGY; BROADCASTING; PRIVILEGE; SPECIAL DAMAGE.

default. To make default is to fail in some duty; *e.g.* to pay a sum due; or failure to take any step required by the rules of procedure; *e.g.* in default of acknowledgment of service (*q.v.*), the plaintiff may, in general, proceed in the absence of the other party to judgment (Ord. 13).

default summons. A summary means of recovering a debt or liquidated demand in the county court.

defeasance. A condition relating to a deed, but contained in a separate instrument, on which being performed the deed is made void.

defeasible. An estate or interest in property, which is liable to be defeated or terminated by the operation of a condition subsequent or conditional limitation.

defective. A person suffering from a state of arrested or incomplete development of mind, including subnormality of intelligence, so that the patient is or will be incapable of living an independent life or of guarding himself against serious exploitation (Mental Health Act 1959, s.127).

defence. A pleading served in the High Court or filed in the County Court in reply to the statement of claim or particulars of claim. It answers the allegations made by admissions or denials. The defendant must deal with each of the plaintiff's allegations; a blanket or general denial is not sufficient. In the High Court a defendant who has entered an acknowledgment of service must serve his defence within 14 days of the time limited for the acknowledgment of service (R.S.C. Ord. 18, r. 2). In the county court a defendant must file a defence within 14 days after the service of the summons on him (C.C.R., Ord. 9, r. 2(1)).

In general, in default of defence a plaintiff may enter judgment without leave (R.S.C. Ord. 19 and C.C.R. Ord. 9, r. 6(1)). See also COUNTERCLAIM.

A defence to a petition for divorce or other matrimonial relief is called an answer. See ANSWER.

Defence Regulations. The regulations made by Her Majesty by Order in Council under the emergency legislation (*q.v.*).

defendant. A person against whom an action, information or other civil proceeding (other than a petition) is brought; also a person being charged with an offence.

defensor. [Roman law.] An unauthorised defender; one that without a mandate undertook the defence of another person who had failed to appear in his own defence.

defensores. [Roman law.] An inferior class of magistrates in provincial towns.

deferment of sentence. With the offender's consent the Crown Court or magistrates' court may defer passing sentence on an offender for up to six months so that the court, in determining sentence, may have regard to the offender's conduct after conviction or to any charge in his circumstances (Powers of Criminal Courts Act 1973, s.1 as amended by Criminal Law Act 1977, s.65(4), Sched. 12).

deferred shares. Deferred or founders' shares in a company are usually of small nominal value but with a right to take the whole or a proportion of the profits after a fixed dividend has been paid on the ordinary shares. The rights of the holders depend on the articles or the terms of issue. Particulars of them must be set out in the prospectus (Companies Act, 1948, Sched. 4). They are now rarely issued.

deforcement. The wrongful holding of lands of another.

defraud. Conspiracy to defraud remains an offence (see CONSPIRACY). A person can be convicted of the offence where it is shown that he had agreed with one or more persons to deprive another by any dishonest means of something that either was his or to which he was or would be or might, but for the perpetration of the fraud, be entitled (*Scott* v. *Commr. of Police for Metropolis* [1974] 1 All E.R. 1032, H.L.).

degree. A step in the line of descent or consanguinity.

dehors. [Without.] Outside the scope of; irrelevant.

del credere agent. An agent for the sale of goods who, in consideration of a higher reward than is usually given, guarantees the due payment of the price of all goods sold by him.

delegated legislation. Legislation by some person or body under authority given to that person or body by statute, *e.g.* Orders in Council, Regulations or Rules. Such delegated or subordinate legislation is controlled by Parliament in that the Orders or Rules are printed and laid before parliament which may then debate them.

delegatus non potest delegare. [A delegate cannot delegate.] A person to whom powers have been delegated cannot delegate them to another. But trustees may appoint agents to do trust business, and are not responsible for their default, if employed in good faith (Trustee Act 1925, s.23).

delivery of a deed. Generally effected by the grantor saying at the time of signing and sealing the deed, "I deliver this as my act and deed." See ESCROW.

delivery order. An order by the owner of goods to a person holding them on his behalf, to deliver them to a person named.

delivery, writ of. A writ of execution to enforce a judgment for the recovery of property other than land or money. It may be either for the return of chattels with the option of paying the assessed value, or for the return without such option (Ord. 45). See also Torts (Interference with Goods) Act 1977, s.3.

demandant. The person bringing a "real" action. See ACTION.

demesme. [Own.] The part of the manor occupied by the lord.

demise. Originally any transfer or succession of a right; now to grant a lease of lands or other hereditaments.

demise of the Crown. The transfer of royal dignity which takes place when one King or Queen succeeds to another; not the *death* of the King or Queen.

demur, to. In pleading, to raise an objection by demurrer (*q.v.*).

demurrage. (1) The detention of a ship beyond the number of days—called lay days—allowing for loading or unloading, and (2) the sum fixed by the contract of affreightment (the charterparty) as payable to the shipowner for such detention.

demurrer. A pleading by which one of the parties alleged that the preceding pleadings of the other party showed no good cause of action or defence. Abolished in 1883. A party by his pleadings may raise any point of law (Ord. 18, r.11). If a pleading raises no reasonable cause of action or defence it may be struck out (Ord. 18, r. 19).

It is still possible in criminal proceedings to demur to the indictment; *i.e.* allege some substantial defect in it. A defendant may plead not guilty in addition to any demurrer (Criminal Law Act 1967). Demurrer in criminal cases is virtually obsolete.

denizen. Originally a natural-born subject of a country; then a person who was an alien born, but who had obtained from the Crown letters patent, called letters of denization, to make him an English subject.

denoting stamp. An embossed Revenue stamp on a document showing or "denoting" the amount of stamp duty paid and stamped on another document in respect of the same matter; *e.g.* on a counterpart of a lease in respect of the lease itself.

deodand. [*Deo*, to God, and *dandam*, to be given.] Formerly if a personal chattel was the immediate and accidental cause of the death of any reasonable creature it was forfeited to the Crown under the name of a deodand. Abolished by the statute 9 & 10 Vict. c. 62.

departure. In pleading, departure is where the second plea contains matter not following the former plea, or a variation from it, which is forbidden (Ord. 18, r. 10).

dependant. See FAMILY PROVISIONS; FATAL ACCIDENTS.

dependency. Territory which has not been formally annexed to the British Crown, but which is in practice governed and represented in relation to other foreign countries by the United Kingdom.

deponent. A person who makes an affidavit or deposition.

deportatio in insulam. [Roman law.] Confinement for life within specified bounds. The person so punished was regarded as civilly dead: a *peregrinus*, no longer a *civis*. He might be recalled and pardoned by the emperor.

deportation. Expulsion from the United Kingdom. Powers of deportation are contained in the Immigration Act 1971, ss. 3–8 (as amended).

deposit. 1. In a contract of sale of land, the deposit is a payment made by way of earnest to bind the bargain. A purchaser who repudiates the contract for good and sufficient reason is entitled to the return of his deposit. If he repudiates it without just and sufficient cause, he forfeits his deposit. The court has a general power to order the return of a deposit (Law of Property Act 1925, s.49(2)). But if the money is not a deposit but a part-payment, it is recoverable by the purchaser even if he is in default. See DEPOSITORS.

A bank is not required to deduct income tax from deposit interest (Board of Inland Revenue Press Notice dated May 31, 1967).

(2) A sum payable by a hirer or debtor as a down payment, *e.g.* under a hire-purchase agreement.

deposit of title deeds, as security for money advanced, creates an equitable charge. By the Law of Property Act 1925, s.2(3), an equitable interest protected by a deposit of title deeds relating to the legal estate is not overreached by a conveyance to a purchaser.

deposition. A statement on oath of a witness in a judicial proceeding: the evidence of witnesses before a magistrate or justices taken down in writing. It must be signed both by the witness and at least one of the committing magistrates. A deposition may be used at the trial instead of calling the witness himself, if he has died in the interval, or has become insane, or is too ill to travel, or is being kept out of the way. The Civil Evidence Act 1968, s.2 enables out-of-court statements to be admitted and the Civil Evidence Act 1972, s.1 enables out-of-court statements of opinion to be admitted.

Depositions *de bene esse* are the depositions on oath of witnesses who are not likely to be able to attend the trial, and cannot be given in evidence without the consent of the opposite party, unless the witness is dead, or beyond the jurisdiction, or incapacitated from attending the trial by sickness or other infirmity. See generally, Ord. 39.

depositors. The Protection of Depositors Act 1963 creates the offence of fraudulent inducement to invest on deposit and provides for the restriction of advertisements for deposits.

depravity. No petition for divorce may be presented to the court before the expiration of three years from the date of the marriage unless a judge so allows on the ground that the case is one of exceptional hardship suffered by the petitioner or of exceptional depravity on the part of the respondent (Matrimonial Causes Act 1973, s.3(1) and (2)). It has been said by the Court of Appeal that the word "depravity" has fallen out of general use "so that it now conveys only a vague idea of very unpleasant conduct . . . in these circumstances it seems to be unnecessary in the great majority of these cases to rely on exceptional depravity with all its unpleasant overtones and difficulties. In practice, when it is alleged, the proposed petitioner often relies for proof of the element of exceptional depravity on the effect of the conduct on him or her" (*C.* v. *C.* [1979] All E.R. 556, C.A. See also *Fletcher* v. *Titt* (1980) 10 Fam. Law. 151, C.A.). See also *Fay* v. *Fay* [1982] 2 All E.R. 922, H.L. where it was said that all that could be said with certainty was that the hardship suffered (or the respondent's depravity) must be shown to be something out of the ordinary.

derelict. A ship which has been abandoned at sea by those in charge of it, with no intention of returning to it, and with no hope of recovering it.

dereliction. (1) The act of abandoning a chattel or movable; (2) the exposure of dry land by the shrinkage of the sea.

derogate. To destroy, prejudice or evade a right or obligation. No one can derogate from his own grant.

descent. The devolution of an interest in land upon the death of the owner of it intestate to a person or persons by virtue of consanguinity with the deceased. The rules of descent prior to 1926 (abolished by the Administration of Estates Act 1925, s.45), were as follows:

(1) To the issue of the last purchaser *in infinitum*.

(2) To the male issue before the female.

(3) Where two or more of the male issue were in equal degree of consanguinity—to the eldest only; where females, they inherited all together (as coparceners, or parceners).

(4) Lineal descendants *in infinitum* represented their ancestor, or stood in the same place as the ancestor had he been living.

(5) On failure of lineal descendants—to the nearest lineal ancestor.

(6) To the father and all the male paternal ancestors and their descendants before the female paternal ancestors of their heirs; to the female paternal ancestors and their heirs before the mother or any of the maternal ancestors (or their descendants); to the mother and the male maternal ancestors (or their descendants) before the female maternal ancestors or their heirs.

(7) To the half blood next after the same degree of the whole blood and their issue when the common ancestor was a male; and next after the common ancestor when a female.

(8) To the mother of the more remote male paternal ancestor and her heirs before the mother of a less remote male paternal ancestor and her heirs; to the mother of the more remote male maternal ancestor and her heirs before the mother of a less remote male maternal ancestor and her heirs.

(9) On a total failure of a purchaser—to the person last entitled, as if he had been the purchaser. See INTESTATE SUCCESSION.

descent case. The doctrine that where a person who had acquired land by disseisin, abatement or intrusion, died seised of the land, the descent of it to his heir took away the real owner's right of entry, so that he could only recover the land by an action.

desertion. (1) Desertion is where a husband or wife voluntarily and without reasonable cause leaves the other spouse against his or her will and with the intention of permanently ending the cohabitation. It is not essential that one or other party should actually depart from the matrimonial home if there is a complete abandonment of all matrimonial duties; desertion is not from a place but from a state of things (*Mummery* v. *Mummery* [1942] P. 107). Where one party's conduct is such as to drive the other party away from the matrimonial home such conduct may be called "constructive desertion" (*Boyd* v. *Boyd* [1938] 4 All E.R. 181), although it would probably also amount to what is now known as unreasonable behaviour (Matrimonial Causes Act 1973, s.1(2)(*b*)). See UNREASONABLE BEHAVIOUR).

Desertion for a continuous period of two years is a ground for showing that the marriage has irretrievably broken down (Matrimonial Causes Act 1973, s.1(2)(*c*)). See DIVORCE.

Magistrates may make a matrimonial order on the ground of desertion (Domestic Proceedings and Magistrates Courts Act 1978).

(2) To desert the armed forces is an offence under the Armed Forces Act 1976.

detainer, writ of. A writ authorising the detention of a man (already in custody for debt, etc.), upon a cause of action other than that upon which he had been arrested originally.

detention centre. Children and young persons may, in lieu of imprisonment be sent to detention centres, or, when the new system is operative, to community homes (*q.v.*).

determinable interest. An estate or interest which may come to an end before its natural termination, or period limited, upon the happening of some contingency. Thus where land is given for a defined or specified period of time of ucertain duration; *e.g.* during widowhood, since 1925, a settlement is created, and an equitable interest conferred, with the powers of a tenant for life.

determine. (1) To come to an end; (2) To decide an issue or appeal.

detinue. Formerly the action by which a person claimed the specific return of goods wrongfully detained or their value. Abolished by the Torts (Interference with Goods) Act 1977 s.1(1). The Tort of conversion has been extended to cover what used to be detinue (1977 Act, s.1(2)). See CONVERSION.

Deus solus haeredem facere potest non homo. [God alone, and not man, can make an heir.]

devastavit. [He has wasted.] Any violation or neglect of the duty of a personal representative to preserve, protect and administer with due diligence the assets of the deceased which involves a wasting of them, and which makes him personally responsible to persons having claims on the assets; *e.g.* creditors and legatees. The personal representative of a deceased defaulter is liable to the extent of the available assets (Administration of Estates Act 1925, s.29).

development. The carrying out of building, engineering, mining and other operations in, on, over or under land, or the making of any material change in the use of any buildings or other land. No development of land may be affected without the permission of a local planning authority (Town and Country Planning Act 1971, s.22).

The Town and Country Planning (Use Classes) Order 1972, specifies 18 use classes. The use of a building specified in one of the use classes may generally, be changed to any other purpose falling within the same use class without planning permission. The Town and Country Planning General Development Order (as amended from time to time) specifies 23 classes of "permitted development." Certain developments have to be advertised.

In addition to planning permission the approval of the local health and building by-law authority must be obtained.

Development for which planning permission has been obtained must be begun and completed reasonably promptly.

If planning permission is refused there is a right of appeal to the Secretary of State for the Environment. Compensation may become payable on refusal of permission for development or on revocation of permission. If the land becomes incapable of reasonably beneficial use the owner may require the local authority to purchase it.

development land. For the purposes of the Community Land Act 1975, "development land" means land which is in the opinion of the authorities concerned (see s.1) is needed for relevant development within 10 years (s.3, Sched. 1). The land may be acquired by agreement or compulsorily at its existing use value (s.25). Persons suffering financial hardship may complain to a financial hardship tribunal (s.27). The object is to bring development land into public ownership (s.17). Charity land (s.25) and National Trust land (s.41) are protected.

development plans. Local planning authorities are charged with the duty of preparing structure and local plans (Town and Country Planning Act 1972, ss.4–18).

deviation. The intentional departure from the due course of a voyage, which discharges the underwriters of a voyage policy of marine insurance, on the gound of the alteration of the nature of the risk, but in certain cases a deviation is justifiable. The carrier is not liable for damage resulting from deviation to save life or property (Carriage of Goods by Sea Act 1924, Art. IV, r.4; Carriage of Goods by Sea Act 1971, Art. IV, r.4).

devilling. Where one counsel hands over his brief to another counsel to represent him in court and conduct the case as if the latter counsel had himself been briefed. Also where pleadings, opinions etc., are drafted by one counsel by way of assistance to the counsel who has not been instructed, who subsequently approves and signs them. Barristers should not be expected to devil without some return, not necessarily financial.

Devil's Own, The. The Inns of Court Regiment of the Territorial Army recruited primarily from members of the legal profession. It obtained its nickname from George III at a review in Hyde Park in 1803. By 1584 the Benchers and members of the Inns of Court had formed armed associations to serve and protect Queen Elizabeth I.

devise. A gift of land or other realty by will, either specific or residuary; to make such a gift. The recipient is a devisee. An executory devise is one limited to take effect in the future on the fulfilment of a condition; *e.g.* on attaining 21, or on marriage.

diem clausit extremum. [He has died.] A special writ of *extendi facias*, or extent in chief, issuing after the death of the King's debtor, against his lands and chattels. It was abolished by the Crown Proceedings Act 1947, s.33. See EXTENT.

dies fasti. [Roman law.] Days on which the Praetor could lawfully exercise his general powers.

dies nefasti. [Roman law.] Days on which the Praetor could not pronounce any of the words *Do, Dico, Addico*; days on which the court did not sit.

dies non (juridicus). A day on which no legal business can be transacted; *e.g.* Sunday, Good Friday, Christmas Day, a bank holiday. See the Bills of Exchange Act 1882, s.92; Banking and Financial Dealings Act 1971, ss.3, 4.

dies utiles. [Roman law.] Days not *nefasti* after the applicant knew of his right and was not unavoidably prevented from going on with his case.

differences. The losses or gains due to changes in prices of stocks, shares, commodities, etc., between the time of making a contract for the purchase or sale thereof, and a subsequent date; *e.g.* the close of a stock exchange account. If the parties intended that no stocks, etc., shall be purchased and delivered, but that "differences" only shall be paid to each other, then the contract is void as a wager; but it is otherwise if the buyer does intend to purchase the shares although, he proposes to resell them before settling day.

digest. A collection of rules of law on concrete cases, as opposed to a code (*q.v.*). The Digest of Justinian was a compilation of the Roman law from the writings of the jurists (A.D. 533).

dignity. A title of honour; in law an incorporal hereditament.

dilapidations. The extent of the repairs necessary to premises at the end of a tenancy.

dilatory plea. Pleas to the jurisdiction of the court; *i.e.* pleas denying the jurisdiction of the court, pleas in suspension, and pleas in abatement.

diligentia. [Roman law.] Diligence; care. There were two grades: (1) *Excata*, all possible diligence; such care as would be taken by good or most thoughtful *paterfamilias*. (2) *Quantum in suis rebus adhibere solitus est*, the diligence or care a man uually employs in his own affairs.

diminished responsibility. Where a person is suffering from such abnormality of mind as substantially impairs his mental responsibility for his acts and omissions in doing or being a party to the killing of another; he is not to be convicted of murder, but of manslaughter. The burden of proof is on the defence, but the standard of proof is not so high as that of the prosecution: *i.e.* beyond reasonable doubt (Homicide Act 1957, s.2). See also the Criminal Procedure (Insanity) Act 1964, s.6.

diplomatic asylum. Sanctuary given in embassies and legations to persons seeking refuge from the State in which they are situated in cases of actual (not apprehended) danger. It is now used of persons admitted to countries not their own, when they fear to remain in their own countries.

diplomatic privileges. The exemption from ordinary law of an accredited representative of a foreign Sovereign. An ambassador or other public minister exercising diplomatic functions and accredited to the Queen by a foreign State or Sovereign is not within the jurisdiction of the English courts during his term of office. The immunity also extends to subordinate officials of the embassy, but can be waived by the ambassador. The present law is contained in the Diplomatic Privileges Act 1964 and the Diplomatic and other Privileges Act 1971.

The International Organisations Act 1968, confers analogous privileges upon certain international organisations and persons connected therewith. See also the European Communities Act 1972, s.4, Sched. 3.

The Diplomatic Immunities (Conferences with Commonwealth Countries and Republic of Ireland) Act 1961 gives diplomatic immunity to representatives of Commonwealth governments, etc., attending conferences with the Government of the United Kingdom and their staffs, their names being included in a list. See EXTRATERRITORIALITY.

directions, summons for. In High Court proceedings the plaintiff must, within one month of close of pleadings, take out a summons for directions (R.S.C., Ord. 25, r.1). The purpose of the summons is, if possible, to deal with all interlocutory matters at the same time. If the plaintiff does not take out a summons the defendant may do so or may apply to dismiss the action (Ord. 25, r.2(4)). For the exceptions to the general rule see Ord. 25, r.1(2). In actions for personal injuries provision is made for automatic directions with no attendance before the Master or District Registrar being necessary (Ord. 25, r.8).

For the procedure in county courts see PRE-TRIAL REVIEW.

Director of Public Prosecutions. His duty is, subject to the superintendence of the Attorney-General, to institute, undertake, or carry on criminal proceedings in any case punishable with death, in important cases referred to him by Government departments and other important or difficult cases. He may give advice to Government departments, clerks to justices and chief officers of police and other persons in any matter of importance or difficulty. He appears for the Crown or the prosecutor on criminal appeals when directed by the court to do so. He may intervene in a privately instituted prosecution with the intent of aborting it in the public interest (*Raymond* v. *Att.-Gen.* [1982] 2 W.L.R. 849, C.A.; see also Prosecution of Offences Act 1979, s.4).

directors. The persons charged with the management of a company. In some respects they are agents of the company, and trustees of the company's money and property, and occupy a fiduciary position. Their appointment, powers, etc., are governed by the articles of association. Companies registered after 1929 must have at least two directors; private companies one (Companies Act 1948, s.176). See also *ibid.* ss.178–204; the Companies Act 1967, ss.15–32; Companies Act 1976, s.21; Companies Act 1980, ss.49–53, 65.

directory. A statute or rule which is not mandatory or imperative, but specifies the way in which a thing should be done. A thing done otherwise is not invalid.

disability. Legal incapacity, either general or special.

disabling statute. One which restricts a pre-existing right.

disaffection. The offence of seducing any members of Her Majesty's forces from his duty or allegiance is punishable under the Incitement to Disaffection Act 1934. See also the Police Act 1964, s.53; Criminal Justice Act 1967, Sched. 5.

disbar. To expel a barrister from his Inn. A barrister may be disbarred on his own application, if, for instance, he desires to become a solicitor. See SENATE OF THE INNS OF COURT AND THE BAR.

discharge. To deprive a right or obligation of its binding force; to release a person from an obligation or prison; thus payment discharges a debt. Rescission, release, accord and satisfaction, performance, judgment, composition with

119

creditors and merger are varieties of discharge. For discharge from bankruptcy see BANKRUPTCY.

disclaimer. A renunciation: the refusal, usually by deed of a proposed trustee to accept the trust. A power, whether coupled with an interest or not, may be disclaimed by deed (Law of Property Act 1925, s.156). Under section 54 of the Bankruptcy Act 1914, the trustee in bankruptcy may disclaim onerous property; *e.g.* a lease. A liquidator has similar powers (Companies Act 1948, s.323).

discontinuance. Where the plaintiff in an action voluntarily puts an end to it. Discontinuance is only applicable to proceedings commenced by writ of summons. The plaintiff may within 14 days after service of defence on him discontinue his action by serving on the defendant a notice to discontinue. Otherwise, a plaintiff cannot discontinue without leave. The effect is that the plaintiff has to pay the defendant's costs, but he may commence another action for the same cause (Ord. 21; Ord. 62, r. 10). A defendant may withdraw his defence at any time. He may discontinue a counterclaim within 14 days after service of a defence to the counterclaim and later by leave of the court. He must pay the costs of the plaintiff (Ord. 21; Ord. 62, r. 3(7)). If all parties consent the action may be withdrawn without the leave of the court (Ord. 21, r. 2(4)).

discovert. A woman who is unmarried or a widow.

discovery of documents. A process whereby the parties to an action disclose to each other all documents in their possession, custody or power relating to matters in question in the action. After the close of pleadings in an action discovery must take place (R.S.C., Ord. 24, r. 1). The court may order either party to file a list of document and, if necessary, to swear an affidavit to verify the list (Ord. 24, r. 3). In personal injury cases the court may order discovery before a writ is issued (Administration of Justice Act 1970, ss.31 and 32(1); Ord. 24, r. 7A). Discovery may be ordered against a person who is not a party to the proceedings (Ord. 24, r. 7A). Failure to comply with an order for discovery may lead to the action being dismissed or a defence being struck out (Ord. 24, r. 16). In personal injury cases discovery must be given of medical or expert evidence unless the court directs otherwise (Ord. 38, r. 37(1)).

As to discovery in county court actions see C.C.R., Ord. 14. A solicitor is under a duty not to use copy documents supplied on discovery for some collateral purpose not reasonably necessary for the proper conduct of his clients case and breach of such duty amounts to a contempt of court even when the documents have been read aloud in open court (*Home Office* v. *Harman* [1982] All E.R. 532, H.L.). See also PILLER, ANTON.

Discrimination. The Race Relations Act 1976 prohibits discrimination on grounds of race (see RACE RELATIONS). The Equal Pay Act 1970 requires equal terms of employment between men and women. The Sex Discrimination Act 1975 prohibits discrimination on grounds of sex or marital status. Discrimination may be direct, indirect or by victimisation. Individual civil actions for breach may be taken in Industrial Tribunals (*q.v.*) or (in cases outside the employment field) County Courts. Enforcement action is also taken by Equal Opportunities Commission (*q.v.*) and the Commission for Racial Equality (*q.v.*).

disentailing deed. An assurance by which a tenant in tail bars his estate so as to convert it into an estate in fee, either absolute or base. The enrolment of such deed, made after 1925, is not necessary (Law of Property Act 1925, s.133).

disgavel. To cause land to cease to be of gavelkind tenure.

dishonestly. In determining whether a person has acted dishonestly a jury has first to decide whether, according to the ordinary standards of reasonable and honest people, what was done was dishonest and secondly whether the accused person must have realised that what he was doing was, by those standards, dishonest. It is dishonest for a person to act in a way which he knows ordinary people consider to be dishonest, even if he feels morally justified in doing what he does (*R.* v. *Ghosh* [1982] 2 All E.R. 689, C.A.).

dishonour. A bill of exchange is dishonoured if the drawee refuses to accept it, or having accepted it fails to pay it (see Bills of Exchange Act 1882, s.47). A banker who without justification dishonours his customer's cheque is liable to him for damages for injury to his credit; but damages may be only nominal in the case of non-traders.

dismissal. An action may be dismissed for want of prosecution; *i.e.* if a plaintiff does not, within the time limited, deliver a statement of claim, take out a summons for direction, give discovery of documents or notice of trial (see Ords. 19, 24, 25).

dismissal of employee. An employee shall be treated as dismissed if, but only if; (a) his contract of employment is terminated by the employer, whether with or without notice; or (b) where a contract for a fixed term expires without being renewed; or (c) the employee terminates the contract, with or without notice, in circumstances such that he is entitled to terminate it without notice by reason of the employer's conduct (Employment Protection (Consolidation) Act 1978, s.55(2)). See also UNFAIR DISMISSAL; WRONGFUL DISMISSAL.

disorderly house. A house in which performances or exhibitions, such as revolting strip-tease acts, amount to an outrage of common decency, tending to corrupt or deprave and call for condemnation and punishment in the public interest. They need not amount to a common nuisance (*R.* v. *Quinn* [1962] Q.B. 245; *R.* v. *Brady and Ram* (1963) 47 Cr.App.R. 169).

disparagement. The bestowing by a lord of an heir in an unsuitable marriage.

dispensing power. The power claimed by the Tudors and Stuarts to give exemption in individual cases from the operation of Act of Parliament. See BILL OF RIGHTS.

disposal of uncollected goods. See UNCOLLECTED GOODS.

disseisin. The wrongful putting out of him that is actually seised of a freehold (Coke).

disqualification from driving. When a person is convicted of certain offences under the Road Traffic Act 1972 he may be disqualified from driving. Certain offences involve mandatory disqualification and disqualification may also follow repeated offences (Transport Act 1981, s.19). See TOTTING UP.

distrain. To seize goods by way of distress (*q.v.*).

distress. The act of taking movable property out of the possession of a wrongdoer, to compel the performance of an obligation, or to procure satisfaction for a wrong committed. It is a mode of legal "self help"; *e.g.* distraining for rent due. Also, the goods so distrained upon. At common law the right was to retain the thing seized until compensation was made, and included no right of sale; the landlord's power of sale of distress for rent is statutory. Distress may be resorted to for collection of taxes and rates (Taxes Management Act 1970, ss.60–62; General Rate Act 1967, ss.96–107 as amended).

distress damage-feasant. The common law remedy of distress damage feasant was abolished by the Animals Act 1971, and replaced by a right to detain and sell trespassing livestock (s.7).

distribution. The division of the personal property of an intestate among his next-of-kin, the rules for which were laid down in the Statute of Distribution (22 & 23 Car. 2, c. 10), now replaced by the Administration of Estates Act 1925. See INTESTATE SUCCESSION.

district auditor. The officer of the Government whose duty it is to disallow items of expenditure by local authorities which are not authorised by law (Local Government Act 1972, ss.156–167). The law was flouted by the councillors of

Clay Cross in Derbyshire but they were absolved by the Housing Finance (Special Provisions) Act 1975.

district council. Urban and rural district councils were created by the Local Government Act 1894. The ceased to exist on April 1, 1974. Counties are divided into districts (Local Government Act 1972, ss.1, 20, Scheds. 1, 4). See also BOROUGH.

district registrars exercise all the authority and jurisdiction of a Master or Registrar (Ord. 32, r. 23). See REGISTRAR.

district registries. Branch offices in the provinces of the Supreme Court of Judicature, in which proceedings may be instituted. If a defendant resides or carries on business within the district, he must enter an acknowledgment of service there, otherwise in London. Proceedings in district registries are regulated by Ord. 32, rr. 23, 24, 26. The practice of the Central Office is followed (Ord. 63, r. 11). An appeal lies to a judge in chambers in London (Ord. 58, r. 4). There are separate district probate registries.

distringas. A writ so called from its commanding the sheriff to distrain on a person for a certain purpose; *e.g.* to enforce appearance to an indictment, information or inquisition in the King's Bench. Abolished by the Administration of Justice (Miscellaneous Provisions) Act 1938, s.11.

distringas notice. Where a person is beneficially interested in any stock, etc., standing in the books of a company, he may file an affidavit and notice specifying the stock, etc., and serve the office copy affidavit and the sealed duplicate notice on the company concerned. If the company thereafter receives an application to deal with the stock, etc., the company must give that person notice and refrain from dealing with the stock, etc., for eight days, during which time that person must proceed for a restraining order, or injunction, against the person in whose name the stock, etc., stands. Otherwise the distringas notice ceases to have effect (see Ord. 50, rr. 11–15). See STOP ORDER.

disturbance. Infringement of a right to an incorporeal hereditament; *e.g.* obstructing an ancient light.

Compensation for disturbance may be payable under the Agricultural Holdings Act 1948 (as amended) and under the Landlord and Tenant Act 1954, s.37, and to persons displaced under the Housing Acts or the Land Compensation Act 1973.

diversity. A plea by a prisoner that he was not the person previously attainted.

divest. To take away an estate or interest which has already vested.

divi fratres. [Roman law.] The Emperors Marcus Aurelius Antoninus and Lucius Aurelius Verus, who reigned together A.D. 161–169.

dividend. The interest payable on the public funds; the payment made out of profits to the shareholders in a company; or the amount payable upon each pound of a bankrupt's liabilites.

divine service. The tenure of an ecclesiastical corporation which is subject to the duty of saying prayers on a certain day, etc.

Divisional Courts. Two or more judges of the High Court sitting together to hear appeals from inferior courts; *e.g.* magistrates' courts. Cases are stated to the Divisional Court on points of law from magistrates' courts. The Divisional Court of the Family Division hears appeals from the Crown Court (*q.v.*) relating to affiliation proceedings (Ord. 56, r. 4A), from magistrates' courts by cases stated in matrimonial proceedings (r. 5) and from county courts and magistrates' courts in matters affecting minors (Ord. 90, r. 9).

divorce. Dissolution of marriage. Before a petition for divorce can be presented the marriage must have subsisted for at least three years unless a judge grants leave on the ground of the petitioner's exceptional hardship or the respondent's exceptional depravity (Matrimonial Causes Act 1973, s.3(1) and (2); see DEPRAVITY). The sole ground for divorce is that the marriage has broken down irretrievably. But a marriage is not to be held to have broken down unless; (a) the respondent has committed adultery and the petitioner finds it intolerable to live with the respondent (see ADULTERY); or (b) the respondent has behaved in such a way that the petitioner cannot reasonably be expected to live with the respondent (see UNREASONABLE BEHAVIOUR); or (c) the respondent has deserted the petitioner for a continuous period of two years immediately preceding the presentation of the petition (see DESERTION); or (d) the parties have lived apart for a continuous period of two years immediately preceding the presentation of the petition and the respondent consents to a decree being granted; or (e) the parties have lived apart for a continuous period of five years immediately preceding the presentation of the petition (Matrimonial Causes Act 1973, s.1). A petition for divorce may be filed in the Divorce Registry (in London) or in a Divorce County Court (elsewhere). Defended suits are transferred to the Family Division of the High Court. For practice see Matrimonial Causes Rules 1977. See COUNTY COURTS; SPECIAL PROCEDURE; FINANCIAL PROVISION.

dock brief. The direct instruction of counsel without the intervention of a solicitor by a prisoner in the dock. Previously a method of ensuring representation of impecunious defendants. Now rendered obselete by the provision of legal aid (*q.v.*).

dock warrant. A document of title issued by a dock company stating that certain goods therein mentioned are deliverable to a person therein named or to his assigns by indorsement.

docket. An epitome or abstract of a judgment, decree, order, etc.

Doctors' Commons. The buildings in which the Ecclesiastical and Admiralty courts, and the College of Advocates practising in those courts, were formerly held.

document. Something on which things are written, printed or inscribed, and which gives information: any written thing capable of being evidence. See the elaborate modern definition in the Civil Evidence Act 1968, s.10(1).

documents: discovery of, list of. See DISCOVERY OF DOCUMENTS.

document of title. A document which enables the possessor to deal with the property described in it as if he were the owner; *e.g.* a bill of lading, dock warrant (see Factors Act 1889, s.1(4)).

Doe, John. Anciently a plaintiff had to find pledges for the prosecution of his suit, but this subsequently became a formality and fictitious names were used, which often rhymed; *e.g.* John Doe and Richard Roe. Later these two "brothers in law" suitably served to play the fictitious parts of plaintiff and casual ejector, respectively, in the old action for ejectment. See EJECTMENT.

dole. A share.

doli capax. [Capable of crime.] See DOLI INCAPAX.

doli incapax. [Incapable of crime.] There is a conclusive presumption that no child under the age of 10 years can be guilty of any offence. A minor between the ages of 10 and 14 years is presumed to be *doli incapax*, but this presumption may be rebutted by evidence of "mischievous discretion," or guilty knowledge that he was doing wrong; except that a boy under 14 cannot be convicted of rape. The principle of law is *malitia supplet aetatem* (*q.v.*).

dolus. [Roman law.] Fraud, wilful injury.

dom. proc. *Domus Procerum* (*q.v.*).

Domesday Book. The great survey of the kingdom, compiled by order of William the Conqueror (1086).

domestic court. Specially constituted Magistrates court comprised of magistrates from the domestic panel. See DOMESTIC PROCEEDINGS.

domestic proceedings. Proceedings before Magistrates under their domestic jurisdiction as set out in Magistrates Court Act 1980, s.65; principally pursuant to the Domestic Proceedings and Magistrates Courts Act 1978. By section 1 of the 1978 Act either party to a marriage may apply to a magistrates court for an order on the ground that the other party; (a) has failed to provide reasonable maintenance for the applicant; or (b) has failed to provide reasonable maintenance or to make proper contribution towards reasonable maintenance for any child of the family; or (c) has behaved in such a way that the applicant cannot reasonably be expected to live with him/her; or (d) has deserted the applicant.

By section 2 the court may order periodical payments for the applicant and/or children and a lump sum not exceeding £500.

The court may make orders as to custody of children and access to children (ss.8–15).

The court may also make an order (similar to an injunction) (*q.v.*) for the protection of a party to the marriage or a child of the family (sometimes called a Protection Order) (ss.16–18). The domestic jurisdiction of magistrates extends to affiliation proceedings. See AFFILIATION.

Apart from proceedings under the Act of 1978 and affiliation proceedings magistrates have domestic jurisdiction principally under the Adoption Act 1976, the Children Act 1975, the Child Care Act 1980, the Guardianship of Minors Act 1971 and 1973 (Magistrates Court Act 1980, s.65).

domestic violence. See INJUNCTIONS.

domicile, or **domicil.** The country in which a person is, or is presumed to be, permanently resident; the place of a person's permanent home. It depends on the physical fact of residence plus the intention of remaining. The civil status of a person, or his legal rights and duties, including capacity to marry, are determined by the law of his domicile. His political status, or nationality, is independent of domicile.

Domicile may be (1) of origin or birth; (2) by operation of law; (3) of choice. To acquire a domicile of choice a person must have a definite determination to abandon the old domicile coupled with an intention to establish a permanent residence in (and actually take up residence in) a new domicile. If a domicile of choice is abandoned the domicile of origin revives until a new domicile of choice is acquired. The burden of proof lies on the person asserting he has acquired a domicile of choice.

Fomerly a woman took the domicile of her husband but under the Domicile and Matrimonial Proceedings Act 1973, the domicile of a married woman is ascertained as in the case of any other person having an independent domicile (s.1). The domicile of a legitimate minor normally follows that of his father (s.3). Where the parents are living apart and the child lives with the mother the child's domicile is that of the mother (s.4).

Dominions. Commonwealth Countries. Autonomous communities within the British Empire, equal in status, in no way subordinate one to another in any aspect of their domestic or internal affairs, though united by a common allegiance to the Crown, and freely associated as members of the British Commonwealth of Nations. See COMMONWEALTH.

dominium. Ownership; lordship.

dominus litis. [Roman law.] The principal in a suit; as opposed to his procurator.

domitae naturae. Of tame disposition. See ANIMALS.

Domus Procerum. The House of the Nobles; the House of Lords.

domus sua cuique est tutissimum refugium. [To every one his house in his surest refuge.] Every man's house is his castle. See *Semayne's Case* (1604) 5 Coke 91.

dona clandestina sunt semper suspiciosa. [Clandestine gifts are always to be regarded with suspicion.]

donatio. [Roman law.] [Gift.] A *donatio inter vivos* (a gift between living persons) when completed was irrevocable except, *e.g.* for ingratitude of the donee. Under Justinian a *donatio* was completed as soon as the donor manifested his intention, whether in writing or not.

Donatio mortis causa. A gift of personal property in anticipation of death. To be a valid gift it must be made in contemplation of the donor's death, be intended to take effect on his death from his existing illness (unless the donor indicates otherwise), and be completed by the delivery at the time to the donee.

donatio propter nuptias. [Roman law.] A settlement made on the wife by the husband of a nature corresponding to the *dos* (*q.v.*).

donee. A gratuitous recipient.

donor. A giver.

doom; dome. A judgment.

dormant funds. Unclaimed funds in court. See the Supreme Court Funds Rules 1975, r. 56; County Courts Funds Rules 1965, rr. 36–39 (as amended).

dos. dower. [Roman law.] The property contributed by a wife, or by anyone else on her behalf to her husband, to enable him to support the expenses of the marriage.

double plea. See DUPLICITY.

double possibility. The rule that a remainder limited to the child of an unborn person, after a life estate to the unborn parent, was void; also known as the old rule against perpetuities. It was abolished by Law of Property Act 1925, s.161, and an equitable interest in land may be given to an unborn person for life with remainder to any issue of that unborn person, provided the perpetuity rule is not infringed.

dower. That portion of lands or tenements which the wife hath for term of her life of the lands or tenements of her husband after his decease, for the sustenance of herself and the nurture and education of her children (Coke). Where a man was seised of land for an estate of inheritance (otherwise than as joint tenant), and died leaving a widow, she was entitled to hold the third part of such land and tenements as were her husband's at any time during the coverture, as tenant in dower for the term of her life.

Under the Dower Act 1833 no widow was entitled to dower out of any land which had been absolutely disposed of by her husband in his lifetime or by his will, or in which he devised any estate or interest for her benefit unless (in the latter case) a contrary intention was declared by the will. A husband might also wholly or partially deprive the widow of dower by a declaration in a deed or will. The right to dower, however, was extended to lands of the husband of which he had not had legal seisin; and to equitable as well as legal estates of inheritance in possession. Dower was abolished by the Administration of Estates Act 1925, s.45(1)(*c*). See ADMEASUREMENT OF DOWER.

dower, writ of. When a widow had no dower assigned to her within the proper time, she had a remedy by "writ of dower *unde nihil habet*." If she had only part of her dower assigned to her, she had a remedy by "writ of right of dower." Both were abolished by the Common Law Procedure Act 1980.

draft. (1) An order for the payment of money, *e.g.* a cheque; (2) a rough copy of a legal document in the course of preparation.

drawback. The refund of duty made on the exportation of goods for which customs duties have been paid on importation, or in which exciseable goods have been incorporated in manufacture.

drawee. The person to whom a bill of exchange is addressed.

drawer. One who signs a bill of exchange as the maker.

driftway. A way affording a right of passage for cattle.

drink and driving. It is an offence to be in charge of a motor vehicle when under the influence of drink or drugs to such an extent as to be incapable of having proper control of the vehicle (Road Traffic Act 1972, s.5(2)). It is also an offence to be in charge of a motor vehicle with alcohol above the prescribed limit (Act of 1972, s.6(1)(b)). See BREATH TEST.

droit. Right or law.

droit administratif. [Administrative law.] That part of the law of France administered by the Conseil D'Etat by which officials are tried for acts done in an official capacity. See RULE OF LAW.

droits of Admiralty. See ADMIRALTY, DROITS OF.

drugs, controlled. Drugs classified by the Misuse of Drugs Act 1971, *e.g.* Cocaine, LSD, Opium, Cannibis (see CANNIBIS). Possession of a controlled drug is an offence (s.5(1)). The maximum penalty depends on the classification of the drug. See POSSESSION OF DRUGS.

drunkenness. Intoxication. Except for offences requiring a specific intent self-induced intoxication resulting from drink or drugs is no defence to a criminal charge. See *R.* v. *Majewski* [1975] 3 W.L.R. 401 (assault); *R.* v. *Howell* [1974] 2 All E.R. 806 (manslaughter). Drunkenness may be a constituent part of an offence: *e.g.* driving a car when under the influence of drink or drugs to such an extent as to be incapable of having proper control of the vehicle (Road Traffic Act 1972, ss.5–13). See DRINK AND DRIVING.

dubitante. [Doubting.]

duces tecum. See SUBPOENA.

Duchy Court of Lancaster. A court formerly held before the Chancellor of the Duchy, concerning all matters of equity and revenue relating to lands holden of the King in right of the Duchy of Lancaster. It was distinct from the Chancery Court of the County Palatine.

duke. The highest rank in the peerage.

dum bene se gesserit. [During good conduct.] *e.g.* A judge of the High Court holds office during good behaviour, subject to removal by the Crown on the address of both Houses of Parliament.

dum casta vixerit. [While she lives chastely.]

dum fuit infra aetatem. [While he was within age.]

dum fuit non compos mentis. [While he was not of sound mind.]

dum sola. [While single or unmarried.]

duplicatio. [Roman law.] [Doubting.] An equitable allegation by a defendant in answer to a *replicatio*.

duplicity. A pleading is double, or open to the objection of duplicity, when it contains more claims, charges or defences than one. It is liable to be struck out as embarassing. An indictment must not be double; *i.e.* no one count should charge the prisoner (except in the alternative) with having committed more than one offence unless part of one act and one entire transaction.

durante absentia. [During absence.]

durante bene placito. [During the pleasure of the Crown.]

durante minore aetate. [During minority.]

durante viduitate. [During widowhood.]

durante vita. [During life.]

duress. Constraint by injury, or imprisonment or threats. An act done under duress is generally invalid. In a criminal case the burden of establishing duress lies on the accused; it is for the prosecution to destroy a defence so established (*R.* v. *Gill* [1963] 1 W.L.R. 841; see also *Abbott* v. *The Queen* [1977] A.C. 755, P.C.; *R.* v. *Graham* [1982] 1 All E.R. 801).

Duress may make a marriage voidable; see NULLITY OF MARRIAGE. See also ECONOMIC DURESS.

dying declaration. A statement admissible in evidence, in trials of homicide, made by the deceased person whose death is the subject of the charge, as to the cause and circumstances of the death; the deceased having at the time abandoned all hope of recovery.

E

e converso. [Conversely.]

E. & O. E. [Errors and omissions excepted.] A declaration on commercial documents intended to protect the maker from liability for mistakes.

ealdorman. An elder. An official who, along with the sheriff and the bishop, was one of the three chief officers of each county.

earl. The title third in the peerage.

Earl Marshal. The Earl Marshal and the Lord High Constable were the two chief officers of the feudal forces under the Norman kings. They jointly presided over the Court of Chivalry (*q.v.*).

earmark. Property is said to be earmarked when it can be identified or distinguished from other property of the same nature: when it can be followed and recovered. Money could only be treated as identifiable at common law if it had not become mixed with other property, but equity developed its own remedy of tracing (*q.v.*).

earnest. A nominal sum given to a vendor as a token that the parties are in earnest in concluding a contract of sale.

easement. A servitude; a right enjoyed by the owner of land over the lands of another: such as rights of way, rights of light, rights of support, rights to a flow of air or water. An easement must exist for the accommodation and better enjoyment of the land to which it is annexed; otherwise it may amount to a mere licence. Easements are created by express grant or prescription (*q.v.*). The dominant tenement is the land owned by the possessor of the easement, and the servient tenement is the land over which the right is enjoyed.

An easement confers no proprietary rights on its owner; if it does it is not an easement. It is a privilege without a profit. A positive easement consists of a right to do something on the land of another; a negative easement restricts the use the owner of the servient tenement may make of his land. An easement may be lost by abandonment; continued non-user may be evidence of an intention to release the easement.

Easements are still capable of existing as legal interests (Law of Property Act 1925, s.1(2)(*a*)). See QUASI-EASEMENT.

Easter offerings. The payments originally due by statute (2 & 3 Edw. 6, c. 13, s. 10) from parishioners to the parish clergy at Easter. They are now mostly paid voluntarily to the clergy by their congregations. The amounts so paid are assessable to income tax.

eat inde sine die. [Let him go without a day.] The dismissal of a defendant from a suit.

Ecclesiastical Commissioners. Established by the Ecclesiastical Commissioners Act 1836 to administer Church property and revenue. See now CHURCH COMMISSIONERS.

Ecclesiastical courts. They are the Arches Court of Canterbury and the Chancery Court of York, the Consistory Courts of the dioceses, the Commissary Court of the diocese of Canterbury, and the Court of Ecclesiastical Causes Reserved. The Judicial Committee of the Privy Council has appellate jurisdiction (Ecclesiastical Jurisdiction Measure 1963, ss.1, 8, 11).

economic duress. Money which one person agrees to pay to another as a result of the payee's coercion by way of something which the law does not regard as legitimate may be recovered as money had and received by subjecting the payer to economic duress. Where such economic duress exists the payee is not entitled to the immunity from action conferred in respect of a trade dispute (*Universe Tankships Inc. of Monrovia* v. *International Transport Workers Federation* [1982] W.L.R. 803, H.L.).

EEC European Economic Community, set up by the Treaty of Rome 1957 (see ROME, TREATY OF). The United Kingdom signed a treaty of accession in 1972. For the objects of the Treaty see Art. 2.

ei incumbit probatio qui dicit, non qui negat. [The burden of proof is on him who alleges, and not on him who denies.]

ei qui affirmat, non ei qui negat, incumbit probatio. [The burden of proof lies on him who affirms a fact, not on him who denies it.]

Eire. Southern Ireland. The Ireland Act 1949 recognised and declared the independence of the Republic of Ireland. Eire ceased to be part of H.M. Dominions, or the Commonwealth, but it is not a foreign country.

ejectment. Originally the action of ejectment was a remedy applicable to a leaseholder wrongfully dispossessed, but owing to the cumbrousness of the old real actions for trying the right to the freehold it was extended to freeholds by means of legal fictions. There was an imaginary lease by the person by the person claiming the freehold to an imaginary "John Doe" who was assumed to be ejected by an imaginary "Richard Roe" (the casual ejector). The claimant, to substantiate the lease, endeavoured to prove his title and the person in possession was allowed to defend on admitting the fictions, and thus the freehold title was put in issue. An action was entitled, *e.g. Doe* d. *Rigge* v. *Bell* (= *Doe*, on the demise or lease of *Rigge* v. *Bell*). It was abolished by the Common Law Procedure Act 1852. See RECOVERY.

ejusdem generis. [Of the same kind or nature.] The rule that where particular words are followed by general words, the general words are limited to the same kind as the particular words. Thus, the Sunday Observance Act 1677, s.1 provides that "no tradesman, artificer, workman, labourer or other person whatsoever shall do or exercise any worldly labour, business, or work of their ordinary callings upon the Lord's Day (works of necessity and charity only excepted)". The words "or other person whatsoever" are to be construed *ejusdem generis* with those which precede them so that an estate agent is not within the section (*Gregory* v. *Fearn* [1953] 1 W.L.R. 974).

Elder Brethren. The Masters of the Trinity House (*q.v.*).

election. Choice. The equitable doctrine of election is to the effect that he who takes a benefit under an instrument must accept or reject the instrument as a whole; he cannot approbate and reprobate. If there is in the will of X a gift of A's property to B, and a gift to A, A can only take the gift by giving his own property or its value to B. Alternatively he can elect to keep his own property and reject the gift.

elections, Parliamentary. Parliamentary elections are dealt with by the Electoral Registers Acts 1949 and 1953; the Representation of the People Act 1949 (a consolidating Act), which deals with the franchise, the conduct of elections and election campaigns and legal proceedings amended by the Representation of the People Act 1969; and the House of Commons (Redistribution of Seats) Acts 1949 and 1958. See CORRUPT PRACTICES.

election petitions. Petitions for inquiry into the validity of elections of Members of Parliment, when it is alleged that the return of a Member is invalid for bribery or any other reason. These petitions are heard by two judges on the rota for the trial of such petitions. They are referred to as the election court (Representation of the People Act 1949, s.110). See also the Representation of the People Act 1969. The place of trial is in the constituency in which the election was held.

elegit. A writ of execution by which a judgment debtor might obtain possession of the debtor's land and hold it until the debt was satisfied out of the rents and profits or otherwise. The issue of writs of elegit was ended by the Administration of Justice Act 1956, s.34 and the writ was finally abolished by the Supreme Court Act 1981, s.141. The modern equivalent remedy is a charging order. See CHARGING ORDER.

elisors. Persons appointed to return a jury for the trial of an action when the jury returned by the sheriff and that returned by the coroner have been successively challenged. See CHALLENGE OF JURORS.

emancipatio. [Roman law.] Freedom from power. (1) By the ancient process of three fictitious sales, each followed by a manumission: abolished by Justinian. (2) By imperial rescript registered by a magistrate (Anastasius). (3) The parent went direct before a judge or magistrate and let his descendant go free from his power (Justinian).

embargo. The provisional seizure or detention by a State of ships or property, generally in its own ports. If only applied by a State to its own ships by virtue of municipal law, it is termed civil embargo; if not, it is hostile embargo, which is a method of international redress short of war.

embezzlement. The felony which consisted of the conversion to his own use by a clerk or servant of property received by him on behalf of his master (Larceny Act 1916, s.17(1)). It now falls within the definition of theft. See THEFT.

emblements. The profits of a crop: such vegetable crops or products as are the annual result of agricultural labour. At common law a tenant for life, or a lessee (or their executors) whose estate was of uncertain duration, on the happening of the contingency which determined his estate (otherwise than by his own act) after crops were sown but before they were reaped, was entitled to re-enter and have the emblements.

This right has been *pro tanto* replaced by the provision of the Agricultural Holdings Act 1948, s.4, that a tenant at a rack-rent whose term ceases by the death, or the cessor of the estate of a landlord entitled for life or any uncertain interest may continue in occupation until a 12 months' notice to quit is given, expiring at the end of a year of the tenancy.

embracery. The common law misdemeanour committed by a person who by any means whatever, except the production of evidence and argument in open court, attempts to influence or instruct any juryman. The Criminal Law Act 1967, s.13, which abolished maintenance and champerty, excepted embracery.

emergency legislation. The laws made in consequence of the outbreak of war in 1939, mainly in the form of Defence Regulations pursuant to the Emergency Powers (Defence) Acts 1939 and 1940. Certain provisions were made permanent by the Emergency Laws (Miscellaneous Provisions) Acts 1947 and 1953. See the Emergency Laws (Repeal) Act 1959 and the Emergency Laws (Re-enactments and Repeals) Act 1964.

emergency powers. Her Majesty may by proclamation declare a state of emergency and make regulations accordingly (Emergency Powers Acts 1920 and 1964), as in the 1955 railway strike.

eminent domain. The right of a Government to take private property for public purposes. In international law the State is regarded not only as having a power of disposition over the whole of the national territory, but also as the representative owner of both the national territory and all other property found within its limits.

emphyteusis. [Roman law.] A grant of land for ever, or for a long period, on condition that an annual rent (*canon*) shall be paid to the grantor and his successors, and that, if the rent be not paid, the grant shall be forfeited.

employer and employee. The relation of employer and employee exists when the employer has the right at the moment to control the manner in which the employee shall act, *e.g.* a clerk is an employee; an opera singer is not. An employer is liable for the act of default of his employee committed in the course of and within the scope of his employment on the ground of implied authority. If the employer himself has no authority to do an act, then the employee can have no implied authority. An employee has implied authority to do all things necessary to protect his employer's property entrusted to his care, but not to arrest a person upon suspicion of an attempt to steal in order to punish the supposed offender.

At common law an employer was not criminally liable for the acts of his employees unless he had authorised them, or aided and abetted them, but by particular statutes the employer may be responsible for acts of his employee even if unauthorised or forbidden, if they are committed within the general scope of his employment.

An independent contractor is not an employee, and the employer is not liable for default, except where (1) the work is unlawful; (2) it must be done in a certain way by statute and the contractor fails to do it in that way; (3) the work is likely to cause injury, when the employer is bound to see that necessary precautions are taken. The employer may be liable if he is in some breach of duty himself as where he employs an incompetent contractor. He cannot rid himself of his own responsibilities by hiring another to carry out the work involved.

The common law duty of an employer to his employee to exercise due care and skill in respect of the adequacy of plant, the competence of fellow employees, and the propriety of the system of work (*Wilsons & Clyde Coal Co.* v. *English* [1938] A.C. 57) has been extended by the Employer's Liability (Defective Equipment) Act 1969. An employer must ensure, so far as is reasonably practicable, the health, safety and welfare at work of all his employees (Health and Safety at Work etc. Act 1974). Sex discrimination is unlawful (Sex Discrimination Act 1975).

An employer may sue one who entices away, imprisons or causes bodily harm to his employee, whereby the employer loses his services. Further, it is a tort for one to induce or procure a breach of contract of service, whereby damage results to the employer but see TRADE DISPUTE.

The Contracts of Employment Act 1972 (as amended by the Employment Protection Act 1975) provides that employers shall normally provide written particulars of the main terms of employment, and the minimum periods of notice required, to persons who have been continuously employed for 26 weeks or more. The minimum period of notice are from one week to four weeks according to service of the employees. An employee can be dismissed without notice in case of misconduct. He can accept payment in lieu of notice. Provision is made for payment of remuneration during a period of notice and for assessing damages if the employer fails to give due notice. See also TRADE DISPUTE; UNFAIR DISMISSAL; REDUNDANCY.

employers' liability. See COMMON EMPLOYMENT; EMPLOYER AND EMPLOYEE.

employment. See EMPLOYER AND EMPLOYEE.

employment agencies. Must be licensed (see Employment Agencies Act 1973).

employment appeal tribunal. A superior court of record to which appeal lies on a question of law only arising from any decision of an Industrial Tribunal (*q.v.*) under the Equal Pay Act 1970, Sex Discrimination Act 1975, Race Relations Act 1976, Employment Protection Act 1975, Employment Protection (Consolidation) Act 1978 and Employment Act 1980, ss.2 and 5 and from certain decisions of the certification officer (*q.v.*). The Tribunal consists of a Judge and two to four appointed members. Further appeal lies, with leave, to the Court of Appeal.

en autre droit. [In the right of another.]

en ventre sa mère. [In the womb of its mother.] A child not yet born. A posthumous child is deemed to be living, or actually born, for the purpose of itself taking any proprietary benefit to which, if born, it would be entitled, but not to secure benefit to some other person (*Elliott* v. *Joicey* [1935] A.C. 209).

enabling Act. A statute legalising that which was hitherto illegal or incompetent.

enactment. An Act of Parliament, or part of an Act of Parliament. As to an Act which repeals and re-enacts a previous enactment see Interpretation Act 1978, s.17(2).

enclosure. See INCLOSURE.

encroachment. The unauthorised extension of the boundaries of land.

encumbrance. A charge or liability, *e.g.* a mortgage.

endorsement. See INDORSEMENT; ENDORSEMENT OF DRIVING LICENCE.

endorsement of driving licence. A person convicted of certain offences under the Road Traffic Act 1972 will have particulars of the offence endorsed on his driving licence together with the number of penalty points (*q.v.*) attributable to that offence. See also TOTTING UP.

endowment. (1) Giving a woman right to dower. (2) Making permanent provision for charity, etc.

enemy. See ALIEN ENEMY.

enfeoff. To invest a person with land by means of a feoffment.

enforcement notice. A means of dealing with a breach of planning control. The notice specifies the breach, the steps required to remedy it and the time for compliance (see Town and Country Planning Act 1971, s.87 and Town and Country Planning (Amendment) Act 1977, s.1). May be registered as a Local Land Charge (*q.v.*) (Local Land Charges Act 1975, s.1).

enfranchise. (1) to make free or to confer a liberty, *e.g.* to confer the right to vote; to enlarge copyhold land into freehold.

(2) Enfranchisement of tenancy or leasehold enfranchisement, *i.e.* procedure whereby a tenant holding a tenancy exceeding 21 years at a rent less than two thirds of the rateable value of the premises may acquire a freehold or extended long lease (see Leasehold Reform Act 1967; Rent Act 1977, Sched. 23; Leasehold Reform Act 1979).

engagement to marry. Betrothal; agreement to marry. See BREACH OF PROMISE.

English information. See INFORMATION.

engrossing. (1) Copying a deed at length in writing or typewriting for execution. (2) Buying in quantity corn, etc., to sell again at a high price; an offence abolished by 7 & 8 Vict. c.24.

engrossment. A deed prior to execution.

enjoyment. The exercise of right.

enlargement. Increasing an estate, *e.g.* when a base fee became united with the reversion or remainder in fee, the base fee was enlarged to the fee simple.

enrol. To enter (or copy) a document on an official record. The Enrolment Office was in the Court of Chancery; later transferred to the Central Office of the Supreme Court.

ens legis. A legal being or entity such as a company.

entail. An estate tail: the interest in real property created prior to 1926 by a grant "to A and the heirs of his body," called a general entail, or "to A and the heirs of his body by his wife J," called a special entail. Tail male or tail female were entails where the property descended exclusively to males or females respectively. The owner of the estate tail was called the tenant in tail, who might bar the entail, and convert the estate tail into a fee simple (see RECOVERY). Where, however, the estate tail was not an estate in possession, as where it was postponed to a tenant for life in possession, the tenant in tail could not completely bar the entail without the consent of the protector of the settlement (*q.v.*). Without such consent the tenant in tail could only bar his own issue, and not the estates in remainder or reversion. He thereby created a base fee (*q.v.*).

Since 1925 estates tail can only subsist in equity, being called "entailed interests," and can only be created by way of trust by using the same expressions as hitherto; but personal property can now be entailed (Law of Property Act 1925, s.130). See ESTATE.

enter. See ENTRY.

entering short. If a bill which is not yet due is lodged by the holder with his bankers, the bankers may enter it short; that is to say, merely note it as having been received for collection in due course, and credit it only when paid.

enticement. The action in tort for damages for inducing by persuasion one spouse to leave the other, or to remain away from that other, without justification. Abolished by the Law Reform (Miscellaneous Provisions) Act 1970, s.5.

entire. (1) A contract or claim of which each part is so connected with the rest that it cannot be separated into several distinct contracts or claims; as opposed to a severable or apportionate contract, etc.; (2) A mail animal which has not been castrated.

entireties. Where an estate was conveyed or devised to a man and his wife during coverture they were tenants by entireties: each was seised of the whole; *i.e. per tout* and not *per my et per tout*. After the Married Women's Property Act 1882 the husband and wife took as joint tenants. Tenancies by entireties were abolished by the Law of Property Act 1925, the property being held on trust for sale (*ibid.* s.36).

entrapment. Enticing a person into committing a crime in order to prosecute him. Generally not a defence to criminal proceedings, but see AGENT PROVOCATEUR.

entry. The act of going on land with the intention of asserting a right in it. See FORCIBLE ENTRY.

entry, writs of. Real actions which lay for one from whom lands were wrongfully withheld. The writ was said to be *in the quibus* when it was against the person who had actually committed the wrong; *in the per and cui* when it was against the heir or grantee of such person; *in the per* where there had been two descents, two alienations or a descent and an alienation since the original commission of the wrong; and *in the post* when the original wrong was still more remote. It was abolished by the Real Property Limitation Act 1833, s.36.

enure. To operate or take effect.

eo instanti. [At that instant.]

eo nomine. [In that name.]

eodem modo quo oritur, eodem modo dissolvitur. [What has been effected by agreement can be undone by agreement.]

eodem modo quid constituitur, eodem modo destruitor. [A thing is made and is destroyed by one and the same means.]

epitome of title. Schedule of documents going back to root of Title, performing the same function as an Abstract of Title. See ABSTRACT OF TITLE.

equal opportunities commission. Set up under Sex Discrimination Act 1975, s.53, its purpose is to work towards the elimination of discrimination and to promote equality of opportunity between men and women. See DISCRIMINATION.

equitable. (1) That which is fair; (2) that which arises from the liberal construction or application of a legal rule or remedy; (3) in particular, that which is in accordance with, or regulated, recognised, or enforced by the rules of equity, as opposed to those of the common law.

equitable assets. Assets available for payment of debts in equity, although not at law. Real property was not generally liable for debts at law, but was liable in equity if devised on trust to pay debts or if charged by the deceased with payment of debts. The Administration of Estates Act 1833, made the deceased's realty assets in equity for payment of his debts. See ASSETS.

equitable assignments. Assignments permitted in equity. No particular form is necessary: it need not even be in writing. All that is necessary is that the debtor should be given to understand that the debt has been made over by the creditor to some third person. If the debtor ignores such a notice he does so at his peril. An equitable assignee of a legal chose in action cannot enforce the right assigned by action, unless the action is in the name of the assignor, or he is joined as a plaintiff, if he consents; or if he does not, as a defendant.

Choses in action were not originally assignable at law, but in equity effect was given to assignments not only of equitable choses in action (*e.g.* an interest in a trust fund) but also of legal choses in action, *e.g.* a debt. In the latter case proceedings were taken in the name of the assignor who was restrained from objecting to the use of his name. See ASSIGNMENT OF CHOSES IN ACTION.

equitable charge. A security for a debt where the lender does not get the legal estate in the property charged: as, where the mortgagor has only an equitable interest, or in the case of informal mortgages, *e.g.* a mortgage by deposit of title deeds. The remedy of an equitable chargee is to apply to the court for the enforcement of his charge by the sale of the property, or the appointment of a receiver, etc., as an equitable mortgagee cannot himself exercise a power of sale or appoint a receiver in the absence of a deed.

equitable defence. A defence available in equity although not at law. By the Judicature Act 1873, when law and equity were fused, it was provided that equitable defences should be available in all courts.

equitable easement. An easement created informally, or not held for a full fee simple or term of years absolute. It is registrable as a land charge, Class D (Land Charges Act 1972, s.2). See EASEMENT.

equitable estates. while having their origin as equitable interests (*q.v.*), now include those limited and future estates and interests which were taken out of the common law of the Property Acts of 1925; *viz.* estates tail, estates for life and all future interests in freehold.

equitable estoppel. See ESTOPPEL; QUASI-ESTOPPEL.

equitable execution. A means of enforcing the rights of a judgment creditor by means of the appointment of a receiver and, if necessary, an injunction to restrain dealings with the judgment debtor's equitable interests. See Ord. 29, r.1; Order 30; Ord. 50.

equitable interests. The interests in property which were created and enforced by the Court of Chancery, where it would have been against conscience to permit the legal owner of property to keep the benefit of property for himself, *e.g.* a trustee had the legal estate in the trust property, but he was compelled to hold the property on behalf of the beneficiaries, whose interests were merely equitable. At first, equitable interests were rights *in personam* (*i.e.* as against the trustee), and subject to the rights of the bona fide purchaser for value without notice. But for certain purposes, an equitable interest is tantamount to a real right, particularly in following trust funds, which the beneficiary can recover. See TRACING. Also in the income tax cases of *Baker* v. *Archer-Shee* [1927] A.C. 844; *Archer-Shee* v. *Garland* [1931] A.C. 212 it was held, in effect, that a life tenant has an interest in specific trust assets.

In consequence, equitable interests are "hybrids," midway between *jura in rem* and *jura in personam*, and are as follows: (1) the trust interest proper; (2) the mortgage relationship; (3) between vendor and purchaser; (4) in agreements for a lease; (5) restrictive convenants; (6) equitable easements; (7) equitable rights to *profits à prendre,* (8) limited owners' charges; (9) licencees' rights (Hanbury, *Modern Equity*).

equitable lien. A lien which exists independently of possession, but cannot be set up against the purchaser of the legal estate for value without notice of the lien; *e.g.* vendor's lien for his purchase-money, and the purchaser's lien for his deposit. See LIEN.

equitable mortgage. See MORTGAGE.

equitable waste. See WASTE.

equities. The right to invoke equitable remedies for fraud, mistake, etc. An equity is weaker than an equitable interest, which will take priority over it, if its owner has no notice of it (Hanbury, *Modern Equity*).

equity. Primarily fairness or natural justice. A fresh body of rules by the side of the original law, founded on distinct principles, and claiming to supersede the law in virtue of a superior sanctity inherent in those principles (Maine). Equity is the body of rules formulated and administered by the Court of Chancery to supplement the rules and procedure of the common law.

By the Judicature Act 1873 the Court of Chancery was amalgamated with the Common Law Courts to form the Supreme Court, and rules of equity are administered in all divisions of the court, and where there is any conflict between the rules of law and equity, equity is to prevail (see the Judicature Act 1925, ss.36–44).

equity, maxims of.
    (1) Equity acts *in personam*.
    (2) Equity acts on the conscience.
    (3) Equity will not suffer a wrong to be without a remedy.
    (4) Equity follows the law.
    (5) Equity looks to the intent rather than the form.
    (6) Equity looks on that as done which ought to be done.
    (7) Equity imputes an intent to fulfil an obligation.
    (8) Equitable remedies are discretionary.
    (9) Delay defeats equities.
    (10) He who comes into equity must come with clean hands.
    (11) He who seeks equity must do equity.
    (12) Equity regards the balance of convenience.
    (13) Where there are equal equities the law prevails.
    (14) Where there are equal equities the first in time prevails.

(15) Equity, like nature, does nothing in vain.
(16) Equity never wants (*i.e.* lacks) a trustee.
(17) Equity aids the vigilant.
(18) Equality is equity.
(19) Equity will not assist a volunteer.
(20) Equity will not permit a statute to be a cloak for fraud.

equity of redemption. (1) The equitable right of a mortgagor to redeem the mortgaged property after the legal right to redeem has been lost by default in repayment of the mortgage money at the due date. (2) The equitable estate or interest of a mortgagor in his mortgaged land in respect of which an equitable right to redeem subsists.

equity to a settlement. The right of a wife to have a settlement on herself of part of her equitable property, which her husband was claiming by suit in a court of equity. Since the Married Women's Property Act 1882 a married woman holds her property separately from her husband, and has no need to invoke this doctrine.

error. Some mistake in the foundation, proceeding, judgment or execution of an action in a court of record, requiring correction either by the court in which it occurred (in case of error of fact), or by a superior court (in case of error in law). To "bring error" was to apply for the rectification required. Abolished by Judicature Act 1873. See APPEAL; MISTAKE.

error, writ of. It lay for substantial defects appearing on the face of the record of a criminal trial. It brought the proceedings from an inferior court to a superior court for review. Abolished by Criminal Appeal Act 1907, s.20(1).

escape. The misdemeanour committed by a person who permits any person in his lawful custody to regain his liberty otherwise than in due course of law. It is an indictable offence to aid a prisoner to escape (Prison Act 1952; Criminal Justice Act 1961, ss.22(1), Sched. 4). Harbouring an escaped prisoner is an offence punishable summarily or on indictment (Act of 1961, s.22(2)).

escheat. The reversion of land to the lord of the fee or the Crown on failure of heirs of the owner or on his outlawry. It is derived from the feudal rule that, where an estate in fee simple comes to an end, the land reverts to the lord by whose ancestors or predecessors the estate was originally created. Escheat was abolished by the Administration of Estates Act 1925, s.45, and the right of the Crown to take as *bona vacantia* was substituted (*ibid*. s.46).

escheator. The officer anciently appointed to enforce the right of escheat on behalf of the Crown.

escrow. A writing sealed and delivered to a stranger (*i.e.* a person not a party to it) to be held by him until certain conditions be performed, *e.g.* payment of money, and then to be delivered to take effect as a deed. See DELIVERY OF DEED. When the conditions of an escrow are satisfied (in the case of lease) rent then becomes payable from the date of its conditional delivery and not the date of satisfaction of the conditions (*Alan Estates* v. *W. G. Stores* [1981] 3 W.L.R. 892, C.A.).

escuage. A variety of tenure by knight's service. It imposed on the tenant the duty of accompanying the King to war for 40 days, or of sending a substitute, or of paying a sum of money which was assessed by Parliament after the expedition.

esquire. The degree next below that of knight. A barrister-at-law is an esquire by virtue of his office.

essence of the contract. An essential condition or stipulation in a contract without which the contract would not have been entered into. Unless a different intention appears from the terms of the contract, time of payment is not of the essence of the contract of sale (Sale of Goods Act 1893, s.10).

essoin; essoign. An excuse made for non-appearance in an action or suit. It was in the nature of an application for time or for an adjournment, made on the first day of term—essoin day.

estate. An interest in land. An absolute estate is one granted without condition or termination. A conditional estate is one liable to divest on the fulfilment of a condition. A contingent estate is one the right to the enjoyment of which will accrue on the happening of some event; and a determinable estate one that is liable to determine on the happening of some event. An estate in expectancy is one which cannot be enjoyed until some future time.

An estate in possession is one which gives the right of present enjoyment, and a vested estate is one the right to the enjoyment of which has accrued. An estate in severalty is one held by a person singly, and an estate in common is one held by several persons jointly in undivided shares. A customary estate is one that existed in manors and boroughs by virtue of local custom: abolished by the Law of Property Act 1922.

An estate in fee simple is one that is granted to a "man and his heirs," and is the greatest estate a subject of the Crown can posses. An estate of freehold is one originally held by a freeman and subject to free services, and of uncertain duration; *e.g.* for life, or for the life of another. An estate of inheritance is one capable of descending to a man's heirs, *i.e.* an estate in fee simple, fee tail or in frankalmoign.

estate agent. Estate agency work consists of things done in the course of a business, pursuant to instructions received from another person who wishes to dispose of or acquire an interest in land, for the purpose of effecting the introduction to the client of a third person who wishes to acquire or dispose of such interest (Estate Agents Act 1979, s.1(1)). The Act of 1979 and orders made thereunder (*inter alia*) empower the Director of Fair Trading to bar unfit persons from such work (s.4) and make provisions to protect client's money (ss.12, 13, 14, and 15).

estate clause. The clause inserted in conveyances after the grant of parcels, conveying "all the estate, right, interest," etc., of the owner. Rendered unnecessary by the Conveyancing Act 1881, s.63, now replaced by the Law of Property Act 1925, s.63.

estate contract. A contract by an estate owner to convey or create a legal estate (Land Charges Act 1972, s.2(4)(iv)).

estate duty. The tax imposed by the Finance Act 1894, s.1, upon the principal value of property, whether real or personal, settled or not, which passed on the death of any person dying after August 1, 1894. Estate duty was abolished in respect of deaths on or after March 13, 1975 (Finance Act 1975, s.49). It is replaced by capital transfer tax (*q.v.*).

estate, legal. One valid against all the world: the estate capable of being created or conveyed at common law. By the Law of Property Act 1925, s.1 the only legal estates capable of subsisting are (1) an estate in fee simple absolute in possession, (2) a term of years absolute. See CHARGE; INTEREST.

estate owner. The owner of a legal estate. A minor is not capable of being an estate owner. See ESTATE.

estate tail. One created by the grant of land to "a man and the heirs of his body" or to a man and specified heirs of his body; *e.g.* the issue of his first wife. The estate tail is derived from the Statute of Westminster II, *De Donis Conditionalibus*, before which a gift of land to a man and the heirs of his body created an estate in fee conditional on his having issue; as soon as the condition was performed the estate became absolute. The statute enacted that in such cases the terms of the gift should be carried out and the land should go to the issue of the donee, and on failure of such issue should revert to the donor. The Fines and Recoveries Act 1833, instituted a disentailing deed for barring the entail, which since the Law of

Property Act 1925, need not be enrolled (s.133). Since 1925, the estate tail can be barred by will (*ibid.* s.176), and will take effect as an equitable interest (*ibid.* s.130).

Estates of the Realm. The Lords Temporal, the Lords Spiritual and the Commons.

estoppel. The rule of evidence of doctrine of law which precludes a person from denying the truth of some statement formerly made by him, or the existence of facts which he has by words or conduct led others to believe in. If a person by a representation induces another to change his position on the faith of it, he cannot afterwards deny the truth of his representation. See QUASI-ESTOPPEL.

(1) Estoppel by record: a person is not permitted to dispute the facts upon which a judgment against him is based.

(2) Estoppel by deed: a person cannot dispute his own deed; he cannot deny the truth of recitals contained in it.

(3) Estoppel *in pais*, or equitable estoppel: estoppel by conduct, *e.g.* a tenant, having accepted a lease, cannot dispute his lessor's title.

(4) Equitable estoppel: a person who stands by and keeps silence when he observes another person acting under a misapprehension or mistake, which by speaking he could have prevented by showing the true state of affairs, can be estopped from later alleging the true state of affairs. Thus an owner of goods who voluntarily allows another to treat them as his own, without protest, whereby a third person is induced to buy them bona fide, cannot recover them from that person. Similarly, if a stranger begins to build on land supposing it to be his own, and the real owner, observing his mistake, abstains from setting him right and leaves him to persevere in his error, equity will not afterwards allow the real owner to assert his title to the land.

Estoppel provides a shield, not a sword: it cannot create a cause of action.

estovers, common of. The right of taking from the woods or waste lands of another person a reasonable portion of his timber or underwood for use in the commoner's tenement.

estrays. Valuable animals found straying in any manor or lordship without an owner. After proclamation and a year and a day they belong to the Crown; or by special grant to the lord of the manor.

estreat. [Extract.] A copy of a record of a court; now used only in connection with fines, forfeitures and recognises.

et seq.: et sequentes. [And those following.]

European Court. The Court of Justice of the European Community (European Communites Act 1972, Sched. 1, Part II). See COURT OF JUSTICE.

European Economic Community. See COMMON MARKET; EEC.

eviction. Dispossession; recovery of land by the course of law. It is an offence to unlawfully deprive or attempt to unlawfully deprive the residential occupier of any premises of his occupation of the premises or any part thereof (Protection from Eviction Act 1977, s.1(2)). Recovery of possession of premises subject to a non-statutorily protected tenancy which has come to an end is unlawful except through the court (s.3(1)). See also Criminal Law Act 1977, ss.6–13.

evidence. All the legal means, exclusive of mere argument, which tend to prove or disprove any matter of fact, the truth of which is submitted to judicial investigation; as follows:

(1) Oral: statements made by witnesses in court.

(2) Documentary: including public and private documents, and statements of relevant facts made by persons in writing (see *infra*).

(3) Conclusive: evidence of a fact which the court must take as full proof of it, and which excludes all evidence to disprove it.

(4) Direct: evidence of a fact actually in issue; evidence of a fact actually perceived by a witness with his own senses.

(5) Circumstantial: evidence of a fact not actually in issue, but legally relevant to a fact in issue.

(6) Real: evidence supplied by material objects produced for the inspection of the court.

(7) Extrinsic: oral evidence given in connection with written documents.

(8) Hearsay: see HEARSAY.

(9) Indirect: circumstantial or hearsay evidence.

(10) Original: evidence which has an independent probative force of its own.

(11) Derivative: evidence which derives its force from some other source.

(12) Parol: oral, extrinsic evidence.

(13) Prima facie: evidence of a fact which the court must take as proof of such fact, unless disproved by further evidence.

(14) Primary evidence of a document is the document itself, or duplicate original.

(15) Secondary: evidence other than the best evidence, and which is rejected if primary evidence is available; *e.g.* oral evidence of the contents of a lost document such as a will.

Evidence must be given in open court *viva voce*, but provision is made where a cause or matter is pending, for depositions to be taken from witnesses who will be unable to attend the hearing (Ord. 39). See PROOF.

ex abundanti cautela. [From excess of caution.]

ex aequo et bono. [In justice and good faith.]

ex cathedra. [From the chair.] With official authority.

ex contractu. [Arising out of contract.]

ex curia. [Out of court.]

ex debito justitiae. A remedy which the applicant gets as of right, *e.g.* a writ of Habeas Corpus.

ex delicto. [Arising out of wrongs.] Actions in tort.

ex diuturnitate temporis omnia praesumuntur esse rite et solennitur acta. [From lapse of time, all things are presumed to have been done rightly and regularly.]

ex dolo malo non oritur actio. [No right of action can have its origin in fraud.]

ex gratia. [As a favour.]

ex maleficio non oritur contractus. [A contract cannot arise out of an illegal act.]

ex mero motu. [Of one's own free will.]

ex nudo pacto non oritur actio. [No action arises from a nude contract.] A contract entered into without consideration cannot be enforced.

ex officio. [By virtue of his office.]

ex parte. An application in a judicial proceeding made: (1) by an interested person who is not a party; (2) by one party in the absence of the other.

ex post facto. [By a subsequent act.] Retrospectively.

ex proprio motu. [Of his own accord.]

ex provisione viri. An estate tail of a wife in lands of her husband or his ancestors. Obsolete.

ex relatione; ex rel. [From a narrative or information.] (1) A report of proceedings not from first hand knowledge; (2) proceedings at the relation or information of a person.

ex turpi causa non oritur actio. [An action does not arise from a base cause.] *e.g.* an illegal contract is void. See ILLEGAL.

exaction. The taking, by an officer of the law, of any fee or reward where none was due.

examination. The interrogation of a person on oath. In court, in general, the evidence of a witness is obtained by oral examination, called the examination-in-chief; he is then examined on behalf of the opposite party in order to diminish the effect of his evidence, called the cross-examination. Then he is again examined by the party calling him in order to give him an opportunity of explaining or contradicting any false impression produced by the cross-examination, called the re-examination, which is confined to matters arising out of the cross-examination.

examination, public. The process by which a bankrupt is examined in open court by the Official Receiver as to events leading to his bankruptcy. On the application of the Official Receiver the court may order that the public examination be dispensed with (Insolvency Act 1976, s.6).

examined copy. A copy of a document sworn to be a true copy by a person who has compared it with the original.

examiner. A person appointed by a court to take the examination of witnesses in an action; that is, to take down the result of their interrogation by the parties or their counsel. An examiner is generally appointed where a witness is in a foreign country, or is too ill or infirm to attend before the court (see Ord. 39).

exception. A saving clause in a deed so that the thing excepted does not pass by the grant. In procedure, to except to a thing was to object to or challenge it.

exchange. Mutual transfer or conveyance of property. An exchange is a place where merchants, dealers or brokers meet to transact business, *e.g.* the London Stock Exchange.

exchange control. A system of legal restrictions to prevent and control payments to persons abroad or transfer of funds out of the United Kingdom (Exchange Control Act 1947). Since October 24, 1979 (December 13, 1979 in the case of Southern Rhodesia) all exchange controls have been lifted.

exchange of contracts. "Where parties enter into an agreement for the sale of real property 'subject to contract,' the contract, in the absence of express agreement to the contrary, is not complete until the parties have exchanged their copies in accordance with ordinary conveyancing procedure" (*Eccles* v. *Bryant* [1947] 2 All E.R. 865, C.A.).

A client impliedly and ostensibly authorises his solicitor to effect exchange in any manner which the law recognises as amounting to exchange. For the position as to the effect of telephone conversations between solicitors see *Domb* v. *Isoz* [1980] 1 All E.R. 942, C.A.

Exchequer. (1) Anciently, the *Scaccarium*, or chess board, from the cloth covering the table. A public office, formerly consisting of two divisions, the Exchequer of Receipt, the Court of Exchequer (*q.v.*). The former managed the royal revenues, receiving and keeping the moneys due to the Crown, and seeing that the payments out were made on proper authority.

(2) The account with the Bank of England into which are paid all Government receipts and revenues. The fund so formed is called the Consolidated Fund, out of which are paid the sums necessary for the public service, as authorised by Parliament, subject to the control of the Comptroller and Auditor General (*q.v.*). See CHANCELLOR OF THE EXCHEQUER.

Exchequer Chamber. There were four Courts of Exchequer Chamber: (1) the Court of Error for the Exchequer; (2) the Court of Equity for the Exchequer; (3) the Court for Errors in the King's Bench; and (4) the Court of Exchequer Chamber, being the assembly of all the judges for considering questions of law. Finally, the Court of Exchequer Chamber (*q.v.*) was a court of error.

excise. A duty of inland revenue chargeable on the manufacture or sale of intoxicating liquors, tobacco, etc. (Customs and Excise Management Act 1979).

exclusion order. (1) Order made under the Prevention of Terrorism (Temporary Provisions) Act 1976 excluding from the United Kingdom persons concerned in the commission, preparation or instigation of acts of terrorism or attempting to enter the country for such purpose.

(2) Order made under the Licensed Premises (Exclusion of Certain Persons) Act 1980, s.1(2) prohibiting a person convicted of an offence on licensed premises who resorted to violence or offered to do so from entering those premises or other specified premises without the express consent of the licensee.

exclusive jurisdiction of the Court of Chancery. Its jurisdiction in cases where no relief was obtainable at law. The jurisdiction comprises trusts, administration of assets and the like.

exeat. [Let him go.]

executed. That which is done. See CONSIDERATION; EXECUTORY.

execution. (1) The act of completing or carrying into effect, particularly of a judgment, effected by writs of execution, orders and notices, which compel the defendant to do or to pay what has been adjudged. Writs of execution are addressed to the sheriff, whose function it is to carry them out. See ATTACHMENT; CHARGING ORDER COMMITTAL; DELIVERY; FIERI FACIAS; POSSESSION; SEQUESTRATION.

(2) The execution of deeds is by the signing, sealing and delivery of them by the parties as their own acts and deeds, in the presence of witnesses. See EQUITABLE EXECUTION; WILLS.

Executive. The Crown in its administrative aspect; the Government Departments and their officials or officers under the Ministers of the Crown. The principal executive body in the Constitution is the Cabinet (*q.v.*).

In principle, the Executive is charged with putting into effect the laws enacted by the Legislature, subject to the judgments and orders of the Judiciary. In practice, the Legislature largely functions at the initiative of the Executive, and the Judiciary cannot interfere in purely administrative matters.

executor. An executor is the person to whom the execution of a will, that is, the duty of carrying its provisions into effect, is confided by the testator. The duties of an executor are to bury the deceased; to prove the will; to collect the estate, and, as necessary, convert it into money; to pay the debts in their proper order; to pay the legacies, and distribute the residue among the persons entitled. The executor may bring actions against persons who are indebted to the testator, or are in possession of property belonging to the estate. When several executors are appointed, and only some of them prove the will, these are called the proving or acting executors. The others are said to renounce probate. An executor is allowed a year to realise the testator's estate (Administration of Estates Act 1925, s.44). See RETAINER.

executor de son tort. [Of his own wrong.] One who, being neither executor nor administrator, intermeddles with the goods of the deceased; he renders himself liable, not only to an action by the rightful executor or administrator, but also to be sued by a creditor or legatee of the deceased. He has all the liabilities, though none of the privileges, of an executor (see Administration of Estates Act 1925, s.28). See DEVASTAVIT.

executory. That which remains to be carried into effect. An executory contract is one which takes the form of promises to be performed in the future.

executory interest. A future estate in lands or personalty which does not depend upon the determination of prior particular estates. An executory devise is an executory interest created by will. An executory interest created under the Statute of Uses is either a springing use, *i.e.* one that comes into being after the happening of some event; or of a shifting use, *i.e.* one that shifts from one person to another on the happening of some event. See USE.

exemplary damages. See DAMAGES.

exemplification. An official copy of a document made under the seal of a court or public functionary.

exemption clause. a clause in a contract excluding or limiting the liability of one or other of the parties. Such clause must be expressly incorporated in the relationship between the parties from the outset (*Thornton* v. *Shoe Lane Parking Ltd.* [1971] 2 Q.B. 163, C.A.). See also *Photo Production Ltd.* v. *Securicor Transport Ltd.* [1980] 2 W.L.R. 283, H.L. A buyer making a consumer purchase from a retailer cannot lose the protection of implied terms and conditions by agreement (Supply of Goods (Implied Terms) Act 1973). See also UNFAIR CONTRACT TERMS.

exequatur. Permission (at discretion) by a Government to the consul of another State to enter upon the discharge of his functions.

exhibit. A document or thing produced for the inspection of the court; or shown to a witness when giving evidence or referred to in a deposition: or a document referred to in, but not annexed to, an affidavit.

exitus. (1) Issue or offspring; (2) the yearly rents and profits of lands and tenements; and (3) a joinder of issue or close of pleadings.

exoneration. Relief from liability; the relieving of one part of the estate of a testator of liability, by throwing it on another part, either by direction of the testator or by operation of law.

exor. An executor.

expatriation. Loss of nationality by renunciation of allegiance, and the acquisition of a foreign nationality. See the British Nationality Act 1964, ss.1, 2.

expectant heir. Everyone who has either a vested remainder or a contingent remainder in a family property, including a remainder in a portion, as well as a remainder in an estate; and everyone who has the hope of succession to the property of an ancestor, either by reason of being the heir-apparent or presumptive, or by reason merely of the expectation of a devise or bequest on account of the supposed or presumed affection of his ancestor or relation.

Bargains with expectant heirs will be set aside unless the purchaser can show that a fair price was paid. See CATCHING BARGAIN.

expectation of life. See LIFE, EXPECTATION OF.

expedit reipublicae ut finis sit litium. [It is in the public interest that the decision of cases should be final.]

expensae litis. [Expenses of the cause.] Costs.

expensilatio. See LITERARUM OBLIGATIO.

expert witness. A person with special skill, technical knowledge or professional qualifications whose opinion on any matter within his cognisance is admitted in evidence, contrary to the general rule that mere opinions are irrelevant; *e.g.* doctors and surgeons, handwriting experts, foreign lawyers. It is for the court to decide whether a witness is so qualified as to be considered an expert.

The procedure for adducing expert evidence is governed by Ord. 38. rr. 35–44. See Practice Direction [1974] 1 W.L.R. 904 and [1979] 1 W.L.R. 290.

In any case to be tried without a jury, the court or judge in his discretion, may appoint an independent expert, called "the court expert," to inquire and report (Ord. 40). The position as to adducing expert evidence in the county court is governed by C.C.R., Ord. 20, rr. 27 and 28.

Expiring Laws Continuance Act. An Act passed to continue, generally until the end of the following year, a number of Acts which otherwise would have expired. The latest of these Acts was the Expiring Laws Continuance Act 1970.

exposure, indecent. See INDECENCY.

express. Direct communication, as opposed to communication by implication, *e.g.* an express trust.

expressio unius personae vel rei, est exclusio alterius. [The express mention of one person or thing is the exlusion of another.] A valuable servant but a dangerous master in the construction of statutes or documents.

expressum facit cessare tacitum. [When there is express mention of certain things, then anything not metioned is excluded.]

expropriation. Compulsorily depriving a person of a right of property belonging to him. Compensation may be promised or paid.

extended sentence. The court may impose an extended sentence on an offender convicted on indictment of an offence punishable with imprisonment of two years or more if the court is satisfied by reason of the offenders previous conduct and the likelihood of his committing further offences that it is expedient to protect the public from him for a substantial time (Powers of Criminal Courts Act 1973, ss.28, 29).

Extendi Facias (Writ of). [That you cause to be extended.] The Writ of Extent.

extent. The writ to recover debts of record due to the Crown, directed to the sheriff, who proceeded to make a valuation of the property of the debtor by means of a statement on oath of a jury. An extent in chief was a proceeding by the Crown for the recovery of a debt of record due to it. An extent in aid was one sued out at the instance and for the benefit of a debtor to the Crown, for the recovery of a debt due to himself, the Crown being merely the nominal plaintiff. An immediate extent was one which issued in urgent cases without the usual preliminary of a *scire facias* (*q.v.*), on proof that the debt was in danger of being lost. Abolished by Crown Proceedings Act 1947, s.33.

extinguishment. The cesser of a right or obligation, particularly by consolidation or merger. An easement is extinguished when the dominant and servient tenements become united in the same person.

extortion. The misdemeanour committed by a public officer, who, under colour of his office, wrongfully takes from any person any money or valuable thing. It was abolished by the Theft Act 1968. See BLACKMAIL.

extortionate. A credit bargain may be considered extortionate and reopened by the court if the debtor, or relatives, are required to make grossly extortionate payments (Consumer Credit Act 1974, ss.137–140).

extradition. The delivery up of a person who has committed a crime in one country by the authorities of another country in which he has taken refuge, to the authorities of the country in which the crime was committed. The law and procedure on the subject is set out in the Extradition Acts 1870 to 1935. The list of extradition crimes is set out in those Acts and other Acts, principally the Aviation Security Act 1982, s.9; the Internationally Protected Persons Act 1978, s.3(1) and the Protection of Children Act 1978, s.1(6).

No such proceedings can be taken unless an extradition treaty has been concluded with the foreign state concerned. No criminal can be extradited for a "political" offence.

An analogous procedure applies to the Commonwealth countries and colonies. See DEPORTATION.

extrajudicial. Outside judicial procedure, *e.g.* distress; a dictum.

extraterritoriality. A legal fiction by which certain persons and things are deemed for the purpose of jurisdiction and control to be outside the territory of the State in which they really are, and within that of some other State. Its principal applications are:

(1) Sovereigns, whilst travelling or resident in foreign countries.

(2) Ambassadors and other diplomatic agents while in the country to which they are accredited.

(3) Public vessels whilst in foreign ports or territorial waters.

(4) The armed forces of a State when passing through foreign territory.

Compare the legal position of members of the naval, military and air forces of certain countries visiting the United Kingdom provided for the Visiting Forces Act 1952. See also DIPLOMATIC PRIVILEGE.

eyre. The justices in eyre were regularly established in 1176, with a delegated power from the King's Great Court or *Aula Regia*, and they made their circuit round the kingdom once in seven years, for the purpose of trying causes, and reviewing the whole working of the local government. They were directed by Magna Carta to be sent into every county once a year; but "as the power of the justices of assize increased so these justices itinerant vanished away" (Coke).

F

f.o.b. Free on board; a price quoted for goods including the cost of placing on board ship. It is a contract of sale of goods where the seller pays the cost of the shipment and makes delivery as soon as the goods are placed on board, the buyer bearing the risk of whether they are lost or not. The seller must give notice to the buyer to enable him to insure the goods. The risk does not pass to the buyer, nor does the property, until the goods are actually on board.

fabric lands. Lands given to provide for the repair of, or to maintain the fabric or structure of, a church. See the Church Property (Miscellaneous Provisions) Measure 1960, s.7.

factor. A mercantile agent; a person who, in the usual course of his business has possession of the goods, or the documents of title to goods, of his principal, with authority to sell, pledge, or raise money on security of the same (Factors Act 1889, s.1(1)). The principal is bound by such sale or pledge even though he has forbidden it, unless there is notice of such prohibition.

factory. A building for the manufacture of goods. The Factories Act 1961, which consolidated the law relating to the safety, health, and welfare of persons employed in a factory, as defined in s.175, and elsewhere as provided in Part VII of the Act, is now amended, and will be increasingly replaced, by the Health and Safety at Work etc. Act 1974, and orders made under it. The Factory Inspectorate is now administered under the 1974 Act as part of the Health and Safety Executive. See HEALTH AND SAFETY EXECUTIVE.

factum. An act or deed.

factum probanda. Facts which require to be proved.

factum probantia. Facts which are given in evidence to prove other facts in issue.

faculty. A licence to do an otherwise unlawful act. See the Faculty Jurisdiction Measure 1964.

failure of record. The unsuccessful plea of a defendant who alleged matter of record in defence.

fair comment. A fair comment on a matter which is of public interest, or is submitted to public criticism, is not actionable as defamation (*q.v.*). The burden of proof is on the defendant setting up the plea. Comment is of the nature of criticism or opinion and must be distinguished from a statement of fact. Fair comment means comment honestly believed to be true, not inspired by any malicious motive, and not irrelevant. It must be based on facts truly stated. The Defamation Act 1952, s.6 provided that a defence of fair comment shall not fail by reason only that the truth of every allegation of fact is not proved, if the expression of opinion is fair comment having regard to such of the facts as are proved.

The "rolled-up plea" was: in so far as the statements complained of are statements of fact, they are true in substance and in fact; and in so far as they consist of comment, they are fair comment on a matter of public interest. This was a plea of fair comment only, and not of justification. The defendant must now, however, furnish particulars of the words alleged to be statements of fact, and also of the facts relied on as supporting the allegation of truth. (Ord. 82, r.3(2)). See also CONTEMPT OF COURT.

fair rent. Since 1968 various Rent Acts have provided for the fixing of a "fair rent" in respect of certain residential tenancies either landlord or tenant may apply. Now governed by Rent Act 1977, Part IV.

fair trading. The Fair Trading Act 1973 set up the office of Fair Trading and laid down a framework of law to eliminate or control unfair consumer practices. See also Competition Act 1980, ss.9, 10, 21–41 and see MONOPOLY.

fair wages resolution. Between 1891 and 1946 Parliament approved Fair Wages Resolutions designed to ensure the inclusion of certain terms as to wages and conditions of work in certain contracts between government departments and private contractors.

fait. [A deed.]

falsa demonstratio non nocet. [A false description does not vitiate a document.] Thus if part of a description is true and part false, if the true part describes the subject with sufficient certainty, the untrue part will be rejected or ignored.

false accounting. This is an indictable offence under the Theft Act 1968, s.17.

false imprisonment. The confinement of a person without just cause or excuse. There must be a total restraint of the person; and the onus of proving reasonable cause is on the defendant.

false pretence. The old offence under the Larceny Act 1916 of obtaining money by false pretences has been repealed (Theft Act 1968, ss.15, 16). For the present position under the Theft Act 1978, ss.1–3 see DECEPTION.

false representation. See MISREPRESENTATION.

false return. An action of damages lies against a person who makes a false return to a writ.

falsification of accounts. See ACCOUNTS, FALSIFICATION OF.

falsify. Where an account is being investigated in the Chancery Division, and the party shows that an item of payment or discharge contained in it is false or erroneous, he is said to falsify it.

familia. [Roman law.] [Family.] It may include: (1) All those persons who were subject to the potestas of the same individual, whether his children, grandchildren, etc., or unconnected in blood, *e.g.* slaves. (2) All descendants of the same ancestors. (3) All persons connected by agnation. (4) The slaves of a *paterfamilias*, or (5) The property of a *paterfamilias*.

family allowances. The weekly allowances for the benefit of every family which includes two or more children. They are replaced by "child benefits." See CHILD BENEFIT.

Family Division. A division of the High Court created by the Administration of Justice Act 1970, s.1, by renaming the Probate, Divorce and Admiralty Division and redistributing the work of that court. See now Supreme Court Act 1981, s.5(1)(c).

family provision. The Inheritance (Provision for Family and Dependants) Act 1975 (replacing the Inheritance (Family Provision) Act 1938, as amended) gives the court power, as respects the death of a person on or after April 1, 1976, to make provision out of his estate for the maintenance of his family and dependants.

Application for such provision must generally be made within 6 months of representation being taken out. County courts have jurisdiction in dealing with estates of a net value not exceeding £30,000. Those classed as dependants and who may apply for financial provision are the deceased's wife, husband or child; a former wife or husband who has not remarried; any person (not being a child of the deceased) who was treated by the deceased as a child of the family in relation to any marriage to which the deceased was a party; and any other person who immediately before the death of the deceased was being maintained, either wholly or partly, by the deceased (1975 Act, s.1).

famosus libellus. [A scandalous libel.]

fast days. Days of general fast may be declared by Royal Proclamation. Such a day is not a business day.

fatal accidents. The Fatal Accidents Act 1976 consolidates the law on this subject. Section 1(1) provides that where death is caused by any wrongful act, neglect or default which (if death had not ensued) would have entitled the person injured to maintain an action and recover damages, the person who would have been liable if death had not ensued shall be liable to an action for damages. The action shall be for the benefit of the dependants of the deceased (s.1(2)). Dependants are the deceased's husband, wife, children, grandchildren, stepchildren, parents, stepparents and grandparents and any person who is the issue of a brother, sister, uncle or aunt of the deceased (s.1(3), (4)).

Neither the remarriage nor the prospect of remarriage of a widow may be taken into account (s.3(2)).

Action must generally be brought within three years (Limitation Act 1939, s.2B; Limitation Act 1975, Sched. 1, para. 1).

Claims may also be made on behalf of the deceased's estate (Law Reform (Miscellaneous Provisions) Act 1934, s.1). For damages for loss of earnings in the "lost years" see *Gammell* v. *Wilson* [1981] 1 All E.R. 578; " . . . the law relating to damages for death recoverable by dependants is neither sensible nor just . . . I join with your Lordships in thinking that it is too late for anything short of legislation to bring the like sense and justice to the law relating to damages for death recoverable by the estate of the deceased" (*Gammell* v. *Wilson, per* Lord Diplock at p. 583).

fauces terrae. A narrow inlet of the sea; a gulf.

fealty. A service which every free tenant (except a tenant in frankalmoign) is in theory bound to perform to his feudal lord. It consisted in the tenant taking an oath of fidelity to the Lord.

federal state. A State with a written constitution which apportions the sovereign power between a central or "federal" legislature on the one hand, and a system of local legislatures on the other, in such a way that each is sovereign within its prescribed sphere, *e.g.* the United States of America. The purpose is to hold minor communities together, or to reconcile national unity and power with the maintenance of State rights; there is union without unity.

fee. Originally a feudal benefice; land granted to a man and his heirs in return for services to be rendered to the grantor.

fee-farm rent. A perpetual rent issuing out of lands held in fee simple, reserved when the lands were granted, and payable by the freeholder. A fee-farm rent is included in the term "rentcharge" (Law of Property Act 1925, s.205(1)(xxiii)) and is now subject to the provisions for extinguishment to be effected by the Rent Charges Act 1977, s.3. See RENTCHARGE.

fee simple. An estate of freehold, held originally by free (not servile) services; an estate of inheritance, being the most extensive interest that a man could have under the King. It implied an absolute inheritance, clear of any condition, limitation or restrictions to particular heirs; it was descendible to heirs general whether male or female, lineal or collateral. See ESTATE.

fee tail. See ENTAIL; ESTATE.

feeble minded. Persons of severe sub-normality. See the Mental Health Act 1959, s.4; Education (Handicapped Children) Act 1970.

feigned issue. A mode of deciding questions of fact, by stating that the parties interested in the matter had made a wager upon the truth or falsehood of the propositions, setting out the fact or facts in dispute, and then having the issue tried by a jury. See now Ord. 18, r.21.

felo de se. One who commits suicide (*q.v.*).

felony. At common law, every species of crime, a conviction for which occasioned the forfeiture of the lands or goods of the offender, and the penalty for which was death (except petty larceny and mayhem). Forfeiture was abolished, however, by the Forfeiture Act 1870. Many offences were made felonies by statute. All distinctions between felony and misdemeanour have been abolished and all indictable offences are governed by the rules relating to misdemeanours (Criminal Law Act 1967, s.1).

feme covert. A married woman.

feme sole. An unmarried woman.

feodum. A fee (*q.v.*).

feoffee to uses. A person to whom a feoffment was made to the use of a *cestui que use*. This vested the legal estate in the feoffee, who held on behalf of the beneficial owner, the *cestui que use*. The Statute of Uses 1535 turned the use into the legal estate, and the *cestui que use* therefore became the legal owner. The feoffee to uses henceforth merely served as a conduit pipe, diverting the flow of the legal estate. The Statute of Uses was repealed by the Law of Property Act 1925.

feoffment. Originally, merely the overt or public delivery of the possession of land by the owner (the feoffor) to the grantee or purchaser (the feoffee), consisting of the ceremony called livery of seisin (*q.v.*). It became usual to put the terms of the conveyance in writing, as a record of the transaction, which was called the charter or deed of feoffment. By the Real Property Act 1845, s.3 a feoffment had to be made by deed. The tortious operation of a feoffment was the granting of a larger estate to the feoffee than the feoffor himself possessed: abolished by the Real Property Act 1845, s.4. Feoffments were abolished by the Law of Property Act 1925, s.51(1).

ferae naturae. [Of a wild nature.] See ANIMALS.

ferry. The right to a ferry is a franchise which can be created only by grant from the Crown, by prescription, or by statute.

feud. (1) A fee (*q.v.*). (2) An enmity or a quarrel.

feudal system. A state of society in which the main social bond is the relation between lord and man, a relation implying on the lord's part protection and defence; on the man's part protection, service, and reverence, the service including service in arms. This personal relation is inseparably involved in a proprietary relation, the tenure of land. The man holds of the lord, the man's service is a burden on the land, the lord has important rights in the land (Maitland).

    The King was the ultimate lord of all land. He granted land to his lords in return for military and other services, ad they in their turn made further similar grants, the process being known ans subinfeudation. The unit of land in the system was the manor, each under its lord, who had a right to services in labour and in kind from the villeins, the servile tenants of the manor, over whom he exercised full jurisdiction. The lord in return owed them a duty of protection. The King had an overriding authority and claimed allegiance both from lords and their tenants.

fi. fa. *Fieri facias* (*q.v.*).

fiat. [Let it be done.] A decree; a short order or warrant of a judge or public officer that certain steps should be taken. In many statutes it is provided that proceedings may not be instituted without the sanction of the Attorney-General. See *e.g.* the Race Relations Act 1965, s.2.

fiat justitia. [Let justice be done.] Formerly, the indorsement of the Home Secretary on a petition of right, without which it could not be proceeded with (Petition of Right Act 1860, s.2). See PETITION OF RIGHT.

fiat justitia, ruat coelum. [Let justice be done, though the heavens fall.]

fictio legis non operatur damnum vel injuriam. [A legal fiction does not work loss or injustice.]

fiction, legal. Any assumption which conceals, or affects to conceal, the fact that a rule of law has undergone alteration, its letter remaining unchanged, it operation being modified (Maine). In English law fictions have played a considerable part. They may be said to be statements or suppositions which are known to be untrue, but which are not allowed to be denied, in order that some difficulty may be overcome, and substantial justice secured. See *e.g.* EJECTMENT.

fideicommissarius. [Roman law.] The *cestui que trust*, the person to whom, by way of trust, the heir is required to give up the whole inheritance, or a share of it.

fideicommissum. [Roman law.] A trust imposed upon the legal heir for the execution of the last wishes of a deceased person.

fidejussor. [Roman law.] A surety; one that binds himself for the promiser. A *fidejussor* might be added in every kind of obligation.

fiduciary. The relationship of one person to another, where the former is bound to exercise rights and powers in good faith for the benefit of the latter; *e.g.* as between trustee and beneficiary. A court of equity will not allow a person in a fiduciary position (unless expressly so entitled) to make a personal profit or to put himself in a position where his duty and his interest conflict.

fieri facias. [Cause to be made.] A writ of execution directing the sheriff to whom it is addressed to levy from the goods and chattels of the debtor a sum equal to the amount of judgment debt and interest. The sheriff makes a seizure and institutes a sale by auction.

fieri feci. The return by a sheriff to the writ of *fieri facias* that he has levied the sum named.

filacers. Officers of the court who filed original writs.

filius nullius. [Son of nobody.] A bastard.

filiusfamilias; filiafamilias. [Roman law.] Son; daughter. Any persons under the *patria potestas* of another.

financial loss. Financial loss incurred by a plaintiff consequential on the negligence (*q.v.*) of a defendant may properly be claimed against the defendant (*Junior Books Ltd.* v. *The Veitchi Co. Ltd.* [1982] 3 W.L.R. 477, H.L.).

financial provision orders. The orders of a financial nature which the court may make on or after granting a decree of divorce, nullity or judicial separation or (in the case of maintenance pending suit) before such decree. They are orders for maintenance pending suit, periodical payments, secured periodical payments, lump sum transfer of property and property adjustment, and similar orders in respect of children (Matrimonial Causes Act 1973, ss.21–24). The principles on which the court will make such orders are set out in section 25 of the 1973 Act. See also *Wachtel* v. *Wachtel* [1973] 1 All E.R. 113.

financial relief. See FINANCIAL PROVISION.

finding. (1) A conclusion upon on inquiry of fact.

(2) The finding and keeping of lost things may constitute theft it the finder at the time of finding believes that the owner can be discovered by taking reasonable steps (Theft Act 1968, s.2(1)(*c*)).

It seems that the finder of a lost article (the owner of which is unknown) on land belonging to another, to which he has lawful access, is entitled to retain the chattel as against the tenant of the land. But it is otherwise if the article is embedded in the soil or in a river on the land, when the tenant of the land is entitled to it: *Elwes* v. *Brigg Gas Co.* (1886) 33 Ch.D. 562; *S. Staffs Water Co.* v. *Sharman* [1896] 2 Q.B. 44.

Provided a lost chattel has not been abandoned, the person with the best right to possession is entitled to retain the chattel as against all, except the true owner. Thus the chimney sweep boy was entitled to the jewel he found in the chimney (*Armory* v. *Delamire* (1721) 1 Str. 505) and the customer to the lost bundle of banknotes on the floor of the shop (*Bridges* v. *Hawksworth* (1851) 21 L.J.Q.B. 15; *Hannah* v. *Peel* [1945] K.B. 509). See TROVER.

fine. (1) A sum of money ordered to be paid to the Crown by an offender, as a punishment for his offence. See the Powers of Criminal Courts Act 1973, s.30(1) and Criminal Law Act 1977, ss.289 and 61.

(2) A money payment made by a feudal tenant to his lord; *e.g.* from a copyholder to the lord of the manor on being admitted to the copyhold estate. But the incidents of copyhold tenure were abolished by the Law of Property Act 1922.

(3) A premium paid for the grant or renewal of a lease, or any foregift, payment, consideration or benefit in the nature of a premium (Law of Property Act 1925, s.205(1)(xxiii)).

(4) A judicial proceeding used for conveying land. A fictitious suit was instituted and compromised with the consent of the court, and an agreement entered into between the parties as to the disposal of the land in question. A note of the proceedings was drawn up by an officer called the chirographer, and a document, called the "chirograph" or "foot" of the fine, which recited the whole proceedings, was enrolled in the records of the court and delivered to the purchaser as a deed of title. A fine was one of the methods of barring an estate tail. It could be used by a person not in possession of the land, but it resulted in the creation of a base fee only. Fines were abolished by the Fines and Recoveries Act 1833.

fingerprints. Previous convictions may be proved by fingerprints (Criminal Justice Act 1938, s.39). Fingerprints include palm prints (Criminal Justice Act 1967, s.33).

finis finem litibus imponit. [A fine puts an end to legal proceedings.]

firearms. For definition see Firearms Act 1968, s.57(1). It is an offence to possess, purchase or acquire such a firearm without holding a firearms certificate (s.1). Shot guns require a shot gun certificate (s.2(1)). Various exemptions are specified in the Act. An honest mistake as to the true nature of a firearm does not avoid liability (*R.* v. *Howells* [1977] Q.B. 614, C.A.). See also Firearms Act 1982.

firm. Persons who have entered into partnership with one another. The name under which their business is carried on is called the firm name (Partnership Act 1890, s.4). An action may be brought by or against a firm in the name of the firm (Ord. 81, r.1). See BUSINESS NAMES.

firma. Victuals, rent, or a farm.

first fruits. Annates (*q.v.*).

first impression. A case which presents to a court of law for its decision a question of law for which there is no precedent.

fish royal. Whale, porpoise and sturgeon, which, when either thrown ashore or caught near the coast, are the property of the Sovereign. The Wild Creatures and Forest Laws Act 1971, s.1, which abolished the prerogative rights of the Sovereign to wild creatures, contains a saving for royal fish.

fishery or piscary. (1) A Royal fishery is the exclusive right of the Crown of fishing in a public river.

(2) A public or common fishery is the right of the public to fish in the sea and in public navigable rivers as far as the tide flows.

(3) A several fishery is an exclusive right of fishing in a particular water, and vested either in the owner of the soil or in someone claiming under him.

(4) Common of fishery is the right of fishing in another man's waters (*e.g.* the lord of the manor) in common with him. It is a *profit à prendre*.

(5) A free fishery is either a Royal fishery granted to a subject, or a common of fishery.

fitness for purpose (sale of goods). See IMPLIED TERMS.

fixed charge. A charge on specific property as, *e.g.* of a company, as contrasted with a floating charge (*q.v.*). See DEBENTURE.

fixtures. Anything annexed to the freehold. Whatever is so annexed, as a general rule, becomes part of the realty, and the property in it immediately vests in the owner of the soil.

Tenant's fixtures are chattels annexed to land or houses, which are removable by the tenant. They are not distrainable for rent, but they may be seized in execution. They are (1) articles either ornamental or of domestic convenience, of the nature of fittings rather than additions to the house itself, and which can be removed entire without substantial damage to the fabric; (2) trade fixtures, *i.e.* fixtures erected for the purpose of carrying on some trade, business or manufacture. They may be removed although damaging the fabric, together with covering erections. Whether a chattel has become a fixture which the tenant has no right to remove depends primarily upon the object and purposes of the annexation of the chattel to the property.

Fixtures affixed to an agricultural holding by a tenant not under an obligation, and for which no compensation is received, may be removed, subject to conditions. See Agricultural Holdings Act 1948, s.13.

Fixtures are capable of being stolen (Theft Act 1968, s.4).

flagrante delicto. [In the commission of the offence.] Provocation due to the sight by a husband of his wife in the act of adultery may reduce murder to manslaughter.

Fleet Registers. Records of marriages clandestinely celebrated in the Fleet Prison (abolished in 1842) and inadmissible in evidence.

Fleta. A commentary on the laws of England of Edward I.

floating charge or security. An equitable charge on the assets for the time being of a going concern. It attaches to the subject charged in the varying condition it happens to be in from time to time. It is the essence of such a charge that it remains dormant until the undertaking charged ceases to be a going concern, or until the person in whose favour the charge is created intervenes.

Debentures issued by a company are often secured by a floating charge on the property, present and future, of the company. A floating charge becomes a specific charge when a receiver is appointed, or possession is taken of any property comprised in the charge, or a winding up commences. It is then said to "crystalise" and preferential debts thereupon become payable (Companies Act 1948, s.94).

floor of the court. That part between the judge's bench and the front row of counsel.

flotsam. Goods lost by shipwreck of cast overboard which remain afloat. If unclaimed they belong to the Crown. They are "wreck" under the Merchant Shipping Acts.

foenus nauticum. [Roman law.] The interest charged for money secured by what corresponded to out bottomry bond.

folcland; folkland. Land held of the King without written title under customary law. (Anglo-Saxon).

folcland; folkland. Land held of the King without written title under customary law the *witenagemot*, for either judicial or legislative purposes.

folcright; folkright. The laws of England in later Anglo-saxon times; the basis of the common law.

foldage. The right of the lord of the manor of having his tenant's sheep to feed on his fields, so as to manure the land, in return for which the lord provides a fold for the sheep.

foldcourse. The right of the lord of the manor of feeding a certain number of sheep on the lands of the tenant during certain times of the year.

folio. In the Rules of the Supreme Court a folio means 72 words (Ord. 1 r.4). The cost of preparing documents and copies in the Supreme Court is now generally based on the size of paper instead of the old number of folios (Ord. 62, App. 2 items 3, 4). Similar rules apply in the county court (C.C.R., App. B, items 3, 4).

foot of a fine. See FINE.

forcible detainer. The misdemeanor committed by a person who, having wrongfully entered upon any land or tenements, detained them with violence or threats. Abolished by Criminal Law Act 1977, s.13(2) and replaced by new offences of entering and remaining on property (ss. 6–10).

forcible entry. Entering land in a violent manner in order to take possession thereof was a crime from 1381. The Criminal Law Act 1977, s.13(1) abolished the common law offence. Section 6 of the Act substitutes new offences.

foreclosure. When a mortgagor has failed to pay off the mortgage debt within the proper time, the mortgagee is entitled to bring an action in the Chancery Division by writ or originating summons asking that a day may be fixed on which the mortgagor is to pay off the debt, and that in default of payment on that day the mortgagor may be foreclosed of his equity of redemption (*q.v.*). The court may make an order for foreclosure nisi (*q.v.*) for payment of the principal with interest and costs, usually within six months, failing which an order absolute will be made, the land thereupon becoming the property of the mortgagee. By section 88(2) of the Law of Property Act 1925, an order absolute vests the legal estate in the mortgagee. The county court has jursidiction in actions up to £30,000 (County Courts Act 1959, s.52).

foreign. Outside the jurisdiction. Thus a "foreign plea" was a plea to the jurisdiction of the court.

foreign attachment. A process whereby a defendant was compelled to appear in the Mayor's Court of the City of London, by attaching property of the debtor in the hands of a third party within the jurisdiction of the court, known as the garnishee. Now obsolete.

foreign currency. Any currency other than sterling. The use of foreign currency in High Court litigation is permitted when justified (*Miliangus* v. *George Frank (Textiles Ltd.)* [1976] A.C. 443, H.L.; *Practice Directions* [1976] 1 W.L.R. 83 and [1977] 1 W.L.R. 197).

Foreign Enlistment Act 1870. The Act making it an offence for any British subject, without the licence of the Crown, to serve in the military or naval service of any foreign State at war with any State which is at peace with England, or to build or equip any ship for the service of any such State, etc.

foreign judgments. May in general be sued on in the English courts. They may also be registered in the High Court (Foreign Judgments (Reciprocal Enforcement) Act 1933; R.S.C. Ord. 71). See also Protection of Trading Interests Act 1980.

foreign jurisdiction. The jurisdiction of a State with regard to its subjects when they are, or the acts done by them are, outside its boundaries. See the Foreign Jurisdiction Acts 1890, 1913.

foreign law is treated as a question of fact to be proved by experts (see the Civil Evidence Act 1972, s.4) but is determinable by the judge and not by the jury (Administration of Justice Act 1920, s.15; Judicature Act 1925, s.102; County Courts Act 1959, s.97).

foreign revenue. The courts of this country will not enforce the revenue laws of foreign Sovereign States.

foreman. The member of a jury who acts as spokesman.

forensic medicine. Medical jurisprudence: "that science which teaches the application of every branch of medical knowledge to the purposes of the law" (Taylor).

foreseeability. "You must take reasonable care to avoid acts or omissions which you can reasonably foresee would injure your neighbour—persons who are so closely and directly affected by my act that I ought reasonably to have them in contemplation as being so affected when I am directing my mind to the acts or omissions which are called in question" (*per* Lord Atkin, *Donoghue* v. *Stevenson* [1932] A.C. 562 at p.579). The test of "reasonable foreseeability" is applied in determining liability in tort, and contract and in murder. See also *The Wagon Mound* [1961] A.C. 388, P.C. and *Hedley Byrne & Co. Ltd.* v. *Heller & Partners Ltd.* [1964] A.C. 465, H.L. See NERVOUS SHOCK; FINANCIAL LOSS.

foreshore. That part of the land adjacent to the sea and which is alternately covered and left dry by the ordinary flow of the tides. The property in the foreshore is prima facie vested in the Crown. Management of the foreshore is in the hands of the Crown Estate Commissioners.

forest. Formerly the exclusive right of keeping and hunting wild beasts and fowls of forest, chase, park, and warren in a certain territory, with laws and officers of its own for the protection of the game. Now, primarily, forests are where timber is grown. National forests are maintained by the Forestry Commissioners. See the Forestry Act 1967, as amended. See also PARK.

forestall. To obstruct a person's way with force and arms; also to raise the price of certain goods by holding up supplies, etc.

forfeiture. The deprivation of a person of his property as a penalty for some act or omission. Formerly, prior to the Forfeiture Act 1870, the goods and chattels of a person convicted of felony were forfeited to the Crown. A dealing with his estate by a feudal tenant in derogation of the right of his lord; *e.g.* a feoffment by a tenant for life, was a ground of forfeiture; the denial of the landlord's title is so still. A forfeiture clause in a lease provides that on the breach of certain covenants the lease shall be at an end and the lessor may re-enter. Equity relieved against forfeitures designed to secure the performance of some collateral act; *e.g.* the payment of rent, when the court could give by way of compensation all that was required.

A lessor cannot enforce a proviso for forfeiture and re-entry unless he serves on the lessee a notice specifying the breach and requiring its remedy, and requiring compensation in money. Breach of a covenant not to deal with or dispose of the land leased formerly operated as a forfeiture, but now the tenant may apply to the court for relief (Law of Property Act 1925, s.146).

Forfeiture of things used to commit a crime may be ordered by the court (Powers of Criminal Courts Act 1973, s.43). See also Forfeiture Act 1982.

forgavel. A quit rent.

forgery. There is now a single new offence of Forgery, defined as the making of a false instrument with the intention that it should be accepted as genuine to the prejudice of another person (Forgery and Counterfeiting Act 1981, s.1). It is an offence to use a false instrument which a person knows or believes to be such (s.3) or a copy thereof (s.4). It is an offence to make, pass or possess counterfeit notes or coins (ss.14–17). The 1981 Act sets out the maximum penalties and makes other provisions, *e.g.* as to powers of search.

forinsecus. [Outside.]

forisfamiliation. Where a son had a portion of his father's estate given to him during his father's lifetime, he was said to be "portioned off."

forjudge. To deprive a person of a thing or right by a judgment.

forma pauperis. See IN FORMA PAUPERIS.

formedon. Writs brought by persons who claimed land under a gift in tail when it was in the possession of a person not entitled to it. Abolished by the Real Property Limitation Act 1833.

forms of action. See ACTION.

formulae. [Roman law.] The Praetorian procedure which superseded the *legis actiones*, under which the Praetor allowed the parties to a dispute to put in writing the issue to be decided by the arbitrators, and then, if the resulting *formula* met with his approval, he authorised the arbitrators to condemn or acquit the defendant according to his discretion. A *formula* was a hypothetical command to a *judex*, to condemn the defendant to pay a sum of money to the plaintiff, if the latter established a right or proved an allegation of fact.

fornication. Voluntary sexual intercourse between man and woman outside the bounds of matrimony. As such, it is not an offence. See ADULTERY.

forthwith. As soon as reasonably can be (*Hillingdon London Borough Council* v. *Cutler* [1968] 1 Q.B. 124).

fortuna. Treasure trove (*q.v.*).

forum. [A place.] A place where disputes may be tried; a court. It is now used as referring to the particular court or courts having jurisdiction in a matter. See LEX FORI.

forum rei. The court of the country in which the thing or person, the subject of an action, is situated.

foster children. See Children Act 1975, ss.95–97 and Foster Children Act 1980.

founders shares. Deferred shares which did not receive a dividend until the preference and ordinary shares had been paid a dividend at a specified rate, but which were entitled to the whole or a substantial part of the balance of the distributable profits. See DEFERRED SHARES.

four corners. Within the four corners of a document, etc., means contained exclusively within the document, etc., itself.

four seas. Within the four seas, meant within the United Kingdom.

Four-day Order. An order for delivery of accounts or answers to inquiries under Ord. 42, r.2.

fourteen day costs. The fixed sum for costs indorsed on a writ claiming a debt or liquidated sum as payable if the sum is paid within fourteen days (see R.S.C., Ord. 6 r.2(1)(*b*)).

fractionem diei non recipit lex. [The law does not recognise any fraction of a day.]

franchise. (1) A liberty or privilege. At common law, a franchise is a royal privilege or branch of the Crown's prerogative, subsisting in the hands of a subject, either by grant or by prescription. It is an incorporeal hereditament. It not only authorises something to be done, but gives the owner the right of preventing others from interfering. Examples are the right to hold a market or maintain a ferry.

(2) The right to elect a Member of Parliament.

frankalmoign. [Free alms.] The free tenures originating in Saxon times, by which church lands were sometimes held, but ecclesiastics often held by military service. It involved no services except praying for the soul of the donor. It is now, in effect, socage tenure.

frank-fee. Freehold land.

frankmarriage (freemarriage). A dowry or gift free from services to a woman about to marry. Land given in frankmarriage created an estate in tail special if it was given to a husband and wife by some blood relation of the wife. It was held by the husband and wife to them and their issue to the fourth degree free of services to the donor.

frankpledge. The system of preserving the peace in force at the time of the Conquest by the compulsory association of men into groups of ten, each member of which was a surety for the others. The "view of frankpledge" was the duty of seeing that these associations were kept in perfect order and number, and was vested in the local courts, especially the Courts Leet. See HEADBOROUGH.

frank-tenement. Freehold.

fraud. In general, fraud is obtaining of a material advantage by unfair or wrongful means; it involves moral obliquity. It must be proved to sustain the common law action of deceit. Fraud is proved when it is shown that a false representation has been made (1) knowingly, or (2) without belief in its truth, or (3) recklessly, careless whether it be true or false. To obtain damages for deceit it must be proved that the defendant intended that the plaintiff should act on the fraudulent misrepresentation, that he did act on it, and suffered damage in consequence. Fraud renders a contract voidable at the option of the injured party. See CONSTRUCTIVE FRAUD.

Certain frauds amount to offences. See the Theft Act 1968, ss.15, 17, 20; the Theft Act 1978, s.1 (see DECEPTION); the Prevention of Fraud (Investments) Act 1958; The Banking Act 1979, ss.1–33, 39; Insurance Companies Act 1974, ss.63, 69.

fraud on a power. The failure to exercise a special power of appointment bona fide to the end intended by the donor. For example, a father having power to appoint an estate to any of his children, appoints it to one on the point of death, he being the child's heir. A fraudulent exercise of an equitable power (*i.e.* not operating to pass the legal estate) is void; a fraudulent exercise of a legal power (*i.e.* one operating to pass the legal estate) is voidable only. Where an appointment is made in favour of a person at least 25 years of age, who is entitled to a share in default of appointment, a purchaser for value without notice of fraud is protected to the extent of that share (Law of Property Act 1925, s.157). See APPOINTMENT, POWER OF.

Frauds, Statute of. See STATUTE OF FRAUDS.

fraudulent conversion. This was a separate offence under the Larceny Act 1916, s.20. It is now included in the offence of theft of which the kernel is dishonest appropriation (Theft Act 1968, s.1).

fraudulent conveyance. Under the Law of Property Act 1925, ss.172, 173 (replacing earlier legislation) every voluntary disposition of land made with intent to defraud a subsequent purchaser is voidable at the instance of that purchaser.

By the Bankruptcy Act 1914, s.1 a fraudulent conveyance, gift, delivery or transfer by a debtor of his property or any part thereof, is an act of bankruptcy.

fraudulent preference. Any payment, conveyance or other advantage given by a debtor to a creditor within six months prior to his bankruptcy, with a view of giving that creditor a preference over the other creditors, is void as against the trustee in bankruptcy (Bankruptcy Act 1914, s.44; Companies Act 1947, s.115(3)).

The same rule to insolvent companies (Companies Act 1948, ss.320, 321).

fraus omnia vitiat. [Fraud vitiates everything.]

free entry. A customs entry for free (*i.e.* non-dutiable) goods.

freebench. An estate analogous to dower, which, by the custom of most manors, the widow of a copyholder had in the land of which her husband was tenant. Freebench was abolished by the Law of Property Act 1922; and the Administration of Estates Act 1925, s.45.

freehold tenure. Under the feudal system land was held by military tenure and socage tenure, which were freehold tenures, being held in return for services which a free man might not think derogatory to perform. In 1660, military tenure was abolished and the land became socage tenure.

There were three estates of freehold: fee simple, fee tail and life estate, and terms of years, or leaseholds (*q.v.*).

freeman. One who possesses the freedom of a borough or city and the accompanying rights and privileges. The rights of freemen of a borough were preserved by the Local Government Act 1972, s.248. Honorary freedom is betowed on persons of distinction as an honour (s.249; S.I. 1974 No. 482, art. 18).

freight. The reward payable to a carrier by sea for the safe carriage and delivery of goods. If the ship is lost or abandoned so that there is no delivery there is no freight, except that freight payable in advance is not then recoverable. The shipowner has a lien on the goods carried for unpaid freight. See DEAD FREIGHT.

fresh disseisin. That disseisin (*q.v.*) which formerly a person might seek to defeat himself by his own power, as where it was not above, *e.g.* 15 days old.

fresh suit. [Pursuit.] The following of a thing or person at once with the intention of reclamation.

friendly societies. Societies established to provide by the voluntary subscriptions of their members, for the relief or maintenance of the members and their families during sickness or old age, and their widows and orphan children. They should be registered under the Friendly Societies Act 1974.

friendly suit. A suit brought between parties by mutual arrangement in order to obtain a decision upon some point in which both are interested.

frith. The peace; a tract of common land.

frithsoken. The right to take the view of frankpledge (*q.v.*).

from. Subject to the context, it ordinarily excludes the day from which time is to be reckoned (*Cartwright* v. *Cormack* [1963] 1 W.L.R. 18). See Ord.3, r.2(2).

frontager. A person owning or occupying land which abuts on a highway, river, or seashore.

fructus industriales. [Fruits of industry.] Crops or produce of the soil which are the result of labour in sowing the seed or in cultivation, such as corn, potatoes, etc. In a sale of *fructus industriales*, on the terms that the owner of the soil is to cut or sever them from the land before delivery, the purchaser acquires no interest in the land, which is like a mere warehouse. See EMBLEMENTS.

fructus naturales. [Fruits of nature.] Crops or produce of the soil which grow naturally like, grass, timber, etc. A contract for the sale of growing grass to be cut by the purchaser later is an agreement relating to an interest in land, and must be in writing; it is otherwise where the seller is to cut.

frustra legis auxilium quaerit qui in legem committit. [He who offends against the law vainly seeks the help of the law.]

frustration. The discharge of a contract rendered impossible of performance by external causes beyond the contemplation of the parties. For example, a contract postponed by Government order would be discharged if the interference was so gross that when the time did arrive to resume work the parties would find themselves in completely different circumstances (*Metropolitan Water Board* v. *Dick Kerr* [1917] 2 K.B. 1). Money paid under a contract which is later frustrated and discharged may be recoverable as in quasi-contract (*The Fibrosa Case* [1943] A.C. 32).

The Law Reform (Frustrated Contracts) Act 1943 provided that where a contract governed by English law becomes impossible of performance or "frustrated" and the parties thereto are discharged from its further performance, all sums paid to any party in pursuance of the contract before the time of discharge are recoverable as money had and received by him for the use of the party by whom the sums were paid. If the sums are unpaid they cease to be payable. But if the party to whom the sums were paid or payable has incurred expenses in or for the purpose of the performance of the contract, the court may allow him to retain or recover (as the case may be) the whole or part of such sums. Also where a party by reason of anything done by another party in or for the purpose of the performance of the contract has obtained a valuable benefit other than money, that other party may recover such sum as the court considers just.

This Act, however, does not apply to any contract to which section 7 of the Sale of Goods Act 1979 applies. This section provides that where there is an agreement to sell specific goods, and subsequently the goods, without any fault on the part of the seller or buyer, perish before the risk passes to the buyer, the agreement is thereby avoided. See also *BP Exploration Co. (Libya) Ltd.* v. *Hunt* [1982] 1 All E.R. 925, H.L.

fugam fecit. [He has made flight.]

full age. A person now attains full age the first moment of his or her 18th birthday (Family Law Reform Act 1969, ss.1, 2). A person who is not of full age may be described as a minor (s.12).

functus officio. [Having discharged his duty.] Thus once a magistrate has convicted a person charged with an offence before him, he is *functus officio*, and cannot rescind the sentence and re-try the case.

fundus cum instrumento. [Roman law.] A farm with its stock and implements of culture including everything on a farm placed there for the purpose of its cultivation and necessary for the cultivation.

fundus instructus. [Roman law.] A farm with furnishings, as well as stock and implements.

further assurance. See COVENANTS FOR TITLE.

furtum conceptum. [Roman law.] Where in a man's house before witnesses something that has been stolen is sought and found. An *actio concepti* lies against the occupier.

furtum oblatum. [Roman law.] Where something that has been stolen is brought to a man's house with the intention that it shall be found there and is so found on formal search in his house. The occupier has an *actio oblati* against the bringer.

155

future estates. Estates limited to come into existence at some future time: contingent remainders, executory interests and future interests in trusts. Since 1925 they exist only as equitable interests.

future property. Property which will be caught by, or subject to, a covenant presently made when it comes into possession at a future date; *e.g.* a covenant to settle after-required property on the trusts of a marriage settlement.

G

gage. A pledge or pawn. See MORTGAGE.

gager de deliverance. To give surety for the delivery of the goods which were in dispute in the action of replevin.

gale. Gavel (*q.v.*).

gambling policies. A person who effects a contract of marine insurance without having a bona fide interest therein commits an offence under the Marine Insurance (Gambling Policies) Act 1909, s.1. See P.P.I.

game. Wild animals, the hunting or taking of which is a sport. In the Game Laws, game consists of hares, pheasants, partridges, grouse, heath or moor game, black-game and bustards. The right to kill game upon any land is vested in the occupier, unless he holds it under a lease or agreement by which the right is reserved to the landlord. But every person killing or taking game, with the exception of ground game (which includes hares and rabbits), is required to take out a yearly excise licence. It is obtainable at a post office (Post Office Act 1969, ss.12, 134, 135).

The Game Laws (Amendment) Act 1960 gives power to the police to arrest persons trespassing in pursuit of game. See POACHING.

gaming. To play at any game of chance, whether lawful or unlawful, for stakes hazarded by the players in money or money's worth. To amount to gaming, the game played must involve the element of wagering, *i.e.* each of the players must have a chance of losing as well as of winning. By the Betting, Gaming and Lotteries Act 1963, s.55(1), and the Gaming Act 1968, s.52(1), "gaming" means the playing of a game of chance for winnings in money or money's worth, and a "game of chance" includes a game of chance and skill combined, but does not include any athletic game or sport.

The Gaming Act 1968 allows commercial gaming to take place under control by licence, registration and permit. Gaming is lawful only in relation to the premises where it is carried on. The only games which are lawful (except on domestic occasions) are games like bridge, whist, piquet, cribbage, bezique, poker or dominoes. Credit for gaming is prohibited. Persons under 18 are debarred from gaming rooms. Gaming on Sundays is restricted. Street gaming is prohibited. Gaming at entertainments not held for private gain ay be lawful. Advertising is restricted. Gaming by means of machines is regulated. Excise licences are chargeable under the Betting and Gaming Duties Act 1972; Finance (No. 2) Act 1975, s.2. Bingo is subject to bingo duty. Gaming on licensed premises is restricted. See LOTTERY.

At common law money won at any game could be recovered by action. By the Gaming Act 1845 all contracts by way of gaming or wagering are void; and money so lost or won cannot be recovered. By the Gaming Act 1892 it was enacted that a person cannot recover commission etc. promised to him for making or paying bets, nor money paid in discharge of the bets of another, but a person employed to make bets on behalf of another cannot retain any winnings. Money or valuables lent for the purpose of gaming or betting are not recoverable. Negotiable instruments given in payment of money so lost are given for an illegal consideration (Gaming Act 1835, s.1) and cannot be sued on, except by a bona fide holder for value. See WAGER. See also the Betting, Gaming and Lotteries (Amendment) Act 1980.

gaming house. Keeping a common gaming house was a common law misdemeanour. Gaming houses are now regulated under the Gaming Act 1968.

gaol delivery. One of the commissions given to the judges or commissioners of assize. It authorised them to try, and (if acquitted) to deliver from custody, every prisoner who should be in gaol for some alleged crime when they arrived at the circuit town. References to a court of gaol delivery are to be construed as references to the Crown Court (Courts Act 1971, Sched. 8).

garnish. (1) to warn. (2) To exact money from prisoners.

garnishee. A debtor in whose hands a debt has been attached, *i.e.* he is warned not to pay his debt to anyone other than the third party who has obtained judgment against the debtor's own creditor. A garnishee order is the order served on a garnishee attaching a debt in his hands (Ord. 49). See ATTACHMENT.

garrotting. Choking, in order to rob. etc.

Garter, Order of. The most distinguished order of knighthood (K.G.).

garth. An enclosure; a yard; a weir or dam.

gavel. Payment of tribute to a superior; rent.

gavelkind. A variety of customary land tenure in Kent. Its principal incidents were (a) the land descended on intestacy to all the sons of the tenant equally; (b) the right of the widow or widower of a deceased tenant to have half the land for dower or curtesy until a second marriage, the widower taking by the curtesy whether issue had been born of the marriage or not; (c) the right of an infant tenant to alien his land by feoffment at the age of 15 years; (d) non-liability to forfeiture on conviction for murder. Gavelkind was abolished by the Law of Property Act 1922 and Administration of Estates Act 1925, s.45.

Gazette. *The London Gazette* is the official organ of the Government for intimating appointments to public offices, and publishing Royal Proclamations, Orders in Council, statutory rules and orders, dissolutions of partnerships, proceedings in bankruptcy, etc. It is admissible in evidence for many purposes.

geld. A tax, payment, tribute or a pecuniary penalty.

gemote; moot. [Anglo-Saxon.] A meeting or assembly.

general average. See AVERAGE.

General Commissioners of Income Tax. Their function is the hearing of appeals against assessments made by the Inspector of Taxes in their Division. They are appointed in England by the Lord Chancellor (Taxes Management Act 1970, s.2).

General Council of the Bar. See SENATE OF THE INNS OF COURT AND THE BAR.

general damages. That kind of damage which the law presumes to follow from the wrong complained of, and which therefore need not be set out in the plaintiff's pleadings. For example, in cases of personal injury resulting from a negligent act, general damages may be recovered for pain and suffering, injury to health and personal inconvenience. See SPECIAL DAMAGES; MEASURE OF DAMAGES.

general issue. See ISSUE.

General Medical Council. The statutory body which registers doctors, and exercises professional discipline over them, the penalty which may be imposed being the removal of the name of a doctor from the Register. In so doing the requirements of natural justice (*q.v.*) ought to be strictly observed. See Medical Acts 1950 and 1969.

157

general sessions. The court of record held by two or more justices of the peace for the trial of offenders, *e.g.* quarter sessions. Courts of quarter sessions were abolished by the Courts Act 1971, s.3.

general ship. A ship which carries the goods of merchants generally under bills of lading, as opposed to a chartered ship which is let to particular persons only under a charterparty.

general warrant. A warrant issued by the Secretary of State for the arrest of such persons as were, for instance, the authors of a seditious libel. No persons were named in such a warrant. In 1765 they were held to be illegal.

general words. Descriptive words added to the parcels clause in a conveyance, to transfer all the rights in the property of the grantor; now rendered unnecessary by the Conveyancing Act 1881, re-enacted with a variation by Law of Property Act 1925, s.62.

generale tantum valet in generalibus quantum singulare in singulis. [When words are general they are to be taken in a general sense, just as words relating to a particular thing are to be taken as referring only to that thing.]

generalia specialibus non derogant. [General things do not derogate from special things.]

generalibus specialia derogant. [Special things derogate from general things.]

Geneva Convention. An international agreement entered into at Geneva in 1864 for the purpose of ameliorating the condition of sick and wounded soldiers in war. It was superseded by the Geneva Convention of 1906. It is under these conventions that the "Red Cross" has been used. See also the Geneva Conventions Act 1957; HAGUE CONVENTIONS.

gestation. The time which elapses between the conception and birth of a child. It is usually about nine months of 30 days each. The time is added, where necessary, to the period allowed under the rule against perpetuities.

gift. A gratuitous grant or transfer of property. For a valid gift there must be an intention to give and such acts as are necessary to give effect to the intention, either by manual delivery of the chattels, or of some token part of the subject-matter, or by such change in possession as would vest possession in the intended donee. It may be made by deed. Equity will not construe an imperfect gift as a declaration of trust (*Richards* v. *Delbridge* (1874) L.R. 18 Eq. 11). See DONATIO MORTIS CAUSA.

Gifts are liable to capital gains tax (*q.v.*) and capital transfer tax (*q.v.*). See BREACH OF PROMISE.

gilda mercatoria. A guild merchant. The association of merchants of a town with the royal grant of the exclusive right of trading and of levying tolls on "foreign" traders.

gilds. Voluntary associations in towns in medieval England for religious and benevolent, or economic purposes. The chief were the Craft and Merchant Gilds. Survivors today are the City Companies.

glebae ascriptitii. Villeins who could not be removed from their holdings provided they performed the prescribed service. See VILLEIN.

glebe. Land attached to a benefice as part of its endowment. By the Endowments and Glebe Measure 1976, s.15 Glebe Land has vested in the Diocesan Boards of Finance.

God's Penny. Earnest (*q.v.*).

going through the Bar. The old practice of the judge of asking, in order of seniority, each barrister who was in court whether he had anything to move.

good behaviour. A person charged with an offence may be ordered to find sureties for good behaviour. A sum is forfeited to the Crown unless such a person is of good behaviour for a certain period. See BIND OVER.

good leasehold title. A title which is approved by the Land Registrar merely as to the leasehold interest, and without prejudice to any estate or interest affecting or in derogation of the title of the lessor to grant the lease (Land Registration Act 1925, ss.8(1), (10)).

goods. All chattels personal other than things in action and money, emblements and things attached to or forming part of the land which are agreed to be severed before sale or under the contract of sale (Sale of Goods Act 1979, s.61).

goodwill. The benefit of advantage which is a business has in its connection with its customers. It is based on the probability that old customers will continue to resort to the old place of business, or continue to deal with the firm of the same name. Goodwill is an asset of a business, and on the sale of a business with goodwill, the purchaser usually obtains the premises and the right to use the name of the old firm, and the right to represent himself as the successor of the old firm. The vendor of a business may be restrained from soliciting his former customer (*Trego* v. *Hunt* [1896] A.C. 7).

Governor, Colonial. The representative of the Crown at the head of the executive of a British colony. His authority is expressly limited to the terms of his commission. He can be sued in his own courts or the High Court for acts committed while in office, but he cannot be held liable for Act of State done within the scope of his authority.

Governor-General. The representative of the Crown at the head of the government of a Commonwealth country. He is a representative of the Crown holding in all essential respects the śame position in relation to the administration of public affairs as is held by Her Majesty in the United Kingdom. He is appointed by the Sovereign on the advice of the country concerned, *e.g.* Canada, Australia, New Zealand.

grace. See ACT OF GRACE; DAYS OF GRACE.

Grand Coustumier du Pays et Duché de Normandie. A collection of the ancient laws and customs of Normandy, the basis of the laws of the Channel Islands.

grand jury. The grand jury was set up by the Assize of Clarendon to present offenders from the neighbourhood and consisted of 12 to 23 persons. Before September 1933 it was summoned at assizes to consider bills of indictment (*q.v.*). By the Administration of Justice Act 1933 grand juries were abolished with some exceptions in respect of London and Middlesex. They were finally abolished by the Criminal Justice Act 1948, s.31(3).

grand serjeanty. A variety of land tenure resembling knight's service, where certain honorary services were rendered to the person of the King, such as carrying his banner or acting as his marshal. These incidents were retained when knight's service were abolished in 1660, and are preserved by the Law of Property Act 1922, s. 136.

grant. (1) The assurance or transfer of the ownership of property, as distinguished from the delivery or transfer of the property itself. A conveyance is a deed of grant. It was the appropriate word for the conveyance of incorporeal hereditaments incapable of livery of seisin. By the Real Property Act 1845 all corporeal hereditaments were deemed to lie in grant as well as in livery. By the Conveyancing Act 1881 the use of the word "grant" was rendered unnecessary, and by the Law of Property Act 1925, s.51, all land lies in grant and is rendered incapable of being conveyed by livery, (*i.e.* delivery).

(2) The allocation of rights, powers, moneys, etc. by the Crown or other authority, to particular persons or for particular purposes.

gratis dictum. [Mere assertion.]

Gray's Inn. One of the Inns of Court (*q.v.*).

Great Council. The *Magnum Concilium*. The assembly of the lords of the kingdom after the Conquest, in place of the Anglo-Saxon Witenagemot, from which developed the House of Lords.

Great Seal. By the Union with Scotland Act 1706 it is provided that there shall be one Great Seal for the United Kingdom, to be used for sealing writs to elect and summon the Parliament, and for sealing all treaties with foreign States, and all public Acts, instruments and orders of State which concern the whole United Kingdom, and in all other matters relating to England, as the Great Seal of England was used before the union. It is in the custody of the Lord Chancellor.

greater hardship. A tenant against whom a landlord brings possession proceedings under Sched. 15, case 9 to the Rent Act 1977, (*i.e.* on the ground that the premises are reasonably required for occupation by the landlord or certain members of his family) may defend such proceedings on the ground that greater hardship would be caused by granting the order for possession than by refusing to grant it (Rent Act 1977, Sched. 15, Pt. III, para. 1).

Greater London Council. See the Local Government Act 1972, s.8, Sched. 2.

green book. The County Court Practice.

Gretna Green. After Lord Hardwicke's Act it was impossible to contract a valid marriage in England without either banns or special licence; but in Scotland it continued to be the law that consent of the parties in the presence of witnesses was sufficient to constitute a valid marriage. Elopements were made to Gretna Green, where the village blacksmith read the English marriage service, and the consent of the parties was expressed by their concurrence in this quasi-ceremony.

But the Marriage (Scotland) Act 1856, s.1 provided that no irregular marriage contracted in Scotland after December 31, 1856, should be valid unless at least one of the parties usually resided or had for the 21 preceding days been in Scotland. See MARRIAGE.

gross indecency. See INDECENCY.

ground rent. See RENT; RENTCHARGE.

groundage. Harbour dues.

guarantee. The person to whom a guarantee is given.

A collateral promise to answer for the debt, default or miscarriage of another, as distinguished from an original and direct contract for the promisor's own act. By the Statute of Frauds, s.4 every guaranty must be in writing, but the consideration need not be stated (Mercantile Law Amendment Act 1856, s.3).

The memorandum of a company limited by guarantee must state that each member undertakes to contribute a specified sum towards the assets of the company in the event of a winding up while he is a member, or within one year after. Such companies are usually formed not for profit but to incorporate clubs or associations.

guarantee payment. The right to a guarantee payment under section 12 of the Employment Protection (Consolidation) Act 1978 arises where an employee is laid off and the employer is obliged to make payments. It does not arise where the failure to provide work is in consequence of a trade dispute (s.13(1)). For the detailed provisions see ss.12–17.

guarantor. The person who binds himself by a guarantee; one who promises to answer for another; a surety (*q.v.*).

guardian. A person having the right and duty of protecting the person, property or rights of one who is without full legal capacity or otherwise incapable of managing his own affairs.

(1) Guardianship in chivalry was the right of the lord to hold the land of an infant tenant until majority.

(2) Guardianship in socage was the right of the next of blood to whom the inheritance could not descend, to the wardship of the land while the heir was under the age of 14.

(3) Guardianship by nature was that exercised by a father over the person of his son and heir apparent.

(4) A guardian by election is one chosen by a minor himself.

(5) A guardian by statute is one appointed by will pursuant to the statute 12 Car. 2, c. 24.

(6) A guardian *ad litem* is a person appointed to defend an action or other proceeding on behalf of a minor or person under a disability (Ord. 80, rr. 2, 3, 6).

The statute law relating to the guardianship of minors has been consolidated by the Guardianship of Minors Act 1971, as amended by the Guardianship Act 1973, a minor being a person who has not attained the age of 18 years (Family Law Reform Act 1969, s.1). Either the father or mother of a minor may, by deed or will, appoint a person to be guardian of the minor after his or her death, to act jointly with the surviving parent (Act of 1971, ss.4, 10, 12). Where there are no parents, a guardian may be appointed by the court (ss.5, 6). A guardian is also the guardian of the minor's estate (Act of 1973, s.7). Father and mother have equal rights of custody of the minor (Act of 1973, s.1). In any proceedings where the custody or upbringing of a minor is in question, the welfare of the minor is the paramount consideration (Act of 1971, s.1; Act of 1973, Sched. 3). On the death of a parent the surviving parent becomes the guardian of a minor either alone or jointly with the guardian appointed by the deceased parent (Act of 1971, s.3). Persons suffering from mental disorder may be placed under the care of a guardian (Mental Health Act 1959, ss.33–35; Local Government Act 1972, Sched. 23, para. 9).

A guardian in tort is one who intrudes on a minor's property and is accountable for profits received.

guardians of the poor. The authority formerly charged with the administration of the Poor Laws. Board of Guardians were abolished by the Local Government Act 1929.

The National Assistance Act 1948 terminated the existing poor law and provided in lieu for the assistance of persons in need by the National Assistance Board and by local authorities.

guillotine. An elaboration of the "Closure" in parliamentary procedure. Definite periods are allotted to the successive stages of a Bill, and at the end of each period the "gullotine" falls and closes the debate in respect of that stage.

guilty. In criminal law, the confession by a person charged with a crime as having committed it, or the finding by a jury after an accused person's trial, that he committed the crime with which he is charged.

H

habeas corpora juratorum. A writ upon which trial of causes at *nisi prius* was had in the Court of Common Pleas. It commanded the sheriff to have before the court at Westminster, or before the judges of assize and *nisi prius*, the bodies of the jurors named in the panel to the writ as having been summoned to make a jury for the trial. It was abolished by the Common Law Procedure Act 1852.

habeas corpus. A prerogative writ directed to a person who detains another in custody and commands him to produce or "have the body" of that person before the court.

(1) *Habeas corpus ad subjiciendum* commands the person to whom it is directed to produce the body of the person detained with the day and cause of his caption and detention, *ad faciendum, subjiciendum et recipiendum* [to do, submit to and receive] whatever the court shall direct. Its use is for testing the legality of an imprisonment.

The Habeas Corpus Act 1679 made the granting of a *habeas corpus* compulsory in the case of a person imprisoned without legal cause being assigned in the warrant of committal, and provided for the speedy trial of persons imprisoned for treason or felony. The Habeas Corpus Act 1816 provided for the issue and return of a *habeas corpus*. The Habeas Corpus Act 1862 enacts that no *habeas corpus* shall issue out of England into any colony or foreign dominion of the Crown where there is a court having authority to issue the writ; subject to this limitation, the writ of *habeas corpus* runs into all parts of the dominions of the Crown.

Application for the writ is made to a Divisional Court of the Queen's Bench Division, or, if no such court is sitting, to a single judge in court. In vacation or when no judge is sitting in court the application may be made to a judge anywhere he can be found. An application on behalf of a minor must be made in the first instance to a judge otherwise than in court (Ord. 54, r. 1).

The Administration of Justice Act 1960, s.14, provided that on a criminal application for *habeas corpus* (which includes applications in respect of persons detained under Mental Health Act 1959, Part V), an order for release of the person restrained may be refused only by the Divisional Court, whether the application is made in the first instance to that court or to a single judge; no second application in respect of the same person on the same grounds can be brought except on fresh evidence. *Ibid.* s.15 provides for an appeal in all *habeas corpus* proceedings.

(2) See also Ord. 54, r. 9 (*habeas corpus ad testificandum* and *habeas corpus ad respondendum*). The writ of *habeas corpus ad satisfaciendum* and *habeas corpus cum causa* (or *ad faciendum et recipiendum*) are obsolete.

habendum. The clause in a conveyance which indicates the estate to be taken by the grantee. Formerly it commenced "To have (*habendum*) and to hold (*tenendum*)."

habere facias possessionem. [That you cause to have possession.] The writ by which the claimant in the old action of ejectment obtained possession of land.

habere facias seisinam. [That you cause to have seisin.] A writ which was formerly addressed to the sheriff requiring him to give seisin of a freehold estate recovered in an action.

habere facias visum. [That you cause to have the view.] A writ which formerly issued in real actions where it was necessary that a view should be had for lands.

habitual criminal. See PERSISTENT OFFENDERS.

haeres legitimus est quem nuptiae demonstrant. [The lawful heir is he whom wedlock shows so to be.]

Hague Conventions. The agreements signed by the Powers in conference at The Hague as to rules of public international law, in 1899, 1904 and 1907. The various treaties on the subject of narcotic drugs were consolidated in 1961. See the Misuse of Drugs Act 1971.

half blood. See BLOOD.

Hallamshire. The Sheffield Division of the county of York was created a separate county by the name of Hallamshire by the Criminal Justice Administration Act 1962, s.3, Sched. 1, Part I. See the Trade Marks Act 1938, s.38.

hallimote; hallmote. The Anglo-Saxon court equivalent to the Court Baron.

handling stolen goods. This is an indictable offence under the Theft Act 1968, s.22, replacing the common law and statutory offences of receiving stolen goods.

handsale. A sale of chattels concluded by the shaking of hands.

handsel. Earnest (*q.v.*) money.

hansard. The term commonly used to describe the Official Report of Parliamentary debates. "There are [*sic*] a series of rulings by this House, unbroken for a hundred years, and most recently affirmed emphatically and unanimously in *Davis* v. *Johnson* [1978] 1 All E.R. 1132, that recourse to reports of proceedings in either House of Parliament during the passage of the Bill that became the Act of Parliament which falls to be construed is not permissible as an aid to its construction" (*Hadmor Productions* v. *Hamilton* [1982] 1 All E.R. 1055, H.L., *per* Lord Diplock).

Hanseatic Laws of the Sea. The maritime law of the Hanse towns collected and published as a code by the Hanseatic League in 1591, and accepted as authoritative throughout northern Europe.

harassment. (1) Of debtors. It is an offence to harass a debtor with demands for payments which are calculated to subject him or members of his family or household to alarm distress and humiliation (Administration of Justice Act 1970, s.40).

(2) Of residential occupiers. If any person with intent to cause the residential occupier of any premises (a) to give up the premises or any part thereof, or (b) to refrain from exercising any right or pursuing any remedy in respect of the premises or any part thereof does acts calculated to interfere with the peace or comfort of the residential occupier or members of his household or persistently withdraws or withholds services reasonably required for the occupation of the premises as a residence he shall be guilty of an offence (Prevention from Eviction Act 1977, s.1(3)).

hard labour. An additional punishment to imprisonment without the option of a fine, introduced by statute in 1706, and unknown to the common law. Abolished by the Criminal Justice Act 1948, s.1.

hardship. See GREATER HARDSHIP; DEPRAVITY.

hawker. A travelling seller of goods (Hawkers Act 1888, s.1 (repealed)).

headborough. The chief of the 10 men who made up a frankpledge; replaced in the fourteenth century by the petty constable.

Health and Safety Commission. The supervisory and advisory body established by the Health and Safety at Work etc. Act 1974, and responsible for seeing that the purposes of the 1974 Act in securing the health and safety of persons at work are fulfilled. It may arrange for research, advice and information. It consists of a Chairman, up to nine Members, and a Secretariat.

Health and Safety Executive. The operational and enforcement arm of the Health and Safety Commission (*q.v.*). It is empowered (Health and Safety at Work etc. Act 1974, s.19) to appoint inspectors, and it administers the former Inspectorates of Factories, Mines and Quarries, Nuclear Installations, Alkali and Clean Air, Explosives, and Agriculture. It is responsible for the Employment Medical Advisory Service set up in 1972.

hearing. A trial or motion for judgment.

hearsay. What someone else has been heard to say: "what the soldier said"; as contrasted with the direct evidence of a witness himself; oral or written statements made by persons not called as witnesses (Phipson). Hearsay evidence is, in general, excluded, but the repetition of another person's statement is sometimes permissible, and there are express exceptions to the rule against hearsay. (See Nokes, *Introduction to Evidence.*)

In criminal proceedings the common law rules as to hearsay still obtain. In civil proceedings the common law rules are abrogated. Hearsay evidence is admissible by virtue (a) of Part I of the Civil Evidence Act 1968, (b) of any other express statutory provision, or (c) of any agreement between the parties (Act of 1968, s.1). Only first-hand hearsay evidence is admissible. Hearsay evidence of opinion is also admissible (Civil Evidence Act 1972, ss.1, 2).

heir or **heir-at-law.** He who succeeded by right of blood to the real property of an ancestor on intestacy. The general rules of descent were laid down in the Inheritance Act 1833. See DESCENT. (1) A customary heir or special heir was one who inherited by virtue of a custom, such as gravelkind or borough-English; (2) an heir general was one who took by descent as fixed by law, as opposed to (3) an heir special or heir in tail, who claimed as issue in tail according to the nature of the estate tail. See ENTAIL.

By the Administration of Estates Act 1925, s.45 all existing modes, rules and canons of descent were abolished, and real estate was assimilated to personal property, and both devolve as laid down by section 46. By the Law of Property Act 1925, s.132 a limitation of real or personal property in favour of the heir, either general or special, which would have conferred on the heir an estate before the Act, confers a corresponding equitable interest on the person who would have been heir but for the Act. See INTESTATE SUCCESSION.

heir apparent. A person who will be heir to his ancestor if he survives him. Properly he is not heir until after the death of his ancestor, for "*nemo est haeres viventis*" [nobody is the heir of a living person].

heir presumptive. A person who would be an heir if the ancestor died immediately (*e.g.* an only daughter); but who is liable to be displaced by the birth of a nearer heir.

heirlooms. Such goods and personal chattels as, contrary to the nature of chattels, go by special custom to the heir or devisee of the owner, along with the inheritance, and not to his executor. The Law of Property Act 1925, s.130(3) provides that when personal estate is directed to be held upon trusts corresponding with the trusts of land in which an entailed interest has been created, a corresponding entailed interest in the personal property is created. A tenant for life may sell heirlooms, and the money arising from the sale is capital money (Settled Land Act 1925, s.67).

Heralds' College. The College of Arms, Incorporated by Richard III in 1483. It is under the jurisdiction of the Earl Marshal and has jurisdiction as to armorial bearings and matters of pedigree.

hereditament. Real property which on an intestacy might have devolved on an heir. Corporeal hereditaments are visible and tangible objects such as lands and houses. Incorporeal hereditaments are intangible objects such as tithes, easements, *profits à prendre*.

hereditas. [Roman law.] Inheritance; the succession in virtue of civil law rights to the whole legal position of a deceased person.

heres. [Roman law.] The universal successor of a deceased person in virtue of his rights under the *jus civile*. He might be appointed by will or take *ab intestato*.

heres fiduciarius. [Roman law.] An heir that has a *fidei commissum* entrusted to him to carry out.

heresy. An ecclesiastical offence, consisting in the holding of a false opinion repugnant to some point of doctrine essential to the Christian faith. It was formerly punishable by death, but the writ *de haeretico comburendo* was abolished by the statute 29 Car. 2, c. 9. The power of the Archbishop of Canterbury to cite any person for heresy was abolished by the Ecclesiastical Jurisdiction Measure 1963, s.82(1).

heriot. The horses and arms of a tenant, or, if he were a villein, the best beast to which the lord was entitled by custom on the death of his tenant. Heriot service consisted of the right of heriot where the tenant died seised of an estate of inheritance, and could only exist as incident to a freehold tenure created before the statute *Quia Emptores*. Suit heriot was where the right was reserved on a grant or lease or freeholds made in modern times. Heriots survived chiefly as an incident of copyhold tenure, but were abolished as a manorial incident subject to compensation by the Law of Property Act 1922, s.128.

High Commission. The court established in 1583, to inquire into all offences against the Acts of Supremacy (1 Eliz. 1, c. 1) and Uniformity (1 Eliz. 1, c. 2) and other offences of wide scope. It was abolished by 16 Car. 1, c. 11.

High Commissioner. The chief representative in the United Kingdom of a Commonwealth country.

High Court of Justice. The High Court of Justice exercises the former jurisdiction of the Court of Chancery, the Courts of Queen's Bench, Common Pleas and Exchequer, the Court of Probate, Divorce and Admiralty, the London Court of Bankruptcy, the Court of Common Pleas at Lancaster, the Court of Pleas at Durham, and the courts of the judges or commissioners of assize. It is a Superior Court of Record, with the Lord Chancellor as President.

The High Court was originally divided into five divisions, *viz.* the Chancery Division, the Queen's Bench Division, the Common Pleas Division, the Exchequer Division, and the Probate, Divorce and Admiralty Division. An Order in Council of 1881 abolished the offices of the Lord Chief Justice of the Common Pleas and the Lord Chief Baron, and consolidated the Queen's Bench, Common Please and Exchequer Divisions into one Division called the Queen's (or King's) Bench Division, under the presidency of a Lord Chief Justice.

The High Court now consists of the Queen's Bench Division (including the Admiralty Court (*q.v.*) and the Commercial Court (*q.v.*) the Chancery Division, and the Family Division (*q.v.*). Sittings of the High Court may be held at any place in England and Wales. See Supreme Court Act 1981, ss.4–7, 19–44, 61–77 and Sched. 1.

high seas. The seas or open salt water beyond the distance of three miles from the coast of any country. The majority of States claim territorial jurisdiction over the seas within three miles of their coasts, but beyond that limit the high seas are said to be free. But there are qualifications to the doctrine. Some countries, *e.g.* Iceland, claim exclusive fishing rights over the seas within 200 miles from their coasts. A State assumes jurisdiction over its own ships, pirates, and foreign vessels which have violated, or are about to violate, its laws, and in time of war exercises the right of visit and search over neutral ships. See TERRITORIAL WATERS. As to offences committed on board ship, see the Consular Relations Act 1968, ss.5, 6.

high treason. See TREASON.

highway. A road or way open to the public as of right for the purpose of passing and repassing. Nuisance in reference to highways is an act or omission whereby the public are prevented from using their right. The ownership of the soil may be private, *e.g.* in the owner of the land adjoining the highway. A highway may be founded on prescription, statute, or by dedication to the public by the owner.

The duty to repair the highway at common law was on the inhabitants of the parish; now under the consolidating Highways Act 1959 the duty to repair is transferred to the Secretary of State for the Environment, or the appropriate local authority, according to the classification of the road. Formerly, a local authority was not liable for injuries caused to users of the highway by its own non-feasance (*e.g.* non-repair of the surface), but this rule is abolished as from August 3, 1964 (Highways (Miscellaneous Provisions) Act 1961, s.1).

As to straying livestock see ANIMALS.

Highway Code. The Code compiled by the Secretary of State for the Environment comprising such directions as appear to him proper for the guidance of persons using roads. Failure to observe it is not of itself an offence, but may be relied upon in any proceedings to establish or negative any liability; *e.g.* for negligence (Road Traffic Act 1972, s.37).

hijacking. See the Hijacking Act 1971; Protection of Aircraft Act 1973; Criminal Jurisdiction Act 1975, s.2.

Hil. Hilary sittings, or Hilary Term which is from January 11 to the Wednesday before Easter Sunday (Ord. 64, r. 1).

Hinde Palmer's Act. The Administration of Estates Act 1869 which abolished the priority of speciality debts in the administration of the estate of a deceased person. Now replaced by the Administration of Estates Act 1925, s.32.

hire-purchase agreement. An agreement for the bailment of goods under which the bailee may buy the goods or under which the property in the goods will or may pass to the bailee. (See the elaborate definitions in the Consumer Credit Act 1974, s.189(1).) Such an agreement differs from a conditional sale inasmuch as the hirer does not agree to buy. He merely has an option to buy on fulfilment of certain conditions, or he may return the goods on payment of the sum stated in the contract.

In practice, in regard, *e.g.* to motor-cars, the buyer selects a car from the seller, who thereupon sells it to a finance house, which then enters into a hire-purchase contract with the buyer. There is then no contract between the car seller and the buyer, but there may be an express warranty as to condition of the car by the seller on which the buyer may sue the seller.

A hire-purchase agreement where the total sum payable by the hirer, less the amount of the deposit, if any, and the total charge for credit does not exceed £5,000 is a consumer credit agreement regulated by the Consumer Credit Act 1974. See s.8. See also UNFAIR CONTRACT TERMS.

historic buildings. The Secretary of State for the Environment and local authorities have extensive powers with regard to the preservation and upkeep of historic buildings under *inter alia* the Historic Buildings and Ancient Monuments Act 1953; Local Authorities (Historic Buildings) Act 1962; Civic Amenities Act 1967; Town and Country Planning Act 1971; Local Government Act 1972; Town and Country Amenities Act 1974; Local Government Act 1974; Housing Act 1974.

holder in due course. One who takes a bill of exchange, complete and regular on the face of it, before it is overdue and without notice of dishonour, in good faith and for value, without notice of any defect of title of the transferor (Bills of Exchange Act 1882, s.29). He holds free from any defect of title of prior parties. A bank which has allowed a customer to draw against unindorsed, uncleared cheques is a holder in due course (*Midland Bank* v. *Harris* [1963] 1 W.L.R. 1021).

holding company. A company which has a subsidiary company, *i.e.* where the holding company is a member of it, and controls the composition of its board of directors, or holds more than half in nominal value of its equity share capital (Companies Act 1948, s.154). Group accounts are to be laid before the holding company in general meeting (*ibid.* ss.150–153).

holding out. A person who "holds himself out" as, or purports to be, of a certain capacity (*e.g.* a partner in a firm), and who is accepted by others as such. When others act on the assumption that he is what he allows himself to be represented to be, he is estopped from denying the truth of such representation.

holding over is where a tenant under a lease continues in possession of land after the determination of his tenancy. He then becomes a tenant at sufferance and at common law was not liable for rent; but where he holds under a periodic tenancy and gives notice to quit, he becomes liable to an action for possession or damages, or to double rent (Distress for Rent Act 1737, s.18). A tenant for life or years who wilfully holds over is liable for double the yearly value (Landlord and Tenant Act 1730, s.1).

A tenancy at sufferance may be converted by implication of law into a tenancy from year to year if the landlord and tenant must be taken to have so agreed, *e.g.* by a yearly rent being paid.

holograph. A deed or will written entirely by the grantor or testator himself.

homage. (1) The tenants of a manor assembled in a customary court. (2) A most honourable and humble service of reverence, which every free tenant for an estate in fee simple or fee tail was bound to perform to his feudal lord by kneeling and saying "I become your man of life and limb." Homage created an obligation of assistance by the tenant to his lord, and of protection by the lord to his tenant. Abolished as an incident of tenure of land by 12 Car. 2, c. 24.

Home Secretary. The Secretary of State at the head of the Home Office. He is the medium of communication between the Crown and its subjects. He is responsible for the maintenance of the public peace, and for the general administration of the criminal law, the police and prisons, and advises the Sovereign in the exercise of the prerogative of mercy. He exercises control over aliens and administers the Extradition Acts, and the Nationality Acts, etc.

homeless person. A person is homeless if he has no accomodation, *i.e.* there is no accomodation which he together with his family is entitled to occupy (Housing (Homeless Persons) Act 1977, s.1(1)). A person is also homeless if he has accommodation but cannot secure entry to it (1977 Act, s.1(2)(*a*)). A person is threatened with homelessness if it is likely that he will become homeless within 28 days (s.1(3)). If a local housing authority are satisfied as a result of inquiries that a person who has applied to them is homeless or threatened with homelessness they are under a duty to secure accommodation for that person (s.4(1) and (5)). Where they are satisfied that there is no priority need (defined in s.2) or that the person is intentionally homeless their duty is to furnish him with advice and appropriate assistance (s.4(2)). For definitions of "intentionally homeless" see *Din* v. *London Borough of Wandsworth* [1981] 3 All E.R. 27; *Islam* v. *London Borough of Hillingdon* [1981] 3 All E.R. 901.

homicide. Unlawfully killing a human being under the [Queen's] peace, the death following within a year and a day. It is punishable by imprisonment for life. See also MURDER.

(1) Felonious homicide. (a) Death caused by an act done with the intention of causing death or bodily harm, or known to be likely to cause death or bodily harm, without legal justification or excuse; (b) Death caused by an omission, amounting to culpable negligence, to discharge a duty tending to the preservation of life, whether accompanied by an intention to cause death or bodily harm or not; (c) Death caused accidentally by an unlawful act.

(2) Excusable homicide. Where the person by whom the homicide is committed is not criminally responsible. It is either by misadventure, or in self-defence.

(3) Justifiable homicide. Where homicide is committed without blame in the execution of a legal duty, or in furtherance of a legal purpose, *e.g.* putting a person to death in pursuance of a legal sentence.

hon. The Honourable. The title of the younger sons of earls; all children of viscounts and barons; justices of the High Court, members of governments and of legislative councils in the colonies; and certain ladies. Right Honourable is the title of Privy Councillors.

honorary services. The services incident to tenure in grand serjeanty or petty serjeanty.

honour. (1) A seignory *in capite* of which several inferior lordships or manors depend; and the land or district included therein. An Honour cannot be created since the statute *Quia Emptores*, except by Act of Parliament. (2) To honour a bill of exchange is to pay it, or to accept it, as may be due. See also MODE OF ADDRESS.

honours. The Queen is the "fountain of honour," but the creation of peers and the conferment of most honours are done on the advice of the Prime Minister. There exists, however, the Political Honours Scrutiny Committee, and trafficking in honours is punishable under the Honours (Prevention of Abuses) Act 1925.

hors de la loi. Outlawed.

Hospitia Cancellariae. [Inns of Chancery.]

Hospitia Curiae. [Inns of Court.]

hospitium. The relation between host and guest; the shelter of an inn. It includes the inn buildings and stables, and may also include a yard or car park.

hostages. See Taking of Hostages Act 1982.

hostile witness. A witness whose mind discloses a bias adverse to the party examining him, and who may, with leave of the court, be cross-examined by the counsel calling him. See Criminal Procedure Act 1865, ss.1, 3.

hotchpot. A blending of properties for the purpose of securing an equal division; a mixture or medley. Where a fund is appointed to be divided amongst a class and one of the class has already received a special or appointed share, that person may be required to add his special share to the fund (for the purpose of computing the share of each beneficiary) before it is distributed, and he is then said to bring his special share into hotchpot.

A "hotchpot provision" is a clause in a settlement, etc., requiring this procedure to be carried out before the beneficiary, who has received prior payments or benefits on account, can share further in the fund to be distributed. See *e.g.* Law of Property Act 1925, s.157, proviso.

House of Commons. The Lower House of Parliament, now consisting of representatives of parliamentary constituencies. By virtue of the House of Commons (Redistribution of Seats) Act 1949 and 1958, and Orders in Council made thereunder, the total membership is 635. Persons disqualified from membership are: aliens; minors; the mentally ill; peers (other than Irish peers (Peerage Act 1963, s.5); ordained clergy of the Church of England or of Ireland, or of Rome; bankrupts; and candidates guilty of corrupt and illegal practices.

Those disqualified under the House of Commons Disqualification Act 1975, are: holders of specified judicial offices; civil servants; members of the armed forces, police forces, foreign legislatures and of certain commissions and tribunals and the holders of specified other offices.

House of Lords. The Upper House of Parliament; the assembly of the lords spiritual and temporal. The lords spiritual are the two archbishops and the senior bishops of the Church of England. Other members of the House are the peers and peeresses in their own right of England, Scotland, Great Britain and the United Kingdom, and the life peers (*q.v.*). (See the Peerage Act 1963, ss.4, 6.) The Lord Chancellor is Speaker and President of the House.

The House of Lords exercises judicial authority in claims of peerage. Any person who succeeds to a hereditary peerage may, within 12 months, by an instrument of disclaimer, disclaim that peerage for his life (Peerage Act 1963, s.1).

The House is the Supreme Court of Appeal from the Court of Appeal in England, and the Superior Courts of Scotland and Northern Ireland. Appeals are heard by the Appellate Committee, which usually consists of five, or three, Law Lords. They give written judgments. In criminal cases the defendant or the prosecutor may appeal to the House of Lords from the decisions of the Criminal Division of the Court of Appeal or the Divisional Court, with leave, if a point of general public importance is involved which ought to be considered by the House (Administration of Justice Act 1960, s.1).

housebreaking. This is no longer a distinct offence. See BURGLARY.

house of correction. A species of prison, originally designed for the confinement of vagrants and paupers refusing to work. Abolished.

housing. The Housing Acts 1957 to 1975.

housing associations. The Housing Act 1964 set up a Housing Corporation to assist housing societies in providing housing accommodation. For the legislation currently governing housing associations, see the Rent Act 1977 ss.86–91, 94(1), 95(1), 96(1)–(3), 97, 141. For the circumstances under which a housing association tenant becomes a protected tenant (*q.v.*) or regulated tenant (*q.v.*) see Rent Act 1977, s.92(1).

hue and cry. The old common law process of pursuing with horn and with voice; all felons and such as have dangerously wounded another. All those who join in a hue and cry are justified in apprehending the person pursued, even though it should turn out that he is innocent. Maliciously or wantonly to raise a hue and cry is a misdemeanour and ground for a civil action.

human rights. The European Convention on Human Rights has been in force since 1953. It created the Commission on Human Rights and the Court of Human Rights. The Commission investigates and tries to conciliate. If this fails the matter may be brought before the court. It has been held that the convention does not have the force of law in the United Kingdom (*Malone* v. *Metropolitan Police Commission* [1979] Ch. 344).

Human Tissue Act 1961 permits the removal of parts of the body of a deceased person for medical purposes if he so requests in writing.

hundred. A district forming part of a county, originally so called because each consisted of a hundred freeholders, or 10 tithings. Each hundred formerly had its court, and was governed by a high constable or bailiff. See also CHILTERN HUNDREDS.

hundred court. The court of the hundred. It was similar to the old county court in jurisdiction and procedure. Judgment was given by the suitors.

hundredor. One of the inhabitants of a hundred who was liable to serve on a jury trying an issue regarding land situate therein.

husband and wife. The old common law rule was that a husband and wife were one person. A husband on his marriage became absolutely entitled to all chattels and *choses in possession* belonging to his wife in her own right, and to a life interest in her inheritable freehold estates. A wife's choses in action did not vest in the husband unless he reduced them into possession. The husband could dispose of his wife's leaseholds during his lifetime without his wife's concurrence. His concurrence was necessary in any disposition by the wife of her real property. In equity, however, property conveyed to trustees or the husband for the "separate use" of the wife became her separate property, disposable by her as if a *feme sole*. The husband had a right to the personal custody of his wife, and to sexual intercourse with her.

The Matrimonial Causes Act 1857 protected property acquired by a wife whilst living apart from her husband under a decree for judicial separation or the protection order. The Married Women's Property Act 1882 provided that thenceforward all the property of a married woman should be her separate property. By the Law of Property Act 1925, s.37 husband and wife are two persons in regard to property acquisitions.

By the Law Reform (Married Women and Tortfeasors) Act 1935, s.1 it was provided, with certain exceptions, that a married woman should be capable of acquiring, holding and disposing of property as if she were a *feme sole*.

Money or property derived from housekeeping allowance belongs normally to the husband and wife in equal shares (Married Women's Property Act 1964).

At common law, husband and wife could not sue each other in tort, but the wife could sue her husband for the protection of her property (Married Women's Property Act 1882, s.12). By the Law Reform (Husband and Wife) Act 1962, s.1, however, each of the parties to a marriage has the same right of action in tort as though they were not married, except that proceedings may be stayed if unwarranted, or if they concern questions of property. A married woman is liable for her own torts, and is subject to bankruptcy law, and to the enforcement of judgments and orders as if a *feme sole* (Law Reform (Married Women and Tortfeasors) Act 1935).

Under the Married Women's Property Acts 1882 and 1893 a married woman had full capacity to contract; but such a contract was only binding on her to the extent of her separate estate. Payment of her debts could not therefore be enforced against her personally; *e.g.* by committal to prison (*Scott* v. *Morley* (1887) 20 Q.B.D. 120). The 1935 Act in effect abolished the distinction between a married woman and a man or single woman in regard to their debts, and a married woman is personally bound by her contract (s.1). A husband is not liable for his wife's contracts (s.3), except her contracts as his agent or for necessaries (s.4).

Husband and wife can be found to have conspired together (see CONSPIRACY). Husbands and wives are criminally liable in respect of offences committed on each other's property as if they were not married (Theft Act 1968, s.30; *R.* v. *Noble* [1974] 1 W.L.R. 894) and have a similar right of action in tort (Law Reform (Husband and Wife) Act 1962). Communications between husband and wife are privileged from disclosure in criminal but not in civil proceedings (Evidence Amendment Act 1853, s.3; Civil Evidence Act 1968, s.16(3)). The evidence of a husband or wife is admissible in any proceedings to prove that marital intercourse did or did not take place between them but neither is compellable in any criminal proceedings to give evidence of such matter (Matrimonial Causes Act 1965, s.43(1); Civil Evidence Act 1968, s.16(4)). Under the Married Women's Property Act 1882 (as amended by the Statute Law (Repeals)Act 1969) questions between husband and wife may be decided summarily and privately by a judge of the High Court or County Court. See also the Matrimonial Causes (Property and Maintenance) Act 1958, s.7.; Matrimonial Proceedings and Property Act 1970, s.39.

At common law, a British woman lost her British nationality if she married an alien. Under the statutory concept of "citizenship" introduced by the British Nationality Act 1948, she is in the same general position as a man. Shortly, the position now is that a British woman who marries an alien retains her British nationality unless she elects to renounce it, while an alien woman who marries a United Kingdom citizen does not automatically acquire British nationality, but by registration can do so. See COERCION; DIVORCE; RESTRAINT ON ALIENATION.

husbandry. Farming.

hush money. Money paid to induce a person to stifle a prosecution, or to refrain from giving evidence or information.

hypnotism includes mesmerism, etc. which produces any form of induced sleep or trance in which the susceptibility of the mind to suggestion is increased (Hypnotism Act 1952, s.6). That Act, as amended regulates the demonstration of hypnotic phenomena for public entertainment.

hypothecation. (1) Pledging a ship or her freight or cargo for the payment of money borrowed by the master. It is either bottomry or *respondentia* (*q.v.*); (2) a charge on property as security for the payment of a sum of money where the property remains in the possession of the debtor.

I

IOU. (I owe you.) A written acknowledgement of a debt. It is not a negotiable instrument.

ibid. (ibidem). [In the same place.]

id certum est quod certum reddi potest. [That is certain which can be made certain.]

idem. [The same.]

identification. (1) To identify a thing or person is to prove that the thing or person produced or shown is the one in question in the proceedings. (2) Identification is the former doctrine that the negligence of the driver of a vehicle was imputed by law to the passenger so as to deprive the passenger of his remedy against third persons, on the ground of contributory negligence. (3) In relation to a road traffic offence the owner of a car may be required to give information as to the identity of the driver (Road Traffic Regulation Act 1967, ss.85, 89, 90 as amended).

idiot. A person in whose case there exists mental defectiveness of such a degree that he is unable to guard himself against common physical dangers. See now MENTAL DISORDER; PATIENT.

ignorantia eorum quae quis scire tenetur non excusat. [Ignorance of those things which everyone is bound to know does not constitute an excuse.]

ignorantia facti excusat; ignorantia juris non excusat. [Ignorance of the fact excuses; ignorance of the law does not excuse.]

ignorantia juris quod quisque scire tenetur non excusat. [Ignorance of the law which everybody is supposed to know does not afford excuse.]

illegal. Unlawful; an act which the law forbids, as to commit a murder, or to obstruct a highway, as opposed to an act or state of things which the law disregards, or does not recognise as capable of giving rise to rights. Thus a contract made *ultra vires* is void, but not illegal. A cheque given in payment of a bet is given for an illegal consideration and the payee cannot sue thereon, but it is not illegal to give the cheque or pay the lost bet. See GAMING.

The following are illegal at common law: (1) Agreements to commit a crime or tort; (2) agreements contrary to public policy; (3) agreements with an alien enemy or which are hostile to a friendly State; (4) agreements injurious to the public service, *e.g.* sale of offices or honours; (5) agreements perverting the course of justice, *e.g.* stifling criminal proceedings, except where civil and criminal remedies co-exist; (6) agreements in abuse of legal process, *e.g.* maintenance and champerty (*q.v.*); (7) immoral contracts; (8) agreements in restraint of marriage; (9) agreements in restraint of trade. See also CORRUPT PRACTICES; LOCUS POENITENTIAE; SEVERANCE.

illusory appointment. See APPOINTMENT, POWER OF.

imbecile. Persons in whose case there exists mental defectiveness which, though not amounting to idiocy, is yet so pronounced that they are incapable of managing themselves or their affairs, or in the case of children, of being taught to do so. See now MENTAL DISORDER; PATIENT.

immemorial. Beyond legal memory: prior to 1 Ric. 1 (1189). Immemorial usage is a practice which has existed time out of mind. See CUSTOM; MEMORY; PRESCRIPTION.

immigration. The Immigration Act 1971 assimilates the control over immigration from Commonwealth countries to that for aliens.

immorality. Contracts based on sexual immorality such as agreements for future illicit cohabitation or a contract to supply goods to a prostitute knowlingly for the purposes of her profession, are void (*Pearce* v. *Brookes* (1866) L.R. 1 Ex. 213).

A conspiracy to corrupt public morals is a common law crime, as by the publishing of advertisements of prostitutes for gain (*Shaw* v. *D.P.P.* [1962] A.C. 220 (*The Ladies Directory*)). See also OBSCENITY: PROSTITUTION.

immunity. The condition of being exempt from some liability to which others are subject, *e.g.* the immunity of a judge in respect of things done or said when exercising his judicial function; the immunity of foreign sovereigns or states from legal process in the United Kingdom (State Immunity Act 1978).

impanel. To enter the names of a jury in the panel (*q.v.*).

imparlance. A conference between plaintiff and defendant with a view to a settlement of an action. In a common recovery (*q.v.*) it was a fictitious proceedings.

impeachment. A solemn accusation of a great public offence, especially against a minister of the Crown. The House of Commons first found the crime, and then as prosecutors supported their charge before the House of Lords, who tried and adjudicated upon it.

Impeachment is practically obsolete, the last being in 1805.

impeachment of waste. Liability for committing waste upon lands. See WASTE.

imperitia culpae adnumeratur. [Inexperience is accounted a fault.]

impertinence. The introduction of unnecessary or immaterial allegations into a pleading which may be struck out on the order of the court or judge (Ord. 18, r. 19).

implead. To prosecute or take proceedings against a person.

implication. The inference from acts done or facts ascertained of the existence of an intention or state of things which may or may not exist in fact, but which is presumed by the law to exist. Examples: an implied warranty, trust or authority; a life estate by implication. See IMPLIED TERM.

implied condition. See IMPLIED TERM.

implied term. A term in a contract which has not been expressly stated but which must be implied to give effect to the presumed intention of the parties. A term may be a condition (*q.v.*) or a warranty (*q.v.*). In the sale of goods certain conditions and warranties are implied by statute (Sale of Goods Act 1979, ss.11(3), 12, 61). See also supply of Goods and Services Act 1982.

implied trust. A trust implied by law as founded upon the unexpressed but presumed intention of the party. It includes resulting trusts (*q.v.*) and constructive trusts (*q.v.*).

importune. It is an offence for a man persistently to solicit or importune in a public place for an immoral purpose (Sexual Offences Act 1956, s.32). Whether the purpose of the importuning is immoral is for the jury to decide (*R*. v. *Grey, The Times*, November 27, 1981).

impossibility. Impossibility of performance of a contract or a condition *ab initio* renders the contract or condition void. Thus where there is a legal or physical impossibility apparent on the face of a contract, or where a condition attached to a legacy is impossible to fulfil, it is void. A contract for the sale of specific goods which have perished at the time without the seller's knowledge is void, and where subsequently the goods without fault of either party, perish before the risk passes to the buyer, the agreement is void.

At common law, impossibility of performance *ex post facto* of a contract was in general no discharge, but certain exceptions were established, as *e.g.* through change of law—"supervening illegality" (*Baily* v. *de Crespigny* (1869) L.R. 4 Q.B. 180); destruction of the subject-matter of the contract (*Taylor* v. *Caldwell* (1863) 3 B. & S. 826); death or illness of the performer in contracts for personal services (*Robinson* v. *Davison* (1871) L.R. 6 Ex. 269). See also FRUSTRATION.

Specific performance of a contract which it is impossible to perform, or the terms of which it is impossible for the court to enforce, will not be decreed.

impossibilium nulla obligato est. [Impossibility is an excuse for the non-performance of an obligation.] See IMPOSSIBILITY.

impotence. Incapacity for normal sexual intercourse. See NULLITY OF MARRIAGE.

impotentia excusat legem. [Impotency excuses law.] To an obligation imposed by law, impossibility of performance is a good excuse.

impound. To put distrained cattle or other goods in a pound or to keep them as security; to seize.

impressment. A power possessed by the Crown of compulsorily taking persons or property to aid in the defence of the country. It was usually exercised until 1815 to obtain seamen for the King's ships.

imprest. Money advanced by the Crown for its use.

imprimatur. [Let it be printed.]

imprisonment. The restraint of a person's liberty by another. It includes confinement in a gaol or house or seizing or holding a man in a street, etc. Imprisonment as a punishment consists in the detention of an offender in prison and subjecting him to discipline for the term of his sentence. See the Criminal Justice Acts 1948 and 1961; Powers of Criminal Courts Act 1973. See FALSE IMPRISONMENT.

imprisonment for debt. Abolished by the Debtors Act 1869, except in the case of the following defaults in payment: (1) of a penalty other than under a contract; (2) of any sum recoverable summarily; (3) into court by a trustee as ordered; (4) by a solicitor of costs awarded against him for misconduct, etc.; (5) for the benefit of creditors of any salary or income as ordered by a court in bankruptcy. Also a judgment debtor may be imprisoned for not more than six weeks for non-payment of a debt if he has the means to pay, but refuses (Debtors Act 1869, s.5).

impropriation. The transfer of the property of an ecclesiastical benefice into the hands of a layman, and the possession by a layman of the property so transferred.

impropriator. A lay rector. See TITHE.

improvement of land. The Improvement of Land Acts 1864 and 1899 provide that certain persons in the possession or receipt of the rents or profits of land may, with the sanction of the Ministry of Agriculture, Fisheries and Food, borrow or advance money for the execution of certain improvements on the land, and obtain an order charging the amount, with interest, on the inheritance or fee of the land. Capital moneys may be expended on improvements under the Settled Land Act 1925, s.84, Sched. 3. The Agricultural Holdings Act 1948, ss.35 *et seq.* provides for compensation for tenants, on termination of tenancy, for both old and new improvements.

impubes. [Roman law.] A person below the legal age of puberty. A male under 14 or a female under 12.

in aequali jure melior est conditio possidentis. [Where the rights of the parties are equal, the claim of the actual possessor is the stronger.]

in ambiguis orationibus maxime sententia spectanda est ejus qui eas protelisset. [In dealing with ambiguous words the intention of him who used them should especially be regarded.]

in Anglia non est interregnum. [In England there is no interregnum.] "The King never dies." For immediately upon the decease of the reigning prince his Kingship, by act of law, without any interregnum or interval, vests in the King's heir (Blackstone).

in articulo mortis. [At the point of death.]

in autre droit. [In the right of another.] An executor holds property in the right of his testator.

in banc. Sittings of the judges of the Queen's Bench, Common Pleas and Exchequer at Westminster for determination of questions of law, prior to the Judicature Acts 1873–1875. See NISI PRIUS.

in bonis. [In the goods of.]

in camera. The hearing of a case in private; *e.g.* in court, the public being excluded; or in the judge's private room. Criminal cases must be heard in public, but divorce causes and civil causes may be heard *in camera* if necessary to secure due administration of justice. It is a usual course in the Chancery Division, where private family matters are involved. In nullity of marriage proceedings, evidence as to sexual capacity is normally to be heard *in camera* (Matrimonial Causes Act 1973, s.48(2)).

in capite. See CAPITE, TENURE IN.

in casu extremae necessitatis onmia sunt communia. [In cases of extreme necessity, everything is in common.]

in commendam. [In trust.]

in conjuctivis oportet utrumque, in disjunctivis sufficit alteram partem esse veram. [In conjunctives both must be true; in disjunctives it is sufficient if one of them be true.]

in consimili casu. [In a like case.] The Statute of Westminster II, 1288 (13 Edw. 1, c. 24), enacted that when a writ was found in Chancery, where original writs were prepared for suitors by the clerks, but in a like case falling under the same right and requiring the same remedy no writ was to be found, the clerks should agree in making a new writ, or, if they could not agree, they were to refer the matter to Parliament. See also ACTION ON THE CASE.

in contractis tacite insunt quae sunt moris et consuetudinis. [The clauses which are in accordance with custom and usage are an implied part of every contract.]

in conventionibus contrahentium voluntas potius quam verba spectari placuit. [In construing agreements the intention of the parties, rather than the words actually used, should be considered.]

in curia. [In open court.]

in custodia legis. [In the custody of the law.]

in esse. [In being.]Actually existing.

in extenso. [At full length.]

in forma pauperis. [In the character of a pauper.] See LEGAL AID.

in futuro. [In the future.]

in gremio legis. [In the bosom of the law.]

in gross. A right that is not appendant, appurtenant, or otherwise annexed to land.

in invitum. [Against a reluctant person.]

in jure non remota causa, sed proxima spectatur. [In law the proximate, and not the remote, cause is to be regarded.]

in limine. [On the threshold.] See POSTLIMINIUM.

in loco parentis. [In the place of a parent.] One who assumes the liability for providing for a minor in the way a parent would do.

in media res. [In the midst of the matter.]

in misericordia. [At mercy.] See AMERCIAMENT.

in nomine. [In the name of.]

in pais. [In the country.] Without legal proceedings or documents. Trial *per pais* means trial by the country, *i.e.* trial by jury. See ESTOPPEL; JURY.

in pari causa potior est conditio possidentis. [Everyone may keep what he has got, unless and until someone else can prove a better title.]

in pari delicto, potior est conditio possidentis. [Where both parties are equally in fault, the condition of the possessor is the best.]

in pari materia. [In an analogous case.]

in perpetuum. [For ever.]

in personam. An act, proceeding or right done or directed against or with reference to a specific person, as opposed to *in rem* (*q.v.*). The right of a beneficiary is primarily a right *in personam* against his trustee. The Court of Chancery acted in personam by means of its decrees compelling, or restraining, specific acts by the person concerned.

in pleno. [In full.]

in posse. A thing which does not actually exist, but which may exist.

in praesenti. [At the present time.]

in propria persona. [In his own proper person.]

in re. [In the matter of.]

in rem. An act, proceeding or right available against the world at large, as opposed to *in personam*. A right of property is a right *in rem*. An Admiralty action is a proceeding *in rem* when the ship itself is arrested and adjudicated upon.

in situ. [In its original situation.]

in specie. In its own form and essence, and not in its equivalent. In coin as opposed to paper money.

in statu quo. [In the former position.]

in terrorem. A condition in a will or gift which is intended to frighten or intimidate; it is void.

in totidem verbis. [In so many words.]

in toto. [Entirely; wholly.]

in transitu. [In course of transit.] See STOPPAGE IN TRANSITU.

incendiarism. Arson (*q.v.*).

incerta persona. [Roman law.] A person that is not a specific living individual; an indeterminate person. A legatee was held to be indeterminate when the testator added him with an indeterminate notion in his mind, as, *e.g.* the man who comes first to my funeral.

inalienable. Not transferable. There is a general rule of law that land must not be rendered inalienable.

incest. Sexual intercourse between a male person and his grand-daughter, daughter, sister, or mother, or between a female person, of or above the age of 16, and her grandfather, father, brother, or son, with her consent and permission. It is immaterial whether the relationship is or is not traced through lawful wedlock, but the accused must know of the relationship. It is a misdemeanour (Sexual Offences Act 1956, ss.10, 11). It is also an offence for a man to incite a girl under the age of 16 years whom he knows to be his grand-daughter, daughter or sister to have sexual intercourse with him (Criminal Law Act 1977, s.45).

incident. A thing appertaining to or following another. Thus a rent may be incident to a reversion, though it may be separated from it; that is, the one may be conveyed without the other.

incidents of tenure. Under the feudal system there were comprised the following incidents of tenure; military service; homage, fealty and suit of court; wardship and marriage; relief and primer seisin; aids, and ascheat and forfeiture. With the abolition of particular tenures by the Statute Quia Emptores, the Tenures Abolition Act 1660, and the Property Acts 1922 and 1925, the incidents of tenure disappeared with them, except that the honourable incidents of grand serjeanty and petty serjeanty were expressly preserved (Law of Property Act 1922, s.136).

incitement. Incitement to commit a crime is a common law misdemeanour, even though the crime be not committed. If the crime be actually committed, the person inciting is equally guilty, in the case of treason or misdemeanour, with the person who commits the crime.

incitement to disaffection. Endeavouring to seduce members of the armed forces from their allegiance (Incitement to Disaffection Act 1934; Public Order Act 1936; Criminal Justice Act 1972, Sched. 5).

inclosure. Inclosure is the act of freeing land from rights of common, commonable rights, and all rights which obstruct cultivation by vesting it in some person as absolute owner. Inclosure may be effected by the lord of the manor, or the tenants by special custom, by prescription, by agreement, or by Act of Parliament. Since the Inclosure Act 1845, inclosures may be effected by the Inclosure Commissioners, now the Ministry of Agriculture, Fisheries and Food.

inclusio unius est exclusio alterius. [The inclusion of one is the exclusion of another.]

income tax. A duty or tax on income or profits. The Income and Corporation Taxes Act 1970 consolidated all the substantive law of income tax (including the tax on short term capital gains) and corporation tax. The Taxes Management Act 1970 consolidated the administrative provisions. The tax is imposed each year by the annual Finance Act. Income tax is levied in respect of income from the sources classified in six Schedules as follows, each Schedule having its own set of rules (Income and Corporation Taxes Act 1970, s.1).

(1) Schedule A (rents, rent charges and other receipts arising out of the ownership of land; s.67).

(2) Schedule B (occupation of commercial woodlands; s.91).

(3) Schedule C (profits arising from public revenue dividends; s.93).

(4) Schedule D (trade or professional profits or gains; also income not chargeable under the other Schedules; s.108).

(5) Schedule E (salaries, wages, annuities, pensions and stipends; s.181).

(6) Schedule F (company dividends and distributions; s.232; Finance Act 1972, s.87).

There are exemptions from the tax in favour of charities etc., and of persons of small means. Reliefs may be claimed by individuals according to their personal circumstances; *e.g.* in respect of children, with the result that the standard rate of tax fixed for any year is not the effective rate of tax charged on the individual's total income.

The income tax year of assessment runs from April 6 to April 5. The tax is managed by the Commissioners of Inland Revenue, Inspectors of Taxes being their subordinate local officers. A person who is aggrieved by the amount of the assessment upon him, or by the refusal of his claim for allowances, may appeal to the local General Commissioners (*q.v.*) or, in certain cases, to the Special Commissioners (*q.v.*). A person who is dissatisfied with the decision of the General or Special Commissioners may, in general, appeal by case stated to the High Court.

incorporation. Merging together to form a single whole; conferring legal personality upon an association of individuals, or the holder of a certain office, pursuant to Royal Charter or Act of Parliament.

incorporeal hereditaments. See HEREDITAMENT.

incriminate. To involve oneself or another in responsibility for a criminal offence. Generally a person cannot be compelled to answer a question which might incriminate him. There are statutory exceptions, *e.g.* Civil Evidence Act 1968, s.14(1); Criminal Damage Act 1971, s.9.

See also CHARACTER, EVIDENCE OF.

incumbent. A rector with cure of souls, vicar, perpetual curate, curate in charge or minister of a benefice.

indebitatus assumpsit. See ASSUMPSIT.

indecency. Whatever openly outrages public decency and is injurious to public morals is a misdemeanour at common law. Public exposure of the person with intent to insult a female is an offence (Vagrancy Act 1824, s.4; Criminal Justice Act 1925, s.42). The similar offence under the Town Police Clauses Act 1847 is complete without intent to insult a female. "Person" here means penis (*Evans* v. *Ewels* [1972] 1 W.L.R. 671). Gross indecency between male persons in public is a misdemeanour punishable with two years' imprisonment (Sexual Offences Act 1956, s.13). Homosexual acts between adults in private are not an offence (Sexual Offences Act 1967).

The Indecency with Children Act 1960 (as amended), provided that any person who commits an act of gross indecency with or towards a child under 14, or invites such child to do such an act, is liable to imprisonment.

indecent assault. An assault consisting of a hostile act accompanied by circumstances of indecency. If committed upon a female, it is a misdemeanour punishable with two years' imprisonment (Sexual Offences Act 1956, s.14); if upon a male, it is a misdemeanour punishable with 10 years' imprisonment (s.15). A female may be guilty under either of these sections (*R.* v. *Hare* [1934] 1 K.B. 354). Consent of a child under 16 is no defence.

indemnify. To make good a loss which one person has suffered in consequence of the act or default of another. See Mercantile Law Amendment Act 1856, s.5. It is an offence to agree with any person to indemnify that person against any liability which the other may incur as a surety for bail (Bail Act 1976, s.9(1)).

indemnity. A collateral contract or security to prevent a person from being damnified by an act or forbearance done at the request of another. See ACT OF INDEMNITY. For indemnity by way of contribution see JOINT TORTFEASORS.

indenture. A document written in duplicate on the same parchment or paper, and divided into two by cutting through in a wavy line. The two parts could be fitted together to prove their genuineness, and were known as counterparts. A deed between parties to effect its objects has the effect of an indenture though not indented or expressed to be an indenture, and any deed, whether or not being an indenture, may be described as a deed simply (Law of Property Act 1925, ss.56(2), 57). See COUNTERPART.

independent contractor. Term used to distinguish a person who contracts to perform a particular task for another and is not under the other's control as to the manner in which he performs the task from an employee of the other. An employer is not normally liable for the torts of an independent contractor and the distinction is also significant in social security law.

indictable offence. An offence which, if committed by an adult, is triable on indictment in the Crown Court whether it is exclusively so triable or triable either by Crown Court or the magistrates court (Criminal Law Act 1977, s.64(1)(*a*)).

indictment. A written accusation of one or more persons of a crime, at the suit of the Queen formerly presented on oath by a grand jury. Indictments were highly technical in form but the Indictments Act 1915 provided that particulars should be set out in ordinary language in which the use of technical terms should not be necessary. An indictment consists of three parts: (1) the commencement indicating the venue; (2) the statement of offence; (3) particulars of the offence. The preferment of a bill of indictment is now regulated by the Indictments (Procedure) Rules 1971. See BILL OF INDICTMENT.

indivisum. That which is held by two persons in common without partition.

indorsement. A writing on the back of an instrument. Indorsement is a mode of transference of bills of exchange, bills of lading, etc., consisting of the signature of the person to whom the instrument is payable on the back of the instrument and delivery to the transferee (called an indorsement in blank). A special indorsement specifies the name of the transferee. See WRIT OF SUMMONS.

inducement, matters of. Introductory statements in a pleading.

industrial and provident societies. A society for carrying on any industries businesses, or trades specified in or authorised by its rules, whether wholesale or retail, including dealings with land, and banking business. When registered such a society becomes a body corporate with limited liability (Industrial and Provident Societies Acts 1965 to 1975, replacing earlier legislation).

Industrial Councils. See WAGES COUNCILS.

industrial injuries. Employees who sustain personal injuries in accidents arising out of and in the course of their employment (or their relatives in the case of death) may claim benefits under the Social Security Act 1975, ss.50–75 and Social Security (Miscellaneous Provisions) Act 1977, ss.9–11.

industrial insurance company. One that grants life assurances for small sums at less periodical intervals than two months (Industrial Assurance Act 1923). See also the Insurance Companies Act 1909, ss.36, 38; and the Industrial Assurance and Friendly Societies Acts, 1948, 1958.

industrial tribunals. Established originally under the Industrial Training Act 1964 their jurisdiction has been gradually increased to deal with many areas of dispute between employer and employee, *e.g.* claims relating to redundancy, unfair dismissal, equal pay or terms of employment. The Chairman of each tribunal is a barrister or solicitor and he sits with two other persons. Appeal lies to the Employment Appeal Tribunal (*q.v.*). See Employment Protection (Consolidation) Act 1978; Industrial Tribunals (Rules of Procedure) Regulations 1980 (S.I. 1980 No. 884).

Ine, Laws of. The earliest laws of the Kingdom of Wessex, probably promulgated between A.D. 688 and 694.

inevitable accident. An accident which cannot be avoided by the exercise of ordinary care, caution and skill.

infamous conduct. The term previously used in respect of disgraceful or dishonourable behaviour by medical men. The position is now covered by the Medical Act 1978, s.7 which gives the General Medical Council the power to deal with cases of "serious professional misconduct".

infamy. A disability which debarred a person from giving evidence. It was incurred at common law by a person on conviction of forgery, perjury, etc.

infans. [Romans law.] A child not yet able to speak. Later, a child under the age of seven.

infant. See now MINOR.

infanti proximus. [Roman law.] A child that can speak but not with understanding (*intellectus*). A child that has not yet passed his seventh year.

infanticide. The killing of a newly born child. The Infanticide Act 1938 provides that where a woman by any wilful act or omission causes the death of her child, being a child under the age of 12 months, but at the time the balance of her mind was disturbed by reason of her not having fully recovered from the effect of giving birth to the child, or by reason of the effect of lactation consequent upon the birth of the child, then she shall be guilty of infanticide and punishable as for manslaughter, if but for the Act she might have been convicted of murder. It is an offence to destroy a child which has not yet had a separate existence (Infant Life Preservation Act 1929). See also CONCEALMENT OF BIRTH.

inferior court. Any court other than the Supreme Court. The inferior courts are amenable to the orders of certiorari, mandamus and prohibition (*q.v.*).

information. A pleading; a step by which certain civil and criminal proceedings are commenced. In Chancery proceedings on behalf of the Crown the information was the statement of facts offered by the Attorney General to the court. In the Exchequer Division there was a proceeding under the equitable jurisdiction of the court to recover damages or money due to the Crown and known as the English Information. The more usual form of proceeding by the Crown to recover a debt was by way of Latin Information on the Revenue side of the King's Bench Division. Latin Informations and English Informations were abolished by the Crown Proceedings Act 1947 (Sched. 1).

In criminal procedure, informations were brought to enforce a penalty or forfeiture under a penal statute. They were abolished by the Criminal Law Act 1967, s.6(6)).

Informations are the normal method of instituting criminal proceedings before justices of the peace (see Magistrates Court Act 1980, s.127). An information is "laid" when it is received at the office of the Clerk to the Justices (*q.v.*) for the relevant area (*R.* v. *Dartford Justices, ex p. Dhesi, The Times*, July 23, 1982, H.L.).

informer. A person who brought an action or some other proceeding for the recovery of a penalty of which the whole or part went to him. The Common Informers Act 1951 abolished common informer procedure and provided that any offence formerly only punishable by common informer proceedings is to be punishable on summary conviction by fine.

infortunium, per. [By misadventure.] See HOMICIDE.

infra. [Below.]

infringement. Interference with, or the violation of, the right of another, particularly the right to a patent or copyright. The remedy is an injunction to restrain future infringements, and an action for the recovery of the damage caused or profits made by the past infringements.

ingenuus. [Roman law.] A free-born man; a man free from the moment of his birth; being born in wedlock the son of parents either freeborn or made free.

inheritance. An estate in land which descends from a man to his heirs. See WILL.

inhibition. (1) A prohibition from proceeding in a cause or matter. (2) An order or entry on the register forbidding for a given time, or until further order, any dealing with lands or charges registered (Land Registration Act 1925, ss.57, 61). (3) An ecclesiastical censure (Ecclesiastical Jurisdiction Measure 1963, s.49).

injunction. An order or decree by which a party to an action is required to do, or refrain from doing, a particular thing. Injunctions are either restrictive (preventive) or mandatory (compulsive). As regards time, injunctions are either interlocutory (or interim) or perpetual. A perpetual injunction is granted only after the plaintiff has established his right and the actual or threatened infringement of it by the defendant; an interlocutory injunction may be granted at any time after the issue of the writ to maintain things *in statu quo*. The High Court may by order (whether interlocutory or final) grant an injunction in all cases in which it appears to the court to be just and convenient to do so (Supreme Court Act 1981, s.37 (1)). On an application for an interlocutory injunction, where there is a serious question to be tried, unless the material before the court fails to disclose that the plaintiff has any real prospect of being granted a permanent injunction at the trial or the court is satisfied that the claim is frivolous or vexatious the court must go on to consider whether the balance of convenience lies in favour of granting or refusing the interlocutory relief sought. No interlocutory injunction will normally be granted where the recoverable damages would be an adequate remedy (*American Cynamid Co.* v. *Ethicon Ltd.* [1975] 1 All E.R. 504, H.L.; R.S.C. Ord. 29, r. 1). Where an action for debt due and owing is brought against a defendant who is not within the jurisdiction but who has assets in this country, the court may grant an *ex parte* or interim injunction to restrain the defendant from removing assets from the jurisdiction pending trial (*Mareva Compania Naviera* v. *International Bulk Carriers Ltd.* [1980] 1 All E.R. 213). This is called a "Mareva Injunction". Order for discovery (*q.v.*) and interrogatories (*q.v.*) may be made in aid of a Mareva injunction (*Bekhor & Co. Ltd.* v. *Bilton* [1981] 2 All E.R. 565). Injunctions may be granted in proceedings for divorce and judicial separation to prevent molestation (pursuant to the courts inherent jurisdiction) or to prevent disposal of assets (Matrimonial Causes Act 1973, s.37). The court may also grant a non-molestation injunction and add a power of arrest by the police in case of breach whether or not a man and woman living together as husband and wife are married (Domestic Violence Act 1976, s.1).

Where an accused person has money in a bank account which the police reasonably believe to have been stolen or fraudulently obtained, the police may apply to the court for an injunction to "freeze" those moneys until trial, to prevent the accused from dissipating them (*Chief Constable of Kent* v. *V. and another*, *The Times*, May 14, 1982, C.A.).

An injunction, once granted, is enforced by committal for contempt of court for any breach.

injuria. [A legal wrong.]

injuria non excusat injuriam. [One wrong does not justify another.]

injurious falsehood. Sometimes called malicious falsehood. A Tort consisting of written or oral falsehoods which are maliciously made or published which are calculated to produce damage and which do result in actual damage. Injurious falsehood can be distinguished from defamation (*q.v.*) in that it is not necessary to show that the falsehood lowers the victim in the estimation of right thinking people, *e.g.* to spread the false rumour that X had retired from practice at the bar would not be defamatory but might cause X financial loss and amount to injurious falsehood (see *Ratcliffe* v. *Evans* [1892] 2 Q.B. 254).

injury. (1) (From Latin Injura). A violation of another's legal rights.
(2) Any disease or impairment of a person's physical or mental condition.

Inner Temple. One of the Inns of Court (*q.v.*).

innkeeper. One who holds himself out as being prepared to receive and entertain travellers, and who is bound to receive and entertain every traveller who presents himself for that purpose and is ready to pay his expenses, provided there be sufficient room in the inn, and no impropriety of conduct in the traveller himself. He has a lien for his charges on all property brought by his guest to the inn, even although it is stolen property. The liability of an innkeeper for the loss, or damage, of guests' property is subject to the Hotel Proprietors Act 1956.

Inns of Chancery. These were legal seminaries attached to the greater bodies, the Inns of Court, to whom their senior students migrated, and from whom they received Readers, or instructors in law. From about 1650 they were entirely in the hands of the attorneys, who did not maintain them for educational purposes, and during the nineteenth century the Inns of Chancery ceased to exist as such.

Inns of Court. The four Inns of Court—Inner Temple, Middle Temple, Lincoln's Inn, and Gray's Inn—are unincorporated voluntary associations with the exclusive right of call to the Bar. They were established in the fourteenth century as hostels and schools of law, outside the walls of the City of London. They stand upon a footing of equality. No precedence, priority or superior antiquity is conceded to, or claimed by, one Inn beyond another. They are not subject to the jurisdiction of the courts, but the judges act as a domestic forum, or as visitors. See SENATE OF THE INNS OF COURT AND THE BAR; SERJEANTS-AT-LAW.

innuendo. That part of an indictment or pleading in proceedings for libel which connects the alleged libel with its subject, or states the latent and secondary defamatory meaning of words which are not on the face of them libellous. It usually commences with the words "meaning thereby." It must be expressly pleaded. An innuendo should not be left to the jury unless it is supported by extrinsic facts (*Lewis* v. *Daily Telegraph* [1963] 1 Q.B. 340).

inofficious testament. [Roman law.] A will which wholly passes over, without assigning sufficient reason, those having strong and natural claims on the testator. Such a will might be set aside.

inops consilii. [Without advice.]

inquest. An inquisition. An inquiry held by a coroner as to the death of a person who has been slain, or has died suddenly, or in prison, or under suspicious circumstances. See CORONER.

inquest of office. An inquiry made by a jury before a sheriff, coroner, escheator, or other officer of the Crown, concerning any matter that entitled the Crown to the possession of lands or tenements, goods or chattels; *e.g.* by reason of an escheat, forfeiture, idiocy, etc. Virtually absolute.

inquiry. In actions in the High Court, if an inquiry is ordered, it is made in Chambers by the Master or other officer who investigates the evidence adduced by the parties, and embodies the result in his certificate.

inquiry, writ of. One of the modes of assessing damages when interlocutory judgment (*e.g.* by default in appearance or pleading) has been obtained by the plaintiff in an action for unliquidated damages. Now abolished.

inquisitio. [Roman law.] Inquiry; made in certain cases by the *Praetor* (or *Praeses*) as preliminary to the confirmation of persons appointed tutors or curators.

inquisitorial procedure. The system of law in countries whose legal systems originate in Roman or Civil Law under which the judge initiates all necessary investigations and summons and examines witnesses and in which a trial is an inquiry by the court. The only common example of such procedure in English Law is a Coroner's Inquest. See CORONERS; CONTRAST ACCUSATORIAL PROCEDURE.

inquisition. (1) An inquiry by a jury, held before an officer or commissioner of the Crown (inquisitor); (2) a formal document recording the result of the inquiry.

insanity. Unsoundness of mind; mental disease. An insane person is *non compos mentis,* and was termed a lunatic. Later the term "person of unsound mind" came into use, and a person might be so found by inquisition. A person of unsound mind is without legal capacity, and is not civilly responsible for his acts, except that he can make a will in a lucid interval. His contract is valid; unless he was incapable of appreciating the nature of the contract, and the other party was aware of it, when the transaction is voidable at his option. Pursuant to the Mental Health Act 1959, an insane person is termed a "patient." When, on the trial of an accused person, the jury find that he did the act (or made the omission) charged but was insane, they must return a special verdict that the accused is not guilty by reason of insanity (Trial of Lunatics Act 1883, s.2; Criminal Procedure (Insanity) Act 1964, s.1). The special verdict under the Act of 1883, was "guilty but insane." See also DIMINISHED RESPONSIBILITY.

An appeal lies to the Court of Appeal against a special verdict (Criminal Appeal Act 1968, ss.12, 13).

Every man is to be presumed sane until the contrary is proved. To establish a defence on the ground of insanity it must be clearly proved that at the time of the committing of the act the party accused was labouring under such a defect of reason from disease of the mind as not to know the nature or quality of the act he was doing, or, if he did know it, that he did not know he was doing wrong (*M'Naghten's Case,* 10 Cl. & Fin. 200). The fact that a person suffers from delusions will not of itself exempt him from punishment, if he knew at the time of committing the crime that he was acting contrary to law.

For the treatment of "patients" and care of their property, see MENTAL DISORDER. See also NULLITY OF MARRIAGE.

insider dealing. Certain dealings in the shares of a company by a person classed as an "insider" have been made a criminal offence by the Companies Act 1980, ss.68–73. To be an insider a person must be (*a*) an individual and not a company and (*b*) "connected" with the company (as defined by ss.68–73), subject to certain specified exceptions. An offence may be committed in the following circumstances:

(a) the dealing must be at a recognised stock exchange (s.68(1)).

(b) the person who deals must be an insider (for definition see above).

(c) he must have knowingly been connected with the company during the preceding six months.

(d) he must have obtained the information by having been connected with the company.

(e) it would be reasonable to expect him not to disclose the information except in the performance of his duties.

(f) the information must be unpublished price sensitive information (as defined in s.73(2)) in relation to the securities.

In England and Wales proceedings may only be instituted by the Secretary of State for Trade and Industry or the Director of Public Prosecutions (s.72(1)).

insolvency. The inability to pay debts in full. Prior to the Bankruptcy Act 1861, bankruptcy only applied to traders, and other persons in a similar condition were said to be insolvent (*q.v.*).

insolvent. A person who is unable to pay his debts as they become due. As to companies, see WINDING UP.

inspection of documents. A party to an action who has served a list of documents must allow the other party to inspect the documents listed, and to take copies thereof. He must, when he serves the list, also serve a notice stating a time within seven days in which the documents may be inspected at a specified place. Objections to production should also be stated, and the grounds thereof.

On failure to comply with the notice, the party requiring production may apply to the judge for an order for production and inspection, which may be enforced by dismissal of the action, or striking out the defence and giving judgment (Ord. 24). See DISCOVERY OF DOCUMENTS.

inspection of property. See PILLER, ANTON.

inspectorship deed. A deed embodying an agreement that the business of a debtor should be carried on under the inspection of the creditor's agents: obsolete.

instalment. A part or portion of the total sum or quantity due, arranged to be taken on account of the total sum or quantity due. See HIRE-PURCHASE AGREEMENT.

instance, court of first. A court in which proceedings are commenced, as distinct from an appellate court.

instrument. A formal legal document in writing; *e.g.* a deed of conveyance.

insurance. A contract whereby a person called the insurer agrees in consideration of money paid to him, called the premium, by another person, called the assured, to indemnify the latter against loss resulting to him on the happening of certain events. The policy is the document in which is contained .the terms of the contract. Insurance is a contract *uberrimae fidei* (of the utmost good faith) and of indemnity only, except in the case of life and accident insurance, when an agreed sum is payable. See the Insurance Companies Act 1974. See also the Policy-holders Protection Act 1975.

intendment of the law. A legal presumption.

intention. The general rule of law is that a person is presumed to intend the natural, reasonable and probable consequences of his acts, whether in fact he intended them or not.

In criminal proceedings the court or jury must decide whether or not the accused did, in all the circumstances of the case, intend or foresee the result of his actions. They are not bound in law to infer intention merely because the result is the natural and probable result of the action taken (Criminal Justice Act 1967, s.8). Intention and act must both normally concur to constitute a crime. But a wrongful intention or guilty mind is not essential in every crime. The mental elements of crimes differ widely, and must be ascertained from the definitions of particular crimes. In most indictable offences, however; *e.g.* homicide and bigamy, a wrongful intention is necessary to constitute a crime. But in many acts prohibited by statute, especially those of an administrative character, there is imposed an absolute liability, and the absence of a wrongful intent is no excuse, *e.g.*breaches of laws and regulations dealing with the revenue, public health and order, etc. See MALICE; MENS REA.

inter alia. [Among others.]

inter arma leges silent. [Between armies the law is silent.] As between the State and its external enemies the laws are silent, and as regards subjects of the State, laws may be silenced by necessity in time of war or disturbance.

inter vivos. [During life: between living persons.]

interdicta. [Roman law.] The procedure by which the Praetor ordered or forbade something to be done, chiefly in disputes about possession or quasi-possession.

interesse termini. [Interest of a term.] The interest which a lessee under a lease at common law had before he entered or took possession of the land demised. By the Law of Property Act 1925, s.149 the doctrine of *interesse termini* was abolished, and leases take effect from the date fixed for the commencement of the term without actual entry.

interest. A person is said to have an interest in a thing when he has rights, titles, advantages, duties, liabilities connected with it, whether present or future, ascertained or potential, provided they are not too remote.

Any direct interest in the subject-matter of legal proceedings disqualifies anyone from acting in a judicial capacity and will invalidate the proceedings if such person so acts, unless such interest is announced to or known by the parties and they waive the right to object. Formerly, the parties to a case, their spouses, and persons with any pecuniary interest in a case, were incompetent witnesses. But now, in general, all persons are competent witnesses and considerations of interest merely affect the weight of their evidence. See HUSBAND AND WIFE.

Interest also signifies a sum payable in respect of the use of another sum of money, called the principal. A judgment debt bears interest at the rate prescribed from time to time. In proceedings in any court for recovery of debt or damages the court has power to award interest on the debt or damages between the date on which the cause of action arose and the date of the judgement (Law Reform (Miscellaneous Provisions) Act 1934, s.3). For the position as to interest on general damages awarded for personal injuries sustained by a plaintiff see *Jefford* v. *Gee* [1970] 1 All E.R. 1202, C.A., *Pickett* v. *B.R. Engineering* [1979] 1 All E.R. 774, H.L. and *Birkett* v. *Hayes* [1982] 2 All E.R. 710, C.A. Interest may run on a default judgment (*Alex Lawrie Factors* v. *M.I.M.* [1981] 3 All E.R. 658) but on an order for costs interest runs only from the date of Taxation (*q.v.*) and not from the date of the order (*K.* v. *K.* [1977] 1 All E.R. 576).

interest reipublicae ne maleficia remaneant impunita. [It is a matter of public concern that wrongdoings are not left unpunished.]

interest reipublicae ne sua re quis male utatur. [It concerns the State that no one should make a wrongful use of his property.]

interest reipublicae ut sit finis litium. [It concerns the State that lawsuits be not protracted.]

interference with goods. See WRONGFUL INTERFERENCE WITH GOODS.

interim order. Some order made in the course of proceedings, not being a final order, *e.g.* an order for financial relief (*q.v.*), made in the course of matrimonial proceedings, intended to last for a limited period only.

interim payment. A plaintiff may at any time after service of writ and time for acknowledgment of service apply to the High Court for an order requiring the defendant to make an interim payment (R.S.C., Ord. 29, r, 10(1)), defined (in r. 9) as a payment on account of any damages, debt or other sum (excluding costs) which the defendant may be held liable to pay to or for the benefit of the plaintiff. Such applications are not restricted to personal injury claims but cover claims of any kind. The plaintiff must show either: (*a*) that the defendant has admitted liability; or (*b*) that there is a judgment for damages to be assessed; or (*c*) that if the action proceeded to trial the plaintiff would obtain judgment for substantial damages.

interlocutory order. While a final order determines the rights of the parties an interlocutory order leaves something further to be done to determine those rights (Ord. 29).

interlocutory proceedings. One taken during the course of an action and incidental to the principal object of the action, namely, the judgment. Thus, interlocutory applications in an action include all steps taken for the purpose of assisting either party in the prosecution of his case; or of protecting or otherwise dealing with the subject-matter of the action, or of executing the judgment when obtained.

international law. The sum of the rules accepted by civilised States as determining their conduct towards each other, and towards each other's subjects. It is law of imperfect obligation inasmuch as there is no sovereign superior to enforce it, but the United Nations set up tribunals to try enemy persons accused of offences against (*inter alia*) international law, committed during the Second World War.

In order to prove an alleged rule of international law it must be shown either to have received the express sanction of international agreement or it must have grown to be part of international law by the frequent practical recognition of States in their dealings with each other. International law is only binding on the courts of this country in so far as it has been adopted and made part of municipal law. See PRIVATE INTERNATIONAL LAW.

interpleader. When a person is in possession of property in which he claims no interest, but to which two or more other persons lay claim, and he, not knowing to whom he may safely give it up, is sued or expects to be sued by one or both, he can compel them to interplead; *i.e.* to take proceedings between themselves to determine who is entitled to it (see Ord. 17). This is called "stakeholder interpleader." Similarly, where any goods, etc., taken in execution by a sheriff are claimed by a third person, the sheriff may apply for interpleader relief.

interpretatio chartarum benigne facienda est ut res magis valeat quam pereat. [The construction of deeds is to be made liberally, that the thing may rather avail than perish.]

interpretation. See the Interpretation Act 1978. See also STATUTORY INTERPRETATION.

interpretation clause. A section in an Act of Parliament or clause in a deed setting out the meaning which is to be attached to particular expressions.

interrogatories. A party to an action may apply to a Master by summons or by notice under the summons for directions for an order giving him leave to serve interrogatories on any other party, and requiring the other party to answer them on affidavit (Ord. 26).

intervener. A person who voluntarily interposes in an action or other proceeding with the leave of the court (Ord. 15, r. 6; Ord. 16).

A person charged with adultery may be allowed to intervene in a suit for divorce or judicial separation (Matrimonial Causes Act 1973, s.49(5)). As to intervention after decree nisi see ss.9, 15. As to intervention in the Admiralty Court, see Ord. 75, r. 17.

intestacy. Dying intestate; *i.e.* without leaving a will. Partial intestacy is the leaving of a will which validly disposes of part only of the property, so that the rest goes as on an intestacy.

intestate succession. The residuary estate of an intestate devolves according to the Administration of Estates Act 1925 and the Intestates' Estate Act 1952 (as amended by the Family Provision Act 1966, s.1), as follows:

(1) If the intestate leaves a surviving spouse, and also leaves issue, the surviving spouse takes all the personal chattels absolutely, £8,750 free of death duties, with interest, and a life interest in half the residue of the estate. The other half of the residue and the reversionary interest is held on the statutory trusts for the issue.

(2) If the intestate leaves no issue, but leaves a parent, brother or sister of the whole blood, the surviving spouse takes the personal chattels absolutely. £30,000 free of death duties, with interest, and one-half of the residue absolutely. The other half of the residue goes to the parents absolutely, or otherwise to the brothers and sisters of their issue on the statutory trusts; if no issue, parents, brothers or sisters of the whole blood, or their issue, the surviving spouse takes all the estate absolutely.

(3) If the intestate leaves no surviving spouse, but leaves issue, then to the issue on the statutory trusts.

(4) If the intestate leaves no issue, then surviving relatives, in their several degrees, become entitled.

The statutory trusts are: for all the children of the intestate, or for all the members of the other class of relative, as the case may be, who are living at the death of the intestate, and attain 21 or marry, in equal shares, but if any of them die before the intestate, all the deceased's issue who survive the intestate and attain 21 or marry take *per stirpes* the share of the deceased (Administration of Estates Act 1925, s.47).

The surviving spouse's life interest (if any) may be redeemed for a capital sum at the election of the spouse, who may require that the matrimonial home may be appropriated in or towards that spouse's interest in the estate.

These rules are modified by the Family Law Reform Act 1969, which gives an illegitimate child a right to succeed on the intestacy of either parent and gives parents the right to succeed on the intestacy of an illegitimate child (s.14). For protection of trustees and personal representatives from late claims, see s.17. See FAMILY PROVISION.

intestatus. [Roman law.] A man dies intestate if he has not made a will at all, or if he has made it wrongly, or if the will he had made has been broken, or become null, or if no one is heir under it.

intimidation. The misdemeanour of using violence or threats to a person, his wife or children, to compel such person to do or abstain from doing any act which he has a legal right to do or abstain from doing (*R.* v. *Jones* (*John*) *and others* (1974) 59 Cr. App. R. 120).

As to the tort of intimidation see *Rookes* v. *Barnard* [1964] A.C. 1129 and the Trade Union and Labour Relations Act 1974, s.13.

intra vires. [Within the power of.] See ULTRA VIRES.

intrusion. Where the tenant for life of an estate dies, and before the heir of the reversioner or remainderman enters, a stranger enters or "intrudes" on the land, the heir's remedies are entry or an action for recovery of the land.

investiture. In the legal sense, the delivery of corporeal possession of land granted by a lord to his tenant; livery of seisin (*q.v.*).

invitee. A person invited to enter the property of another. An invitee is a person who comes on the occupier's premises with his consent, on business in which the occupier and he have a common interest. At common law, an invitee, using reasonable care on his own part for his own safety, is entitled to expect that the occupier shall on his part use reasonable care to prevent damage from unusual danger which he knows or ought to know. By the Occupiers' Liability Act 1957, s.2 the occupier must take reasonable care to see that a visitor will be reasonably safe in using the premises.

invito beneficium non datur. [Roman law.] A benefit is not conferred upon anyone against his consent.

ipsissima verba. [The identical words.]

ipso facto. [By the mere fact.]

Ireland. By the Ireland Act 1949 Eire became the independent Republic of Ireland, but Northern Ireland's constitutional position was declared and affirmed.

irregularity. The departure from, or neglect of, the proper formalities in a legal proceeding. They may be waived or consented to by the other party, or rectified by the court on payment of costs occasioned.

issuable. A pleading which raised a substantial question of fact or law, a judgment or verdict on which would determine the action on its merits.

issue. (1) The issue of a person consists of his children, grandchildren, and all other lineal descendants. At common law, a gift "to A and his issue" conferred a life estate only because of the failure to use the appropriate word "heirs." The Wills Act 1837, s.29 provided that in a will the words "die without issue" are to be construed as meaning a want or failure of issue in the lifetime, or at the death of, the party, and not an indefinite failure of issue, unless a contrary intention appears by the will. Since 1925, "issue" has been construed as a word of purchase (*q.v.*). See MALE ISSUE.

(2) "Issues" is the technical name for the profits of land taken in execution under a writ of distringas (*q.v.*).

(3) When the parties to an action have answered one another's pleadings in such a manner that they have arrived at some material point or matter affirmed on one side and denied on the other, the parties are said to be "at issue."

(4) A "general issue" was a plea used where the defendant wished to deny all the allegations in the declaration or the principal fact on which it was founded: such is a plea of not guilty to an indictment.

J

jactitation of marriage. Where a person boasts or gives out that he or she is married to someone, whereby a common reputation of their marriage may ensue; in such a case the person aggrieved may present a petition praying a decree of perpetual silence against the jactitator.

jeopardy, in. In danger of being convicted on a criminal charge. See AUTREEFOIS ACQUIT.

jetsam. Goods which are cast into the sea and there sink and remain under water.

jettison. The throwing overboard of goods from necessity to lighten the vessel in a storm, or to prevent capture.

joinder of causes of action. A plaintiff may without the leave of the court, join in one action several causes of action, even if in the alternative, against the same defendant including other causes of action with a claim for the recovery of land (Ord. 15, r. 1) subject to the power of the court to order separate trials where joinder may embarrass or delay the trial or is otherwise inconvenient (r. 5).

joinder of parties. All persons may be joined in one action as plaintiffs or defendants where the claim is in respect of the same transaction or series of transactions and common questions of law or fact arise (Ord. 15, r. 4).

joint account. Where two or more persons advance money and take the security to themselves jointly, each is in equity deemed to be separately entitled to his proportion of the money, so that on his death it passes to his personal representatives and not to his surviving co-lenders. The Law of Property Act 1925, s.111 made it sufficient to say that the money is advanced by the lenders out of money belonging to them on a joint account. This is simply conveyancing machinery, however, and does not conclude the question whether the survivor is entitled beneficially to the whole of the money, or must hold part as trustee for the representatives of the deceased mortgagee.

A joint account in business is one that can be operated by any or all of the persons concerned, either singly or collectively as may be arranged and agreed, *e.g.* a joint banking account.

joint and several obligation. An obligation entered into by two or more persons, jointly and severally, so that each is liable severally, and all liable jointly, and a creditor or obligee may sue one or more severally, or all jointly, at his option.

joint custody. An order for custody of children (*q.v.*) in which custody is awarded jointly to the parents so that they share the legal responsibility for the upbringing of the children and both must consent to any major decision affecting the children, *e.g.* education or religious persuasion. In such a case it would be necessary to specify which parent had care and control of the child. See CUSTODY OF CHILDREN, CARE AND CONTROL.

joint obligation. A bond or covenant or other liability entered into by two or more persons jointly, so that all must sue or be sued upon it together. A judgment against one joint contractor, even though unsatisfied is generally (but not in all circumstances) a bar to any action against the others; a release given to one joint contractor releases all (*Kendall* v. *Hamilton* (1879) 4 App. Cas. 504). But one joint obligor who pays a joint debt is entitled to contribution from the others.

joint stock company. See COMPANY.

joint tenancy. The ownership of land in common by several persons where there is a right of survivorship, *i.e.* where on the death of one joint owner the land as a whole vests in the survivors, and can only be disposed of by will by the last surviving owner. Every joint tenant is seised or possessed of the joint property *per my et per tout,* that is, by every part and by the whole. The four unities of joint tenancy which must exist, or the tenancy will be in common, are:

(1) Possession. Each joint tenant must be entitled to the possession of the whole of the land.

(2) Interest. Each joint tenant must have the same estate or interest in the land.

(3) Title. Each joint tenant must have the same title, *i.e.* take in virtue of the same instrument.

(4) Time. Each joint tenant must have an estate for the same time.

By section 36 of the Law of Property Act 1925 where a legal estate, not being settled land, is beneficially limited to, or held in trust for, any persons as joint tenants, it shall be held on trust for sale.

Equity leans against a joint tenancy, *i.e.* it will hold, where possible, joint tenants at law to be tenants in common in equity.

As to a conveyance by the survivor of joint tenants, see the Law of Property (Joint Tenants) Acts 1964.

joint tortfeasors. [Joint wrongdoers.] Persons are joint tortfeasors in cases of (1) vicarious liability; (2) agency; (3) common action, *i.e.* they must in fact or law, have committed the same wrongful act. Joint tortfeasors are jointly and severally responsible for the whole damage. At common law a judgment obtained against one joint wrongdoer released all the others, even if it was unsatisfied. This rule was abolished by the Law Reform (Married Women and Tortfeasors) Act 1935, s.6(1)(*a*).

At common law one joint tortfeasor had no right of contribution or indemnity from another joint tortfeasor. This rule was abolished by the Law Reform (Married Women and Tortfeasors) Act 1935, s.6(1)(*c*), and the position is now governed by the Civil Liability (Contribution) Act 1978. Any person liable in respect of damage suffered by another person may recover contribution in respect of the same damage, whether the other person's liability is joint with the first person's liability or not (Act of 1978 s.1(1)).

The amount recoverable is such as is just and equitable having regard to each party's responsibility for the damage (s.2(3)).

jointress. A woman entitled to a jointure (*q.v.*).

jointure. A provision made by a husband for the support of his wife after his death: originally an estate in joint tenancy of a husband and wife, granted to them before marriage, as provision for the wife. A legal jointure was a competent livelihood of freehold for the wife of lands or tenements, etc., to take effect presently in possession or profit after the decease of her husband for the life of the wife at the least (Coke).

An equitable jointure is a rentcharge or annuity payable by the trustees of a marriage settlement to the wife for her life if she should survive her husband, the rentcharge or annuity being generally secured by powers of distress and entry, and by the limitation of the settled lands to trustees for a long term of years.

journals of Parliament. The records made in the House of Lords from 1509 and the House of Commons from 1547 of business done, but not of speeches made. The journals of the House of Lords, but not those of the House of Commons, are public records.

joy riding. The term commonly applied to the offence of taking a motor vehicle or other conveyance for one's own or another's use without the consent of the owner or other lawful authority, or driving a vehicle or allowing oneself to be carried in it knowing it to have been taken without authority (Theft Act 1968, s.12).

judge. An officer of the crown who sits to administer Justice according to law. Judges are Lords of Appeal in Ordinary (House of Lords) Lords Justices of Appeal (Court of Appeal), Puisne Judges (High Court), Circuit Judges (Crown Court and county court) and Recorders (Part-time Crown Court and county court).

A judge is generally appointed from the ranks of practicing barristers but a solicitor may be appointed a Recorder and thereafter a Circuit judge. Judges of the High Court and above may only be removed from office on address by both Houses of Parliament.

judge advocate. The Judge Advocate-General is the adviser of the Secretary of State for Defence in reference to courts-martial and other matters of military law. The Judge Advocate of the Fleet holds an analogous post in regard to the Navy. Both these offices were provided for by the Courts-Martial (Appeals) Act, 1951. Every military court-martial is attended by an officiating judge advocate whose functions are to superintend the trial and advise the court on points of law and procedure. At naval courts-martial, the Judge Advocate of the Fleet, or a deputy judge advocate acts, if so required.

Judge Ordinary. The President of the Family Division.

judge's order. An order made by a judge in chambers in the Chancery Division so called to distinguish it from a Master's order.

Judges' Rules. Rules for the guidance of the police in interrogating persons suspected of, or charged with, an offence or crime, *e.g.* when a caution should be given that what is said may be taken down and used in evidence, and the form that written statements by an accused should take. See Practice Note (C.C.A.) (Judges' Rules) [1964] 1 W.L.R. 152. The admissibility of an alleged confession does not depend upon whether or not there has been compliance with the Judges' Rules but on whether it is shown that the confession was made voluntarily (*R.* v. *Prager* [1972] 1 W.L.R. 260).

judgment. The decision or sentence of a court in a legal proceeding. Also the reasoning of the judge which leads him to his decision, which may be reported and cited as an authority, if the matter is of importance, or can be treated as a precedent (*q.v.*).

As to the entry of judgment in proceedings, see Ord. 42, r. 5.

judgment creditor. One in whose favour a judgment for a sum of money is given against a judgment debtor.

judgment debtor. One against whom judgment is given for a sum of money, and for which his property is liable to be taken in execution at the instance of the judgment creditor.

judgment summons. The process used to procure the committal (*q.v.*) of a judgment debtor.

judgments, extension of. The reciprocal enforcement of judgments. The process by which judgments obtained in the courts of one country may be enforced, by registration, in the courts of another country. See the Administration of Justice Act 1920, Part II, and the Foreign Judgments (Reciprocal Enforcement) Act 1933 (see Ord. 71, r. 1, notes).

judicatum solvi stipulatio. [Roman law.] A stipulation whereby a plaintiff took security at the beginning of a suit for satisfaction of the judgment.

(1) Before Justinian. In a real action commenced by *formula petitoria* the defendant was required to give the *cautio judicatum solvi*—a security with sureties. In a personal action, the defendant sued in his own name did not give security.

(2) Under Justinian. The defendant if sued in his own name was required to give security that he would appear personally and remain in court to the end of the trial.

Judicature Acts. The Judicature Act 1873, which took effect in 1875, amalgamated the then existing superior courts into the Supreme Court of Judicature (*q.v.*) consisting of the Court of Appeal and the High Court of Justice. It also provided for the fusion of law and equity, with the supremacy of equity in case of conflict (s.25).

The Judicature Acts were re-consolidated by the Supreme Court of Judicature (Consolidation) Act 1925 (usually referred to as the Judicature Act 1925). See now Supreme Court Act 1981.

judici officium suum excedenti non paretur. [Effect is not given to the decision of a judge delivered in excess of his jurisdiction.]

judicia publica. [Roman law.] Public prosecutions: so called, because generally it was open to any citizen to institute them and carry them through.

Judicial Committee. The Committee of the Privy Council constituted by the Judicial Committee Act 1833. It has power to entertain an appeal from any

Dominion or Dependency of the Crown in any matter, civil or criminal, except where its jurisdiction has been excluded as regards a particular country. Appeals may require the special leave of the Privy Council. It is the final court of appeal from the Ecclesiastical Courts and Prize Courts. The Judicial Committee has also a "domestic" jurisdiction in hearing appeals from certain professional organisations that have power to strike a member off its register, *e.g.* the General Medical Council.

The *ex officio* members of the Judicial Committee include persons who hold or have held the office of Lord President or Lord Chancellor, the Lords of Appeal in Ordinary, and not exceeding six senior judges or ex-judges of self-governing Dominions of the Crown, if members of the Privy Council.

The Judicial Committee does not formally deliver judgment, but the decision of the Committee is given in one speech, and the Queen is advised accordingly. An order in Council is issued to give effect thereto. Formerly dissenting opinions were not disclosed but this is no longer the case. See *e.g. Public Prosecutor* v. *Oie Hee Koi* [1968] A.C. 829.

judicial notice. The courts take cognisance or notice of matters which are so notorious or clearly established that formal evidence of their exercise is unnecessary: and matters of common knowledge and everyday life; *e.g.* that there is a period of gestation of approximately nine months before the birth of a child.

judicial review. An application to the High Court for (*a*) orders of mandamus (*q.v.*), Prohibition (*q.v.*) or certiorari (*q.v.*), or (*b*) a declaration or injunction in proceedings for judicial review or (*c*) an injunction restraining a person acting in a public office when not entitled to do so is by a procedure known as an application for judicial review (Supreme Court Act 1981, ss.29, 30, 31; R.S.C., Ord 53). The new procedure reforms the procedure relating to administrative law and creates a uniform system for the exercise by the High Court of its supervisory jurisdiction over inferior courts, Tribunals and public bodies and persons. By the new procedure the applicant merely applies for judicial review and need not specify which particular remedy he seeks.

The remedy of judicial review is concerned not with the decision of which review is sought but with the decision making process (*R.* v. *Chief Constable of North Wales Police, ex p. Evans, The Times*, July 24, 1882, H.L.).

judicial separation. A petition for judicial separation may be presented to the Family Division by either party to a marriage. The grounds on which the court may grant a decree are the same as for a decree of divorce (*q.v.*) but the court is not concerned to consider whether the marriage has broken down irretrievably (Matrimonial Causes Act 1973, s.17). After the decree the petitioner is not bound to cohabit with the respondent.

judicial trustee. A trustee appointed by the court under the Judicial Trustees Act 1896.

judicium Dei. [The judgment of God.] Trial by ordeal.

junior barrister. A barrister who is not a Queen's Counsel.

jura eodem modo destituuntur quo constituuntur. [Laws are abrogated by the same means by which they were made.]

jura publica anteferenda privatis. [Public rights are to be preferred to private.]

jura regalia. [Sovereign rights.] Such rights were exercised under royal grant by the Lords Marchers (*q.v.*).

jurat. A memorandum at the end of an affidavit stating where and when the affidavit was sworn, followed by the signature and description of the person before whom it was sworn (Ord. 41, rr. 1, 3).

juratores sunt judices facti. [Juries are the judges of fact.]

juris praecepta sunt haec: honeste vivere, alterum non laedere, suum cuique tribuere. [These are the precepts of the law: to live honestly, to hurt no one, and to give to every man his own.] (Justinian.)

juris ultrum. A writ or action by an incumbent to recover possession of land held by him in right of the church.

jurisdiction. (1) The power of a court or judge to entertain an action, petition or other proceeding. (2) The district or limits within which the judgments or orders of a court can be enforced or executed. The territorial jurisdiction of the High Court of Justice is over England and Wales.

In general, the court may take cognisance of acts committed or matters arising abroad, but in practice the defendant must be within the jurisdiction at the time the writ is served, except in cases where leave is given for service out of the jurisdiction (Ord. 11).

jurisprudence. The science or theory of law. The study of the principles of law. The philosophical aspect of the knowledge of law (Cicero). The knowledge of things human and divine, the science of the just and the unjust (Ulpian). Jurisprudence as a formal science was developed in England by Hobbes, Bentham and Austin. Sir Henry Maine fostered the study of the historical development of law and comparative jurisprudence, the purpose being "to aim at discovering the principles regulating the development of legal systems, with a view to explain the origin of institutions and to study the conditions of their life" (Vinogradoff).

Jurisprudence is the scientific synthesis of the essential principles of law (C.K. Allen). See LAW.

jurisprudentia. [Roman law.] Law learning, the learning of the *jurisprudentes* (men skilled in the law).

jury. [Lat. *jurare,* to swear.] A body of sworn men summoned to decide questions of fact in a judicial proceeding. The jury in origin was a body of neighbours summoned by some public officer to give, upon oath, a true answer to some question (Maitland). The jury is the principal criterion of truth in the law of England (Blackstone). They originally testified to and decided issues of fact of their own knowledge. With the introduction of sworn witnesses the jury became exclusively the judges of fact.

The sworn inquest was apparently introduced by the Normans into England from the procedure of the Carlovingian Kings of France. The inhabitants of a district were summoned by a royal officer to testify and to declare or decide matters of fact relating to property and offences.

Henry II inaugurated the assize (*q.v.*) in lieu of trial by battle for deciding disputed questions of property rights. It was summoned to answer certain specific questions only. The *jurata,* or jury proper, replaced battle, the ordeal, and compurgation as a method of proof.

The statute law relating to juries, jurors and jury service was consolidated by the Juries Act 1974.

The mode of trial is normally fixed by the order on the summons for directions, or order giving leave to defend under Ord. 25. In the Queen's Bench Division neither party has a right to a jury except in cases of fraud, libel, slander, malicious prosecution, or false imprisonment (Administration of Justice (Miscellaneous Provisions) Act 1933, s.6(1); Ord. 33, r. 5). In other cases the action may be tried at the discretion of the judge with or without a jury. In the Chancery Division trial is without a jury.

There is a right to trial by jury in criminal matters in cases which are triable only on indictment or those which are triable either on indictment or summarily (Criminal Law Act 1977, s.14(*a*), (*c*)). For a definitive list of such offences see the Act of 1977, Scheds. 1, 2, 3.

Where a juror dies or is discharged during a criminal trial, the trial may continue provided the number of the jury is not less than nine. On a trial for murder or for any offence punishable with death the consent in writing of the prosecution and the accused is necessary. Alternatively, the court may discharge the jury (Juries Act 1974, s.16). The verdict of the juries in the Crown Court or the High Court need not be unanimous. See the Courts Act 1971, s.39. In a civil action the court may, with the consent of the parties, accept a majority verdict (Juries Act 1974, s.17).

jus. [Roman law.] In its widest sense includes a moral as well as legal obligations. It means (1) "law" as opposed to *lex* (a statute); (2) a right; (3) relationship; (4) the court of a magistrate.

jus accrescendi. [Roman law.] The right of accrual.

jus accrescendi inter mercatores pro beneficio commercii locum non habet. [The right of survivorship among merchants, for the benefit of commerce, does not exist.] See JOINT TENANCY.

jus aedilicium. [Roman law.] The rules of law as stated in the edicts published by the *curule aediles* and administered by them. It was included in the *jus honorarium*.

jus canonicum. [Canon law.]

jus civile. [Roman law.] (1) The law peculiar to a particular State, *e.g.* Rome. (2) The old law of Rome as opposed to the later *jus praetorium*.

jus disponendi. [Roman law.] The right of disposing; the right of alienation.

jus ex injuria non oritur. [A right does not arise out of a wrong.]

jus gentium. [Roman law.] The law of nations. The law common to all peoples. The rules of private law, recognised generally by different nations.

jus honorarium. [Roman law.] Magisterial law, *jus praetorium* and *jus aedilicium*.

jus in personam. A right against a specific person.

jus liberorum. [Roman law.] The special rights granted to the mother of three or four children; or to the father.

jus mariti. [The right of a husband.] See HUSBAND AND WIFE; INTESTATE SUCCESSION.

jus naturale. [Roman law.] The law that nature has taught all living things (Justinian). The law supposed to be constituted by right reason, common to nature and to man; the principles deducible from the *jus gentium*.

jus non scriptum. [Roman law.] The unwritten law. The law that use has approved (Justinian).

jus postliminii. See POSTLIMINIUM.

jus potestatis. See PATRIA POTESTAS.

jus praetorium. [Roman law.] The rules of law as stated in the Praetor's edict and administered by the Praetor. Part of the *jus honorarium*.

jus privatum. [Roman law.] That part of the law which related to causes between private individuals; divided into three parts, according as it related to persons, things, or actions.

jus publicum. [Roman law.] That part of the law concerning public affairs; that which dealt with causes between the State and private individuals. It comprised ecclesiastical law, constitutional law, and criminal law.

jus publicum privatorum pactis mutari non potest. [Public law is not to be superseded by private agreements.]

jus quaesitum tertio. [Rights on account of third parties.] A contract cannot confer rights on a third party. Only a party to a contract can sue on it. But rights may be conferred on third parties by way of trust, if so intended. But see the Third Parties (Rights against Insurers) Act 1930.

jus scriptum. [Roman law.] The written part of the law consisting of statutes, decrees of the *plebs* and of the senate, decisions of emperors, edicts of magistrates and answers of jurisprudents.

jus spatiandi et manendi. The right to stray and remain. *Jus spatiandi* is the right of perambulation. The right to use a garden is an easement (*Re Davies, Powell* v. *Maddison* [1956] Ch. 131).

jus tertii. [The right of a third person.] A defendant cannot plead that the plaintiff is not entitled to possession as against him because a third party is the true owner, except where the defendant is acting with the authority of the true owner.

jus tripertitum. [Roman law.] The threefold law, *e.g. jus privatum* was *tripertitum,* as composed of the *jus naturale, jus gentium* and the *jus civile.*

justice. The upholding of rights, and the punishment of wrongs, by the law. See also JUSTITIA.

justices of the peace. (Magistrates.) Persons appointed by the Crown to be justices within a certain area (*e.g.* a county) for the conservation of the peace, and for the execution of other duties. They are said to act ministerially in cases of indictable offences, where they merely initiate the proceedings by issuing a warrant of apprehension, taking the depositions, and committing for trail. They act judicially in all cases where they have summary jurisdiction, whether criminal or civil. On the hearing of appeals from magistrates' courts and on proceedings on committal for sentence, justices sit with the judge of the Crown Court (*q.v.*). See MAGISTRATES.

justiciar. The chief political and legal officer of the Norman and Plantagenet kings. He was *ex officio* regent when the King went overseas, and presided over the Curia Regis (*q.v.*). The office ceased to exist during the reign of Henry III.

justicias facere. To hold pleas; to exercise judicial functions.

justification. (1) The plea in defence of an action which admits the allegations of the plaintiff but pleads that they were justifiable or lawful. For example, in libel a plea of justification admits the publication of the defamatory words, but pleads that they are true in substance and in fact. (2) In procedure, bail or sureties for the defendant in an action were said to justify when they satisfied the plaintiff or the court that they were sufficient.

justitia. [Roman law.] Justice. The constant and perpetual wish to give each man his due (Justinian).

juvenile courts. Special courts sitting apart from the ordinary criminal courts, and consisting of persons whose names are on a special panel for the purpose, for the trial of children and young persons under 17. It must exclude all persons except those directly concerned in the case, and press representatives.The parent or guardian of the child or young person charged must attend, who may be ordered to pay any fine and costs. The words "conviction" and "sentence" must not be used (Children and Young Persons Act 1933, ss.45 *et seq.*).

See Justices of the Peace Act 1949, s.11; Magistrates' Courts Act 1952, s.112.

The constitution and place of sitting of juvenile courts is provided for in Children and Young Persons Act 1963, s.17, Sched. 2.

juvenile offenders. (1) a child, *i.e.* under 14 years; (2) a young person, *i.e.* over 14 and under 17 years. Charges against juvenile offenders which are dealt with summarily must be heard by a juvenile court (*q.v.*). See BORSTAL INSTITUTIONS; COMMUNITY HOMES; DETENTION CENTRE; REMAND.

K

K.C. King's Counsel. See QUEEN'S COUNSEL.

kangaroo. The power of the Chairman of a Committee of the Whole House of Commons of choosing which amendments shall be discussed. Those he "jumps over" are left undiscussed.

keeping house. Confining oneself to one's house. It is an act of bankruptcy.

Keys, House of. The Legislative Assembly of the Isle of Man.

King's (Queen's) Bench. See COURT OF KING'S (QUEEN'S) BENCH.

King's (Queen's) Chambers. Those portions of the British territorial waters which are inclosed within headlands so as to be cut off from the open sea by imaginary straight lines drawn from one promontory to another.

King's (Queen's) Coroner and Attorney. Originally this officer was concerned with deaths in the King's Bench Prison (now abolished). In 1892 the office was merged in that of Master of the Crown Office.

King's Widow. The widow of a tenant *in capite* of the King.

Knight. The lowest title of dignity. It is not hereditary. Knights are of the following orders: Garter, Thistle, St. Patrick, Bath, St. Michael and St. George, Star of India, Indian Empire, Royal Victorian, British Empire, and last, Knights Bachelor.

An obsolete order is that of Knight Banneret, who, created by the King in the field, ranked after a baronet.

Knight's service, tenure by. Where a man held land of another or of the Crown by military service, of which the principal varieties were escuage, grand serjeanty, castleward and cornage. It had five incidents, namely, aids, relief, wardship, marriage and escheat; the King's tenants *in capite ut de corona* were further liable to primer seisin and fines for alienation. Tenure by knight's service was converted into common socage by the statute (1660) 12 Car. 2, c. 24.

know-how. The putting together and applying in practice of the principles of some branch of engineering, technology or manufacturing technique, by one who has been initiated in it. It indicates the way in which a skilled man does his job (*Stevenson Jordan and Harrison* v. *Macdonald and Evans* [1952] 1 T.L.R. 101, C.A.). It is defined for tax purposes in the Income and Corporation Taxes Act 1970, s.386(7).

The sale of "know-how" by one concern to another involves initiating the purchaser into the way of working, or the carrying on of processes, by the seller. It includes the sale of information as to secret processes. Unless there is an outright sale of information as to secret processes. Unless there is an outright sale to the purchaser, and the seller's withdrawal from the business, and his agreement not to use the know-how to the prejudice of the purchaser, the proceeds of sale will be chargeable to income tax (*Evans Medical Supplies, Ltd.* v. *Moriarty* (1957) 37 T.C. 540; *I.R.C.* v. *Rolls-Royce Ltd.* [1962] 1 W.L.R. 425; *English Electric Co. Ltd.* v. *Musker* [1963] T.R. 13).

L

L.S. *Locus sigilli* (*q.v.*).

Labourers, Statute of. The statute 23 Edw. 3, passed in 1349 after about half the population had died of the Black Death. It enacted that everyone under sixty, except traders, craftsmen, those with private means and land owners, should work for anyone willing to employ them at the wages paid from 1340 to 1346.

laches. Negligence or unreasonable delay in asserting or enforcing a right. The equitable doctrine that delay defeats equities, or that equity aids the vigilant and not the indolent. A court of equity has always refused its aid to stale demands, where a party has slept upon his rights and acquiesced for a great length of time. Nothing can call forth this court into activity but conscience, good faith and reasonable diligence; when these are wanting the court is passive and does nothing.

When an equitable right is analogous to a legal right which is subject to a period of limitation in bringing actions to enforce it, the court of equity may by analogy apply the same provision to the equitable right.

laesaw majestatis, crimen. [The crime of injured majesty.] Treason.

lagan. When goods are cast into the sea as jetsam, and afterwards the ship perishes, and such goods are so heavy that they would sink to the bottom, and the mariners, to the intent to have them again, tie to them a buoy or cork or such other thing as will not sink so that they may find them again (*Sir Henry Constable's Case* (1601) 5 Co. Rep. 106*a*).

Lammas. August 1.

Lammas Lands. Lands held by a number of holders in severalty during a portion of the year. After the severalty crop has been removed they are commonable also to other classes of commoners. The date of opening them is now August 12.

Lancaster, County Palatine of. See PALATINE COURT.

land. Comprehendeth any ground, soile, or earth whatsoever. It legally includeth also all castles, houses, and other buildings; also water (Coke). Land includes land of any tenure, and mines and minerals, whether or not held apart from the surface, buildings or parts of buildings (whether the division is horizontal, vertical or made in any other way) and other corporeal hereditaments; also a manor, an advowson, and a rent and other incorporeal hereditaments, and an easement, right, privilege or benefit in, or over, or derived from land; but not an undivided share in land (Law of Property Act 1925, s.205(1) (ix)). In respect of Acts of Parliament passed after 1978, "land" includes buildings and other structures, land covered with water and any estate, interest, easement, servitude or right in or over land (Interpretation Act 1978, s.5, Sched. 1).

land charges. Under the Land Charges Act 1972 (as amended by the Finance Act 1975, Sched. 12 and the Local Land Charges Act 1975, s.17, Sched. 2) the following registers are kept at the Land Registry at Kidbrooke, London, S.E.3:

(1) land charges;
(2) pending actions;
(3) writs and orders affecting land;
(4) deeds of arrangement affecting land;
(5) annuities (but this is now closed and the entries transferred to land charges Class E. (below) (Act of 1972, s.1).

The register of land charges is made up as follows (s.10):

Class A: statutory land charges.

Class B: similar charges not made on the application of any person, if created or conveyed after 1925 and not being local land charges (*q.v.*).

Class C: (not being a local land charge) (i) puisne mortgages, (ii) limited owner's charges, (iii) general equitable charges, (iv) estate contracts, if created after 1925, or acquired after that date.

Class D: (not being a local land charge) (i) Inland Revenue charges for capital transfer tax, (ii) restrictive covenants created after 1925, except covenants in leases, (iii) equitable easements, rights and privileges created after 1925.

Class E: annuities created before 1926 and registered after 1925.

Class F: charges affecting any land by virtue of the Matrimonial Homes Act 1967.

Such charges are in general void against a purchaser if arising since 1925 and unregistered, or if not registered within 12 months of the first conveyance after 1925.

See LOCAL LAND CHARGE.

land, compulsory acquisition. Land may be acquired statutorily for public purposes, *e.g.* for planning (*q.v.*). The Land Compensation Act 1961 consolidates the law relating to the assessment of compensation on compulsory acquisition. See also the Land Compensation Act 1973.

land registration. The Land Registry, London, was established by the Land Registry Act 1862. The Land Transfer Act 1875 provided for the voluntary registration of title to freeholds and leaseholds, and for the compulsory registration of writs, deeds, notices and charges relating to land.

Under the Land Transfer Act 1897, the registration of title to land was made compulsory for the city and county of London.

In the Land Registration Act 1925, as amended by the Land Registration Act 1936, there are provisions for the extension of the compulsory area, and the law relating to land registration was amended and codified. Orders in Council have been made extending compulsory registration.

The Register is in three parts: (1) The property register, which describes and identifies the land and states the estate for which it is held; (2) the proprietorship register states whether the title is absolute, good leasehold, qualified or possessory; and indicates any restrictions on dealing with the land; (3) the charges register sets out mortgages, restrictive covenants and adverse notices. A land certificate is given to a registered proprietor.

Registers of deeds and wills relating to land have been kept in Middlesex, Yorkshire and the Bedford Level. The Bedford Level Registry was closed in 1920. The Middlesex Deeds Registry was closed in 1940 (Middlesex Deeds Act 1940). The Yorkshire Deeds Registries were closed by the Law of Property Act 1969, s.16. Instruments which do not affect the legal estate need not be registered (Law of Property Act 1925, s.11). See LAND CHARGES.

land tax. A tax formerly payable annually in respect of the beneficial ownership of land. The tax was originally levied in 1692 under the statute 4 Will. & Mary, c. 1, and was made redeemable by the Land Tax Perpetuation Act 1798.

The Finance Act 1949, Part V provided for the stabilisation and compulsory redemption of land tax. Land tax was finally abolished by the Finance Act 1963, s.68.

land values duties. Duties imposed by the Finance (1909–10) Act 1910, Part I. They have all been abolished (Finance Act 1920, s.57; Finance Act 1967, Sched. 16. Part VIII).

landlord and tenant. The relation of landlord and tenant depends upon contract and is created by the landlord allowing the tenant to occupy the landlord's house or land for a consideration termed rent, recoverable by distress. Exclusive possession of the premises must be granted, for a defined term. The contract is embodied in a lease (*q.v.*) or in a tenancy agreement, for short terms.

In the absence of express agreement, the landlord impliedly contracts with the tenant to give him possession and guarantee him against eviction by any person having a title paramount to that of the landlord. The tenant impliedly contracts with the landlord to pay the rent, not to commit waste, and to give up possession at the end of the tenancy. Liability for repair is a matter of express stipulation or covenant. Under the Housing Act 1957, where houses are let at certain low rents there is an implied condition that it is fit for human habitation and that the landlord will maintain it in this condition. Local authorities have extensive powers in regard to houses let to tenants.

The security of tenure of tenants of residential premises has been statutorily protected under various Acts, the most recent of which is the Rent Act 1977 (see also HARRASSMENT). Agricultural tenants may be protected under the Rent (Agriculture) Act 1976 and the Agricultural Holdings (Notices to Quit) Act 1977. Business tenants may have security of tenure under Part II of the Landlord and Tenant Act 1954. For the position of tenants of local authority residential accomodation see the Housing Act 1980.

Lands Clauses Acts. These Acts form a code under which land can be compulsorily acquired for public or quasi-public purposes, but only by way of the incorporation of the Acts with a special Act passed for a particular purpose.

Lands Tribunal. The tribunal established by the Lands Tribunal Act 1949 (in place of official arbitrators and others) to determine questions relating to compensation for the compulsory acquisition of land and other matters, including the discharge or modifications of restrictive covenants under Law of Property Act 1925, s.84, and appeals from the local valuation courts. Appeal is by way of case stated to the Court of Appeal. See also the Law of Property Act 1969, s.28.

lapse. As a general rule, when a person to whom property has been devised or bequeathed dies before the testator, the devise or bequest fails or lapses, and the property falls into residue, except that a lapsed share of residue does not fall into residue, but devolves as upon an intestacy. But if land is given to a person in tail who dies before the testator, leaving issue capable of taking under the entail, the land goes as if the devisee had died immediately after the testator (Wills Act 1837, s.32). And if the testator bequeaths (or devises) property to a child or other descendant of himself, and such descendant dies leaving issue who survive the testator, the legacy (or devise) does not lapse but takes effect as if the person to whom the gift was made had died immediately after the testator (*ibid.* s.33). But this rule does not apply if land is devised to children as joint tenants, or to children as a class, or to children by reason of a special power of appointment. It applies to illegitimate children or other issue (Family Law Reform Act 1969, s.16).

Proceedings lapse in the event of the death of a defendant in criminal proceedings, or where no step is taken in an action within the appropriate time.

larceny. The offence of larceny at common law was abolished by the Theft Act 1968, s.32 and by Sched. 3, Part I, the Larceny Acts 1861 and 1916 were repealed. See THEFT.

lata culpa dolo aequiparatur. [Roman law.] Gross negligence is equivalent to fraud.

latitat. See BILL OF MIDDLESEX.

law. A law is an obligatory rule of conduct. The commands of him or them that have coercive power (Hobbes). A law is a rule of conduct imposed and enforced by the Sovereign (Austin). But *the* law is the body of principles recognised and applied by the State in the administration of justice (Salmond). Blackstone, however, maintained that a rule of law made on a pre-existing custom exists as positive law apart from the legislator or judge, and Maine pointed out that there is law in primitive societies. Savigny regarded law as itself subject to evolution and as no arbitrary expression of the will of the law giver. Ihering found the end of law in the "delimitation of interests," and Vinogradoff saw law as a set of rules imposed and enforced by a society with regard to the attribution and exercise of power over persons and things. De Montmorency regarded law ultimately as the rules which bind men together in society in its struggle against natural environment: "Adaptation to environment is the condition of survival. Custom was the method by which man adapted himself to environment. To break custom was to face death. Coercion is a weapon of law which law has forged, but it is not the basis of law." Anson disposed of the difficulties of Austin thus: "When the State has attained to regularity in definition and enforcement of rules of conduct, then we get the positive law with which Austin delighted to torment himself and his readers." See CODE.

Law Commission. The Law Commission was set up to promote the systematic development, simplification and modernisation of the law (Law Commissions Act 1965).

Law List. An annual publication containing lists of barristers, solicitors and legal executives. The inclusion of a solicitor's name therein is prima facie evidence that he holds the prescribed certificate for the current year.

Law Lords. The Lord Chancellor, the Lords of Appeal in Ordinary (*q.v.*), ex-Lord Chancellors, and other peers who have held high judicial office. They sit in the Appellate Committee of the House of Lords to hear appeals. See also JUDICIAL COMMITTEE.

law merchant. The custom of merchants as settled by judicial decisions. It had its origin in the international usages of merchants, and some part of it was borrowed from Roman law. It was administered in special courts, such as courts of the markets and fairs; *e.g.* courts of *pie poudre*. Before the time of Lord Mansfield, all the evidence in mercantile cases was left to the jury, the custom of merchants being treated as a question of fact. When so proved a mercantile custom became part of the general law. Lord Mansfield separated the law from the facts in his charges to the jury, and henceforward the law merchant became assimilated to the common law. See COMMERCIAL CAUSE.

law of nations. International law or public international law.

law of nature. The *jus naturale*. The Roman conception of a hypothetical law of a bygone state of nature or golden age, and believed to exist in part in all then existing bodies of law; to be ascertained by segregating the principles common to many or all of them, *i.e.* the *jus gentium*. The *jus naturale* or law of nature is simply the *jus gentium* or law of nations seen in the light of a particular theory—stoic philosophy (Maine).

Law of Property Acts. The name given to the following group of Acts (and the Acts amending them): Law of Property Act 1925; Administration of Estates Act 1925; Land Charges Act 1925; Land Registration Act 1925; Settled Land Act 1925; Trustee Act 1925; Universities and College Estates Act 1925. The Law of Property Act 1922, was drafted by a committee set up by Lord Birkenhead when Lord Chancellor to reform the law and rid it of the traces of the feudal system, and is consequently known as Lord Birkenhead's Act. It was due to come into operation on January 1, 1925, but was postponed, and finally only came into effect as amended by the Law of Property (Amendment) Act 1924, with regard to the abolition of copyhold tenure, as from January 1, 1926. The rest of the Act was split up into Acts dealing with particular subjects, as above, with effect from January 1, 1926.

Law Officers of the Crown. The Attorney General and the Solicitor-General. See the Law Officers Act 1944.

law reform. See LAW COMMISSION.

law report. A published account of a legal proceeding, giving a statement of the facts, and the reasons the court gave for its judgment. The Law Reports (see below) give an account of the arguments of counsel. There is a "headnote" or "short points" to law reports for the convenience of users, but they may be misleading. Reports by barristers are cited in arguments as precedents. Regular law reporting appears to have commenced in the thirteenth century with the Year Books (*q.v.*). In 1865 the Council of Law Reporting commenced a series of reports covering all the superior courts, known as the Law Reports. Reports in *The Times* and in professional journals may be cited if a case is not officially reported. The Stationery Office "Tax Cases" give revised shorthand reports of the judgments. The official Weekly Law Reports give promptly published reports of decided cases, some only of which will appear in the Law Reports. See APPENDIX: LAW REPORTS AND THEIR ABBREVIATIONS.

The Judicial Proceedings (Regulation of Reports) Act 1926 prohibits the publication of indecent matter by the Press in relation to judicial proceedings.

Law Society. Formed in 1825, incorporated in 1831, and entrusted with the custody of the roll of solicitors, 1888, since when no person can be admitted as a solicitor unless he has obtained from the society a certificate that he has passed certain examinations (Solicitors Act 1974). The Law Society is entrusted with the control and regulation of the solicitors' profession. See DISCIPLINARY COMMITTEE.

lawful in a statute is normally permissive, but may confer legal rights, the resistance to which, or the infringement of which by others would be wrongful.

lay days. The days which are allowed by a charterparty for loading and unloading the ship. If the vessel is detained beyond the period allowed, demurrage becomes payable.

lay impropriator. A lay person or corporation who is in possession of the revenues of an ecclesiastical living.

lay-fee. Lands held in fee of a lay lord, as distinguished from lands held in frankmoign.

Le Roy (or La Reine) le veult. [The King (or the Queen) wishes it.] The form of the royal assent to Bills in Parliament.

Leader, or leading counsel. Queens Counsel (*q.v.*).

leading case. A judicial decision or precedent (*q.v.*) settling the principles of a branch of law. For example, the case of *Coggs* v. *Bernard* is one of the most celebrated ever decided in Westminster Hall, since the elaborate judgment of Lord Holt contains the first well-ordered exposition of the English law of bailments.

leading questions. Questions which directly or indirectly suggest to a witness the answer he is to give, or which put disputed matters to the witness in a form admitting of the answer "Yes" or "No." The general rule is that leading questions are allowed in cross-examination, but not in examination-in-chief.

League of Nations. The society or association of States established by Part I of the Treaty of Peace between the Allied and Associated Powers, and Germany, signed at Versailles, June 28, 1919. The League has been superseded by the United Nations following the Second World War.

Leapfrog. An appeal from the High Court or Divisional Court direct to the House of Lords, thereby "leapfrogging" the Court of Appeal. A certificate must be granted by the trial judge, all parties must agree and the House of Lords must give leave (Administration of Justice Act 1969, ss.12–15).

lease. A conveyance or grant of the possession of property to last during the life of a person, or for a term of years or other fixed period, and usually with the reservation of a rent. It is essential that a lease shall specify the period during which the lease is to endure, and the beginning and end of the term. The person who grants the lease is called the lessor, and the person to whom it is granted the lessee. A lease must be for a less estate or term than the lessor has in the property, for if it comprises his whole interest it is a conveyance or assignment and not a lease. Complete possession as against others must be granted. Where a person who is himself a lessee grants a lease of the same property to another person for a shorter term, it is called an underlease or sublease or a derivative lease. Leases might formerly be created orally or in writing, or by deed, but by the Law of Property Act 1925, ss.51–55, for the purposes of creating a legal estate all leases are to be by deed, except leases taking effect in possession for a term not exceeding three years at the best rent obtainable without taking a fine (or premium), which may be made orally or in writing. A lease void because not made by deed may be enforceable in equity under the doctrine of part performance (*Walsh* v. *Lonsdale* (1882) 21 Ch.D. 9). Leases come to an end by

199

expiry, notice, forfeiture, surrender, merger, or by becoming a satisfied term, by being enlarged into a fee simple or by disclaimer. See ESTATE; FORFEITURE; LEASEHOLD; REVERSION; TERM OF YEARS.

lease and release. A mode of conveying freehold land which was in common use from 1536 to 1841. It was used to evade the Statute of Enrolments (27 Hen. 8, c. 16), passed to prevent land from being conveyed secretly by bargain and sale (*q.v.*). The Act required only bargains and sales of estates of inheritance or freehold to be enrolled, and therefore it soon became the practice on a sale of land for the vendor to execute a lease to the purchaser for a year by way of bargain and sale, which under the Statute of Uses (27 Hen. 8, c. 10), gave him seisin of the land without entry or enrolment, and then the vendor released his reversion to the purchaser by a deed known as a release, thus vesting in him the fee simple in possession without entry or livery of seisin. The lease and the release were executed on the same day, the release being dated for the following day and being executed after the lease. The consideration for the lease was a nominal sum of five or ten shillings, which was never paid, the real consideration being stated in the release. In 1841 the statute 4 Vict. c. 21 made a release effectual without the preliminary lease for a year, and in 1845 the Real Property Amendment Act 1845 made a deed of grant sufficient for the conveyance of all corporeal hereditaments. Conveyance by bargain and sale was finally abolished by the Law of Property Act 1925, s.51(1).

lease by estoppel. If a person makes a lease of land in which he has no interest, and he afterwards acquires the land, he is estopped or precluded from denying the existence of the lease.

leaseholds. Lands held under a lease for years. They are personal estate, being chattels real. Leaseholds are transferable by assignment and the assignee is liable to the lessor on the covenants in the lease which run with the land so long as he holds under the lease. But the original lessee remains liable to the lessor on the covenants, notwithstanding any assignment, and is entitled to be indemnified by the assignee. In a conveyance of leaseholds for valuable consideration by a beneficial owner, a covenant as to the validity of the lease is implied. Since 1925 a mortgage of leaseholds can only be by sub-demise of a term shorter by one day than the term of the lessee, or by a deed of charge by way of legal mortgage (Law of Property Act 1925, s.86). Leaseholds, on the death of the lessee, vest in his personal representatives.

When there is a residue unexpired of not less than 200 years of a term originally created for at least 300 years, unaffected by trust or right of redemption in favour of a reversioner, and subject to no rent of money value, the term may be enlarged into a fee simple by deed; provided it is not liable to be determined by re-entry for condition broken, and is not a sub-demise out of a superior term itself incapable of enlargement (Law of Property Act 1925, s.153).

Under a contract to grant or assign a term of years, the intended lessee or assign has no right to call for the title to the freehold or leasehold reversion, as the case may be (*ibid.* s.44). See LANDLORD AND TENANT.

Tenants on long leases were given the right to acquire the freehold by the Leasehold Reform Act 1967 (as amended).

Leave and licence. Permission. In an action for trespass it is a good defence to plead that the act complained of was done with the "leave and licence," *i.e.* the permission, of the plaintiff.

leave to defend. The leave granted to a defendant whether conditional or unconditional, under Ord. 14, who can show he has a good defence on the merits. The Master gives all necessary direction as to the further conduct of the action.

legacy. A gift of personal property by will. The person to whom the property is given is called the legatee, and the gift or property is called a bequest. The legatee's title to the legacy is not complete until the executor has assented to it. (1) A specific legacy is a bequest of a specific part of the testator's personal estate; (2) A demonstrative legacy is a gift of a certain sum directed to be paid out of a specific fund; (3) A general legacy is one payable only out of the general assets of the testator. See ABATEMENT OF LEGACIES.

legacy duty. An *ad valorem* duty on all legacies of personal property other than leaseholds. It was abolished by the Finance Act 1949, s.27.

legal aid. Legal aid is now governed by the Legal Aid Act 1974 as amended by the Legal Aid Act 1979, and regulations made thereunder. The scheme gives to persons whose disposable income and capital fall within the limits prescribed from time to time assistance and/or representation in legal proceedings of most kinds. An applicant for civil legal aid must show that he has reasonable grounds for asserting or defending a claim. The scheme in civil cases is administered by the Law Society but assessment of means is carried out by the Supplementary Benefits Commission. In criminal cases application for legal aid is made to the Magistrates. Overall responsibility for legal aid rests with the Lord Chancellor. In criminal proceedings a defendant's legal aid application form may not be used in cross examination as to credit where the application form is not evidence in the case (*R.* v. *Winter* [1980] Crim. L.R. 659, C.A.; *R.* v. *Stubbs* [1982] 1 All E.R. 424, C.A.).

See also CHARGE, STATUTORY.

legal estate; legal fiction; legal memory. See ESTATE; FICTION; MEMORY.

legal executive. Solicitor's unadmitted staff, previously known as managing clerks. The Institute of Legal Executives prescribes examinations, regulations etc. Legal Executives have a right of audience in chambers (*i.e.* not in open court) and a limited right of audience in open court in the county court (County Courts (Right of Audience) Direction 1978.

legal tender. Tender or offer of payment in a form which a creditor is obliged to accept. Bank of England notes and gold coins are legal tender for the payment of any amount. Cupro-nickel and bronze coins are legal tender for relatively small amounts (Coinage Act 1971, s.2). A creditor is not obliged to give change; the exact sum due must be tendered.

legatarius partiarius. [Roman law.] A legatee to whom the testator had in his will instructed his heir to give a definite share of his universal succession (*hereditas*), called a legacy of partition (*legatum partitionis*) because the legatee divided the inheritance with the heir.

legatum. [Roman law.] A legacy; any gift from a deceased person.

legatum generis. [Roman law.] A legacy of a thing in general terms as belonging to a class; *e.g.* a slave.

legatum nominis. [Roman law.] A legacy of a debt.

legatum optionis. [Roman law.] A legacy of choice, where the testator directs the legatee to choose from among his slaves or other property.

legatum partitionis. [Roman law.] A legacy where the legatee divided the inheritance with the heir. See LEGATARIUS PARTIARIUS.

legatum poenae nomine. [Roman law.] A legacy by way of penalty, to constrain their heir to do or not to do something.

leges posteriores priores contrarias abrogant. [Later laws abrogate prior contrary laws.]

legitimacy. The condition of being born in lawful wedlock. Every child born of a married woman during the subsistence of the marriage is presumed to be legitimate but this presumption may be rebutted. By the Legitimacy Act 1926, where the parents of an illegitimate person marry or have married one another, if the father was at the date of the marriage domiciled in England or Wales, it renders that person, if living, legitimate from the commencement of the Act, or from the date of the marriage, whichever last happens, unless the father or mother was married to a third person when the illegitimate child was born. By the Legitimacy Act 1959, s.1, however, the provisions of the 1926 Act were extended to cases where either or both of the parents were married when the child was born.

A legitimated person is, after his legitimation, in the same position as if he had been legitimate when born, In regard to property, however, a legitimated person, his spouse or issue may only claim if their title is subsequent to the date of legitimation. An illegitimate child and the mother are entitled to succeed to each other's property on intestacy.

Where a decree of nullity is granted in respect of a voidable marriage, the legitimacy of a child is not affected by the annulment of the marriage of its parents (Matrimonial Causes Act 1973, s.16). The child of a void marriage is treated as the legitimate child of his parents if at the time of the act of intercourse resulting in the birth, or at the time of the celebration of the marriage, if later, both or either of the parties reasonably believed that the marriage was valid (Legitimacy Act 1976, s. 1).

Any person claiming that he or his parents or any remoter ancestor became or has become a legitimated person may apply by petition to the High Court or the county court for a decree to that effect (Matrimonial Causes Act 1973, s.45).

After 1975 or after the date of an adoption order whichever is later, the effect of an adoption order is to prevent an adopted child from being illegitimate (Children Act 1975, Sched. 1, para. 3) but this does not prevent an adopted child being legitimated under the Act of 1926, if either natural parent is the sole adoptive parent (Act of 1975, Sched. 1, para. 13). For the rules of construction of instruments concerning property, see para. 12.

legitimatio. [Roman law.] Children of concubinage could be legitimated:
(1) *Per subsequens matrimonium;* by the subsequent marriage of the parents; (2) By offering to the *curia* (*per oblationem curiae*), *i.e.* by making a son a *decurio,* a member of the magisterial class; (3) By rescript of the emperor (Justinian).

lesbianism. Unnatural sexual practices between women. An imputation of lesbianism is an imputation of unchastity within the Slander of Women Act 1891 (*Kerr* v. *Kennedy* [1942] 1 K.B. 409). In *Spicer* v. *Spicer* [1954] 1 W.L.R. 1051 it was held that it might amount to cruelty to a husband. Today it might be regarded as unreasonable behaviour and thus a ground for divorce.

lessee. One to whom a lease is granted.

lessor. One who grants a lease.

letter of credit. An authority by one person to another to draw cheques or bills of exchange (with or without a limit as to amount) upon him, with an undertaking to honour the drafts on presentation. An ordinary letter of credit contains the name of the person by whom the drafts are to be negotiated or cashed: when it does not do so, it is called an open letter credit.

letter of request. A method of obtaining evidence in foreign countries established by diplomatic correspondence. Letters of request are issued at the office of the Master's Secretary (Ord. 70).

letters of administration. Where a person possessed of property, whether real or personal, dies intestate, or without an executor, the Family Division will grant to a proper person an authority under the seal of the court, called letters of administration by which the grantee, the administrator, becomes clothed with powers and duties similar to those of an executor (Judicature Act 1925, s.150, as amended). In addition to the oaths by the administrator, he enters into a bond (s. 167).

If the deceased has made a will, but failed to appoint executors, the court will grant letters of administration with the will annexed (*cum testamento annexo*) to a person interested in the estate; *e.g.* a devisee, legatee, or the trustees of a settlement of land made previously to the death (s.166). Since 1925, probate or administration may not be granted to more than four persons in respect of the same property, and if there is a minority, or a life interest arises, administration is to be granted, either to a trust corporation (*e.g.* the Public Trustee) with or without an individual, or to not less than two individuals (s.160). A trust corporation may be granted probate or administration, and either solely or jointly with any other person (s.161).

Where the deceased dies wholly intestate, administration is, except in special circumstances, *e.g.* insolvency, granted to persons interested in the residuary estate, on application made by them, or to trustees of the settlement in respect of the settled land (s.162).

Administration may be granted *pendente lite* to an administrator subject to the control of the court, and who has not the power of distributing residue (s.163). If a personal representative to whom a grant has been made resides abroad for 12 months after the death, special administration may be granted to a creditor or other person interested (s.164). Where a minor is sole executor, administration with the will annexed is to be granted to his guardian or other person until majority (s.165). Probate and letters of administration are capable of transferring a legal estate to personal representatives (Law of Property Act 1925, s.11(2)).

letters of marque (or **mart**). Extraordinary commissions issued, either in time of war or peace, by the Lords of the Admiralty, or the vice-admirals of a distant province, to the commanders of merchant ships, authorising reprisals for reparation of the damages sustained by them through enemies at sea. They were either "special," to make reparation to individuals, or "general," when issued by the government of one State against all the subjects of another. Letters of countermarque were issued as a reprisal for the issue of letters of marque.

letters patent. Grants by the Crown of lands, franchises, etc., contained in charters or instruments not sealed up but exposed to open view with the Great Seal pendent at the bottom, and usually addressed to all the subjects of the realm. See PATENT.

levant and couchant. [Risen and lain down.] When land to which a right of common of pasture is annexed can maintain during the winter by its produce, or requires, to plough and manure it, a certain number of cattle, those cattle are said to be levant and couchant on the land.

levari facias. A writ of execution which commanded the sheriff to levy a judgment debt on the lands and goods of the debtor by seizing and selling the goods, and receiving the rents and profits of the lands until the debt was satisfied. It was superseded by the writ of *elegit* (*q.v.*).

levy. To raise money compulsorily, *e.g.* by means of a distress, or by taxes.

lex Angliae sine Parliamento mutari non potest. [The law of England cannot be changed except by Parliament.]

lex domicilli. The law of the place of a person's domicile (*q.v.*).

lex fori. The law of the forum or court in which a case is tried. More particularly the law relating to procedure or the formalities in force (adjective law) in a given place.

Lex Hortensia (187 B.C.). [Roman law.] It provided that *plebiscita* should bind the whole people equally with *leges*.

lex hostilia. [Roman law.] It permitted an action of theft to be brought on account of persons who were among the enemy or away in the service of the commonwealth or who were in the *tutela* of some person bringing the action.

lex loci celebrationis. [The law of the place where a marriage is celebrated.]

lex loci contractus. [The law of a place where a contract is made.] It may be uncertain, *e.g.* where the parties are travelling by the Orient Express to Istanbul.

lex loci solutionis. [The law of the place of performance.]

lex mercatoria. [The law merchant] (*q.v.*).

lex non cogit ad impossibilia. [The law does not compel the impossible.]

lex non requirit verificari quod apparet curiae. [The law does not require that which is apparent to the court to be verified.]

lex non scripta. [The unwritten law.] The common law.

lex posterior derogat priori. [A later Act overrules an earlier one.]

Lex Regia. [Roman law.] The statute by which the people vested the supreme power in the emperor.

lex rei situs. [The law of the situation of the thing.]

lex scripta. [The written law.] Statute law.

lex situs. [The law of the place where property is situated.] The general rule is that lands and other immovables are governed by the *lex situs.*

lex spectat naturae ordinem. [The law has regard to the order of nature.]

lex talionis. The primitive law embodied in the phrase "an eye for an eye, a tooth for a tooth."

liability. Subjection to a legal obligation; or the obligation itself. He who commits a wrong or breaks a contract or trust is said to be liable or responsible for it. Liability is civil or criminal according to whether it is enforced by the civil or criminal courts. A contingent liability is a future unascertained obligation.

liable. One who incurs legal liability.

libel. Defamation (*q.v.*) by means of writing, print, or some permanent form. The publication of false defamatory words, etc., is a tort actionable without proof of special damage. It is a defence to an action for libel (1) that there was no publication; (2) that the words used were incapable of a defamatory meaning; (3) that the words used were true in substance and in fact (justification); (4) that the publication was privileged. Broadcasting by wireless telegraphy is publication in a permanent form (Defamation Act 1952, s.1). Privilege may be absolute or qualified, and qualified privilege may be lost by proof of express or actual malice (*q.v.*).

The Defamation Act 1952, s.4 provides for an offer of amends to be made in cases of unintentional defamation, which will operate to determine the proceedings if accepted, and if not accepted, as a defence. Section 7 deals with qualified privilege of newspapers.

Libel, but not slander, is also a crime (misdemeanour), the essence of which is the danger to the public peace, so it is only necessary to prove publication to the prosecutor; publication to a third person is unnecessary. To be libellous, the matter must be calculated to provoke a breach of the peace by casting upon the prosecutor an injurious imputation. Defences: (1) publication on a privileged occasion; (2) the matter was fair comment on a matter of public interest; (3) publication was accidental, or without authority or knowledge; (4) justification; *i.e.* the libel was true and its publication for the public benefit.

A public libel is one which tends to produce evil consequences to society, because it is blasphemous, obscene, or seditious. The publication of such a libel is a misdemeanour.

In an action for libel, sufficient particulars of the publications complained of must be given to enable them to be identified (Ord. 82).

libertas. [Roman law.] Freedom; the capacity to possess the rights and to fulfil the duties of a free person.

libertas directa. [Roman law.] The setting free of his own slave by a master, as when he appointed his slave as a tutor. Either the testator accompanied the appointment with express enfranchisement or the law implied his intention to do so.

libertas fideicommissaria. [Roman law.] Where the testator appointed as a tutor another man's slave, entrusting his heir to purchase and enfranchise the slave.

libertinus. [Roman law.] A freedman; a man who had been set free from lawful slavery by manumission. They fell originally into three classes: (1) Full Roman citizens; (2) *Latini Juniani;* (3) *Dedititii.*

liberty. An authority to do something which would otherwise be wrongful or illegal. Formerly used in the sense of franchise (*q.v.*) denoting both a right or rights, and the place where they are exercisable.

liberum tenementum. A freehold or frank tenement.

libripens. [Roman law.] A scalesman.

licence. An authority to do something which would otherwise be inoperative, wrongful, or illegal; *e.g.* to enter on land which would otherwise be a trespass. A licence passes no interest, and a mere licence is always revocable. A licence coupled with an interest which is in the nature of grant; *e.g.* of sporting rights, is irrevocable until the benefit granted has been enjoyed. A contractual licence, whether or not coupled with an interest, may be irrevocable, depending on the construction of the terms of the contract between the parties. If the time of enjoyment is not limited, the giving of reasonable notice of revocation will be necessary. See BARE LICENSEE.

licence, marriage. See MARRIAGE.

licensed victualler. A publican; a person selling intoxicating liquors under a justices' licence (Licensing Act 1964, s.1).

licensee. One to whom a licence (*q.v.*) is given.

licet dispositio de interesse futuro sit inutilis, tamen fieri potest declaratio praecedens quae sortiartur effectum, interveniente novo actu. [Although the grant of a future interest is inoperative, yet it may become a declaration precedent, which will take effect on the intervention of some new act.] See LEASE BY ESTOPPEL.

lie. An action "lies" if, on the facts of the case, it is competent in law, and can properly be instituted or maintained.

lien. The right to hold the property of another as security for the performance of an obligation. A common law lien lasts only so long as possession is retained, but while it lasts can be asserted against the whole world. An equitable lien exists independently of possession; *i.e.* it may bind property not in possession at the time the obligation is incurred, but it cannot avail against the purchaser of a legal estate for value without notice of the lien.

A possessory lien is the right of the creditor to retain possession of his debtor's property until his debt has been satisified. A particular lien exists only as a security for the particular debt incurred, while a general lien is available as a security for all debts arising out of similar transactions between the parties. Thus a solicitor has a lien on his client's papers to secure his costs.

A charging lien is the right to charge property in another's possession with the payment of a debt or the performance of a duty. A maritime lien is a lien on a ship or freight, either possessory, arising out of contracts of carriage, or charging, arising out of collision or other damage. A vendor's lien is the right of a seller to retain the property till payment of the purchase price.

lieu, in. In the place of.

life estate. A "mere" freehold, as not being an estate of inheritance. It arises by grant or operation of law for the benefit of a person for the rest of his own life.

Since 1925 it can exist in freeholds only in equity, under a trust, as a "life interest." See TENANT FOR LIFE.

life, expectation of. A person who is injured by another's negligence may recover, as an independent head of damage, compensation for the loss of his normal expectation of life (*Flint* v. *Lovell* [1935] 1 K.B. 354). He may also recover, as a separate head of damage, damages for the loss of earnings during the "lost years" (*Pickett* v. *British Rail Engineering Ltd.* [1980] A.C. 136). The personal representatives of a person killed may similarly recover damages for the deceased loss of expectation of life (usually an award of a conventional amount—see *McCann* v. *Sheppard* [1973] 1 W.L.R. 540, C.A.) and may also recover damages for the loss of earnings during the "lost years" (*Gammell* v. *Wilson* [1981] 1 All E.R. 578, H.L.).

life in being. See PERPETUITIES.

life peer. Although the Crown may have power by its prerogative to create a peer for life, yet such grant does not confer a right to sit and vote in the House of Lords (*Wensleydale Case* (1856) 5 H.L.C. 958). By the Appellate Jurisdiction Act 1876, there were created Lords of Appeal in Ordinary, with the dignity of Baron and the right to sit and vote in the House of Lords for life. Also, the Life Peerages Act 1958, provided for the creation of peers or peeresses for life, with the right to sit and vote in the House.

life, presumption of. Once the fact of life on a given date has been established, the law will presume its continuance unless there be evidence, or a presumption of fact recognised by the law, to the contrary effect.

ligan. See LAGAN.

light. There is no right at common law to the unobstructed access of light to one's windows, but such a right might be acquired by prescription (Prescription Act 1832). That Act stipulated uninterrupted enjoyment of the access of light for 20 years. The Rights of Light Act 1959 provided that an owner of land may prevent the acquisition of a right to light over his land by registration of a notice in the local land charges register.

limitation. To limit an estate is to mark out the extreme period during which it is to continue, and the clause by which this is done in a conveyance is called a limitation. See WORDS OF LIMITATION.

limitation of liability. The imposition of a maximum amount of liability for loss or damage of, *e.g.* a carrier, by contract, or more particularly, by statute, See also LIMITED COMPANY.

limitation, statutes of. The statute which prescribes the periods within which proceedings to enforce a right must be taken or the action barred is now the Limitation Act 1980 which is a Consolidating Act. The time limits prescribed in respect of actions founded on the following matters are as indicated: tort (other than one causing personal injuries: six years (s.2); simple contract: six years (s.5); specialty: 12 years (s.8(1)); contribution: two years from date of right to recover (s.10); action for personal injuries: three years from either the cause of action arising or the date of knowledge of the injured person, whichever be the later (s.11(4)). If the injured person dies before the expiration of the limitation period the period is three years from the date of death or from the date of knowledge of the personal representative (s.11(5)).

Fatel Accidents Acts: three years from the date of death or from the date of knowledge of the person for whose benefit the action is being brought (s.12(2)); recovery of land: 12 years (s.15); redemption actions: 12 years (s.16); mortgagee's actions: 12 years from the date of accrual of the right to receive the money (s.20). The date from which time begins to run may be postponed for disability, fraudulent concealment or mistake (see Part II of the Act). There is also discretion to exclude the time limits in certain cases involving personal injury and death (see s.33). In cases involving the equitable jurisdiction of the court the timelimits do not normally apply (s.36). The defendant must plead the statutes if he intends to rely on them; the court will not of its own motion take notice that an action is out of time.

limited company. For the division of limited companies into Private Companies and Public Limited Companies see COMPANY.

A limited company is an Incorporated Company with limited liability. Such a company may either have the liability of its members limited by the memorandum to the amount, if any, unpaid on the shares respectively held by them ("a company limited by shares") or to such amount as the members may respectively undertake to contribute to the assets of the company in the event of its being wound up ("a company limited by guarantee"). See COMPANY.

limited owner. The owner of an interest in property less than the full fee simple; *e.g.* a tenant for life.

limited owner's charge. A charge in favour of a tenant for life or statutory owner who has discharged death duties (Land Charges Act 1972, s.2(1), Class C (ii)).

limited partnership. See PARTNERSHIP.

Lincoln's Inn. One of the Inns of Court (*q.v.*).

linea recta semper praefertur transversali. [The direct line is always preferred to the collateral.]

liquid assets. Cash in hand or at bank, and readily realisable property.

liquidated. Fixed or ascertained. A debt is liquidated when paid, and a company when wound up.

liquidated damages. A genuine covenanted pre-estimate of damages for an anticipated breach of contract, as contrasted with a penalty (*q.v.*). The sum fixed as liquidated damages is recoverable; a penalty is not, but only the damages actually incurred.

liquidated demand. Every writ indorsed with a claim for a debt or liquidated demand only, must state the amount claimed and also bear a prescribed indorsement for costs in case the defendant may elect to pay within eight days after servive (Ord. 6, r. 2(1)(*b*)). Also it must give sufficient particulars to disclose the nature of the contract giving rise to the claim.

liquidator. A person appointed to carry out the winding up of a company. The duties of a liquidator are to get in and realise the property of the company, to pay its debts, and to distribute the surplus (if any) among the members. The chief difference between a liquidator in a winding up by the court and a liquidator appointed in a voluntary winding up is that the former cannot as a rule take any important step in the winding up without the sanction of the court. In the Companies Act 1948, ss.237–251 deal with liquidations in a winding up by the court, and s.303 in a voluntary winding up. The court may appoint and remove a liquidator in a voluntary winding up (s.304).

lis. A suit or action, where there is an issue between parties in dispute.

lis alibi pendens. [A suit pending elsewhere.] Actions may be stayed on this ground.

lis mota. Existing or anticipated litigation. See ANTE LITEM MOTAM.

lis pendens or **lite pendente.** A pending suit, action, petition or matter, particularly one relating to land. A *lis pendens* may be registered under the Land Charges Act 1972, s.5.

literarum obligatio (or **expensilatio**). [Roman law.] Created by an entry in the account books (*codex*) of the creditor, with the consent of the debtor, charging the debtor as owing a certain sum.

litigant in person. One who sues or defends without legal representation. Every litigant in person is entitled to be accompanied by another person who may assist or quietly advise the litigant but who has no right to address the court. As to Arbitration in the county court see COUNTY COURT and as to costs see COSTS IN CIVIL PROCEEDINGS.

litigation. The parties before the court are wholly answerable for the conduct of their own cases. Litigation is a game in which the court is umpire (Pollock).

Littleton, Thomas. Serjeant-at-law 1453, Judge of the Common Pleas 1466, knighted 1475 and died August 23, 1481. He wrote the celebrated "Treatise on Tenures," upon which Coke wrote a commentary.

livery. Formerly when an infant heir of land held *in capite ut de corona,* he was obliged on attaining 21 to sue livery, that is, to obtain delivery of the possession of the land, for which he paid half-a-year's profit of the land.

livery of seisin. An "overt ceremony," which was formerly necessary to convey an immediate estate of freehold in lands or tenements. It was the transfer of the feudal possession of the land.

There are two kinds of livery of seisin, *viz.* a livery in deed and a livery in law. A livery in deed is where the feoffor is on the land to be conveyed, and orally requests or invites the feoffee to enter, or formally hands to him any object, such as a branch or twig of a tree, and declares that he delivers it to him, by way of seisin of the land. "A livery in law is when the feoffor saith to the feoffee, being in view of the house or land, 'I give you yonder land to you and your heires, and go enter into the same, and take possession thereof accordingly,' and the feoffee doth accordingly in the life of the feoffor enter" (Coke).

The Real Property Act 1845 required a feoffment (*q.v.*) to be evidenced by deed, unless made by an infant under a custom. The Law of Property Act 1925, s.51(1) provided that since 1925 all lands and all interests therein lie in grant, and are incapable of being conveyed by livery of seisin. See GRANT.

livestock. See ANIMALS.

Lloyd's. An association of underwriters and insurance brokers in the City of London, incorporated by Lloyd's Act 1871.

local authority. A body charged with the administration of local government (*q.v.*); a county council, the Greater London Council, a district council, a London borough council, a parish council or (in Wales) a community council (Local Government Act 1972, s.270(1)). Meetings are open to the public (Public Bodies (Admission to Meetings) Act 1960; Local Government Act 1972, s.100).

Complaints of maladministration may be made to the Commission for Local Administration under the Local Government Act 1974, ss.23–34.

local government. The system under which the administration of the local affairs of the whole of England and Wales is in the hands of parish meetings, and parish (or in Wales, community), district and County Councils, the Greater London Council and the Common Council of the City of London, called local authorities (*q.v.*). They exercise important functions in regard to public health, education, highways, rating and valuation, town planning, housing, etc. (See the Local Government Act 1972, the Local Government (Records) Act 1962, the Local Government (Finance) Act 1982, the Local Government (Miscellaneous Provisions) Act 1982.)

local land charge. A charge binding on land registrable in the local land charges registers kept by local authorities (Local Land Charges Act 1975).

location of offices. A bureau was set up under the Location of Offices Bureau Order (S.I. 1963 No. 792) to encourage decentralisation.

Locke King's Act. The Real Estate Charges Act 1854 which enacted that the heir should take mortgaged land subject to the mortgage debt. Replaced by Administration of Estates Act 1925, s.35.

loco citato. [At the passage quoted.]

locus in quo. [The place in which.]

locus poenitentiae. [A place (or opportunity) of repentance.] The interval between the time money is paid or goods are delivered for an illegal purpose and the time the illegal purpose is carried out. During this interval the person who has so paid the money or delivered the goods may recover them back. See ILLEGAL.

locus regit actum. [The place governs the act.] The validity of an act depends on the law of the place where it is done; *e.g.* marriage.

locus sigilli. [The place of the seal.]

locus standi. [A place of standing.] The right to be heard in court or other proceeding.

lodger. A person who occupies rooms in a house of which the general possession remains in the landlord, as shown by the fact that he retains control over the street or outer door.

log or **log-book.** A record of happenings in and to a ship, including its speed and progress. See Merchant Shipping Act 1970, s.68.

loiter. To idle in the street for an unlawful purpose. Loitering contrary to the Vagrancy Act 1824 is no longer an offence (see ATTEMPT) but loitering for purposes of prostitution is an offence (Street Offences Act 1959, s.1).

London Gazette. The official journal of government. Certain notices, *e.g.* petitions for winding up a limited company must be advertised in it.

Long Vacation. The period usually during August and September, when the Supreme Court (*q.v.*) does not transact business. A Vacation Court usually sits to deal with urgent business. Pleadings are not to be served during the long vacation except with leave of the court or the consent of all parties (Ord. 18, r, 5).

lord. (1) A person of whom land is held by another as his tenant. The relation between the lord and the tenant is called tenure, and the right or interest which the lord has in the services of his tenant is called a lordship or seignory. (2) A peer of the realm.

Lord Advocate. The chief law officer of the Crown in Scotland.

Lord Campbell's Act. The Fatal Accidents Act 1846.

Lord Chamberlain. See CHAMBERLAIN, LORD.

Lord Chancellor. See CHANCELLOR, LORD HIGH.

Lord Chief Justice of England. The President of the Queens Bench Division (*q.v.*) and the second senior judge in the High Court ranking only after the Lord Chancellor. An *ex officio* judge of the Court of Appeal and the President of the Criminal Division of the Court of Appeal. When sitting in the Court of Appeal ranks over the Master of the Rolls (*q.v.*) (see generally Supreme Court Act 1981, ss.2(2), 3(2), 4(1), 5(1)(*b*) and 13(1)). In him are merged the old offices of Chief Justice of Queens Bench, Chief Baron of the Exchequer and Chief Justice of Common Pleas.

Lord High Admiral. See ADMIRAL.

Lord High Steward. Formerly, when a person was impeached, or when a peer was tried on indictment for treason or felony before the House of Lords, one of the lords was appointed Lord High Steward, who presided *pro tempore,* or, in the absence of such an appointment, the Lord Chancellor presided. If the House of Lords was not sitting, the Court of the Lord High Steward was instituted by commission from the Crown, to which were summoned all the peers of Parliament. The Lord High Steward was the sole judge.

Lord Keeper of the Great Seal. Now the Lord Chancellor.

lord lieutenant. The office of "lieutenants of counties" was created for the purpose of having a representative of the Crown in each county to keep it in military order. For this purpose he had the power of raising militia. The appointment to the office is made by the Crown, and it is held for life, or during good behaviour. (See Local Government Act 1972, s.218(1).)

Lord President of the Council. The President of the Privy Council. The office is held by such person, being a member of one House of Parliament or the other, as the Queen in Council, from time to time, orally declares to be the Lord President of the Council. It is of Cabinet rank.

Lord Privy Seal. The officer who affixed the Privy Seal to documents, especially letters patent, which were to pass the Great Seal. The Great Seal Act 1884, s.3 abolished the use of the Privy Seal, and the Lord Privy Seal has now no official duties. The office carries Cabinet rank.

Lord Steward of the Queen's Household. He originally presided over the court of the Lord Steward of the King's Household. He supervises the servants and the arrangements of the Royal Household.

Lord Treasurer or **Lord High Treasurer and Treasurer of the Exchequer.** The office dates from the earliest Norman period. After 1612 it was sometimes put in commission, and since 1714 it has always been in commission. The Commissioners constitute the Treasury Board, which now never meets. See TREASURY.

Lords Justices of Appeal. The designation of the ordinary judges of the Court of Appeal (*q.v.*).

lords marchers. Until the conquest of Wales in 1282 the English kings permitted their nobles to conquer and hold such parts of Wales as they could. Each noble, known as a Lord Marcher, was given *jura regalia,* or sovereign rights, within the area held by him.

Lords of Appeal in Ordinary. Law Lords appointed for the purpose of hearing appeals; they must have held some high judicial office for two years, or have been practising barristers or advocates for at least 15 years; they are barons for life, and are entitled to sit and vote in the House of Lords (Appellate Jurisdiction Acts, 1876, 1913, 1929 and 1947). Their maximum number is 11 (Administration of Justice Act 1968).

loss. See TOTAL LOSS.

lost or not lost. Words inserted in a maritime policy of insurance to prevent the operation of the rule that if a ship is lost at the time of insurance, the policy is void, although the assured did not know of the loss. See the Marine Insurance Act 1906, s.6(1).

lost years. See FATAL ACCIDENTS; LIFE, EXPECTATION OF.

lottery. A distribution of prizes by lot or chance without the use of skill. By the Betting, Gaming and Lotteries Act 1963 (as amended by the Gaming Act 1968 and the Lotteries Act 1975), all lotteries which do not constitute gaming are unlawful (Act of 1963, s.41), except where otherwise provided in the Act of 1963 (ss.38, 48–50). Exempt are small lotteries, incidental to certain entertainments (s.43), private lotteries (s.44), lotteries of art unions (s.46), lotteries promoted by registered societies or local authorities (Act of 1975). Restrictions are imposed on the conduct in or through a newspaper, or in connection with a trade or business, or the sale of any article to the public, of certain competitions (Act of 1963, s.47). Amusements with prizes may also be exempt (ss.48, 49, as amended).

lump sum. A payment which may be ordered as between husband and wife on or after the grant of a decree of divorce, judicial separation or nullity of marriage (Matrimonial Causes Act 1973, s.23(1) (*c*)). A lump sum may also be ordered for the benefit of the children (Act of 1973 s.23(1)(*f*)). The essence of a lump sum is that it is a capital sum (as opposed to periodical payments of maintenance). Only one lump sum order may be made, although the order may specify payment of more than one sum on different dates. Magistrates Courts have jurisdiction to order limited lump sums in the exercise of their domestic jurisdiction (Domestic Proceedings and Magistrates Courts Act 1978, s.2(1)(*b*)).

See FINANCIAL PROVISION ORDERS, DOMESTIC PROCEEDINGS.

lunatic. This term is no longer used. The Mental Health Act 1959 uses the term "patient." See MENTAL DISORDER.

In legal proceedings a patient can only sue by his "next friend," or defend by his guardian *ad litem,* who must act by a solicitor (Ord. 80). See COURT OF PROTECTION.

Lyndhurst's Act (Lord). The Marriage Act 1835 which provided that any marriage after 1835 between persons within the prohibited degrees of affinity should be null and void.

M

M.R. Master of the Rolls (*q.v.*).

magistrate. A judicial officer having a summary jurisdiction in matters of a criminal or quasi-criminal nature; a justice of the peace. Stipendiary magistrates are appointed to act in certain populous places with wider powers than ordinary justices, and receive a salary. See JUSTICES OF THE PEACE.

magistrates' court. A court of summary jurisdiction or examining justices, including a single examining justice (Justices of the Peace Act 1949, s.44(1)); any justice or justices of the peace acting under any enactment or by virtue of his or their commission or under the common law (Magistrates' Courts Act 1952, s.124(1)).

Magna Carta. The charter originally granted by King John, and afterwards re-enacted and confirmed by Parliament more than 30 times. The charter now in force is the statute 9 Hen. 3, with which our statute book commences. It contained provisions to protect the subject from abuse of the Royal prerogative in the matter of arbitrary arrest and imprisonment, and from amercements, purveyance and other extortions (see McKechnie, *Magna Carta*).

Magnum Concilium. The Great Council (*q.v.*).

maiden assize, etc. One at which there was no prisoner for trial.

mainprize. Taking into the hand; the process of delivering a person to sureties or pledges (mainpernors) who undertook to produce him again at a future time. Bail applied only to cases where a man was arrested or imprisoned, while a man could be mainperned not only in such cases, but also, *e.g.* in an appeal of felony. Mainpernors were not bound by recognisances to the Crown, and they could not relieve themselves of responsibility by seizing and remitting to custody the man for whom they had gone security.

maintenance. The supply of the necessaries of life for a person. A maintenance clause in a deed of settlement is the provision of income for such a purpose.

On a petition for divorce, nullity of marriage or judicial separation either party to the marriage may be ordered to make periodical payments for the maintenance of the other from the presentation of the petition to the determination of the suit (Matrimonial Causes Act 1973, s.22). After the decree, permanent financial provision may be ordered to be made (ss.23–33, 37–40). Maintenance agreements are subject to the jurisdiction of the court (ss.34–36). Maintenance may be obtained from the estate of a deceased spouse under the Inheritance (Provision for Family and Dependants) Act 1975. See PERIODICAL

PAYMENTS; FINANCIAL PROVISION ORDERS; DOMESTIC PROCEEDINGS; WILFUL NEGLECT TO MAINTAIN.

maintenance and champerty. The offence of maintenance was abolished by the Criminal Law Act 1967, s.13. That Act provides that no person shall be liable in tort for maintenance or champerty (s.14).

maintenance pending suit. Formerly known as "alimony pending suit." After a petition for divorce, judicial separation or nullity of marriage has been filed one party may apply for an order that the other make payments for his or her maintenance (Matrimonial Causes Act 1973, s.22). Such an order will expire on decree nisi (*q.v.*) in the case of judicial separation or decree absolute (*q.v.*) otherwise.

making off without payment. A person who, knowing that payment on the spot for any goods supplied or service done is required or expected of him, dishonestly makes off without having paid with intent to avoid payment commits an offence (Theft Act 1978, s.3).

mala fides. [Bad faith.] See BONA FIDE.

mala grammatica non vitiat chartam. [Bad grammar does not vitiate a deed.]

mala in se; mala prohibita. *Mala in se* are acts which are wrong in themselves, such as murder, as opposed to *mala prohibita*, acts which are merely prohibited by law, *e.g.* smuggling. A distinction not now of great importance, except that the doctrine of *mens rea* has apparently more application to the former class than the latter.

mala praxis. Where a medical practitioner injures his patient by neglect or want of skill, giving rise to a right of action for damages.

male issue. This is a term of art, meaning male descendants claiming exclusively through the male line, although it will yield to a contrary indication in the context. "Male descendants" is a term of ordinary speech, though it may mean "male issue" in its context (*Re Du Cros' Settlement Trusts* [1961] 1 W.L.R. 1252).

maledicta expositio quae corrumpit textum. [It is a bad exposition which corrupts the text.]

Malfeasance. The doing of an unlawful act, *e.g.* a trespass.

malice. Ill-will or evil motive: personal spite or ill-will is sometimes called actual malice, express malice, or malice in fact. In law an act is malicious if done intentionally without just cause or excuse. So long as a person believes in the truth of what he says and is not reckless, malice cannot be inferred from the fact that his belief is unreasonable, prejudiced or unfair (*Horrocks* v. *Lowe* [1972] 1 W.L.R.1625). Malice in the law of tort is a constituent of malicious prosecution, defamation, malicious falsehood, and conspiracy. But an act otherwise legal is not made wrongful by an improper motive (*Mayor of Bradford* v. *Pickles* [1895] A.C. 587).

malice aforethought. The element of *mens rea* in the crime of murder. It includes an intention to kill a person, and it is immaterial whether there was in mind either no particular person or a different person from the one killed. It also includes an intention to do an act likely to kill from which death results.

malicious falsehood. See INJURIOUS FALSEHOOD.

malicious injuries to property. The Malicious Damage Act 1861, which dealt with this, has been repealed and replaced by the Criminal Damage Act 1971. See CRIMINAL DAMAGE.

malicious injury to the person. An indictable offence, the punishment for which is imprisonment for life (Offences against the Person Act 1861, s.18).

malicious prosecution. The tort consisting of the institution of criminal or bankruptcy proceedings against another (or liquidation proceedings against a company) or to procure the arrest and imprisonment of another by means of judicial process, civil or criminal, or to cause execution to issue against the property of a judgment debtor, maliciously and without reasonable and probable cause, by which that other suffers damage to his fame, person, or property, provided that the proceedings terminate in the other's favour, so far as that may be possible. Damage must be pleaded and proved (*Berry* v. *British Transport Commission* [1962] 1 Q.B. 306).

maliciously. See MALICE.

malitia supplet aetatem. [Malice supplements age.] See DOLI INCAPAX.

mandamus. [We command.] A high prerogative writ which issued in the King's name from the High Court of Justice on application to the Kings Bench Division to some person or body to compel the performance of a public duty. It was replaced by an order of Mandamus which is now comprised in the procedure known as Judicial Review. Applications for judicial review are made to the Divisional Court. See JUDICIAL REVIEW.

mandatarius terminos sibi positos transgredi non potest. [A mandatory cannot exceed the limits imposed upon him.]

mandatary. The receiver of a mandate (*q.v.*).

mandate. (1) A direction, request, or authoritative command. Thus a cheque is a mandate by the drawer to his banker to pay the amount to the transferee or holder of the cheque. (2) The authority which was conferred on "advanced nations" by the Covenant of the League of Nations, Art. 22, to administer, as Mandatories on behalf of the League, former enemy colonies and territories which were inhabited by peoples not yet able to stand by themselves under the strenuous conditions of the modern world, applying the principle that the well-being and development of such peoples formed a sacred trust of civilisation. See TRUST TERRITORIES.

mandatory. See INJUNCTION.

mandatum. See BAILMENTS.

mandavi ballivo. [I have commanded the bailiff.] Where a sheriff receives a writ which has to be executed within a place which is a liberty (*q.v.*), he commands the bailiff of the liberty to execute the writ.

manor. A district of land of which the freehold was vested in the lord of the manor, of whom two or more persons, called freeholders of the manor, hold land in respect of which they owed him certain free services, rents or other duties. Hence every manor must have been at least as old as the Statute of Quia Emptores and consisted of demesne lands, the right to hold a court baron, and the right to the services of free tenants in fee, who were liable to escheat and owed attendance at the Court Baron. With the enfranchisement of copyholds since 1925, effected by the Law of Property Act 1922, and the extinguishment of manorial incidents, manors have ceased to exist.

manorial incidents. Incidents of land held on copyhold tenure in respect of which the tenants were liable to the lord of the manor.

The following manorial incidents were temporarily saved from the effect of the general enfranchisement of copyhold lands effected by the Law of Property Act 1922, (1) quit rents, chief rents, etc.; (2) fines, reliefs, heriots and dues; (3) forfeitures other than those for the conveyance of an estate of freehold in the land, and for alienation without licence; (4) rights of timber.

Certain incidents, such as rights to mines and minerals; and rights of common, were preserved indefinitely. See the Law of Property Act 1922, Part VI.

manslaughter. The crime of unlawful homicide; (a) where death is caused accidentally by an unlawful act; or where death is caused by culpable negligence;

(b) where death is caused by an act done in the heat of passion, caused by provocation (*q.v.*). Manslaughter is an indictable offence, punishable by imprisonment for life (Offences against the Person Act 1861, s.5). Upon an indictment for murder the jury, if they find that malice aforethought has not been proved, can bring in a verdict of manslaughter. Causing death by reckless or dangerous driving is an indictable offence punishable with imprisonment for five years (Road Traffic Act 1972, s.1, Sched. 4 as amended by Criminal Law Act 1977, s.50(1)), but still amounts to manslaughter even though it is also a statutory offence (*Re Gail Anne Jennings, The Times*, August 2, 1982, H.L.).

mansuetae naturae. [Tame by nature.] Animals such as a dog, cow, or horse. See ANIMALS.

manumissio. [Roman law.] The giving of his freedom to a slave; setting him free from the "hand" or *potestas* of his master.

manus. [Roman law.] Hand: marital power. A woman was subjected to the manus of her husband by (1) *Confarreatio* (A religious ceremony); (2) *Coemptio* (fictitious sale); (3) *Usus* (cohabitation).

marches. The boundary between England and Wales and that between England and Scotland. See LORDS MARCHERS.

marchet; marcheta; merchetum. A fine which some tenants had to pay to their lord for liberty to give away their daughters in marriage.

mareva. See INJUNCTION.

marginal notes. The notes printed at the side of sections of an Act of Parliament. They are not part of the Act, but it is permissible to consider a marginal note to ascertain the mischief at which an Act is aimed (*Stephens* v. *Cuckfield R.D.C.* [1960] 2 Q.B. 373).

maritagium. The power which the lord had of disposing of his infant ward in marriage. Also land given as a marriage portion: a dowry.

marital rights. Formerly the right of a husband to property of his wife during marriage, *jus mariti* (*q.v.*). It is now used as synonymous with conjugal rights.

market overt. [Open market.] Market overt in ordinary market towns is only held on the special days provided for by charter or prescription; but in the City of London every weekday is market day and every shop is a market overt. The goods must be such things only as the seller professes to trade in and the sale must be made openly between sunrise and sunset (*Reid* v. *Commissioner of Police of the Metropolis* [1973] 1 Q.B. 551).

The doctrine of market overt is that all sales of goods made therein, except horses, are not only binding on the parties, but also on all other persons: so that if stolen goods are sold in market overt, the purchaser, if acting in good faith, acquires a valid title to them against the true owner (Sale of Goods Act 1979, s.22(1)). But the court has power to make orders for restitution or for compensation (Theft Act 1968, s.28; Criminal Justice Act 1972, s.6, Scheds.5, 6).

markets and fairs. At common law a market or a fair is a franchise or privilege to establish meetings or persons to buy and sell, derived either from Royal grant or from prescription implying such grant.

Marlebridge, Statute of. The Statute of Marlborough, 52 Hen. 3, c. 1. Its new short title is Distress Act 1267.

marque. See LETTERS OF MARQUE.

marquis; marquess. The rank in the peerage next below that of duke, dating from 1386. The wife of a marquis is styled marchioness.

marriage. Marriage is essentially the voluntary union for life of one man and one woman to the exclusion of all others, subject to the rules as to consanguinity or affinity and capacity to perform the duties of matrimony prevailing in the place of domicile of the parties, and subject to the formalities required either by the law of England or the place where the marriage takes place. But a potentially polygamous marriage, if valid by the law of the parties' domicile (*e.g.* a Hindu marriage in India), is valid in English law. See, *e.g.* the Matrimonial Causes Act 1973, ss.11, 74.

An agreement to marry is a contract, but failure to complement it does not now give rise to an action. See BREACH OF PROMISE. Marriage means (a) the act of marrying in the ceremony of marriage, and (b) the status of marriage or being married.

Under the canon law, adopted by the common law, marriage could be by (1) a public celebration of the marriage service in a church, known as a celebration *in facie ecclesiae*; (2) by a clandestine celebration anywhere conducted by one in priest's orders. The statute 26 Geo. 2, c. 33 (Lord Hardwicke's Act), provided that any marriage celebrated after 1754 without publication of banns or licence duly granted or celebrated elsewhere than in the parish church or public chapel should be null and void in the absence of a special licence from the Archbishop of Canterbury.

The statute law is contained in the Marriage Acts 1949 to 1970. The Act of 1949, provided, principally, that marriages within the scheduled prohibited degrees should be void (s.1), see AFFINITY; marriages of persons under 16 are void (s.2); marriages of persons under 18 may be subject to consents (s.3); a marriage may be solemnised between the hours of eight in the forenoon and six in the afternoon (s.4); and a marriage according to the rites of the Church of England may be solemnised (a) after the publication of banns of matrimony; (b) on the authority of a special licence of marriage granted by the Archbishop of Canterbury; (c) on the authority of a licence of marriage granted by a competent ecclesiastical authority (a "common licence"), or on the authority of a certificate issued by a superintendent registrar (s.5). See REGISTRATION OF MARRIAGE.

The Marriage (Enabling) Act 1960 enables a valid marriage to be contracted between a man and a woman who is the sister, aunt, or niece of a former wife of his (whether living or not) or was formerly the wife of his brother, uncle or nephew (whether living or not).

A void marriage is one where the parties went through a marriage ceremony but there was lacking some necessary ingredient of a valid marriage: it is void *ab initio*, and is regarded as never having taken place. A voidable marriage is a valid subsisting marriage until a decree of nullity is pronounced as, *e.g.* for failure to consummate the marriage.

A clergyman of the Church of England or the Church in Wales is not bound to solemnise the marriage of a divorced person whose former spouse is still living or permit such a marriage in his church (Matrimonial Causes Act 1965, s.8(2)).

Where a man and a woman have lived together as man and wife there is a rebuttable presumption that they lived together in consequence of a valid marriage (*Re Taylor* [1961] 1 W.L.R. 9).

A person born biologically male cannot contract a valid marriage as a woman despite a sex-change operation (*Corbett* v. *Corbett* (*orse Ashley*) [1971] P. 110).

Proceedings for a declaration as to the validity of a marriage or as to a person's matrimonial status are assigned to the Family Division of the High Court (Administration of Justice Act 1970, s.1, Sched. 1).

"Marriage" was formerly also the right of a guardian by tenure to bestow his ward in marriage.

marriage settlement. A conveyance of property for the benefit of the parties to, and the prospective issue of, a marriage. A marriage settlement is made by means of a vesting deed and a trust instrument.

Ante-nuptial and post-nuptial settlements can be varied by the court when pronouncing a decree of divorce or nullity or judicial separation (Matrimonial

Causes Act 1973, s.4). They may also be varied under the Inheritance (Provision for Family and Dependants) Act 1975, s.2(1)(*b*).

marriage-brocage. A contract to procure a marriage between two persons for reward. Such a contract is void (see *Hermann* v. *Charlesworth* [1905] 2 K.B. 123).

married woman. See HUSBAND AND WIFE.

marshal. In the Queen's Bench Division of the High Court, a marshal is an officer who attends each judge on circuit in a personal capacity. The Marshal of the Admiralty Court is entrusted with execution of warrants and orders of the court.

marshalling. (1) As between creditors. Where there are two creditors of the same debtor, and one creditor has a right to resort to two funds of the debtor for payment of his debt, and the other creditor has the right to resort only to one fund, the court will order the first creditor to be paid out of the fund against which the second creditor has no claim, so far as that fund will extend, so as to leave as much as possible of the second fund for payment of the second creditor. If the first creditor has already paid himself out of the second fund, the court will allow the second creditor to stand in his shoes and resort to the first fund to the extent to which the second fund has been exhausted by the first creditor.

(2) As between beneficiaries. If any beneficiary is disappointed of his benefit under the will through a creditor being paid out of the property intended for that beneficiary, he may recoup himself by going against any property which ought to have been used to pay debts before his property was resorted to.

(3) As between legatees, where certain legacies are charged on real estate and others not, a case for marshalling arises where the realty is specifically devised.

martial law. Originally the law administered in the court of the Constable and Marshal. Now it means the suppression of ordinary law and the temporary government of a country or parts of it by military tribunals (Dicey). Martial law is the assumption by officers of the Crown of absolute power, exercised by military force for the suppression of an invasion and the restoration of order and lawful authority. Where actual war is raging acts done by the military authorities are not justiciable by the ordinary tribunals (*Ex parte Marais* [1902] A.C. 109).

There is usually a proclamation made that a state of martial law exists, but the courts will determine whether there exists such a state of war as renders martial law necessary. Acts of Indemnity are always passed to legalise the acts done during war or while martial law prevails.

master and servant. See now EMPLOYER AND EMPLOYEE.

Master in Lunacy. Now the Master of the Court of Protection (*q.v.*).

Master of the Crown Office. A Master of the Supreme Court who files criminal informations in the Court of Queen's Bench upon the relation or complaint of private persons. See INFORMATION.

Master of the Mint. The Chancellor of the Exchequer (Coinage Act 1971, s.4).

Master of the Rolls. The President of the Civil Division of the Court of Appeal (*q.v.*) (Supreme Court Act 1981, s.3(2)). Originally keeper of the records and assistant to the Lord Chancellor. In the reign of Edward I he acquired judicial authority. By the Judicature Act 1881 he became a judge of the Court of Appeal. Today he is the senior member of the Court of Appeal (Civil Division) and thus this country's most important civil judge outside the House of Lords.

Masters in Chancery. They were assistants of the Lord Chancellor, and of the Master of the Rolls. They sat in chambers for the discharge of functions which were partly ministerial and partly judicial. The Court of Chancery Act 1852 abolished the Masters and provided for the appointment of eight Chief Clerks (*q.v.*).

Masters of the Supreme Court. These consist of (1) the Masters in the Chancery Division; (2) the Masters of the Queen's Bench Division, who superseded the Masters of Queen's Bench, Common Pleas and Exchequer; (3) the Masters of the Supreme Court who carry out the taxation of the costs of all cases in the Chancery and Queen's Bench Divisions. The jurisdiction of a Master is, with some exceptions, that of a Judge in Chambers. See APPEAL.

mate's receipt. The receipt given by the mate for goods shipped on board, which are later given to the master of the ship so that he may sign the bills of lading for the goods.

matricide. The crime of mother-murder.

matrimonial causes. Suits for divorce, nullity of marriage, judicial separation, and jactitation of marriage.

matrimonial home. The place where husband and wife have lived together. A spouse who has no right by virtue of any estate, interest, contract of enactment to occupy the matrimonial home is given protection from eviction or exclusion by the Matrimonial Homes Act 1967; Matrimonial Proceedings and Property Act 1970, s.38; Law of Property Act 1969, Sched. 2, Part II; Land Charges Act 1972, Scheds. 3, 5. The matrimonial home may be the subject of a property adjustment order (Matrimonial Causes Act 1973, s.24).

matrimonial proceedings in magistrates' courts. See DOMESTIC PROCEEDINGS.

matrimonium. [Roman law.] Matrimony, the marriage-tie. See NUPTIAE.

mayhem. Violently depriving another of the use of a member proper for his defence in fight, such as an arm, a leg, an eye, etc. It was both a civil injury and a criminal offence.

Mayor's and City of London Court. A new court formed in 1921 by the amalgamation of the Mayor's Court of London and the City of London Court (Mayor's and City of London Court Act 1920). The court was abolished but, in effect, revived with normal county court jurisdiction (Courts Act 1971, s.42, Sched. 5).

me judice. [In my opinion.]

measure of damages. See DAMAGES; REMOTENESS OF DAMAGE.

measures. By the Church of England Assembly (Powers) Act 1919 every measure prepared by the Church Assembly with the assistance of the Legislative Committee of the Church Assembly is submitted to the Ecclesiastical Committee, consisting of 15 members of each House of Parliament, who consider the measure and report on it, especially with relation to the constitutional rights of all Her Majesty's subjects. The report, after communication to the Legislative Committee, and with its concurrence, is made to Parliament, and the measure is laid before Parliament, which has no power to amend it. On a resolution passed by both Houses it is presented for the Royal Assent and has the effect of a statute.

The Church Assembly has been renamed the General Synod of the Church of England and reconstituted (Synodical Government Measure 1969).

The Ecclesiastical Jurisdiction Measure 1963 reformed and reconstructed the system of ecclesiastical courts (*q.v.*) of the Church of England, and replaced the existing enactments relating to ecclesiastical discipline.

medical inspection. May be required in cases of Nullity of Marriage (*q.v.*) where it is alleged that the marriage has not been consummated. See Matrimonial Causes Rules 1977, rr. 30 and 31.

medical jurisprudence. This term has been replaced by forensic medicine (*q.v.*).

mediums. Any person who for reward (and not solely for entertainment) with intent to deceive, purports to act as a spiritualistic medium, or to exercise any powers of telepathy or clairvoyance, or uses any fraudulent device in so doing, commits an offence (Fraudulent Mediums Act 1951).

meetings, public. Offensive words and behaviour in public places or at public meetings conducive to breach of the peace, or disorderly conduct designed to break up public meetings, are offences under the Public Order Act 1936, the Public Meetings Act 1908, and Public Order Act 1963. See also the Race Relations Act 1965, s.6.

melior est conditio possidentis et rei quam actoris. [The position of the possessor is the better; and that of the defendant is better than that of the plaintiff.]

memorandum. A note of the particulars of any transaction or matter. A clause inserted in a policy of marine insurance to prevent the underwriters from being liable for injury to goods of a peculiarly perishable nature and for minor damages. It begins as follows: "N.B.—Corn, fish, salt, fruit, flour and seed are warranted free from average, unless general or the ship be stranded." See also ASSOCIATION, MEMORANDUM OF.

memorial. An abstract of the material parts of a deed, with the parcels at full length, and concluding with a statement that the party desires the deed to be registered, which is left at the Land Registry for registration. See LAND REGISTRATION.

memory. "Living memory" is time whereof the memory of man runneth not to the contrary, *i.e.* the period for which evidence can be given by the oldest living available witnesses.

"Legal memory" runs from the accession of Richard I, in 1189, because the Statute of Westminster 1 (3 Edw. 1, c. 39) fixed that period as the time of limitation for bringing certain real actions.

menaces. Threats of injury to persons or property, including third persons, to induce the person menaced to part with money or valuable property, *e.g.* threats to accuse of immorality or misconduct. An unwarrantable demand with menaces constitutes blackmail (*q.v.*).

mens rea. [Guilty mind.] An evil intention, or a knowledge of the wrongfulness of an act. There is a presumption that it is an essential ingredient in every criminal offence, liable to be displaced either by the words of the statute, or by the subject-matter with which it deals. Many minor statutory offences, however, are punishable irrespective of the existence of *mens rea*; the mere intent to do the act forbidden by the statute is sufficient *mens rea*. If a particular intent or state of mind is an ingredient of a specific offence, that must be proved by the prosecution; but the absence of *mens rea* generally is a matter of defence. See INTENTION; MALICE.

mental disorder. Mental illness, arrested or incomplete development of mind, psychopathic disorder, and any other disorder or disability of mind. "Psychopathic disorder" is divided into severe subnormality, subnormality, and psychopathic disorder. "Severe subnormality" means a state of arrested or incomplete development of mind, which includes subnormality of intelligence, and which renders the patient incapable of living an independent life or of guarding himself against serious exploitation. "Subnormality" means a state of arrested or incomplete development of mind, which includes subnormality of intelligence, but which requires or is susceptible to medical or special treatment or training. "Psychopathic disorder" means a persistent disorder or disability of mind, whether or not including subnormality of intelligence, which results in abnormally aggressive or seriously irresponsible conduct which requires or is susceptible to medical treatment (Mental Health Act 1959, s.4).

mercantile agent. A person having in the customary course of his business as such agent, authority either to sell goods, or to consign goods for the purpose of sale, or to raise money on the security of goods including pledging them (Factors Act 1889, s.1).

mercantile law. The branch of English law which has succeeded to the "Law Merchant." It comprises usually partnership, companies, agency, bills of exchange, carriers, carriage by sea, insurance, sale, bottomry and *respondentia*, debt, guaranty, stoppage *in transitu*, lien and bankruptcy.

merchandise marks. See TRADE DESCRIPTION.

merchantable, marketable. Where goods are sold in the course of business there is, in general, an implied condition that they are of merchantable quality (Sale of Goods Act 1979, s.14(2); Supply of Goods (Implied Terms) Act 1973, s.3).

merger. That operation of law which extinguishes a right by reason of its coinciding with another and greater right in the same person, *e.g.* a life estate is merged in or swallowed by the reversion when the two interests come into the hands of the same person. A right of action on a simple contract debt is merged in the right of suing on a bond for the same debt, and a right of action is merged in a judgment in the sense that no further action may be brought on the debt, but only on the judgment. A special characteristic of the debt, however, such as being as preferential claim in bankruptcy, is not lost merely because judgment is obtained in respect of the debt.

In equity, merger is a question of intention. If the benefit of a charge on property, and the property subject to the charge, vest in the same person, then equity will treat the charge as kept alive or merged according to whether it be of advantage or not to the person entitled. The Law of Property Act 1925, s.185, provided that there is no merger at law if there would have been none in equity.

Business mergers are subject to the Fair Trading Act 1973, ss.57–77.

metropolitan stipendiary magistrate. Full time professionally qualified magistrate who sits alone. He can do all things for which two Justices of the Peace are normally required (see Justices of the Peace Act 1979, ss.31–34).

merits. The real matters in question as opposed to technicalities. An affidavit of merits is an affidavit showing that a defendant has a substantial ground of defence to an action.

Merton, Statute of. The statute 20 Hen. 3, cc. 1–11, enacting that children born before the marriage of their parents were illegitimate, in connection with which the Barons declared *"Nolumus leges Angliae mutari."* [We will not have the laws of England changed.] That is, the barons refused to agree to the adoption of the canon law rule of legitimation by subsequent marriage. See LEGITIMACY.

mesne. Middle, intervening or intermediate. See PROCESS.

A mesne lord was one who held of a superior lord.

mesne profits. The profits lost to the owner of land by reason of his having been wrongfully dispossessed of his land. A claim for mesne profits is usually joined with the action for recovery of possession of the land (Ord. 13, rr. 4, 5).

messuage. A house, including gardens, courtyard, orchard and outbuildings.

metes and bounds. By measurement and boundaries.

Middle Temple. One of the Inns of Court (*q.v.*).

Middlesex Registry. A registry of deeds and wills relating to land situate in the county of Middlesex to facilitate proof of title. It was transferred in 1891 to the Land Registry in London. Provision was made by the Land Registration Act 1936 for the closing of the Middlesex Deeds Registry, finally provided for by the Middlesex Deeds Act 1940. See also the Land Registration and Land Charges Act 1971, s.14. See LAND REGISTRATION.

military law. The law to which persons in the military service of the Crown are subject.

militia. The force which was raised after the Restoration of 1660 as a substitute for those which had been raised under the commissions of array and lieutenancy, was superseded by the Territorial Forces after 1907. See the Reserve Forces Act 1966.

mind. The state of a man's mind is as much a fact as the state of his digestion (*per* Bowen L.J., *Edgington* v. *Fitzmaurice* (1885) 29 Ch. D. 459, at p.483). See MENS REA.

minimum lending rate. Instituted in 1972 to replace Bank rate. It represented the published minimum rate at which the Bank of England would lend to the discount market. It ceased to be published on August 20, 1981.

minister. A "Servant of the King"; a member of the Cabinet, or a holder of high office under the Crown who vacates it on a change of Government. Every act of the Crown must be done through Ministers, who can be personally sued in law for their own acts. The constitutional doctrine of Ministerial responsibility is that every member of the Cabinet who does not resign is absolutely responsible for all that is done at Cabinet meetings; that is, Ministers are collectively responsible to Parliament. But the individual Minister is responsible for all the acts of his own Department.

The functions, styles, and titles of ministers may be altered under the Ministers of the Crown Act 1975. The number of ministers entitled to sit in the House of Commons is 95 (House of Commons (Disqualification) Act 1975, s.2, Sched. 2).

ministerial act. An act or duty which involves the exercise of administrative powers or the carrying out of instructions (*e.g.* the arrest of a person) as opposed to a judicial or discretionary act.

minor. A person under the age of 18 years. He becomes of full age from the first moment of the 18th anniversary of his birth (Family Law Reform Act 1969, ss.1, 9). An infant may be described as a minor (s.12). A minor has not full legal capacity.

In Roman law, the age of minority extended from puberty (12 or 14) up to 25 years.

The Infants Relief Act 1874 provided that contracts entered into by infants for the repayment of money lent or goods supplied other than necessaries, and all accounts stated shall be null and void and incapable of ratification on the attainment of full age.

By the Betting and Loans (Infants) Act 1892 a promise after majority to repay money borrowed during minority is void as against all parties thereto, except to the extent of any money actually lent after majority. Other contracts are voidable by the minor unless for necessaries (*q.v.*) or for his benefit, being a service or apprenticeship agreement (*Clements* v. *L. & N.W. Ry.* [1894] 2 Q.B. 482).

Betting circulars are not to be sent to minors (Betting, Gaming and Lotteries Act 1963, s.22; Family Law Reforms Act 1969, Sched. 1, Part IV). See also the Consumer Credit Act 1974, s.50.

Contractual obligations attaching to property of which a minor becomes possessed are binding so long as he possesses the property, but he may repudiate the property and with it the obligations within a reasonable time after attaining majority (*London & North Western Ry.* v. *M'Michael* (1850) 5 Ex. 114). A minor may take up shares in a limited company and may repudiate all liability on attaining majority (*Hamilton* v. *Vaughan Sherrin Co.* [1894] 3 Ch. 589), but the minor cannot recover money paid for them unless there has been a total failure of consideration (*Steinberg* v. *Scala* (*Leeds*) *Ltd.* [1923] 2 Ch. 452). If a minor has paid for property and has consumed it or altered its condition, he cannot recover money paid for it (*Valentini* v. *Canali* (1889) 24 Q.B.D. 166). The other party to a contract, if adult, is bound (*Holt* v. *Ward* (1732) 2 Str. 937).

A minor is liable in tort, but where a tort arises out of a contract a minor is not liable in tort as an indirect way of enforcing an invalid contract (*Leslie* v. *Shiell* [1914] 3 K.B. 607). Where a minor induces another to contract with him by fraudulently representing that he is of full age, the minor must make equitable restitution, but is not liable in tort for deceit: see however, *Stocks* v. *Wilson* [1913] 2 K.B. 35.

A minor cannot make a will (Wills Act 1837, s.7) but by *ibid.* s.11, and the Wills (Soldiers and Sailors)Act 1918 (as amended by the Family Law Reform Act 1969, s.3), if he is a soldier in actual military service, or a seaman at sea, he may make a valid will.

By the Law of Property Act 1925, s.1 a legal estate in land cannot be held by a minor, nor may he be an estate owner; *ibid.* s.205(2). In regard to land which it is desired that the minor should hold beneficially, a trust for sale or a settlement as may be appropriate must be created in accordance with the Settled Land Act, 1925. On an intestacy, the administrator holds on trust for sale, and even if the sole beneficiary is a minor he cannot take an absolute interest until he becomes of age or marries under that age (Administration of Estates Act 1925, s.47).

A minor cannot be an executor (Judicature Act 1925, s.165). A minor sues by a "next friend" and defends by a guardian *ad litem* (Ord. 80). See also CHILD.

minor interests. Interests not capable of being disposed of or created by registered dispositions, and capable of being overriden by the proprietors, unless protected as provided by the Land Registration Act 1925, and all rights and interests which are not registered or protected on the register, and are not overriding interests (Land Registration Act 1925, s.3(xv)).

minutes. (1) Notes or records of business transacted at a meeting. (2) Copies of a draft order or decree before being embodied in a formal judgment of the court.

misadventure. An accident or mischance, unexpected and undesigned, arising out of a lawful act. See HOMICIDE.

miscarriage. In its legal sense means a failure of justice.

mischief of the statute. The wrongs intended to be redressed by a statute; the gist or real purpose and object of it. The mischief of the statute is often to be found from the preamble and sometimes from the marginal notes (*Stephens* v. *Cuckfield R.D.C.* [1960] 2 Q.B. 373).

misdemeanour. An indictable offence. All distinctions between misdemeanour and felony have been abolished and all indictable offences (including piracy) are now governed by the rules relating to misdemeanours (Criminal Law Act 1967, s.1).

misdescription. An error, mistake, or misstatement in the description of property. A misdescription affecting the title, value or character of land in a contract of sale may be (1) substantial, so that the property purchased is not that which it was intended to purchase, or (2) slight, so that compensation in money would be proper. In (1) the misdescription is a defence to an action for specific performance, and a ground for rescission; the purchaser cannot be compelled to take the property. The purchaser may, however, at his option, generally compel specific performance of the contract with an abatement of the purchase price. The vendor cannot enforce the contract where he has been guilty of fraud or misrepresentation.

misdirection. When the judge improperly or erroneously directs or informs the jury as to the law or the evidence they have to consider in arriving at their verdict. The withdrawal of evidence, or of a question, from the jury which might have influenced their decision is misdirection. A judge sitting alone can misdirect himself, as where, *e.g.* he puts the wrong questions to himself to answer. Misdirection is a ground of appeal for a new trial in a civil action if some substantial wrong or miscarriage of justice is thereby occasioned.

misericordia. [Mercy.] See AMERCIAMENT.

misfeasance. Misfeasance is the improper performance of a lawful act, *e.g.* where there is negligence or trespass. A misfeasor is a person who is guilty of a misfeasance.

misjoinder. Where persons are wrongly joined as plaintiffs or defendants in an action, *i.e.* where persons are made parties who ought not to be. No action can now be defeated by a misjoinder or non-joinder of parties, and the court may of its own motion, or on application, order a party to cease to be a party (Ord. 15, r. 6).

misnomer. A mis-naming. An amendment in consequence can be made in either civil or criminal causes.

misprision. (1) Misprision of treason, is where a person who knows that some other person has committed high treason does not within a reasonable time give information thereof to a judge of assize or justice of the peace. At common law the punishment is imprisonment for life and forfeiture of the offender's goods. (2) Misprision of felony was the concealment of knowledge of the commission of a felony. It was a common law misdemeanour. The offence has lapsed with the abolition of the distinction between felony and misdemeanour. See FELONY; MISDEMEANOUR.

misrepresentation. A statement, or conduct, which conveys a false or wrong impression. A false or fraudulent misrepresentation is one made with knowledge of its falsehood, and intended to deceive. A negligent misrepresentation is one made with no reasonable grounds for believing it to be true. An innocent misrepresentation is one made with reasonable grounds for believing it to be true, as where an honest mistake is made. A fraudulent misrepresentation is actionable as a tort.

When a person has been induced to enter into a contract by misrepresentation, he may in general either (1) affirm the contract and insist on the misrepresentation being made good, if that is possible; or (2) rescind the contract if it is still executory, and if all parties can be restored to their original positions; or (3) bring an action for damages; or (4) rely upon the misrepresentation as a defence to an action on the contract.

A contract may be rescinded on the ground of misrepresentation even if innocent (Misrepresentation Act 1967, s.1). Specific performance will not be decreed if a definite untrue representation has been relied on. See FRAUD. Liability for misrepresentation may only be excluded from a contract if the clause satisfies the test of reasonableness (Unfair Contract Terms Act 1977, ss.8, 11, Sched. 2).

mistake. A mistake in a written document may, in a proper case, be rectified by the court. A mistake as to the provisions of English law is, in general, immaterial: everyone is presumed to know the law. A mistake of fact is in a better position. Thus if a person signs a document believing it to be of another sort, he may plead *non est factum* [it is not his deed]. But unilateral mistake as a general rule, has no legal effect, *e.g.* an error of judgment as to the value of a thing. Mistake, however, avoids a contract if as to (1) the nature of the contract itself (*Lewis* v. *Clay* (1898) 77 L.T. 653); (2) the identity of the person contracted with, where this is material (*Cundy* v. *Lindsay* (1878) 3 App. Cas. 459); (3) the subject-matter of the contract, or the identity of the thing contracted for (*Raffles* v. *Wichelhaus* (1864) 2 H. & C. 906; *Bell* v. *Lever Bros.* [1932] A.C. 161); (4) the intention or promise of one party known to the other party (*Webster* v. *Cecil* (1861) 30 Beav. 62). Mistake is usually no defence in an action of tort. In criminal law, mistake of law is no excuse, but mistake of fact (which if true would have justified the act) is a good defence (*R.* v. *Tolson* (1889) 23 Q.B.D. 168).

Money paid under mistake of fact may be recovered, as money had and received to the use of the person paying it (*Jones* v. *Waring and Gillow* [1926] A.C. 670), but money paid under mistake of law is not recoverable, except where paid to an officer of the court (*Ex p. James* (1874) L.R. 9 Ch. App. 614) or in case of fraud.

mitigation. Where a defendant or prisoner whose responsibility or guilt is not in dispute proves facts tending to reduce the damages or punishment to be awarded against him, he is said to show facts in mitigation of damages, or of sentence, as the case may be.

In general, it is the duty of the party whose legal rights have been infringed to act reasonably in mitigation of damages.

mittimus. [We send.] *e.g.* a writ.

mixed fund. A fund consisting of the proceeds of both real and personal property.

mobilia sequuntur personam. [Movables follow the person.] Thus the law of a man's domicile governs the descent of his personal property.

mobility allowance. Benefit payable to a person suffering from a physical disablement so that he is unable or virtually unable to walk (Social Security Act 1975).

mock auction. One not conducted in good faith. The Mock Auctions Act 1961 prescribes penalties for the promotion or conduct of them.

mode of address. For the correct way to address judges, recorders, etc., see *Lord Chief Justice's Practice Direction* [1982] 1 All E.R. 320.

modo et forma. A denial that the thing alleged in the pleading of the other side had been done *modo et forma* [in the manner and form] alleged. This put the opposite party upon strict proof of every averment.

modus. The payment of tithes otherwise than by a tenth of the yearly increase of land, *e.g.* by a payment of twopence per acre.

modus et conventio vincunt legem. [Custom and agreement overrule law.] Within ever decreasing limits, the parties to a contract can make their own rules.

modus legem dat donationi. [Agreement gives law to the gift.] *e.g.* the agreement for the transfer of land settles the conditions upon which the land is to be held.

molest. To pester or interfere with someone. For remedies against molestation see INJUNCTION.

money. The medium of exchange, and measure of value. "Money" is construed widely when used in wills, as including cash in hand or at bank, and it may be investments.

money bill. A bill which in the opinion of the Speaker of the House of Commons contains provisions dealing with finance and taxation.

A money bill can only originate in the House of Commons, and any bill certified by the Speaker to be a money bill must be presented for the Royal Assent at the end of the session in which it passes the Commons, whether it is or it not passed by the Lords (Parliament Act 1911).

money had and received. Money which is paid to one person which rightfully belongs to another, as where money is paid by A to B on a consideration which has wholly failed, is said to be money had and received by B to the use of A, and is recoverable by action by A. See QUASI-CONTRACT.

moneylender. A moneylender was defined for the purpose of the Moneylenders Acts 1900 and 1927, as any person whose business is that of moneylending, or who advertises or announces himself or holds himself out in any way as carrying on that business; but not including pawnbrokers, friendly societies, bodies authorised by law to lend money, bankers, or bodies exempted by the Department of Trade (Moneylenders Act 1900, s.6).

Moneylenders as a separate class have almost disappeared from the law and have been swallowed up in the Consumer Credit Act 1974. A loan by a moneylender is a "personal credit agreement." It may amount to a "use credit" or a "debtor-creditor-supplier agreement." See the Act of 1974, ss.8, 11 and the examples in Sched. 2. A moneylender must be licensed by the Director-General of Fair Trading (s.21). Extortionate bargains may be reopened by the county court (ss.137–140, 189(1)). As to advertising, see ss.43–47.

monopoly. A licence or privilege allowed by the Sovereign for the sole buying and selling, making, working, or using of anything whatsoever. Monopolies were made illegal by the Statute of Monopolies (21 Jac. 1, c. 3), except in the case of patents for new inventions, etc. Ancient franchises (*q.v.*) are not within the statute.

A commercial monopoly is where the supply of a certain commodity is controlled by one manufacturer, trader, or group. See RESTRICTIVE TRADE PRACTICES.

Investigations into alleged monopolies are carried out by the Monopolies and Mergers Commission under the Fair Trading Act 1973.

monstrans de droit. [Manifestation of right.] A remedy which a subject had when the Crown was in possession of property belonging to him, and the title of the Crown appeared from facts set forth upon record. In such a case the claimant might present a *monstrans de droit*, either showing that upon the facts as recorded he was entitled to the property, or setting forth new facts showing that he was entitled. It was superseded by the Petition of Right, and abolished by the Crown Proceedings Act 1947, Sched. 1.

month. A month is either a lunar month of 28 days, or a calendar month. A month at common law meant a lunar month, but in ecclesiastical and mercantile law a calendar month. Now, unless a contrary intention appears, "month" means calendar month (Interpretation Act 1978, ss.5, 22 and 23; Law of Property Act 1925, s.61; R.S.C., Ord. 3, r. 1).

In calculating the period of a month or months that have elapsed after a certain event, *e.g.* a notice, the period ends on the corresponding date in the appropriate subsequent month irrespective of whether some months are longer than others (*Dodds* v. *Walker* [1981] 1 W.L.R. 1027, H.L.).

moots. A meeting of the members of an Inn of Court in Hall at which points of law arising in a given case were argued by selected barristers before the benchers who in turn gave their opinions thereon. They were an essential part of professional legal education until about the end of the seventeenth century. They still survive on a voluntary basis at Gray's Inn, where one of the benchers is appointed "Master of the Moots," and amongst law students elsewhere.

moral defectives. See MENTAL DISORDER.

morally wrong is distinguishable from legally wrong (*Sofaer* v. *Sofaer* [1960] 1 W.L.R. 1173). See also IMMORALITY.

moratorium. The general postponement of payment of debts authorised by statute, *e.g.* as on the outbreak of war in 1914.

moratur in lege. [He tarries in the law.] A demurrer.

morganatic marriage. Marriage between a royal or noble person and one of lower rank in which the children do not inherit the royal or noble rank.

mortgage. [Norman-French, *mort,* dead, and *gage,* a pledge, from low Latin, *vadium*] A mortgage originally denoted a pledge of land under which the creditor took the rents and profits for himself, so that it was dead or profitless to the debtor, as opposed to a pledge under which the rents and profits went in reduction of the debt (*vif gage, vadium vivum*).

A legal mortgage is a transfer of a legal estate or interest in land or other property for the purpose of securing the repayment of a debt. An equitable mortgage is one which passes only an equitable estate or interest, either (1) because the form of transfer or conveyance used is an equitable one, that is, operates only as between the parties to it, and those who have notice of it, *e.g.* a deposit of title deeds, or (2) because the mortgagor's estate or interest is equitable, that is, consists merely of the right to obtain a conveyance of the legal estate.

Prior to 1926 a mortgage was ordinarily effected by an absolute conveyance followed by a proviso for redemption, by which the mortgagee agreed to reconvey the property to the mortgagor on payment of the debt and interest by a certain date. Formerly, if the money was not paid on the day, the mortgage became irredeemable at common law, but the mortgagor had an equity of redemption until foreclosure or sale. The right of foreclosure entitled the mortgagee to compel the mortgagor either to pay off the debt within a reasonable time or to lose his equity of redemption.

By s.85 of the Law of Property Act 1925, a mortgage of an estate in fee simple may only be made by a demise for a term of years absolute, subject to a provision for cesser on redemption, or by a charge by deed expressed to be by way of legal mortgage. A first or only mortgagee takes a term of 3,000 years from the date of the mortgage, and a second or subsequent mortgagee takes a term commencing from the date of the mortgage one day longer. By *ibid.* s.86, a mortgage of a term of years absolute may only be made either by a sub-demise for a term of years absolute less by one day at least than the term vested in the mortgagor, or by a charge by deed expressed to be by way of legal mortgage.

The object of the changes in the law was to secure to the mortgagor a legal estate, and not a mere equity of redemption as hitherto. See EQUITY OF REDEMPTION; CLOG ON EQUITY OF REDEMPTION; OPTION MORTGAGE.

mortgagee. The person to whom property is mortgaged; the lender of the mortgage debt.

mortgagor. The person who mortgages his property as security for the mortgage debt; the borrower.

mortmain. The alienation of land to corporations, whereby the benefit of the incidents of tenure was lost, because "a corporation never dies." Land could not be conveyed to corporations except by statutory authority or by licence of the Crown (7 Edw. 1, stat. 2, c. 13 and 15 Ric. 2, c. 5, replaced by the Mortmain and the Charitable Uses Act 1888). An assurance or conveyance to a corporation not authorised to hold land rendered the land liable to forfeiture to the Crown. The law of mortmain was abolished by the Charities Act 1960, s.38.

mortuary. A place for the reception of dead bodies before interment.

mortuum vadium. [A mortgage (*q.v.*).]

mote. A meeting or assembly. See FOLCMOTE.

motion. An application to a court or a judge for an order directing something to be done in the applicant's favour. Ordinarily a motion is to be made only after a notice has been given to the parties affected, but in certain cases it may be made *ex parte*. Certain proceedings are by way of originating motion. See Ord. 5, r. 5, Ord. 8 notes.

motor insurance bureau. A company formed by motor insurers in 1946 operating within the terms of two agreements with the Secretary of State for the Environment dated November 22, 1972. Provision is made to meet the claims of: (a) victims of uninsured drivers; (b) victims of drivers who cannot be traced; and (c) victims of foreign motorists visiting Britain. Only claims for personal injuries are met.

movables. Personal property, *e.g.* goods, as opposed to "immovables" (*e.g.* land) or real property.

mulier. [Latin, *mulier*, a wife.] A woman, virgin, wife, or a legitimate child.

multifariousness. A demurrer to a bill in Chancery that it attempted to embrace too many objects or causes of suit. See JOINDER OF CAUSES OF ACTIONS.

municipal corporation. Formerly the local government authority of a borough, consisting of a mayor, aldermen and councillors, which had been incorporated by royal charter. Municipal corporations were regulated by the Municipal Corporations Acts 1835 and 1882 and the Local Government Act 1933. Outside London, they ceased to exist on April 1, 1974 (Local Government Act 1972, s.1(11)). See DISTRICT COUNCIL.

municipal law. The law of a state or country, as opposed to international law; internal law.

muniments. [*Munio,* to defend or fortify.] Title deeds and other documents relating to the title to land.

murder. The crime of unlawful homicide with malice aforethought; as where death is caused by an unlawful act done with the intention to cause death or bodily harm, or which is commonly known to be likely to cause death or bodily harm. Death must result in a year and a day. The burden of proving malice (either express, or by implication) rests upon the prosecution (*Woolmington* v. *D.P.P.* [1935] A.C. 462). Malice is implied by a proved intention to inflict grievous bodily harm (*D.P.P.* v. *Smith* [1961] A.C. 290).

Where a person kills another in the course or furtherance of some other offence, the killing does not amount to murder unless done with the same malice aforethought (express or implied) as is required for a killing to amount to murder when not done in the course of furtherance of another offence (Homicide Act 1957, s.1(1)).

In cases of homicide, provocation (*q.v.*)will reduce the offence from murder to manslaughter. A person found not guilty of murder may be found guilty of manslaughter (Criminal Law Act 1967, s.6). As to bail in murder cases see *R.* v. *Vennege* (note) [1982] 1 All E.R. 403. See CONSTRUCTIVE MALICE; DIMINISHED RESPONSIBILITY; REPRIEVE.

mutatis mutandis. [The necessary changes being made.]

mute. A prisoner who, being arraigned for treason, or misdemeanour, either makes no answer at all, or with such matter as is not allowable. In the first case, a jury must be sworn to try whether the prisoner stands mute of malice (*i.e.* obstinately) or by visitation of God (*e.g.* being deaf or dumb). If he is found mute by visitation of God, the trial proceeds as if he had pleaded not guilty; if he is found mute of malice, or if he will not answer directly to the indictment, it formerly exposed him to the *peine forte et dure* (*q.v.*); now the court, under the Criminal Law Act 1967, s.6(1)(c), orders a plea of not guilty to be entered, and the trial proceeds accordingly.

Mutiny Act. The Bill of Rights (1 Will. & M., sess. 2, c. 2) declares that the raising or keeping a standing army within the kingdom in time of peace, unless it be with the consent of Parliament, is illegal. Consequently, an Act of Parliament was passed annually to legalise the Army for the year, called the Mutiny Act, and containing rules for its regulation, later replaced by the Army Act 1955, which is continued on an annual basis by orders made under the Armed Forces Act 1976, s.1.

mutual credits. Where there have been mutual credits, mutual debts or other mutual dealings between a debtor and a creditor, only the balance is to be claimed or paid in the debtor's bankruptcy proceedings (Bankruptcy Act 1914, s.31).

mutuum. A bailment (*q.v.*) consisting of the loan of personal chattels to be consumed by the borrower and to be returned to the lender similar in kind and quantity.

N

N.P. Nisi prius (*q.v.*).

nam; namium. The taking or distraining of the goods of another.

name and arms clause. The clause, sometimes inserted in a will or settlement by which property is given to a person, for the purpose of imposing on him the condition that he shall assume the surname and arms of the testator or settlor, with a direction that if he neglects to assume or discontinues the use of them, the estate shall devolve on the next person in remainder. A name and arms clause which is sufficiently certain is valid. See, *e.g. Re Neeld* [1969] 1 W.L.R. 998.

name, change of. A person may change his surname (*e.g.* by deed poll) but not his Christian name, which can only be changed by Act of Parliament or by the Bishop at confirmation. A deed poll for change of name by a British subject whose permanent place of residence is in the United Kingdom may be enrolled (Judicature Act 1925, s.218; Enrolment of Deeds (Change of Name) Regulations 1949 (S.I. 1949 No. 316), 1969 (S.I. 1969 No. 1432) and 1974 (S.I. 1974 No. 1937).

A company may change its name by special resolution with the consent of the Board (now Department) of Trade (Companies Act 1948, s.18).

national assistance. The National Assistance Act 1948, was passed to terminate the existing poor law and to provide for the assistance of persons in need by the National Assistance Board, and to provide further for disabled, sick, and aged persons, etc. It has been frequently amended.

National Health Service. The principal Act is the National Health Service Act 1946, which has been amended by subsequent Acts the latest of which is the National Health Service Reorganisation Act 1973.

national insurance. Social security under the National Insurance Acts and the National Insurance (Industrial Injuries) Acts has been replaced by the scheme under the Social Security Act 1975. Claimants for the various benefits may appeal from the decision of an Insurance Officer to a National Insurance Local Tribunal consisting of a legally qualified chairman and two lay members. Further appeal lies to a Social Security Commissioner and thence, on a point of law, to the High Court.

national parks. See CONSERVATION.

National Trust for the preservation of places of historic interest or natural beauty was incorporated by the National Trust Act 1907. It is a charity.

nationality. The character or quality arising from membership of some particular nation or State, which determines the political status and allegiance of a person. It may be acquired by birth, descent, naturalisation (*q.v.*), conquest or cession of territory, or (if a woman) by reason of marriage. See BRITISH SUBJECT; NATURALISATION.

nations, law of. International Law (*q.v.*).

natural child. The child of one's body; or an illegitimate child.

natural justice. The rules and procedure to be followed by any person or body charged with the duty of adjudicating upon disputes between, or the rights of others, *e.g.* a government department. The chief rules are to act fairly, in good faith, without bias, and in a judicial temper; to give each party the opportunity of adequately stating his case, and correcting or contradicting any relevant statement prejudicial to his case, and not to hear one side behind the back of the other. A man must not be judge in his own cause, so that a judge must declare any interest he has in the subject-matter of the dispute before him. A man must have notice of what he is accused. Relevant documents which are looked at by the tribunal should be disclosed to the parties interested.

In short, not only should justice be done, but it should be seen to be done; see *Local Government Board* v. *Arlidge* [1915] A.C. 120; *Errington* v. *Minister of Health* [1935] 1 K.B. 249; *Board of Education* v. *Rice* [1911] A.C. 179, *per* Lord Loreburn at p. 182; *R.* v. *City of Westminster Assessment Committee* [1941] 1 K.B. 53. *Ridge* v. *Baldwin* [1964] A.C. 40.

The rules of natural justice do not apply to administrative acts (*Schmidt* v. *Secretary of State for Home Affairs* [1969] 2 Ch. 149).

natural law. The law of nature; law as the emanation of the Divine Providence, rooted in the nature and reason of man. It is both anterior and superior to positive law.

natural persons. Human beings, as distinguished from artificial persons or corporations recognised by the law, *e.g.* companies.

natural rights. Fundamental rights common to the law of all civilised peoples, *e.g.* right of personal liberty, of ownership and possession of property, freedom of speech, etc.

naturales liberi. [Roman law.] Natural children. (1) Children not born in lawful wedlock, as opposed to *legitimi*; (2) children born as opposed to adopted.

naturalisation. When a person becomes the subject of a state to which he was before an alien. Certificates of Naturalisation as a British Citizen (*q.v.*) may be granted to persons of full age and capacity who fulfil certain requirements set out in the British Nationality Act 1981, Sched. 1; whereupon, on taking the oath of allegiance, such persons become British Citizens (Act of 1981, ss.6 and 42; Sched. 5).

The qualification required for naturalisation as a British citizen set out in Sched. 1 to the Act of 1981 may be summarised as relating to residence, character, language and intentions. A person may also acquire British Dependant Territories citizenship (*q.v.*) by naturalisation (Act of 1981, s.18; Sched. 1).

Navigation Acts. Various statutes (especially 12 Car. 2, c. 18) passed for the encouragement and protection of British shipping by excluding foreign ships from trading with British colonies and even with Great Britain. Now repealed.

Navy. The discipline of the Navy is regulated by the Naval Discipline Act 1957.

ne exeat regno. A writ which issues from the High Court of Justice (in the Chancery Division) to restrain a person from going out of the kingdom without licence of the Crown or leave of the court. It is a high prerogative writ, which was originally applicable to purposes of State only, but was afterwards extended and confined to absconding debtors. For the modern practice see *Felton* v. *Callis* [1969] 1 Q.B. 200 and R.S.C., Ord. 45, r. 1 (notes thereto).

nec tempus nec locus occurrit regi. [Neither time nor place affects the King.]

nec vi, nec clam, nec precario. [Not by violence, stealth, or entreaty.] User as of right, in order to found a title by prescription to an easement, must be *longus usus nec per vim, nec clam, nec precario* [long use not by violence, stealth or entreaty].

necessaries. Minors (and mental patients) normally incapable of making a binding contract, can contract to buy necessaries, *i.e.* goods suitable to the condition in life of such [minor] and to his actual requirements at the time of the sale and delivery (Sale of Goods Act 1979, s.3).

Any rule of law or equity conferring on a wife authority, as agent of necessity of her husband, to pledge his credit or to borrow money on his credit was abrogated by the Matrimonial Proceedings and Property Act 1970, s.41.

For ships, the term "necessaries" means such things as are fit and proper for the service in which the ship is engaged, and such as the owner, being a prudent man, would have ordered if present. The master may hypothecate the ship for necessaries supplied abroad so as to bind the owner.

necessitas inducit privilegium quoad jura privata. [Necessity gives a privilege as to private rights.] See NECESSITY.

necessitas non habet legem. [Necessity knows no law.]

necessitas publica major est quam privata. [Public necessity is greater than private.] A maxim favoured by the Executive (*q.v.*).

necessity. The invasion of the private rights of others may possibly be justified and defended on the grounds of necessity. Thus to destroy property in the path of a conflagration to halt it, or to enter on property and damage it in time of war may be justified as for the commonweal. Similarly, acts injurious to others may be done in the defence of a man's own property which is in imminent danger. Thus a farmer may shoot a savage dog which is attacking his sheep. The test is whether there was reasonable necessity for doing the act done in the circumstances existing at the time (*Cresswell* v. *Sirl* [1948] 1 K.B. 241). Necessity may be an excuse for committing what would otherwise be a criminal offence if the act or omission which is in question was necessary to prevent the execution of an illegal purpose. But mere personal necessity is no justification for a crime, *e.g.* hunger (*R.* v. *Dudley and Stephens* (1884) 14 Q.B.D. 273). See ANIMALS; RIGHT OF WAY.

neck verse. The words *Miserere mei Deus*, with which the fifty-first Psalm begins. A prisoner was entitled to benefit of clergy (*q.v.*) if he could read or recite these words.

negative pregnant. A literal denial in pleading which does not go to the substance of the allegation. Where a traverse is of a negative averment so that it is clear that it is intended to set up an affirmative case, particulars of the affirmative case ought to be delivered (*I.R.C.* v. *Jackson* [1960] 1 W.L.R. 873).

neglect to maintain. See WILFUL NEGLECT TO MAINTAIN.

negligence. A tort, actionable at the suit of a person suffering damage in consequence of the defendant's breach of duty to take care to refrain from injuring him.

Negligence is the omission to do something which a reasonable man, guided upon those considerations which ordinarily regulate the conduct of human affairs, would do, or doing something which a prudent and reasonable man would not do (*per* Alderson B., *Blyth* v. *Birmingham Waterworks Co.* (1856) L.R. 11 Ex. 781, at p. 784). Negligence is simply neglect of some care which we are bound to exercise towards somebody (*per* Bowen L.J., *Thomas* v. *Quartermaine* (1887) 18 Q.B.D. 685, at p. 694). You must take reasonable care to avoid acts or omissions which you can reasonably foresee would be likely to injure your neighbour. Who then in law is my neighbour? The answer seems to be—persons who are so closely and directly affected by my act that I ought reasonably to have them in contemplation as being so affected when I am directing my mind to the acts or omissions which are called in question (*per* Lord Atkin, *Donoghue* v. *Stevenson* [1932] A.C. 562, at p. 580).

The degree of care which the law requires is that which is reasonable in the circumstances of the particular case. The standard is the foresight and caution of the ordinary or average prudent man, *i.e.* the man in the street, or on the Clapham omnibus, who takes the magazines at home, and in the evening pushes the lawn mower in his shirt sleeves (see *per* Greer L.J., *Hall* v. *Brooklands Auto-Racing Club* [1933] 1 K.B. 205, at p.224). But the standard of care is higher where a person puts a dangerous object attractive to children in a place where they may have access to it. Persons professing special skill must use such skill as is usual with persons professing such skill.

The burden of proving negligence is on the plaintiff who alleges it, and there must be reasonable evidence of negligence for the case to be left to the jury, but where the maxim *res ipsa loquitur* (*q.v.*) applies, the plaintiff merely proves the accident.

The Court of Appeal held in *Re Polemis* [1921] 3 K.B. 560 that a person guilty of negligence was liable in damages for all the direct consequences of such negligence, even though such consequences could not reasonably have been foreseen. But in *The Wagon Mound* [1961] A.C. 338 the Judicial Committee of the Privy Council refused to follow *Re Polemis*, and held that damage must be reasonably foreseeable for there to be liability in negligence but not necessarily the precise sequence of events. See CONTRIBUTORY NEGLIGENCE. See also FINANCIAL LOSS.

negotiable instrument. An instrument the transfer of which to a transferee who takes in good faith and for value passes a good title, free from any defects or equities affecting the title of the transferor. The most important kinds of negotiable instruments are bills of exchange, cheques and promissory notes. Negotiability may be conferred by custom or statute, and restricted or destroyed by the holder of the instrument.

Negotiability is also used popularly as equivalent to transferability.

negotiate. To transfer for value by delivery or indorsement.

negotiorum gestio. Interference of one in the affairs of another merely from benevolence and without authority. In English law a man so interfering (1) has no claim on the other in respect of what he may do; (2) is liable for the wages of anyone whom he may employ; (3) must have the skill and knowledge necessary for whatever he takes it on himself to do.

nem. con.: nemine contradicente. [No one saying otherwise.]

nem. dis.: nemine dissentiente. [No one dissenting.]

neminem oportet legibus esse sapientiorem. [It is not permitted to be wiser than the laws.]

nemo admittendus est inhabilitare seipsum. [Nobody is to be permitted to incapacitate himself.]

nemo agit in seipsum. [No one can take proceedings against himself.]

nemo contra factum suum proprium venire potest. [No one can go against his own deed.]

nemo dat qui non habet. [No one gives who possesses not.]

nemo debet bis puniri pro uno delicto. [No one should be punished twice for one fault.]

nemo debet esse judex in propria causa. [No one can be judge in his own cause.] A judge may not have any pecuniary or personal interest in a case which he tries. If he has some interest he must declare it, *e.g.* shares in a company which is party to an action.

nemo est haeres viventis. [No one is the heir of anyone who is alive.]

nemo ex proprio dolo consequitur actionem. [No one obtains a cause of action by his own fraud.]

nemo ex suo delicto meliorem suam conditionem facere potest. [No one can improve his position by his own wrongdoing.]

nemo plus juris ad alium transferre potest, quam ipse haberet. [The title of an assignee can be no better than that of his assignor.]

nemo potest esse simul actor et judex. [No one can be at once suitor and judge.]

nemo potest facere per alium, quod per se non potest. [No one can do through another what he cannot do himself.]

nemo potest plus juris ad alium transferre quam ipse habet. [No one can transfer a greater right to another than he himself has.]

nemo prohibetur pluribus defensionibus uti. [No one is forbidden to use several defences.]

nemo tenetur ad impossibile. [No one is required to do what is impossible.]

nemo tenetur se ipsum accusare. [No one is bound to incriminate himself.]

nervous shock. Injury to health due to nervous shock is a form of bodily harm for which damages may be claimed (*Hambrook* v. *Stokes* [1925] 1 K.B., pp. 153–156, *per* Atkin L.J.). But for the defendant to be liable he must owe a duty to the plaintiff to take care with respect to him, and the fact that the defendant would suffer injury from nervous shock as a result of the defendant's act must have been reasonably foreseeable by him, *i.e.* the plaintiff must have been within the area of potential danger (*Bourhill* v. *Young* [1943] A.C. 92). However in *McLoughlin* v. *O'Brien* [1982] 2 All E.R. 298, H.L. it was held that a plaintiff who had not been at the scene of an accident might recover damages for nervous shock brought on by injury caused not to herself but to a near relative, or the fear of such injury.

new towns. The New Towns Act 1946, provided for the creation of new towns by means of development corporations. This and subsequent legislation were consolidated in the New Towns Act 1965, amended by the Statutory Corporations (Financial Provisions) Act 1974 and the New Towns Acts 1975 and 1980.

new trial. Application for a new trial or to set aside a verdict, finding, or judgment is to the Court of Appeal and is heard as an appeal (Ord. 59, r. 11). Grounds for a new trial are (*a*) misdirection of the jury or himself by the judge, or improper admission or rejection of evidence by the judge, provided substantial injustice was caused; (*b*) verdict against weight of the evidence; (*c*) discovery of fresh evidence; (*d*) excessive or inadequate damages. See also VENIRE DE NOVO.

next friend. A minor or patient (*q.v.*) who desires to bring an action must, as a rule do so through the intervention of a person called a next friend, generally a relation. He must act by a solicitor (Ord. 80).

next-of-kin. The nearest blood relatives. Strictly those who are next in degree of kindred to a deceased person. The degrees of kindred are reckoned according to the Roman law, both upwards to the ancestor and downwards to the issue, each generation counting for a degree. Thus, from father to son, is one degree, and from brother to brother is two degrees, namely, one upwards to the father and one downwards to the other son.

Formerly, the "next-of-kin" of a person who had died intestate signified those persons who were entitled to his personal property, after payment of his debts, under the Statute of Distribution (22 & 23 Car. 2, c. 10), repealed by the Administration of Estates Act 1925. See INTESTATE SUCCESSION.

next presentation. The right to present to the *first* vacancy of a benefice, which, under the old law, the owner of an advowson (*q.v.*) could grant to another. Since the Benefices Act 1898, however, the whole interest of the grantor must pass, so that the right of next presentation is a right of the owner of the advowson (*q.v.*) for the time being. But a priest cannot present himself to a living the right to the presentation to which is vested in himself, or his wife, or person on their behalf (Benefices Act 1898 (Amendment) Measure 1923). See also the Pastoral Measure 1968, ss.32, 67–73.

nihil: nil. [Nothing.] No goods.

nihil facit error nominis cum de corpore constat. [A mistake as to the name has no effect when there is no mistake as to who is the person meant.]

nisi. A decree, order, rule, declaration, or other adjudication of a court is said to be made *nisi* when it is not to take effect unless the person affected by it fails to show cause against it within a certain time, that it, unless he appears before the court, and gives some reason why it should not take effect. See ABSOLUTE; DECREE NISI.

nisi prius. A trial at *nisi prius* was a trial by a jury before a single judge, either at the sittings held for that purpose in London and Middlesex, or at the assizes. Formerly all common law actions were tried at the bar, that is, before the full court, consisting of several judges; and, therefore, the writ for summoning the jury commanded the sheriff to bring the jurors from the county where the cause of action arose to the court at Westminster. But when the statute 13 Edw. 1 directed the justices of assize to try issues in the county where they arose, the sheriff was thenceforth commanded to bring the jurors to Westminster on a certain day, "unless before that day" (*nisi prius*) the justices of assize came into the county.

noise. Where noise or vibration amount to a nuisance, the local authority may serve an abatement notice. Contravention of the notice is an offence. Alternatively the local authority may obtain an injunction (Control of Pollution Act 1974, ss.58, 70, 73). An occupier of premises who is aggrieved by noise etc. may complain to the magistrates (ss.59, 70). Specific provisions apply to construction sites (ss.60, 61). The use of loudspeakers in streets is restricted. Ice-cream etc. vans are partially exempt (s.62). Noise from model aircraft is within the Act (s.73(4)). For penalties see ss.74, 87(2).

Compensation for noise from the use of public works may be claimed under the Land Compensation Act 1973.

nolle prosequi. An acknowledgment or undertaking entered on record by the plaintiff in an action, to forbear to proceed in the action, either wholly or partially; superseded by the modern practice of discontinuance. In criminal prosecutions by indictment or information, a *nolle prosequi* to stay proceedings may be entered by leave of the Attorney-General at any time before judgment; it is not equivalent to an acquittal and is no bar to a new indictment for the same offence. The powers of the Attorney-General are not subject to control by the court (*R.* v. *Comptroller of Patents* [1899] 1 Q.B. 909, at p.914).

nolumus leges Angliae mutari. [We will not have the laws of England changed.] See MERTON, STATUTE OF.

nominis umbra. [The shadow of a name.] *e.g.* a one-man company.

non aliter a significatione verborum recedi oportet quam cum manifestum est aliud sensisse testatorem. [There should be no departure from the ordinary meaning of words except in so far as it appears that the testator meant something different.]

non assumpsit. [He did not promise.] The plea to an action of *assumpsit* (*q.v.*).

non cepit modo et forma. [He did not take in the manner and form (alleged).] The plea to the action of replevin (*q.v.*).

non compos mentis. [Not sound in mind.] See MENTAL DISORDER; PATIENT.

non constat. [It does not follow.]

non culpabilis. [Not guilty.]

non debet, cui plus licet, quod minus est non licere. [It is lawful for a man to do a less thing if he is entitled to do a greater thing.]

non est factum. [It is not his deed.] The old common law defence which permitted a person who had executed a written document in ignorance of its character to plead that notwithstanding the execution "it is not his deed." See, *e.g. Saunders* (*Executrix in the Estate of Rose Maud Gallie*) v. *Anglia Building Society* [1971] A.C. 1004.

non est inventus. [He has not been found.] The return which a sheriff has to make upon a writ commanding him to arrest a person who is not within his bailiwick.

non liquet. [It is not clear.]

non observata forma infertus adnullatio actus. [Non-observance of the prescribed formalities involves the invalidity of the proceeding.]

non obstante. [Notwithstanding.] About the year 1250, the Crown began to issue licences to do such a thing *non obstante* any law to the contrary. The Bill of Rights enacted that any dispensation *non obstante* should be wholly void and without effect.

non obstante veredicto. [Notwithstanding the verdict.] Upon an application for a new trial the Court of Appeal may set aside the judgment of the court below and enter judgment notwithstanding the verdict (Judicature Act 1925, s.50; Ord. 59, rr. 2, 11).

non omittas propter libertatem. A clause inserted in writs of execution, directing and authorising the sheriff "not to omit" to execute the writ by reason of any liberty or district in which the sheriff had no power to execute process unless he had special authority.

non omne quod licet honestum est. [All things that are lawful are not honourable.]

non placet. [It is not approved.]

non possessori incumbit necessitas probandi possessiones ad se pertinere. [A person in possession is not bound to prove that what he possesses belongs to him.]

non potest rex gratiam facere cum injuria et damno aliorum. [The king cannot confer a favour on one man to the injury and damage of others.]

non pros.; non prosequitur. [He does not follow up.] Judgment *non pros.* was available for the defendant in an action when the plaintiff failed to take the proper steps within the prescribed time. See Ord. 34, r. 2.

non quod voluit testator, sed quod dixit, in testamento inspicitur. [Not what the testator wished, but what he said, is considered in construing a will.]

non refert an quis assensum suum praefert verbis, an rebus ipsis et factis. [It matters not whether a man gives his assent by his words, or by his acts and deeds.]

non refert quid notum sit judici, si notum non sit in forma judicii. [It matters not what is known to the judge, if it be not known judicially.]

non sequitur. [It does not follow.]

non solent quae abundant vitiare scripturas. [Surplusage does not vitiate writings.]

non videntur qui errant consentire. [Those who are mistaken are not deemed to consent.] See MISTAKE.

non videtur consensum retinuisse si quis ex praescripto minantis aliquid ammutavit. [He is not deemed to have consented who has altered anything at the command of anyone using threats.]

nonagium; nonage. The ninth part of the movables of a deceased which was anciently paid for pious uses to the clergy of his parish.

nonfeasance. The neglect or failure to do some act which ought to be done, *e.g.* failing to keep in repair the highway (*q.v.*). The exemption from civil liability enjoyed by the highway authority was abrogated by the Highways (Miscellaneous Provisions) Act 1961, s.1(1), but the absence of negligence is a defence (s.1(2)(3)).

non-intromittant clause. A clause in the charter of a borough which exempted the borough from the jurisdiction of the justices of the peace appointed for the county in which the borough was situated.

non-joinder. The omission of a person who ought to be made party to an action. The court, however, has a discretion in the matter, and an action cannot be defeated merely by reason of non-joinder (Ord. 15, r. 6).

nonsuit. Formerly, the abandonment of a case at the trial, before the jury had given their verdict, whereupon judgment of nonsuit was given against the plaintiff. Now used where the judge withdraws the case from the jury and directs a verdict for the defendant. At any time up to verdict the plaintiff may elect, as of right, to be non-suited. Non-suit still applies in the county court.

noscitur a sociis. [The meaning of a word can be gathered from the context.]

not guilty. The appropriate plea to an indictment where the prisoner wishes to raise the general issue, *i.e.* when he wishes to deny everything and to let the prosecution prove what they can. It was also a plea used in common law actions of tort under the old practice, when the defendant simply denied that he had committed the wrong complained of. Under the present system of pleading, a defendant must deal specifically with all allegations made by the plaintiff which he does not admit.

not negotiable. When these words are endorsed on, *e.g.* a cheque the meaning is that the holder has no better right than a previous holder. See NEGOTIABLE INSTRUMENT.

not proven. A verdict returnable in Scotland only, not in England or Wales, meaning that the charge has not been proved.

Notary Public. A person who attests the execution of any deeds or writings, or makes certified copies of them in order to render the same authentic, especially for use abroad. He is appointed to his office by the Archbishop of Canterbury, and can be removed from office by the Court of Faculties.

notation. Making a memorandum of some special circumstance on a probate or letters of administration.

note of a fine. See FINE.

notice. Knowledge or cognisance. To give notice is to bring matters to a person's knowledge or attention. Notice is either actual (express) or constructive. Constructive notice is where knowledge of the fact is presumed or imputed by law, *i.e.* (1) where it would have come to the knowledge of a person's agent as such if proper inquiries had been made; (2) where in the same transaction it has come to the knowledge of a person's counsel, solicitor, or other agent, as such, or would have done so if such inquiries and inspections had been made as ought reasonably to have been made; (3) where it would have come to a person's own knowledge if proper inquiries had been made (Law of Property Act 1925, s.199(1)(ii)).

The doctrine of notice is that a person who acquires an estate, even although for valuable consideration, with notice of a prior equitable right, takes subject to that right. But a purchaser is not prejudically affected by notice of any instrument capable of registration under the Land Charges Act 1972, and void or unenforceable because of non-registration (Law of Property Act 1925, s.199(1)(i)). Where an intending lessee or assign is not entitled to call for the title to the freehold or leasehold reversion, he is not, since 1925, affected with notice of anything affecting such title contained in the deeds (Law of Property Act 1925, s.44(5)).

By the Law of Property Act 1925, s.198, registration under the Land Charges Act 1972 of instruments and matters required to be so registered constitutes actual notice of such instrument or matter and of the fact of such registration to all persons and for all purposes connected with the land affected. A purchaser may rescind the contract on discovering an undisclosed land charge (Law of Property Act 1969, s.24, reversing the rule in *Re Forsey and Hollebone's Contract* [1927] 2 Ch. 379). Compensation for loss due to undisclosed land charges may be claimed under s.25.

If a chose in action is assigned to two or more persons in succession, the one who first gives notice to the debtor will be entitled to the debt provided that at the date when he took his assignment he had no notice of any prior assignment (*Daerle* v. *Hall* (1823) 3 Russ. 1). By the Law of Property Act 1925, s.137 the rule was extended to equitable interests in land and capital money. See JUDICIAL NOTICE.

notice (employment). For the minimum periods of notice to be given as between employer and employee see Employment Protection (Consolidation) Act 1978, Pt. IV.

notice of intended prosecution. See the Road Traffic Act 1972, s.179; *Groome* v. *Driscoll* [1969] 3 All E.R. 1638 n.

notice of trial. A party to an action who sets it down for trial must, within 24 hours after doing so, notify the other parties that he has done so (R.S.C., Ord. 34, r. 8 (1)).

An action must be set down for trial by the plaintiff within the period named in the order for directions failing which the defendant may apply to set down or that the action be dismissed (Ord. 34, r. 2). See *Practice Direction* [1979] 3 All E.R. 193.

notice of writ of summons, etc. In an action in the High Court, when the plaintiff has obtained leave (under Ord. 11, r. 1) to serve the defendant out of the jurisdiction, notice of the writ, and not the writ itself is served in accordance with Ord. 11, r. 3.

notice to admit. Any party, within 14 days after the action has been set down for trial, can call upon the opposite party to admit any document or fact which is material, on pain of paying the costs occasioned by proof (Ord. 27). See ADMISSION.

notice to proceed. In any cause or matter in which there has been no proceeding for a year, the party who desires to proceed must before taking any step give the opposite party a month's notice of his intention to proceed (Ord. 3, r. 6).

notice to produce. At any time before the trial of an action, any party to an action may give any other party notice to produce for his inspection any document referred to in pleadings or affidavits; and on refusal to produce it without good cause, an order for production and inspection may be obtained from the court (Ord. 24, rr. 11, 12). See DISCOVERY.

notice to quit. Where there is a tenancy of land or tenements from year to year, or other like indefinite period, a notice to quit is required to enable either the landlord or the tenant to determine the tenancy without the consent of the other. The notice must be strictly correct, or it will be void. It must specify the correct date or time for the termination of the tenancy; it must be unconditional and relate to the whole of the premises. For the information which must be contained in a notice to quit premises let as a dwelling see Notices to Quit Regulations 1975 (S.I. 1975 No. 2196).

notice to treat. The notice which a public body having compulsory powers for the purchase of land is bound to give to the persons interested in any land which it is empowered and desires to purchase. See COMPULSORY ACQUISITION.

noting. A minute or memorandum made by a notary on a bill of exchange which he has presented, and which has been dishonoured. It consists of his initials and charges and the date, and, in the case of foreign bills, is preparatory to a formal protest.

nova constitutio futuris formam imponere debet, non praeteritis. [A new law ought to regulate what is to follow, not the past.]

Nova Statuta. The statutes from the year 1327 to 1483.

novatio. [Roman law.] The renewal or re-making of an existing obligation; the transmutation of an obligation so that it ceases to exist and is renewed as a new obligation. The preceding obligation may have been contracted in any form and with any subject; the new obligation must be *verbis* or *literis* and it must bind either civilly or naturally.

novation. A tripartite agreement whereby a contract between two parties is rescinded in consideration of a new contract being entered into on the same terms between one of the parties and a third party. A common instance is where a creditor at the request of the debtor agrees to take another person as his debtor in the place of the original debtor. It involves the substitution of one party to a contract by another person, and its effect is to release the obligations of the former party and to impose them on the new party, as in the case of a change in the membership of a partnership firm. The creditors of the old firm will usually be deemed to have accepted the new firm as their debtor by continuing to trade with the new firm as if it were identical with the old.

novel disseisin. See ASSIZE OF NOVEL DISSEISIN.

novellae. See CORPUS JURIS CIVILIS.

novus actus interveniens. [A new act intervening.] The intervention of human activity between the defendant's act and its consequences. The doctrine that A is not liable for damage done to B if the chain of causation between A's act and B's damage is broken by the intervention of the act of a third person. B's damage is then said to be too remote. If, however, the intervening act is a direct or foreseeable consequence of the defendant's act, then the doctrine does not apply, nor does it where the intervening actor is not fully responsible, or if his act is intentionally procured by the defendant.

nudum pactum. [A nude contract.] An agreement made without consideration and upon which, unless it be under seal, no action will lie.

nuisance. An inconvenience materially interfering with the ordinary comfort physically of human existence, not merely according to elegant or dainty modes and habits of living, but according to plain and sober, simple notions among the English people (*per* Knight-Bruce V.-C. in *Walter* v. *Selfe* (1851) 4 De G. & Sm. 332).

A public or common nuisance is an act which interferes with the enjoyment of a right which all members of the community are entitled to, such as the right to fresh air, to travel on the highways, etc. The remedy for a public nuisance (which is a misdemeanour) is by indictment, information, or injunction at the suit of the Attorney-General, and in certain cases by summary process, or abatement (*q.v.*). If special damage is caused to an individual, he has an action for damages or injunction against the wrongdoer. A claim in respect of public works may be made under the Land Compensation Act 1973, ss.1–19. Recurring public nuisances may be restrained by a prosecution order issued by the local authority followed, if necessary, by a nuisance order made by the justices (Public Health (Recurring Nuisances) Act 1969). See also the Public Health Act 1936, s.94.

A private nuisance is a tort consisting of (1) any wrongful disturbance or interference with a person's use or enjoyment of land or of an easement or other servitude appurtenant to land; (2) the act of wrongfully causing or allowing the escape of deleterious things into another person's land, *e.g.* water, smoke, smell, fumes, gas, noise, heat, vibrations, electricity, disease-germs, animals, and vegetation. Nuisance is commonly a continuing injury, and is actionable only at the suit of the person in possession of the land injuriously affected by it: there must be actual damage to the plaintiff. The remedy for a private nuisance is either by abatement (*q.v.*) or by action for damages, injunction or mandamus.

nul tiel record. The plea or defence that "no such record" as that alleged by the plaintiff exists.

nulla bona. [No goods.] The return made by a sheriff to a writ or warrant authorising him to seize the chattels of a person, when he has been unable to find any to seize.

nulla pactione effici potest ut dolus praestetur. [By no contract can it be arranged that a man shall be indemnified against responsibility for his own fraud.]

nulla poena sine lege. [No punishment except in accordance with the law.]

nullity of marriage. When a marriage is void, or voidable, the party not in fault may present a petition to the divorce registry or a divorce county court, for a decree of nullity of the marriage.

A marriage which took place before August 1, 1971, is void *ab initio* (a) if either party is at the time of marriage under the age of 16; (b) unless both parties were capable of understanding the nature of the contract; (c) if the parties are within the prohibited degrees of relationship; (d) if one of the parties has previously contracted a valid marriage which is still subsisting; (e) if one of the parties is induced to take part in the ceremony by threats or is under a mistake as to the identity of the other party, or as to the nature of the ceremony or is in a state of intoxication; (f) if there is lack of proper form in the ceremony of marriage. See MARRIAGE.

A marriage which took place before August 1, 1971 is voidable if (a) there is impotence or incapacity to consummate the marriage at the time of marriage (in this case a petition may be presented by the impotent party); (b) there is refusal to consummate the marriage; (c) either party was at the time of marriage a patient (*q.v.*), or a mental defective, or subject to recurrent fits of insanity or epilepsy; (d) the respondent was at the time of marriage suffering from venereal disease in a communicable form; (e) the respondent at the time of marriage was pregnant by some person other than the petitioner (Matrimonial Causes Act 1965, s.9(1); Matrimonial Causes Act 1973, Sched. 1, Part II).

A marriage which takes place after July 31, 1971, is void *ab initio* (a) if the parties are within the prohibited degrees of relationship (see AFFINITY); (b) if either party is under the age of 16; (c) if the parties have knowingly married in disregard of the rules relating to marriage (see MARRIAGE); (d) if at the time of the marriage either party was already lawfully married; (e) if the parties are not respectively male and female; (f) if in the case of a polygamous marriage entered into outside England and Wales, either party was domiciled in England and Wales (Matrimonial Causes Act 1973, s.11).

A marriage which takes place after July 31, 1971, is voidable (a) if the marriage has not been consummated owing to the incapacity of either party or owing to the wilful refusal of the respondent to consummate it; (b) for lack of valid consent; (c) if, at the time of the marriage the respondent was suffering from venereal disease; (d) if at the time of marriage the wife was pregnant by some person other than her husband (Matrimonial Causes Act 1973, s.12).

Whatever the date of the marriage the court may not grant a decree on the ground that the marriage is voidable (a) if the petitioner, knowing that it was open to him to have the marriage avoided, led the respondent reasonably to believe that he would not seek to do so, or (b) it would be unjust to the respondent to grant a decree. Without prejudice to the above, the court may not grant a decree on the grounds of non-consent, venereal disease or pregnancy unless proceedings are instituted within three years of the date of the marriage. The court may not grant a decree on the grounds of venereal disease or pregnancy if the petitioner knew the facts at the time of the marriage (s.13).

A decree granted in respect of nullity after July 31, 1971, in respect of a voidable marriage operates only from the time the decree is made absolute (s.16). See also the Legitimacy Act 1959, s.2. Every decree of nullity is in the first instance a decree nisi (Matrimonial Causes Act 1973, ss.1(5), 15). Satisfactory arrangements must be made for any children (ss.41–44). One of the parties must be domiciled in England and Wales (Domicile and Matrimonial Proceedings Act 1973, s.5). The evidence of either party is admissible to prove or disprove marital intercourse (Matrimonial Causes Act 1973, s.48(1)). Evidence on the subject of capacity is heard in camera (s.48(2)).

nullius filius. A bastard (*q.v.*).

nullum crimen nulla poena sine lege. [There is no crime nor punishment except in accordance with law.]

nullum simile est idem. [A thing which is similar to another thing is not the same as that other thing.]

nullum tempus aut locus occurrit regi. [Time never runs against the Crown.]But see the Crown Proceedings Act 1947 and the Law Reform (Limitation of Actions, etc.) Act 1954.

nullus videtur dolo facere qui suo jure utitur. [A malicious or improper motive cannot make wrongful in law an act which would be rightful apart from such motive.] See MALICE.

nunc pro tunc. [Now for then.] As when the court directs a proceeding to be dated as of an earlier date than that on which it was actually taken.

nuncupative will. See WILL.

nuptiae. [Roman law.] Marriage, the ceremonies with which the legal tie was formed; the union of a man and a woman involving unbroken harmony in the habits of life.

nuptiae, justae. [Roman law.] Legal marriage. That union of the sexes which gave the father *potestas* over the children born to him by his wife. Conditions of *justae nuptiae*: (1) Consent of the parties duly expressed; (2) Puberty; (3) *Connubium* (the legal power of contracting marriage).

nuptias non concubitus sed consensus facit. [It is consent, not cohabitation, which makes a marriage.]

O

oaths. An oath is a religious asserveration by which the party calls his God to witness that what he says is the truth, or that what he promises to do he will do. Evidence is given on oath "for the law presumeth that no man will forswear himself for any worldly thing." An affirmation may be made instead of an oath; see AFFIRM. See generally Oaths Act 1978. See also PERJURY.

obiter dictum. [A saying by the way.] An observation by a judge on a legal question suggested by a case before him, but not arising in such a manner as to require decision. It is therefore not binding as a precedent. But there is no justification for regarding as *obiter dictum* a reason given by a judge for his decision because he has given another reason also.

obligatio civilis. [Roman law.] A statutory obligation, or one recognised by the *jus civile*.

obligatio literarum. See LITERARUM OBLIGATIO.

obligatio praetoria, or **honoraria.** [Roman law.] An obligation established by the Praetor in the exercise of his jurisdiction.

obligatio verborum. See VERBORUM OBLIGATIO.

obligation. A duty: the bond of legal necessity which binds together two or more determinate individuals. It is limited to legal duties arising out of a special personal relationship existing between them, whether by reason of a contract or a tort, or otherwise, *e.g.* debtor and creditor. See LIABILITY.

obligee. One to whom a bond is made.

obligor. One who binds himself by bond.

obscene. A publication, the tendency of which is to deprave and corrupt those whose minds are open to immoral influences, and into whose hands it is likely to fall (*per* Cockburn C.J. in *R. v. Hicklin* (1868) L.R. 3 Q.B. 360, at p. 371). Obscene publications or libels were punishable with fine or imprisonment, being misdemeanours at common law.

By the Obscene Publications Act 1959 (as amended by the Obscene Publications Act 1964 and the Criminal Justice Act 1967, s.25), an article is deemed to be obscene if its effect (or if composite, the effect of any one of its items) is, if taken as a whole, such as to deprave or corrupt persons likely to read, see, or hear the contents of it (Obscene Publications Act 1959, s.1). Section 4 provided that a person should not be convicted if it is proved that the publication of the article in question is justified as being for the public good on the ground that it is in the interest of science, literature, art or learning, and that the opinion of experts may be admitted. Premises may be searched and obscene articles seized and forfeited (Obscene Publications Act 1964, s.3). But a warrant is to be issued only on an information laid by the Director of Public Prosecutions or by a constable (Criminal Justice Act 1967, s.25).

Sending obscene articles through the post is an offence under the Post Office Act 1953, s.11 (as amended). For restrictions on use of obscene cinematograph material see Criminal Law Act 1977, s.53.

obtaining credit. See DECEPTION; BANKRUPTCY.

occupancy. The taking possession of a *res nullius* or ownerless thing.

occupant. See TENANT PUR AUTRE VIE.

occupatio. [Roman law.] The taking possession of a thing belonging to nobody (*res nullius*) but capable of being owned.

occupation. (1) The exercise of physical control or possession of land; having the actual use of land: (2) Taking possession of enemy territory by the armed forces.

occupiers liability. See DANGEROUS PREMISES.

of course. A writ or a step in an action or proceeding which the court has no discretion to refuse, provided the proper formalities have been observed. An order *of course* is one made on an *ex parte* application to which a party is entitled as of right on his own statement, and at his own risk.

offence. Generally synonomous with crime.

offensive weapons. It is an offence to possess firearms or ammunition without a certificate from the Chief Officer of Police (Firearms Act 1968). Other offensive weapons are proscribed by the Prevention of Crime Act 1953 and the Restriction of Offensive Weapons Acts 1959 and 1961.

offer. The offer of a promise which when accepted constitutes an ageement. The formula of a true offer is "I promise, if you will in return make a certain promise or do a certain act." It must be distinguished from an invitation to others to make offers, *e.g.* as by an auctioneer. An offer may be withdrawn or revoked at any time before it has been unconditionally accepted; or it may be rejected; or lapse because of the death of the offeror, or by non-acceptance within a reasonable time.

An acceptance of an offer "subject to contract," does not constitute a binding contract, because it is not unconditional.

office. (1) Offices are either public or private, a public office being one which entitles a man to act in the affairs of others without their appointment or permission.

(2) Office premises means a building, or part, used for office purposes, including administration, clerical work, handling money, and telephone and telegraph operating (Offices, Shops, and Railway Premises Act 1963, s.1(1)(2)). The main object of that Act is to set standards of health, welfare and safety for employees in such premises. The Act was amended by the Health and Safety at Work etc. Act 1974.

office copy. A copy made by an officer appointed for that purpose, and sealed with the seal of his office. It is admissible in evidence (Ord. 38, r. 10).

office, inquest of. See INQUEST OF OFFICE.

official receivers. Officers appointed by the Board (now Department) of Trade, who act in bankruptcy and in the winding up of companies. See Bankruptcy Act 1914, Part III.

official referee. See REFEREE.

official secrets. The Official Secrets Acts, 1911, 1920, 1939, were passed to prevent breaches of official confidence (for which there was no penalty at common law), and to counter espionage and sabotage (*Chandler* v. *D.P.P.* [1964] A.C. 763). See also the European Communities Act 1972, s.11 (Euratom information).

Official Solicitor. Formerly the Official Solicitor of the Court of Chancery: transferred to the High Court by the Judicature Act 1873, s.77. He acts generally where his services are required by the Supreme Court as solicitor; *e.g.* in connection with persons committed for contempt, lunacy matters, or in taking a grant of administration. See Judicature Act 1925, s.129.

Official Trustee of Charity Lands; Official Trustee of Charitable Funds. The Charities Act 1960, s.3, provided for the appointment of an Official Custodian of Charities, who takes the place of these Trustees.

Old Bailey. Now the Central Criminal Court (*q.v.*).

Oleron, Laws of. A collection of customs of the sea compiled in the twelfth century at Oleron, an island off the west coast of France.

ombudsman. The popular name (derived from Scandinavia) of the Parliamentary Commissioner appointed under the Parliamentary Commissioner Act 1967 to investigate complaints of administrative action and the parallel Commissions for Local Administration (*q.v.*).

omne quod inaedificatur solo cedit. [Everything which is built into the soil is merged therein.]

omne testamentum morte consummatum est. [Every will is completed by death.] A will is ambulatory until death.

omnes licentiam habent his, quae pro se indulta sunt, renunciare. [Everyone has liberty to renounce those things which are granted for his benefit.]

omnia praesumuntur contra spoliatorem. [All things are presumed against a wrongdoer.] As in *Armory* v. *Delamirie* (1722) 1 Strange 504, where jewels were presumed, as against a wrongful possessor, to be of the finest quality.

omnia praesumuntur legitime facta donec probetur in contrarium. [All things are presumed to have been legitimately done, until the contrary is proved.]

omnia praesumuntur rite et solemniter esse acta. [All acts are presumed to have been done rightly and regularly.]

onerous. A right of property, *e.g.* a lease, in which the obligations attaching to it counterbalance or exceed the advantage to be derived from it.

onus probandi. [The onus of proof (*q.v*).]

op. cit. The book previously cited.

open contract. A contract for the sale of property which merely specifies the names of the parties, a description of the property, and a statement of the price. The rights and duties of the parties under an open contract are: (1) duty of vendor (a) to show title for 15 years; (b) to abstract and produce documents; (c) to convey the identical property he has agreed to sell; (2) obligation of purchaser (a) to bear the cost of producing certain documents; (b) to examine the abstract at his own expense; (c) to complete the contract.

operative part. The part of an instrument which carries out the main object, as opposed recitals.

oppression. The common law misdemeanour committed by a public officer, who, under colour of his office, wrongfully inflicts upon any person any harm or injury. See also the Companies Act 1948, s.210.

optima est lex quae minimum relinquit arbitrio judicis; optimus judex qui minimum sibi. [That system of law is best which confides as little as possible to the discretion of a judge; that judge the best who trusts as little as possible to himself.]

optima legum interpres est consuetudo. [Custom is the best interpreter of the law.]

optimus interpres rerum usus. [The best interpreter of things is usage.]

option. A right of choice; a right conferred by agreement to buy or not at will any property within a certain time. An option, exercisable by notice in writing, is not validly exercised by the posting of a letter which is not received (*Holwell Securities* v. *Hughes* [1974] 1 W.L.R. 155).

option mortgage. Type of mortgage (*q.v.*) established by Housing Subsidies Act 1967 as amended by Housing Act 1974, s.119, Sched. II under which the mortgagor pays a lower rate of interest than normal but is granted no income tax relief.

oratio. [Roman law.] An address by the emperor to the senate, stating what he wished them to embody in a *senatus consultum*.

Orcinus. [Roman law.] Pertaining to *Orcus* (Pluto) the nether world, or death; a freedman who had received freedom directly from the will of his master, having been the slave of the testator at the date of the will as well as at the time of his death.

ordeal. The most ancient mode of trial: it involved an appeal to the supernatural or the *judicium Dei*. The ordeal by fire consisted of taking up in the hand a piece of red-hot iron, or of walking barefoot and blindfold over red-hot plough-shares. If the party was unhurt he was innocent; if otherwise, he was guilty. Ordeal by hot water was performed by plunging the arm in boiling water, with similar consequences. The cold water ordeal consisted of throwing the offender in a pond or river; if he sank he was innocent, and if he floated he was guilty. The ordeal was abolished in the reign of Henry III, and was ultimately replaced by the trial by jury.

order. A command or direction; used in law with particular reference to courts of justice. The directions of a court in a proceeding or matter other than a decree of judgment are termed "orders." The code of procedure of the Supreme Court consists of Orders subdivided into rules.

order and disposition. See REPUTED OWNERSHIP.

Order in Council. An Order made by the Queen "by and with the advice of Her Majesty's Privy Council," for the purposes of government, either in virtue of the royal prerogative, as, *e.g.* declarations of war and peace, the Queen's Regulations for the Army and Navy, and legislation for Crown Colonies and Protectorates; or under statutory authority. The latter may be termed subordinate legislation and is much used in modern times for giving the force of law to the administrative regulations and provisions drawn up by Government Departments. See STATUTORY INSTRUMENTS.

ordinance. (1) Formerly an Act of Parliament which lacked the consent of one of the three elements, Crown, Lords, and Commons. (2) A declaration of the Crown lacking the authority of Parliament.

ordinary. The bishop of a diocese when exercising the ecclesiastical jurisdiction annexed to his office, he being *judex ordinarius* within his diocese.

original writ. See WRIT.

originating summons. Proceedings may be begun by originating summons, as well as by writ, motion, or petition (Ord. 5). Proceedings suitable for commencement by originating summons are where the principal question is the construction of an Act, statutory instrument, deed, will, contract or other document or some other question of law, and where there is unlikely to be any substantial dispute of fact.

Originating summons issue in the Queen's Bench Division as well as in the Chancery Division, except that claims in tort (other than trespass to land) or for fraud, infringement of patents, personal injury, and fatal accidents cases must be begun by writ (Ords. 5, 28).

ouster. The deprivation of a person of his freehold.

ousterlemain. A writ directing the possession of land to be delivered out of the hands of the Crown into those of a person entitled to it. It was the mode by which an heir in ward of land held of the Crown *ut de honore* obtained possession of it on attaining majority. It also meant a judgment on a *monstrans de droit*, deciding that the Crown had no title to a thing which it had seized.

outgoings. Necessary expenses and charges. A receiver must apply moneys received by him, in the first place, in discharge of all rents, taxes, rates and outgoings affecting the mortgaged property (Law of Property Act 1925, s.109(8)(i)).

outlawry. An outlaw was a person who was put out of the protection of the law by judgment of outlawry. In effect it was a conviction; there was attainder, forfeiture of chattels, and escheat of realty after the King's "year, day and waste." Where an indictment had been found against a person and summary process proved ineffectual to compel him to appear, process of outlawry might be issued. Outlawry was subsequently extended to civil proceedings, *e.g.* trespass. Outlawry proceedings have long been obsolete and were finally abolished by Administration of Justice (Miscellaneous Provisions) Act 1938, s.12. See PROCESS.

outstanding. The legal estate in land was said to be outstanding when it had been conveyed to a mortgagee, and had not been reconveyed to the mortgagor when the mortgage debt had been cleared off. Similarly, an outstanding term is a term of years which has not come to an end although the purpose for which it was created has been realised. See SATISFIED TERM.

over. In conveyancing, gifts or limitations "over" are limitations intended to take effect on the cessation or failure of prior estates.

overdue. A bill of exchange is said to be overdue when the time for its payment has passed or, if it is a bill payable on demand, when it appears to have been in circulation for an unreasonable length of time (Bills of Exchange Act 1882, s.36 (3)). Anyone taking an overdue bill takes it subject to the equities of prior holders (*ibid.* s.36(2)).

overreaching clause. A clause in a resettlement which saves the powers of sale and leasing annexed to the estate for life created by the original settlement, when it is desired to give the tenant for life the same estate and powers under the resettlement; so called because it provides that the resettlement shall be overreached by the exercise of the old powers.

overreaching conveyance. A conveyance which enables the owner of an estate which is subject to equitable interests, or charges, to convey it to another free from such interests or charges which are thereby shifted from the land to the purchase of money. See CURTAIN PROVISIONS.

overriding interests. The incumbrances, interests, rights, and powers not entered on the register, but subject to which registered dispositions take effect under the Land Registration Act 1925 (see *ibid.* s.3 (xvi)).

overriding trust. A trust which takes precedence of other trusts previously declared.

overt act. An open act; an act capable of being observed, and from which an intention may be deduced. See TREASON.

ownership. The right to the exclusive enjoyment of a thing (Austin). Strictly, it denotes the relation between a person and any right that is vested in him (Salmond). Ownership is absolute or restricted. Absolute ownership involves the right of free as well as exclusive enjoyment, including the right of using, altering,

242

disposing of or destroying the thing owned. Absolute ownership is of indeterminate duration. (Land is in strictness not subject to absolute ownership because it cannot be destroyed, and because of the theory that all land is ultimately held of the Crown.) Restricted ownership is ownership limited to some extent; as, for example, where there are several joint owners, or a life tenancy, or where the property is charged with the payment of a sum of money, or subject to an easement. Beneficial ownership is the right to the enjoyment of a thing as contrasted with the legal or nominal ownership. Ownership is always subject to the rule that a man must so use his own property as not to injure his neighbour. See REPUTED OWNERSHIP.

oyer and terminer. [To hear and determine.] A commission to the judges to try offences committed in a certain area. References to a court of oyer and terminer are to be construed as references to the Crown Court (Courts Act 1971, Sched. 8).

P

P.A.Y.E. [Pay as you earn.] The system of collection of income tax by deductions made by the employer from emoluments assessable to tax under Income and Corporation Taxes Act 1970, ss.204, 205, paid to the employee, in such a way, by reference to tax tables, that the periodical deductions of tax keep pace as far as possible with the accruing liability to tax of the employee.

P.C. Privy Council.

PLC. See COMPANIES.

P.P.I. [Policy proof of interest.] A policy of marine insurance where the assured has no insurable interest. It is void (Marine Insurance Act 1906, s.4). It is an offence to effect a contract by way of gambling on loss of maritime perils (Marine Insurance (Gambling Policies) Act 1909).

pace. [By permission of.]

pacta dant legem contractui. [Agreements constitute the law of contract.]

pacta quae contra leges constitutionesque vel contra bonos mores fiunt, nullam vim habere, indubitati juris est. [It is undoubted law that agreements which are contrary to the laws and constitutions, or contrary to good morals, have no force.]

pains and penalties. See BILL OF PAINS AND PENALTIES.

pais. See IN PAIS.

Palatine Court. The jurisdiction of the Court of Common Pleas at Lancaster and the Court of Pleas at Durham was transferred to the High Court (Judicature Act 1925, ss.18, 19). The Court of Chancery of the County Palatine of Lancaster was merged with the High Court by the Courts Act 1971, s.41. The Vice-Chancellor of the County Palatine became a circuit judge with precedence next to the High Court judges (Sched. 1, paras. 1, 4).

Pandects. The Digest of Justinian. See CORPUS JURIS CIVILIS.

panel. The list of the persons who have been summoned to serve as jurors for the trial of all actions at a particular sittings.

paper office. An office of records. (1) In Whitehall. (2) In the Old Court of King's Bench.

paper, special. A list kept in the Queen's Bench Division of matters set down for argument on points of law, awards in the form of a special case and other matters. See Directions given by the Lord Chief Justice on December 9, 1958, art. 1(2)(g); Ord. 34, r. 4, notes.

parage; paragium. Equality of blood, name, or dignity.

paramount. Superior.

paraphernalia. Such apparel and personal ornaments given to a married woman by her husband as were suitable to her condition in life; they remained the property of the husband unless the wife survived the husband, when she kept them for herself. The husband might dispose of them during his life, and they were liable for his debts, on his death, after other assets had been exhausted.

paravail. Inferior or subordinate.

parcels. Parts or portions of land. The part of an instrument following the operative words which contains a description of the property dealt with.

parcener; parcenary. The equivalents of coparcener and coparcenary.

pardon. The release by the Crown of a person from punishment incurred for some offence. A pardon may be granted in bar, or (2) after conviction, in which case it may be pleaded in arrest of judgment or in bar of execution, so that the offender is discharged from punishment. Some offences, however, cannot be pardoned; *e.g.* a common nuisance while it remains unredressed: and a pardon cannot be pleaded to a parliamentary impeachment.

parent. Father or mother of a child. Parents are not liable for their children's torts unless the tort occurs by reason of the parents negligence or authorisation. By Children Act 1975, s.26, an adopted person aged 18 may obtain a copy of his original birth certificate showing his natural parents.

pares. Peers, equals.

pari passu. [With equal step.] Equally, without preference.

parish. The unit of local government, formerly co-incident with the ecclesiastical parish. Parish meetings and councils were created by the Local Government Act 1894. Rural parishes, boroughs and urban districts became parishes as a result of the Local Government Act 1972, s.1, Sched. 1. Every parish in England has a parish meeting and in most cases a parish council (s.9). A parish may, by resolution take on itself the status of a town with a town mayor and town council. The parish meeting will thereupon become the town meeting (s.245). Former boroughs may regain the status of boroughs. See BOROUGH

park. Strictly an enclosed chase (*q.v.*). See also the National Parks and Access to the Countryside Act 1949. Franchises of park were abolished by the Wild Creatures and Forest Laws Act 1971.

Parliament. The sovereign legislative authority in the Constitution consisting of the Queen, the House of Lords, and the House of Commons. Originally all legislation required the assent of both Houses of Parliament. Bills, other than a money (or finance) Bill, may be introduced into either House. With regard to money Bills (which are introduced in the House of Commons), it was a convention that the House of Lords might reject, but could not amend, them. The Parliament Act 1911 was enacted to enable, exceptionally, legislation to be effected by the King and Commons alone. Thus if the House of Lords fail within one month to pass a Bill which, having passed the Commons, is sent up endorsed by the Speaker as a money Bill before the end of the session, it may be presented for the Royal assent without the consent of the House of Lords. With regard to non-money Bills, the Act provided in effect for a suspensory veto for the House of Lords.

The Parliament Act 1911 was amended by the Parliament Act 1949 which reduced the "suspensory period" from three to two successive sessions: the 1949 Act itself was passed under the 1911 Act provisions without the consent of the House of Lords.

The duration of Parliament is for five years, but it has the power of prolonging its own life by Act of Parliament.

parliamentary agents. Persons (usually solicitors) who transact the technical business involved in passing private Bills through the Houses of Parliament.

Parliamentary Commissioner. See OMBUDSMAN.

parliamentary committees. A committee of the whole House, whether in the Lords or the Commons, is really the House of Lords or the House of Commons, as the case may be, presided over by a chairman instead of by the Lord Chancellor or the Speaker. The standing or sessional committees and the select committees consist in each House of a certain number of Members who perform various functions in connection with Bills. Joint committees consist of equal numbers of Members of each House.

parliamentary franchise. The right to vote at elections of Members of Parliament. The persons entitled to vote in any constituency are those resident there on the qualifying date who are British subjects of full age and not subject to any legal incapacity to vote, and registered there in the register of parliamentary electors. Such persons may vote in only one constituency (Representation of the People Act 1948, s.1). The following are disqualified: aliens, minors, patients (*q.v.*), idiots, peers, returning officers, persons serving sentences of imprisonment, and persons convicted of electoral offences.

The Representation of the People Act 1949 consolidated the law relating to the parliamentary franchise. See ELECTIONS, PARLIAMENTARY.

parochial church councils. Bodies corporate to whom have been transferred the functions of vestries in matters relating to the affairs of the church: Parochial Church Councils (Powers) Measures 1956, amended by the Synodical Government Measure 1969, s.6. See also the Pastoral Measure 1968, Sched. 3, para. 12.

parol. Verbal or oral; not in writing or under seal.

parole. The release on licence of a prisoner serving his sentence. Such licence may be revoked. The Home Secretary either grants or refuses parole or may refer to the Parole Board (Criminal Justice Act 1967, ss. 59–64; Criminal Justice Act 1972, s. 35; *Practice Note* [1976] 1 All E.R. 271, C.A.).

parricide. The killing of a father.

parson. The ecclesiastical officer in charge of a parish church. He is a corporation sole. His house is called the parsonage.

part performance. The equitable doctrine that where a contract is not enforceable for want of some formality, if the contract has been partly carried into effect by one of the parties (the plaintiff) the other (the defendant) cannot set up the informality. Thus section 40 of the Law of Property Act 1925 requires contracts for the sale or other disposition of land to be in writing, but the section expressly recognises the doctrine of part performance, so that if the purchaser has gone into possession of the land, equity will enforce the contract. The acts of the plaintiff in part performance of a contract must be unequivocally and exclusively referable to a completed agreement (*Maddison* v. *Alderson* (1883) 7 App. Cas. 467) and must be such that it would amount to fraud in the defendant to take advantage of the want of writing. Evidence must be given of the terms of the contract.

particeps criminis. One who has a share in a crime: an accessory.

particular average. See AVERAGE.

particular estate. An estate which preceded a reversion or remainder: thus a grant to A for life with remainder to B and his heirs gave A a particular estate and B a reversionary estate.

particulars. The details of the claim or the defence in an action which are necessary in order to enable the other side to know what case they have to meet. Further and better particulars may be ordered at the discretion of the court on such terms as may be just (see Ord. 18, r. 12).

parties. Persons suing or being sued (see Ord. 15).

partition. The division of land owned by persons jointly among the owners in severalty. Partition was either voluntary by deed or compulsory by order of the court. Until the Partition Act 1968, the court had no power to order a sale and division of the proceeds instead of a partition of the property itself. By the operation of the Law of Property Act 1925 land belonging to joint owners is vested in trustees on trust for sale, with power to postpone the sale, and the Partition Acts are repealed.

partnership. The relation which subsists between persons carrying on business in common with a view to profit (Partnership Act 1890, s.1). The relationship between the members of an incorporated company is not that of partnership. A partnership firm is not a separate legal entity in English law. The rights of partners between themselves are governed by the partnership agreement, or deed of partnership.

In general, every partner is entitled and bound to take part in the conduct of the business, unless it is otherwise agreed between them. Every partner is liable for the debts of the partnership to the whole extent of his property. As between the partners, each partner is bound to contribute to the debts in proportion to his share of the profits, unless otherwise agreed. As regards third persons, the act of every partner, within the ordinary scope of the business, binds his co-partners, whether they have sanctioned it or not. The relation between the partners being personal, no one of them can put a stranger in his place without the consent of the others. Where no time for the duration of the partnership is fixed, it is called a partnership at will, and may be dissolved at the pleasure of any partner. Dissolution takes place ordinarily by bankruptcy, or by the death of a partner, or on an order of dissolution being made by the court on the ground of the insanity, incapacity, misconduct of a partner, or of the hopeless state of the business (Partnership Act 1890, ss.32–35; Ord. 81).

A limited partnership is one in which, although there must be one or more partners responsible for all the liabilities of the partnership, there may be one or more partners who are under no liability if they contribute an agreed sum for partnership purposes, provided that they take no part in the management, and that the partnership is registered as a limited partnership (see the Limited Partnership Act 1907). For limitation on the number of persons in a partnership, see the Companies Act 1948, ss.429, 434; Companies Act 1967, ss.119–121. See also Banking Act 1979, s.51(2), Sched. 7.

part-owners. Persons who are entitled to property, *e.g.* a ship, in common.

party. A person who takes part in a transaction or legal proceeding.

party-wall. A wall adjoining property belonging to different owners. In the absence of evidence to the contrary, tenancy in common of the wall was presumed. By the Law of Property Act 1925, s.38(1), a party-wall or structure shall be and remain severed vertically as between the respective owners, each of whom shall have the requisite rights of support and user over the rest of the structure.

party and party. See COSTS.

Pasch. [The Passover.] Easter.

passage. The right of way over private water: an easement.

passim. [In various places; everywhere in the book.]

passing off. The pretence by one person that his goods are those of another. Where a person sells goods, or carries on business, etc., under such a name, mark, description, or otherwise in such a manner as to mislead the public into believing that the goods or business, etc., are that of another person, the latter person has a right of action in damages or for an account, and for an injunction to restrain the defendant for the future.

passport. The document (in book form) issued by the Foreign Office to responsible persons who contemplate travelling abroad, containing particulars enabling the bearer to be identified, and a request to all concerned to allow the bearer to pass without let or hindrance and to afford him all necessary assistance and protection.

It is a misdemeanour to forge or to make false statements for procuring a passport (Criminal Justice Act 1925, s.36 as amended by the Criminal Justice Act 1967, s.92(8)). The offence is triable summarily (Magistrates' Court Act 1952, Sched. 6).

In international law, it means primarily the document issued by a belligerent to a diplomatic representative of an enemy State after the outbreak of war, to enable him to return to the country he represents, by virtue of the right of immunity of diplomatic representatives.

pasture, common of. The right of feeding beasts on the land of another. Common of pasture appendant was the right which every freehold tenant of a manor possessed to feed his cattle used in agriculture (*i.e.* horses, cattle, and sheep) upon the lord's waste, provided they were levant and couchant on the tenant's freehold land.

Common of pasture appurtenant is a right annexed to certain land, by virtue of which the owner of those lands feeds cattle on the soil of another person.

Common because of vicinage is where the tenants of two adjoining places, or the owners of two contiguous pieces of land, have from time immemorial "intercommoned," *i.e.* allowed each other's cattle to stray and pasture on each other's land, or on a waste or open field lying between their lands.

Common of pasture in gross differs from the foregoing varieties of common in being unconnected in any way with the tenure of occupation of land.

patent. (1) Letters patent from the Crown, *e.g.* conferring a Peerage. (2) The right conferred by letters patent of the exclusive use and benefit of a new invention capable of industrial application. See generally Patents Act 1977 and Patents Rules 1978. A patent is obtained by making application accompanied by specifications to the Patents Office. The normal duration of a patent is 20 years and this may not be extended (1977 Act, s.25). A patent once granted may be revoked (s.72(1)). For the system of European Patents now incorporated in to English Law see 1977 Act, Pt. II, ss.79–95.

The 1977 Act established a Patents Court which is part of the Chancery Division (s.96(1)) to deal with such proceedings relating to patents and other matters as may be prescribed by rules of court. The court has taken over the jurisdiction of the former Patents Appeal Tribunal. Infringement of a Patent is actionable; for definition of infringement see section 60.

pater est quem nuptiae demonstrant. [He is the father whom marriage indicates.]

paterfamilias. [Roman law.] One invested with *patria potestas* over another; a man *sui juris* or not under the authority of another.

paternity. Any presumption of law as to legitimacy or illegitimacy may in civil proceedings be rebutted on a balance of probabilities rather than by proof beyond a reasonable doubt (Family Law Reform Act 1969, s.26) and a blood test may be ordered (ss.20–25).

patient. A person who by reason of mental disorder (*q.v.*) is incapable of managing his own affairs. It is the term used since the passing of the Mental Health Act 1959, in lieu of lunatic, or person of unsound mind. A patient can only sue by his next friend, or defend by his guardian *ad litem* (Ord. 80).

patria. A jury of neighbours. See JURY.

patria potestas. [Roman law.] The rights enjoyed by the head of a Roman family (*paterfamilias*) over his legitimate children. It was acquired by (1) birth, (2) legitimation, (3) adoption. It was lost (1) by death of the *paterfamilias*, (2) by loss of status of parent or child, (3) by promotion of the son to the patriciate, (4) by emancipation.

patrial. The term formerly used in the Immigration Act 1971, s.2 to denote a person with a right of abode in the United Kingdom. The term is now replaced by the term "British citizen" (*q.v.*) (British Nationality Act 1981, s.39 and Sched. 4 amending the 1971 Act).

patriciatus. [Roman law.] The patriciate; from the time of Constantine, the highest rank at court.

patrimonium. [Roman law.] Things *in nostro patrimonio* are things belonging to individuals. Things *extra nostrum patrimonium* are things belonging not to individuals but to all men (*communes*), to the State (*publicae*), to corporate bodies (*universitatis*), or to no one (*nullius*).

patronage. The right of presenting to a benefice (*q.v.*).

Patronage Secretary. The Chief Government Whip. See WHIPS.

pauper. (1) A person in receipt of relief under, formerly, the poor laws. (2) A person suing or defending an action *in forma pauperis* (*q.v.*). See LEGAL AID.

pauperies. [Roman law.] Mischief occasioned by an animal; damage done without *injuria*, or wrong intent, on the part of the doer. See ACTIO NOXALIS.

pawn. To pledge a chattel as security for debt; *i.e.* to part with its possession to the lender. A special property is conferred on the pawnee, who has the power of sale in default of redemption. The surplus, after satisfying the debt, belongs to the pawnor. It is a tort for the pawnee to retain the goods after payment or tender of the debt. See BAILMENTS.

pawnbroker. A person who carries on the business of taking goods and chattels in pawn. The Pawnbrokers Acts 1872 to 1960 were repealed by the Consumer Credit Act 1974, and replaced by ss.114–122 which relate to what the Act calls "regulated agreements" which cover a wider range of transactions than are traditionally associated with the concept of pawnbroking. The county court has power to re-open extortionate bargains (ss.137–140, 189 (1)).

payee. The person to whom a bill of exchange is payable.

Paymaster-General. The officer who makes the payments out of public money required for the Government Departments, by issuing drafts on the Bank of England.

payment into court. The deposit of money with an official or banker of a court of justice for the purposes of proceedings pending in the court.

(1) In any action for debt or damages the defendant may at any time after appearance upon notice to the plaintiff pay into court a sum of money in satisfaction of the claim. See Ord. 22.

(2) In the Chancery Division payment into court is also a mode by which a person may relieve himself from the responsibility of distributing or administering a fund in his hands; *e.g.* as a trustee. See Ord. 92.

peace. In early times criminal matters and offences against public order were within the jurisdiction of local lords and local courts, and the King's Court exercised jurisdiction over offences committed within the vicinity of the King himself: committed "*contra pacem Domini*," or "against the peace of our Lord the King." By a fiction that the King's peace extended to the highways and ultimately over the whole realm, the King's Court acquired its comprehensive jurisdiction. See BREACH OF THE PEACE.

pecuniary advantage. See DECEPTION.

peer. (1) An equal; trial by peers was the solemn trial of a vassal by his fellow vassals in the court of their lord. (2) A Member of the House of Lords. The

per infortunium

privilege of peerage, *i.e.* the right of a peer to be tried on a charge of felony by the House of Lords, was abolished by the Criminal Justice Act 1948, s.30.

Peers, in order of precedence, are dukes, marquesses, earls, viscounts and barons. See Peerage Act 1963. See also LIFE PEER; HOUSE OF LORDS.

peine forte et dure. The torture inflicted upon a prisoner indicted for felony who refused to plead and submit to the jurisdiction of the court. Heavy weights were applied to his body until he consented to be tried by pleading "guilty" or "not guilty," or until he died.

After the procedure by appeal of felony, ordeal, and compurgation had become obsolete there was no suitable mode of proof for the graver crimes. Consequently the judges sought to persuade the alleged criminal to "put himself on his country", *i.e.* to abide the decision of a jury of his neighbours. The alternative was the *peine forte et dure.* A prisoner who refused to plead escaped the attainer and forfeiture of property which resulted from conviction of felony.

In 1772 the statute 12 Geo. 3, c. 20 abolished the *peine forte et dure* and made refusal to plead to a charge of felony equivalent to a plea of guilty; subsequently by 7 & 8 Geo. 4, a plea of not guilty was to be entered.

penal action. An action for a penalty imposed by statute as a punishment, recoverable by any person who will sue for it. See QUI TAM, etc.

penal servitude. The punishment substituted for transportation by the Penal Servitude Acts 1853 and 1857. It might be for life or any period not less than three years. It was abolished by the Criminal Justice Act 1948, s.1, which substituted imprisonment for it.

penalty. (1) A punishment, particularly a fine or money payment. (2) The nominal sum payable (*a*) by an obligor on breach of the condition in a bond; (*b*) on breach of a term in a contract. In each case only the sum representing the actual loss can be recovered, as equity will relieve against a penalty.

Whether a sum specified in a contract as being payable on breach thereof is a penalty or an agreed sum for damages is a question of construction of the contract judged as at the time of the making of it. The use of the term "penalty" or "liquidated damages" is not conclusive.

penalty points. When a person's driving licence is endorsed with particulars of a road traffic offence the endorsement includes details of the number of penalty points attributable to that offence (Transport Act 1981, s.19; Sched. 7). See also TOTTING UP.

pendente lite. [While litigation is pending.] After an action has been commenced, and before it has been disposed of.

pending action. An action which has not been tried. A pending action relating to land may be registered as a Land Charge (*q.v.*) in the register of pending actions (Land Charges Act 1972, s.17(1)).

peppercorn. See RENT.

per. [As stated by.]

per, actions in the. See ENTRY, WRITS OF.

per annum. [By the year.]

per autre vie. [For the life of another.] See TENANT PUR AUTRE VIE.

per capita. [By heads.] Individually. Distribution of the property of an intestate is *per capita* if it is divided amongst all entitled to it in equal shares. See PER STIRPES.

per cur.: per curiam. [By the court.]

per incuriam. [Through want of care.] A decision of the court which is mistaken. A decision of the court is not a binding precedent if given *per incuriam; i.e.* without the court's attention having been drawn to the relevant authorities, or statutes.

per infortunium. [By mischance.] See HOMICIDE.

249

per mensem. [By the month.]

per minas. [By menaces (*q.v.*).]

per my et per tout. [By the half and by the whole.] See JOINT TENANCY.

per pro.: per procurationem. [As an agent.] On behalf of another.

per quod. [Whereby.]

per quod consortium et servitium amisit. [Whereby he lost her society and services.] An action for damages by a husband lay against any person who committed a tortious act or breach of contract against his wife, whereby he was deprived for any period of her society or services. In so far as the action lay for enticement of a spouse, or a child it was abolished by the Law Reform (Miscellaneous Provisions) Act 1970, s.5.

per se. [By itself.] Taken alone.

per stirpes. [By stock or branches.] Distribution of the property of an intestate is *per stirpes* if it is divided amongst those entitled to it according to the number of stocks of descent; that is, if it is divided equally amongst the surviving children of an intestate individually, and the descendants of deceased children collectively, so that the descendants of a deceased child take that child's share between them.

per totam curiam. [By the whole court.]

perambulation. The act of walking over the boundaries of a district or piece of land, either for the purpose of determining them or of preserving evidence of them.

peremptory. An order or writ which admits of no excuse for non-compliance.

performance. The doing of that which is required by a contract or condition. A contract is discharged by performance. Where a person covenants to do an act, and he does some other act of a kind to be available for the performance of his covenant, he is presumed to have had the intention of performing the covenant, because "Equity imputes an intention to fulfil an obligation." This doctrine applies (1) where there is a covenant to purchase and settle lands, and a purchase is in fact made (see *Lechmere* v. *Earl of Carlisle* (1733) 3 P. Wms. 211); (2) where there is a covenant to leave personalty to A and the covenantor dies intestate, and property thereby comes in fact to A (see *Blandy* v. *Widmore* (1716) 1 P. Wms. 323). See SPECIFIC PERFORMANCE.

Performing Rights Tribunal was constituted by the Copyright Act 1956 to adjudicate in certain disputes about licences for the public performance, including broadcasts, of literary, dramatic or musical works. It is under the supervision of Council on Tribunals. (See also the Performers' Protection Acts, 1963 and 1972.)

periculum rei venditae, nondum traditae, est emptoris. [Roman law.] A thing sold but not yet delivered, is at the risk of the purchaser.

periodical payments. Payments ordered to be made, *e.g.* weekly or monthly by one person for the maintenance of another. See FINANCIAL PROVISION.

perils of the seas refers only to fortuitous accidents or casualties of the seas, and does not include the ordinary action of the wind and waves (Marine Insurance Act 1906, Sched. 1, r. 7), *e.g.* foundering of a ship at sea, collisions, unintentional standing, etc.

perjury. False swearing. The making on oath by a witness or interpreter in a judicial proceeding of a statement material in that proceeding, which he knows to be false or which he does not believe to be true. Perjury is a misdemeanour, but no conviction can be made on the evidence of one witness only. See the Perjury Act 1911.

perpetua lex est, nullam legem humanam ac positivam perpetuam esse, et clausula quae abrogationem excludit, ab initio non valet. [It is an everlasting law, that no positive and human law shall be perpetual, and a clause which excludes abrogation is invalid from its commencement.]

perpetuation of testimony. A proceeding originally by Bill in Chancery to place on record evidence material for establishing a future claim to property or title. (See now Ord. 39, r. 15; Ord. 77, r. 14.)

perpetuity. A disposition of property by which its absolute vesting is postponed for ever. Perpetuities are contrary to the policy of the law, because they "tie up" property and prevent its free alienation. The rule against perpetuities forbids any disposition by which the absolute vesting of property is or may be postponed beyond the period of the life or lives of any number of persons living at the time of the disposition, and the further period of 21 years after the death of the survivor, with the possible addition of the period of gestation (*Cadell* v. *Palmer* (1833) 1 Cl. & Fin. 372). The "lives in being" must be those referred to in the disposition and must be ascertainable. If there is no reference to lives in being, the period is 21 years.

Under the Perpetuities and Accumulations Act 1964, a settlor or testator may specify a period not exceeding 80 years as the perpetuity period (s.1). ss.2–12 remove a number of technical difficulties arising out of the rule against perpetuities. See also the Children Act 1975, Sched. 3, para. 43. See Morris and Leach, *Rule against Perpetuities*.

persistent offenders. Where an offender is convicted on indictment of an offence punishable with imprisonment for a term of two years or more, the court, if satisfied, by reason of his previous conduct and of the likelihood of his committing further offences, that it is expedient to protect the public from him for a substantial time, may impose an extended term of imprisonment (Powers of Criminal Courts Act 1973, ss.28, 29). This supersedes the sentences of preventive detention and corrective training authorised by the Criminal Justice Act 1948, s.21.

person. The object of rights and duties, that is, capable of having rights and of being liable to duties. Persons are of two kinds, natural and artificial. A natural person is a human being; an artificial person is a collection or succession of natural persons forming a corporation. "Individual" denotes a human being.

persona. [Roman law.] (1) A human being. (2) A being or entity capable of enjoying legal rights, or subject to legal duties; *e.g.* a person or corporation. (3) A man's political and social rights collectively; his legal capacity.

persona designata. A person pointed out or described as an individual, as opposed to a person ascertained as a member of a class, or as filling a particular character.

persona extranea. [Roman law.] A person outside one's family.

persona incerta. See INCERTA PERSONA.

persona publica. [Roman law.] A public officer; a notary.

personal action. An action *in personam*, as opposed to an action *in rem*. See ACTION.

personal injuries. See DAMAGES; LIMITATIONS, STATUTES OF.

personal property. Movable property; goods and chattels. Movable property, if lost or taken, could not as of right be recovered from the wrongful possessor; the latter had the option of paying its value as damages in lieu. The action against the wrongdoer was called a personal action, and the property in question personal property. Leasehold interests in land are personal property.

personal representative. An executor or administrator. By section 55(1)(xi) of the Administration of Estates Act 1925, "personal representative" means the executor original or by representation or administrator for the time being of a deceased person.

By the Administration of Estates Act 1925, s.1: (1) Real estate to which a deceased person was entitled for an interest not ceasing on his death, shall on his death, and notwithstanding any testamentary disposition thereof, devolve from time to time on the personal representative of the deceased in like manner as, before 1926, chattels real devolved. (2) The personal representatives for the time being of a deceased person are deemed in law his heirs and assigns within the meaning of all trusts and powers. (3) The personal representatives shall be the representative of the deceased in regard to both real and personal estate.

personalty. Personal property: used particularly in regard to the estate of a deceased. Pure personalty is personal property unconnected with land. Mixed personalty is personal property consisting of interest in land, such as leaseholds.

personation. The act of representing oneself to be someone else, whether living or dead, real or fictitious.

perverting the course of justice. It is an offence to act in a way which has a tendency and is intended to pervert the administration of justice (*R.* v. *Vreones* [1891] 1 Q.B. 360; *R.* v. *Rowell* [1978] 1 W.L.R. 132). The Crown may not prove the offence by basing its case on other alternative crimes which cannot be proved (*Tsang Ping-Nam* v. *The Queen* [1981] 1 W.L.R. 1462, P.C.).

petition. A written statement addressed to the Crown, a court or public officer, setting forth facts on which the petitioner bases a prayer for remedy or relief. Proceedings for divorce or nullity, in bankruptcy, in the House of Lords and Privy Council are commenced by petition. An originating petition is also one of the methods of initiating proceedings in the Chancery Division where required by statute (Ord. 9).

The right of the subject to petition the Crown or Parliament was affirmed by the court in the case of the Seven Bishops (12 St.Tr. 183), and in the Bill of Rights. But violent and tumultuous petitioning is forbidden by the statute 13 Car. 2, st. 1, c. 5.

petition of right. (1) The mode by which a subject could claim relief from the Crown for certain kinds of injury arising from the acts of the Crown or its servants, *e.g.* an illegal seizure of goods, or a claim for breach of contract. The petition could be presented in any of the divisions of the High Court on the Home Secretary granting his fiat for that purpose (Petition of Right Act 1860, s. 1); proceedings by way of Petition of Right were abolished by the Crown Proceedings Act 1947, s. 23, Sched. 1. See CROWN PROCEEDINGS. (2) The statute 1627, 3 Car. 1, c. 1.

Petty Bag Office. The principal office on the common law side of the Court of Chancery, under the management of the Clerk of the Petty Bag (*q.v.*). Out of it issued all original writs.

petty serjeanty. A form of tenure, which consisted in the rendering of some minor personal service to the lord, such as yielding him yearly a sword or pair of gilt spurs. The Act 1660, 12 Car. 2, c. 24, did not affect its incidents, which are expressly preserved by the Law of Property Act 1922, s. 136.

petty sessional court or **petty sessions.** A court of summary jurisdiction consisting of two or more justices when sitting in a petty sessional court-house, and including the Lord Mayor or any alderman of the City of London, or any salaried magistrate when sitting in any place where he is authorised by law to do alone any act for which two justices are required. They are now called "magistrates' courts."

picketting. The posting of persons in the vicinity of a place of work during a trade dispute in order to persuade others not to work, to communicate information about the trade dispute or to obstruct them from working. There is no "right to picket" as such. Persons picketting may be guilty of criminal offences or be liable to civil action unless they fall within the protection conferred by section 15 of the Trade Union and Labour Relations Act 1974 (substituted by Employment Act 1980, s. 16(1)), *i.e.* on those simply attending at or near their own place of work in furtherance or contemplation of a trade dispute (*q.v.*). See SECONDARY PICKETTING.

Piller, Anton. The High Court has inherent power to make an order for the detention and preservation of the subject matter of a cause and the documents relating thereto. Application for such order may be made *ex parte*. Such order may compel one party to permit the other to enter his premises and is often called an Anton Piller order (*Anton Piller K.G.* v. *Manufacturing Processes Ltd.* [1976] 1 All E.R. 779; R.S.C. Ord. 29, r. 2). Such an order may be made in the course of ancillary relief proceedings after divorce or judicial separation (*Emanuel* v. *Emanuel and Vale* [1982] 2 All E.R. 342).

pin money. An allowance made by a husband to a wife for her dress and personal expenses. It may be secured by settlement, or it may be given voluntarily.

pipe. A "roll" in the Exchequer, also known as the Great Roll. It consisted of the accounts relating to the hereditary revenues of the Crown.

pipe-lines. The construction and control of cross-country pipe-lines is regulated by the Pipe-lines Act 1962, as amended. See also the Petroleum and Submarine Pipe-Lines Act 1975.

piracy. (1) The act of robbery on the seas within the jurisdiction of the admiral, and not being an act of war. Certain acts also constitute piracy by statute. Piracy is punishable with imprisonment for life, unless it is accompanied by attempted murder, or violence dangerous to life, in which case the punishment is death (Piracy Act 1837, s.2). Actual robbery is not an essential element in the crime of piracy *jure gentium* (in international law). A frustrated attempt to commit a piratical robbery is equally piracy *jure gentium* (see *Re Piracy Jure Gentium* [1934] A.C. 586). Piracy *Jure gentium* is defined in the Tokyo Convention Act 1967, s.4, Sched. Arts. 15–17. It extends to acts of piracy against aircraft. The Act supplements the common law (*Cameron* v. *H.M.Advocate*, 1971 S.C. 50). (2) The infringement of copyright.

piscary. Fishery (*q.v.*).

placita. [Pleas.]

plaint. The cause for which the plaintiff complained against the defendant and for which he obtained a writ or summons.

plaintiff. One who brings an action at law.

planning. At common law a landowner could develop his land as he liked. Since, however, the Housing, Town Planning, etc., Act 1909 local authorities have had increasing powers of control of the use and development of land. The modern scheme of development control was instituted by the principal Act, the Town and Country Planning Act 1947, as amended by the Acts of 1954 and 1959, and the Caravan Sites and Control of Development Act 1960. The law is now contained in the Town and Country Planning Act 1971, as amended by the Town and Country Planning (Amendment) Act 1972 and the Local Government Act 1972, s.182, Sched. 16. Development (*q.v.*) is controlled by the need for planning permission first being obtained by application to the local planning authority (the appropriate council), subject to appeal to the Secretary of State for the Environment. Planning permission is allowed for minor development, without application, by the Town and Country Planning General Development Order 1963. Where planning permission is refused, compensation may be payable.

If development is carried out without planning permission, an enforcement notice is served by the local planning authority, subject to appeal to the Secretary of State. There are penalties for non-compliance with an enforcement notice. The display of advertisements on land is controlled, and trees and buildings of special interest are subject to preservation orders.

planning blight. Land the value of which is adversely affected by a proposal contained in a development plan (*q.v.*) for its acquisition at some future time by a public authority. Owner-occupiers who suffer hardship by being unable to sell their land at a reasonable price may serve a notice on the local authority requiring the authority to purchase the land.

plantations. The early name for British colonial possessions in America, *e.g.* in the West Indies.

plea. The reply to a "plaint"; a mode of defence in an action at law. In a criminal prosecution the prisoner has to plead to the indictment, which he may do (1) by pleading to the jurisdiction, that is, alleging that the court has no jurisdiction to try him; (2) by a demurrer (*q.v.*); or (3) by some plea in bar, either a general plea, "guilty," or "not guilty," or a special plea, such as "autrefois acquit." The accused may plead not guilty in addition to any demurrer or special plea. He may plead not guilty of the offence charged but guilty of another offence of which he might be found guilty on the indictment (Criminal Law Act 1967, s.6).

Formerly in a civil action pleas were of two kinds, dilatory and peremptory. The former included pleas to the jurisdiction, pleas in suspension, *e.g.* an allegation of infancy, and pleas in abatement; the latter consisted of pleas in bar which showed a substantial defence to the action, either by traverse or by confession and avoidance (*q.v.*). Pleas have been superseded by the Statement of Defence.

plea bargain. An arrangement by which a defendant to criminal proceedings may agree to plead guilty to one or more charges in return for the prosecution extending some advantage to him, *e.g.* dropping another charge. Such a bargain will be closely scrutinised by the court and a judge should never indicate what sentence he has in mind to induce a defendant to change his plea. The principles to be observed are set out in *Practice Direction of Court of Appeal* [1976] Crim. L.R. 561.

plead. To make a plea (*q.v.*).

pleader. (1) An advocate. (2) One who draws pleadings.

pleadings. Written or printed statements delivered alternately by the parties to one another, until the questions of fact and law to be decided in an action have been ascertained, *i.e.* until issue is joined. The pleadings delivered (a) by the plaintiff, (b) by the defendant, are as follows: (1)(i) statement of claim; (ii) defence. (2)(i) reply. There also exist 2(ii) rejoinder, 3(i) surrejoinder; (ii) rebutter; (4) surrebutter; but they are seldom used. No pleading subsequent to reply may be served without the leave of the court (Ord. 18, r. 4).

Every pleading must state facts and not law, it must state the material facts only and in a summary form, and it must not state the evidence by which the facts are to be proved. Facts not denied specifically or by necessary implication, or stated to be not admitted, are taken to be admitted except as against persons under disability (Ord. 18). See COUNTERCLAIM.

pleas in abatement. Pleas which showed that in criminal proceedings the presecutor, or in civil proceedings the plaintiff, had committed some formality which prevented him from succeeding. Now obsolete owing to the powers of amending pleadings.

pleas of the Crown. Offences averred to have been committed *contra pacem Domini Regis, coronam et dignitatem suam* [against the peace of our Lord the King, his crown and dignity], which were triable only in the King's Courts, as distinguished from offences which could be tried in the local courts; *e.g.* the county court. A general term for criminal prosecutions. See PEACE.

pledge. The transfer of the possession (but not ownership) of a chattel as security for the payment of a debt or performance of an obligation. On default being made the chattel may be sold.

plene administravit. The defence set up by an executor or administrator when sued upon a debt of his testator, that he has fully administered the deceased's estate and that he has no assets to satisfy the claim.

plenipotentiary. Having full powers.

plus-petere, plus-petitio, pluris petitio. [Roman law.] Where the plaintiff claims more than he is entitled to. This might be done in four ways: *re, tempore, loco, causa.*

poaching. The offence of unlawfully taking or destroying game on another man's land. See the Night Poaching Act 1828; Poaching Prevention Act 1862; Game Laws (Amendment) Act 1960. Criminal Law Act 1977, ss.15, 30, 65(4), Sched. 1, Sched. 12.

poena. [Roman law.] A penalty, the punishment of an offence: generally inflicted for delicts. It is not confined to a money payment, as is *multa*, a fine, but may extend to the *caput* of the offender, and is not left to the discretion of the judge, but is attached to or appointed for each particular delict.

police court. A petty sessional court (*q.v.*), held in London and in other cities by a magistrate: now called a magistrates' court.

police, obstruction of. It is an offence to unlawfully obstruct a constable in the execution of his duty (Police Act 1964, s.51). The prosecution must prove that there was an obstructing of a constable, that the constable was acting in the execution of his duty, and that the person obstructing did so wilfully (*Rice* v. *Connolly* [1966] 2 All E.R. 651). To give a person a warning so that he may postpone the commission of a crime until the danger of detection has passed in an obstruction within section 51 of the Act (*Green* v. *Moore* [1982] 1 All E.R. 428, Div. Ct.).

policy of assurance. An instrument containing a contract of insurance, and called a marine, fire, life or accident policy, according to the nature of the insurance. An unvalued policy is where the value of the thing insured is not stated; a valued policy is where the value is stated (Marine Insurance Act 1906, ss.27, 28).

political offence. An offence committed in connection with or as part of political disturbances. The Extradition Act 1870, s.3 provides that a fugitive offender shall not be surrendered by this country for a political offence. Genocide is not an offence of a political nature (Genocide Act 1969, s.2(2)). See also Suppression of Terrorism Act 1978, Sched. 1. for offences *e.g.* murder, rape, which are not to be regarded as political offences.

poll. Taking a vote at an election, or on a motion. At a general meeting of members of a company, etc., questions are decided in the first place by a show of hands, but there is a right of members to demand a poll, unless expressly excluded, and, if demanded, it must be taken. The usual method is to require the persons present in person (or, normally, by proxy) to sign a paper headed "for" or "against" the motion. The poll is taken by counting these votes.

poll-tax. A tax upon every poll or head, that is to say, upon every person.

pollution. See Prevention of Oil Pollution Act 1971; Control of Pollution Act 1974; Dumping at Sea Act 1974.

polygamy. A system of marriage whereby one is allowed to have several spouses. Such a marriage may be recognised by the English courts in some circumstances (Matrimonial Causes Act 1973, s.47). See also *Quazi* v. *Quazi* [1979] 3 All E.R. 897, H.L.).

pone. A writ whereby a cause pending in the old county court of the sheriff was removed into the Common Pleas or King's Bench.

pool betting duty. See the Betting and Gaming Duties Act 1972, ss.1–12, 14, Sched. 1; Finance Act 1972, s.58; Finance (No. 2) Act 1975, s.2.

poor law. The law which related to the public or compulsory relief of the indigent poor. By the Poor Relief Act 1601 overseers of the poor were appointed in every parish to provide for the relief of paupers settled there, and to levy a rate on property therein. The system of overseers being unsatisfactory, the statute 22

Geo. 3, c. 83, authorised any parish to appoint guardians in lieu of overseers, and also to enter into a voluntary union with one or more other parishes.

By the Poor Law Amendment Act 1834 the general management of the poor was placed under the Poor Law Commissioners, whose functions were transferred by the Poor Law Board Act 1847 to the Poor Law Board, and in 1871 to the Local Government Board (since 1919 the Ministry of Health). By the Rating and Valuation Act 1925, ss.1, 62, overseers were abolished and their functions transferred to rating authorities. The poor law was consolidated by the Poor Law Act 1930 and terminated by the National Assistance Act 1948. See NATIONAL ASSISTANCE.

poor person. See LEGAL AID.

poor rate. The rate formerly levied by the overseers for the relief of the poor.

port. (1) A city or town (Anglo-Saxon). (2) A harbour or other stretch of water available for the loading and unloading of goods on ships. The Commissioners of Customs and Excise may by order appoint and name as a port for the purposes of customs and excise any specified area in the United Kingdom (Customs and Excise Act 1952, s.13), and approve fit places for the loading and unloading of goods therein: referred to as "approved wharves" (*ibid.* s.14).

portion. The provision made for a child by a parent or one *in loco parentis*; the gross sums of money provided in a strict settlement for the children, other than the eldest son, on their attaining 21, or, if females, marrying before that age. See SATISFACTION.

portreeve. The chief magistrate of a town.

positive law. That part of law which consists of rules imposed by a sovereign on his subjects: law proper as opposed to moral law, and so on (Austin). See LAW.

posse comitatus. [The power of the county.] An assemblage of the able-bodied male inhabitants of a county, except peers and clergymen. The sheriff of the county could summon it either to defend the county against the King's enemies or to enforce the King's writ.

possessio. [Roman law.] Legal possession. The detention or physical apprehension of a thing with the intention of holding it as one's own (*detentio*, together with *animus possidendi*). It was protected by interdicts.

possessio civilis. [Roman law.] Civil possession; possession capable of ripening into ownership by *usucapio, i.e.* if it was (1) free from *vitium*; (2) held *ex justa causa*; (3) bona fide.

possessio naturalis. [Roman law.] Natural possession; where a person possessed a thing not *ex justa causa* and bona fide. It was not protected by interdicts.

possession. Physical detention coupled with the intention to hold the thing detained as one's own (Maine). The continuing exercise of a claim to the exclusive use of a material object (Salmond). Possession has two elements: (1) the *corpus*, or the thing possessed; (2) the *animus possidendi*, the intention to appropriate to oneself the exclusive use of the thing possessed.

Immediate possession is possession retained personally; mediate possession or custody is possession retained for or on account of another. Incorporeal possession is the possession not of a material thing, but of a legal right. Constructive possession is possession in contemplation of law as opposed to *de facto* possession or actual possession in fact.

Possession is prima facie evidence of ownership. "Possession is nine-tenths of the law" means that possession is good against all the world except the true owner. Possession ripens into ownership by effluxion of time. Adverse possession of land (*i.e.* not by agreement with the owner) for 12 years destroys the title of the owner and vests it in the possessor. The holder of a negotiable instrument, a factor, and a seller in market overt, can give a better title than he himself has, provided the buyer takes in good faith and for value.

possession money. The fee to which a sheriff's officer is entitled for keeping possession of property under a writ of execution.

possession of drugs. It is an offence to have in ones possession a controlled drug (Misuse of Drugs Act 1971, s.5(1)). For the drug to be in a person's possession that person must know that the drug is within his control (*Warren* v. *Metropolitan Police Commissioner* [1969] A.C. 256). The quantity of drug must be such as to amount to something, and this is a question of fact for the jury; however, it does not have to be usable. The question is not usability but possession (*R.* v. *Boyeson* [1982] 2 All E.R. 161, H.L.). See DRUGS, CONTROLLED.

possession, order for. For the cases in which the court must or may order a tenant of residential premises to give possession to the landlord see Rent Act 1977, Sched. 15.

possession, writ of. The writ which commands the sheriff to enter the land and give possession of it to the person entitled under a judgment (Ord. 47, 44. rr. 1, 2).

possessory action. A real action to recover the possession of land.

possessory title. See POSSESSION.

possibility. A future event the happening of which is uncertain; an interest in land which depends on the happening of such an event. A possibility is said to be either bare or coupled with an interest. Thus, the expectation of an eldest son of succeeding to his father's land was a bare possibility, which was not capable of transfer. If land was conveyed to A for life, and if C should be living at his death, then to B in fee, B's contingent remainder was a possibility coupled with an interest, which might be transferred. See DOUBLE POSSIBILITY.

possidere pro herede. [Roman law.] To possess in the belief that one is heir.

possidere pro possessore. [Roman law.] To possess the part or the whole of an inheritance without any right, and with the knowledge that one is not the owner.

post litem motam. After litigation has been in contemplation. See LIS MOTA.

postea. A formal statement, indorsed on the *nisi prius* record, which gave an account of the proceedings at the trial of the action.

postliminium. [Beyond the threshold.] The doctrine of the Roman law that persons captured by the enemy were, on their return, deemed to revert to their original status, on the fiction that no capture had occurred. The doctrine has been adopted by international law as the rule by which persons, property and territory tend to revert to their former condition on the withdrawal of enemy control.

post-mortem examination. A medical examination of a corpse in order to discover the cause of death. It may be ordered by a coroner under section 21 of the Coroners Act 1887. It may be made without an inquest (Coroners (Amendment) Act 1926, s.21). See also the Human Tissue Act 1961, s.2.

post-obit. A money bond conditioned for payment at or after the death of some person other than the giver of the bond.

postumus. [Roman law.] (1) A child of a testator, born after his death, who, if born in his lifetime, would have been under his *potestas*, and entitled to succeed him if he died intestate; (2) a child of a testator conceived before the date of the will, but born a *suus heres* after the date of the will, and before the testator's death. This was called a *postumus Vellaeanus*, from *lex Junia Vellaea*, which provided that the testator might institute or exclude such a child.

postumus alienus. [Roman law.] A posthumous stranger; a posthumous child that would not have been under the testator's power if born in his lifetime.

potior est conditio defendentis. [The condition of a defendant is the better.] *i.e.* the onus of proof is on the plaintiff.

potior est conditio possidentis. [The condition of a possessor is the better.] *i.e.* the onus is on a claimant to prove a superior title in himself to that of the possessor.

pound. A place where goods which have been seized as distress are placed by the distrainor, and in which the goods are in the custody of the law. A pound is either overt (open overhead) or covert (closed in).

poundage. (1) A fee of so much in the pound. (2) Formerly a customs duty on the value of imports other than wine. See TONNAGE.

pound-breach. The offence of taking of goods out of a pound before the distrainor's claim has been satisfied. Once goods are impounded, they are *in custodia legis*, and a pound must be respected by all persons; ignorance that goods are impounded is no defence. See RESCUE.

power. The ability conferred on a person by law to determine, by his own will directed to that end, the legal relations of himself or others (Salmond). A power is the converse of disability. It differs from a right in that there are no accompanying duties. Powers are public, *i.e.* when vested by the State in its agent or employee, or private, when conferred by one person on another. General powers are those which are by law incident to an office; *e.g.* of solicitor or trustee; special powers are those conferred specially; *e.g.* by a power of attorney, or a power of sale. See SALE, POWER OF.

power of appointment. A power which enables the donee to create or modify estates or interests in property. It confers the right of alienation as opposed to that of enjoyment; that is, the power enables the donee to declare in whom and in what manner the property is to vest, but gives him no right of ownership over it. A power was said to be legal when it passed the legal estate in land, and equitable when it passed an equitable estate or interest. Legal powers are (*a*) appendant or appurtenant when the donee has an estate in the land and the power is to take effect wholly or in part out of that estate; (*b*) in gross, where the donee may exercise the power for his own benefit; (*c*) collateral or naked, where he cannot.

By the Law of Property Act 1925, s.1(7) every power of appointment is to operate only in equity, except that vested in a legal mortgagee or estate owner in right of his estate. See also APPOINTMENT, POWER OF.

power of attorney. A formal instrument by which one person empowers another to represent him, or act in his stead, for certain purposes; usually in the form of a deed poll, and attested by two witnesses. The donor of the power is called the principal or constituent; the donee is called the attorney (Powers of Attorney Act 1971). The attorney is not entitled to exercise his powers for his own benefit, *e.g.* draw cheques on the principal's account to pay his own debts (see *Reckitt* v. *Barnett, Pembroke and Slater* [1929] A.C. 176).

practice. Procedure (*q.v.*) That which pertains to the actual conduct of legal proceedings and is governed by the Rules of the Supreme Court.

practice court. The Bail Court (*q.v.*).

practice directions. Statements by the judiciary, usually noted in the law reports, intended to guide the courts and the legal profession on matters of practice and procedure.

practising certificate. The certificate taken out annually by a solicitor (*q.v.*) from the Law Society which entitles him to practise as a solicitor.

praecipe. (1) A species of original writ, which required the sheriff to command the defendant either to do a certain thing or to show cause why he had not done it. (2) A slip of paper on which a party to a proceeding writes the particulars of a document which he wishes to have prepared or issued; he then hands it to the officer of the court whose duty it is to prepare or issue the document.

praedia stipendiaria. [Roman law.] Provincial lands belonging peculiarly to the Roman people, and paying taxes (*stipendia*).

praedium dominans. [Roman law.] The land in favour of which a servitude existed over the land of another.

praedium serviens. Land subject to a servitude in favour of the owner of adjoining land.

praefectus urbi. [Roman law.] The city prefect or governor. His civil jurisdiction extended to 100 miles around Rome and his criminal jurisdiction throughout Italy. An appeal lay to him from the Praetor.

praemunire. The offence of directly or indirectly asserting the supremacy of the Pope over the Crown of England, as by procuring excommunication or bulls from Rome, contrary to the Statute of Praemunire (16 Ric. 2, c. 5). The writ employed commenced with the words praemunire facias [that you cause to be forewarned].

praepositus. [One put in front.] A person in authority.

praeses. [Roman law.] The president or governor of a province; a *legatus Caesaris* being the governor of a province reserved by the emperor.

praesumptio. See PRESUMPTION.

praetor. [Roman law.] The consul whose special function was to administer justice in the city (*Praetor Urbanus*). A second Praetor was appointed to deal with cases between citizens and aliens, or between aliens alone (*Praetor Peregrinus*). Although theoretically the Praetor merely administered the law, his powers of interpretation and amendment developed the law. He applied, as far as possible, the rules of natural justice (*naturalis aequitas*). On taking office he issued an edict stating the rules by which he would be guided.

The Praetors achieved (1) admission of aliens to Roman law; (2) the supersession of formalism by rules giving effect to the intention of the parties: (3) change of the law on intestate succession from the basis of *potestas* to blood.

preamble. The recitals set out in the beginning of a statute showing the reason for the Act.

precatory words. Words of wish, hope, desire or entreaty accompanying a gift, that the donee will dispose of the property in some particular way, which may show that a trust was intended. The modern tendency is against construing precatory words as a trust. See *Re Adams and Kensington Vestry* (1884) 27 Ch. D. 394.

Precedence, Patent of. Letters patent whereby the Crown assigns to some person a rank higher than that to which he would otherwise be entitled.

precedent. A judgment or decision of a court of law cited as an authority for deciding a similar set of facts; a case which serves as an authority for the legal principle embodied in its decision. The common law has developed by broadening down from precedent to precedent.

A case is only an authority for what it actually decides. "The only use of authorities or decided cases is the establishment of some principle which the judge can follow out in deciding the case before him" (*per* Sir George Jessel M.R.; *Re Hallett* (1880) 13 Ch. D. 712).

An original precedent is one which creates and applies a new rule; a declaratory precedent is one which is merely the application of an already existing rule of law. An authoritative precedent is one which is binding and must be followed; a persuasive precedent is one which need not be followed, but which is worthy of consideration. Decisions of the House of Lords or the Court of Appeal are authoritative precedents. The High Court, however, will usually follow its own decisions (unless they are distinguishable). American or Commonwealth judgments, etc., are persuasive precedents. See RATIO DECIDENDI; STARE DECISIS.

In conveyancing or drafting, a precedent is a copy of an instrument used as a guide in preparing another similar instrument.

precept. An order or direction given by one official person or body to another, requiring some act to be done, *e.g.* the payment of a sum of money. As to precepts to rating authorities, see the Local Government Act 1972, s.149.

pre-emption. The right of purchasing property before or in preference to other persons. In international law, pre-emption is the right of a government to purchase, for its own use, the property of the subjects of another Power *in transitu*, instead of allowing it to reach its destination.

preference shares. Shares in a joint stock company which are entitled to a fixed rate of dividend payable in preference to the dividend on the ordinary shares. Unless preference shares are made preferential as to capital they rank *pari passu* with the ordinary shares on a winding-up. They are presumed to be cumulative. See SURPLUS ASSETS.

preferential payments. The payment of debts in priority to others in distributing or realising an estate, as in the distribution of a bankrupt's estate (Bankruptcy Act 1914, s.33); of a deceased insolvent's estate (Administration of Estates Act 1925, s.34, Sched. 1, Pt. I); in the winding up of a company (Companies Act 1948, s.319), and out of any assets coming to the hands of a receiver taking possession under a floating charge (*ibid.* s.94). See also Insolvency Act 1976, s.1, Sched. 1, Pt. I.

They are such debts as: (1) one year's rates and taxes; (2) four months' wages or salaries of clerks, employees, or workers; (3) other debts given priority by statute, *e.g.* contributions under the Social Security Act 1975, s.153, amounts payable under the Employment Protection Consolidation Act 1978. These debts rank equally amongst themselves, and if the assets are insufficient to pay them in full, they abate in equal proportions.

The right of a personal representative to prefer creditors was abolished by the Administration of Estates Act 1971, s.10.

prejudice. Injury. A statement which is made "without prejudice" for the purpose of settling a dispute cannot be construed as an admission of liability or given in evidence.

preliminary act. A sealed document giving particulars of a collision between vessels, which must be filed by the solicitors for each party in an Admiralty action for damages for collision. It is not opened, except by special order, until the pleadings are completed (Ord. 75, r. 18).

premises. That which has been stated before. (1) In a conveyance, when the property has been fully described, it is generally referred to in the subsequent parts of the deed as "the premises hereinbefore described." From this, "premises" has acquired the sense of land or buildings. (2) That part of a deed which precedes the *habendum*.

premium. (1) A sum payable in advance of or over and above the consideration for an agreement. Unlawful premiums may be recovered by action (Rent Act 1977, ss.119–127). (2) The consideration for a contract of assurance.

prender. The power of taking a thing without its being offered.

prerogative, royal. Those exceptional powers and privileges of the Sovereign in virtue of the Crown, *e.g.* the command of the Army, or the treaty-making power. The prerogative appears to be both historically and as a matter of actual fact nothing else than the residue of arbitrary authority which at any given time is legally left in the hands of the Crown (Dicey, *Law of the Constitution*).

prerogative writs. Writs which issued from the superior courts for the purpose of preventing inferior courts, or officials, from exceeding the limits of their legitimate sphere of action, or of compelling them to exercise their functions in accordance with the law, to assure the full measure of justice to the King's subjects. These writs were: (1) Habeas Corpus; (2) Certiorari; (3) Prohibition;

(4) Mandamus; (5) Quo Warranto; (6) Ne Exeat Regno; (7) Procedendo. They were within the jurisdiction of the King's Bench Division.

By the Administration of Justice (Miscellaneous Provisions) Act 1938, s.7 orders of mandamus, prohibition and certiorari were substituted for the corresponding writs. For the modern procedure see JUDICIAL REVIEW.

prescribe. (1) To claim a right by prescription. (2) To lay down authoritatively.

prescription. The vesting of a right by reason of lapse of time. Negative prescription is the divesting of a right by the same process. In Roman law the *praescriptio* was a clause placed at the head of the formula or pleadings (*prae*, before and *scribere*, to write). *Praescriptio* was also a variety of *usucapio, i.e.* a mode of acquiring property by undisturbed possession for a certain length of time.

At common law, a title by prescription was acquired by the enjoyment of a right from time immemorial, or time out of mind, from which an original grant was implied. Such user would be presumed from evidence of long actual user, but the presumption might be rebutted by proof that the enjoyment had in fact commenced within legal memory. The doctrine of the lost modern grant overcame this difficulty by presuming from long user that an actual grant of the easement or profit was made at some time subsequent to 1189, but prior to the user supporting the claim, and that unfortunately this grant had been lost.

The Prescription Act 1832 enacts that in the case of rights of common and other *profits à prendre*, the period of enjoyment as of right required to establish the title is 30 years, subject to an extension in case the person against whom it is claimed was under disability during part of that period; but enjoyment for 60 years establishes an absolute right. In the case of rights of way and watercourses the terms are respectively 20 and 40 years, and of light, enjoyment for 20 years gives an absolute right. Where a person claiming a right by prescription proves that it has been enjoyed by him and his predecessors in title in virtue of certain lands, he is said to prescribe in a *que* estate. Prescription in gross arises where a person claims that he and his ancestors have from time immemorial exercised a right to *profits à prendre* over the land of another. See ANCIENT LIGHTS; MEMORY; SQUATTER'S TITLE.

present. To tender or offer, *e.g.* to present a bill of exchange for acceptance or payment to the acceptor.

presentment. A report by a jury or members of a court of facts and matters peculiarly within their own knowledge or observation. Thus, formerly, at the Customary Court of a manor, events relating to the copyhold lands were presented by the tenants for the information of the lord; indictments were presented by grand juries, after hearing evidence upon which they decided that there was a case against the accused on which he should stand his trial.

presumption. A conclusion or inference as to the truth of some fact in question, drawn from other facts proved or admitted to be true.

(1) Irrebuttable or conclusive presumptions (*praesumptiones juris et de jure*) are absolute inferences established by law; evidence is not admissible to contradict them: they are rules of law. See, *e.g.* DOLI INCAPAX.

(2) Rebuttable presumptions of law (*praesumptiones juris*) are inferences which the law requires to be drawn from given facts, and which are conclusive until disproved by evidence to the contrary, *e.g.* the presumption of the innocence of an accused person.

(3) Presumptions of fact (*praesumptiones hominis vel facti*) are inferences which may be drawn from the facts, but not compulsorily.

presumption of death. Any married person who alleges that reasonable grounds exist for supposing the other party to the marriage to be dead may petition to have it presumed that the other party is dead and to have the marriage dissolved (Matrimonial Causes Act 1973, s.19(1)). Absence of seven years where the petitioner has no reason to believe the other party has been living within that period shall be evidence that the other party is dead unless the contrary be proved (1973 Act, s.19(3)).

preventive detention. See PERSISTENT OFFENDERS.

previous convictions. Generally in criminal proceedings evidence may not be introduced as to a defendant's previous convictions save where the defendant puts his own credit in issue or impugns the character of an opposing witness. The protection is withdrawn when a defendant gives evidence against any other person charged in the same proceedings (Criminal Evidence Act 1979, s.1(1)). In such a case it must be objectively decided whether the co-defendants evidence either support the prosecution case or undermines the other defendants defence; mere denial of participation in a joint venture is not of itself evidence "against" the other defendant (*R.* v. *Varley* [1982] 2 All E.R. 519, C.A.).

pricking for sheriffs. The practice of appointing sheriffs by the Sovereign pretending to prick their names with a bodkin, as a survival from the days when the selection was by change.

prima facie case. [Of first appearance.] A case in which there is some evidence in support of the charge or allegation made in it, and which will stand unless it is displaced. In a case which is being heard in court, the party starting, that is, upon whom the burden of proof rests, must make out a prima facie case, or else the other party will be able to submit that there is no case to answer, and the case will have to be dismissed.

primage. A small payment made by the owner or consignee of goods to the master of the vessel in which they are shipped, for his care.

Prime Minister. He takes the office of First Lord of the Treasury. He is the leader of the political party in a majority in the House of Commons, charged by the Sovereign with the formation of a government. As chairman of the Cabinet , he is the executive head of the Government. He takes precedence next after the Archbishop of York.

primer seisin. A payment of a year's profits due by a tenant of land held of the Crown *in capite ut de corona* if he succeeded to it by descent when of full age.

primo loco. [In the first place.]

primogeniture. [*Primo-genitus*, first-born.] The rule of inheritance according to which the eldest male in the same degree succeeded to the ancestor's land to the exclusion of the others.

Prince of Wales. The eldest son of the reigning Sovereign is always created Prince of Wales and Earl of Chester by patent. He is Duke of Cornwall by inheritance during the life of the Sovereign. Since the accession of James I, the heir apparent has been by inheritance Duke of Rothesay, Earl of Carrick, and Baron Renfrew, Lord of the Isles and Great Steward of Scotland.

principal. (1) A principal of the first degree is the actual perpetrator of a crime; a principal of the second degree is one who is present, aiding and abetting. The abolition of the distinction between felony and misdemeanour has the result that principals of either degree and accessories before the fact are treated as principal offenders (Criminal Law Act 1967, s.1).

(2) A principal is one who authorises another to act on his behalf, called the agent. If an agent purports to act on his own behalf, his principal is called an undisclosed principal. In general, the third party can sue the undisclosed principal when he discovers his existence.

(3) A principal debtor is one who owes a debt which is guaranteed by a surety.

(4) A sum of money put out at interest.

principum placita. [Roman law.] The enactments of constitutions of the emperors. "What the emperor determines has the force of a statute."

priority. Precedence; the right to enforce a claim in preference to others. Mortgages affecting a legal estate in land made after 1925, whether legal or equitable (not being a mortgage by deposit of documents), other than a mortgage of registered land, rank according to date of registration as a land charge (Law of Property Act 1925, s.97). Equitable claims rank in order of the time of creation. However, "where the equities are equal the law prevails," so that the bona fide purchaser of a legal estate without notice of an earlier equity takes priority over the earlier equity.

Where there are successive assignments of an equitable chose in action, priorities are determined by the order in which notice is given to the person by whom the fund is distributable. This rule, known as the rule in *Dearle* v. *Hall*, is extended by the Law of Property Act 1925, to equitable interests in land. See PREFERENTIAL PAYMENTS.

priority notice. See the Land Charges Act 1972, s.11.

prisage. A former hereditary revenue of the Crown, consisting in the right to take a certain quantity from cargoes of wine imported into England, later converted into a pecuniary duty called butlerage.

prisons. The Home Secretary has general control over prisons. The functions of the Prison Commissioners were transferred to the Home Secretary by Order in Council under the Criminal Justice Act 1961, s.24. Prisoners are deemed to be in the legal custody of the Prison Governor. Sentences of imprisonment may be remitted for good conduct, and certain prisoners may be released on parole or given temporary or conditional discharge. The enactments relating to prisons were consolidated by the Prison Act 1952, as amended. See ESCAPE.

prison-breach. The offence of breaking out of prison by force.

private company. See COMPANIES.

private international law. Conflict of laws. The body of rules for determining questions of jurisdiction, and questions as to the selection of the appropriate law, in civil cases which present themselves for decision before the courts which involve a "foreign element." Its objects are to prescribe the conditions under which the court is competent to entertain such a suit; to determine for each class of case the particular internal system of law by reference to which the rights of the parties must be ascertained; to specify the circumstances in which a foreign judgment can be recognised as decisive of the question in dispute, and when the right vested in a creditor by a foreign judgment can be enforced by action in England. (Cheshire.)

privateers. Vessels belonging to private owners which in time of war were furnished with a commission from the State, known as letters of marque, empowering them to carry on war against the enemy, and to capture enemy vessels and property. Privateering is and remains abolished (Declaration of Paris 1856).

privatorum conventio juri publico non derogat. [An agreement between private persons does not derogate from the public right.]

privatum commodum publico cedit. [Private good yields to public good.]

privatum incommodum publico bono pensatur. [Private loss is compensated by public good.]

privilege. An exceptional or extraordinary right, immunity or exemption blonging to a person in virtue of his office or status, *e.g.* the immunity from arrest of ambassadors, Members of Parliament or barristers on circuit.

A man attacks the reputation of another at his own risk, but a defamatory statement is privileged as follows. (1) A statement is absolutely privileged when no action will lie for it even if it is made with malice (*q.v.*), *e.g.* statements made in the course of judicial proceedings. (2) Qualified privilege is where a person is not liable to an action for defamation unless he is guilty of malice, *e.g.* statements made in the course of duty, reports or proceedings, etc.

In the law of evidence, the following matters are protected from disclosure on the grounds of privilege: (1) professional confidences; (2) title-deeds, etc., of a stranger to the action; (3) matrimonial communications; (4) criminating questions. See CROWN PRIVILEGE.

Privileges, Committee for. A committee of the House of Lords concerned with claims to peerages and the privileges of peers.

Privileges, Committee of. A committee of the House of Commons concerned with questions of privilege of the House and its members.

privilegium clericale. [Benefit of clergy (*q.v.*).]

privilegium non valet contra rempublicam. [A privilege avails not against the State.]

privity. The relationship in which a person stands to a transaction in which he is a party, or to some other party with whom he is connected.

Privity of contract is the relation which exists between the immediate parties to a contract (*q.v.*) which is necessary to enable one person to sue another on it.

Privity of estate is that which exists between lessor and lessee, lessor and assignee (but not lessor and underlessee), tenant for life and remainderman or reversioner, etc. Privity of estate is required for a release by enlargement. Thus, if A grants land to B for life, and B grants a lease to C, and then A executes a release to C, this is void as a release, because there is no privity between A and C. An original lessee is always liable to the lessor on the covenants of a lease, but an assignee is only liable, and entitled to the benefit of the covenants, so long as he holds and until he further assigns the lease, because thereupon there ceases to be any privity between him and the lessor.

privy. One who is a party to, or had a share or interest in something.

Privy Council. Nominally, the principal council of the Crown, consisting of persons of distinction, nominated by the Crown to the office, and bearing the title "Right Honourable."

Members of the Cabinet are always Privy Councillors, as the Cabinet itself evolved from the Privy Council. See JUDICIAL COMMITTEE.

Privy Purse. A sum voted by Parliament as part of the Civil List for the personal use of the Queen.

Privy Seal. A seal employed by the Crown, chiefly as an authority to the Lord Chancellor to affix the Great Seal to documents. It was abolished in 1884.

prize. Property captured from an enemy at sea. The Prize Act 1948 extinguished the prerogative right to make grants of prize money to captors of prize, and to grant prize bounty.

prize courts. Courts specially constituted for the purpose of deciding questions of maritime capture in time of war according to international law. The procedure of the British Prize Court is regulated by the Naval Prize Acts 1864 to 1916. It is exercised by the Admiralty Court (*q.v.*). Appeals from the Admiralty Court acting as a Prize Court lie to the Judicial Committee of the Privy Council (Judicature Act 1925, s.27(1)).

prize fight. A fight between two men with ungloved fists until one of them can fight no more: it constitutes an indictable misdemeanour.

pro confesso. [As if conceded.]

pro forma. [As a matter of form.]

pro hac vice. [For this occasion.] An appointment which is for a particular occasion only.

pro indiviso. [As undivided.]

pro interesse suo. [As to his interest.]

pro rata. [In proportion.]

pro tanto. [For so much; to that extent.]

probabilities, balance of. See PROOF.

probate. A certificate granted by the Family Division of the High Court of Justice to the effect that the will of a certain person has been proved and registered in the court and that administration of his effects has been granted to the executor proving the will, he having first sworn faithfully to administer them and to exhibit a true inventory and render a just account when called on. The copy of the will is termed the "probate copy."

Probate may be granted either in solemn form or in common form. Probate in solemn form is only employed when there is or is likely to be a dispute as to the validity of the will, and in such a case the person who wishes its validity to be established commences an action against the person who disputes it. Probate in common form is granted in ordinary cases as a matter of course on the executor swearing and filing affidavits. By the Administration of Estates Act 1925, s.2 the rules of law as to probate in case of chattels real apply to real estate (Ord. 76). Contentious probate business is assigned to the Chancery Division (Judicature Act 1925, s.56(1)(*bb*); Administration of Justice Act 1970, s.1(6), Sched. 2, para. 8).

Probate, Divorce and Admiralty Division. The Division of the High Court of Justice under the President which exercised jurisdiction in matters formerly within the exclusive cognisance of the Court of Probate (*q.v.*), the Court for Divorce and Matrimonial Causes (*q.v.*), and the Court of Admiralty (see Judicature Act 1925, s.4(3)). See ADMIRAL.

It has been re-named the Family Division. Admiralty and prize jurisdictions have been transferred to the Admiralty Court which is part of the Queen's Bench Division. Probate (other than non-contentious or common form probate business) has been transferred to the Chancery Division (Administration of Justice Act 1970, ss.1, 2).

probate duty. A stamp duty payable on the personal property over the value of £100 in this country of anyone in respect of whom a grant of probate or letters of administration should be obtained (Customs and Inland Revenue Act 1881). Replaced by estate duty.

probation of offenders. A court by or before which a person of or over 17 years of age is convicted of an offence (not being an offence the sentence for which is fixed by law) may, instead of sentencing him, make a probation order, *i.e.* an order requiring him to be under the supervision of a probation officer for not less than six months or more than three years. A probation order can only be made with the offender's consent. If the offender fails to comply with the probation order or commits another offence he will be liable to be sentenced for the original offence (Powers of Criminal Courts Act 1973, ss.2, 12, 13). Breach of a probation order may be dealt with by fine, a community service order or requirement to attend at an attendance centre (s.6). As to further offences see s.8. Conditional discharge may be substituted for probation (s.11).

procedendo. A prerogative writ which issued (1) when the judge of an inferior court delayed the parties to a proceeding before him, by not giving judgment for one side or the other, when he ought to do so; or (2) when a cause had been removed from an inferior court to a superior court improperly or on insufficient grounds, and the superior court thought fit to remit or remove it back to the inferior court.

procedure. The formal steps to be taken in an action or other judicial proceeding, civil or criminal. Procedure is governed by the *lex fori* (see *Leroux* v. *Brown* (1852) 12 C.B. 801).

process. A form of proceeding taken in a court of justice for the purpose of giving compulsory effect to its jurisdiction. The process of the Supreme Court of Judicature consists of writs, originating summonses, motions and petitions (Ord. 5). Formerly, original process was the original writ issued out of Chancery; mesne process was the name for the writs issued out of the common law courts in the course of proceedings; and final process the writs to enforce execution. See SERVICE OF PROCESS.

proclamation. The King cannot by his Proclamation create any offence which was not an offence before. But the King, for prevention of offences, may by proclamation admonish his subjects that they keep the laws (*The Case of Proclamations* (1610) 12 Rep. 74). See EMERGENCY POWERS; PREROGATIVE.

proctors. In the Ecclesiastical and Admiralty Courts proctors discharged duties similar to those of solicitors and attorneys in other courts. By the Judicature Act 1873, s.87 proctors were entitled solicitors of the Supreme Court.

The Solicitors Act 1974 allows solicitors to appear in ecclesiastical courts (ss.19, 89(6)).

procuration. (1) Agency. The abbreviations "*per proc.*" or "*p.p.*" following a signature upon a bill of exchange indicate that the signatory signs only as an agent. Such signature binds the principal only in so far as the agent signs within the limits of his authority, and does not make the agent personally liable (Bills of Exchange Act 1882, ss.25, 26).

(2) Of women and girls. The provision or procuring of women and girls for the purposes of illicit intercourse is punishable under the Sexual Offences Act 1956, ss.2, 3, 4, 22, 23.

procurator. [Roman law.] An agent appointed by a mandate to act for another in a single, or in all, actions. He might be appointed under any conditions or arrangements; no special words were needed. The procurator superseded the *cognitor* (*q.v.*).

Procurator-General. The Treasury Solicitor (*q.v.*).

prodigus. [Roman law.] A prodigal; a person who cannot be trusted to look after his own property. A curator would then be appointed.

profits à prendre. Right of taking the produce or part of the soil from the land of another person, *e.g.* rights of common, of pasture, of vesture and herbage.

prohibition. A writ formerly issuing out of the High Court to restrain an inferior court from exceeding its powers. Prohibitions were of three kinds. (1) An absolute prohibition was peremptory, and wholly tied up the inferior jurisdiction. (2) A temporary prohibition (a prohibition *quousque*) was operative only until a particular act was done, and was *ipso facto* discharged on the act being done. (3) A limited or partial prohibition (a prohibition *quoad*) extended only to that part of the proceeding which exceeded the jurisdiction of the inferior court, allowing it to proceed as to the residue.

The writ of prohibition was replaced by an order of prohibition (Ord. 53) which was used not only to restrain an inferior court from exceeding its jurisdiction, or acting contrary to the rules of natural justice, but also to control a minister or public authority in the exercise of their judicial or quasi-judicial functions. For the modern procedure see JUDICIAL REVIEW.

prolixity. The allegation of facts at unnecessary length, either in a pleading or affidavit. The party offending may be ordered to pay the costs thereby occasioned (Ord. 41, r. 6, notes).

prolocutor. A Speaker.

promise. The expression of an intention to do or forbear from some act. To have legal effect, a promise must either be under seal, when it forms a covenant, or must form part of a contract; that is, be made in consideration of something done or to be done. See BREACH OF PROMISE.

promissory note. An unconditional promise in writing, made by one person to another, signed by the maker, engaging to pay on demand, or at a fixed or determinable future time, a sum certain in money to, or to the order of, a specified person or to bearer (Bills of Exchange Act 1882, s.83(1)).

promoter. Anciently, the persons who laid themselves out to bring, as common informers, penal and popular actions. Now it generally means a person who procures the passing of a private Act of Parliament, who "floats" a company, or arranges a sporting event.

proof. (1) A fact is said to be proved when the court is satisfied as to its truth, and the evidence by which that result is produced is called the proof. The general rule is that the burden of proof lies on the party who asserts the affirmative of the issue or question in dispute. When that party adduces evidence sufficient to raise a presumption that what he asserts is true, he is said to shift the burden of proof: that is, his allegation is presumed to be true, unless his opponent adduces evidence to rebut the presumption. In criminal cases the standard of proof was formerly that the Jury must find the case proved "beyond reasonable doubt." It is now more usually the case that the jury is told that it must be sure of the defendants guilt. In civil cases, while the burden of proof of a fact generally remains on the person asserting that fact, the court makes its decision on "the balance of probabilities."

(2) To prove a debt is to establish the existence of a debt due from a bankrupt's estate. To prove a will is to obtain Probate of it.

(3) Proof also means the standard of strength of spirituous liquors. See the Alcoholic Liquors Duties Act 1979, ss.2, 4.

proper law of a contract. The system of law (*i.e.* whether of this country or another) by which a contract is to be interpreted. See PRIVATE INTERNATIONAL LAW.

property. That which is capable of ownership; also used as meaning a right of ownership, as "the property in the goods."

General property is that which every absolute owner has. Special property may mean: (1) that the subject-matter is incapable of being in the absolute ownership of any person, *e.g.* wild animals; (2) that the thing can only be put to a particular use, *e.g.* in the case of a bailment.

property adjustment order. See FINANCIAL PROVISION ORDERS.

property tax. See the Income and Corporation Taxes Act 1970, ss.67–79.

propositus. The person put forward, when there is a class ascertained by their relationship to a certain person, *e.g.* as regards the children of A, A is the propositus.

propound a will. To institute an action for obtaining probate in solemn form. See PROBATE.

proprietary rights. Rights of property; rights of ownership.

proprietas nuda; proprietas deducto usufructu. [Roman law.] Bare ownership; ownership without *usufruct*.

prorogation. The bringing of a session of Parliament to an end by an exercise of the royal prerogative. Bills lapse on a prorogation and must be reintroduced in the new session.

prosecutor. A person who takes proceedings against another in the name of the Crown; usually either the person injured, or the police, or in graver crimes the Director of Public Prosecutions.

prospectus. A document setting forth the nature and objects of an issue of shares, debentures, or other securities created by a company or corporation, and inviting the public to subscribe to the issue. See Companies Act 1948, s.455. See also *ibid.* ss.37–46.

267

prostitution. It is an offence, punishable with fine and imprisonment, for a common prostitute to loiter or solicit in a street or public place for the purpose of prostitution (Street Offences Act 1959, s.1). It is a misdemeanour for a man, knowingly to live wholly or in part on the earnings of prostitution (Sexual Offences Act 1956, ss.30–32; Street Offences Act 1959, s.4; *Shaw* v. *D.P.P.* [1962] A.C. 220). Prostitution is not confined to sexual connection, but includes participation in physical acts of indecency with men (*R.* v. *Webb* [1964] 1 Q.B. 357). See IMMORALITY.

protected tenancy. A tenancy under which a dwelling house, or part of a dwelling house, is let as a separate dwelling. Unless it falls within one of the exceptions specified in the Rent Act 1977 it is protected by the Act as to the grounds on which the landlord may recover possession and the rent payable.

protection. See COURT OF PROTECTION.

protection order. See DOMESTIC PROCEEDINGS.

protective award. An award made by an Industrial Tribunal on the ground that an employer has failed to consult trade union representatives with regard to redundancies whereby the employer is ordered to pay remuneration to employees for a specified period (Employment Protection Act 1975, ss.99 and 101).

protective trust. A trust for life, or any less period, of the beneficiary, which is to be determined in certain events such as the bankruptcy of the beneficiary, whereupon the trust income is to be applied for the maintenance, etc., of the beneficiary and his family at the absolute discretion of the trustees (see Trustee Act 1925, s.33).

Illegitimate children may benefit (Family Law Reform Act 1969, s.15(3)). As to capital transfer tax, see the Finance Act 1975, Sched. 5, para. 18.

A person may now, however, make a settlement of his own property on himself defeasible in the event of his bankruptcy.

protector of a settlement. A person without whose consent a tenant in tail cannot bar the entail except as against his own issue, nor a tenant in base fee enlarge his estate into a fee simple. In the absence of a protector specially appointed by the settlor, the original owner of the first life estate is the protector (Fines and Recoveries Act 1833, s.22). By the Law of Property Act 1925 estates tail take effect as equitable interests, and all statutory provisions relating to estates tail in real property shall apply to entailed interests in personal property (s.130).

protectorate, British. An area the soil of which does not belong to the Crown, but the foreign relations of which are subject to its control, based on agreement by treaty, grant, capitulation, etc. The Crown legislates for protectorates by Order in Council (Foreign Jurisdiction Act 1890, s.1). The inhabitants rank as "British protected persons" (*q.v.*). (See the British Protectorates, Protected States and Protected Persons Order in Council 1974.)

protest. (1) An express declaration by a person doing an act that the act is not to give rise to an implication which it might otherwise cause, *e.g.* that payment of money is not to imply a debt.

(2) A solemn declaration by a notary stating that he has demanded acceptance or payment of a bill, and that it has been refused, with the reasons, if any, given by the drawee or acceptor for the dishonour. The object of a protest is to give satisfactory evidence of the dishonour to the drawer or other antecedent party; but it is not necessary except in the case of a foreign bill.

(3) A written statement by the master of a ship, attested by a notary public or consul, of the circumstances under which an injury happened to his ship or cargo.

(4) A payment under protest is one made by A on demand by B, where A denies the money is due from him, with a view to its later recovery.

prothonotary. A principal notary; a chief clerk. The title was borne by three officers of the Common Pleas and by one officer of the King's Bench, who were analogous to the modern Master.

protocols. The minutes or records of the proceedings of an international conference, or drafts, signed by the delegates, to serve as the basis for the final instrument.

province. A district subject to an Archbishop's jurisdiction. England is divided into the two provinces of Canterbury and York.

Provisional Orders. Orders made by a Minister, in pursuance of statutory powers, on the application of a local authority or statutory undertaker, in place of private Bills. They are inoperative until confirmed by an Act of Parliament.

proviso. A clause in a deed or other instrument beginning "provided always that" (in Latin, *proviso semper*).

proviso (criminal appeals). By applying the proviso to section 2(1) of the Criminal Justice Act 1968 the Court of Appeal (Criminal Division) or the House of Lords may dismiss an appeal even if satisfied that the appellant has succeeded on a point of law if they consider that no miscarriage of justice has actually occurred.

provocation. Acts which are sufficient to prevent the exercise of reason and to deprive a reasonable man of his self-control, so negativing the existence of malice, and thus reducing the crime of homicide from murder to manslaughter.

Where on a charge of murder there is evidence of provocation, the question whether the provocation was enough to make a reasonable man do as he did is to be left to the jury to determine, they take into account all that was both done and said (Homicide Act 1957, s.3). However in *R. v. Camplin* [1978] A.C. 705 it was held that the jury is required to consider the effect of the provocation on a person of the age, sex and characteristics of the accused and not merely on a hypothetical "reasonable man."

Provost-Marshal. An officer appointed by general officers commanding to secure the prompt repression of all offences committed abroad, to arrest and detain for trial persons subject to military law committing offences, and to execute punishments ordered by courts-martial. In the Navy, a senior member of the ship's police is appointed provost-marshal when a court-martial is to be held. He arrests the accused and produces him to the court.

proxy. A lawfully constituted agent; a person deputed to vote for another. Under the Companies Act 1948, it denotes (1) a person appointed to represent another at a meeting or number of meetings; (2) the instrument containing the appointment.

prudentium responsa. [Roman law.] The answers of the wise. The opinions of the jurisconsults; restricted by the Law of Citation (A.D. 426) to Papinian, Paul, Gaius, Ulpian and Modestinus.

pubertas. [Roman law.] The legal age of puberty, 14 for males and 12 for females. *Plena pubertas* was fixed at 18, when the body was regarded as fully developed.

pubertati proximi. [Roman law.] Children in the stage prior to puberty.

public authorities. Bodies exercising public functions such as local authorities (*q.v.*). The Law Reform (Limitation of Actions, etc.) Act 1954, s.1 assimilated proceedings against public authorities to other cases.

public document. A document made for the purpose of the public making use of it, *e.g.* registers kept by public officers, judicial records, etc. A record kept for the information of the Crown and the executive, however, is not a public document and production of it in court can be refused if it is considered contrary to the public interest to produce it. The contents of a public document are proved by producing the document itself for inspection from the proper custody and identifying it as what it purports to be, or an examined copy. An entry by a public officer in a public document is presumed to be true when made and is receivable as evidence accordingly.

public examination. See EXAMINATION, PUBLIC.

public-house. Premises licensed for the sale of intoxicating liquor over the counter as in a shop. No one has a right to insist on being served. See INNKEEPER.

public lending right. A scheme under which authors are enabled to receive annual payments in respect of loans of their books from Public libraries (Public Lending Right Scheme 1982 (Commencement) Order 1982 (S.I. 1982 No. 719)).

public limited company. See COMPANIES.

public meeting. A public meeting may be held on private property by licence, but there is no right to cause obstruction to a highway (*Arrowsmith* v. *Jenkins* [1963] 2 Q.B. 561). To create disorder in order to prevent the transaction of business at a lawful meeting is an offence punishable summarily (Public Meeting Act 1908; Public Order Acts 1936 and 1963; Criminal Law Act 1977, ss.15, 30, 31).

No public meeting can be held within one mile of Westminster Hall during a session of Parliament (Seditious Meetings Act 1817).

A lawful assembly is not rendered unlawful merely because the participants know that the unlawful acts of other persons hostile to the assembly will probably cause a breach of the peace (*Beatty* v. *Gillbanks* (1882) 9 Q.B.D. 308; 15 Cox C.C. 138), but the participants in an otherwise lawful assembly whose procedure is calculated to incite or provoke a breach of the peace may be restrained from holding their meetings (*Wise* v. *Dunning* [1902] 1 K.B. 167). See also *Thomas* v. *Sawkins* [1935] 2 K.B. 249; *Duncan* v. *Jones* [1936] 1 K.B. 218.

Newspaper reports of public meetings enjoy qualified privilege (Defamation Act 1952, s.7(1), Sched., Part II, para. 9).

public mischief. At common law a misdemeanour committed by a person wilfully interfering with the course of justice by an act or attempt which tends to the prejudice of the community. Since it was held that such cases should be regarded as part of the law of conspiracy (*R.* v. *Newland* [1954] 1 K.B. 529) and the offence of conspiracy at common law is abolished (Criminal Law Act 1977, s.5(1); see CONSPIRACY), the offence seems no longer to exist. Wasting police time is a separate statutory offence (Criminal Law Act 1967, s.5). See also PERVERTING THE COURSE OF JUSTICE.

public nuisance. Causing substantial annoyance to the subjects of the Crown by exposing to danger, or in other ways affecting injuriously, their lives, health, property or morals, is a common law misdemeanour. See IMMORALITY.

public officer. (1) The holder of a public office under the Crown, or public agent. (2) An officer of a joint stock company or corporation, such as a director.

public order. It is an offence to use threatening, abusive, or insulting words or behaviour in public with intent to provoke a breach of the peace, or whereby a breach of the peace if likely to be caused: Public Order Act 1936, s.5, as amended by the Public Order Act 1963. The 1936 Act also proscribed private uniforms and armies (ss.1–3; Criminal Jurisdiction Act 1975, Sched. 5). See also Race Relations Act 1976, s.70(2).

public policy. Certain classes of acts are said to be against public policy, or against the policy of the law, when the law refuses to enforce or recognise them on the ground that they have a mischievous tendency so as to be injurious to the interests of the State or the community. Thus, trading with an enemy, marriage-brocage contracts, and agreements in general restraint of marriage or trade, are instances of acts against public policy (see *Egerton* v. *Brownlow* (1853) 4 H.L.C. 1). However, "you are not to extend arbitrarily those rules which say that a given contract is void as being against public policy, because if there is one thing which, more than another, public policy requires, it is that men of full age and competent understanding shall have the utmost liberty of contracting" (*per* Jessel M.R., *Printing, etc., Co.* v. *Sampson* (1875) L.R. 19 Eq. 462, at p. 465. See also *Fender* v. *Mildmay* [1938] A.C. 1).

A disposition in favour of illegitimate children not in being when the disposition takes effect is not against public policy (Family Law Reform Act 1969, s.15(7)).

It is contrary to public policy to disclose in evidence the source of information given to the police, but not to journalists. See also CROWN PRIVILEGE; ILLEGAL; RESTRICTIVE TRADE PRACTICES.

Public Prosecutor. The Director of Public Prosecutions (*q.v.*).

Public Records. The General Records of the Realm which are kept at the Record Office in the custody of, formerly, the Master of the Rolls but now, by virtue of the Public Records Act 1958, the Lord Chancellor. Copies purporting to be sealed with the seal of the Record Office are admissable as evidence (s.9). Public records are not available for public inspection until 30 years old (s.5; Public Records Act 1967).

Public Trustee. The official appointed by the Lord Chancellor under the Public Trustee Act 1906. He is a corporation sole, and the State is responsible for his breaches of trust. He may act as a custodian, ordinary or judicial trustee, either solely, or jointly.

publication. For the purposes of the Copyright Act 1956 publication in relation to any work means the issue of copies of the work to the public.

In any action of libel or slander the plaintiff must show that the defamatory words were actually published, that is to say, brought to the knowledge of some person other than the plaintiff. In criminal proceedings for libel, however, publication to the prosecutor himself is sufficient.

publici juris. [Of public right.] *e.g.* the right to light and air.

puis darrein continuance. A plea in which the defendant pleaded some matter of defence which had arisen "since the last continuance" or adjournment. See Ord. 18, r. 9.

puisne. [Later born, or younger.] A puisne judge means a judge of the High Court of Justice other than the Lord Chancellor, the Lord Chief Justice of England, and the President of the Family Division. The puisne judges are styled "Justices of the High Court" (Supreme Court Act 1981, s.4(2)).

puisne mortgage. Any legal mortgage not protected by a deposit of documents of title (Land Charges Act 1972, s.2, Class C.).

pupillus. [Roman law.] A person *sui juris*, under the age of puberty, whose affairs are managed, and whose want of legal capacity is supplied, by a tutor.

pur autre vie. [For the life of another.] See TENANT PUR AUTRE VIE.

purchase. To acquire land by lawful act, *e.g.* by conveyance, gift or devise, as opposed to title by act of the law, such as descent, dower, curtesy, inclosure, partition; and to title by wrong, as in disseisin.

purchaser. (1) One who acquires land by purchase (*q.v.*). (2) The opposite party, in a transaction of sale, to the vendor. (3) In the Law of Property Act 1925, s.205(1)(xxvi), "purchaser" means a purchaser in good faith for valuable consideration and includes a lessee, mortgagee, etc.

purgation. To make clean: the modes by which a man accused of crime acquitted himself. They were compurgation, the ordeal, and trial by battle.

purpresture. Inclosure.

purveyance. The Crown's prerogative right, at an appraised price, to buy up provisions and other necessaries for the Royal Household, and of impressing horses and vehicles for the royal use.

purview. That part of a statute which provides or enacts, as opposed to the preamble; the scope or policy of a statute.

putative father. The person alleged to be the father of a bastard child in proceedings for an affiliation order.

Q

Q.C. Queen's Counsel. (*q.v.*)

Q.V.(Quod vide). [Which see.]

qua. [In the capacity of; as.]

quae non valeant singula, juncta juvant. [Words which are of no effect by themselves are effective when combined.]

quaelibet concessio fortissime contra donatorem interpretanda est. [Every grant is to be construed as strongly as possible against the grantor.]

qualified property. The interest of a bailee in the goods bailed. The bailee has the right to possession, and the rights annexed to possession. He is therefore said to have a special or qualified property or ownership in the goods, as contrasted with the general property or ownership of the owner.

qualified title. A title registered subject to an excepted estate, right, or interest arising before a specified date or under a specified instrument, or otherwise particularly described in the register (Land Registration Act 1925, s.7).

quality. (1) The nature of an estate (*q.v.*) as regards the certainty of its duration. (2) Status.

quality or fitness. As to the implied undertakings of quality or fitness on a sale of goods, see the Sale of Goods Act 1979, s.14; Supply of Goods (Implied Terms) Act 1973, ss.3, 7(2), 10; Consumer Credit Act 1974, Sched. 4, para. 35.

quamdiu se bene gesserit. [During good behaviour.]

quando acciderint. [When it happens.] A judgment to be levied when assets come into the hands of a personal representative *in futuro*. It may be given where the personal representative, on being sued for a debt of the deceased person, pleads *plene administravit* (*q.v.*).

quando aliquid mandatur, mandatur et omne per quod pervenitur ad illud. [When anything is commanded, everything by which it can be accomplished is also commanded.]

quando aliquid prohibetur fieri, prohibetur ex directo et per obliquum. [When the doing of anything is forbidden, then the doing of it either directly or indirectly is forbidden.]

quando duo jura in una persona concurrunt, aequum est ac si essent diversis. [When two titles concur in one person, it is the same as if they were in different persons.]

quando jus domini regis et subditi concurrent, jus regis praeferri debet. [When the titles of the King and of the subject concur, that of the King is to be preferred.]

quando lex aliquid alicui concedit, concedere videtur id sine quo res ipsa esse non potest. [When the law gives anything to anyone, it gives also all those things without which the thing itself could not exist.]

quando plus fit quam fieri debet, videtur etiam illud fieri quod faciendum est. [When more is done than ought to be done, then that is considered to have been done which ought to have been done.]

quantity. The nature of an estate (*q.v.*) with regard to the time of its duration.

quantum meruit. [As much as he has earned.] Where one person has expressly or impliedly requested another to render him a service without specifying any remuneration, but the circumstances of the request imply that the service is to be paid for, there is implied a promise to pay *quantum meruit, i.e.* so much as the party doing the service deserves. If a person by the terms of a contract is to do a certain piece of work for a lump sum, and he does only part of the work, or something different, he cannot claim under the contract, but he may be able to claim on a *quantum meruit,* as, *e.g.* if completion has been prevented by the act of the other party to the contract.

A claim on a *quantum meruit* also arises when work has been done and accepted under a void contract believed to be valid (*Craven-Ellis* v. *Cannons Ltd.* [1936] 2 K.B. 403).

A claim on a *quantum meruit* may be indorsed on a writ as a debt or liquidated demand under Ord. 6, r.2.

quantum ramifactus. [The amount of damage suffered.]

quantum valebant. [As much as they were worth.] An action analogous to *quantum meruit* (*q.v.*), but brought in regard to goods supplied.

quarantine (40 days). (1) The period which persons coming from a country or ship in which an infectious disease is prevalent are obliged to wait before being permitted to land. Dogs and cats brought into this country must be quarantined for nine months. (2) The period during which a widow was entitled to remain in her husband's dwelling-house after his death.

quare impedit. [Wherefore he hinders.] An ancient writ which lies by him who being in possession of an advowson of a church is disturbed in his presentation of it (Coke). It was abolished by the Common Law Procedure Act 1860.

quarta Antonina or **quarta d. Pii.** [Roman law.] An adrogated son under puberty if disinherited, or emancipated wihout lawful cause, received back all the property he had brought to the adrogator or acquired for him; and also one-fourth of the adrogator's property, as enacted by Antoninus Pius.

quarter sessions. A court of record held before two or more justices of the peace as often as necessary, and at least four times a year (except London), for execution of the authority given them by the commission of the peace and certain statutes. Courts of quarter sessions were abolished on January 1, 1972 (Courts Act 1971, s.3). The appellate etc. jurisdiction of the court has been transferred to the Crown Court; administrative functions were transferred to local authorities (ss.8, 56, Scheds. 1, 8–10).

quarter-days. Christmas Day (December 25), Lady Day (March 25), Midsummer Day (June 24) and Michaelmas (September 29).

quash. To discharge or set aside, *e.g.* a wrongful conviction.

quasi. [As if it were.]

quasi-contract. The term is an abbreviation of the *obligatio quasi ex contractu* of Roman law. It is an obligation not created by, but similar to that created by contract, and is independent of the consent of the person bound. Thus, in Roman law, if a person left his property without anyone to look after it, a stranger might undertake the care of it, and had a right of action against the owner for his expenses (*actio negotiorum gestorum*). Compare salvage (*q.v.*) in English law.

The basis of the action for money had and received is thought to be rooted in quasi-contract on the footing of an implied promise to repay (see *per* Lord Sumner in *Sinclair* v. *Brougham* [1914] A.C. 398). The other view is that in the action for money had and received liability is based on unjust benefit or enrichment, *i.e.* that action is applicable wherever the defendant has received money which, in justice and equity, belongs to the plaintiff under circumstances which render the receipt of it by the defendant a receipt to the use of the plaintiff.

But Lord Porter in *Reading* v. *Att.-Gen.* [1951] A.C. 507 at p.514 said that, as yet, the doctrine of unjust enrichment forms no part of English law. But perhaps an implied contract to repay should be found in favour of the plaintiff where the defendant has been improperly enriched at his expense (Sir C. K. Allen). But the *rationale* of quasi-contract is still undetermined (Cheshire and Fifoot).

quasi-easement. The implied right of the grantee of part of a tenement to all those easements which are necessary to the reasonable enjoyment of his property, and which are at the time of the grant enjoyed by the grantor in respect of the whole tenement for the benefit of the part granted (see *Wheeldon* v. *Burrows* (1879) 12 Ch.D. 71).

quasi-entail. This exists when an estate *pur autre vie* is limited to a person and the heirs of his body.

quasi-judicial. Executive powers or functions which involve the exercise of a discretion and the making of a decision in a judicial manner; as *e.g.* where a Minister makes an order after consideration of the findings of an inquiry which involves the hearing of evidence. See NATURAL JUSTICE.

quasi-trustee. A person who, without authority, has taken it on himself to act as a trustee, and is held liable as though he were a trustee.

que estate. See PRESCRIPTION.

Queen. A Queen Regnant is a reigning Sovereign in her own right. A Queen Consort is the wife of the Sovereign; and Queen Dowager or Queen Mother is the widow of a deceased Sovereign.

Queen Anne's Bounty. By the statute 2 & 3 Anne, c. 20, the Governors of the Bounty of Queen Anne for the Augmentation of the Maintenance of the Poor Clergy were appointed to receive the first fruits and tenths, hitherto payable to the Crown, and apply them for the benefit of the poor clergy. The First Fruits and Tenths Measure 1926, however, provided for the extinguishment or redemption of first fruits and tenths. The Tithe Act 1925 transferred to Queen Anne's Bounty ecclesiastical tithe rentcharge (Tithe Act 1936; and see Sched. 8). By the Church Commissioners Measure 1947, Queen Anne's Bounty and the Ecclesiastical Commissioners were united under the name of the Church Commissioners.

Queens Bench Division. One of the three Divisions of the High Court, consisting of the Lord Chief Justice (*q.v.*) and puisne judges (*q.v.*).
See Supreme Court Act 1981, s.5(1)(*b*); Sched. 1(2).

Queen's Counsel. Barristers "learned in the law" who have been appointed Counsel to Her Majesty on the recommendation of the Lord Chancellor. They wear silk gowns, sit within the bar, and take precedence in court over "utter barristers" (*i.e.* outer barristers; junior barristers). A licence or permission to plead is not now required when a Q.C. is instructed to appear on behalf of a defendant against the Crown. He is called a "leader" when he is retained to conduct a case in court, and lead the "juniors" instructed to appear with him.

Queen's evidence. A prisoner who, instead of being put upon trial, is permitted by the Crown to give evidence againt those associated with him in crime, on the understanding that he will go free, is said to turn Queen's evidence. See ACCOMPLICE.

Queen's proctor. The Treasury Solicitor who represents the Crown in the Family Division. His main function is to intervene to show cause why a decree nisi should not be made absolute because material facts have not been disclosed (Matrimonial Causes Act 1973, ss.8, 9, 15). He shows cause by entering an appearance in the suit and filing his plea setting out his case.
His assistance may be invoked by the court itself by investigating the circumstances of a case, or to argue a difficult point of law (Matrimonial Causes Act 1973, s.8). Counsel are instructed for the latter purpose.

Queen's regulations and orders for the Army are issued by the Crown, for the government of the Army, the command of the Army being a branch of the Royal Prerogative.

Queen's Remembrancer performed duties connected with recoveries of penalties and debts due to the Crown; he kept the documents relating to the passing of lands to and from the Crown; and he had functions in connection with English Bills. See BILL OF COMPLAINT. He was transferred to the Central Office and made a Master of the Supreme Court. His duties as Queen's Remembrancer now consist, *inter alia,* of certain functions connected with the selection of sheriffs (*q.v.*), the swearing in of the Lord Mayor of London, and proceedings by the Crown on the Revenue side of the Queen's Bench Division. He is the Senior Master (Judicature Act 1925, s.122; Courts Act 1971, s.26(3)).

querela. Any civil proceedings in any court. See AUDITA QUERELA.

qui facit per alium facit per se. [He who acts through another is deemed to act in person.] A principal is liable for the acts of his agents.

qui haeret in litera haeret in cortice. [He who sticks in the letter sticks in the bark.] *i.e.* he does not get at the substance or the meaning.

qui jure suo utitur neminem laedit. [He who exercises his legal right inflicts upon no one any injury.]

qui jussu judicis aliquod fecerit non videtur dolo malo fecisse quia parere necesse est. [He who does anything by command of a judge will not be supposed to have acted from an improper motive; because there is an obligation to obey.]

qui omne dicit nihil excludit. [He who says everything excludes nothing.]

qui per alium facit, per seipsum facere videtur. [He who does anything by another is deemed to have done it himself.]

qui prior est tempore potior est jure. [He who is first in time has the strongest claim in law.]

qui sentit commodum sentire debet et onus; et e contra. [He who enjoys the benefit ought also to bear the burden; and vice versa.]

qui tacet consentire videtur. [He who is silent is deemed to consent.] A party's silence will render statements made in his presence evidence against him of their truth, when he is reasonably called on to reply, *e.g.* A said to B: "You know you always promised to marry me, and now you don't keep your word." B kept silent. *Held,* this was admissible in evidence to prove the promise of marriage (*Bessela* v. *Stern* (1887) 2 C.P.D. 265).

qui tam pro domino rege quam pro si ipso in hac parte sequitur. [Who sues on behalf of our Lord the King as well as for himself.] An action brought by an informer. See PENAL ACTION.

qui vult decipi decipiatur. [If a man wants to be deceived, then let him be deceived.]

quia emptores. [Because purchasers.] The statute 18 Edw. 1, c. 1—the statute of Westminster III—which commences with these words. It enacted that every freeman should be at liberty to sell his lands, but that the purchaser should hold them of the feoffor's lord and not of the feoffer. The statute therefore abolished subinfeudation (*q.v.*), and made the future creation of manors, etc., impossible.

quia timet. [Because he fears.] A *quia timet* action is one by which a person may obtain an injunction to prevent or restrain some threatened act being done which, if done, would cause him substantial damage, and for which money would be no adequate or sufficient remedy.

quicquid plantatur solo, solo cedit. [Whatever is affixed to the soil belongs to the soil.]

275

quicquid solvitur, solvitur secundum modum solventis; quicquid recipitur, recipitur secundum modum recipientis. [Whatever is paid, is paid according to the intention or manner of the party paying; whatever is received, is received according to the intention or manner of the party receiving.]

quid pro quo. [Something for something.] Consideration (*q.v.*).

quiet enjoyment. The right of a grantee of property (and of any person deriving title from him) to enter upon and remain in enjoyment of the property without any lawful interruption or disturbance by or on behalf of the person conveying the property to him, or by, through, or under any person through whom the person conveying derives title, otherwise than by purchase for value (Law of Property Act 1925, Sched. 2, Part I). See COVENANTS FOR TITLE.

quietare. To quit, discharge or save harmless.

quietus. A discharge granted by the Crown or its officer to a person indebted to the Crown, *e.g.* an accountant or sheriff.

quietus redditus. [Quit rent.] See RENT.

quilibet potest renunciare juri pro se introducto. [Every man is entitled to renounce a right introduced in his favour.]

quit rent. See RENT.

quittance. An acquittance (*q.v.*).

quo ligatur, eo dissolvitur. [Whatsoever binds can also release.]

quo minus. [By which the less.] The initial words of the writ by means of which the Court of Exchequer obtained its extended jurisdiction. It permitted the plaintiff to plead that he was debtor of the King, and by reason of the cause of action pleaded he had become less able to pay his fictitious debt to the King.

quo warranto. [By what authority.] A high prerogative writ by the Crown against one who claimed or usurped any office, franchise or liberty, to inquire by what authority he supported his claim. It lay also in cases of non-user, or mis-user, of a franchise, or where any public trust was executed without authority. The writ was supplanted by the "information in the nature of a writ of *quo warranto*," which could be brought with the leave of the court, at the relation of a private person. It was a civil proceeding (Judicature Act 1925, s.48). These informations were abolished by the Administration of Justice (Miscellaneous Provisions) Act 1938, s.9 and proceedings by way of injunction substituted. Applications for injunctions similar to quo warranto proceedings should now be brought as applications for judicial review under Ord. 53 (see JUDICIAL REVIEW).

quoad hoc. [Regarding this.]

quod ab initio non valet, in tractu temporis non convalescit. [That which is bad from the beginning does not improve by length of time.]

quod aedificatur in area legata cedit legato. [That which is built on ground that is devised passes to the devisee.]

quod contra legam fit, pro infecto habetur. [What is done contrary to law is deemed not to have been done at all.]

quod fieri non debet, factum valet. [A thing which ought not to have been done may nevertheless be perfectly valid when it is done.]

quod non apparet non est. [That which does not appear does not exist.]

quod nullius est, est domini regis. [That which is the property of nobody, belongs to our Lord the King.]

quod per me non possum, nec per alium. [What I cannot do in person, I cannot do by proxy.]

quod prius est verius; et quod prius est tempore potius est jure. [What is first is truer; and what is first in time is better in law.]

quod semel meum est amplius meum esse non potest. [What is once mine cannot be more fully mine.]

quod semel placuit in electione, amplius displicere non potest. [Where election is once made it cannot be revoked.]

quorum. [Of whom.] The minimum number of persons which constitutes a valid formal meeting.

quoties in verbis nulla est ambiguitas ibi nulla expositio contra verba expressa fienda est. [When in the words there is no ambiguity then no interpretation contrary to the actual words is to be adopted.]

quousque. [Until.] When a copyhold tenant died intestate his heir was bound to come to the lord of the manor for admittance within a certain time and pay the fine due on admittance. If he did not appear the lord might seize the land "quousque" (*i.e.* until he did appear) and enjoy the rents and profits in the meantime.

R

R.: Reg., the Queen; or **R.: Rex,** the King.

race relations. The Race Relations Act 1976:

(a) defines racial discrimination (s.1(1)), discrimination by way of victimisation (s.2(1)) and ('racial grounds') and groups (s.3);

(b) makes racial discrimination unlawful in the employment field (ss.4–16), in education (ss.17–19), and in provision of goods, facilities or services (ss.20–27);

(c) set up the commission for Racial Equality and defined its powers and duties (ss.43–52). The commission must work towards the elimination of discrimination, promote equality of opportunity and monitor the working of the Act. Detailed procedures are laid down for investigations of complaints and proceedings for breaches of the Act;

(d) amends the Public Order Act 1936 by stating that a person commits an offence if he publishes or distributes or uses in public words or written matter which is or are threatening, abusive or insulting, where hatred is likely to be stirred up against any racial group in Great Britain by the matter or words in question (s.70).

rack-rent. The rent at which a property is worth to be let by the year in the open market, *i.e.* what a tenant, taking one year with another, might fairly and reasonably be expected to pay, the tenant paying tenant's rates and taxes, and the landlord doing repairs.

railways. For the British Railways Board see the Transport Act 1962; Transport Act 1968; Railways Act 1974.

Railway and Canal Commission. A court established by the Railway and Canal Traffic Act 1888, having jurisdiction in matters directly relating to railways and canals, and also as regards the construction of telegraphs and the water supply of London. It was abolished by the Railway and Canal Commission (Abolition) Act 1949, which transferred its functions to the High Court.

rank. (1) A claim to a prescriptive payment, such as a *modus* (*q.v.*), which is excessive, and therefore void. (2) Order in precedence, or priority.

rape. (1) Divisions of the county of Sussex, *viz.* Chichester, Arundel, Bramber, Lewes, Pevensey and Hastings. They appear to have been military governments in early Norman times. (2) A man commits rape if he has unlawful sexual intercourse with a woman who at the time of the intercourse does not consent, knowing that she does not consent or being reckless as to whether she consents

(Sexual Offences (Amendment) Act 1976, s.1(1). For a definition of "reckless" see *R.* v. *Pigg* [1982] 1 W.L.R. 762, C.A.). Limitations are placed on cross-examination of a complainant regarding her sexual experience (Act of 1976, s.2(1); *R.* v. *Viola, The Times,* May 13, 1982) and on reporting of names of parties (s.4). Maximum penalties are life imprisonment for rape and seven years' imprisonment for attempted rape. For the purpose of this offence intercourse is deemed complete upon proof of penetration (Sexual Offences Act 1956, s.44). Other than in most exceptional circumstances, rape must be punished by an immediate custodial sentence (*R.* v. *Roberts* [1982] 1 All E.R. 609, C.A., *per* Lord Lane C.J.).

rate. A sum assessed or made payable by a local authority in respect of the occupation of property in proportion to its value (*pro rata,* hence "rate"). Provision was made by the Rating and Valuation Act 1925 for the consolidation of the various pre-existing rates, *e.g.* poor rate, district rate, into one "general rate" for a district. The law is contained in the Local Government Act 1974, s.11 *et seq. See also* LOCAL GOVERNMENT.

rate of exchange. Where the consideration for a contract is expressed in a foreign currency but damages have to be awarded by the English Courts, the court must determine the currency of the contract and award damages in that currency, any conversion to sterling for the enforcement of the judgment being carried out at the commencement of the enforcement proceedings (*The Despina R.* [1979] 1 All E.R. 421, H.L.).

ratification. The act of adopting a contract, or other transaction, by a person who was not bound by it originally, *e.g.* because it was entered into by an unauthorised agent. Ratification cannot take place where the party who professes to ratify a transaction was not in existence when it took place (*Kelner* v. *Baxter* [1866] L.R. 2 C.P. 174), nor unless the agent manifested the intention to contract on behalf of the pincipal at the time (*Keighley, Maxted & Co.* v. *Durant* [1901] A.C. 240). See PRINCIPAL.

Ratification of a treaty is a formal ceremony whereby some time after a treaty has been signed, solemn confirmations of it are exchanged by the contracting parties. No treaty is, normally, binding without ratification.

ratio decidendi. [The reason (or ground) of a judicial decision.] It is the *ratio decidendi* of a case which makes the decision a precedent for the future.

ratione soli. [By reason only.]

ratione tenurae. By reason or in respect of his tenure.

ravishment. The tortious act of taking away a wife from her husband, or a ward from her guardian. Popularly, rape (*q.v.*).

re. [In the matter of.]

real property. [*res,* a thing.] Lands, tenements, and hereditaments. Immovable property which could be recovered by a real action.

real representative. The person on whom the real property of a deceased person devolved immediately upon death. The Land Transfer Act 1897, s.1 enacted that realty should vest in the personal repesentative, *i.e.* an executor or administrator of a deceased person.

The Administration of Estates Act 1925, s.13 provided that representation may be granted in respect of real estate, either separately, or together with personal estate, or in respect of realty only, where there is no personalty, or in respect of a trust estate only.

real securities. Securities charged on land.

realty. Real property (*q.v.*).

rebut. To repel, defeat or take away the effect of something, *e.g.* to disprove a presumption.

rebutter. See PLEADINGS.

recaption. A remedy by act of the party which may be resorted to when a man has deprived another of his goods, or wrongfully detains his wife, child, or servant: then the person injured may lawfully claim and retake them, but not so as to cause a breach of the peace.

receditur a placitus juris potius quam injuriae et delicta maneant impunita. [We dispense with the forms of law rather than that crimes and wrongs should be unpunished.]

receipt. An acknowledgment of the receipt of money paid in discharge of a debt. A receipt under hand alone is in general only prima facie evidence, but a receipt under seal amounts to an estoppel, and is conclusive.

receiver. (1) A person appointed by the court on an interlocutory application, to receive the rents and profits of real estate, or to get in personal property affected by proceedings in lieu of the person then having the control of the property, to protect the property until the right of the parties have been ascertained. In an action for the dissolution of a partnership a receiver is frequently appointed to realise the partnership assets. A receiver is an officer of the court and generally has to give security for the due performance of his duties. See Ord. 30.

(2) In bankruptcy the official receiver may be appointed interim receiver, at any time after the presentation of the petition, if that course be necessary for the preservation of the estate, and it is his duty to act as interim receiver after adjudication until a trustee is appointed (Bankruptcy Act 1914, ss.8, 74).

(3) A mortgagee has the power, when the mortgage money has become due, to appoint a receiver (Law of Property Act 1925, ss.101, 109).

(4) A receiver by way of equitable execution is appointed by the court to enable a judgment creditor to obtain payment of his debt, when the debtor is in possession of property, or has an interest in property which cannot be reached by ordinary process of execution (Ord. 51).

(5) A person authorised by the Court of Protection (*q.v.*) to manage the affairs of a mental patient.

receiver of wreck. A person appointed by the Board (now Department) of Trade under the Merchant Shipping Act 1894 to take steps for the preservation of any vessel stranded or in distress within his district, and if necessary receive and take possession of it.

receiving order. The order made by the court, on presentation of a bankruptcy petition, for the protection of the debtor's estate, constituting the official receiver the interim receiver of the property of the debtor, and restraining all legal proceedings against the person or property of the bankrupt in respect of any debt provable in the bankruptcy (Bankruptcy Act 1914, ss.3, 7 *et seq.*).

receiving stolen property. See HANDLING STOLEN PROPERTY.

recitals. Statements introduced to explain or lead up to the operative part of an instrument. They are generally divided into narrative recitals, which set forth the facts on which the instrument is based; and introductory recitals, which explain the motive for the operative part. A recital commences with "Whereas."

reckless driving. A person who drives a motor vehicle on a road recklessly is guilty of an offence (Road Traffic Act 1972, ss.1, 2, as substituted by Criminal Law Act 1977, s.50(1)). The court must be satisfied (1) that the defendant drove in such a manner as to create an obvious and serious risk of physical injury to another road user or doing substantial damage to property and (2) that he did so without having given any thought to the possibility of such risk or, having recognised the risk, had nonetheless gone on to take it (*R. v. Lawrence* [1981] 1 All E.R. 974, H.L.).

recognisance. An obligation or bond acknowledged before some court of record or authorised officer, and afterwards enrolled in some court of record (*q.v.*). The person bound by it is called the conusor (or cognisor), and the person in whose favour it is made, the conusee (or cognisee). The object of a recognisance is to secure the performance of some act by the conusor, such as to appear in court, to keep the peace, or be of good behaviour. See BINDING OVER. For the powers of the court in relation to forfeited recognisances see the Powers of Criminal Courts Act 1973, ss.31, 32. See BAIL.

recognitors. The jurors in an assize of novel disseisin or the like.

reconversion. The notional or imaginary process by which a prior constructive or notional conversion is annulled or discharged, and the notionally converted property restored in contemplation of equity to its original quality.

Reconversion by operation of law occurs where there is no act or declaration of the parties: if the obligation to lay out money in land and the right to call for the money vest in the same person, the obligation is at an end, and the property is "at home" or reconverted.

reconveyance. The deed of conveyance by which the mortgagee's estate in mortgaged land revested in the mortgagor on payment of the mortgage debt. Since January 1, 1926, a mortgage, whenever executed, may be discharged by a receipt, in the prescribed form indorsed on, written at the foot of, or annexed to, the mortgage deed (Law of Property Act 1925, s.115); there is no need for reassignment because when the money secured by a mortgage has been discharged the mortgage term becomes a satisfied term and ceases (*ibid.* s.116).

record. (1) An authentic memorial peserved by a court or the legislature. (2) Formerly the official statement of the writ and pleadings for the use of the judge in a common law action. See PUBLIC RECORDS.

record, conveyances by. Conveyances of land effected by a judicial or legislative act, as evidenced by the record, *e.g.* fines, or an Act of Parliament.

record, trial by. Where in an action one party alleged and the other party denied the existence of a record, there was the issue known as *Nul Tiel* record (*q.v.*), and the court would thereupon order a trial by inspection and examination of the record. Failing proof of the record, judgment was given for the party who had denied its existence.

recordari facias loquelam. A writ used to remove a suit from an inferior court not of record into one of the superior courts of common law.

recorded delivery. In general, the Recorded Delivery Service Act 1962, provides that any document or thing which by any enactment is required to be sent by registered post, may be sent either by registered post or by the recorded delivery service. See also the Post Office Act 1969, s.5.

recorder. Prior to 1972, a barrister, of five years' standing at the least, appointed by the Crown under the Municipal Corporations Act 1882, to act as a justice of the peace and sole judge in a borough court of quarter sessions.

Courts of quarter sessions were abolished by the Courts Act 1971, and their criminal jurisdiction transferred to the Crown Court (*q.v.*). The Recorders of London, Liverpool and Manchester became circuit judges (Courts Act 1971, s.16, Sched. 2). The offices of the other recorders lapsed. Paid recorders may be appointed to act as part time judges of the Crown Court. A recorder so appointed must be a barrister or solicitor of 10 years' standing (ss.4, 21). Honorary recorders may be appointed (s.54). Recorders are addressed in court as 'Your Honour.' Limitations are placed on a recorder practising at a court where he also sits. The Recorder of London is the judge of the Central Criminal Court (s.4(7)).

recovery. (1) Proceedings for the recovery of land from a person wrongfully in possession of it, are taken either in the High Court of Justice or in the county court, or before justices. In the High Court the proceedings are a substitute for the old action of ejectment (*q.v.*).

(2) A common recovery was a mode of barring estates tail. It was a judgment in a collusive suit brought by a friendly plaintiff or "demandant" against the tenant in tail. As a first step the tenant in tail conveyed his life estate to the "tenant to the *praecipe*" to allow of the writ of *praecipe* being served upon him. The tenant to the *praecipe* then vouched (*i.e.* called on) the tenant in tail to warranty, who in turn vouched the "common vouchee" (the crier of the court) on the fiction that the land had been conveyed by the common vouchee to him with warranty of title. The common vouchee admitted the fiction and craved leave to "imparl" with the tenant in tail (*i.e.* confer with him out of court). He remained out of court and judgment was given against him by default, to the effect that the land belonged to the plaintiff and that the common vouchee must give land of equal value to the tenant to the *praecipe*. The common vouchee being a man of straw, no land was forthcoming, but the land of the tenant in tail went to the plaintiff under the judgment, freed from the estate tail and the remainders and reversions expectant on it, and then the plaintiff conveyed it back to him in fee simple. Common recoveries were abolished by the Fines and Recoveries Act 1833, which substituted a simple disentailing assurance.

rectification. The correction of an error in a register or instrument, *e.g.* a conveyance or settlement, on the ground of mutual mistake, *e.g.* a clerical error, or an error in draftmanship. The court may, in such a case, at its discretion, allow the instrument to be rectified. An action may be brought in the Chancery Division for rectification (Judicature Act 1925, s.56); but every Division can give effect to a claim for rectification in any action before it.

recto de dote. A writ of right of dower which lay for a widow who alleged that she had received only part of her dower and claimed the residue against the heir of her husband.

recto de dote unde nihil habet. A writ which lay for a widow who had received no part of her dower.

rector. An officer of the Church having a benefice with cure of souls and an exclusive title to the emoluments of the living, *e.g.* tithes (*q.v.*). Since the Reformation lay rectors with vicars to perform the cure of souls have been possible; they are termed Lay Impropriators.

reddendo singula singulis. [Giving each to each.] A clause in an instrument is so read when one of two provisions in one sentence is appropriated to one of two objects in another sentence, and the other provision is similarly appropriated to the other object. Thus, "I devise and bequeath all my real and personal property to A," will be construed *reddendo singula singulis* by applying "devise" to "real property" and "bequeath" to "personal property."

reddendum. That which is to be paid or rendered. That clause in a lease which specifies the amount of the rent and the time at which it is payable.

redditus. Rents.

redemption. The paying off of a mortgage debt or charge upon property whereby the equitable interest and legal estate merge: the "buying back" of the property. An action for redemption is one brought by the mortgagor to compel the mortgagee to reconvey the property on payment of the debt and interest. See EQUITY OF REDEMPTION.

reduction into possession. The act of exercising the right conferred by a chose in action, so as to convert it into a chose in possession; thus a debt is reduced into possession by payment.

reduction of capital. A company limited by shares or guarantee and having a share capital, may, if so authorised by its articles, by special resolution reduce its capital, which must be confirmed by an order of the court on petition in the Chancery Division. The company may be required to add the words "and reduced" to its name (Companies Act 1948, ss.66–71A).

redundancy. Dismissal of employee whose job has ceased to exist. Subject to minimum periods of employment and other regulations such dismissal employees are entitled to redundancy payments to compensate for loss of the job. See Employment Protection (Consolidation) Act 1978, Pt. VI.

re-entry. See RIGHT OF ENTRY.

reeve. An officer or steward, *e.g.* the shire-reeve or sheriff.

re-examination. See EXAMINATION.

re-exchange. See RATE OF EXCHANGE.

re-extent. A second execution by extent in respect of the same debt. See EXTENT.

referee. (1) A person to whom a question is referred for his decision or opinion; an arbitrator. Official referees were appointed under the Administration of Justice Act 1956, but the office was abolished by the Courts Act 1971, s.25 and the functions of official referees are discharged by circuit judges.

(2) Referees on private bills are members appointed by the House of Commons to report on questions of *locus standi* (*q.v.*) arising on private bills.

reference. The decision of a question by a referee (*q.v.*). See REFEREE.

reference in case of need. The name of a person indorsed on a bill of exchange to whom the bill may be presented if it is dishonoured (Bills of Exchange Act 1882, s.15).

referendum. The submission to the electorate of a proposed legislative Measure or Act, *e.g.* Referendum Act 1975, Scotland Act 1978, Wales Act 1978.

refresher. A fee paid to a counsel on the trial of an action in addition to the fee originally marked on his brief.

refreshing memory. A witness may refresh his memory while under examination, by referring to a document or memorandum made by himself, although it is not itself admissible as evidence. A witness may refresh his memory from a note written by someone else as long as he adopts it as his own, particularly if he does so by signing it (*Gorves* v. *Redbart* [1975] R.T.R. 268).

regalia. (1) The royal prerogative, or rights. (2) The Crown jewels. See JURA REGALIA.

Regency Acts provide for the exercise by a certain named person or persons, of limited Royal powers while the Sovereign is under 18 years or incapacitated by illness, absence, etc., *e.g.* the Regency Act 1953.

register of writs. The collection of the various original writs.

registered office. A company must have a registered office to which communications and notices may be addressed, notice of the situation of which, and of any change therein, must be given to the Registrar of Companies (Companies Act 1976, s.23). Service of a writ or process on a company is effected by leaving it or sending it by post to the company's registered office.

registrar. Originally an officer responsible for keeping a register, *e.g.* an officer of the Chancery Division responsible for keeping records and drawing up orders. Today the duties of registrars of the Family Division, bankruptcy registrars, county court registrars and High Court district registrars are almost wholly judicial and consist of hearing and determining interlocutory applications (*q.v.*) and some final hearings, with all the powers of a judge save for the power to commit to prison.

Registrar-General of Births, Deaths, and Marriages. The officer established by the Births and Deaths Registration Act 1836, s.2. His offices are called the General Register Office, see the Registration Service Act 1953 (a consolidating Act).

registration as British citizens, etc. A minor (*q.v.*) may become a British citizen (*q.v.*) by registration (British Nationality Act 1981, s.3). Any minor may be so registered at the discretion of the Home Secretary(s.3(1)). Certain minors born outside the United Kingdom are entitled to registration as of right if certain conditions are fulfilled (as to which see s.3(2)–(6)). A British Dependent Territories citizen (*q.v.*), a British Overseas citizen (*q.v.*), a British subject (*q.v.*) or a British protected person (*q.v.*) may also apply for registration as a British citizen under the requirements of section 4 of the Act of 1981. British Overseas Citizenship, British Dependent Territories Citizenship and the status of British subject may also be acquired by registration (see respectively ss.27 and 28, 17, and 32 and 33 of the Act of 1981).

registration of births and deaths. The Acts are consolidated in the Births and Deaths Registration Act 1953. See also the Legitimation (Re-registration of Birth) Act 1957, s.1(2); Criminal Justice Act 1967, Sched. 3, Part I; Family Law Reform Act 1969, s.27; Children Act 1975, s.93.

Registration of Business Names Act 1916. See BUSINESS NAMES.

registration of land. See LAND CHARGES; LAND REGISTRATION.

registration of marriage. Every marriage solemnised in England must be registered, if celebrated according to the rites of the Church of England, by the clergyman who solemnised it, and in other cases generally by the registrar (Marriage Act 1949, ss.53–67).

registration of title. See LAND REGISTRATION.

regnal years. See the Table of Regnal Years of the English Sovereigns, *post.*

regrating. Buying corn, etc., in any market so as to raise the price, and then selling it again in the same place.

Regulae Generales. [General Rules.] The Rules of the Supreme Court.

regulated tenancy. A protected tenancy (*q.v.*) or statutory tenancy (*q.v.*) which is not a controlled tenancy (*q.v.*) (Rent Act 1977, s.18(1); see also ss.44, 62, 66 and 67).

rehabilitation of offenders. See SPENT CONVICTION.

re-hearing. The re-arguing of a cause or matter which has been already adjudicated upon. Every appeal to the Court of Appeal is by way of re-hearing, and hence the court may receive fresh evidence *i.e.* normally if not previously available, and review the whole case (Ord. 59, r.3). But a re-hearing does not mean that the case is tried all over again: an appeal is normally a re-hearing on the documents (including the judge's notes and the transcript, if any, of the shorthand notes of the evidence).

re-insurance. The act of an insurer in relieving himself of part or the whole of the liability he had undertaken by insuring the subject-matter himself with other insurers.

Re-insurance was formerly illegal, but the Marine Insurance Act 1906, s.9(1) provides that an insurance may be effected in respect of the interest of an insurer under a contract of marine insurance.

reinstatement. When an Industrial Tribunal finds that an employee was unfairly dismissed it may order reinstatement, *i.e.* that the employer treat the employee as if he had never been dismissed (Employment Protection (Consolidation) Act 1978, s.69(2)).

rejoinder. See PLEADINGS.

relation back. The doctrine by which an act is made to produce the same effect as if it had occurred at an earlier time. Thus, an adjudication in bankruptcy relates back to the act of bankruptcy on which the receiving order was made.

If a person has an authority to enter on land, and after entering he abuses the authority, he becomes a trespasser *ab initio,* because his wrongful act relates back to the time of his entry.

relator. The private person whose name was inserted in the proceedings formerly taken in an action by way of information (*q.v.*) in Chancery. Now used to mean the person at whose suggestion or information an action is instituted by the Attorney-General, *e.g.* in a case of public nuisance. See Ord. 15, r. 11. Where the Attorney-General decides not to consent to relator proceedings his decision is final and a private individual has no remedy (*Gouriet* v. *Union of Post Office Workers* [1977] 3 W.L.R. 300).

release. (1) The giving up, discharge, or the renunciation of rights or claims against another. When trustees or executors have wound up an estate they usually require a release from the persons beneficially entitled before handing over or dividing it, in order to clear themselves of responsibility. A release may take the form of a covenant not to sue. (2) The discharge by a person of his interest in land in favour of the person in possession, thus vesting the entire legal estate in the possessor. See LEASE AND RELEASE.

relegatio. [Roman law.] Banishment. A prohibition from entering Rome or elsewhere.

relegation. Exile or banishment short of outlawry.

relevant. A fact so connected, directly or indirectly, with a fact in issue in an action or other proceeding that it tends to prove or disprove the fact in issue. Any two facts so related to each other that according to the common course of events one either taken by itself or in connection with other facts proves or renders probable the past, present or future existence or non-existence of the other (Stephen). Evidence must be relevant to be admissible.

relicta verificatione. [Verification abandoned.] Down to 1856, a defendant who had pleaded a plea which was demurred to, could withdraw it by entering a *relicta verificatione*. See COGNOVIT ACTIONEM.

relief. (1) A payment which a tenant of full age was bound to pay to the feudal lord on succeeding to the land by descent. By the common law it was an incident to the service of every free tenure, and is sometimes called relief service. It usually consisted of one year's rent. Reliefs incident to knight's service were abolished by the statute 1660, 12 Car. 2, c.24. A customary relief was one due by the special custom of some manors on every descent, and in some cases on every purchase, of freehold tenements held of the manor. See MANORIAL INCIDENTS. (2) The remedy sought by the plaintiff in an action, *e.g.* a decree or damages. (3) Allowances from an individual's total income before computing the tax payable (Income and Corporation Taxes Act 1970, ss.5–27, as amended).

remainder. A remnant of an estate in lands or tenements, expectant upon a particular estate created together with the same at one time (Co.Litt. 93A). Thus if A, a tenant in fee simple, grants land to B for life, and after B's decease to C and his heirs, C's interest is termed a remainder in fee expectant on the decease of B. No tenure exists between the particular tenant (B) and the remainderman (C). Since 1925, remainders can only be created and subsist as equitable interests (Law of Property Act 1925, s.1(1), (3), Sched. 1, Part I).

A vested remainder is one ready to come into possession the moment the prior estate determines. See CONTINGENT REMAINDER.

remand. To adjourn a hearing to a future date, and to order that the defendant, unless admitted to bail, be kept in custody in the meantime. Instead of being sent to remand centres or remand homes, children and young persons in trouble are to be sent to community homes (Children and Young Persons Act 1969, ss.35–59, Sched. 6).

remanent pro defectu emptorum. [They are left on my hands for want of buyers.] A return made by a sheriff with regard to goods taken under a *fieri facias*.

remanet. An action in the Queen's Bench Division which has been set down for trial at one sitting, but has not come on, so that it stands over to the next sittings.

remedy. The means by which the violation of a right is prevented, redressed, or compensated. Remedies are of four kinds: (1) by act of the party injured, the principal of which are defence, recaption, distress, entry, abatement and seizure; (2) by operation of law, as in the case of retainer and remitter; (3) by agreement between the parties, *e.g.* by accord and satisfaction, and arbitration; and (4) by judicial process, *e.g.* action or suit.

remembrancers. The three officials of the Exchequer known as the Queen's Remembrancer (*q.v.*), the Lord Treasurer's Remembrancer, and the Remembrancer of the First Fruits. The Remembrancer of the City of London represents the Corporation before parliamentary committees; he accompanies the sheriffs when they wait on the Sovereign in connection with any address from the Corporation; and he is bound to attend all Courts of Aldermen and Common Council when required. See QUEEN'S REMEMBRANCER.

remise. To release or surrender.

remission. (1) The reference of a case by a higher court to a lower, *e.g.* by the High Court to the county court. (2) The forgiveness of a debt. (3) The pardon of an offender by the remission of his sentence of imprisonment.

remitter is where a man hath two titles to lands or tenements, *viz.* one a more ancient title, and another a more latter title; and if he comes to the land by a latter title, yet the law will adjudge him in by force of the elder title, because the elder title is the more sure and more worthy title (Litt. § 659).

remoteness. A disposition of property which is not to take effect within the period allowed by the rule against perpetuities (*q.v.*) is said to be void for remoteness.

remoteness of damage. Damage which results from an act of the defendant, but which cannot be said to be caused by the defendant. If a defendant has been negligent and damage results therefrom which otherwise would not have occurred, prima facie he is liable in damages for it. Consequences which could not have been foreseen by a reasonable man are too remote. It is not enough that the damage was the direct consequence of a negligent act (*The Wagon Mound* [1961] A.C. 388, not following *Re Polemis* [1921] 3 K.B. 560). The same rule applies in nuisance (*Overseas Tankship (U.K.)* v. *Miller Steamship Co.* [1967] 1 A.C. 617). See NOVUS ACTUS INTERVENIENS.

In case of breach of contract, the damages should be such as may fairly and reasonably be considered either arising naturally, *i.e.* according to the usual course of things from such breach of contract itself, or such as may reasonably be supposed to have been in the contemplation of the parties, at the time they made the contract, as the probable result of the breach of it (*per* Alderson B. in *Hadley* v. *Baxendale* (1854) L.R. 9 Ex. 341, at p. 354). Otherwise the damage will be too remote. See DAMAGES; FINANCIAL LOSS.

render. To yield or pay. Some kinds of heriots were said to lie in render, that is, the tenant was bound to give the heriot to the lord. See MANORIAL INCIDENTS; PRENDER.

rent. A periodical payment due from a tenant of land or other corporeal hereditament to the owner or lord which is recoverable by distraint in the event of non-payment. It is usually payable in money but it may be reserved in kind. A peppercorn rent is a nominal rent which serves as an acknowledgment of the tenancy. See DISTRESS.

Rent service is always incident to tenure; it is that which is due when one man holds land of another by fealty (or any other service) and rent. It is called a rent service because it has some corporeal service annexed unto it, which at least is fealty (Co.Litt. 142A); but at the present day fealty is never exacted.

Quit rents were rents due usually from the tenants of manors, in lieu and in discharge of services. If a rent is severed from the reversion (as where either is assigned without the other) it becomes a rent in gross. A rack-rent is a rent of the full annual value of the land, or near it. See RACK-RENT.

When land is leased to a person on condition that he erects certain buildings on it, the rent reserved (which is small in comparison with the rent of the land when built on) is called the ground-rent.

rentcharge. Any annual or periodic sum charged on or issuing out of land except rent reserved by lease or tenancy or any sum payable by way of interest (Rent Charges Act, 1977 s.1). The creation of new rentcharges is now prohibited, with limited exceptions (Act of 1977, s.2(1) and (3)); existing rentcharges will be extinguished over a period of 60 years from 1978 (s.3) and may be redeemed (ss.8 to 10). "Rentcharge" includes groundrent and fee farm rent.

rent rebates. See the Housing Finance Act 1972, ss.18–26; the Furnished Lettings (Rent Allowances) Act 1973 and the Rent Act 1974.

rent restriction. The control of rent and mortgage interest had its origin in the Increase of Rent and Mortgage Interest (War Restrictions) Act 1915. The law was consolidated in the Increase of Rent and Mortgage Interest (Restrictions) Act 1920, which was frequently amended. Tenancies were subjected to a fresh control at the outbreak of the Second World War by the Rent and Mortgage Interest Restrictions Act 1939. Control is now governed by the Rent Act 1977. See also Prevention from Eviction Act 1977.

rent tribunal. A tribunal for adjudicating on differences between landlord and tenant as to rent (see Rent Act 1977, Pt. V, Sched. 13).

renunciation. A disclaimer. A document by which a person appointed by a testator as his executor, or a person who is entitled to take out letters of administration to the effects of an intestate in priority to other persons, renounces or gives up his right to take out probate or letters of administration; the document is filed in the probate registry.

renvoi. The doctrine regarding the choice of law where the law of more than one country may be applicable. It is to the effect that if a judge is seized of a case in country A, whose law requires him to apply the law of country B, and the rules for choice of law in country B refer to the law of country A, then the judge in country A must apply the law of country A. In short, the reference to the law of the country means a reference to the whole of its law, including its private international law which deals with choice of law.

An alternative is the foreign court theory: or the English doctrine of *renvoi,* under which an English judge who is referred by English law to a foreign legal system, must apply whatever law a court in that foreign country would apply, which would depend upon whether that foreign legal system recognised the doctrine of *renvoi* or not. (See Cheshire, *Private International Law.*)

repatriation. The resumption of a nationality which has been lost; or the sending of an alien back to his own country. See EXPATRIATION.

repeal. The abrogation of a statute or part of a statute by a subsequent statute. It may be either express, *i.e.* specially enacted, or it may be implied, *i.e.* the necessary result of the subsequent enactment. The repeal of a repealing enactment does not revive the enactment originally repealed (see the Interpretation Act 1978, ss.15, 17). See STATUTE LAW REVISION.

repleader. A judgment in an action when the pleadings had failed to raise a definite issue, that the pleadings be begun again.

replegiari facias. The writ of replevin (*q.v.*).

replevin. Judicial redelivery to their owner of chattels alleged to have been wrongfully seized. It is a remedy available to a bailiff. Power to grant replevin, irrespective of the value of the goods, is vested exclusively in the registrar of the county court (see *Swaffer* v. *Mulcahy* [1934] 1 K.B. 608; County Courts Act 1959, ss.104–106). For an analagous and more modern remedy for recovery of goods see WRONGFUL INTERFERENCE WITH GOODS.

replication; reply. If the plaintiff desires to deliver a reply, he must deliver it within fourteen days from the service of the defence (Ord. 18). If no reply is served there is implied joinder of issue on the defence (Ord. 18, r.14(1)). See PLEADINGS.

reply. (Pleading.) Plaintiff's answer to defence or counterclaim.

reply, right of. The right of counsel in a case to have the last word, or make the last speech to the jury, before the judge's summing-up.

report. A judge may refer an issue to a master or registrar for inquiry and report (R.S.C., Ord. 36; C.C.R., Ord. 19, Pt. II).

representation. (1) One person is said to represent another when he takes his place. Thus, an agent represents his principal, and an executor his testator. In intestacy, the rule of representation is that by which the children or other descendants of a deceased person who, if he had lived, would have taken property by virtue of an intestacy, stand in his place, so as to take that property. Under the Administration of Estates Act 1925, s.47, the issue of any child of an intestate who predeceased the intestate take the share which their parent would have taken if living at the death of the intestate; and the same rule is extended to the issue of relatives of the intestate.

(2) A representation is a statement or assertion of fact made by one party to a contract to the other, before or at the time of the contract, of some matter or circumstance relating to it. But a representation of belief, expectation, or intention may be a representation of fact, for "the state of a man's mind is as much a matter of fact as the state of his digestion" (*per* Bowen L.J., *Edgington* v. *Fitzmaurice* (1885) 29 Ch.D. 459, at p. 483). A representation made during the making of a contract of sale may be: (a) A mere expression of opinion, or simply "puffing" by a seller of his goods; it is then inoperative. (b) A warranty (*q.v.*). (c) A condition (*q.v.*) as constituting part of the description of the thing sold, and an essential term of the contract. If false or fraudulent it may avoid the contract. It may create an estoppel (*q.v.*). Rescission of a contract and damages may be claimed for an innocent misrepresentation. See the Misrepresentation Act 1967. See MISREPRESENTATION.

representative. A person who takes the place of another. The executor or administrator of a deceased person is called his personal representative, because he represents him in respect of his personal estate. The personal representative is also the real representative where there is realty. See REAL REPRESENTATIVE.

representative action. One brought by a member of a class of persons on behalf of himself and the other members of the class. The writ of summons must be indorsed with a statement showing in what capacity the plaintiff sues (Ord. 6, r. 3). Where there are numerous persons having the same interest, one may sue or be sued on behalf of the others (Ord. 15, r.12).

reprieve. The suspension of the execution of a sentence. The Home Secretary exercises the prerogative of mercy on behalf of the Crown.

reprisal. (1) A recaption (*q.v.*). (2) Every species of means, short of war, employed by one State to procure redress for an injury committed by another State. It includes embargo and retorsion (*q.v.*).

republication. The re-execution by the testator of a will or codicil previously revoked.

repudiation. Words or conduct indicating that a person does not intend to be or does not regard himself as being bound by an obligation, *e.g.* a contract.

repugnant. Contrary to, or inconsistent with.

reputation. Matters of public and general interest, such as the boundaries of counties or parishes, rights of common, etc., are allowed to be proved in evidence by general reputation, *e.g.* by the declarations of deceased persons made *ante litem motam,* by old documents, etc., notwithstanding the general rule against secondary evidence.

reputed ownership. The doctrine that if the circumstances in which property is in a trader's possession, order or disposition, are such as to lead to a fair and reasonable inference amongst persons likely to have dealings with him, that he is the owner, and if the real owner is a consenting party, that property is said to be in his reputed ownership, and on the trader becoming bankrupt, that property is divisible among his creditors (Bankruptcy Act 1914, s.38). For the position as to goods subject to hire purchase, consumer hire agreement or conditional sale agreement see Act of 1914, s.38A.

requisitions on title. When a contract for the sale of real property has been entered into, and the vendor's solicitor has delivered the abstract of the title to the purchaser, the latter's solicitor goes through the abstract, and if there are any apparent defects in or questions as to the vendor's title, he puts his objections into writing and delivers them to the vendor. These are called requisitions, because they require the vendor to remove the defects or doubts pointed out.

res. [Things.]

res accessoria sequitur rem principalem. [Accessory things follow principal things.]

res furtivae. [Stolen goods.]

res gestae. The facts surrounding or accompanying a transaction which is the subject of legal proceedings; or, all facts so connected with a fact in issue as to introduce it, explain its nature, or form in connection with it one continuous transaction. Evidence of words used by a person may be admissible on the ground that they form part of the *res gestae,* which might otherwise be inadmissible as hearsay.

res integra. A point, governed neither by any decision nor by any rule of law, which must be decided upon principle.

res inter alios acta alteri nocere non debet. [A transaction between others does not prejudice one who was not a party to it.]

res ipsa loquitur. [The thing speaks for itself.] The maxim applies whenever it is so improbable that such an accident would have happened without the negligence of the defendant, that a reasonable jury could find without further evidence that it was so caused (see *Scott* v. *London and St. Katherine's Docks Co.* (1865) 3 H. & C. 596). For example, in *Byrne* v. *Boadle* (1863) 2 H. & C. 722, a barrel of flour rolled out of an open doorway on the upper floor of the defendant's warehouse and fell upon the plaintiff, a passer-by in the street below. It was held that this of itself was sufficient evidence of negligence to go to a jury. The maxim throws on to the defendant the burden of disproving negligence (*Swan* v. *Salisbury Construction Co.* [1966] 1 W.L.R. 204).

res judicata pro veritate accipitur. [A thing adjudicated is received as the truth.] A judicial decision is conclusive until reserved, and its verity cannot be contradicted. *Res judicata* presupposes that there are two opposing parties, that there is a definite issue between them, that there is a tribunal competent to decide the issue, and that within its competence, the tribunal has done so. Once a matter or issue between parties has been litigated and decided, it cannot be raised again between the same parties, but other parties are not so bound. A conviction in criminal proceedings is not strictly *res judicata* in civil proceedings, but the conviction is admissible in evidence and it will be presumed that the convicted person committed the offence unless the contrary is proved (Civil Evidence Act 1968, s.11).

res nova. A matter not yet decided.

res nullius. A thing which has no owner. See BONA VACANTIA.

res sic stantibus. [Things standing so, or remaining the same.] Agreements or treaties, etc., may be entered into on the basis that existing circumstances remain substantially unaltered. See FRUSTRATION.

res sua nemini servit. [No one can have an easement over his own property.]

rescission. Abrogation or revocation, particularly of a contract. In a sale of land there is usually an express condition of sale under which, in case the purchaser makes and persists in any objection or requisition which the vendor is unable or unwilling to comply with, the vendor may by notice in writing rescind the sale, and return the deposit to the purchaser and so escape liability to pay damages for breach of contract. If a party is entitled to rescind a contract owing to a misrepresentation having been made, he must notify the other party of his intention by pleading invalidity as a defence to proceedings to enforce the contract, or by bringing a suit for having the contract judicially set aside. Rescission is only allowed where restitution is possible. A contract may be rescinded on the ground of an innocent misrepresentation (Misrepresentation Act 1967).

rescous. Rescue (*q.v.*).

rescue. (1) The act of forcibly and knowingly freeing a person from an arrest or imprisonment. (2) The act of forcibly taking back goods which have been distrained and are being taken to the pound. If the distress was unlawful, the owner may lawfully rescue the goods; if the distress was lawful, the rescuer is liable to an action by the distrainor. See POUND-BREACH.

rescue cases. Those dealing with liability for damages ensuing from the voluntary assumption of risk, *e.g.* stopping horses bolting in the street. See *Haynes* v. *Harwood* [1935] 1 K.B. 146.

reservation. A clause of a deed whereby the feoffor, donor, lessor, grantor, etc., doth reserve some new thing to himself out of that which he granted before. And this doth most commonly and properly succeed the *tenendum* (Sheppard's *Touchstone*). The commonest instance of a reservation is the rent in an ordinary lease. See DEED.

resiant. A resident in a manor.

residence. The place of a person's home or habitation; the place where he abides; the place from which the affairs of a company are directed. It is of importance as determining domicile and liability to taxation. In general, the courts have jurisdiction over persons resident within the territorial limits of the court's powers. A company is resident for tax purposes in the country where its central management and control are exercised (*Unit Construction Co.* v. *Bullock* [1960] A.C. 351).

residuary devisee. The person named in a will who is to take any real property remaining after satisfying the specific gifts of real property in the will.

residuary legatee. Prima facie, this means the person entitled under a will to the balance of personal estate remaining after paying the debts, expenses, and legacies bequeathed by the will, but his meaning may be extended, if the context of the will so requires, so as to include the real estate as well. In that case, the term is equivalent to "residuary beneficiary."

residue. That which remains of a deceased person's estate after payment of debts, funeral and testamentary expenses, legacies, and annuities. Where a testator does not effectually dispose of the residue of his property he dies intestate as to it, *i.e.* if a share of residue lapses, it does not fall into residue, but goes to the next-of-kin.

Residue is ascertained when the administration of the deceased's estate is so far completed that the nature and value of the residue can bé determined. A personal representative who has completed administration, holds the residue on trust for residuary legatees or next-of-kin; he ceases to be a personal representative and becomes a trustee (*Attenborough* v. *Solomon* [1913] A.C. 76).

resolution. A resolution is an expression of opinion or intention by a meeting. Resolutions of the members of a company are either ordinary, special, or extra-ordinary. An ordinary resolution is one passed by a simple majority in number at an ordinary meeting.

An extraordinary resolution is one which has been passed by a majority of not less than three-fourths of such members as being entitled so to do vote in person or (where proxies are allowed) by proxy at a general meeting of which notice specifying the intention to propose the resolution as an extraordinary resolution has been duly given (Companies Act 1948, s.141(1)).

A special resolution is one which has been passed by such a majority as is required for the passing of an extraordinary resolution (*i.e.* three-fourths), and at a general meeting of which not less than 21 days' notice, specifying the intention to propose the resolution as a special resolution, has been duly given; provided that, if all the members entitled to attend and vote at any such meeting so agree, a resolution may be proposed and passed as a special resolution at a meeting of which less than 21 days' notice has been given (*ibid.* s.141(2)). Special resolutions are required for, *inter alia,* the alteration of a company's objects, articles, or name, and for the reduction of its capital.

In bankruptcy proceedings, an ordinary resolution is one decided by a majority in value of the creditors present (personally or by proxy) at the meeting, and voting on the resolution. A special resolution is one passed by a majority in number and three-fourths in value of the creditors present (personally or by proxy) at the meeting, and voting on the resolution (Bankruptcy Act 1914, s.167).

resoluto jure concedentis resolvitur jus concessum. [The grant of a right comes to an end on the termination of the right of the grantor.]

respite. To discharge or dispense with.

respondeat ouster. [Let him answer over.] A judgment formerly given when a defendant or prisoner failed to substantiate a plea, and which ordered him to plead again. See PLEA.

respondeat superior. [Let the principal answer.] Where the relation of employer and employee exists, the employer is liable for the acts of the employee committed in the course of his employment. See EMPLOYER AND EMPLOYEE.

respondent. A person against whom a petition is presented, a summons issued, or an appeal brought.

respondentia. The making of the cargo on board a ship security for the repayment of a loan. See HYPOTHECATION; BOTTOMRY.

restitutio in integrum. [Restoration to the original position.] The remedy administered by courts of equity in rescinding a contract or otherwise placing parties in the position they occupied before entering into a transaction.

restitution of conjugal rights. The right of action for restitution of conjugal rights was abolished by the Matrimonial Proceedings and Property Act 1970, s.20.

restitution. (1) The writ by which a defendant, successful in an appeal, is restored to all he has lost by the execution of the judgment which is reversed; the writ by which stolen goods were formerly restored to their true owner.

(2) The trial court has power to order that stolen goods or the proceeds thereof be restored to the owner or their value be paid to the owner from money taken from the person convicted on his apprenhension. The last named power may also be exercised in favour of an innocent purchaser who has been ordered to restore stolen goods to the true owner (Theft Act 1968, s.28; Criminal Justice Act 1972,

s.6, Sched. 5). If there is any doubt about the title to the property, the order is suspended for 28 days and, if there is an appeal, the order is suspended until the determination of the appeal. If the appeal is successful the order for restitution is annulled. The Court of Appeal may annul or vary the order (Theft Act 1968, s.28(5), Sched. 3, Pt. III; Criminal Appeal Act 1968, ss.30, 42; Criminal Damage Act 1971, s.8(2)).

restraint of marriage. A contract, or disposition, the object of which is to restrain a person from marrying at all, or not to marry anyone except a specific person, is void as against public policy.

restraint of trade. Contractual interference with individual liberty of action in trading, which as a general rule is void as being contrary to public policy. Such a restriction will be valid, however, if it is reasonable in reference to the interests of the parties concerned, and of the public, and if it is so framed as to protect the party in whose favour it is imposed, without being injurious to the public (see *per* Lord Macnaghten in *Maxim-Nordenfelt Gun Co.* v. *Nordenfelt* [1894] A.C. 535). Restraints of trade may be reasonable not only in protection of a purchaser of a business, but of an employer from improper use of trade secrets, confidential information, etc., by an employee when he leaves his service. But a mere covenant not to compete with the employer, by an employee, will not be upheld.

restraint on alienation: restraint on anticipation. A clause restraining anticipation (*q.v.*) was generally introduced into a settlement of property on a woman in order to protect her from the influence of her husband by preventing her from depriving herself of the benefit of future income. By the Law Reform (Married Women and Tortfeasors) Act 1935, however, a restraint upon anticipation of property of a married woman could not be imposed unless pursuant to an obligation incurred before 1936, or unless it was contained in a will executed before 1936 of a testator who died before 1946. Existing restraints continued in force. The Married Women (Restraint upon Anticipation) Act 1949 abolished any restraint upon anticipation or alienation attached to the enjoyment of property by a woman which could not have been attached to enjoyment by a man. Where property was given to a married woman to her separate use without power of disposing of it, by means of a restraint on anticipation, she had the power of a tenant for life under the Settled Land Act 1925 (see ss.1, 20, 25). See ANTICIPATION.

restrictive covenant. See COVENANT.

restrictive indorsement. An indorsement on a bill of exchange which prohibits the further negotiation of the bill, or expresses that it is a mere authority to deal with the bill as thereby directed, and not a transfer of the ownership thereof, *e.g.* "Pay X only," or "Pay X, or order, for collection" (Bills of Exchange Act 1882, s.35(1)).

restrictive trade practices. The Restrictive Trade Practices Act 1956 provided for the registration and judicial investigation of certain restrictive trading agreements, which are to be prohibited if found contrary to the public interest. The Act established the Restrictive Practices Court, which is a superior court of record, and the office of Registrar, whose duty is to take proceedings before the court in respect of agreements which he has registered. Information agreements were brought within and certain agreements of national importance were excepted from the Act by the Restrictive Trade Practices Act 1968. The functions of the Registrar were transferred to the Director General of Fair Trading by the Fair Trading Act 1973. See also the Consumer Credit Act 1974, Sched. 4, para. 17 and the European Communities Act 1972, s.10; Restrictive Trade Practices Acts 1976 and 1977; Competition Act 1980, ss.25–30.

rests. The period for which accounts are balanced and interest is ascertained and charged, and added to the principal sum, *e.g.* half-yearly.

result. A thing is said to result when, after having been ineffectually or only partially disposed of, it comes back to its former owner or his representatives, *e.g.* property subject to a trust which fails returns to the author of the trust under a resulting trust. See RESULTING TRUST.

resulting trust. An implied trust where the beneficial interest in property comes back, or results, to the person (or his representatives) who transferred the property to the trustee or provided the means of obtaining it. The chief kinds are (1) Where the expressed trusts do not exhaust the whole beneficial interest: but a resulting trust in the case of a voluntary conveyance is not implied forj the grantor merely because the property is not expressed to be conveyed for the use or benefit of the grantee (Law of Property Act 1925, s.60(3)). (2) Where on a purchase property is conveyed into the name of someone other than the purchaser, there is a resulting trust in favour of the man who advances the purchase money: but not where it would defeat the policy of the law, or where there is a presumption of advancement. (3) In cases of joint purchases or mortgages, on the death of one of the persons advancing a part of the money, there is often a resulting trust in favour of his representatives. (4) In case of mutual wills. See also the Perpetuities and Accumulations Act 1964, ss.12, 15(5).

resulting use. Where property, prior to 1926, was conveyed to a person without any mention of a use, and without any consideration, the property was held to the use of the grantor, which use was "executed" by the Statute of Uses so that the legal estate immediately revested in and remained in the grantor, and the grantee took nothing.

retail. The sale of goods in small quantities to the public, as in a shop.

resumption. The taking again of lands by the owner.

retainer. (1) The right of the executor or administrator of a deceased person to retain out of the assets sufficient to pay any debt due to him from the deceased in priority to the other creditors whose debts are of equal degree. The right was abolished by the Administration of Estates Act 1971, s.10.

(2) The engagement of a barrister or solicitor to take or defend proceedings, or to advise or otherwise act for the client.

retire. To take up a bill of exchange and extinguish it by paying what is due.

retorsion. A form of retaliation, unfriendly, but not affording a cause of war, consisting of the adoption of measues directed against an offending nation analogous to those to which exception is taken, *e.g.* the imposition of a diffeential tariff.

retour sans protêt. [Return without protest.] A direction in case a bill of exchange is dishonoured, that it shall not be "protested." See PROTEST.

retraction. A withdrawal of a renunciation (*q.v.*).

return. A report. Thus, the sheriff executing a writ of execution has to report to the court what he has done in pursuance of it (see R.S.C. App. A, Form No. 53 and Ord. 46, r. 9). A writ is said to be returnable at a certain time when the return must be made by that time.

Every company formed under the Companies Acts, and having a share capital, is bound to send in an annual return to the Registrar of Companies, giving the address of its registered office (or where registers are kept), a list of its shareholders, and a summary of shares issued, calls paid, directors, charges secured on the company's property, etc., and annexed thereto (including private companies) a certified copy of the balance sheet and auditors report (Companies Act 1948, ss.124, 127, 129; Companies Act 1967, s.2). An annual return has also to be made by a company not having a share capital (Act of 1948, s.125).

returning officer. A person responsible for the conduct of an election. For parliamentary elections he is the sheriff or mayor (Representation of the People Act 1949, s.17). His duties are discharged by the registration officer (*ibid.* s.18).

returnus brevium. [The Return of Writs.] The manorial right of making returns to writs addressed to residents within the manor.

reus. [Roman law.] Any party to a case, including a stipulator.

reversal. The setting aside of a judgment on appeal.

reversion. Where land is granted by the owner for a less estate or interest than he himself has, his undisposed-of interest is termed the reversion, because the land will revert to the owner on the determination of the particular estate, *e.g.* where a tenant in fee simple grants the land to another person for a term of years, for life, or in tail.

The estate created by the grant is called the particular estate, and tenure exists between the reversioner (the owner of the reversion) and the tenant. See also Perpetuities and Accumulations Act 1964, ss.12, 15(4).

reversionary interest. Any right in property the enjoyment of which is deferred; *e.g.* a reversion or remainder, or analogous interests in personal property.

reverter. A reversion (*q.v.*).

revesting. The vesting of property again in its original owner, *e.g.* stolen property.

review of taxation. The reconsideration of taxed costs on the application of a dissatisfied party. See Ord. 62, r.33.

revival. The renewal of rights which were at an end or in abeyance by subsequent acts or events *e.g.* a will once revoked may be revived by republication.

revocation. Recalling, revoking, or cancelling.

(1) Revocation by act of the party is an intentional or voluntary revocation, *e.g.* of authorities and powers of attorney and wills (Wills Act 1837, s.20).

(2) A revocation in law is produced by a rule of law, irrespective of the intention of the parties. Thus, a power of attorney, or the authority of an agent, is in general revoked by the death of the principal.

(3) By an order of the court, *e.g.* when a grant of probate or letters of administration has been improperly obtained, it may be revoked by the court at the instance of a person interested.

(4) In the law of contract, an offer may be revoked at any time before acceptance, but the revocation must be communicated to the offeree to be operative (*Byrne* v. *Van Tienhoven* (1880) 5 C.P.D. 344).

reward. (1) Of persons active in the apprehension of offenders (Criminal Law Act 1826, ss.28–30; Criminal Law Act 1967, Sched. 2, para. 3, Sched. 3, Part III). (2) Advertising a reward for the return of stolen goods, "no questions asked" is an offence (Theft Act 1968, s.23).

rex non potest peccare. [The King can do no wrong.]

rex nunquam moritur. [The King never dies.]

rex quod injustum est facere non potest. [The King cannot do what is unjust.]

Rhodes, Law of. A code of sea laws compiled at a very early date in the Island of Rhodes, and declared by the Roman emperors to be binding on the world at large.

rider. (1) Anciently a rider-roll meant an additional clause on a separate piece of parchment which was added to the parchment roll containing an Act of Parliament. Now, a rider is an addition in the form of a new clause added to a Bill; amendments, etc., by means of a separate sheet of paper to a legal document. (2) A recommendation to mercy added by a jury to their verdict.

right. An interest recognised and potected by the law, respect for which is a duty, and disregard of which is a wrong (Salmond). A capacity residing in one man of controlling, with the assent and assistance of the State, the actions of others (Holland).

A right involves (1) a person invested with the right, or entitled; (2) a person or persons on whom that right imposes a correlative duty or obligation; (3) an act or forbearance which is the subject-matter of the right; (4) an object, that is, a person or thing to which the right has reference; and (5) a title or reason for the right becoming vested in the owner. Rights are perfect and imperfect; positive and negative; real and personal; proprietary and personal; *in re propria* and *in re aliena;* principal and accessory; and legal and equitable (Salmond).

right of action. The right to bring an action. Thus a person who is wrongfully dispossessed of land has a right of action to recover it. It is used also as equivalent to *chose in action (q.v.).*

right of entry. The right of taking or resuming possession of land by entering on it in a peaceable manner. A right of entry is usually reserved in a lease in respect of breaches of covenant. After 1925 all rights of entry affecting a legal estate may be made exercisable by any person and the person deriving title under him (Law of Property Act 1925, s.4(3)). See ENTRY.

right of way. The right of passing over land of another. A right of way is either public or private. A public right is called a highway (*q.v.*). Rights of way are of various kinds and may be for limited purposes only, *e.g.* a footway, horseway, carriageway, way to church, agricultural way, etc. Any person who uses a highway for any purpose other than that of passage (including purposes ordinarily incidental thereto) becomes a trespasser. See DEDICATION.

A private right of way is either an easement or a customary right. A way of necessity is a right of way which arises where a man having a close surrounded with his own land grants (or devises) the close to another; the grantee has a right of way to the close over the grantor's land, otherwise he cannot derive any benefit from the grant (or devise). Similarly, where the grantor keeps the close and grants the surrounding land, a way of necessity is implied in his favour.

right to begin. The right of counsel of first addressing the court or jury. It belongs to the party on whom the onus of proof rests. In criminal cases the prosecution always begins. See PROOF.

riot. There are five necessary elements of a riot: (1) number of persons, three at least; (2) common purpose; (3) execution or inception of the common purpose; (4) an intent to help one another by force if necessary against any person who may oppose them in the execution of their common purpose; (5) force or violence not merely used in demolishing, but displayed in such a manner as to alarm at least one person of reasonable firmness and courage (*per* Phillimore J. in *Field* v. *Receiver of Metropolitan Police* [1907] 2 K.B. 859). "Appear to alarm" may be enough. Riot is a common law misdemeanour.

The Riot Act 1714 under which rioters could be called upon to disperse (commonly but inaccurately called "reading the Riot Act") was repealed by the Statute Law Repeals Act 1973. But the Riot Act and its repeal did not affect the common law duty of justices to suppress a riot or the right of private persons to do the same.

Compensation is payable to persons whose property has been damaged by riot (Riot Damages Act 1886; Police Act 1964, Scheds. 9, 10). For procedure see the Riot (Claims for Compensation Regulations) 1921 (S.I. 1921 No. 1536). See ROUT; UNLAWFUL ASSEMBLY.

riparian. Property, or States, bounded by rivers.

risk note. A contract, signed by the consignor, which makes a transport undertaking instead of being liable as carriers (*q.v.*), liable only for such loss or injury as results from the wilful misconduct of themselves or their employees.

road traffic. See the Road Traffic Regulation Act 1967, as amended; the Road Traffic Act 1972; the Local Government Act 1972, s.35, Sched. 6 para. 20; the Road Traffic Act 1974; the Transport Act 1981.

robbery. Stealing by force. See the Theft Act 1968, s.8. The offence of robbery at common law was abolished by s.32.

Roe, Richard. See DOE, JOHN.

rolls. In ancient times records were written on pieces of parchment stitched together so as to form a long continuous piece, which was rolled up when not in use. The Parliament Rolls are the records of the proceedings of Parliament, especially Acts of Parliament.

root of title. See TITLE.

rout. An unlawful assembly which has made some motion towards the execution of the common purpose of the persons assembled. It is, therefore, intermediate between an unlawful assembly (*q.v.*) and a riot (*q.v.*). It is a common law misdemeanour.

Royal Assent. The assent of the Crown to a Bill in Parliament becoming law as an Act of Parliament. It woild be unconstitutional for the Crown to refuse the Royal Assent. An Act of Parliament is duly enacted if Her Majesty's assent thereto being signified by Letters Patent under the Great Seal, signed by Her Majesty's own hand (a) is pronounced in the presence of both Houses in the House of Lords in the customary manner or (b) is notified to each House of Parliament seated separately, by the Speaker of that House. The power of Her Majesty to declare Her Royal Assent in person in Parliament and the manner in which an Act of Parliament is required to be endorsed in Her Majesty's name remain unaffected (Royal Assent Act 1967).

The Crown Office Rules Order 1967 (S.I. 1967 No. 802), prescribes the forms to be used for Letters Patent signifying the Royal Assent.

Forms: (1) Public Bills, *Le Roy [La Reine] le veult* [The King (Queen) wishes it.]

(2) Money Bills, *Le Roy [La Reine] remercie ses bons sujets, accepte leur bénévolence, et ainsi le veult* [The King (Queen) thanks his (her) good subjects, accepts their benevolence, and also wishes it.]

(3) Private Bills, *Soit fait comme il est désiré* [Let what is desired be done.]

(4) Refusal of consent, *Le Roy (La Reine) s'avisera* [The King (Queen) will consider.]

An Act of Parliament, unless otherwise provided commences to operate from the date of the Royal Assent (Acts of Parliament (Commencement) Act 1793), with effect from the last moment of the previous day (Interpretation Act 1889, s.36(2)).

royal title. "Elizabeth the Second, by the Grace of God of the United Kingdom of Great Britain and Northern Ireland and of Her other Realms and Territories Queen, Head of the Commonwealth, Defender of the Faith."

rule. (1) A regulation made by a court of justice or a public office with reference to the conduct of business therein. Rules made under the authority of an Act of Parliament have statutory effect. Rules of court are made by the judges for the regulation of practice and procedure. (2) An order or direction made by a court of justice in an action or other proceeding. A rule is either—(i) absolute in the first instance, or (ii) *nisi, i.e.* calling upon the opposite party to show cause why the rule applied for should not be granted. If no sufficient cause is shown, the rule is made absolute; otherwise it is discharged. (3) A principle of the law, *e.g.* the rule against perpetuities, or the rule in *Howe* v. *Lord Dartmouth.*

rule of law. The doctrine of English law expounded by Dicey, in *Law of the Constitution,* that all men are equal before the law, whether they be officials or not (except the Queen), so that the acts of officials in carrying out the behests of the executive government are cognisable by the ordinary courts and judged by the ordinary law, as including any special powers, privileges or exemptions attributed to the Crown by prerogative or statute.

So far as offences are concerned, an offender will not be punished except for a breach of the ordinary law, and in the ordinary courts: there is here an absence of the exercise of arbitrary power. Further, the fundamental rights of the citizen; the freedom of the person, freedom of speech, and freedom of meeting or association, are rooted in the ordinary law, and not upon any special "constitutional guarantees."

running days. A charterparty includes all days, whether working or non-working, as well as Sundays and holidays. But custom may, as in the City of London, make either "running days" or "days" equivalent to working days.

running down case. An action for damages against the driver or owner of a vehicle for colliding with another vehicle or person. See ACCIDENT CASES.

running with the land. See COVENANT.

ruptum. [Roman law.] Broken. In the *lex aquilia, ruptum* means *corruptum* or spoliation in any way. "Not only breaking and burning, but also cutting and crushing and spilling, and in any way destroying or making worse are included under this term."

S

S.C. Same case.

S.I. Statutory instruments (*q.v.*).

S.-G. Solicitor-General.

S.R. & O. Statutory Rules and Orders (*q.v.*).

sac. Jurisdiction.

safe conduct. A pass issued to an enemy subject by a belligerent State.

safe system of work. At Common Law an employer is under a duty to provide a safe system of work for employees (*Wilsons & Clyde Coal* v. *English* [1938] A.C. 57). A statutory duty is imposed by Health and Safety at Work Act 1974, s.2.

sale. A transfer of a right of property in consideration of a sum of money.

sale, power of. The right of a person to sell the property of another, and apply the proceeds in satisfaction of a debt or claim due to him from that other; usually conferred by statute. Thus a mortgagee has a power of sale of the mortgaged property, where the mortgage is made by deed, as soon as the mortgage money has become due (Law of Property Act 1925, s.101(1)(i)).

sale of goods. A contract for the sale of goods is a contract whereby the seller transfers or agrees to transfer the property in goods to the buyer for a money consideration called the price (Sale of Goods Act 1979, s.2(1)). Every sale includes an agreement, the payment of the price and the delivery of the property. The property in the goods sold is transferred at the time when the parties intend it to pass, which is usually when the agreement is concluded. In the case of an agreement for the sale of unascertained goods, *e.g.* 10 sheep to be selected from a flock, the property does not pass until the goods are ascertained and appropriated to the contract.

Where the transfer of the property in the goods is to take place at a future time, or subject to some condition thereafter to be fulfilled, the contract is called an agreement to sell (*ibid.* s.2(5)).

sale or return. A contract whereby the buyer has the right of returning the goods to the seller within a reasonable time.

salus populi est suprema lex. [The welfare of the people is the paramount law.]

salvage. Compensation allowed to persons (salvors) by whose assistance a ship or cargo or the lives of persons belonging to her are saved from danger or loss at sea. The assistance must be voluntary and salvors have a retaining lien for their remuneration on the property rescued. The Admiralty Courts will assess the amount payable as salvage (Judicature Act 1925, s.22).

salvo jure. [Without prejudice.]

sanction. The penalty or punishment provided as a means of enforcing obedience to law.

sanctuary. Consecrated places in which neither the civil nor criminal process of the law could be executed: abolished by 21 Jac. 1, c.28, s.7.

sans frais. [Without expense.]

sans nombre. A right of common of pasture where the number of beasts is not fixed.

sans recours. [Without recourse.] Where an agent so signs a bill of exchange, he is not personally liable on it (Bills of Exchange Act 1882, s.16).

satisfaction. The extinguishment of an obligation by performance, *e.g.* the payment of a debt. A judgment may be satisfied by payment or execution. The equitable doctrine of satisfaction relates to the doing of an act in substitution for the performance of an obligation.

(1) Satisfaction of debts. If A, after contracting a debt, makes a will giving B a pecuniary legacy equal to or greater than the debt, the legacy is considered a satisfaction of the debt unless a contrary intention appears.

(2) Satisfaction of portions. When a father or a person *in loco parentis* has covenanted to provide a portion (*q.v.*) and subsequently by will provides a portion, or subsequently makes a gift in the nature of a portion, the second provision is presumed to be wholly or *pro tanto* in substitution for the first.

Equity leans against satisfaction of debts but favours satisfaction of portions. See ADEMPTION; ACCORD AND SATISFACTION.

satisfied term. Where property subject to a long term of years vested in trustees (*e.g.* to secure portions) was sold to a purchaser so that the purposes for which the term was created were fulfilled, the term became a "satisfied term." The purchaser, however, might require the term to be assigned by the trustees to his own trustees in trust for himself, his heirs and assigns "in trust to attend the inheritance" in order to keep the term in existence to protect himself against any undisclosed incumbrances affecting the fee simple, but created subject to the term. This procedure was rendered unnecessary by the Satisfied Terms Act 1845 (8 & 9 Vict. c. 112), now superseded by Law of Property Act 1925, s.5. See TERM OF YEARS.

scaccarium. The exchequer.

scandalous. The allegation in pleading of anything unbecoming the dignity of the court to hear, or contrary to good manners or which unnecessarily charges some person with crime or immorality. It may be struck out (Ord. 18, r.19).

scandalum magnatum. The former offence of making defamatory statements regarding persons of high rank, such as peers, judges or great officers of State.

Schedule. An appendix to an Act of Parliament or an instrument.

scheme or arrangement. A proposal for dealing with his debts by an insolvent debtor, by applying his assets or income in proportionate payment of them (except preferential debts which will normally have to be given priority) which is agreed to by his creditors, or the requisite majority of them. In bankruptcy, the court has power to approve a scheme of arrangement in lieu of the debtor being adjudged bankrupt (Bankruptcy Act 1914, s.16). With regard to schemes of arrangement entered into by a company see Companies Act 1948, s.306.

scienter. Knowledge; an allegation in a pleading that a thing has been done knowingly; the knowledge of the owner of an animal of its mischievous disposition. Liability for animals is now governed by the Animals Act 1971. See ANIMALS.

scilicet. [That is to say; to wit.]

scintilla juris. [A spark or fragment of a right.] The doctrine that a possibility of seisin remained in a feoffee to uses where there was a shifting use. Thus suppose a grant to B and his heirs, to the use of A and his heirs, until an event, and then to C and his heirs. Although the first use was executed and the legal estate vested in A and his heirs, there was always a "possibility" of seisin remaining in B and his heirs, so that on the happening of the event specified the legal estate would "flash back" to B and then instantly vest in C and his heirs on execution of the second use. Abolished by the Law of Property Amendment Act 1867, s.7.

scire facias. A writ founded upon some record, such as a judgment or letters patent, etc., directing the sheriff to warn the person against whom it was brought to show cause why the person bringing it should not have advantage of the record, etc.; or where it was used to repeal letters patent, etc., why the record should not be annulled. Abolished by the Crown Proceedings Act 1947, Sched. 1.

scot and lot. The rates formerly payable by the inhabitants of a borough.

scribere est agere. [To write is to act.]

scrip. A certificate issued by a newly formed company or the issuers of a loan, acknowledging that the person named or the holder is entitled to certain shares, bonds, etc. Scrip certificates are negotiable instruments.

script. A draft of a will or codicil, or written instructions for the same. If the will is destroyed a copy of its contents becomes a script.

scrutiny. An inquiry into the validity of votes recorded at an election.

scutage. Escuage (*q.v.*).

scuttling. The intentional casting of a ship away, for the sake of the insurance money, etc.

seal. A solemn mode of expressing consent to a written instrument by attaching to it wax impressed with a device; but any act done with the intention of sealing is sufficient. By the Law of Property Act 1925, s.73 where a deed is executed it must be signed or marked, and sealing alone is not sufficient.

search. By international law warships of a belligerent have the right to visit and search merchant vessels in order to ascertain whether the ship or cargo is liable to seizure.

This right may be exercised in any waters except the territorial waters of a neutral State, but it must be the work of commissioned ships. The purpose of the visit, which is effected usually by sending on board the ship officers to examine the ship's papers, is to discover the nationality of the vessel, and whether, if neutral, the ship is liable to detention for carriage of contraband, violation of blockade, or enemy service. If the visiting officers are dissatisfied, search follows, and, if warranted, detention of the ship is made, followed by sending in the ship to port with a prize crew on board. See BLOCKADE.

search warrant. An order under the hand of a justice of the peace authorising a named person to enter a specified building and to look for and seize certain specified objects. Search warrants for stolen goods may be issued at common law, and in respect of offences under the Theft Act 1968, under s.26 of that Act. Special powers are contained in a number of statutes to issue warrants to search for documents, etc.

searches. Examination by a purchaser of records and registers for the purpose of finding incumbrances affecting the title to the property. Under the Land Charges Act 1972, s.3, an official search may be made and a certificate of the result issued.

seas. See PERILS OF THE SEAS.

seat belts. The Secretary of State for Transport may make regulations requiring persons driving or riding in motor vehicles to wear seat belts (Road Traffic Act 1972, s.33A inserted by Transport Act 1981, s.27(1)).

seaworthiness. The fitness of a vessel in all respects to undertake a particular voyage which is a matter of concern to shipowners who contract for carriage of goods by sea, and marine insurance underwriters. If there is loss or damage to ship or cargo on a voyage, where the Carriage of Goods by Sea Act 1971, applies, there is an implied warranty that due diligence has been used to make the ship seaworthy, and to secure that the ship is properly manned, equipped and supplied, and to make the holds in which goods are carried fit and safe. The effect of a breach of the warranty of seaworthiness is not to displace the whole of the contract of carriage as in deviation (*q.v.*) but to nullify the exceptions from liability of the shipowner in so far as the loss results from unseaworthiness (*The Europa* [1908] P. 84).

seck. Dry. Where there is no tenure created and consequently no incidents such as the right of distress and escheat. See RENT CHARGE.

secondary picketting. Picketting (*q.v.*) not protected by statute, *e.g.* not in furtherance of a trade dispute (*q.v.*) or not at or near a person's place of work. A person involved in secondary picketting may be liable to civil action or criminal prosecution, *e.g.* for conspiracy or obstruction. See PICKETTING.

Secret Service. This is attached to the Home Office with the right of access, where necessary, to the Prime Minister, who answers questions in the House of Commons.

secret trusts. Where there is a bequest or devise of property by a testator to a person who has expressly or impliedly agreed to hold the property in trust for another or others, that person will be compelled to carry out the trust. If the testator gives the property to A with an express direction in the will itself that A is to hold upon trust without the trusts being disclosed by any will or codicil, A must carry out a trust communicated to him before or at the time of the making of the will (*Re Blackwell* [1929] A.C. 318). A secret trust is not enforced unless communicated in the testator's lifetime; it must be definite, and not illegal.

Secretary of State. The expression means "one of Her Majesty's Principal Secretaries of State for the time being" (Interpretation Act 1978, s.5), *e.g.* the Home Secretary and Foreign Secretary. They may sit in the House of Commons. Each Secretary of State can do anything which any one of the others is empowered to do. He is assisted by one or more Ministers of State and one or more Under-Secretaries of State.

secta. A following. (1) A service, due by custom or prescription, which obliged the inhabitants of a particular place to make use of a mill, kiln, etc. (2) The followers or witnesses whom the plaintiff brought into court with him to prove his case.

secta curiae. Suit and service done by tenants at the court of the lord.

secta regalis. The obligation to attend twice a year at the Sheriff's Tourn.

secure tenancy. A tenancy of a dwelling house let as a separate dwelling where (a) the landlord is a local authority, the commission for New Towns, a development corporation, the Housing Corporation or a housing Trust and (b) the tenant is an individual and occupies the dwelling house as his only or principal home (Housing Act 1980, s.28). A secure tenancy attracts security of tenure and the landlord may only recover possession on one of the grounds specified in the Housing Act 1980, s.34.

security. A possession such that the grantee or holder of the security holds as against the grantor a right to resort to some property or some fund for the satisfaction of some demand, after whose satisfaction the balance of the property or fund belongs to the grantor. There are two owners, and the right of the one has precedence of the right of the other. Debentures, but not shares, of a company are securities.

security for costs. A defendant may apply at any stage of an action, after he has appeared, for security for his costs to be given by the plaintiff on the grounds that the plaintiff is ordinarily resident out of the jurisdiction; that the plaintiff is a nominal plaintiff suing for the benefit of another; or that the plaintiff's address is not stated, or stated incorrectly, in the writ (Ord. 23).

security for good behaviour. See SURETIES OF THE PEACE AND GOOD BEHAVIOUR.

security of tenure. A tenancy where the right of continued occupation by the tenant is protected by some statute is said to attract security of tenure, *e.g.* the position of protected tenants (*q.v.*) under the Rent Act 1977 and Prevention from Eviction Act 1977, secure tenants (*q.v.*) under Housing Act 1980 and business tenants under Landlord and Tenant Act 1954, Pt. II.

secus. [Otherwise.]

sedition. The misdemeanour of publishing orally or otherwise any words or documents with the intention of exciting disaffection, hatred, or contempt against the Sovereign, or the Government and constitution of the kingdom, or either House of Parliament, or the administration of justice, or of exciting Her Majesty's subjects to attempt, otherwise than by lawful means, the alteration of any matter in Church or State, or of exciting feelings of ill-will and hostility between different classes of Her Majesty's subjects.

seditious libel. The publication, in any form constituting a libel, of any seditious matter.

seduction. (1) An action for damages in tort could be brought by a parent (or employer) for loss of services of his daughter (or employee) owing to her seduction and consequent illness. The cause of action was abolished by the Law Reform (Miscellaneous Provisions) Act 1970, s.5.

(2) Anyone who maliciously and advisedly endeavours to seduce any member of Her Majesty's forces from his duty or allegiance to Her Majesty is guilty of an offence under the Incitement to Disaffection Act 1934, s.1.

seignory. A lordship. The interest of one who has tenants holding of him in fee simple.

seised in demesne as of fee. One in whom an immediate freehold in severalty was vested for an estate in fee simple.

seisin. Feudal possession; the relation in which a person stands to land or other hereditaments, when he has in them an estate of freehold in possession. It is formal legal ownership as opposed to mere possession or beneficial interest. Seisin in deed is actual possession of land. Seisin in law is that which an heir had when his ancestor died intestate seised of land, and neither the heir nor any other person had taken actual possession of the land. See LIVERY OF SEISIN.

seisina facit stipitem. [Seisin makes the stock of descent.] The old rule was that when a person died intestate as to his land, it descended to the heir of the person who was last seised of it. See DESCENT.

semble. [It appears.] Used in law reports and text books to introduce a proposition of law which is not intended to be stated too definitely, as there may be doubt about it.

semestria. [Roman law.] Half-yearly ordinances, the records of the half-yearly imperial council of senators.

semper in dubiis benigniora praeferenda. [In doubtful matters the more liberal construction should always be preferred.]

semper praesumitur pro legitimatione puerorum. [It is always to be presumed that children are legitimate.]

semper praesumitur pro negante. [The presumption is always in favour of the negative.]

Senate of the Inns of Court and the Bar. This came into being at the end of July 1974 as a result of a resolution at an Extraordinary General Meeting of the Bar on June 3, 1973. The former Senate of the Four Inns of Court is merged with it. The offices of the Senate are at 11, South Square, Gray's Inn. The Senate has a number of Standing Committees including a Professional Conduct Committee whose functions are to investigate and sift complaints, to prefer and prosecute disciplinary charges, and to make recommendations on matters of professional etiquette to the Bar Committee of the Bar Council (see below). Any charge of professional misconduct against a barrister is heard and determined by an *ad hoc* Committee of the Senate.

Within the framework of the Senate there is a new Bar Council, which is an autonomous body not subject to the directions of the Senate.

The Council of Legal Education continues as an educational charity on behalf of the Inns of Court.

sentence. The judgment of a court, particularly in an ecclesiastical or criminal cause.

separate estate. Property given to a married woman to her separate use as if she were a *feme sole*. She was entitled to the income of it, and could charge it, or dispose of it by deed or will, unless she was restrained from anticipation or alienation, without the consent of her husband. The doctrine was invented in equity to overcome the common law rule, that a married woman was incapable of owning property apart from her husband, which was abolished by the Married Women's Property Act 1882, s.2. The Law Reform (Married Women and Tortfeasors) Act 1935, s.2 abolished the doctrine of separate estate of a married woman, and her property now belongs to her in all respects as if she were a *feme sole*. See also the Law Reform (Husband and Wife) Act 1962, s.3(2). Restraint on anticipation was abolished by the Married Women (Restraint upon Anticipation) Act 1949.

separation (divorce). See DIVORCE.

separation deed. A deed made between the husband and a trustee for the wife, and generally containing provisions for the allowance by the husband of an annuity for the wife, for his indemnification by the trustee against the wife's debts, for the custody and education of the children, etc. It is avoided by subsequent reconciliation and cohabitation.

separation order. See DOMESTIC PROCEEDINGS; JUDICIAL SEPARATION.

sequela villanorum. The possessions of a villein, which were at the disposal of the lord.

sequestration. Legal process consisting of the temporary deprivation of a person of his property. It is a writ or commission directed to certain persons (usually four in number and one of them being usually a sheriff's officer) nominated by the person prosecuting the judgment, and empowering them to enter upon the real estate of the disobedient person, and receive the rents and profits thereof, and take his chattels, and keep them in their hands, until he performs the act required (Ord. 45, r. 1; Ord. 46, r. 5). See ASSISTANCE, WRIT OF.

Serjeants-at-Arms. Officers of the Crown, whose duty is nominally to attend the person of the Sovereign, to arrest traitors, and so on. Two of them attend the House of Parliament to execute the commands of each House.

Serjeants-at-Law. Barristers of superior degree of the Order of the Coif, to which they were called by writ under the Great Seal. They formed an Inn called

301

Serjeants' Inn, with buildings in Fleet Street and Chancery Lane. Formerly they were supposed to serve the Crown (hence their name, serjeants or *servientes ad legem*); they had a right of exclusive audience in the Court of Common Pleas; and every judge of the Superior Courts of Common Law had to be a Serjeant. This rule was abolished by the Judicature Act 1873, s.8. The degree of Queen's Counsel supplanted that of Serjeant, and Old Serjeants' Inn (in Chancery Lane) was sold in 1877. See COIF.

serjeanty. (Norman-French, *serjantie*; Latin, *serviens,* a servant.) Service: a form of tenure. See GRAND SERJEANTY; PETTY SERJEANTY.

service. (1) The duty due from a tenant to his lord. Services were (i) spiritual, *e.g.* as in tenure by frankalmoign; (ii) temporal, (a) free, (b) base or villein. (2) The relationship of a servant to his master.

service of process. A writ of summons and all other originating processes must be served personally on each defendant (Ord. 10, r. 1). However provision is made for service by post (Ord. 10, r. 1(2)(*a*)), by insertion through the defendant's letter box (Ord. 10, r. 1(2)(*b*)) or on the defendant's solicitor empowered to accept service (Ord. 10, r. 1(4)). Personal service means leaving a copy of the document with the defendant (Ord. 65, r. 2). Every writ served must be accompanied by an acknowledgment of service (Ord. 10, r. 1(6)). Service may be effected at any hour of the day or night, save on a Sunday when, in cases of urgency, leave of the court may be granted (Ord. 65, r. 10). Substituted service may be ordered where it is impracticable to serve the writ, etc., personally (Ord. 65, r. 4). Service out of the jurisdiction is effected under Ord. 11.

In the county court service is generally by post (C.C.R., Ord. 7, r. 1). Where personal service is required service may be by the court bailiff or the party or his solicitor or agent (Ord. 7, r. 2).

servient tenement. A tenement subject to a servitude or easement (*q.v.*).

servitium. Services.

servitude. An easement (*q.v.*).

servitus. [Roman law.] Slavery. An institution of the *jus gentium* by which, contrary to nature, a man becomes the property of a master.

servus ordinarius. [Roman law.] A slave holding some special post in the establishment as cook, baker, etc.

servus poenae. [Roman law.] A penal slave: a convict, *e.g.* slaves sent to the mines, or condemned to fight with wild beasts. Abolished by Justinian.

servus vicarius. [Roman law.] An attendant or assistant of a *servus ordinarius:* often purchased by the latter out of his *peculium.*

session. The period between the opening of Parliament and its prorogation (*q.v.*).

Session of the peace. A sitting of justices of the peace for the exercise of their powers. There are petty and special sessions. See Justices of the Peace Act 1949; Magistrates' Courts Act 1952.

set down. A request in the proper form to the appropriate officer to list a case for hearing. For the procedure in the High Court see Ord. 34.

set-off. A claim in a liquidated amount by the defendant to a sum of money as a defence to the whole or part of a money claim made by the plaintiff, which may be included in the defence and set off against the plaintiff's claim, whether or not it is added as a counterclaim (*q.v.*) (Ord. 18, r. 17).

There can, in general, be no set-off against the Crown (Ord. 77, r. 6).

settle. (1) To draw up a document and decide upon its terms, *e.g.* a partnership deed may be settled by counsel. (2) To compromise a case. (3) To create a settlement (*q.v.*).

settled acount. See ACCOUNT, SETTLED.

settled land. Land limited to several persons in succession, so that the person for the time being in the possession or enjoyment of it has no power to deprive the others of their right of future enjoyment. Under the Settled Land Act 1925, s.1, settled land is land:

(1) Limited in trust for any person by way of succession.

(2) Limited in trust for any person in possession, (a) for an entailed interest; (b) for an estate subject to an executory limitation over; (c) for a base or determinable fee; (d) being a minor.

(3) Limited in trust for a contingent estate.

(4) Limited to or in trust for a married woman with a restraint on anticipation (but see RESTRAINT ON ANTICIPATION).

(5) Charged with any rentcharge for the life of any person.

See TENANT FOR LIFE.

settlement. The instrument or instruments by which land is settled; where property is limited upon trust for any persons by way of succession.

A compound settlement is the description of a number of documents, *e.g.* deeds and wills, extending over a period, by means of which land is settled.

A marriage or ante-nuptial settlement is an instrument executed before a marriage, and wholly or partly in consideration of it, for the purpose of regulating the enjoyment and evolution of real or personal property.

A strict settlement is one which is designed to retain estates in the family. It proceeds (1) To provide for the wife by securing the payment to her of two annuities; the one, pin-money, payable during her husband's lifetime; the other a jointure, payable after his death. (2) To provide for the payment of gross sums of money (portions) to such of the younger children of the marriage as attain their majority. (3) To provide that the property so charged should go as a whole to the eldest son.

A voluntary settlement is one not made for valuable consideration.

several. Separate: as opposed to "joint."

severalty. Property is said to belong to persons in severalty when the share of each is ascertained (so that he can exclude the others from it) as opposed to joint ownership, ownership in common, and coparcenary, where the owners hold in undivided shares.

severance. Where a transaction is composed of several parts, and it is possible to divide it up so as to preserve part and disregard the other part, the contract is said to be severable. Thus if one of the promises is to do an act which is either in itself a criminal offence or *contra bonos mores* (*q.v.*), the whole contract is void, but if the objectionable part is only subsidiary, then it may be treated as struck out and the contract enforced without it.

sewer. Originally an open trench or channel for carrying off surplus water from land near the sea or from marshy ground.

sex change. A marriage may be declared void on the ground that the parties are not respectively male and female (Matrimonial Causes Act 1973, s.11(*c*); see NULLITY OF MARRIAGE) but it has been held that the sex of an individual is fixed at birth and cannot be changed by medical or surgical means (*Corbett* v. *Corbett (Orse. Ashley)* [1970] 2 All E.R. 33).

sex discrimination. See the Sex Disqualification (Removal) Act 1919; Sex Discrimination Act 1975. See DISCRIMINATION.

sexual offences. Rape, unlawful sexual intercourse with mental defectives, girls under 13, or girls 13 or over but under 16; indecent assault upon a female of any age, or upon a male person; the abduction of an unmarried female, whether under 16, or under 18 if with intent that she shall have unlawful sexual intercourse with a man or men; incest; sodomy; permitting the defilement of girls under 16; procuration of females by threats, fraud or drugs; detention of females

303

in brothels, permitting a child or young person to be in a brothel, living on the earnings of prostitution, and importuning by male prostitutes (Sexual Offences Act 1956; Sexual Offences (Amendment) Act 1976; Criminal Law Act 1977 s.54). Indecent photography of children is also an offence (Protection of Children Act 1978). See also PROSTITUTION.

shack, common of. The right of owners of adjacent fields to pasture their cattle after the crop has been gathered over the whole extent.

share. A definite portion of the capital of a company; it is personal property. Shares may be, *e.g.* preference, ordinary, deferred, or founders' shares. The ownership of a share entitles the owner to receive a proportionate part of the profits of the company, and to take part in the management in accordance with the articles of association, which also regulate the mode in which shares may be transferred. Shares may be converted by a limited company into stock (*q.v.*).

share certificate. An instrument under the seal of the company, certifying that the person therein named is entitled to a certain number of shares; it is not a negotiable instrument. A share warrant to bearer is a certificate under the seal of the company, stating that the bearer of the warrant is entitled to a certain number or amount of fully paid-up shares or stock; it is a negotiable instrument. See SCRIP.

sharepushing. Sharehawking: calling from house to house to sell shares. The Prevention of Fraud (Investments) Act 1958 prohibits dealing in securities without licence from the Board (now Department) of Trade. See also the Banking Act 1979, ss. 1–20; the Criminal Justice Act 1972, Sched. 5.

sheriff. The chief officer of the Crown in the county. He is appointed by the Crown every year and must hold some land within the county. The duties of sheriffs include the charge of parliamentary elections, the execution of process issuing from the High Court and the criminal courts, and the levying of forfeited recognisances. A high sheriff is appointed for every county and for Greater London (other than the City of London) (Local Government Act 1972, s.219). The sheriffs of the City of London are two in number and are elected by the City corporation. Formerly, the sheriff had judicial duties to perform as judge of the Sheriff's County Court. He also held a court of record, called the Sheriff's Tourn, which had the same functions and jurisdiction as the Court Leet (*q.v.*) (Sheriffs Act 1887). See PRICKING FOR SHERIFFS.

Where a claim is made to any money, goods or chattels being taken by a sheriff in execution, or to the proceeds or value thereof by some third person, the sheriff may apply to the court by way of interpleader (*q.v.*).

shew cause. When an order, rule, decree or the like has been made *nisi,* the person who appears before the court and contends that it should not be allowed to take effect is said to shew cause against it. See RULE.

shifting use. See USE.

ship. A vessel cannot be registered as a British ship unless she belongs wholly to British subjects, or to a corporation formed under and subject to the laws of, and having its principal place of business in, the British Commonwealth. The ownership of every registered ship is divided into 64 shares, all of which may belong to one person, but not more than 64 persons can be registered as part-owners of any one ship. Not more than five persons may be registered as joint-owners of any ship or share (Merchant Shipping Act 1979).

ship's husband. The agent of the owners in regard to the management of all affairs of the ship in the home port.

ship's papers. A ship's registry certificate, bill of lading, bill of health, charterparty and log, which show the character of the ship and cargo.

shire. The county.

shire-reeve or **shire clerk.** The sheriff.

shoplifting. To steal goods from a shop. Not a distinct offence as it amounts to theft contrary to Theft Act 1968, ss. 1, 7.

shops. Shop premises means a shop, or a building, or part, where retail or wholesale trading is carried on, or where goods are delivered by the public for repair or treatment, and also solid fuel sale depots (Offices, Shops and Railway Premises Act 1963, s.1(3)). The main object of that Act is to set standards of health, welfare and safety for the employees working in such premises.

short cause. Simple actions which can be tried as short causes in a summary manner, *i.e.* not exceeding four hours are inserted in the "Short-Cause List." The order may be made by a Master at the hearing of the summons under Ord. 14.

shorthold tenancy. A tenancy granted for not less than one and not more than five years (Housing Act 1980, s.52). It is protected during its subsistence but the landlord may recover possession at its expiry date (Rent Act 1977, Sched. 15, Pt. II, case 19 inserted by Housing Act 1980, s.55(1)).

sic utere tuo ut alienum non laedas. [So use your own property as not to injure your neighbour's.] See NUISANCE.

sign manual. The signature or "royal hand" of the Queen, as distinguished from the signing of documents by the signet.

signature. A person signs a document when he writes or marks something on it in token of his intention to be bound by its contents, commonly by subscribing his name. Illiterate people commonly sign by making a cross. Corporations sign by means of the corporate seal.

signet. A seal with which certain documents are sealed by a principal Secretary of State on behalf of the Queen. The signet is the principal of the three seals by the delivery of which a Secretary of State is appointed to his office.

signing judgment. The proper term is "entering judgment." See Ord. 42, rr. 4, 5; Masters' Practice Directions, 19, 20.

similiter. [In like manner.] That set form of words used by the plaintiff or defendant in an action by which he signified his acceptance of the issue tendered by his opponent.

simony. The selling of such things as are spiritual, by giving something of a temporal nature for the purchase thereof (Stephen). Selling the next presentation to a living was simony. The Simony Act 1713 was repealed by the Statute Law (Repeals) Act 1971. See ADVOWSON; NEXT PRESENTATION.

sine die. [Without day.] Indefinitely. See EAT INDE SINE DIE.

sittings. The sittings of the Supreme Court are four in number: the Hilary Sittings, commencing on January 11, and ending on the Wednesday before Easter Sunday; the Easter Sittings commencing on the second Tuesday after Easter Sunday and ending on the Friday before Spring Bank Holiday; the Trinity Sittings commencing on the second Tuesday after Spring Bank Holiday and ending on July 31, and the Michaelmas Sittings commencing on October 1, and ending on December 21 (Ord. 64, r. 1).

Sittings of the High Court may be held at any place in England and Wales (Courts Act 1971, s.2).

six clerks. Officials of the Court of Chancery who acted as intermediaries between solicitors and the court.They were abolished in 1842 and their duties were transferred to the Clerk of Enrolments and to the Clerks of Records and Writs (*q.v.*).

slander. Defamation (*q.v.*) by means of spoken words or gesture. It is a tort and not a crime and is not actionable without proof of special damage, except in four cases when the words are said to be actionable *per se, i.e.*: (1) Imputing a crime punishable with imprisonment. (2) Imputing contagious venereal disease. (3) Disparaging a person in his office, profession, calling, trade or business, whether or not the words are spoken of him in the way of his office, etc. (Defamation Act 1952, s.2). (4) Imputing unchastity to a woman (Slander of Women Act 1891). See LIBEL.

The publication of words in the course of the performance of a play is, in general, treated as publication in a permanent form (Theatres Act 1968, ss. 4, 7).

slander of title. A false and malicious statement about a person, his property, or business which inflicts damage, not necessarily on his personal reputation, but on his title to property, or on his business, or generally on his material interests (Winfield). Examples are false allegations that a house is haunted; that a lady engaged to be married is married already; or that goods are liable to a lien or infringe a patent or copyright. It includes slander of goods: a false and malicious depreciation of the quality of the merchandise manufactured and sold by the plaintiff (*White* v. *Mellin* [1895] A.C. 154). Slander of title is not actionable unless special damage (*q.v.*) results from it, or unless the words are calculated to cause damage to the plaintiff in respect of his office, profession, calling, trade or business (Defamation Act 1952, s.3). See MALICIOUS FALSEHOOD.

slip. A memorandum containing the agreed terms of a proposed policy of marine insurance, and initialled by the underwriters. The insurance cover commences from the moment the slip is signed. See the Marine Insurance Act 1906, ss. 21, 22.

slip rule. Clerical mistakes, accidental omissions, etc., in judgments and orders may be corrected by the court at any time on application by motion or summons (Ord. 20, r. 11).

small claims. The term commonly applied to cases involving less than £500 dealt with in County Courts under the arbitration procedure. See COUNTY COURTS.

small holding. Small holdings are regulated under the Agriculture Act 1970, ss. 37–65, as amended by the Agriculture (Miscellaneous Provisions) Act 1972, ss. 9, 26, Sched. 6 and the Local Government Act 1972, ss. 131, 272, Sched. 30.

smuggling. The offence of importing or exporting prohibited goods, or of importing or exporting goods and fraudulently evading the duties imposed on them. Goods so imported are liable to confiscation, and the offenders are liable to forfeit treble the value of the goods, or the penalty of £100, whichever is the greater; or to imprisonment for two years, or both (Customs and Excise Management Act 1979).

socage. A variety of tenure with fixed and certain services, as distinguished from frankalmoign and knight's service.

Socage was originally of two kinds, free socage and villein socage, according as the services were free or base. Free socage was of two kinds, socage *in capite* and common socage, but the former has been abolished. Common free socage is the modern ordinary tenure. Villein socage is now represented by tenure in ancient demesne (*q.v.*).

solicitor. A person employed to conduct legal proceedings or to advise on legal matters. To enable a person to practise as a solicitor, he must (a) be admitted as a solicitor, (b) have his name on the roll of solicitors and (c) have in force a practising certificate issued by the Law Society (Solicitors Act 1974, ss. 1, 28). Solicitors are not only bound to use reasonable diligence and skill in transacting the business of their clients, but they also occupy a fiduciary position towards their clients. They are officers of the court.

A solicitor has a lien on documents of which he has possession in his capacity of solicitor, *e.g.* title deeds, until his proper costs are paid. Also any court in which a solicitor has been employed to prosecute or defend any suit, matter or proceeding may make a charging order on the property recovered or preserved through his instrumentality for his taxed costs therein.

The law was consolidated in the Solicitors Act 1974.

The immunity of a barrister from claims in negligence may extend to a solicitor doing litigation work which could have been done by counsel (*Rondel* v. *Worsley* [1969] 1 A.C. 191 but see *Saif Ali* v. *Sidney Mitchell & Co.* [1980] A.C. 198).

solicitor, change of. A notice of change is filed in the appropriate office by the party changing his solicitor, and the serves on the other parties, and on the former solicitor, copies of that notice (Ord. 67).

Solicitor-General. The second of the law officers. He is a member of the House of Commons. The office is conferred by patent at the pleasure of the Crown.

solvent. In a position to pay debts as they become due.

solvit ad diem. The plea by the defendant, in an action on a bond, bill, etc., that he had "paid on the day" the money was due.

solvitur ambulando. The question is resolved by action.

solvitur in modum solventis. [Money paid is to be applied according to the wish of the person paying it.]

sounding in damages. An action which is brought to recover damages, as opposed to an action for debt. For the plaintiff to succeed he must prove he suffered some damage.

sovereignty. The supreme authority in an independent political society. It is essential indivisible and illimitable (Austin). However, it is now considered both divisible and limitable. Sovereignty is limited externally by the possibility of a general resistance. Internal sovereignty is paramount power over all action within, and is limited by the nature of the power itself. In the British Constitution the Sovereign *de jure* is the Queen or Crown. The legislative sovereign is the Queen in Parliament, which can make or unmake any law whatever. The legal sovereign is the Queen and the Judiciary. The executive sovereign is the Queen and her Ministers. The *de facto* or political sovereign is the electorate: the Ministry resign on a defeat at a general election.

Speaker. The Speaker of the House of Commons is the member of the House through whom it communicates with the Sovereign, and who presides over the proceedings of the House and enforces obedience to its orders. He is elected, subject to the approval of the Crown, on the frst day that a new Parliament assembles.

speaking order. An order which tells its own story, and is intelligible; so that if it is in error, it could by certiorari (*q.v.*) be quashed.

special case. Under Ord. 33, r. 3 the court can if necessary, order that any question or issue arising in the action, whether of fact or law or both, and whether or not raised by the pleadings, shall be tried before, at, or after the trial of the cause or matter. Previous provision for an arbitrator to state a special case on a point of law has been abolished (Arbitration Act 1979, s.1(1)) and replaced by appeal to the High Court (see Ord. 73, r. 2; see also ARBITRATION).

Special Commissioners of Income Tax are salaried officials appointed by the Treasury. Appeals which raise questions of law or which may be prolonged are usually brought before them.

special damage. Damage of a kind which is not presumed by law, but must be expressly pleaded and proved.

Slander (*q.v.*) is not (with some exceptions) actionable without proof of special damage. Also, in an action for slander of title, or other malicious falsehood, it shall not be necessary to allege or prove special damage if the words are calculated to cause pecuniary damage to the plaintiff and are published in writing or other permanent form; or are calculated to cause pecuniary damage to the plaintiff in respect of any office, profession, calling, trade or business held or carried on by him (Defamation Act 1952, s.3).

An action will lie for a public nuisance at the instance of a person who has suffered special damage (over and above that suffered as a member of the public) as a result of the nuisance.

special jury. Where a trial by jury was ordered, either party could formerly insist upon a special jury drawn from a panel of persons with a higher property qualification than common jurors. Special juries have been abolished (Juries Act 1949, ss. 18, 19; Courts Act 1971, s.40).

special licence. See MARRIAGE.

special pleader. See PLEADER.

special procedure list. The name given to those divorce cases dealt with by the registrar (*q.v.*) reading the affidavit of the Petitioner and certifying that the Petitioner has proved the contents of the petition and is entitled to a decree. All undefended divorces are now dealt with in this way so that the description is to some extent a misnomer (see Matrimonial Causes Rules 1977, r.33(3)).

special resolution. See RESOLUTION.

special verdict. See VERDICT.

specialia generalibus derogant. [Special words derogate from general ones.]

specialty. A contract under seal. A specialty debt is one due under a deed.

specific performance. Where damages would be inadequate compensation for the breach of an agreement, the contractor may be compelled to perform what he has agreed to do by a decree of specific performance, *e.g.* in contracts for the sale, purchase or lease of land, or for the recovery of unique chattels (*i.e.* not obtainable in the market). Specific performance will not be decreed of contracts of personal service, but a defendant may be restrained by injunction from the breach of a negative stipulation in such a contract, *e.g.* a covenant not to give services elsewhere during the term of the contract. The making of a decree is in the discretion of the court. Actions for the specific performance of contracts relating to real estate are assigned to the Chancery Division. Where appropriate a court may, by way of interim relief, order specific performance by granting an interlocutory mandatory injunction to enforce a contractual obligation (*Astro Exito Navegacion S.A.* v. *Southland Enterprise Co. Ltd., The Times*, April 8, 1982, C.A.).

specificatio. The making of a new article out of the chattel of one person by the labour of another.

specification. The statement in writing describing the nature of an invention, required under the Patents Act 1949.

spent conviction. A conviction which, after a "rehabilitation period" of between five and 10 years (depending on the sentence) need not be disclosed and which may not be referred to in open court without leave of the judge. Some convictions, depending on the sentence, can never be "spent" (Rehabilitation of Offenders Act 1974).

spes successionis. A mere hope of succeeding to property, *e.g.* on the part of the next-of-kin of a living person who will take his property if he happens to die intestate. See EXPECTANT HEIR.

sponsus. [Roman law.] Betrothed. The man who intended to marry a woman stipulated with the person that was to give her in marriage that he would do so, and on his part promised to marry her. *Sponsa* was the woman thus promised; *sponsus* the man who promised to marry her. *Sponsalia* denoted the proposal and promise of marriage.

spouse. A husband or wife. See HUSBAND AND WIFE.

springing use. See USE.

spurii. [Roman law.] Bastards: persons born out of lawful marriage.

squatter. Summary proceedings for claiming possession of land (R.S.C. Ord. 113; C.C.R. Ord. 24 may be taken against squatters. All persons on the premises should be evicted (*R.* V. *Wandsworth County Court* [1975] 1 W.L.R. 1314; *Swordheath Properties Ltd.* v. *Floyd* [1978] 1 W.L.R. 551). For criminal liability SEE FORCIBLE ENTRY.

squatter's title. The title acquired by one who, having wrongfully entered upon land, has occupied it without paying rent or otherwise acknowledging any superior title for such time that he acquires an indefeasible title (see *Re Nisbet and Pott's Contract* [1910] 1 Ch. 1).

A squatter is bound by burdens binding the land, *e.g.* restrictive covenants. The squatter in possession has a good title against all but the true owner. To establish a good title in himself, a squatter must show who was the true owner, and that he has been barred by lapse of time. See LIMITATION, STATUTES OF.

stabit praesumptio donec probetur in contrarium. [A presumption will stand good until the contrary is proved.]

stakeholder. A person with whom money is deposited pending the decision of a bet or wager; or one who holds money or property which is claimed by rival claimants, but in which he himself claims no interest. Where money is placed in the hands of a stakeholder to abide the result of a wager the money is recoverable from the stakeholder either before or after the determination of the wager if the money has not been paid over to the winner, and even after the money has been paid to the winner, if before payment the authority to pay was withdrawn by the party seeking to recover (see Ord. 17). See INTERPLEADER.

stallage. A payment for the exclusive occupation of a portion of the soil within a market.

stamp duties. Revenue raised by means of stamps affixed to written instruments such as conveyances, leases, etc. Stamps are either impressed or adhesive. Impressed stamps are required for the most part, the adhesive stamps being permitted for small amounts of duty. The impressed stamps are made by the Inland Revenue when an instrument is tendered for stamping. Stamp duties are either fixed in amount, or *ad valorem,* that is, proportionate to the value of the property dealt with by the instrument. Such instruments cannot in general be received in evidence in civil proceedings unless duly stamped. Counsel do not take stamp objections, but the court may; if so, the document may be duly stamped under penalty, unless it is one, such as a bill of exchange, which cannot be stamped after execution. See the Stamp Duties Management Act 1891 and the Stamp Act 1891.

Standing Orders. Rules and forms regulating the procedure of each House of Parliament.

stannaries. Parts of Devon and Cornwall where any tin works are in operation. Civil actions in respect of mining matters might formerly be brought in the Stannary Court, which was abolished in 1896. See the Stannaries Acts 1869 and 1887.

staple towns. The seaports from which wool, leather, tin and lead (collectively termed the staple) were exported, and which were regulated by the Statute of the Staple. The merchants of those towns, the Staplers, had, from the reign of Edward I, a monopoly in the staple. In each staple town the mayor of the staple held Staple Courts.

Star Chamber. The *Aula Regis* sitting in the Star Chamber at Westminster, with a residuary jurisdiction after the severance of the Courts of Common Law and

Chancery. It acted as a "court of equity" in criminal matters. By the statute 1487, 3 Hen. 7, c. 1, a court was constituted to consist of the chief officers of State and the two Chief Justices, with jurisdiction over unlawful combinations, riots and assemblies, and offences of sheriffs and jurors; later extended to offences against Royal Proclamations. This court appears to have become assimilated in the Court of Star Chamber. The Star Chamber was abolished by the Statute 1640, 16 Car. 1, c. 10.

stare decisis. The "sacred principle" of English law by which precedents are authoritative and binding, and must be followed. See PRECEDENT; RATIO DECIDENDI.

State. The organised community: the central political authority.

In international law a State is a people permanently occupying a fixed territory, bound together into one body politic by common subjection to some definite authority exercising, through the medium of an organised government, a control over all persons and things within its territory, capable of maintaining relations of peace and war, and free from political external control.

statement of claim. A written or printed statement by the plaintiff in an action in the High Court, showing the facts on which he relies to support his claim against the defendant, and the relief which he claims. It may be indorsed on the writ (Ord. 6, r. 2). If not, it must be served within 14 days after acknowledgment of service by the defendant (Ord. 18, r. 1). In default, the defendant may apply to dismiss the action for want of prosecution (Ord. 19, r. 1). The plaintiff may amend the statement of claim once without leave (Ord. 20, r. 2).

In a commercial cause the "points of claim" correspond to the statement of claim.

statement of defence. See DEFENCE.

status. The legal position or condition of a person, *e.g.* a minor, married woman, bankrupt, or British national. The status of a person is an index to his legal rights and duties, powers and disabilities.

status de manerio. The state of a manor: the assembly of the tenants in the court of the lord to do suit.

status quo. The state in which things are, or were.

statute. An Act of Parliament, particularly a public Act. Statutes are of the following kinds: (1) declaratory, when they do not profess to make any alteration in the existing law, but merely to declare or explain what it is; (2) remedial, when they alter the common law; (3) amending, when they alter the statute law; (4) consolidating, when they consolidate several previous statutes relating to the same subject-matter; (5) disabling or restraining, when they restrain the alienation of property; (6) enabling, when they remove a restriction or disability; (7) penal, when they impose a penalty or forteiture; (8) codifying. See STATUTORY INTERPRETATION.

statute law revision. Statute Law Revision Acts were passed every few years since 1861, to remove from the statute book Acts, or parts of Acts, which had become obsolete. On the recommendations of the Law Commission (see the Law Commissions Act 1965), Statute Law (Repeals) Acts were passed in 1969, 1971 and 1973. The legal effect of anything repealed by the Acts remains notwithstanding the repeal.

statute merchant. A bond acknowledged before the chief magistrate of some trading town pursuant to the statute *De Mercatoribus*, 13 Edw. 1.

Statute of Frauds 1677 (29 Car. 2, c. 3). Passed for the prevention of frauds and perjuries. It enacted (ss. 1 and 2) that leases of lands, tenements or hereditaments (except leases not exceeding three years, reserving a rent of at least two-thirds the value of the land) shall have the force of leases at will only, unless they are put in writing and signed by the parties or their agents. Section 3 required assignments and surrenders of leases and interests in land (not being copyholds, etc.) to be in writing. Section 4 enacted that no action shall be brought upon any special promise by an executor or administrator to answer damages out of his own estate, or upon a guarantee, or upon an agreement made in consideration of marriage, or upon any contract for sale of lands, etc., or any interest in or concerning them, or upon any agreement that is not to be performed within a year, unless the agreement is in writing and signed by the party to be charged, or his agent. Sections 7 and 9 required declarations or creations of trusts of lands, etc., and all assignments of trusts, to be in writing, signed by the party, but s.8 exempted trusts arising by implication of law. Sections 10 and 11 made the lands of a *cestui que trust,* when in the hands of his real representative, liable to his judgments and obligations.

It is now largely repealed and replaced by later enactments.

Statute of Uses 1535 (27 Hen. 8, c. 10). See USE.

Statute of Westminster 1931 was passed to define the constitutional position of the Dominions. In regard to legislation, by section 2 no Dominion legislation after 1931 is void or inoperative on the ground of repugnancy to the law of England, and a Dominion Parliament has power to repeal Imperial legislation in so far as it is part of the law of the Dominion. By section 4 no Imperial legislation is to extend to a Dominion as part of the law of the Dominion, unless it is expressly declared in the Act that the Dominion has requested and consented to the enactment.

statute staple. A bond acknowledged before the mayor of the staple (*q.v.*) to provide a speedy remedy for recovering debts.

statutes of distribution. See DISTRIBUTION.

statutes of limitation. See LIMITATION, STATUTES OF.

statutory declaration. A written statement of facts which the person making it (the declarant) signs and solemnly declares to be true before a commissioner or magisterial officer. The Statutory Declarations Act 1835 substitutes declarations for oaths in many cases. The expression statutory declaration means a declaration under that Act (Interpretation Act 1978, s.5). Making a false statutory declaration is a misdemeanour (Perjury Act 1911).

statutory duty. A duty, or liability, imposed by some statute (*q.v.*).

statutory interpretation. The courts frequently have to interpret (*i.e.* decide the meaning of) statutes, particularly where they are not clear. Where possible the words of the statute must be interpreted literally, save where this would produce unintended consequences or absurdity. The courts may not use Hansard (*q.v.*) as a guide to Parliament's intention. See HANSARD.

statutory instruments. In general, where the power of subordinate legislation is conferred upon Her Majesty in Council, or on a Secretary of State, any document by which that power is exercised is to be known as a statutory instrument (Statutory Instruments Act 1946; Laying of Documents before Parliament (Interpretation) Act 1948). See also STATUTORY RULES AND ORDERS.

statutory owner. The trustees of the settlement (except where they have power to convey in the name of the tenant for life) or other persons who, during a minority, or when there is no tenant for life, have the powers of a tenant for life (Settled Land Act 1925, s.117(1)(xxvi)).

statutory rules and orders. Regulations made by the Queen in Council, Government Departments, or other authorities pursuant to Acts of Parliament. They are superseded by statutory instruments (*q.v.*).

statutory tenant. A tenant who is entitled to remain in possession of a rent-controlled house or premises by virtue of the Rent Acts, after his contractual tenancy has expired. The term includes the widow and members of the family of a deceased tenant (see Rent Act 1977, s.2(1)(a), (2)).

statutory trusts. Land held upon the "statutory trusts" is held upon trust to sell and to stand possessed of the net proceeds of sale, after payment of costs, and of the net rents and profits until sale after payment of rates, taxes, costs of insurance, repairs and other outgoings, upon such trusts, and subject to such powers and provisions, as may be requisite for giving effect to the rights of the persons interested in the land (Law of Property Act 1925, s.35). See INTESTATE SUCCESSION.

Statutum de Mercatoribus. The Statute of Acton Burnel, which established the Statute Merchant (q.v.).

stay of execution. The suspension of the operation of a judgment or order (see Ord. 47).

stay of proceedings. Suspension of proceedings in an action, which may be temporary until something requisite or ordered is done, or permanently, where to proceed would be improper. The court has an inherent jurisdiction to stay all proceedings which are frivolous and vexatious, or an abuse of the process of the court, or taken for the purpose of delay, or otherwise, or where the claim or defence set up rests upon no solid basis (see Ord. 18, r. 19). The Supreme Court has a general power to stay any proceedings (Judicature Act 1925, s.41). See VEXATIOUS ACTIONS.

stealing. See THEFT.

stet processus. [Stay of proceedings.] An entry on the record in an action in the old common law courts.

steward. Formerly an officer of the Crown, or of a feudal lord, who acted as keeper of a court of justice; as, for example, the Lord High Steward (q.v.), or the steward of a lord of a manor.

stint. A limit, as in the right to pasture a limited number of animals on land.

stipendiary magistrate. A salaried magistrate with the powers of a justice of the peace, except that a stipendiary can do all things for which two ordinary justices are required. See Justices of the Peace Act 1979, ss. 13–16.

stipulatio. [Roman law.] A verbal contract formed by question and answer. One party proposed a question (*stipulatio*) and the other responded to it (*promissio*). In the time of Gaius it was necessary to use a certain solemn form of words; but before Justinian, the question and answer could be embodied in any words to express the meaning of the parties. The contract was unilateral, the *promissor* only being bound, and the parties had to be present when the contract was entered into.

stirpes. Stocks or families. See PER STIRPES.

stock. (1) A family. (2) The capital of a company was formerly called its "joint-stock" meaning the common or joint fund contributed by the members. (3) A fund or capital which is capable of being divided into and held in any irregular amount. See COMPANY.

Stock Exchange. An association of stockbrokers and stockjobbers. The Governing body is the Committee, who can enforce the rules upon members by disciplinary powers. As between themselves the members carry out transactions according to the customs and usages of the Exchange. Power to suspend dealings is conferred on the Treasury by the Banking and Financial Dealings Act 1971, s.2.

stock transfers. The Stock Transfer Act 1963 provides for simplified transfers of securities.

stockbroker. A member of the London Stock Exchange, or a provincial Stock Exchange, who effects sales and purchases of stocks and shares with other members of his Exchange on behalf of clients. The client who employs a stockbroker is bound by the customs and usages of the Exchange, although he is ignorant of them, and he must indemnify the stockbroker for any liability he incurs under them, unless they are unlawful or unreasonable.

stockjobber. The members of the Stock Exchange who carry stocks and shares on their books, and make a market for the stockbrokers. They quote different prices for buying and selling; the jobbers "turn" is the difference between the two.

stop order. In Chancery practice, when a fund (in cash, stock or other securities) is in court in a cause or proceeding, any person claiming an interest in it, *e.g.* a judgment creditor, may apply to the court for an order to prevent it from being paid out or otherwise dealt with, without notice to the applicant (see Ord. 50, r. 10). See also rr. 11–15.

stoppage in transitu. The right which an unpaid vendor has to resume the possession of goods sold upon credit and to retain them until tender of the price where the vendee has become insolvent before they come into his possession, or that of his agent.

The right of stoppage lasts only so long as the goods are in transit, and is not affected by any sale or disposition of the goods by the buyer, unless the seller has assented thereto, or unless the seller has parted with documents of title to the goods which have been transferred to a person who takes them in good faith and for value. See Sale of Goods Act 1979, ss. 44–47; *Lickbarrow* v. *Mason* (1788) 2 T.R. 63.

stranding. Does not occur when a vessel takes the ground in the ordinary and usual course of navigation, so that she will float again on the flow of the tide; but it occurs if the vessel takes the ground by reason of some unusual or accidental occurrence, *e.g.* in consequence of an unknown and unusual obstruction, or on being driven on to rocks.

stranger. One not party or privy to an act or transaction.

strict liability. Liability without fault. Where a man acts at his peril and is responsible for accidental harm, independently of the existence of either wrongful intent or negligence; as, for example, in the liability for escape of dangerous things. This term supersedes the term "absolute liability" (in view of the admitted exceptions to that rule): see *Read* v. *Lyons & Co.* [1947] A.C. 156.

strict settlement. See MARRIAGE SETTLEMENT; SETTLEMENT.

strike. Withdrawal or cessation of labour by employees. Such action may expose participants to civil action or criminal liability unless the action is in contemplation or furtherance of a trade dispute as defined by statute. See TRADE DISPUTE; PICKETTING.

striking out pleadings. This takes place when the court makes an order to that effect, either for the purpose of amendment (*q.v.*) or to compel one of the parties to do some act. Thus, if a defendant fails to comply with an order for discovery, he is liable to have his defence struck out, the court may give judgment, or make such other order as it thinks fit (Ord. 24, r. 16). See STAY OF PROCEEDINGS.

strip-tease. See DISORDERLY HOUSE.

stuprum. [Roman law.] Any connection between a man and an unmarried free woman otherwise than in concubinage.

sub colore juris. [Under colour of the law.]

sub judice. [In course of trial.]

sub modo. [Under condition or restriction.]

sub nom. : sub nomine. [Under the name.]

sub voce. [Under the title.]

subduct. To withdraw.

subinfeudation. The grant of the whole or part of his land by a tenant in fee simple to another to hold of him as his tenant so that the relation of tenure with its incidents of fealty, etc., was created between them. Subinfeudation was abolished by the Statute Quia Emptores (*q.v.*) (18 Edw. 1, c. 1).

subject to contract. An offer made "subject to contract" means that no legally binding agreement or contract shall exist until a formal contract (usually in or recorded by writing) has been completed. The words usually occur in relation to sale and purchase of land (as to whose formalities see CONTRACT). (See *Law* v. *Jones* [1974] Ch. 112, C.A.; *Tiverton Estates* v. *Wearwell Ltd.* [1975] Ch. 146, C.A.)

submission. A submission to arbitration is an instrument by which a dispute or question is referred to arbitration pursuant to an agreement between the parties. For the Arbitration Acts to apply it must be in writing. See ARBITRATION; REFERENCE.

subornation of perjury. The offence of procuring a person to commit perjury, punishable as perjury (*q.v.*).

subpoena. A writ issued in an action or suit requiring the person to whom it is directed to be present at a specified place and time, and for a specified purpose, under a penalty (*sub poena*). They are tested in the name of the Lord Chancellor. The varieties in use are: (1) the *subpoena ad testificandum,* used for the purpose of compelling a witness to attend and give evidence; (2) the *subpoena duces tecum,* used to compel a witness to attend in court or before an examiner or referee, to give evidence and also bring with him certain documents in his possession specified in the subpoena. See Ord. 38, rr. 14–19. For enforcing attendance of a witness in chambers, see Ord. 32, r. 7.

Subpoenas are not issued in criminal proceedings for the purpose of which a witness summons may be issued (Criminal Procedure (Attendance of Witnesses) Act 1965, s.8).

subrogation. The substitution of one person or thing for another, so that the same rights and duties which attached to the original person or thing attach to the substituted one. If one person is subrogated to another, he is said to "stand in that other's shoes." *e.g.* creditors are subrogated to the executors' right of indemnity against the estate where a business is carried on under the authority of the will; a person paying the premium on a policy of insurance belonging to another may be subrogated to that other; and an insurer is subrogated to the rights of the insured on paying his claim.

subscribe. To "write under"; to sign or attest; to apply for shares, etc.

subsidiary company. See HOLDING COMPANY.

subsidy. Originally, import and export duties granted to the King; later, any tax imposed by Parliament; now, popularly, as synonymous with subvention.

substantive law. The actual law, as opposed to adjectival or procedural law.

substratum. [Bottom or basis.] It is a ground for winding up a company that its "substratum" has gone, *i.e.* that it is impossible to carry on the business for which the company was incorporated.

substituted service. See SERVICE.

subtraction. The neglect or refusal to perform a duty or service, *e.g.* pay a tithe.

succession. Where property passes on the death of a corporation sole to his successor; "for as the heir doth inherit to the ancestor, so the successor doth succeed to the predecessor" (Co. Litt. 8B). See INTESTATE SUCCESSION.

succession duty. A duty which was first imposed by the Succession Duty Act 1853 on gratuitous acquisition, on death, of property in respect of which no legacy duty (*q.v.*) was payable unless specially exempted. Abolished by the Finance Act 1949, Part III.

sue. To bring an action, suit or other civil proceeding against a person.

sufferance wharf. A place appointed by the Commissioners of Customs and Excise for the lading and unlading of goods liable to Customs duties. Now, an "approved wharf" (Customs and Excise Act 1952, s.14). See also the Finance Act 1966, s.10.

suggestio falsi. An active misrepresentation, as opposed to a *suppressio veri,* or passive misrepresentation (*q.v.*).

sui generis. [Of its own kind; the only one of its kind.]

sui juris. [Roman law.] One of full legal capacity. An independent person not subject to any of the three forms of authority, *potestas, manus, mancipium.* In English law, a person who can validly contract and bind himself by legal obligation uncontrolled by any other person.

suicide. Formerly the felony of self-murder. By the Suicide Act 1961 the rule of law whereby it is a crime for a person to commit suicide was abrogated, and the offence was created of complicity, whereby a person who aids, abets, counsels or procures the suicide of another is punishable by 14 years' imprisonment.

suicide pact. Where two (or more) persons agree to commit suicide and there is a survivor, he is guilty of manslaughter if he killed another party to the pact in pursuance of it (Homicide Act 1957, s.4; Suicide Act 1961, ss. 2, 3, Sched. 2).

suing and labouring clause. The clause in a policy of marine insurance, as follows: "In case of any loss or misfortune, it shall be lawful for the assured, their factors, servants, and assigns, to sue labour, and travel, for, in, or about the defence, safeguard, and recovery of the said goods, and merchandises, and ship, etc., or any part thereof, without prejudice to the insurance; to the charges whereof we will contribute each one according to the rate and quantity of his sum herein insured" (see Marine Insurance Act 1906, s.78).

suit. Any legal proceeding of a civil kind brought by one person against another; an action, particularly in equity or for divorce.

A bond or recognisance given to a public officer as security is said to be put in suit when proceedings are taken to enforce it.

suit of court. A service theoretically due from every tenant of land forming part of, or held of, a manor, and consisting in the duty of attending the courts held by the lord. It was abolished by the Law of Property Act 1922 as from January 1, 1926. See MANORIAL INCIDENTS.

suit of the peace. A prosecution.

summary judgment. The procedure under Order 14 whereby a plaintiff who takes out a summons for judgment supported by an affidavit verifying the cause of action and stating that there is no defence, may, by order, enter judgment without trial.

It does not apply to a claim for libel, slander, malicious prosecution, false imprisonment, fraud, or claim against the Crown. The application is made after the defendant enters an acknowledgment of service, and after service of the statement of claim. Similar provisions now apply in the county court (see C.C.R., Ord. 9, r. 14).

summary proceedings. Criminal offences are divided into three classes, *viz.* : (1) those triable on indictment only (*i.e.* at Crown Court); (2) those triable summarily only (*i.e.* by Magistrates); (3) those which may be tried either way (Criminal Law Act 1977, ss. 14–16; Sched. 3). Summary proceedings are therefore class (2) above and such of class (3) as are dealt with by Magistrates.

Summer time. See the Summer Time Act 1972.

summing-up. A recapitulation by the judge of the evidence adduced in an action, drawing the attention of the jury to the salient points. A defective summing-up in a criminal case may be a ground for quashing the conviction by the Court of Appeal.

summons. A document issued from the office of a court of justice, calling upon the person to whom it is directed to attend before a judge or officer of the court. In the High Court of Justice a summons is a mode of making an application to a judge or master in chambers for the decision of matters of procedure prior to, or in lieu of, the hearing of an action in court, *e.g.* a summons for directions (*q.v.*). See ORIGINATING SUMMONS.

summons for directions. See DIRECTIONS.

summum jus summa injuria. [Extreme law is extreme injury.] The rigour of the law, untempered by equity, is not justice but the denial of it.

super visum corporis. [Upon view of the body.] See CORONER.

supercargo. A person employed by charterers of ships to go on the ship for the purpose of looking after cargo shipped by them and of selling it abroad.

superficies solo cedit. [Whatever is attached to the land forms part of it.] Actual physical attachment is not essential, *e.g.* a dry stone wall is part of the land.

superior court. Defined in Contempt of Court Act 1981, s.19 as the Court of Appeal, the High Court, the Crown Court, the Courts Martial Appeal Court, the Restrictive Practices Court, the Employment Appeal Tribunal, and any other court exercising powers equivalent to those of the High Court, including the House of Lords in its appellate capacity.

supersedeas. A writ which stays or puts an end to a proceeding.

superstitious uses. A trust which has for its object the propagation of the rites of a religion not tolerated by the law, and which is therefore void. It is otherwise if the trust is for saying masses for the dead (*Bourne* v.*Keane* [1919] A.C. 815; *Re Caus* [1934] Ch. 162).

supervision order. An order placing a minor under the supervision of a local authority or probation officer (Children and Young Persons Act 1969, s.7; Criminal Law Act 1977, s.65(4), Sched. 12; Powers of Criminal Courts Act 1973, s.26; Matrimonial Causes Act, 1973, s.44).

Supply, Committee of. See COMMITTEE OF THE WHOLE HOUSE.

support, right of. Every proprietor of land is entitled to so much lateral support from his neighbour's land as is necessary to keep his soil at its natural level, that is, his neighbour must not excavate so close to the the boundary as to cause the land to fall or subside. Similarly the owner of the surface is entitled to vertical support as against the owner of the subsoil, that is, the owner of the subjacent land must not cause subsidence of the surface unless he has an easement entitling him to do so. The right does not extend to the case of land, the weight of which has been increased by buildings, unless it can be shown that the land would have sunk if there had been no buildings on it, or unless an easement has been acquired by twenty years' uninterrupted enjoyment. See *Dalton* v. *Angus* (1881) 6 App. Cas. 740; *Darley Main Colliery Co.* v. *Mitchell* (1886) 11 App. Cas. 127.

suppressio veri. [Suppression of the truth.] Misrepresentation.

supra. [Above.]

Supreme Court of Judicature. The court formed by the Judicature Act 1873, whose constitution and jurisdiction are now defined by the Supreme Court Act 1981. The Supreme Court consists of the Court of Appeal, the High Court of Justice and the Crown Court (Act of 1981, s.1(1)).

sur. [Upon.] Used to point out on what the old real actions were founded, *e.g.* "sur disseisin," was to recover the land from a disseisor.

surcharge. (1) To surcharge a common is to put more cattle thereon than the pasture and herbage will sustain, or than the commoner has a right to do. (2) In taking or auditing accounts, to surcharge is to disallow an unauthorised item of expenditure and make the accounting party liable for it personally. See also ACCOUNT SETTLED.

sureties of the peace and good behaviour. A person may be ordered to find sureties for his keeping the peace or to be of good behaviour on a complaint being made under section 91 of the Magistrates' Courts Act 1952, in addition to his own recognisances. This process is called "binding over" (*q.v.*).

surety. A person who binds himself, usually by deed, to satisfy the obligation of another person, if the latter fails to do so; a guarantor.

If a surety satisfies the obligation for which he has made himself liable, he is entitled to recover the amount from the principal debtor. If one of several sureties is compelled to pay the whole amount or more than his share, he is entitled to contribution (*q.v.*) from his co-sureties. A surety is entitled to the benefit of all the securities which the creditor has against the principal. If the creditor releases the principal debtor, this will discharge the surety from liability, unless the creditor reserves his right against the surety.

surplus assets. What is left of a company's property after payment of debts and repayment of the whole of the preference and ordinary capital. Whether the preference shareholders are entitled to share in surplus assets is a question of construction, but the courts will not readily hold that the preference shareholders have bartered away their rights as contributories.

surplusage. A superfluity or excess; in pleading, the allegation of unnecessary matter. See STRIKING OUT PLEADINGS.

surprise may be a ground for setting aside a contract, judgment or order if substantial injustice has been done.

surrebutter; surrejoinder. See PLEADINGS.

surrender. The yielding up of an estate for life or for years in land, so that it merges in the reversion or remainder. Surrender must be by deed, or may be by operation of law, *e.g.* if a lessee accepts a new lease incompatible with his existing lease, this operates as a surrender in law of the latter. A mortgagee or mortgagor in possession has power to accept surrenders of leases, subject to the conditions in section 100(5) of the Law of Property Act 1925.

Surrender to the lord of the manor to the use of the intended transferee was the principal mode of alienating copyholds (*q.v.*).

surtax. The additional income tax charged upon an individual whose total income for any year exceeded a stated amount (Income and Corporation Taxes Act 1970). As a separate tax it has ceased to exist and in lieu thereof income tax is charged at different rates according to the individual's total income (Finance Act 1971, ss. 32–35).

survivorship. The right of a person to property by reason of his having survived another person who had an interest in it, *e.g.* on the death of one of two joint tenants the whole property passes to the survivor. See COMMORIENTES.

sus. per coll. (suspendatur per collum.) [Let him be hanged by the neck.]

suspended sentence. A sentence of imprisonment which is not to take effect immediately but only on the happening of another event, *e.g.* conviction for another offence punishable by imprisonment. The sentence of imprisonment ordered must not exceed two years and the period of suspension must be between one and two years (Powers of Criminal Courts Act 1973, ss. 22–25). The court may also impose a partly suspended sentence, *i.e.* an order that part of a sentence of imprisonment shall be served in prison and part held in suspense (Criminal Law Act 1977, s.47 and Sched. 9).

syndic. A person appointed by a corporation to act for it as regards a particular matter.

synod. An ecclesiastical council. See the Synodical Government Measure 1969; Synodical Government (Special Majorities) Measure 1971, and the Synodical Government (Amendment) Measure 1974.

T

tabula in naufragio. [Plank in the shipwreck.] In the doctrine of tacking (*q.v.*) the legal estate was the plank on which the third mortgagee could save himself in the shipwreck while the second mortgagee was drowned.

tabulae. [Roman law.] Tablets.

tabularius. [Roman law.] A public notary.

tacking. The priority of mortgagees over the same property is determined by the order in which the mortgages were made. Prior to 1926, this order might be disturbed by the process of adding a subsequent mortgage to an earlier mortgage or a further advance by the earlier mortgagee to his mortgage, when both would take the priority of the earlier, provided there was no notice of intervening mortgages at the time of the subsequent mortgage was made. This was known as tacking. Thus a third mortgagee, who had no notice of a second mortgage at the time his mortgage was made, might subsequently acquire the first mortgage and the legal estate and squeeze out or postpone the second mortgagee. By section 94 of the Law of Property Act 1925 tacking was abolished, except that a prior mortgagee has the right to make further advances to rank in priority to subsequent mortgages, where such is made (a) by arrangement with the subsequent mortgagees; or (b) without notice of the subsequent mortgages; or (c) under an obligation in the mortgage deed.

tail. See ENTAIL; ESTATE.

tales (pr. Tal'es). [Such.] Where a jury is summoned and found to be insufficient in number, the judge was empowered to award a *tales de circumstantibus*, that is, in command the sheriff to return so many other men duly qualified as should be present or could be found. The jurors so added were called talesmen. By the Juries Act 1974 the court itself has power to make up the required numbers of a full jury from any persons in the vicinity of the court (ss.6, 11(2)).

tallage. Taxes.

tally. A stick of rectangular section across one side of which were cut notches denoting payments. The stick being split lengthwise so that on each half there was one half of each notch, the debtor retained one half of the stick as evidence of the payment and the creditor kept the other half as a record. They were used in the Exchequer (*q.v.*) from the earliest times.

tattooing. It is an offence punishable by fine on summary conviction to tattoo a person under the age of 18 years except for medical reasons (Tattooing of Minors Act 1969).

taxation. The imposition of duties for the raising of revenue. Direct taxes are imposed upon the individual, usually according to his ability to pay, *e.g.* income tax; indirect taxes are levied upon certain articles of popular consumption; *e.g.* customs and excise duties. See also VALUE ADDED TAX.

taxation of costs. The process of examining and, if necessary, reducing the bill of costs of a solicitor. In the Supreme Court, taxation is carried out by taxing masters, registrars of the principal registry of the Family Division and the

Admiralty Registrar (Ord. 62, rr. 12—15). In the county court taxation is a function of the registrar (C.C.R. Ord 38 r.2). See also COSTS.

tellers. (a) Four officers of the Exchequer who received all moneys due to the King. (2) Counters of votes.

temporalities. The properties and possessions of a bishop in his see.

tenancy in common. Where two or more persons are entitled to land in such a manner that they have an undivided possession but several freeholds: that is, no one of them is entitled to the exclusive possession of any part of the land, each being entitled to occupy the whole in common with the others. It is distinguished from joint tenancy by the fact that on the death of any one of them his share passes, not to the survivors, but to his devisee, who then becomes tenant in common with the survivors. By the Law of Property Act 1925, ss.1(6) and 34 no undivided share in land is capable of being created, except as equitable interests under a settlement, or as that of a joint tenant upon the statutory trusts for sale. See JOINT TENANCY.

tenant. One who holds land. In theory of law "all the lands and tenements in England in the hands of subjects are holden mediately, or immediately of the King" (Coke). Popularly a lessee of land or buildings for occupation, agriculture, etc. See ESTATE.

tenant at sufferance. One who has originally come into possession of land by a lawful title, and holds such possession after his title has determined. See HOLDING OVER.

tenant at will is where lands or tenements are let by one man to another, to have and to hold to him at the will of the lessor, by force of which lease the lessee is in possession. In this case the lessee is called tenant at will, because he hath no certain nor sure estate, for the lessor may put him out at what time it pleaseth him (Litt. s.68). His tenancy is determined, and he can be ejected, as soon as notice to that effect is given. See TENANT FROM YEAR TO YEAR.

tenant by copy of court roll. A copyholder. See COPYHOLD.

tenant by curtesy. See TENURE BY CURTESY OF ENGLAND.

tenant for life. One who is entiled to land or tenements for the term of his own life. The person of full age who is for the time being beneficially entitled under a settlement to possession of settled land for his life, is for the purposes of the Settled Land Act 1925, s.19(1), the tenant for life of that land, and the tenant for life under that settlement. His interest ceases on his death and does not pass to his legal personal representatives. Since 1925 a life interest can only exist in equity. A tenant for life has the legal estate in settled lands vested in him, and at the same time he is tenant for life in equity (Settled Land Act 1925, s.4(2)).

A tenant for life is entitled to the rents and profits of the lands during his life, but is not entitled to commit voluntary waste (*q.v.*) unless made unimpeachable for waste. He is not liable for permissive waste, unless he is under an express duty to repair. A tenant for life unimpeachable for waste has no right to commit equitable waste, unless expressly authorised by the trust instrument (Law of Property Act 1925, ss.135).

The powers of the tenant for life as regards the settled land include: (1) power of sale or exchange; (2) power to grant leases; (3) power to mortgage; (4) power to accept leases of other land. These powers may have to be exercised under an order of the court or with the consent of the trustees, or after notice to the trustees, and the moneys arising from the exercise of these powers will have to be treated, either wholly or in part, as capital moneys, *e.g.* invested in trustee securities on the trusts of the settlement, or expended in repairs to the settled land, etc. (see the Settled Land Act 1925).

tenant for years. One who holds for a term of years certain; a lessee.

tenant from year to year. A tenant of land whose tenancy can only be determined by a notice to quit expiring at that period of the year at which it commenced. In the case of ordinary tenancies from year to year (in the absence of any provision to the contrary) a six months' notice to quit is required, or two quarters' notice where the term begins on one of the quarter days. Whenever one person holds land of another, and there is no express limitation or agreement as to the term for which it is to be held then, if the rent is payable with reference to divisions of the year (*e.g.* quarterly), the tenancy is deemed to be a tenancy from year to year. See NOTICE TO QUIT.

tenant in tail after possibility of issue extinct. Where tenements are given to a man and his wife in special tail, if one of them die without issue, the survivor is tenant in tail after possibility of issue extinct, because there is no possibility of issue being born capable of inheriting the estate. Such a tenant canot bar the entail and is not impeachable for waste (Fines and Recoveries Act 1833, s.18; continued permanently in force by the Expiring Laws Act 1925). See Law of Property Act 1925, s.176(2). See ESTATE.

tenant pur autre vie. A tenant for the life of another. If A granted land to B during the life of C and B died before C, then there was no one entitled to the land because A had parted with his right during C's life. Anyone might enter and occupy during C's life and was called a "general occupant." But B's heir might enter and occupy, and was called the "special occupant." By the Statute of Frauds, s.12, however, a tenant *pur autre vie* might dispose of his interest by will; otherwise it formed part of his personal estate (see Wills Act 1837, ss.3, 6). Since 1926, a tenancy *pur autre vie* can only exist in equity, and on the death of the tenant *pur autre vie* during the life of the *cestui que vie*, the property is held in trust for the person entitled to the deceased's property, whether under his will, or on intestacy, as the case may be. See CESTUI QUE VIE.

tenant to the praecipe. One against whom a praecipe or writ was issued in a real action. See RECOVERY.

tenant-right. (1) the right of a tenant in agricultural districts to claim a beneficial interest in the land, notwithstanding the expiration of his lease, *e.g.* a right to the return of a portion of the amount spent on manuring. (2) Tenant-right estates are a kind of customary freeholds.

tenants in chief. Those who held their land directly from the King; they normally held by knight service.

tender. An offer, *e.g.* by a debtor to his creditor of the exact amount of the debt. The offer must be in money, which must be actually produced to the creditor, unless by words or acts he waives production. If a debtor has made a tender and continues ready to pay, he is exonerated from liability for the non-payment, but the debt is not discharged. See LEGAL TENDER; PAYMENT INTO COURT.

tenement. (1) A thing which is the subject of tenure (*q.v.*) *i.e.* land. (2) A house, particularly a house let in different apartments.

tenendum. [To be held.] The clause in a deed of conveyance of land which formerly indicated the tenure by which the grantee was to hold the land of the grantor, but which now simply says that the land is to be held by the grantee, without mentioning of whom.

tenor. (1) The general import of a document. (2) The period of time, as expressed in a bill of exchange, after which it is payable.

Tenterden's Act (Lord). The Statute of Frauds Amendment Act 1828, which enacted that there must be in writing and signed; a promise to pay, or an acknowledgment of a debt (s.1), and any representation as to the character or means of another with the intent that such person may obtain credit, money or goods (s.6).

tenths. (1) The tenth part of the annual profit of an ecclesiastical benefice. See ANNATES; QUEEN ANNE'S BOUNTY. (2) The tax consisting of one-tenth of every man's whole personal property, formerly levied by the Crown.

tenure. The mode of holding of occupying land, or an office, etc. No person except the Sovereign can be the absolute owner of land in England; all lands in the hands of subjects are held of some superior, and mediately or immediately of the Crown. The possessor is merely a tenant. The manner of his possession is called tenure, and the extent of his interest is called an estate (*q.v.*).

The varieties of tenure were: (1) Temporal or lay tenures by which land was held by secular persons. They were of two kinds according as their services were originally free or base. The frank or freehold tenures were: (a) knight's service with its varieties of grand serjeanty, escuage, castle ward and cornage, all of which have been converted into common socage (statute 12 Car. 2, c.24); and (b) free socage with its varieties of petty serjeanty, burgage tenure, borough-English and gravelkind. The base, villein or customary tenures were (a) pure villeinage, which existed in the form of copyhold and customary freehold tenures; and (b) the obsolete privileged villeinage or villein socage, from which is derived tenure in ancient demesne. The customary tenures were converted into socage tenures by the Law of Property Act 1922, Part. V. (2) Ecclesiastical or spiritual tenures; tenant in frankalmoign and tenure by divine service (*q.v.*). See INCIDENTS OF TENURE.

tenure by curtesy of England. The life estate of a husband in the land of his deceased wife, provided he had issue by her, born alive, and capable of inheriting. Abolished by the Administration of Estates Act 1925, s.45(1).

tenure, security of. A tenant's possession of property under a lease or letting cannot be determined simply by notice to quit, or at the end of the period of the lease in the following cases: (1) business premises; (2) agricultural holdings; (3) under the Rent Acts.

term. (1) A portion of the year during which alone judicial business could be transacted. By the Judicature Acts 1873 and 1875 the division of the year into terms was abolished, the year being divided into sittings (*q.v.*) and vacations (*q.v.*). See now Judicature Act 1925, ss.52, 53.

(2) The fixed period for which a right is to be enjoyed.

(3) "Keeping Term" is the dining in hall of an Inn of Court the requisite number of times, in the course of qualifying for call to the Bar.

term of years. An estate or interest in land limited to a fixed number of years, as in the case of an ordinary lease for seven years. A long term of years is often granted as security for the performance of an obligation, *e.g.* to secure portions to younger children under a marriage settlement. (Since 1925, portions terms normally take effect in equity.) Under the Law of Property Act 1925 a mortgage may be made by the lease of the land for a term of 3,000 years. A term of years absolute is one of the only two corporeal interests in land which, since 1925, are capable of subsisting or being conveyed or created at law (*ibid.* s.1(1)). See LEASEHOLDS.

terminus a quo. [The starting point.]

terminus ad quem. [The finishing point.]

termor. One who holds land for a term of years.

terra. Land.

terre-tenant. [Land holder.] One who has the seisin of land.

territorial waters. Such parts of the sea adjacent to the coast of a country as are deemed by international law to be within the territorial soveriegnty of that country (the "three-mile limit" as regards the United Kingdom). By the Territoral Waters Jurisdiction Act 1878, passed in consequence of the decision in

R. v. *Keyn* (1876) L.R. 2 Ex.D. 63 (*The Franconia*), it is enacted that an offence committed by any person within territorial waters (*i.e.* within one marine league of the coast from low-water mark), shall be an offence within the Admiral's jurisdiction, although committed on a foreign ship. British fishing limits have been extended to 20 miles (Fishery Limits Act 1976, s.1).

terrorism. The use of violence for political ends. See Prevention of Terrorism (Temporary Provisions) Act 1976, Suppression of Terrorism Act 1978, Taking of Hostages Act 1982.

test case. An action the result of which is applicable to other similar cases which are not litigated.

testament. A will of personal property, A formal will usually begins: "This is the last will and testament of me, A. B. etc." But "testamentary" applies to wills generally.

testamenti factio. [Roman law.] Capacity to take any part in making a will or any benefit under a will.

testamenti, secundum tabulas. [Roman law.] According to the tables or terms of the will. *Contra tabulas testamenti*, in opposition to the provisions of the will.

testamentum. [Roman law.] A will. There were the following varieties: (a) *Calatis comitiis*, made in time of peace in the *comitia curiata* twice a year. (b) *Procinctum*, made in time of war in the field by the army in fighting order. (c) *Per aes et libram*: By the copper and scales. The testator alienated by *mancipatio* his estate in early times to the heir, and *temp.* Gaius, to another person (*familiae emptor*) who represented the heir. The testator then announced his wishes orally or by written tablets, called the *nuncupatio*. (d) *Praetorianum.* The Praetors protected by *boborun possessio* the persons intended to be benefited, if the will was sealed by seven witnesses, although there had been no*nuncupatio.* (e) *Triperitum:* Of triple origin. From the civil law was derived the necessity for the witnesses' presence together at the same time; from the Imperial Constitutions the signatures (*subscriptiones*) of the testator and witnesses; from the Praetorian edict the seals and the number of seven witnesses. (f) *Millitare.* A will made by a soldier on active service, in writing or orally, without any formality.

testamentum destitutum. [Roman law.] An abandoned will, *i.e.* when no one entered on the inheritance. One of the forms of *testamentum irritum.*

testate. Having made a will. See also INTESTACY.

testator. One who makes a will.

testatum. The part of an indenture beginning with the words "Now this indenture witnesseth."

testatum writ. A writ which is issued into a county other than that in which the venue is laid.

teste. Formerly the concluding part of a writ, so called because it began with the words "witness ourselves" (in latin *Teste Meipso*). Abolished by S.I. 1979 No. 1716 (see now R.S.C., Ord. 6, r.1, App. A, Form 1).

testimonium. The clause at the end of a deed or will which commences "In witness, etc."

testimony. The evidence of a witness given *viva voce* in court.

theft. The law relating to larceny, robbery, burglary, receiving stolen goods and kindred offences has been restated in the Theft Act 1968. Offences involving deception are dealt with the Theft Act 1978. A person is guilty of theft if he dishonestly appropriates property belonging to another with the intention of permanently depriving the other of it whether or not the appropriation is made for gain or for the thiefs' own benefit. The words "thief" and "steal" are to be construed accordingly (Act of 1968, s.1). The meaning of expressions used in section 1 is amplified by sections 2–6. A person guilty of theft is liable to imprisonment for a term not exceeding 10 years (Act of 1968, s.7). For mode of trial see Criminal Law Act 1977, s.16, Sched. 3, para. 28 and Theft Act 1978, s.4(1).

See BLACKMAIL; BURGLARY; DECEPTION; HANDLING STOLEN GOODS; ROBBERY.

theftbote. Hush-money (*q.v.*) for larceny.

Thellusson Act. The Accumulations Act 1800. See ACCUMULATION.

thesaurus non competit regi, nisi quando memo scit qui abscondit thesaurum. [Treasure does not belong to the King, unless no one knows who did it.]

third party. (1) One who is a stranger to a transaction or proceeding. Where a defendant claims to be entitled to contribution or indemnity over against any person not a party to an action, or some question or issue between plaintiff and defendant should properly be determined between plaintiff, defendant and third party, the defendant may issue a third-party notice against such third-party. No leave is required to issue a third-party notice where the action is begun by writ and the notice is issued before defence is served (Ord. 16, r.1).

(2) A "third party risk policy" is a policy of insurance against liability in repsect of injury caused by the insurer or his servants to the property or persons of others. See the Road Traffic Act 1972, ss.143–158, 162, 166, 167; Road Traffic Act 1974, Sched. 6, para. 20, Sched. 7. A motor-car owner is liable in damages to an injured third party for breach of the statutory duty to insure.

threats. The common law offence of obtaining property by threats was abolished by the Theft Act 1968, s.32. See now BLACKMAIL. Threats to destroy or damage property constitute an offence. See CRIMINAL DAMAGE.

ticket of leave. See PAROLE BOARD.

tied-house. A public-house subject to a covenant, made with the freeholder or lessor of the premises, to obtain all supplies of alcoholic liquor from a particular brewer.

timber. Properly only oak, ash and elm of mature age; but timber now includes all trees used for building. Timber is part of the realty until severed. Cutting timber is waste (*q.v.*). See ESTOVERS.

time. Judicial acts and acts in the law relate back to the first moment of the day on which they are done; acts of the parties, where necessary, will be assigned to the part or time of the day when they were actually done. Where an act is required to be done within a specified period after or from a specified date, the period begins immediately after that date. Where the act is required to be done within or not less than a specified period before a specified date, the period ends immediately before that date. Where the act is required to be done a specified number of clear days before or after a specified date, at least that number of days must intervene between the day on which the act is done and the specified date (Ord. 3, r.2). Certain days are excluded from short periods of time. Time may be enlarged or abridged by the court, or by consent (Ord. 3, r.5).

time bargain. An option (*q.v.*).

time immemorial. Term used to denote a time before legal memory. The statute of Westminster 1275 fixed it at 1189.

tipstaff. An officer, in the nature of a constable, attached to the Supreme Court. Since the abolition of imprisonment on mesne process, the functions of the tipstaves have been confined to arresting persons guilty of contempt of court.

tithe. The payment due by the inhabitants of a parish for the support of the parish church, generally payable to the person of the parish. Originally tithe was payable in kind and consisted of the tenth part of all yearly profits; from the soil *praedial tithes*), from farm stock (mixed tithes), and from personal industry (personal tithes). Rectorial or great tithe is payable to the rector, vicarial or little tithe to the vicar, and lay tithe to a layman. Ecclesiastical tithe is attached to a benefice or ecclesiastical corporation. When land came into the hands of the monastries the tithe was appropriated and the cure of souls was deputed to a vicar. The Tithe Act 1925 vested ecclesiastical tithe in Queen Anne's Bounty (*q.v.*).

Tithes generally were commuted for a rentcharge, formerly varying with the price of corn. However, by the Tithe Act 1936, all tithe rentcharge was extinguished and was replaced by "redemption annuities" payable to the Crown for 60 years, the owners of the tithe rentcharge being compensated by issues of Government Stock. The Finance Act 1962, s.32 provided for the compulsorily redemption of tithe annuities charged on land whenever such land is sold. Tithe rentcharge annuities under the Acts of 1936 and 1951 were finally abolished by the Finance Act 1977, s.56.

Tithe Redemption Commission. The body established to administer the redemption of tithe rentcharge under the Tithe Act 1936. It was dissolved on April 1, 1960, and its functions transferred to the Inland Revenue.

tithing. A local division or distinct forming part of a hundred (*q.v.*), and so called because every tithing formerly consisted of 10 freeholders with their families. The tithing man was the chief member of a tithing. See FRANKPLEDGE; HEAD BOROUGH.

title. (1) The right to ownership of property; "a vestive fact" (Salmond). A title may be: (a) original, where the person entitled does not take from any predecessor; *e.g.* a patent, copyright, etc.; and (b) derivative, where the person entitled takes the place of a predecessor, by act of the parties or by operation of law. A title by wrong or tort occurs in the case of wrongful possession, disseisin, etc., and is liable to be defeated by the person rightfully entitled, until the wrongful title has become absolute by lapse of time.

A marketable title to land is one which formerly went back 40 years (Vendor and Purchaser Act 1874, s.1), then 30 years (Law of Property Act 1925, s.44) and now 15 years (Law of Property Act 1969, s.23). The contract of sale may stipulate that the title shall commence at a more recent date. The conveyance or other document with which the title commences is called the root of title, and if the vendor shows that he has the title which he is bound to prove, he is said to show a good title. See ABSOLUTE TITLE; ABSTRACT OF TITLE; COVENANTS FOR TITLE.

(2) An appellation or address of honour or dignity.

(3) A description or heading, *e.g.* of an action at law.

title-deeds. The documents and instruments conferring or evidencing the title to land. They "savour of the realty" and pass with the land under a conveyance except deeds relating to the part of the estate retained by the vendor. In such case the vendor must acknowledge the buyer's right to production, and undertake their safe custody (Law of Property Act 1925, s.64). The rule of law whereby, in any legal proceedings, a person other than a party to the proceedings could not be compelled to produce any deed or other document relating to his title to land was abrogated by the Civil Evidence Act 1968, s.16(1)(*b*).

toft. Land on which a building which has decayed once stood.

toll. A payment for passing over a highway, bridge, ferry, etc. The right to demand tolls frequently forms part of franchise (*q.v.*).

Toll traverse was a sum payable for passing over the private soil of another; toll thorough for passing over the public highway.

tolt. A writ by which anciently a cause could be removed from the Court Baron to the Sheriff's County Court; and thence by a writ of Pone to the Court of Common Pleas.

Tolzey Court of Bristol. Originally the court of the bailiffs of the Hundred of Bristol. Its jurisdiction included mixed and personal actions to any amount, provided the cause of action arose within the city. The court was abolished on January 1, 1972, by the Courts Act 1971, s.43. See also Sched. 5, para. 12.

tomlin order. An order which records that an action is stayed by the agreement of the parties on terms set out in a schedule (see *Practice Note* [1927] W.N. 276; *Noel* v. *Becker (Practice Note)* [1971] 1 W.L.R. 355, C.A.).

tonnage. A duty on imported wines, imposed by Parliament, in addition to prisage (*q.v.*). The duty was at the rate of so much for every tun or cask of wine. See POUNDAGE.

tonnage-rent. The rent reserved by a mining lease or the like consisting of a royalty on every ton of minerals gotten in the mine.

tontine. A loan the subscribers to which receive annuities with the benefit of survivorship.

Torrens Title. A title to land under the system of registration of title which was introduced in South Australia, in 1858, by Sir Robert Torrens, the first Premier. It was subsequently adopted in the rest of Australia, and in Canada, and is the foundation of the system of registration of title established in England under the Land Transfer Acts. See LAND REGISTRATION.

tort. [Crooked (conduct); a wrong.] An act which causes harm to a determinate person, whether intentionally or not, being the breach of a duty arising out of a personal relation or contract, and which is either contrary to law, or an omission of a specific legal duty, or a violation of an absolute right (Sir F. Pollock). A civil wrong for which the remedy is a common law action for unliquidated damages, and which is not exclusively the breach of a contract, or the breach of a trust or other merely equitable obligation (Salmond).

tortfeasor. One who commits a tort. See JOINT TORTFEASORS.

tortious. Wrongful. As to tortious feoffments, see FEOFFMENT.

total loss. In marine insurance the total loss of the subject-matter insured may be either actual or constructive. Actual total loss arises where the ship or cargo is totally destroyed or damaged that it can never arrive in specie at its destination. There is a constructive total loss where the subject-matter insured is reasonably abandoned on account of its actual total loss appearing to be unavoidable, or because it could not be preserved from actual total loss without an expenditure which would exceed its total value (Marine Insurance Act 1906, s.60). See ABANDONMENT.

toties quoties. As often as something happens.

totting up. Term applied to the procedure for disqualification from driving for repeated driving offences whereby each offence carries certain penalty points and disqualification must normally follow the achieving of a certain number of points (Road Traffic Act 1972, s.93; Transport Act 1981, s.19 and Sched. 7).

towage. Remuneration for towing a vessel which may be decreed in an Admiralty action.

town. A collection of houses which has, or has had, a church and celebration of divine service, sacraments and burials.
   A parish may, by resolution, take on itself the status of a town (Local Government Act, 1972, s.245).

town and country planning. See NEW TOWNS; PLANNING.

tracing. The equitable right of beneficiaries to follow assets to which they are entitled, or other assets into which they have been converted, into the hands of those who hold them. Thus, where executors make a mistaken distribution the next-of-kin must go first against them; but they also have a direct claim in equity against those to whom the residuary estate has been wrongly distributed (*Ministry of Health* v. *Simpson* [1951] A.C. 251).

trade. The business of selling with a view to profit goods which the trader has either manufactured or himself purchased. See FIXTURES.

Trade, Board of. In theory, a committee of the Privy Council (Interpretation Act 1889, s.12). The Secretary for Trade is President of the Board of Trade. The Board of Trade is now known as the Deartment of Trade.

trade boards. See NOW WAGES COUNCILS.

trade description. A false trade description is one which is false or misleading in a material respect as regards the goods to which it is applied. A "trade description" is elaborately defined in section 2 of the Trade Description Act 1968, which replaced the Merchandise Marks Acts 1887 to 1953.

trade dispute. A dispute (primarily) between employer and employees concerning the terms and conditions of employment or between workers and workers. In cases of strikes (q.v.) or picketting (q.v.) an act may render a person liable to civil action or criminal liability unless the act is in contemplation or furtherance of a trade dispute as defined by Trade Union and Labour Relations Act 1974, s.29(1).

trade mark. A distinctive mark or device affixed to or accompanying an article intended for sale for the purpose of indicating that it is manufactured, selected or sold by a particular person or firm. It may be registered with the Comptroller-General of Patents, Designs and Trade Marks (see the Trade Marks Act 1938). See MERCHANDISE MARKS.

trade unions. Originally friendly societies consisting of artisans engaged in a particular trade, such as carpenters, bricklayers, etc.; they in course of time acquired the character of associations for the protection of the interests of workmen. Being in restraint of trade they were illegal associations at common law, but, by the Trade Union Act 1871, this doctrine was abolished, and provisions were made for the registration of trade unions, for the regulations to be contained in their rules, and for the appointment of trustees in whom the property of the union is to vest, etc. But (ibid. s.4) no agreements between the members as to the conditions on which they are to work, or as to the payment of subscriptions or application, of the funds, are enforceable in any court of law. The Trade Disputes Act 1906, provided: (1) An act done in pursuance of an agreement or combination by two or more persons shall not, if done in contemplation or furtherance of a trade dispute, be actionable unless the act, if done without any such agreement or combination, would be actionable. (2) Persons acting in contemplation or furtherance of a trade dispute may attend at or near a house or work for the purpose of peacefully obtaining or communicating information or of peacefully persuading any person to work or abstain from working. (3) Liability was removed for interfering with another person's business, etc., in contemplation or furtherance of a trade dispute. (4) Actions of tort against trade unions were prohibited. The definition of a trade union is now contained in section 28 of the Trade Union and Labour Relations Act 1974. See also CLOSED SHOP; TRADE DISPUTE; PICKETTING.

transcript. (1) An official copy of proceedings in a court, *e.g.* an account; (2) the transcription of the shorthand note of the proceedings at a hearing.

transfer. The passage of a right from one person to another (i) by virtue of an act done by the transferor with that intention, as in the case of a conveyance or assignment by way of sale or gift, etc.; or (ii) by operation of law, as in the case of forfeiture, bankruptcy, descent, or intestacy. A transfer may be absolute or conditional, by way of security, etc. See BLANK TRANSFER; STOCK TRANSFERS.

transfer of actions. Actions may be transferred from one Division of the High Court to another on application and order (Ord. 4), and between the High Court and county court (q.v.).

transire. The pass issued by the Collector of Customs for the goods loaded in a coasting ship in port, and without which the ship cannot sail (Customs and Excise Act 1952, s.59).

transit in rem judicatam. [It passes into (or becomes) a *res judicata*.] When a person has obtained a judgment in respect of a given right of action, he cannot bring another action for the same right, but must take proceedings to enforce his judgment. See MERGER.

transport. The Transport Act 1962 dismembered the British Transport Commission, and established the British Railways Board; London Transport Board; British Transport Docks Board, British Waterways Board, and the Holding Company. See also the Transport Act 1968, the Transport Holding Company Act 1972, the Transport (London) Act 1969, the Transport Act 1981.

transportation. The former punishment for felonies consisting of sending the convict to, *e.g.* Australia, to be there kept in hard labour. It was replaced by penal servitude (*q.v.*).

traverse. To deny an allegation of fact in pleading. See NEGATIVE PREGNANT.

treason. Breach of allegiance. There existed formerly both high treason and petty treason. Under the Treason Act 1351 high treason was limited to seven heads: (1) imagining the death of the King, or of his Queen, or of their eldest son and heir; (2) violating the King's consort, or the King's eldest daughter unmarried, or the wife of the King's eldest son and heir; (3) levying war against the King in his realm; (4) adhering to the King's enemies in his realm, giving them aid or comfort in the realm, or elsewhere; (5) counterfeiting the King's seals or money; (6) importing counterfeit money; (7) slaying the Chancellor or the judges. In all prosecutions for treason some overt act must be alleged and proved. In view of the doctrine of constructive treason (*q.v.*), treason was further defined by the Treason Act 1795. The principal treasons are now therefore (1) compassing etc., the death, or any harm tending to the death, wounding, imprisonment or restraint of the King; (2) levying war against the King in his realm; (3) being adherent to the King's enemies in the realm, giving them aid or comfort in the realm, or elsewhere (see *R. v. Casement* [1917] 1 K.B. 98).

The Treason Act 1800 provided that in cases of high treason where the acts charged were the killing of the King or any direct attempt against his life, or whereby his life might be endangered or his person suffer bodily harm, the person charged should be indicted, arraigned and tried in the same manner as if he stood charged with murder. The Treason Act 1945, amended the Act of 1800 to make it of general application to all cases of treason.

Petty treason was where a servant killed his master, a wife her husband, or an ecclesiastical person his superior. It was converted into the crime of murder by the statute 9 Geo. 4, c.31, s.2.

treason felony. The Treason Felony Act 1848 provides that treason felony consists in an intention to depose or levy war upon the Sovereign or compel him to change his measures or counsels, or to terrorise either House of Parliament, or to incite any foreigner to invade the King's dominions, coupled with an expression of such intention by any printing or writing or by open and advised speech or by any overt act. The maximum penalty is imprisonment for life.

treasure trove. Any money, coin, plate or bullion found hidden in the earth or other private place which contains a substantial amount of gold or silver. If it does not contain a substantial amount of gold or silver it is not treasure trove; this is an issue of fact for the Coroner's Jury to decide in each case (*Att.-Gen. of the Duchy of Lancaster* v. *G.E. Overton (Farms) Ltd.* [1982] 1 All E.R. 524, C.A.). Treasure trove belongs to the crown unless the owner appears to claim it. The right of the crown is not an incident of the Sovereign by virtue of the Royal Prerogative (*Lord Advocate* v. *Aberdeen University* 1963 S.L.T. 361).

treasury, or the Lords Commissioners of the Treasury. The Treasury is the Government Department which administers the revenue of the State in accordance with the votes of the House of Commons. The political heads of the Treasury are the Chancellor of the Exchequer, the Paymaster-General, the Chief Secretary, the Parliamentary Secretary and the Financial Secretary. The Parliamentary Secretary is the Chief Whip. See EXCHEQUER; PRIME MINISTER; WHIPS.

Treasury Bills. Under the Treasury Bills Act 1877 the Treasury, when authorised by any other Act to raise money, may do so by means of bills (known as Treasury Bills) payable not more than 12 months after date. See also National Loans Act 1968.

Treasury Solicitor. The legal adviser to the Treasury and certain other Government Departments. The post is held normally by a barrister (see the Treasury Solicitor Act 1876). He is a corporation sole. The Treasury Solicitor is also Her Majesty's Procurator-General (proctor) who acts for the Crown in the Prize Court, and the Queen's Proctor (*q.v.*).

treaty. (1) The negotiations prior to and leading up to a contract or agreement. (2) An agreement between the governments of two or more States. The treaty-making power is part of the Royal Prerogative, but the private rights of a subject of this country are not affected by a treaty unless its terms are embodied in an Act of Parliament.

trespass. [To pass beyond.] A trespass is a wrong or tort. The action of trespass became common at the time of Edward I, and was in the nature of a criminal proceeding: the court punished the defendant as well as compensated the plaintiff. Maitland called it that fertile mother of actions. It developed into the misdemeanour (*q.v.*), and by way of its extension, the action of trespass on the case, it gave rise to many of the doctrines of the common law. Where an injury was immediate, trespass would lie; where it was consequential, an action of trespass on the case would lie.

The chief varieties of trespass originally were: (1) Trespass *vi et armis* [with force and arms]: injuries to the person accompanied with actual force or violence, as in the case of battery and imprisonment, and the forcible entry on another man's land. (2) Trespass *quare clausum fregit* [because he (the defendant) broke or entered into the close or land] of the plaintiff, without lawful authority. (3) Trespass *de bonis asportatis* [the wrongful taking of chattels.] See ACTION ON THE CASE.

trespass ab initio. [Trespass from the beginning.] He who enters on the land of another, by authority of law (not of a party), and is subsequently guilty of an abuse of that authority by committing a wrong of misfeasance against that other person, is deemed to have entered without authority, and is therefore liable as a trespasser *ab initio* for the entry itself and for all things done thereunder not otherwise justified (see *The Six Carpenters' Case* (1610) 8 Rep. 146*b*).

trespasser. One who goes on land without invitation of any sort and whose presence is either unknown to the proprietor, or, if known, is practically objected to (*per* Lord Dunedin, *Addie* v. *Dumbreck* [1929] A.C. 358). An occupier owes to a trespasser a duty to take such steps as common sense or common humanity would dictate to exclude or warn or otherwise, within reasonable and practicable limits, to reduce or avert any danger (*British Railways Board* v. *Herrington* [1972] A.C. 877). A person crossing the land of another by reason of a right of way may nevertheless be a trespasser if he exceeds or abuses his right to pass and repass (*Harrison* v. *Duke of Rutland* [1893] 1 Q.B. 142). A reasonable degree of force may be used in order to prevent a trespasser from entering, or to restrain him after entry, or to eject him.

Where there are children trespassing on his land, because of their natural disposition to mischief and meddling, the occupier, by effective warning or protection, must keep them from injuring themselves, by, *e.g.* playing with alluring but potentially dangerous things.

trial. The examination and decision of a matter of law or fact by a court of law. Trial by judge and jury is the characteristic feature of the English legal system, but the absolute right to trial by jury (*q.v.*) in a civil action no longer exists. The place and mode of trial is as directed by the order made on the summons for directions (Ord. 36, r.1), or order giving leave to defend under Ord. 14.

A trial by jury consists of the operation of calling and swearing the jury, of a speech by the counsel for the plaintiff, the examination, cross-examination and re-examination of his witnesses: a speech by the counsel for the defendant, followed by the examination, cross-examination and re-examination of his winesses, and a summing up of their evidence by him: the reply or speech by the plaintiff's counsel: the summing up of the whole case by the judge for the jury: and, last, the jury's verdict.

An action must be set down for trial by the plaintiff within the period directed, otherwise the defendant may set it down or apply to dismiss the action (Ord. 36, r.4). A plaintiff who has commenced an action with a writ may, on the ground that the defendant has no defence to the plaintiff's claim apply to the court for summary judgment (Ord. 14). See also SUMMARY PROCEEDINGS.

trial at bar. Formerly a trial before several judges and a jury; a trial by a Divisional Court.

trial by battle. See APPEAL OF FELONY; BATTLE, TRIAL BY.

Triers or **triors.** Persons appointed by the court to decide challenges to jurors. See CHALLENGE OF JURORS.

tribunals. Bodies with judicial or quasi-judicial functions set up by statute and existing outside the usual judicial hierarchy of Supreme Court and County Courts, *e.g.* Industrial Tribunals, National Insurance Local Appeal Tribunals, Rent Tribunals. In most cases chairman are barristers or solicitors appointed by the Lord Chancellor and sit with laymen representing special interests. Appeal may lie to further statutory creations and ultimately to the High Court. The Council on Tribunals was created in 1958 to keep under review the constitution and working of the Scheduled Tribunals, and to report on their constitution and working, and to consider and report on other administrative tribunals, and procedures. It is continued in being by the Tribunals and Inquiries Act 1971 (consolidating the Tribunals and Inquiries Act 1958 and 1966).

Trinity House. The Corporation of the Trinity House of Deptford Strond. It received its charter from Henry VIII in 1514. It has been entrusted with many duties relating to pilotage and lighthouses, beacons and sea marks. The Masters of Trinity House are known as Elder Brethren, and they may sit as assessors in the Admiralty Court.

trinoda necessitas. Anciently, the service of repairing the highways, building castles, and repelling invasions.

triplicatio. [Roman law.] Triplicate. An equitable allegation by a plaintiff in answer to a *duplicatio*.

trover. A species of action on the case *(q.v.)*, which originally lay for the recovery of damages againt a person who had found another's goods and wrongfully converted them to his own use. Subsequently the allegation of the loss of the goods by the plaintiff and the finding of them by the defendant was merely fictitious, until the Common Law Procedure Act 1852 abolished these fictitious allegations and substituted a new form of declaration: "that the defendant converted to his own use, or wrongfully deprived the plaintiff of the use and possession of the plaintiff's goods." The action then became the remedy for any wrongful interference with or detention of the goods of another, and was called the action of conversion *(q.v.)*. See CONVERSION.

In an action of trover the plaintiff could recover only the value of the goods, not the goods themselves. See TRESPASS.

Truck Acts. The Truck Acts 1831, 1887, 1896, 1940, were passed to abolish the "truck" system, or the practice of employers in paying their employees in tokens exchangeable for goods. Under these Acts, the full amount of a workman's wages must actually be paid to him in cash, without any unauthorised deductions, and any contract as to the manner in which any part of the wages is to be expended is illegal. But union contributions may legally be deducted under an agreement between the employer, the union and the employee (*Williams* v. *Butlers* [1975] 1 W.L.R. 946).

Notwithstanding the Truck Acts, the Payment of Wages Act 1960 provided that it may be agreed between employer and employee that his wages should be paid into his bank account, or by cheque, postal, or money order.

The Truck Acts are enforced by officers appointed by the Secretary of State (S.I. 1974 No. 1887).

true bill. See INDICTMENT.

trust. A relation or association between one person (or persons) on the one hand and another person (or persons) on the other, based on confidence, by which property is vested in or held by the one person, on behalf of and for the benefit of another. The holder of the property is the trustee, and the beneficial owner is the *cestui que trust*. The trustee has a right *in rem* in the property, the *cestui que trust* has a right *in personam* against the trustee or those who take from the trustee with notice of the trust. The beneficiary not only has the right to have the trust administered by the trustee, but he has also an interest in the specific trust property and assets themselves, and he may be able to follow them into the hands of a person not entiled to them. See TRACING.

The practice of one person holding property on behalf of another, or to the "use" of another, grew up owing to the fact that land was originally not devisable by will, and that certain religious orders could not hold property themselves. The Statute of Uses 1535 abolished uses, and the trust was gradually instituted in its stead. The Courts of Common Law took no cognisance of trusts, which were developed under the equitable jurisdiction of the Chancellor and the Court of Chancery.

No special form of words is necessary to create a trust, if that intention is shown or can be inferred, but the words must be so used that they are imperative; and the subject-matter of the trust and the objects or persons intended to have the benefit of the trust must be certain. Trusts may be expressed, *i.e.* created by clear words, or implied by law. In wills, an executed trust is one in which the limitations are complete; one where the testator has been his own conveyancer. An executory trust is one in which the limitations are incomplete and intended to serve as a guide or draft of the intentions of the testator. See CONSTRUCTIVE TRUST; EQUITABLE INTERESTS; TRACING.

The court has jurisdiction to vary trusts on the application of persons interested, notwithstanding the effect may be to avoid tax (Variation of Trusts Act 1958).

trust corporation. The Public Trustee or a corporation either appointed by the court in any particular case, or entitled by rules made under Public Trustee Act 1906, s.4(3) to act as custodian trustee (Law of Property Act 1925, s.205(1) (xxxviii)): extended by Law of Property (Amendment) Act 1926, s.3 to include the Treasury Solicitor, the Official Solicitor, trustee in bankruptcy, etc.

trust for sale, in relation to land, means an immediate binding (*i.e.* imperative) trust for sale, whether or not excercisable at the request or with the consent of any person, and with or without a power at the discretion to postpone the sale (Law of Property Act 1925, s.205(1) (xxxix). See *Re Parker* [1928] Ch. 247).

trust instrument. The instrument whereby the trusts of settled land are declared (Settled Land Act 1925, s.117(1) (xxxi)). It also (a) appoints or constitutes trustees of the settlement; (b) contains the power, if any, to appoint new trustees of the settlement; (c) sets out any powers intended to be conferred by the settlement in extension of those conferred by the Settled Land Act; (d) bears any *ad valorem* stamp duty payable in respect of the settlement (*ibid*. s.4(3)).

trust territories. The territories in Asia Minor belonging to Turkey, and the German Colonies in Africa which, after the First World War were administered under Mandate (*q.v.*) from the League of Nations, and ultimately the Trusteeship Council of the United Nations.

trustee. A person who holds property on trust for another. The Trustee Act 1925, repealed and replaced the Trustee Act 1893, and provided generally for the appointment, powers and discharge of trustees, but the prime duty of a trustee is to carry out the terms of the trust and preserve safely the trust property. He must use the utmost diligence in discharging the trust duties, and as regards the exercise of his discretion, he must act honestly, and use as much diligence as a prudent man of business would exercise in dealing with his own affairs. Otherwise the trustee may be liable for breach of trust and will have to make good personally the loss thereby incurred by the trust estate. In certain cases, however, the trustee may be excused his breaches of trust (*ibid*. s.61), and may plead the Limitations Act 1939, s.19(2) as regards income. See also BARE TRUSTEE.

The power of investment of the trust funds of trustees was provided for in the Trustee Act 1925, ss.1–11, but the Trustee Investments Act 1961 opened up a wider field of investment, but ensured an even balance in the holdings of trusts between "narrower-range" and "wider-range" securities. The former are specified in Parts I and II, and the latter in Part III of Schedule I. A trustee may invest in Part I without advice, while as regards Part II and III he must take financial advice.

Part I contains Defence Bonds, Savings Certificates, deposits in Savings Banks, etc.

Part II contains local authority loans; building society deposits; mortgages.

Part III contains United Kingdom company securities; shares in building societies; units of a unit trust scheme.

trustee de son tort. One who intermeddles in a trust without authority, and is held liable to account as a trustee.

trustee in bankruptcy. A person in whom the property of a bankrupt is vested in trust for the creditors; his duty is to discover, realise and distribute it among the creditors, and for that purpose to examine the bankrupt's property, accounts, etc.; to investigate proofs (*q.v.*) made by creditors, and to admit, reject or reduce them according to circumstances (Bankruptcy Act 1914, s.19).

Where a trustee in bankruptcy has received during the bankruptcy moneys which in the view of the court it is not honest for him, as an officer of the court, to retain, the court may order him to refund (*Ex p. James* (1874) L.R. 9 Ch. App. 609).

Trustee Savings Banks. Banks for the deposit of small savings at interest. Their business is regulated by the Trustee Savings Banks Act 1969, as amended.

turbary, common of. The right of digging peat for fuel upon another man's ground.

turpis causa. See EX TURPI CAUSA NON ORITUR ACTIO.

tutela. [Roman law.] Tutelage; guardianship. The public and unpaid duty imposed by the civil law on one or more persons of managing the affairs of a person under the age of puberty.

tutor. [Roman law.] A person on whom the civil law has imposed the duty of *tutela*. There were the following varieties: (a) *Atilianus* or *Juliatitanus*. A tutor given to

331

a pupil without one. (b) *Dativus*. A tutor appointed by an authorised magistrate. (c) *Fiduciarius*. A tutor holding office as if on a trust committed to him by the father. If a *paterfamilias* emancipated a descendant, and then died, leaving male descendants alive, such male descendants become the fiduciary tutors of those emancipated. (d) *Honorarius*. Tutors excluded from the actual administration of a pupil's property. (e) *Legitimus*. A statutory tutor who succeeded to the office under the provisions of some statute or the Twelve Tables. (f) *Onerarius*. A tutor who actually administered a pupil's property. (g) *Testamentarius*. A tutor appointed by will.

U

uberrimae fidei. [Of the fullest confidence.] A contract is said to be *uberrimae fidei* when the promise is bound to communicate to the promisor every fact and circumstances which may influence him in deciding to enter into the contract or not. Contracts of insurance of every kind are of this class. To a certain extent contracts for the sale of land, for family settlements, for the allotment of shares in companies, and (after the relationship has been entered into), contracts of suretyship and partnership, are also within this principle.

ubi aliquid, conceditur, conceditur et id sine quo res ipsa esse non potest. [Where anything is granted, that is also granted without which the thing itself is not able to exist.]

ubi easem ratio ibi idem jus. [Like reasons make like law.]

ubi jus ibi remedium. [Where there is a right, there is a remedy.] See, *e.g. Ashby* v. *White* (1703) 2 Ld. Raym. 955.

ubi remedium ibi jus. [Where there is a remedy there is a right.] The maxim of early law before development.

ultima voluntas testatoris cst perimplenda secundum veram intentionem suam. [Effect is to be given to the last will of a testator according to his true intention.]

ultra vires. [Beyond the power.] An act in excess of the authority conferred by law, and therefore invalid, *e.g.* a company's powers are limited to the carrying out of its objects as set out in its memorandum of association, including anything incidental to or consequential upon those authorised objects, and the shareholders cannot, by any purported ratification of the company's acts, make any other contract valid; any such contract is *ultra vires* and void (*Ashbury Carriage Co.* v. *Riche* (1875) L.R. 7 H.L. 653). The doctrine is restricted, in favour of a person dealing with a company in good faith, by the European Communities Act 1972, s.9.

umpire. In an arbitration, the person who supersedes the arbitrators if they cannot agree (Arbitration Act 1950, ss.8–10).

uncertainty. Failure to define or limit with sufficient exactitude; a gift by will, or a trust, will be void for uncertainty.

A pleading will be struck out as being embarrassing for uncertainty (Ord. 18, r.19).

unchastity. An imputation of unchastity to a woman or girl is actionable *per se* (Slander of Women Act 1891). See DEFAMATION; LESBIANISM.

uncollected goods, disposal of. A person in possession of goods belonging to another may give that person written notice that the goods are ready for delivery and specifying the amount payable by that person in respect of the goods. If notice is given and the owner is not traced provision is made for the sale of the goods (Torts (Interference with Goods) Act 1977, Sched. 1; s.12(3)).

unconscionable bargain. A catching bargain (*q.v.*).

uncontrollable impulse. Irresistible impulse does not in itself affect criminal liability, but may be evidence of insanity; but it may be taken into account in trials for murder in determining the diminished responsibility of the accused under Homicide Act 1957, s.2.

unde nihil habet. [Whence she has nothing.] See DOWER, WRIT OF.

underlease. A lease granted by a lessee or tenant for years; the latter is called the underlessor, and the person to whom the underlease is granted is called the underlessee. The underlessee is not liable to the original lessor on the covenants, etc., of the original lease. By the Law of Property Act 1925, s.146(5)(*d*) "underlease" includes an agreement for an underlease where the underlessee has become entitled to have his underlease granted.

undertaking. A promise, especially a promise in the course of legal proceedings by a party or his counsel, which may be enforced by attachment or otherwise in the same manner as an injunction.

undertaking for safe custody of documents. When given, in writing, by a person retaining documents of title, it imposes on ever possessor of the documents, so long as he has possession or control of them, an obligation to keep them safe, whole, uncancelled and undefaced, unless prevented from so doing by fire, or other inevitable accident (Law of Property Act 1925, s.64(9)).

underwriter. (1) A person who joins with others in entering into a policy of insurance as insurer. Except where an insurance is effected with a company, a policy of marine insurance is generally entered into by a number of persons, each of whom makes himself liable for a certain sum, so as to divide the risk; they subscribe or underwrite the policy in lines one under the other.

(2) Subscribers to a public issue of shares by a company, who offer to take shares not taken up by the public in consideration of a commission at a rate disclosed in the prospectus.

undivided share. Where land belongs to its owners jointly or in common. Since 1925 an undivided share in land is not capable of being created except under a trust instrument, as settled land, or behind a trust for sale (see Law of Property Act 1925, s.34; Settled Land Act 1925, s.36).

undue influence. The equitable doctrine that where a person enters into an agreement or makes a disposition of property under such circumstances as to show or give rise to the presumption that he has not been allowed to exercise a free and deliberate judgment on the matter, the court will set it aside. Such a presumption chiefly arises in cases where the parties stand in a relation implying mutual confidence, *e.g.* parent and child, guardian and ward, trustee and *cestui que trust*, legal adviser and client. But it may normally be rebutted by showing that the transaction was in fact reasonable and entered into in good faith, upon independent advice (see *Allcard* v. *Skinner* (1887) 36 Ch.D. 145).

It is not the law that in no circumstances can a solicitor who prepared a will for a testator take a benefit under it, but that fact creates a suspicion: it may be slight and easily dispelled; but it may be so grave that it can hardly be removed (*Wintle* v. *Nye* [1959] 1 W.L.R. 284).

undue preference. Where an insolvent debtor within the three months preceding his bankruptcy, pays a creditor in full. It is a ground for the suspension of, or attaching conditions to, the bankrupt's discharge (Bankruptcy Act 1914, s.26(3)(*i*)).

unemployment benefit. See the Social Security Act 1975, ss.14–20; Social Security Pensions Act 1975.

unenforceable. That which cannot be proceeded for, or sued on, in the courts, *e.g.* a contract may be good, but incapable of proof owing to want of form. The effect is that as the contract, though unenforceable, is valid and subsisting, a transferee of property under such a contract can obtain a good title, and a deposit paid may be retained. Similarly a new contract, although unenforceable itself, may effect the discharge of a previous contract which it abrogated (*Morris* v. *Baron & Co* [1918] A.C. 1).

unfair contract terms. By the Unfair Contract Terms Act 1977 the right of the parties to a contract to avoid or limit their liability under the contract or otherwise may be limited. First, liability for negligently causing the death of or personal injury to any person may not be excluded or restricted (s.2(1)). Secondly liability arising from negligence in the manufacture or distribution of consumer goods may not be reduced or excluded (s.5). Otherwise any exclusionism must satisfy the test of reasonableness (s.2(2)). The reasonableness test requires any term which it governs to be fair and reasonable in the circumstances which were, or ought reasonably to have been, known to or in the contemplation of the parties when the contract was made (s.11(1); see also s.11(2), Sched. 2).

unfair dismissal. When an employee can prove that he has been dismissed (see DISMISSAL OF EMPLOYEE) the burden of proving the reason for the dismissal is on the employer (Employment Protection (Consolidation) Act 1978, s.57(1)(*a*)). The determination of whether the dismissal was fair or unfair depends on whether, having regard to the reason shown by the employer, the employer acted reasonably or unreasonably in treating it as a sufficient reason for dismissing the employee (Act of 1978, s.57(3) as amended by Employment Act 1980, s.6). Subject to limited exceptions, certain reasons for dismissal are automatically unfair, *viz.* (1) reasons relating to Trade Union activity or membership or refusal to join a union in certain situations (Act of 1978, s.58); (2) redundancy (*q.v.*) where selection was for inadmissible reason or in contravention of procedure (s.59); (3) pregnancy (s.60). Claims for unfair dismissal are dealt with by Industrial Tribunals (*q.v.*). Remedies are compensation, re-instatement and re-engagement (see Act of 1978, Pt. V).

Uniformity, Act of. See ACT OF UNIFORMITY.

union membership. See CLOSED SHOP.

United Kingdom. England, Wales, Scotland and Northern Ireland (Ulster), but not including the Channel Islands or the Isle of Man.

United Nations. Established by Charter at San Francisco on June 26, 1945. It is based on the sovereign equality of all its Members and establishes machinery to enable them to settle their disputes, maintain international peace and co-operate together for the general welfare. Power is given to Her Majesty by the United Nations Act 1946 to give effect by Order in Council to measures not involving the use of armed force, including the apprehension, trial and punishment of persons offending against the Order.

universal succession. In Roman law, the succession of the heir to all the deceased had. It is now used where one corporation succeeds entirely to another.

universitas. [Roman law.] A corporate body. *Universitas juris* was the totality of the rights and duties inhering in any individual man, and passing to another as a whole at once; an estate or inheritance.

University Courts. Courts held by the Universities of Oxford and Cambridge pursuant to Royal Charters confirmed by 13 Eliz. 1, c.29.

unjust enrichment. See Goff and Jones, *Law of Restitution*; QUASI-CONTRACT.

unlawful assembly. The common law misdemeanour consisting of the assembly of three or more persons with intent to commit by open force a crime, or in such a manner as to give just ground to apprehend a breach of the peace. See PUBLIC MEETING.

unlawful combination. See TRADE UNIONS.

unliquidated. Unascertained, *e.g.* damages left to a jury to determine.

uno flatu. [With one breath.]

unreasonable behaviour. Under Matrimonial Causes Act 1973, s.1(2)(*b*) a petition for divorce may be presented on the ground that the marriage has irretrievably broken down and that the respondent has behaved in such a way that the petitioner cannot reasonably be expected to live with the respondent.

Proceedings on similar grounds may be instituted in Magistrates Courts (see DOMESTIC PROCEEDINGS; *Bergin* v. *Bergin* (1982) 126 S.J. 623, D.C.).

For guidance as to interpretation see *Livingstone-Stallard* v. *Livingston-Stallard* [1974] C.L.Y. 1070.

unsolicited goods. Goods sent to any person without any prior request made by him or on his behalf. See the Unsolicited Goods and Services Act 1971.

unsound mind. This term is now superseded by "patient" (*q.v.*).

usage. A uniformity of conduct of persons with regard to the same act or matter. A usage may harden into custom (*q.v.*).

usance. The period for which bills on a foreign country are by the practice of merchants almost invariably drawn.

use. The technical noun "use" is derived from the Latin *opus* (benefit). It is a word which has mistaken its own origin (Maitland).

Before 1536, if A conveyed land by feoffment to B, with the intention, express or implied, that B should not hold it for his own benefit, but for the benefit of a third person C, or of A himself, then B was said to hold the land "to the use," that is, for the benefit, of C or A. At common law the feoffee to uses (B) was the owner of the land, the seisin or legal estate being in him. In the Court of Chancery, on the other hand, he was merely the nominal owner; he was bound to allow the *cestui que use* (C), or the feoffor (A), to have the profits and benefit of the land. The "use" or beneficial ownership was treated like an estate. It was devisable by will, although the land was not. A conveyance to uses enabled interests in land to be created ad transferred with a flexibility and secrecy unknown to the common law; and it enabled the owners of land to evade inconvenient incidents of tenure.

The Statute of Uses was passed (27 Hen. 8, c.10) in 1536 to abolish uses by providing that where a person was seised of an estate of freehold to the use of another, the use should be converted into the legal estate, and the *cestui que use* should become the legal owner. But the Statute failed to destroy uses and equitable interests owing to the decision in *Jane Tyrrel's Case* (1557) Dyer 155a, where it was held that if there was a use following on a use, the Statute executed the first use, and was then exhausted, so that the legal estate vested in the first *cestui que use*, who held on behalf of the second, who still had an equitable estate. The second use came to be known as a trust. A use had only to be expressed to shift the legal estate without formality.

An executed use is one which takes effect immediately, as where land is conveyed to A and his heirs to the use of B ad his heirs. An executory use is one which is to take effect at some future time. A springing use is an executory use which is to come into existence on the happening of some event, *e.g.* to A and his heirs to the use of B and his heirs on the death of C. A shifting use is an executory use which shifts from one person to another on the happening of some event, *e.g.* to A and his heirs to the use of B and his heirs, and on the death of C, to X and his heirs. The Statute of Uses was repealed by the Law of Property Act 1925.

use and occupation. A claim for use and occupation arises where a person has used and occupied the land of another with his permission, but without any actual lease or agreement for a lease at a fixed rent.

use classes. For purposes of the Town and Country Planning Act 1971, a material change in the use of any buildings or other land is development (s.22(1)). The Town and Country Planning (Use Classes) Order 1972, specifies 18 different classes of use and provides that land, etc., used for a purpose within a certain class may be used for another purpose within the same class without the need to obtain planning permission.

user. The use, enjoyment, or benefit of a thing, *cf.* USAGE.

uses to bar dower. A form of conveyance of land prior to the Dower Act 1833 for preventing the wife's right to dower attaching to the land. The purchaser reserved only a life estate to himself.

usher. An official appointed to keep silence and order in a court and attend upon the judge. See BLACK ROD.

usufruct. [Roman law.] The right of using and taking the fruits of something belonging to another. It was understood to be given for the life of the receiver, the usufructuary, unless a shorter period was expressed, and then it was to be restored to the owner in as good condition as when it was given except for ordinary wear and tear.

usurpation. The use by a subject of a royal franchise without lawful warrant.

usury. Originally meant interest. By Acts of Parliament known as the Usury Laws (repealed in 1854) interest above certain rates was prohibited. Usury hence came to mean only illegal or excessive interest.

ut res magis valeat quam pereat. [It is better for a thing to have effect than to be made void.] See *Roe* v. *Tranmarr* (1757) Willes 682.

uterine. Born of the same mother, but not of the same father.

uti possedetis. [Roman law.] As you possess. A decree of the Praetor that the ownership of property in question should remain in the person in possession.

utlis actio. [Roman law.] An action granted by the Praetor, in the exercise of his judicial authority by means of an extension of an existing action (*actio directa*) to person or cases that did not come within its original scope.

utilis annus. [Roman law.] A year of *dies utiles*, made up by reckoning in succession only the days on which the plaintiff could bring his action, *i.e.* when the Praetor sat, and on which neither party was unable to appear in person or by procurator.

utrum. See ASSIZE UTRUM.

utter. To attempt to pass off a forged document, die or seal, etc., or counterfeit coin, as genuine when it is known to be forged. See FORGERY.

utter barrister. [Outer barrister.] A barrister who has not been called within the bar, *i.e.* is not a Queen's Counsel.

V

vacation. The periods of the year during which the courts are not sitting, and chambers of the Supreme Court of Judicature are closed for ordinary business. There are, however, certain kinds of business which may be transacted during vacation (*e.g.* applications for injunctions, for extension of time, etc.), and for this purpose two vacation judges attend. Provision is made for the trial or hearing during the Long Vacation of urgent causes, actions, or matters and appeals (see Ord. 64). See SITTINGS.

vadium. [Roman law.] A pledge or security. In English law, a *vivum vadium* was a mortgage in which the lender took the rents and profits of the land in satsifaction of both the principal and interest of his loan: a *mortuum vadium* was a mortgage in which he took them in satisfaction of the interest only.

vagabond or **vagrant.** wanderers or idle fellows. The term includes: (1) idle and disorderly persons; *e.g.* persons who refuse to work, unlicensed pedlars, beggars, etc.; (2) rogues and vagabonds; *e.g.* fortune-tellers, persons without visible means of subsistence, sellers of obscene prints, etc.; (3) incorrigible rogues; *e.g.* persons twice convicted of being rogues and vagabonds, persons who escape from imprisonment as rogues and vagabonds, etc.; (4) persons gaming or betting in a public street; (5) persons persistently soliciting in public places for immoral purposes; (6) or that while lodging they have caused damage to property or infection with vermin, etc. (see the Vagrancy Acts 1824–1898 and 1935). For the modern position see ATTEMPT.

value. Valuable consideration, as in "purchaser for value," etc.

Value Added Tax. This tax (VAT) was introduced by the Finance Act 1972 (as amended). It is a tax payable in reality by the ultimate consumer. VAT is a tax on the supply of all goods and services in the United Kingdom, some supplies are exempt. Exports and some items such as books and food are Zero-rated. Imports are taxed and VAT is collected as if it were a customs duty. Purchase tax was abolished. See also the Finance Act 1973, ss.4–9; Counter-Inflation Act 1973, s.12; Finance Act 1974, ss.5, 6; Finance Act 1975, ss.17–24.

valued policy. See POLICY OF ASSURANCE.

variance. A discrepancy between a material statement in the writ and in a pleading; or between a statement in a pleading and the evidence adduced in support of it at the trial. Amendment (*q.v.*) of the pleadings (*q.v.*) may be allowed.

vastum. Waste (*q.v.*).

venditioni exponas. [That you expose for sale.] When a writ of *fieri facias* has been issued and the sheriff returns that he has taken goods, but that they remain in his hands for want of buyers, this writ may be sued out (Ord. 46, r.1) to compel a sale of goods for any price they will fetch.

vendor. A seller. Under a contract for sale of real property a vendor is bound to show a good title to the interest which he has contracted to sell, to deliver an abstract of title and supply evidence in support of the accuracy thereof, to convey the property free from encumbrances, execute a conveyance and hand over to the purchaser the title deeds. See OPEN CONTRACT; TITLE.

venire de novo. A writ issued by the Queen's Bench on a writ of error (*q.v.*) from a verdict given in an inferior court vacating the verdict and directing the sheriff to summon jurors anew. In civil cases this procedure is replaced by that relating to new trial (*q.v.*). In criminal matters, however, the court of trial may still, before verdict, discharge the jury and direct a fresh jury to be summoned, and even after verdict, if the findings are too imperfect to amount to a verdict at all. The Court of Appeal, where it holds that the trial of the appellant was a nullity, may order that the appellant be tried on the indictment. The Courts Act 1971, Sched. 4, para. 4, provides that a writ or order of *venire de novo* shall no longer be addressed to the sheriff and shall be in such form as the court considers appropriate. For guidance as to the circumstances in which the Court of Appeal may order a *venire de novo* see *R.* v. *Rose* [1982] 2 All E.R. 731, H.L.

venire facias ad respondendum. A writ to summon a person, against whom an indictment for a misdemeanor was found, to appear and be arraigned for the offence. A warrant is now issued instead.

venue. The place where a case is to be tried; the neighbourhood from which jurors are to be summoned. The common law rule is that the venue must be laid (that is, the indictment must be preferred in a court having jurisdiction) in the county where the offence was committed, but a person charged with an indictable offence may be tried where he was apprehended or is in custody, or where he has appeared to a summons, provided hardship is not caused to him. The venue is now sufficiently indicated by stating the court of trial at the commencement of an indictment. In civil actions, venue is now abolished (Ord. 33, r.4).

verba accipienda sunt secundum subjectam materiem. [Words are to be interpreted in accordance with the subject-matter.]

verba chartarum fortius accipiuntur contra proferentem. [The words of deeds are to be interpreted most strongly against him who uses them.]

verba cum effectu accipienda sunt. [Words are to be interpreted in such a way as to give them some effect.]

verba fortius accipiuntur contra proferentem. [Words must be construed against those who use them.]

verba generalia restringuntur ad habilitatem rei vel aptitudinem personae. [General words are restricted to the nature of the subject-matter or the aptitude of the person.]

verba intentioni, non e contra, debent inservire. [Words ought to be made subservient to the intent, and not the other way about.]

verba ita sunt intelligenda ut res magis valeat quam pereat. [Words are to be understood that the object may be carried out and not fail.]

verba posteriora, propter certitudinem addita, ad priora, quae certitudine indigent, sunt referenda. [Subsequent words, added for the purpose of certainty, are to be referred to preceding words which need certainty.]

verba relata hoc maxime operantur per referentiam ut in eis inesse videntur. [Words to which reference is made in an instrument have the same operation as if they were inserted in the instrument referring to them.]

verborum obligatio. [Roman law.] A verbal obligation, contracted by means of a question and answer; *stipulatio (q.v.)*.

verdict. The answer of a jury on a question of fact in civil or criminal proceedings (*vere dictum* = Truly said). In civil cases the verdict of a jury must be unanimous unless the parties agree to accept a majority verdict (Juries Act 1974, s.17). In criminal cases majority verdicts may be accepted in certain circumstances (Juries Act 1974, s.17; see also *Practice Direction* [1970] 1 W.L.R. 916). A general verdict is where, in a civil case, there is a finding for the plaintiff or defendant or in a criminal case, the finding is either guilty or not guilty. A special verdict is where certain facts are found proved but the application of the law to the facts so found is left to the court. Such special verdicts should only be returned in the most exceptional cases (*R. v. Bourne* (1953) 34 Cr.App.R. 125).

A person may be found guilty of an offence other than the one specifically charged provided the allegations on the indictment amount to or include an allegation of that other offence (Criminal Law Act 1967, s.6). As to the powers of the Court of Appeal see the Criminal Appeal Act 1968, s.3(1),(2). The jury may return a special verdict that the accused is not guilty by reason of insanity (Criminal Procedure (Insanity) Act 1964).

When the prosecution offers no evidence the judge may order that a verdict of not guilty be recorded (Criminal Justice Act 1967, s.17).

verge. The compass of the King's Court within which the coroner of the county had no jurisdiction.

vest. To clothe with legal rights.

vested. An estate is said to be vested in possession when it gives a present right to the immediate possession of property; while an estate which gives a present right to the future possession of property is said to be vested in interest.

vesting assent. The instrument whereby a personal representative, after the death of a tenant for life or statutory owner, vests settled land in a person entitled as tenant for life or statutory owner (Settled Land Act 1925, s.117(1)(xxxi)).

vesting declaration. A declaration in a deed of appointment of new trustees by the appointor that any estate or interest in the trust property is to vest in the new trustees. After 1881 the declaration operated to vest the property without any conveyance, and in a deed made after 1925 the effect is the same even if there is no such declaration, except in cases of mortgages, shares in companies, and land held subject to a covenant not to assign the lease (Trustee Act 1925, s.40).

When a compulsory purchase order has come into operation, a public authority may acquire the land by vesting declaration (Town and Country Planning Act 1968, s.30, Sched. 3; Land Commission (Dissolution) Act 1971, Sched. 2, para. 2, App. A).

vesting deed. An instrument whereby settled land is conveyed to, or vested in, a tenant for life or statutory owner (Settled Land Act 1925, s.117(1)(xxxi)). A vesting deed for giving effect to a settlement, or for conveying settled land to a tenant for life, is called a principal vesting deed. It contains (1) a description of the settled land; (2) a statement that the settled land is vested in the person or persons to whom it is conveyed (or in whom it is declared to be vested) upon the trusts from time to time affecting the settled land; (3) the names of the trustees of the settlement; (4) any additional powers conferred by the trust instrument, which operate as powers of a tenant for life; (5) the name of the person for the time being entitled to appoint new trustees (Settled Land Act 1925, s.5(1)).

vesting instrument. A vesting deed, a vesting assent, or where the land affected remains settled land, a vesting order (Settled Land Act 1925, s.117(1)(xxxi)).

vesting order. An order of a court under which property passes as effectually as it would under a conveyance; *e.g.* vesting property in trustees. See Trustee Act 1925, ss.44 *et seq.*

vestry. The assembly of the whole of a parish for the dispatch of the affairs and business of the parish, the repair of the church etc., formerly commonly held in the vestry adjoining to or belonging to the church. The local governmental functions of the vestries have been transferred to parish meetings and councils, and other local authorities.

The work of the vestry relating to the affairs of the church is now performed by parochial church councils.

Vetera Statuta. The *Antiqua Statuta* (*q.v.*).

vexatious actions. The High Court may, at any stage of proceedings, order to be struck out or amended any pleading or indorsement or writ on the ground that it discloses no reasonable cause of action or defence; is scandalous, frivolous or vexatious; it may prejudice or embarass a fair trial; or it is otherwise an abuse of the process of the court (Ord.18, r. 19). See also VEXATIOUS LITIGANT; ABUSE OF PROCESS.

vexatious litigant. The Attorney General (*q.v.*) may apply to the High Court for an order preventing anyone who has instituted vexatious legal proceedings or made vexatious applications in any legal proceedings from instituting or continuing any legal proceedings without leave of the court (Supreme Court Act 1981, s.42).

vi et armis. [With force and arms.] See TRESPASS.

vicar. A delegate; the incumbent of a parish church not being a rector (*q.v.*).

vicarious liability. Liability which falls on one person as a result of an action of another, *e.g.* the liability of an employer for the acts and omissions of his employees.

Vice-Admiralty Courts. Courts having Admiralty jurisdiction in British possessions overseas. They acted under commissions from the Crown authorising governors of colonies to exercise such powers as in England appertained to the Lord High Admiral. The Colonial Courts of Admiralty Act 1890 provided for the establishment of Colonial Courts of Admiralty with a right of appeal to the Queen in Council in all British possessions to which it was applied by Order in Council.

Vice-Chancellor. The first Vice-Chancellor was appointed in 1813 to relieve the Lord Chancellor of some of his duties as a judge of first instance of the Court of Chancery; in 1841 two more Vice-Chancellors were appointed. They were transferred to the Chancery Division of the High Court of Justice by the Judicature Act 1873.

The title was revived in favour of the senior judge of the Chancery Division in 1970 and the Vice Chancellor is now vice president of the Chancery Division (the Lord Chancellor being president) (Supreme Court Act 1981, s.5(1)(*a*)) and *ex officio* a judge of the Court of Appeal (Act of 1981, s.2(2)(*g*)).

vice-comes. The sheriff.

videlicet. [Namely; that is to say.]

view. If an action or other proceeding concerns an immovable thing, such as land or houses, the judge and jury may view such property (Ord.35 r. 8). In any criminal case the judge may order that the jury or some of them (called "viewers") may view a place.

view of frankpledge. See FRANKPLEDGE.

vigilantibus, non dormientibus, jura subeniunt. [The laws give help to those who are watchful and not to those who sleep.] See LACHES.

vill. A township or parish.

villein. Serf. (Latin, *villanus*, appertaining to a *villa*, or farm.) They belonged principally to lords of manors, and were either *villeins regardant*, that is, annexed to the manor or land, or else they were *in gross*, or at large, that is, annexed to the person of the lord; thus, where a lord granted a villein regardant by deed to another person, he became a villein in gross. Villeins could not leave their lord without his permission, nor acquire any property; but they could sue anyone except their lord, and were protected against atrocious injuries by him.

villein socage. See SOCAGE.

villein tenure. See SERVICE; TENURE.

villeinage. The status of a villein; villein tenure.

vindicatio. [Roman law.] A real action, especially the real action by which a title to real property could be made out, brought by the owner (*dominus*) against the person in possession.

violenta praesumtpio aliquando est plena probatio. [Violent presumption is often proof.]

vir et uxor censentur in lege una persona. [Husband and wife are considered one person in law.] See HUSBAND AND WIFE.

vis major. Irresistible force; *e.g.* a storm, earthquake, or armed forces. One of the "excepted perils" in a policy of marine insurance.

viscount. The fourth in rank of the peers; he ranks above a baron and below an earl. The title dates from 1440.

vivary. Fish-ponds, or waters in which fish are kept.

viz. *Videlicet* (*q.v.*).

vocatio in jus. [Roman law.] A summons before a magistrate.

void. Of no legal effect; a nullity; *e.g.* an agreement for an immoral consideration. A contract may be void on the face of it, or evidence may be required to show that it is void. But when an illegal contract has been executed, money paid either in consideration or performance of the contract cannot be recovered back. See also NULLITY OF MARRIAGE.

voidable. An agreement or other act which one of the parties to it is entitled to rescind, and which until that happens, has full legal effect; *e.g.* in case of fraud in a contract. If, however, the party entitled to rescind the contract affirms the contract, or fails to exercise his right of rescission within a reasonable time, so that the position of the parties becomes altered; or if he take a benefit under the contract or if third parties acquire rights under it, he will be bound by it. See UNENFORCEABLE. See also NULLITY OF MARRIAGE.

voire dire. A preliminary examination of a witness by the judge in which he is required to "speak the truth" with respect to the questions put to him; if his imcompetency appears, *e.g.* on the ground that he is not of sound mind, he is rejected.

volenti non fit injuria. [That to which a man consents cannot be considered an injury.] No act is actionable as a tort at the suit of any person who has expressly or impliedly assented to it; no one can enforce a right which he has voluntarily waived or abandoned.

The maxim applies to (1) intentional acts which would otherwise be tortious; *e.g.* taking part in a boxing match; (2) running the risk of accidental harm which would otherwise be actionable as negligence; *e.g.* watching motor racing (*Hall* v. *Brooklands Auto-racing Club* [1933] 1 K.B. 205), or show jumping (*Woodridge* v. *Sumner* [1963] 2 Q.B. 43). Consent, express or implied, may negative the existence of *mens rea* in crime: thus a person can effectively consent to certain acts being done; *e.g.* a surgical operation, or seduction, which would otherwise be criminal acts. But if an act is itself unlawful and criminal it cannot be rendered lawful because the person to whose detriment it is done consents to it. No person can license another to commit a crime (*R.* v. *Donovan* [1934] 2 K.B. 498, at p.507).

Consent must be real, and given without force, fear, or fraud, because fraud vitiates consent. There is no consent where a man acts under the compulsion of legal or moral duty (*Haynes* v. *Harwood* [1935] 1 K.B. 146). Mere knowledge of a risk does not amount to consent; the maxim is *volenti*— not *scienti—non fit injuria*; but it cannot apply in the absence of negligence (*Woodridge* v. *Sumner*, *supra*). Where a term in a contract or notice purports to exclude or restrict liability for negligence a person's agreement to or awareness of such term is not of itself to be taken as indicating his voluntary acceptance of any risk (Unfair Contract Terms Act 1977, s.2(3)).

voluntary. Without valuable consideration. A voluntary gift, conveyance, or contract is valid if under seal. A voluntary conveyance is avoided if the owner becomes bankrupt within two years, or within 10 years unless he was fully solvent at the time of the conveyance, irrespective of the land conveyed (Bankruptcy Act 1914, s.42). A voluntary conveyance of land was void until 1893, if the grantor afterwards conveyed the land to a purchaser for value. Now the Law of Property Act 1925, s.173 provides that a voluntary disposition of land with intent to defraud is voidable as against a subsequent purchaser for value.

voluntary indictment. One preferred by the direction or with the consent of a High Court judge.

voluntas in delictis non exitus spectatur. [In crimes, the intention, and not the result, is looked to.]

voluntas reputabatur pro facto. [The will is to be taken for the deed.]

voluntas testatoris est ambulatoria usque ad extremum vitae exitum. [The will of a testator is ambulatory (or revocable) down to the very end of his life.]

volunteer. (1) A person who gives his services without any express or implied promise of remuneration. He is liable in damages if he performs a voluntary act improperly, but not if he neglects to perform it at all. If he interferes in the affairs of others, in general, he takes on himself the risk of injury. A person who of his own volition assists others at their work and is injured may be in the position of a trespasser (see *Degg* v. *Midland Ry.* (1857) 1 H. & N. 773): it is otherwise where he has volunteered to assist in an emergency (*Cutler* v. *United Dairies* [1933] 2 K.B. 297); or where he has a common interest with the defendant. Thus in some circumstances a volunteer may be entitled to have reasonable care taken for his safety.

(2) A person who is an object of bounty under a will or settlement as opposed to one who gives valuable consideration. Equity does not assist volunteers (see *Ellison* v. *Ellison* (1802) 6 Ves. 656).

vouch. To call upon or summon. A voucher is a document which evidences a transaction; *e.g.* a receipt for money. As to "voucher to warranty," see RECOVERY.

W

wager. A promise to give money or money's worth upon the determination or ascertainment of an uncertain event; the consideration for such a promise is either something given by the other party to abide the event, or a promise to give upon the event determining in a particular way (Anson). The essence of gaming and wagering is that one party is to win and the other to lose upon a future event, which at the time of the contract is of an uncertain nature—that is to say, if an event turns out one way A will lose, but if it turns out the other way he will win (*Thacker* v. *Hardy* (1878) 4 Q.B.D. 685, at p. 695). See BETTING; GAMING.

At common law wagers were enforceable, unless it would have been contrary to public policy to enforce them; *e.g.* wagers as to the sex of a person, but wagers were rendered void by the Gaming Act 1845, s.18, which provided that no action should be brought to recover any money or thing won upon a wager. See GAMING.

wager of law. Compurgation (*q.v.*).

wagering policy. A policy effected on a ship, etc., in which the insurer has no insurable interest. See INTEREST; P.P.I.

wages. Money payable by an employer to an employee in respect of services at, usually weekly intervals.

wages council. See the (consolidating) Wages Council Act 1959 (as amended). The Secretary of State may convert wages councils into statutory joint industrial councils (Employment Protection Act 1975, s.90) and may abolish the latter (s.93).

waifs. (*bona waviata.*) Stolen goods which are waived or thrown away by the thief in his flight, for fear of being apprehended. They belong to the owner, if he follows and apprehends the thief or prosecutes him to conviction; otherwise they belong to the Crown.

waive; waiver. A person is said to waive a benefit when he renounces or disclaims it, and he is said to waive a tort or injury when he abandons the remedy which the law gives him for it. A waiver may be either express or implied. In the torts of detinue and conversion the party aggrieved may elect to waive the tort and sue on a implied contract for the price of the goods, or for money had and received, and if the action is pursued to judgment, this will amount to a waiver of the tort and so far a subsequent action in tort.

wapentake. A hundred (*q.v.*).

war. The power to declare war is part of the Royal Prerogative. As to the existence of a state of war, the certificate of a Secretary of State (on behalf of the Crown) that Her Majesty is still in a state of war with a named country is conclusive and binding on the court even though hostilities may have ceased and the enemy has surrendered.

The effect of war on a contract with an enemy is to abrogate any right to further performance of the contract, other than the right to the payment of a liquidated sum of money which is treated as a debt which survives the war. Accrued rights are not affected, although the right of suing is suspended.

ward of court. A ward is a minor who is under the care of a guardian (*q.v.*). Formerly, if an action or suit relative to a minor's estate or person, and for his benefit was instituted in the Chancery Division, the minor thereupon became a ward of court. But the Law Reform (Miscellaneous Provisions) Act 1949, s.9, a minor can be made a ward of court only by virtue of an order of the court to that effect; except that where an application is made for such an order, the minor thereupon becomes a ward of court, but ceases to be so if no order is made in accordance with the application. A ward of court may, on an order being made, cease to be such. Proceedings in relation to the wardship of minors are assigned to the Family Division of the High Court (Administration of Justice Act 1970, Sched. 1).

A ward of court cannot be taken out of the jurisdiction of the court, nor can any change be made in his or her position in life, without leave of the court. Thus marrying a ward of court without the consent of the court is a contempt.

wardmote. Formerly a court of the wards of the City of London.

wards. Local government divisions. See the Local Government Act 1972, ss.6, 16, 17, Sched. 2, para. 7.

wardship. The status or condition of being a ward. Anciently, wardship was the right to the custody of the land or ofthe person of an infant heir of land. See WARD OF COURT.

warehouse receipt. A document of title to goods lying in a warehouse, signed or certified by or on behalf of the warehouse keeper.

warrant. An authority under hand and seal, used in executing process in civil and criminal cases, *e.g.* a warrant signed by a magistrate ordering some person to be arrested and brought before the court or empowering a constable to enter premises and search (see SEARCH WARRANT), or a warrant issued by a county court registrar (*q.v.*) by way of execution against the goods of a judgment debtor.

warranty. A guaranty or assurance. An agreement with reference to goods which are the subject of a contract of sale, but collateral to the main purpose of such contract, the breach of which gives rise to a claim for damages, but not to a right to reject the goods and treat the contract as repudiated (Sale of Goods Act 1979 s.61(1)).

Whether a stipulation in a contract of sale is a condition, the breach of which may give rise to a right to treat the contract as repudiated, or a warranty, depends in each case on the construction of the contract; a stipulation may be a condition though called a warranty in the contract (*ibid.* s.11(3)).

For implied warranties on the sale of goods, see the Sale of Goods Act 1979, s.12.

In marine insurance a warranty is in fact a condition; *e.g.* that the ship is seaworthy. See Marine Insurance Act 1906, ss. 33–41.

An action for breach of warranty of authority may be brought against an agent who acts in excess of the authority granted him by his principal (*Collen* v. *Wright* (1857) 8 E. & B. 647).

Formerly warranty was a covenant by the feoffor or donor of land to defend the feofee or donee in the possession of the land, and to given him land of equal value if he was evicted from it.

warren. The privilege of keeping and killing hares and rabbits on a piece of ground. Franchises of free warren were abolished by the Wild Creatures and Forest Laws Act 1971.

waste. (1) Uncultivated land. *e.g.* manorial waste or that part of a manor which is subject to the tenant's rights of common. (2) Whatever does lasting damage to the freehold or inheritance of land, or anything which alters the nature of the property. Voluntary waste is an offence of commission, such as pulling down a house, converting arable land into pasture, opening new mines or quarries, etc. Permissive waste is one of omission, such as allowing a house to fall for want of necessary repairs.

If a limited owner is given power to commit waste, he is said to be unimpeachable for waste. Wanton destruction, *e.g.* cutting down ornamental timber or destruction of the mansion-house (*Vane* v. *Lord Barnard*, 2 Vern. 738), by an owner unimpeachable for waste may be restrained as equitable waste (see Law of Property Act 1925, s.135). Ameliorating waste consists in altering the property by improvements.

wasting assets. Property with only a limited existence; *e.g.* leaseholds. Where residuary personalty is given by will to trustees on trust for persons in succession, it is the duty of the trustees (unless the will shows a contrary intention) to realise such parts of the estate as are wasting, perishable, or unauthorised by the will or the general law, or reversionary, and invest the proceeds in authorised investments. This is the rule in *Howe* v. *Lord Dartmouth* (1802) 7 Vest. 117, the object of which is to secure that successive beneficiaries should enjoy the same thing.

watch and ward. "Watch" is the duty of apprehending rioters and robbers by night; "ward" by day.

watch committee. The committee of a council which controls the police.

water gavel. A rent paid for water or for fishing rights.

water-bailiff. An official who enforces the Salmon Fishery Acts, etc.

watercourse. The right of watercourse is the right of receiving or discharging water through another person's land, and is an easement.

waveson. Floating wreckage: flotsam (*q.v.*).

way. See RIGHT OF WAY.

way-going crop. A crop which has been sown or planted during a tenancy, but is not ready for gathering until after its expiration. A custom that the tenant should have the way-going crop, where not repugnant to the lease, may be good (*Wigglesworth* v. *Dallison* (1779) 1 Doug. 201). See EMBLEMENTS.

wayleave. A right of way over or through land for the carriage of minerals from a mine or quarry, or wires on pylons, or the like; generally created by express grant or by reservation.

wedding presents. In the absence of evidence to the contrary, it may be assumed that wedding presents originating from one side of the family were intended for the husband and those from the other side were intended for the wife (*Samson* v. *Samson* [1960] 1 W.L.R. 190).

weight of evidence. Where the evidence given at a hearing inclines in favour of one party, and the jury find in favour of the other party, the verdict is said to be against the weight of the evidence. The jury's verdict will not be disturbed, however, unless the jury could not properly, on a reasonable view of the evidence, have found as they did.

Weights and Measures Act 1963. This is a comprehensive Act which sets up a Commission on Units and Standards, and which *inter alia* includes certain units of the metric system as units of measurement in the United Kingdom. Local authorities are the local weights and measures authorities. See also Weights and Measures Act 1977 and 1979.

Welfare Report. In proceedings for divorce or judicial separation the court may at any time refer to a court welfare officer for investigation and report any matter arising concerning the welfare of a child (Matrimonial Causes Rules, 1977, r.95(1)). Such report, when obtained, is for the use of the court and the parties only; to public or reveal its contents to a third party may constitute contempt of court (see *Practice Direction* [1982] 1 All E.R. 512).

Welsh language. Welsh may be spoken by any party, witness or other person in any legal proceedings in Wales or Monmouthshire subject to such prior notice as may be required by rules of court (Welsh Language Act 1967, s.1).

Welsh mortgage. The coveyance of an estate as security for a loan, redeemable at any time on payment of the debt without payment of interest by the borrower, or account of the rents and profits receivable by the lender, who is let into possession from the beginning, and who takes the rents in lieu of interest.

wer; wergild. Compensation for personal injury. [Anglo-Saxon.]

Westminster, Statute of (1931). See STATUTE OF WESTMINSTER 1931.

Westminster the First, Statute of. The 51 chapters passed in 1275.

Westminster the Second, Statute of. The 50 chapters passed in 1285, the first of which is the statute *De Donis*, etc. See ESTATE.

Westminster the Third, Statute of. Passed in 1290, commencing *quia emptores* (*q.v.*).

whipping. A form of the common law punishment for misdemeanours: abolished by the Criminal Justice Act 1948, s.1.

whips. (From the hunting term "whipper-in" of a pack of hounds.) The party officials whose duty it is to see that their party is as fully respresented as possible at parliamentary divisions (*i.e.* when a vote is taken).

A "three-line whip" is an urgent, imperative call to a member to attend the House and vote.

Whit Monday. This is no longer a bank holiday. The last Monday in May is substituted as a bank holiday (Banking and Financial Dealings Act 1971, s.1 Scheds. 1, 2).

white book, the. Colloquial description of the Supreme Court Practice, *i.e.* a book published periodically containing (*inter alia*) the Rules of the Supreme Court with detailed notes thereon, which is in daily use by the courts and legal practioners.

wilful default. See ACCOUNT ON THE FOOTING OF WILFUL DEFAULT.

wilful refusal to consummate. See NULLITY OF MARRIAGE

will. A disposition or declaration by which the person making it (the testator) provides for the distribution or administration of property after his death. It is always revocable by him.

Formerly "will" signified a testamentary disposition of land, as opposed to a testament or will of personalty. Minors and patients are incapable of making wills. A married woman has complete testamentary power with regard to all her property. No particular form of words is required to make a valid will so long as the testator's intention can be ascertained; otherwise its provisions will fail from uncertainty.

A will must in ordinary cases be in writing, and signed at the foot or end by the testator, or by someone in his presence and by his direction, and the signature must be made or acknowledged by the testator in the presence of two or more witnesses, who must be present together at the same time, and must attest and subscribe the will in the presence of the testator (Wills Acts 1837, s.9; Wills Act

Amendment Act 1852). A devise or bequest to an attesting witness, or to his or her wife or husband, does not affect the validity of the will, but the gift is void (Wills Act 1837, s.15). A gift to an attesting witness is saved if the will is also attested by two independent witnesses (Wills Act 1968). See ATTESTATION CLAUSE.

A nuncupative will is a declaration by the testator without any writing before a sufficient number of witnesses. They are invalid except those made by soldiers or seamen on active service (see the Wills (Soldiers and Sailors) Act 1918, and the Navy and Marines (Wills) Acts of 1930, 1939, and 1953). See PROBATE.

A will may be revoked by (1) another later will; (2) by destruction, burning or tearing by the testator, or by some person in his presence and by his direction, with the intention of revoking it (Wills Act 1837, s.20). The doctrine of dependent relative revocation is that the intention to revoke the will must be absolute: if it is only conditional; *e.g.* upon the coming into force of some other disposition of the property in question, then the condition must be fulfilled; if it is not fulfilled the original will is not revoked; (3) a will is revoked by marriage (*ibid.* s.18), but a will made after 1925 and expressed to be made in contemplation of marriage is not revoked by the solemnisation of the marriage contemplated (Law of Property Act 1925, s.177).

The Wills Act 1963 applies to testators who died after January 1, 1964, and seeks to secure that if the testator complies with the formal requirements of any system of law which he may reasonably assume to be applicable, his will will be treated as formally valid. In general the effect of the Act is that a will will be held to be validly executed as regards form it if satisfies the requirements of the internal law of any of the following: the place where it was made; the place of the testators domicile; the county of the testator's nationality; the place where he had his habitual residence, or, so far as it disposes of immovable property, the place where the property is situated.

winding-up. The operation of putting an end to the carrying on of the business of a company or partnership, realising the assets and discharging the liabilities of the concern, settling any question of account or contribution between the members, and dividing the surplus assets (if any) among the members.

The winding up of a partnership is either voluntary, *i.e.* by agreement between the partners), or by order of a court made in an action for the dissolution of the partnership.

Companies are wound up under the Companies Act 1948 as follows: compulsory winding-up by the court; voluntary winding-up without the intervention of the court, being either a member's or a creditor's voluntary winding-up; and voluntary winding-up under the supervision of the court: *ibid.* s.211, and Part V.

Wisby, Laws of. The code of maritime law drawn up at the Hanse town of Wisby, in the island of Gotland, about the fourteenth century.

witchcraft. A capital offence: abolished by the Witchcraft Act 1735, itself repealed by the Fraudulent Mediums Act 1951. See MEDIUMS; CONJURATION

wite. A penalty for murder, etc. [Anglo-Saxon.] See BLODWYTE.

witenagemot. The mote or meeting of the wise men. In Anglo-Saxon times it was the great council, consisting of bishops, abbots, ealdormen and other notables, which was associated with the King in the government of the country. See GREAT COUNCIL.

withdrawal. A party may withdraw an acknowledgment of service at any time with leave. The plaintiff in any action begun by writ may without leave withdraw any particular claim made by him therein not later than 14 days after service of defence. The defendant may without leave withdraw his defence, or any part of it at any time, or withdraw any particular claim made in his counterclaim not later han 14 days after service of a defence to the counterclaim. An action may be withdrawn without leave before trial by production of a written consent signed by all parties (Ord. 21). See DISCONTINUANCE.

withdrawal of a juror. At the trial of an action, when neither party wishes to proceed further, they may, by consent, withdraw a juror upon which the hearing comes to an end. The action, however, is not at an end; and if the terms agreed upon between the parties are not complied with, the action can be restored and tried. The court may, in certain cases, order a juror to withdraw (Juries Act 1974, s.11(6)).

withernam. [A taking again.] See CAPIAS IN WITHERNAM.

without day. See EAT INDE SINE DIE.

without prejudice. When negotiations, or letters written in the course thereof, are stated to be "without prejudice" this means that proposals made and not accepted are not later to be admissible in evidence at the instance of the other party, but if they are accepted a complete contract is established. The maker of the proposal may always waive the privilege attaching to his own proposals but where part of a "without prejudice" letter is introduced into evidence the whole of the letter becomes admissible (*Great Atlantic Insurance Co.* v. *Home Insurance Co.* [1981] 1 W.L.R. 529, C.A.). See also CALDERBANK LETTER.

without recourse to me. An agent who so indorses a bill of exchange protects himself from liability.

witness. A person who makes a *viva voce* statement to a judicial tribunal on a question of fact. Witnesses require to be sworn before their evidence is given, unless they choose to make a solemn affirmation. The general rule is that all persons are competent to give evidence, provided they have sufficient mental understanding. Every witness has a right to refuse to answer questions the answers to which would have a tendency to expose him to criminal proceedings, or to a forfeiture or penalty.

The court, however, where there is any pending matter, may order evidence to be taken by an examiner which is incorporated in depositions (Ord. 39).

Young children may give evidence unsworn when the court is satisfied that they do not understand the nature of an oath, but are possessed of sufficient intelligence to justify the reception of the evidence and to understand the duty of speaking the truth (Children and Young Persons Act 1933, s.38). Such testimony must, however, be corroborated by sworn testimony. See AFFIRM; EVIDENCE; HOSTILE WITNESS; OATHS.

witnessing part. The testatum (*q.v.*).

woolsack. The seat on which the Lord Chancellor sits in his capacity of Speaker of the House of Lords. It is not technically part of the House. When the Lord Chancellor votes as a peer, he votes from the Woolsack; but if he desires to speak as a peer, he leaves the Woolsack and goes to his place in the House.

words of limitation. Words in a conveyance or will which have the effect of marking out the duration of an estate. Thus, in a grant to A and his heirs, the words "and his heirs" are words of limitation. Formerly these words were essential to pass the fee simple, both in legal and equitable interests (*Re Bostock* [1921] 2 Ch. 469). The Conveyancing Act 1881, s.51 authorised the use of the words "in fee simple," but any other words, including "in fee," passed only a life estate (*Re Ethel and Mitchell* [1901] 1 Ch. 945). No words of limitation are necessary since 1925: a conveyance passes the whole interest of the grantor, unless a contrary intention is expressed (Law of Property Act 1925, s.60).

To create an estate tail by deed, it was necessary that "words of procreation" should be used as "to A and the heirs of his body." Since 1925 an entailed interest may be created by way of trust in any property by the use of like words (Law of Property Act 1925, s.130).

words of purchase. Words which denote the person who is to take an estate or interest in land in his own right. They are to be contrasted with words of limitation (*q.v.*). See PURCHASE.

workmen's compensation. The system of workmen's compensation was superseded by the National Insurance (Industrial Injuries) Act 1946, and is now part of social security under the Social Security Act 1975. See also the Industrial Injuries and Diseases (Old Cases) Act 1975.

wounding and maiming. Aggravated forms of battery (*q.v.*). See MALICIOUS INJURIES TO THE PERSON; MAYHEM.

wreck. If a ship was lost at sea, and the cargo or a portion of it came to land, the goods saved belonged to the Crown. This privilege was frequently granted to lords of manors. The owners of shipwrecked goods were allowed to reclaim them within a year and a day, if they could identify them. At the present day, "wreck" includes jetsam, flotsam (*q.v.*), ligan and derelict. It is the duty of receivers of wreck to preserve wreck, and if it is not claimed by the owner within a year, then to sell it and pay the proceeds into the Exchequer.

Wreck Commissioners. Persons appointed by the Lord Chancellor under the Merchant Shipping Act 1970 to hold investigations at the request of the Department of Trade into shipping casualties.

writ. A document in the Queen's name and under the seal of the Crown, a court or an officer of the Crown, commanding the person to whom it is addressed to do or forbear from doing some act. An original writ was anciently the mode of commencing every action at common law. It issued out of the common law side of the Chancery under the Great Seal. A judicial writ is any writ which is issued by a court under its own seal, as follows: (1) writs originating actions and other proceedings; (2) interlocutory writs, issued during the course of an action before final judgment; (3) writs of execution. See PREROGATIVE WRITS; WRIT OF SUMMONS.

writ of right. A real action which lay to recover lands in fee simple, unjustly withheld from the rightful owner. It might be brought in any case of disseisin. There were also writs in the nature of writs of right, such as the writ of dower (*q.v.*).

writ of summons. A process issued in the High Court at the instance of the plaintiff for the purpose of giving the defendant notice of the claim made against him and of compelling him to acknowledge service and answer it if he does not admit it. It is the first step in an action. It is issued from the Central Office or from a district registry.

A writ of summons may be in general form or indorsed with a statement of claim. The original writ is sealed and given to the person issuing it. The duplicate is filed. The title to the writ should contain the full name of the plaintiff, and his adress must be indorsed. The defendant's full name and address should be given in the body of the writ. The plaintiff's solicitor indorses his own name and his business address within the jursidiction which is his address for service. A writ requires to be personally served (but see SERVICE OF PROCESS). Writs not served within 12 months may be renewed by leave. Concurrent writs, which are copies of the original writ bearing the same date, may be issued (Ord. 6). The statement of claim may either be indorsed upon the writ, or be served with it, or within fourteen days of acknowledgment of service (Ord. 18, r.1). See ACKNOWLEDG-MENT OF SERVICE.

writing. The following contracts are required to be in writing: (1) Bills of exchange, promissory notes, and acceptances; (2) Assignments of copyright (Copyright Act 1956); (3) Contracts of marine insurance (Marine Insurance Act 1906); (4) Acceptances or transfers of shares in a company.

wrong. A violation or infringement of a right. A private wrong or tort (*q.v.*) is an offence against an individual; a public wrong or crime (*q.v.*) is an offence against the community.

wrongful dismissal. An employee has at common law a claim in damages for unjustifiable dismissal. He has also a statutory right not to be unfairly dismissed. See UNFAIR DISMISSAL.

wrongful entry into life. A disabled child (by its next friend) sued a doctor and Area Health Authority on the ground that the mother should have been advised to have an abortion and claimed damages for wrongful entry into life, *i.e.* for allowing it to have been born. It was held that the statement of claim would be struck out and that English law did not recognise such a cause of action (*McKay v. Essex Health Authority* [1982] 2 All E.R. 922, C.A.).

wrongful interference with goods. See CONVERSION.

Y

year. A year consists of 12 calendar months; that is, 365 days in ordinary years, and 366 in leap-year. (1) The historical year has for a very long period begun on January 1. (2) The civil, ecclesiastical and legal year, used by the Church and all public instruments, began at Christmas, until the end of the thirteenth century. In and after the fourteenth century, it commenced on March 25, and so continued until January 1, 1753 (Calendar (New Style) Act 1750). (3) The regnal year commences on the Sovereign's accession. (See Ord. 6, r. 8(1).) See TABLE OF REGNAL YEARS, *post*. The income tax year ends on April 5 (Income and tion Taxes Act 1970, s.2(2)).

Year Books. A series of reports of cases written in the Anglo-Norman language, commencing in the thirteenth century and extant either in manuscript copies or in print from 1290 to 1535—with very few gaps. It is generally agreed that they were notes of cases taken by apprentices to the law.

year, day, and waste. The right which the Crown had to hold the lands of felons for a year and a day, and commit waste (*q.v.*) thereon.

yeoman. He that hath free land of forty shillings by the year: who was anciently thereby qualified to serve on juries, vote for knights of the shire, and do any other act where the law requires (*Blackstone*).

yield. To perform a service due by a tenant to his lord. It survives in the phrase "yielding and paying" the rent reserved in a lease.

York-Antwerp Rules. The rulse for adjustment of general average drawn up at conferences of the International Law Association at York (1864), and Antwerp (1877). They were revised in 1890, 1924, and 1950. The application of the York-Antwerp Rules, if desired, must stipulated in the contract.

Yorkshire Deed Registry. A registry of deeds and wills relating to land in each of the three ridings of Yorkshire. If a deed or will was not registered it was void as against a subsequent purchaser for value, who had registered his deed. By the Law of Property Act 1925, s.11 instruments which did not deal with the legal estate did not require registration; and land registered under the Land Registration Act 1925 was exempt from the local county registry. The Yorkshire deeds registries were closed by the Law of Property Act 1969, s.16.

young person. A person of 14 and upwards, and under 17 (Children and Young Persons Act 1933, s.107).

LAW REPORTS

AND THEIR ABBREVIATIONS

This list shows the corresponding volume of the "English Reports" or the "Revised Reports" in which the various series may be found. In the last column the "English Reports" volume appears without bracket, whilst the "Revised Reports" volume is indicated by a square bracket [50].

The supplementary list of abbreviations compiled by Professor Glanville L. Williams, with references to the "English Reports" (7 C.L.J. 262) has, with his kind permission, been incorporated in this list.

★	= Current Series.	K.B.	= King's Bench.
Adm.	= Admiralty.	L.C.	= Land Court.
All	= All Courts.	L.S.	= Locus Standi.
Bail Ct.	= Bail Court.	M.C.	= Magistrates Cases.
Bky.	= Bankruptcy.	N.P.	= Nisi Prius.
C.C.	= Crown Cases.	P. & D.	= Probate and Divorce.
C.P.	= Common Pleas.	P.C.	= Privy Council.
C.S.	= Court of Session.	Pat. Cas.	= Patent Cases.
Ch.	= Chancery.	Q.B.	= Queen's Bench.
Co. Cts.	= County Courts.	R.C.	= Rolls Court.
Crim.	= Criminal Cases.	[R.R.]	= Revised Reports.
E.R.	= English Reports (Reprint).	Rail. Ca.	= Railway and Canal Cases.
Ecc.	= Ecclesiastical.	Reg.	= Registration Cases.
Elec.	= Election.	Sc. Cts.	= Scottish Courts.
Ex.	= Exchequer.	Sett.	= Settlement Cases.
H.L.	= House of Lords.	Sh. Ct.	= Sheriff Court.
Just.	= Justiciary.	V.C.	= Vice-Chancellor's Court.

ABBR.	REPORTS	SERIES	VOLS.	PERIOD	E.R. [R.R.]
A. & E.	Adolphus & Ellis	K.B.	12	1834–1840	110–3
A. & E. (N.S.)	See "Queen's Bench Reports."				
A. & H.	Arnold & Hodges	K.B.	1	1840–1841	—
A. & N.	Alcock & Napier (Ir.)	K.B.	1	1831–1833	—
A.B.	Anonymous at end of "Benloe"	K.B.	1	1515–1628	73
A.C.	See "Law Reports."				
A.B.C.	Australian Bankruptcy Cases	Bky.	★	1928–date	—
A'Beckett	Judgments of the Supreme Court of New South Wales for the District of Port Phillip—A'Beckett	—	1	1846–1851	·—

Law Reports

ABBR.	REPORTS	SERIES	VOLS.	PERIOD	E.R. [R.R.]
Arnot Cr. C.	Arnot's Criminal Cases (Scotland)			1536–1784	
Asp. Mar. Law Cas.	Aspinall's Maritime Law Cases	Adm.	22	1870–1940	—
Atk.	Atkyns	Ch.	3	1736–1755	26
Aust.	Austin	Co. Ct.	1	1867–1869	—
Aust. Jur.	Australian Jurist.			1870–1874	
B.	Beavan	R.C.	36	1838–1866	48–55
B. & A.	Barnewall & Alderson	K.B.	5	1817–1822	106
B. & Ad.	Barnewall & Adolphus	K.B.	5	1830–1834	109–10
B. & Arn.	Barron & Arnold	Elec.	1	1843–1846	—
B. & Aust.	Barron & Austin	Elec.	1	1842	—
B. & B.	Broderip & Bingham	C.P.	3	1819–1822	129
B. & B.	Ball and Beatty (Irish)	Ch.		1807–1814	
B. & C.	Barnewall & Cresswell	K.B.	10	1822–1830	107–9
B. & C. Pr. Cas.	British & Colonial Prize Cases	Adm.	3	1914–1922	—
B. & C.R.	Bankruptcy and Companies (Winding-up) Cases	Bky.	20	1918–1941	—
B. & F.	Broderick & Freemantle	Ecc.	1	1840–1864	—
B. & G.	Brownlow & Goldesborough	C.P.	2	1569–1625	123
B. & I.	Bankruptcy and Insolvency Cases	Bcy.		1853–1855	
B. & L.	Browning & Lushington	Adm.	1	1863–1865	167
B. & Mac.	Browne & Macnamara (see "Railway and Canal Traffic Cases.")				
B. & P.	Bosanquet & Puller	C.P.	3	1796–1804	126–7
B. & P., N.R.	Bosanquet & Puller, New Reports	C.P.	2	1804–1807	127
B. & S.	Best & Smith	K.B.	10	1861–1871	121–2[1]
B.C.	British Columbia Law Reports	All	63	1867–1947	—
B.C.C.	Bail Court Cases (by Lowndes & Maxwell)	Bail Ct.	1	1852–1854	—
B.C.C.	Brown Chancery Cases (by Belt)	Ch.	4	1778–1794	28–9
B.C. (N.S.W.)	New South Wales Bankruptcy Cases	Bky.	9	1890–1899	—
B.C.R.	Bail Court Reports (by Saunders & Cole)	Bail Ct.	2	1846–1848	[82]
B.C.R.	Lowndes & Maxwell	Bail Ct.	1	1852–1854	—
B.D. & O.	Blackburn, Dundas & Osborne (Ir.)	N.P.	1	1846–1848	—
B.G.	British Guiana Law Reports			1890–1896	
B.H.C.	Bombay High Court Reports			1862–1875	
B.L.R.	Bengal Law Reports			1868–1875	
B.M.	Burrow	K.B.	5	1756–1772	97–8
B. Moore	Moore	C.P.	12	1817–1827	[19–29]
B.N.C.	Bingham New Cases	C.P.	6	1834–1840	131–3
B.N.C.	Brooke's New Cases	K.B.	1	1515–1558	73[2]

[1] Vols. 7–10 do not appear in the E.R., being after 1865.

[2] The volume called "Brooke's New Cases" in the E.R. should for preference be designated "Marsh Brook" (abbreviated Mar. Br.) It is a translation of "Brooke's New Cases" (otherwise called "Bellewe's Petit Brook, Cases tempore H.V.III"), but it is arranged alphabetically, whereas the original work is arranged chronologically.

ABBR.	REPORTS	SERIES	VOLS.	PERIOD	E.R. [R.R.]
B.P.C.	Brown's Parliamentary Cases	H.L.	8	1702–1801	1–3
B.P.N.R.	Bosanquet & Puller's New Reports	C.P.	2	1804–1807	127
B.R.A.	Butterworth's Rating Cases	—		1913–1931	—
B.R.H.	Cases, temp. Hardwicke	K.B.	1	1733–1738	95
B.S.	Brown's Supp. to Dictionary of Decisions	C.S.	5	1622–1780	—
B.T.R.	British Tax Review	—	★	1956–date	—
B.T.R.L.R.	Brewing Trade Review Law Report	—	22	1913–1957	—
B.W.C.C.	Butterworth's Workmen's Compensation Cases	—	41	1908–1946	—
Bac. Abr.	Bacon's Abridgment	—	8	—	—
Bac. Rep.	Bacon's Decisions by Ritchie	Ch.		1617–1621	
Bah. L.R.	Bahamas Law Reports		1	1900–1906	
Bail Ct. Rep.	Bail Court Reports (by Saunders & Cole)	Bail. Ct.	2	1846–1848	[82]
	See also: Lowndes and Maxwell			1852–1854	
Ball & B.	Ball & Beatty, t. Manners (Ir.)	Ch.	2	1807–1814	[12]
Banks & Ins.	Bankruptcy & Insolvency	Bky.	2	1853–1855	—
Bar. & Arn.	Barron & Arnold	Elec.	1	1843–1846	—
Bar. & Aust.	Barron & Austin	Elec.	1	1842	—
Barn.	Barnardiston	K.B.	2	1726–1734	94
Barn.	Barnardiston, temp. Harwicke	Ch.	1	1740–1741	27
Barn. & Adol.	Barnewall & Adolphus	K.B.	5	1830–1834	109–10
Barn. & Ald.	Barnewall & Alderson	K.B.	5	1817–1822	106
Barn. & Cress	Barnewall & Cresswell	K.B.	10	1822–1830	107–9
Barn. C.	Barnardiston, temp. Hardwicke	Ch.	1	1740–1741	27
Barnard.	Barnardiston	K.B.	2	1726–1734	94
Barnard. Ch.	Barnardiston, temp. Hardwicke	Ch.	1	1740–1741	27
Barnard Ch. Rep.	Barnardiston, temp. Hardwicke	Ch.	1	1740–1741	27
Barnard. K.B.	Barnardiston	K.B.	2	1726–1734	94
Barnes	Barne's Notes of Cases	C.P.	1	1732–1760	94
Batt.	Batty (Ir.)	K.B.	1	1825–1826	—
Beat.	Beatty (Ir.) temp. Manners and Hart	Ch.	1	1813–1830	—
Beav.	Beavan	R.C.	36	1838–1866	48–55
Beav. & W.	Beavan & Walford	Rail. Ca.	1	1846	—
Bel.	Bellewe	K.B.	1	1378–1400	72
Bell	Bell (Sc.)	H.L.	7	1842–1850	—
Bell App.	Bell (Sc.)	H.L.	7	1842–1850	—
Bell, C.	Bell (Sc.)	CS.	1	1790–1792	—
Bell, C.C.	Bell	C.C.	1	1858–1860	169
Bell. Cas. t. Hen. VIII	Brooke's New Cases	K.B.	1	1515–1558	73[1]
Bell. Cas. t. R. II.	Bellewet Richard II	K.B.	1	1378–1400	72
Bell. Fol.	Bell (Sc.)	C.S.	1	1794–1795	—
Bell Oct.	Bell (Sc.)	C.S.	1	1790–1792	—
Bellewe's Ca., temp. Hen. VIII	Brooke's New Cases	K.B.	1	1515–1558	73[1]

[1] See note on p.353.

ABBR.	REPORTS	SERIES	VOLS.	PERIOD	E.R. [R.R.]
Bellewe's Ca., temp. R. II	Bellewet Richard II	K.B.	1	1378–1400	72
Bell's Dict.	Bell's Dictionary of Decisions (Sc.)	C.S.	2	1808–1833	—
Belt Bro.	Brown (by Belt)	Ch.	4	1778–1794	28–9
Belt. Supp.	Vesey Senior Supp.	Ch.	1	1747–1756	28
Ben. & D.	Benloe & Dalison	C.P.	1	1486–1580	123[1]
Ben. in Keil	Benloe	K.B.	1	1530–1627	73
Bendl.	Benloe	K.B.	1	1515–1628	73
Benl.	Benloe & Dalison	C.P.	1	1486–1580	123[1]
Benl.	Benloe	K.B.	1	1530–1627	73
Benl. & Dal.	Benloe & Dalison	C.P.	1	1486–1580	123[1]
Benne	7 Modern Reports	K.B.	1	1702–1745	87
Beor	Queensland Law Reports	All	1	1876–1878	—
Ber.	Berton's Reports, New Brunswick	All	1	1835–1839	—
Bern.	Bernard Church Cases (Irish)			1870–1875	
Bidd.	Bidder's Locus Standi Reports 1.			1920–1936	
Bing.	Bingham	C.P.	10	1822–1834	130–1
Bing., N.C.	Bingham, New Cases	C.P.	6	1834–1840	131–3
Bitt. Cha. Cas.	Bittleston's Chamber Cases	K.B.	1	1883–1884	—
Bl., D. & Osb.	Blackham, Dundas & Osborne (Ir.)	N.P.	1	1846–1848	—
Bl. H.	Blackstone H.	C.P.	2	1788–1796	126
Bl. R. (Bl. W.)	Blackstone, W.	K.B.	2	1746–1780	96
Bla.	Blackstone, W.	K.B.	2	1746–1780	96
Black.	Blackerby	M.C.	1	1327–1716	—
Black.	Blackstone, W.	K.B.	2	1746–1780	96
Black. H.	Blackstone, H.	C.P.	2	1788–1796	126
Black R. (Black W.)	Blackstone, W.	K.B.	2	1746–1780	96
Blackst.	Blackstone, W.	K.B.	2	1746–1780	96
Bli.	Bligh	H.L.	4	1818–1821	4
Bli., N.S.	Bligh, New Series	H.L.	11	1827–1837	4–6
Bli., O.S.	Bligh	H.L.	4	1818–1821	4
Bomb. L.R.	Bombay Law Reporter.	All	★	1899–date	—
Bos. & Pul.	Bosanquet & Puller	C.P.	3	1796–1804	126–7
Bos. & Pul. N.R.	Bosanquet & Puller, New Reports	C.P.	2	1804–1807	127
Bosw.	Boswell Reports on Literary Properties (Scotland)			1773	
Bott.	Bott	Sett.	2	1761–1827	—
Bott's P.L.	Bott	Sett.	2	1560–1833	—
Br. & Col. Pr. Cas.	British and Colonial Prize Cases			1914–1919	
Br. Sup.	Brown's Supp. to Dictionary of Decisions	C.S.	5	1622–1780	—
Br. Syn.	Brown's Synopsis of Decisions	C.S.	4	1540–1827	—
Brac.	Bracton's Note Book	K.B.	3	1217–1240	—
Bridg.	Bridgman, J.	C.P.	1	1614–1621	123
Bridg. O.	Bridgman, O.	C.P.	1	1660–1667	124
Brn.	Brownlow & Goldesborough	C.P.	2	1569–1624	123
Bro. & Mac.	Brown & Macnamara	Rail Ca.	1	1855	—
Bro. C.C.	Brown's Chane. Rep.	Ch.	4	1778–1794	28–9
Bro. Ch.	Brown's Chane. Rep.	Ch.	4	1778–1794	28–9

[1] See Wallace's "The Reporters," 4th ed., p. 118, n. 2.

ABBR.	REPORTS	SERIES	VOLS.	PERIOD	E.R. [R.R.]
Bro. N.C.	Brooke's New Cases	K.B.	1	1515–1558	73
Bro. P.C.	Brown's Parliamentary Cases	H.L.	8	1702–1801	1–3
Bro. Syn.	Brown's Synopsis of Decisions	C.S.	4	1540–1827	—
Brod. & B.	Broderip & Bingham	C.P.	3	1819–1822	129
Brod. & Frem.	Broderick & Fremantle	Ecc.	1	1840–1864	—
Brooke	Brooke	Ecc.	1	1850–1872	—
Broun	Broun (Sc.)	Just.	2	1852–1845	—
Brown. & Lush	Browning & Lushington	Adm.	1	1863–1865	167
Brownl.	Brownlow & Goldesborough	C.P.	2	1569–1625	123
Bruce	Bruce (Sc.)	C.S.	1	1714–1715	—
Buch.	Buchanan	C.P.	1	1800–1813	—
Buch.	Buchanan Supreme Court, Cape of Good Hope, Reports.			1868–1879	
Buck	Buck	Bky.	1	1816–1820	—
Bulst.	Bulstrode	K.B.	3	1610–1638	80–1
Bunb.	Bunbury	Ex.	1	1713–1741	145
Burma L.R.	Burma Law Reports.			1948–date	
Burr.	Burrow	K.B.	5	1756–1772	97–8
Burr. S.C.	Burrow	Sett.	1	1732–1776	—
Burrell	Burrell	Adm.	1	1648–1840	167
Burt. Cas.	Burton's Cases with Opinions			1700–1795	
Bus.L.Rev.	Business Law Review	★		1980–date	—
C. & A.	Cooke & Alcock (Ir.)	K.B.	1	1833–1834	—
C. & D.	Corbett & Daniell	Elec.	1	1819	—
C. & D.C.C.	Crawford & Dix Circuit Reports (Irish)	—	3	1839–1846	—
C. & E.	Cababe & Ellis	N.P.	1	1882–1885	—
C. & F.	Clark & Finelly	H.L.	12	1831–1846	6–8
C. & J.	Crompton & Jervis	Ex.	2	1830–1832	148–9
C. & K.	Carrington & Kirwan	N.P.	3	1843–1853	174–5
C. & L.	Connor & Lawson, t. Sugden (Ir.)	Ch.	2	1841–1843	—
C. & M.	Carrington & Marshman	N.P.	1	1841–1842	174
C. & M.	Crompton & Meeson	Ex.	2	1832–1834	149
C. & P.	Carrington & Payne	N.P.	9	1823–1841	171–3
C. & P.	Craig & Phillips, temp. Cottenham	Ch.	1	1840–1841	41
C. & R.	Clifford & Rickards	L.S.	3	1873–1884	—
C. & R.	Cockburn & Rowe	Elec.	1	1833	—
C. & S.	Clifford & Stephens	L.S.	2	1867–1872	—
C.A.R.	Commonwealth (Australia) Arbitration Reports	—	★	1905–date	—
C.B.	Common Bench	C.P.	18	1845–1856	135–9
C.B., N.S.	Common Bench, New Series	C.P.	20	1856–1865	140–4
C.B.R.	Canadian Bankruptcy Reports		★	1920–date	—
C.C.	See Law Reports Crown Cases				
C.C.C.	Choyce Cases in Chancery	Ch.	1	1557–1606	21
C.C.C.	Cox's Criminal Cases	Crim.	31	1843–1941	—
C.C.C. Sess Pap.	Central Criminal Ct. Sessions Papers	Crim.	—	1834–1913	—
C.C. Chron.	County Courts Chronicle	Co. Ct.	12	1847–1920	—
C.C.R.	See "Law Reports"				
C. Home	Clerk Home (Sc.)	C.S.	1	1735–1744	—
C.L.J.	Cambridge Law Journal	—	★	1921–date	—

ABBR.	REPORTS	SERIES	VOLS.	PERIOD	E.R. [R.R.]
C.L.J.	Canada Law Journal			1855–1922	—
C.L.B.	Commonwealth Law Bulletin		★	1974–date	—
C.L.R.	Common Law Reports	K.B.	3	1853–1855	—
C.L.R.	Commonwealth Law Reports	All	★	1903–date	—
C.L.R.	Cyprus Law Reports		★	1883–date	—
C.L.T.	Canadian Law Times	All	42	1881–1922	—
C.L.Y.B.	Current Law Year Book	—	★	1947–date	—
C. M. & H.	Cox, Macrae & Hertslet	C.C.	3	1847–1858	—
C. M. & R.	Crompton, Meeson & Roscoe	Ex.	2	1834–1835	149–50
C.P.	See "Law Reports"				
C.P.C.	Cooper, C.P., Practice Cases	Ch.	1	1837–1838	47
C.P.D.	See "Law Reports"				
C.P.D.	Cape Provincial Division, S.A.			1910–1946	—
C.P.L.	Current Property Law	—	—	1952–1953	—
C.R.R.	Chief Registrar's Reports (Fr. Soc.)				
C. Rob.	Robinson, Christopher	Adm.	6	1799–1808	165
C.S. & P.	Craigie, Stewart & Paton (Sc.)	H.L.	6	1726–1821	—
C.T.	Cape Times				
C.t. N.	Eden	Ch.	2	1757–1766	28
C.W.N.	Calcutta Weekly Notes			1896–date	—
Ca. Prac. C.P.	Cooke's Practice Cases	C.P.	—	1706–1747	125
Ca. Sett.	Cases of Settlements and Removals	K.B.	—	1710–1742	—
Ca. temp. F.	Cases temp. Finch	Ch.	1	1673–1681	23
Ca. temp. Hard.	Cases, temp. Hardwicke	K.B.	—	1733–1738	95
Ca. temp. Holt.	11 Modern Reports	K.B.	—	1702–1710	88
Ca. temp. King	See "Select Cases in Chancery."				
Ca. temp. Lee	Cases temp. Lee	Ecc.		1752–1758	
Ca. temp. Talbot	Cases temp. Talbot	Eq.	1	1733–1738	25
Cab. & Ell.	Cababe & Ellis	K.B.	—	1882–1885	—
Cairns Dec.	Cairn's Decisions Albert Assurance Arbitration			1871–1875	
Cal.	Calthrop's Customs and Liberties of London	K.B.	—	1609–1618	80
Cal. L.J.	Calcutta Law Journal			1905–date	—
Cal. W.N.	Calcutta Weekly Notes			1896–date	—
Cald.	Caldecott	M.C.	—	1776–1785	—
Camp.	Campbell	N.P.	4	1807–1816	170–1
Can. B. Rev.	Canadian Bar Review	—	★	1923–date	—
Can. Com. R.	Canadian Commercial Law Reports	—	4	1901–1903	—
Can Cr. Cas.	Canadian Criminal Cases	Crim.	★	1898–date	—
Can. Ex. R.	Canadian Exchequer Reports	Ex.	21	1895–1922	—
Can. L.J.	Canada Law Journal			1855–1922	—
Can. L. Rev.	Canadian Law Review	—	6	1901–1907	—
Can. L.T.	See C.L.T.				
Can. Sup. Ct.	Canada Supreme Court Reports	All	64	1876–1922	—
Car. & K.	Carrington & Kirwan	N.P.	3	1843–1853	174–5
Car. & M.	Carrington & Marshman	N.P.	1	1841–1842	174
Car. & P.	Carrington & Payne	N.P.	9	1823–1841	171–3
Carp. P.C.	Carpmael	Pat. Cas.	2	1602–1840	—
Cart.	Carter	C.P.	1	1664–1674	124

ABBR.	REPORTS	SERIES	VOLS.	PERIOD	E.R. [R.R.]
Cart. B.N.A.	Cartwright's Constitutional Cases, Canada	—	5	1868–1896	—
Carth.	Carthew	K.B.	1	1687–1700	90
Cartm.	Cartmell's Trade Mark Cases			1876–1892	
Cary	Cary	Ch.	1	1557–1604	21
Cas. B.R. [t. W. III.]	12 Modern Reports	K.B.	1	1690–1702	88
Cas. C.R.	12 Modern Reports	K.B.	1	1690–1702	88
Cas. Ch.	9 Modern Reports	Ch.	1	1722–1755	88
Cas. Eq. Abr.	Equity Cases Abridged	Ch.	2	1667–1744	21–2
Cas. K.B. t. Hard	Kelynge (W.)	Ch.	1	1730–1734	25
Cas. L. Eq.	10 Modern Reports	K.B.	1	1710–1725	88
Cas. Sett	Cases of Settlements	K.B.	1	1710–1742	—
Cas. t. Hard., [by Lee]	Cases temp. Hardwicke	K.B.	1	1733–1738	95
Cas. t. Maccl.	10 Modern Reports	K.B.	1	1710–1725	88
Cas. t. Q. Anne	11 Modern Reports	K.B.	1	1702–1731	88
Cas. t. Talb.	Talbot, Cases in Equity	Ch.	1	1733–1738	25
Cass. L.G.B.	Casson's Decisions of Local Government Board			1902–1916	
Ch.	See "Law Reports."				
Ch. & P.	Chambers and Pretty, Cases on the Finance Act 1910				
Ch. App.	See L.R.Ch. Appeals				
Ch.Ca.	Cases in Chancery	Ch.	3	1660–1697	22
Ch.D.	See "Law Reports."				
Cham. Rep.	Chambers Reports, Upper Canada	All	29	1849–1882	—
Chan. Cas.	Cases in Chancery	Ch.	3	1660–1697	22
Chan. Chamb.	Chancery Chambers Reports, Upper Canada	Ch.	4	1857–1872	—
Chan. Rep. C.	Reports in Chancery	Ch.	1	1615–1712	21
Charl. Cha. Ca.	Charley's Chamber Cases	—	2	1875–1876	—
Charl. Pr. Ca.	Charley's New Practice Cases	—	3	1875–1881	—
Chip.	Chipman's Reports, New Brunswick	All	1	1825–1838	—
Chit.	Chitty	Bail Ct.	2	1770–1822	[22–3]
Cho. Ca. Ch.	Choyce Cases in Chancery	Ch.	1	1557–1606	21
Cl. & F.	Clark & Finnelly	H.L.	12	1831–1846	6–8
Clay.	Clayton's York Assizes	—	1	1631–1650	—
Cliff.	Clifford's Southwark	Elec.	1	1796	
Cliff. & Rick	Clifford & Rickards	L.S.	3	1873–1884	—
Cliff. & Steph.	Clifford & Stephens	L.S.	2	1867–1872	—
Co.	Coke	K.B.	13	1572–1616	76–7
Co. Ct. Chr.	County Courts Chronicle	Co. Ct.	47	1847–1920	—
Co. Ct. Rep.	County Courts Reports	Co. Ct.	34	1860–1920	—
Co., G.	Cooke's Practice Cases	C.P.		1706–1747	125
Co. Rep.	Coke	K.B.	13	1572–1616	76–7
Coch.	Cochran, Nova Scotia Reports	All Cts.	1	1859	—
Cockb. & R.	Cockburn & Rowe	Elec.	1	1833	—
Col. C.C.	Collyer, temp. Bruce, V.-C.	Ch.	2	1844–1846	63
Coll. N.C.	Collyer, temp. Bruce, V.-C.	Ch.	2	1844–1845	63
Coll., P.C.	Colles (Supp. vol. to Bro. P.C.)	H.L.	1	1697–1713	1
Colles, P.C.	Colles (Supp. vol. to Bro., P.C.)	H.L.	1	1697–1713	1

					E.R. [R.R.]
ABBR.	**REPORTS**	**SERIES**	**VOLS.**	**PERIOD**	
Colly.	Collyer, temp. Bruce, V.-C.	Ch.	2	1844–1845	63
Colquit	1 Modern Reports	K.B.	1	1669–1670	86
Colt.	Coltman	Reg.	1	1879–1885	—
Com.	Comyns	K.B.	2	1695–1740	92
Com. Cas.[1]	Commercial Cases	All	45	1895–1941	—
Com. Dig.	Comyns Digest		8		
Com. Law Rep.	Common Law Reports	K.B.	3	1853–1855	—
Com. Rep.	Comyns	K.B.	2	1695–1741	92
Comb.	Comberbach	K.B.	1	1685–1698	94
Comm. A.R.	Commonwealth Arbitration Reports, Australia		★	1905–date	—
Con. & L.	Connor & Lawson (Ir.), temp. Sugden	Ch.	2	1841–1843	—
Conr.	Conroy's Reports Ex.	Ex.		1652–1788	
Conv. (N.S.)	Conveyancer and Property Lawyer (New Series)	—	★	1936–date	—
Coo. & Al.	Cooke & Alcock (Ir.)	K.B.	1	1833–1834	—
Cooke	Cooke's Practice Cases	C.P.	1	1706–1747	125
Coop.	Cooper, G., temp. Eldon	Ch.	1	1815	35
Coop., C.C.	Cooper, C.C. temp. Cottenham	Ch.	2	1846–1848	47
Coop., G.	Cooper, G., temp. Eldon	Ch.	1	1815	35
Coop. P.C.	Cooper, C.P., Practice Cases	Ch.	1	1837–1838	47
Coop., temp. Brough	Cooper, C.P., temp. Brougham	Ch.	1	1832–1834	47
Coop., temp. Cott.	Cooper, C.P., temp. Cottenham	Ch.	2	1846–1848	47
Corb. & Dan.	Corbett & Daniell	Elec.	1	1819	—
Coup.	Couper (Sc.)	Just.	5	1868–1885	—
Cowp.	Cowper	K.B.	2	1774–1778	98
Cox	Cox's Equity	Ch.	2	1783–1796	29–30
Cox & Atk.	Cox & Atkinson	Reg.	1	1843–1846	—
Cox & M'C.	Cox, Macrae & Hertslet	C.C.	3	1847–1858	—
Cox, C.C.	Cox's Criminal Cases	Crim.	31	1843–1941	—
Cox Cty. Ct. Cas.	Cox County Court Cases			1860–1919	
Cox Jt. Stk.	Cox Cases referring to Joint Stock Companies			1864–1872	
Cox M.C.	Cox	M.C.	27	1859–1920	—
Cr. & Dix	Crawford & Dix's Irish Circuit Reports	—	3	1839–1846	—
Cr. & Dix Ab. Ca.	Crawford & Dix's Notes of Cases (Ir.)	—	1	1837–1838	—
Cr. & Ph.	Craig & Phillips, temp. Cottenham	Ch.	★	1840–1841	41
Cr.App.R.	Criminal Appeal Reports	Crim.	★	1908–date	—
Cr.App.R.(S.)	Criminal Appeal Reports (Sentencing)		★	1979–date	—
Cr. S. & P.	Craigie, Stewart & Paton (Sc.)	H.L.	6	1726–1821	—
Creasy	Creasy's Reports, Ceylon			1859–1870	—
Cress.	Cresswell	Bky.	1	1827–1829	—
Crim. L.R.	Criminal Law Review	Crim.	★	1954–date	—
Cripps' Cas.	Cripps' Church and Clergy	Ecc.	1	1847–1850	—
Cro. Car. (3)	Croke	K.B.	1	1625–1641	79[2]
Cro. Eliz. (1)	Croke	K.B.	1	1582–1603	78[2]
Cro. Jac. (2)	Croke	K.B.	1	1603–1625	79[2]

[1] Incorporated in T.L.R. until 1952.

[2] "According to the lettering on the spines of Volumes 78 and 79, '1 & 2 Cro.' are Cro. Eliz., '3 Cro.' is Cro. Jac., and '4 Cro.' is Cro. Car. But this has never been the standard mode of

Law Reports

ABBR.	REPORTS	SERIES	VOLS.	PERIOD	E.R. [R.R.]
Crockford	Crockford, Maritime Law Reports	Adm.		1860–1871	
Croke	See "Cro.Car., Eliz. and Jac."				
Croke	Keilway	K.B.	1	1496–1531	72
Cromp.	Star Chamber Cases, by Crompton			1881	
Cromp. & Jer.	Crompton & Jervis	Ex.	2	1830–1832	148–9
Cromp. & M.	Crompton & Meeson	Ex.	2	1832–1834	149
Cromp., M. & R.	Crompton, Meeson & Roscoe	Ex.	2	1834–1835	149–50
Crow	Crowther's Reports, Ceylon			1863	
Ct. of S.	"See Session Cases"				
Cunn.	Cunningham, temp. Harwicke	K.B.	1	1734–1736	94
Curt.	Curteis	Ecc.	3	1834–1844	163
D.	Session Cases, 2nd Series [Dunlop] (Sc.)	C.S.	24	1838–1862	—
D.	Denison	C.C.	2	1844–1852	169
D.	Dyer, ed. Valiant	K.B.	3	1513–1582	73
D. & B.	Dearsly & Bell	C.C.	1	1856–1858	169
D. & C.	Dow & Clark's Appeals	H.L.	2	1827–1832	6
D. & Ch.	Deacon & Chitty	Bky.	4	1832–1835	—
D. & E.	Durnford & East's Term Reports	K.B.	8	1785–1800	99–101
D. & G.	Diprose and Gammon, Reports of Law Affecting Friendly Societies			1801–1897	
D. & J.	De Gex & Jones, temp. Cranworth, Chelmsford & Campbell	Ch.	4	1857–1859	44–45
D. & J.B.,	De Gex & Jones' Reports	Bky.	1	1857–1859	—
D. & L.	Dowling & Lowndes	Bail Ct.	7	1843–1849	[67–82]
D. & Mer.	Davison & Merivale	K.B.	1	1843–1844	[64]
D. & R.	Dowling & Ryland	K.B.	9	1821–1827	[23–30]
D. & R.M.C.	Dowling & Ryland	M.C.	4	1822–1827	—
D. & R.N.P.	Dowling & Ryland	N.P.	1 pt.	1822–1823	171
D. & S.	Drewry & Smale, temp. Kindersley	V.C.	2	1860–1865	62
D. & Sm	De Gex & Smale, temp. Knight-Bruce & Parker	V.C.	5	1846–1852	63–4
D. & W.	Drury & Walsh (Ir.)	Ch.	2	1837–1840	—
D. & W.	Drury & Warren (Ir.)	Ch.	4	1841–1843	—
D.F. & J.	De Gex, Fisher & Jones, temp. Campbell	Ch.	4	1860–1862	45
D.F. & J.B.	De Gex, Fisher & Jones	Bky.	1	1859–1861	—
D.G.	De Gex	Bky.	2	1844–1850	—
D.J. & S.	De Gex, Jones & Smith	Ch.	4	1862–1866	46
D.J. & S.B.	De Gex, Jones & Smith	Bky.	1	1862–1865	—
D.L.R.	Dominion Law Reports	All	★	1912–date	
D.M.	Davison & Merivale	K.B.	1	1843–1844	[64]
D.M. & G.	De Gex, Macnaghten & Gordon	Ch.	8	1851–1857	42–44
D.M. & G.B.	De Gex, Macnaghten & Gordon	Bky.	9 pts.	1851–1857	—

citation. Originally Cro. Jac. and Cro. Car. were published before Cro. Eliz., and the three volumes were therefore labelled '1,' '2,' '3,' in that order. Later, however, the regnal order of time asserting itself, they become '2,' '3,' and '1' respectively. It was not until 1790–1792 that Cro. Eliz. was published as two volumes, and I cannot find that this has since affected the mode of citation."—C.L.J., vii, p. 262.

ABBR.	REPORTS	SERIES	VOLS.	PERIOD	E.R. [R.R.]
D.N.S.	Dowling's New Series	Bail Ct.	2	1841–1842	[63–5]
D.P.C.	Dowling's Practice Cases	Bail Ct.	9	1830–1840	[36–61]
D.R.A.	De-Rating Appeals	All	★	1930–date	—
Dal.	Benloe & Dalison	C.P.	1	1486–1580	123[1]
Dal. in Keil.	Dalison's Reports in Keilwey			1533–1664	—
Dale	Dale's Judgments	Ecc.	1	1868–1871	—
Dalr.	Dalrymple (Sc.)	C.S.	1	1698–1718	—
Dan.	Daniell (Equity), temp. Richards	Ex.	1	1817–1823	159
Dan. & L.	Danson & Lloyd	M.C.	1	1828–1829	[34]
Das.	Dassent's Bankruptcy Reports		1	1853–1855	
Dav. P.C.	Davies	Pat. Cas.	1	1785–1816	—
Davies (Davis or Davy)	Davis (Ir.)	K.B.	1	1604–1612	80
Day Elect. Cas	Day's Election Cases			1892–1893	
De Coly	De Colyar, County Court Cases			1867–1882	
De G. & J.	De Gex & Jones, temp. Cranworth, Chelmsford & Campbell	Ch.	4	1857–1859	44–5
De G. & J. By.	De Gex & Jones' Appeals	Bky.	1	1857–1859	—
De G. & Sm.	De Gex & Smale, temp. Knight-Bruce & Parker	V.C.	5	1846–1852	63–4
De G.F. & J.	De Gex, Fisher & Jones, temp. Campbell	Ch.	4	1860–1862	45
De G.F. & J. By.	De Gex, Fisher & Jones	Bky.	1	1859–1861	—
De G.J. & S.	De Gex, Jones & Smith	Ch.	4	1862–1866	46
De G.J. & S. By.	De Gex, Jones & Smith's Reports	Bky.	1	1862–1865	—
De G.M. & G.	De Gex, Macnaghten & Gordon	Ch.	8	1851–1857	42–44
De G.M. & G. By	De Gex, Macnaghten & Gordon	Bky.	9 pts.	1851–1857	—
De Gex	De Gex	Bky.	2	1844–1850	—
Dea. & Ch.	Deacon & Chitty	Bky.	4	1832–1835	—
Dea. & Sw.	Deane & Swabey	Ecc.	1	1855–1857	164
Deac.	Deacon	Bky.	4	1835–1840	—
Deane. Ecc. Rep. B.	Deane & Swabey	Ecc.	1	1855–1857	164
Dears. & B. C.C.	Dearsley & Bell	C.C.	1	1856–1858	169
Dears. C.C.	Dearsley	C.C.	1	1852–1856	169
Deas & And.	Deas & Anderson (Sc.)	C.S.	5	1829–1833	—
Del.	Delane's Decisions			1832–1835	
Den. & P.	Denison and Pearce	C.C.	2	1844–1852	169
Den. C.C.	Denison and Pearce	C.C.	2	1844–1852	169
Dick.	Dickens	Ch.	2	1599–1798	21
Dirl.	Dirleton (Sc.)	C.S.	1	1665–1677	—
Dod. (Dods.)	Dodson, temp. Scott	Adm.	2	1811–1822	165
Donn.	Donnelly	Ch.	2	1836–1837	47
Donn.Ir.Land Cas.	Donnell Irish Land Cases (Ir.)			1871–1876	
Dor.	Dorion's Reports, Quebec	Q.B.		1880–1886	
Doug.	Douglas	Elec.	4	1774–1776	—
Doug.	Douglas	K.B.	4	1778–1785	99
Dow.	Dow.	H.L.	6	1812–1818	3
Dow. (Dow. P.C.; Dow. P.R.)	Dowling's Practice Cases	Bail Ct.	9	1830–1841	[36–61]
Dow. & Cl.	Dow & Clark's Appeals	H.L.	2	1827–1832	6

[1] See Wallace's "The Reporters," 4th ed., p. 118, n. 2.

Law Reports

ABBR.	REPORTS	SERIES	VOLS.	PERIOD	E.R. [R.R.]
Dow. & L.	Dowling & Lowndes	Bail Ct.	7	1843–1849	[67–82]
Dow. & Ry.	Dowling & Ryland	K.B.	9	1821–1827	[24–30]
Dow. & Ry. N.P.	Dowling & Ryland	N.P.	1 pt.	1822–1823	171
Dow. & Ry. M.C.	Dowling & Ryland	M.C.	4	1822–1827	—
Dow. N.S.	Dow & Clark's Appeals	H.L.	2	1827–1832	6
Dow. N.S.	Dowling's New Series	Bail Ct.	2	1841–1843	[63–5]
Dr.	Drewry's Reports, temp. Kindersley	V.C.	4	1852–1859	61–2
Dr. & Sm. (Drew. & Sm.)	Drewry & Smale, temp. Kindersley	V.C.	2	1860–1865	62
Dr. & Wal.	Drury & Walsh (Ir.)	Ch.	2	1837–1840	—
Dr. & War.	Drury & Warren (Ir.)	Ch.	4	1841–1843	—
Dr. t. Nap.	Drury, temp. Napier (Ir.)	Ch.	1	1858–1859	—
Dr. t. Sug.	Drury, temp. Sugden (Ir.)	Ch.	1	1843–1844	—
Draper	Draper's Upper Canada King's Bench Reports	K.B.	1	1829–1831	—
Drew.	Drewry Reports, temp. Kindersley	V.C.	4	1852–1859	61–2
Drink.	Drinkwater	C.P.	1	1840–1841	[60]
Dunc.Mer.Cas	Duncan Mercantile Cases			1885–1886	
Dunlop	Session Cases, 2nd Series (Sc.)	C.S.	24	1838–1862	—
Dunning	Dunning	K.B.	1	1753–1754	—
Durie	Durie (Sc.)	C.S.	1	1621–1642	—
Durn. & E.	Durnford & East's Term Reports	K.B.	8	1785–1800	99–101
Dy.	Dyer, ed. Valiant	K.B.	3	1513–1582	73
E.	East's Term Reports	K.B.	16	1800–1812	102–4
E. & A.	Ecclesiastical and Admiralty Reports (Spinks)	Ecc. Ad.	2	1853–1855	164
E. & A.R.	Error and Appeal Reports, Ontario	All	3	1846–1866	—
E. & B.	Ellis & Blackburn	Q.B.	8	1851–1858	118–120
E. & E.	Ellis & Ellis	Q.B.	3	1858–1861	120–1
E. & I. App.	Law Reports, House of Lords Appeals				
E. & Y.	Eagle & Young	Tithe	4	1204–1825	—
E.A.C.A.	East Africa Court of Appeal Reports		★	1934–date	
E.A.L.R.	East Africa Law Reports		9	1897–1921	
E.B. & E.	Ellis, Blackburn & Ellis	Q.B.	1	1858	120
E.C.R.	European Court Reports	—		1954–date	—
E.D.C.	Eastern District Court Reports, Cape of Good Hope			1880–1909	—
E.D.L.	South African Law Reports, Eastern District.			1910–1946	—
E.G.	Estates Gazette	—	★	1858–date	—
E.L.R.	Eastern Law Reporter, Canada			1906–1914	
E.L.R.	European Law Review			1975–date	—
E.P.C.	English Prize Cases (Ed. Roscoe)		2	1745–1859	
E.R.	English Reports	All	176	1220–1865	1–176
E.R.L.R.	Eastern Region of Nigeria Law Reports		★	1956–date	
Ea. (East)	East's Term Reports	K.B.	16	1800–1812	102–4
Ec. & Mar.	Notes of Cases in Ecclesiastical and Marriage Courts			1841–1850	

ABBR.	REPORTS	SERIES	VOLS.	PERIOD	E.R. [R.R.]
Ecc. & Ad.	Spinks	Ecc. & Ad.	2	1853–1855	164
Ed.	Eden	Ch.	2	1757–1766	28
Edgar	Edgar (Sc.)	C.S.	1	1724–1725	—
Edw.	Edwards	Adm.	1	1808–1812	165
El. & Bl.	Ellis & Blackburn	Q.B.	8	1851–1858	118–20
El. & El.	Ellis & Ellis	Q.B.	3	1858–1861	120–1
El. B. & El.	Ellis, Blackburn & Ellis	Q.B.	1	1858	120
Elch.	Elchies (Sc.)	C.S.	2	1733–1754	—
Eng. Judg.	English Judges (Sc.)	C.S.	1	1665–1661	—
Eq.	See "Law Reports."				
Eq. Ab.	Equity Cases Abridged	Ch.	2	1667–1744	21–2
Eq. Ca. Abr.	Equity Cases Abridged	Ch.	2	1667–1744	21–2
Eq. Cas.	9 Modern Reports	K.B.	1	1722–1755	88
Eq. Rep.	Gilbert, Equity Reports	Ch.	1	1705–1727	25
Eq. Rep.	Common Law and Equity Reports	K.B.	3	1853–1855	—
Esp.	Espinasse	N.P.	6	1793–1807	170
Eur. Ass. Arb.	European Assurance Arbitration			1872–1875	
Evans	Evans	K.B.	2	1756–1788	—
Ex.	Exchequer Reports (Welsby, Hurlstone & Gordon)	Ex.	11	1847–1856	154–6
Ex.	See "Law Reports"				
Exch. Rep., W.,H. & G.	Exchequer Reports (Welsby, Hurlstone & Gordon)	Ex.	11	1847–1856	154–6
F.	Faculty Decisions, Court of Session				
F.	Session Cases, 5th Series [Fraser] (Sc.)	C.S.		1898–1906	—
F. & F.	Foster & Finlayson	N.P.	—	1858–1867	175–6
F. & S.	Fox & Smith (Ir.)	K.B.	1	1822–1824	—
F. & S.	Fox & Smith	Reg.	1	1886–1895	—
F.B.C.	Fonblanque	Bky.	1	1849–1852	—
F.B.R.	Full Bench Rulings—Bengal: North West Provinces				
F.C.	Faculty Collection (Sc.)	C.S.	38	1738–1841	—
F.L.	Family Law		★	1971–date	—
F.L.R.	Family Law Reports		★	1980–date	—
F.L.R.	Federal Law Reports	—	★	1956–date	—
F.L.R.	Fiji Law Reports			1875–1959	
F.M.S.R.	Federated Malay States Reports			1899–1941	
F.S.R.	Fleet Street Patent Law Reports	—	★	1963–date	
Falc.	Falconer (Sc.)	C.S.	2	1744–1751	—
Falc. & Fitz.	Falconer & Fitzherbert	Elec.	1	1835–1838	—
Farresley	7 Modern Reports	K.B.	1	1733–1745	87
Ferg.	[Ferguson of] Kilkerran's Session Cases (Sc.)	C.S.	1	1738–1752	—
Ferg.	Ferguson Consistorial Decisions			1811–1817	
Fin.(Fin.H.)	Reports, temp. Finch.	Ch.	1	1673–1681	23
Fin. Dig.	Finlay's Irish Digest			1769–1771	
Fin. Pr.	Finch's (T.) Precedents	Ch.	1	1689–1723	24
Fin. T.	Finch's (T.) Precedents	Ch.	1	1689–1723	24
Finch Cas. Contr.	Finch's Cases on Contract			1886	
Fitzg.	Fitzgibbon	K.B.	1	1727–1732	94
Fl. & K.	Flanagan & Kelly (Ir.)	Ch.	1	1840–1842	—

ABBR.	REPORTS	SERIES	VOLS.	PERIOD	E.R. [R.R.]
Fol. Dic.	Folio Dictionary (Kames & Woodhouselee) (Sc.)	C.S.	5	1540–1796	
Fol. P.L.C.	Foley's Poor Law Cases			1556–1730	
Fonbl.	Fonblanque New Reports	Bky.	1	1849–1852	—
Foord	Foord's Supreme Court Reports, Cape Colony			1880	—
For.	Forrester's Chancery Reports	Ch.		1733–1738	25
Forbes	Forbes' Decisions (Sc.)	C.S.	1	1705–1713	—
Forr.	Forrest	Ex.	1	1800–1801	145
Forr.	Talbot, Cases In Equity	Ch.	1	1734–1738	25
Fors. Cas. & Op.	Forsyth Cases And Opinions on Constitutional Law			1704–1856	
Fort. (Fortes.)	Fortescue	K.B.	1	1695–1738	92
Fost. (Foster)	Foster	C.C.	1	1743–1761	168
Fost. & Fin.	Foster & Finlason	N.P.	4	1856–1867	175–6
Fount.	Fountainhall (Sc.)	C.S.	2	1678–1712	—
Fox	Fox Registration Cases			1886–1895	
Fox. & S.	Fox & Smith (Ir.)	K.B.	1	1822–1824	—
Fox & Sm. R.C.	Fox & Smith	Reg.	1	1886–1895	—
Fr. E.C.	Fraser	Elec.	2	1776–1777	—
Free.	Freeman (ed. by Hovenden)	Ch.	1	1660–1706	22
Free. Ch.	Freeman (ed. by Hovenden)	Ch.	1	1660–1706	22
Free. K.B.	Freeman (ed. by Smirke)	K.B.	1	1670–1704	89
Fult.	Fulton's Supreme Court Reports, Bengal			1842–1844	—
G.	Gale	Ex.	2	1835–1836	—
G. & D.	Gale & Davison	Q.B.	3	1841–1843	[55–62]
G. & J.	Glyn & Jameson	Bky.	2	1819–1828	—
G.C.D.C.	Gold Coast Divisional Court Reports.			1921–1931	—
G.W.L.	South Africa Law Reports Griqualand West			1910–1946	—
Gal. & Dav.	Gale & Davison	Q.B.	3	1841–1843	[55–62]
Gaz. Bank	Gazette of Bankruptcy			1861–1863	
Gaz. L.R.	Gazette Law Reports, New Zealand	All	—	1898–1953	—
Geld. & Ox.	Geldert & Oxley, Decisions, Nova Scotia			1866–1875	—
Geld. & R.	Geldert & Russell Reports, Nova Scotia			1895–1910	—
Gif. (Giff.)	Giffard	V.C.	5	1857–1865	65–6
Gil. (Gilb.)	Gilbert, Equity Reports	Ch.	1	1706–1726	25
Gil. (Gilb.)	Gilbert, Cases in Law and Equity	K.B.	1	1713–1714	93
Gil. & Fal.	Gilmour Falconer (Sc.)	C.S.	1	1661–1666 1681–1886	— —
Gl. & J.	Glyn & Jameson	Bky.	2	1819–1828	—
Glan. El. Cas.	Glanville Election Cases	Elec.	1	1623–1624	—
Glas.	Glascock (Ir.)	All	1	1831–1832	—
Godb.	Godbolt	K.B.	1	1574–1638	78
Good. Pat.	Goodeve Abstract of Patent Cases			1785–1883	
Gould. (Gold., Goldes.)	Gouldsborough	K.B.	1	1586–1601	75
Gow	Gow's Cases	N.P.		1818–1820	171
Grant	Grant's Upper Canada Chancery Reports	Ch.	29	1849–1882	—

ABBR.	REPORTS	SERIES	VOLS.	PERIOD	E.R. [R.R.]
Grant E. & A.	Grant's Error and Appeal Reports, Ontario	All	3	1846–1866	—
Green Sc. Cr. Cas	Green Criminal Cases, Scotland			1820	—
Greer	Greer—Irish Land Cases			1872–1903	
Greg.	Gregorowski High Court Reports, Orange Free State			1883–1887	—
Gren.	Grenier's Reports, Ceylon			1872–1874	—
Grif. P.L.C.	Griffith London Poor Law Cases			1821–1831	
Grif. Pat. C.	Griffin's Patent Cases			1866–1887	
Guth. Sh. Cas.	Guthrie (Sc.)	Sh. Ct.	2	1861–1885	—
Gwil.	Gwillim Tithe Cases	—	4	1224–1824	—
H.	Hare, t. Wigram, Knight-Bruce, Turner & Page-Wood	V.C.	11	1841–1853	66–8
H. & B.	Hudson & Brooke (Ir.)	K.B.	2	1827–1831	—
H. & C.	Hurlstone & Coltman	Ex.	3	1862–1866	158–9
H. & H.	Horn & Hurlstone	Ex.	2	1838–1839	[51]
H. & J.	Hayes & Jones (Ir.)	Ex.	1	1832–1834	—
H. & M.	Hay & Marriott	Adm.	1	1776–1779	165
H. & M.	Hemming & Miller	V.C.	2	1862–1865	71
H. & N.	Hurlstone & Norman	Ex.	7	1856–1862	156–8
H. & P.	Hopwood & Philbrick	Reg.	1	1863–1867	—
H. & R.	Harrison & Rutherford	C.P.	1	1865–1866	—
H. & T. (H. & Tw.)	Hall & Twells, temp. Cottenham	Ch.	2	1849–1850	47
H. & W.	Harrison & Wollaston	K.B.	2	1835–1836	[47]
H. & W.	Hurlstone & Walmsley	Ex.	1	1840–1841	[58]
H.B. (H.Bl.)	Blackstone, H.	C.P.	2	1788–1796	126
H.C.R.	High Court Reports, India			1910–1913	—
H.C.R., N.W.F.	High Court Reports, North West Frontier.				
H.K.L.R.	Hong Kong Law Reports			1905–date	
H.L.	See "Law Reports."				
H.L. Cas.	House of Lords Cases (Clark)	H.L.	11	1847–1866	9–11
Ha.	Hare, t. Wigram, Knight-Bruce, Turner and Page-Wood	V.C.	11	1841–1853	66–8
Ha. & Tw.	Hall & Twells, temp. Cottenham	Ch.	2	1849–1850	47
Had.	Haddington's Reports (Scotland)	C.S.		1592–1624	—
Hag. Adm.	Haggard (Admiralty)	Adm.	3	1822–1838	166
Hag. Con.	Haggard (Consistory)	Ecc.	2	1789–1821	161
Hag. Ecc.	Haggard (Ecclesiastical)	Ecc.	4	1827–1833	162
Hailes	Hailes (Sc.)	C.S.	2	1766–1791	—
Hale Ecc.	Hale's Ecclesiastical Reports			1583–1736	
Hale Prec.	Hale's Precedents in Ecclesiastical Cases			1475–1640	
Han.	Hanson Bankruptcy	—	3	1915–1917	—
Hann.	Hannay's Report, New Brunswick			1867–1871	
Har. & Ruth	Harrison & Rutherford	C.P.	1	1865–1866	—
Har. & Woll.	Harrison & Wollaston	K.B.	2	1835–1836	[47]
Harc.	Harcase (Sc.)	C.S.	1	1681–1691	—
Hard.	Hardres	Ex.	1	1655–1669	145
Hard.	Kelynge, W.	Ch.	1	1730–1734	25

ABBR.	REPORTS	SERIES	VOLS.	PERIOD	E.R. [R.R.]
Hardw.	Cases, temp. Hardwicke	K.B.	1	1733–1738	95
Hare	Hare	V.C.	11	1841–1853	66–8
Hare (App.)	Hare (Appendix)	V.C.	2[1]	1852–1853	68[1]
Harm.	Harman's Upper Canada Common Pleas Reports	C.P.	32	1850–1882	—
Harr. & Hodge.	Harrison & Hodgins' Upper Canada Municipal Reports	—	1	1845–1851	—
Harr. & Woll.	Harrison & Wollaston	K.B.	2	1835–1836	[47]
Hats.	Hatsell Parliamentary Precedents			1290—1818	
Hav.Ch.Rep.	Haviland's Chancery Reports, Prince Edward Island	—	1	1850–1872	—
Haw.	Haward's Star Chamber Cases			1593–1609	
Hay	Hayes (Ir.)	Ex.	1	1830–1832	—
Hay. & J.	Hayes & Jones (Ir.)	Ex.	1	1832–1834	—
Hay & M.	Hay & Marriott	Adm.	1	1776–1779	165
Hayes	Hayes (Ir.)	Ex.	1	1830–1832	—
Hem. & M.	Hemming & Miller	V.C.	2	1862–1865	71
Hemmant.	Hemmant Sel. Cases in the Exchequer Chamber, (Selden Society)			1377–1460	
Herm.	Hermand Consistorial Decisions (Scotland)			1684–1777	—
Het. (Hetl.)	Hetley	C.P.	1	1627–1631	124
Ho. Lords C.	House of Lords Cases (Clark)	H.L.	11	1847–1866	9–11
Hob. (Hob. R.)	Hobart	K.B.	1	1603–1625	80
Hodg.	Hodgins' Election Cases Ontario	—	1	1871–1879	—
Hodges	Hodges	C.P.	3	1835–1837	[42–3]
Hog.	Hogan, temp. M'Mahon (Ir.)	Ch.	3	1816–1834	—
Holt	Holt's Judgments in *Ashby* v. *White* and *Re Patey et al.*	KB.	1	1704–1705	—
Holt. Adm. Ca.	Holt's Admiralty Cases	Adm.	1	1863–1867	—
Holt, Eq.	Holt	V.C.	1	1845	71
Holt, N.P.	Holt	N.P.	1	1815–1817	171
Home (Cl.)	Clerk Home (Sc.)	C.S.	1	1735–1744	—
Hop. & C.	Hopwood & Coltman	Reg.	2	1868–1878	—
Hop. & Ph.	Hopwood & Philbrick	Reg.	1	1863–1867	—
Horn & H.	Horn & Hurlstone	Ex.	2	1838–1839	[51]
Hov. Supp.	Hovenden's Supplement (See Vesey, Jun.)	Ch.	2	1789–1817	34
How. C.	Howard's Chancery Practice (Ir.)			1775	
How.Po.Ca.	Howard Popery Cases (Ir.)			1720–1773	
How.St.Tr.	See "State Trials."				
Hub.	Hobart	K.B.	1	1603–1625	80
Hud. & Br.	Hudson & Brooke (Ir.)	K.B.	2	1827–1831	—
Hume	Hume (Sc.)	C.S.	1	1781–1822	—
Hunt's A.C.	Hunt's Annuity Cases	Q.B.	1	1776–1796	—
Hurl. & Colt	Hurlstone & Coltman	Ex.	3	1862–1866	158–9
Hurl. & Gord.	Hurlstone & Gordon	Ex.	2	1854–1856	156
Hurl. & Nor.	Hurlston & Norman	Ex.	7	1856–1862	156–8
Hurl. & Walm.	Hurlstone & Walmsley	Ex.	1	1840–1841	[58]
Hut. (Hutt.)	Hutton	C.P.	1	1588–1639	123

[1] Appendices will be found in vols. 9 and 10.

ABBR.	REPORTS	SERIES	VOLS.	PERIOD	E.R. [R.R.]
Hyde.	Hyde's Reports, Bengal				
I.A.	Law Reports, Indian Appeals			1872–1875	—
I.C.L.Q.	International & Comparative Law Quarterly	—	★	1952–date	—
I.C.R.	Industrial Cases Reports	—	—	1972–date	—
I.C.R.	Irish Circuit Reports	—	1	1841–1843	—
I.J.	Irish Jurist	All	18	1849–1866	—
I.J.	Irish Jurist	All	★	1935–date	—
I.L.J.	Industrial Law Journal	—	—	1972–date	—
I.L.Q.	International Law Quarterly		4	1947–1951	—
I.L.R.	Indian Law Reports—Allahabad: Bombay: Calcutta: Lahore: Lucknow: Madras: Nagpur: Patna: Rangoon.				
I.L.R.	International Law Reports			1950–date	
I.R.L.R.	Industrial Relations Law Reports	—	—	1972–date	—
I.T.R.	Industrial Tribunal Reports	—	—	1966–date	
Imm. A.R.	Immigration Appeal Reports	—	—	1972–date	—
Ind. C. Aw.	Industrial Court Awards		★	1919–date	
Ind. App.	See "Law Reports."				
I.R.	Irish Reports	All	★	1838–date	—
	First Series				
I.L.R.	Irish Law Reports	K.B.	13	1838–1850	—
I.Eq.R.	Irish Equity Reports			1838–1850	—
	Second Series				
I.C.L.R.	Irish Common Law Reports	K.B.	17	1850–1866	—
I.Ch.R.	Irish Chancery Reports	Ch.	17	1850–1866	—
	Third Series				
I.R.C.L.	Irish Reports, Common Law	K.B.	11	1866–1878	—
I.R. Eq.	Irish Reports, Equity	Ch.	11	1866–1878	—
	Fourth Series				
L.R.Ir.	Law Reports, Ireland	All	32	1878–1893	—
	Fifth Series				
I.R.	Irish Reports	All	★	1894–date	—
Ir. Cir.	Irish Circuit Reports	—	1	1841–1843	—
Ir. Eccl.	Irish Reports by Milward	Ecc.	1	1819–1843	—
Ir. L. Rec.	Irish Law Recorder	Eq.	4	1827–1831	—
Ir. L.T.	Irish Law Times	All	★	1867–date	—
Ir. Law Rec., N.S.	Law Recorder, New Series (Ir.)	All	6	1833–1838	—
Ir. R. Reg. App.	Irish Reports, Registration Appeals	Reg.	1	1868–1876	—
Ir. W.L.R.	Irish Weekly Law Reports	All	8	1895–1902	—
Irv.	Irvine (Sc.)	Just.	5	1851–1868	—
I.S.L.L.	International Survey of Legal Decisions on Labour Law			1925–1938	
J.	Scottish Jurist (Sc.)	C.S.	46	1829–1873	—
J. & C.	Jones & Cary (Ir.)	Ex.	1	1838–1839	—
J. & H.	Johnson & Hemming	V.C.	2	1859–1862	70
J. & La T.	Jones & La Touche (Ir.)	Ch.	3	1844–1846	—
J. & S.	Jebb & Symes (Ir.)	Q.B.	2	1838–1841	—
J. & S.	Judah and Swan Reports, Jamaica			1839	
J. & W.	Jacob & Walker	Ch.	2	1819–1821	37

ABBR.	REPORTS	SERIES	VOLS.	PERIOD	E.R. [R.R.]
J.B.L.	Journal of Business Law	—	★	1957–date	—
J. Bridg.	Bridgman J.	C.P.	1	1614–1621	123
J.C.	Justiciary Cases (Sc.)	Just.	★	1916–date	—
J. Kel.	Kelyng, Sir John	C.C.	1	1662–1669	84
J.L.R.	Jamaica Law Reports	—	6	1953–1955	
J. Leg. Hist.	Journal of Legal History		★	1980–date	—
J.P.	Justice of the Peace and Local Government Review	All	★	1837–date	—
J.P.L.	Journal of Planning Law	—	6	1948–1953	—
J.P.L.	Journal of Planning and Property Law	—	19	1954–1972	—
J.P.L.	Journal of Planning and Environment Law	—	★	1973–date	—
J.P. Sm	Smith, J.P.	K.B.	3	1803–1806	[7–8]
J.R.	N.Z. Jurist Reports	All	2	1973–1875	—
J.R.(N.S.)	N.Z. Jurist Reports, New Series	All	4	1875–1878	—
J.S.P.T.L.	Journal of the Society of Public Teachers of Law			1924–1938, 1947–1980	—
J.S.W.L.	Journal of Social Welfare Law		★	1978–date	—
J. Shaw	John Shaw (Sc.)	Just.	1	1848–1852	—
Jac.	Jacob	Ch.	1	1821–1822	37
Jac. & W.	Jacob & Walker	Ch.	2	1819–1921	37
James & Mont.	Jameson & Montagu Bankruptcy Reports	—		1821–1828	
James Sel. Cas	James' Select Cases, Nova-Scotia	—	1	1853–1855	—
Jebb	Jebb (Ir.)	C.C.	1	1822–1840	—
Jebb & B.	Jebb & Burke (Ir.)	Q.B.	1	1841–1842	—
Jebb & S.	Jebb & Symes (Ir.)	Q.B.	2	1838–1841	—
Jenk.	Jenkins	Ex.	1	1220–1623	145
Jer. Dig.	Jeremy's Digest	All Cts.	23	1829–1851	—
Jo.	Jones (Ir.)	Ex.	2	1834–1838	—
Jo. & La T.	Jones & La Touche (Ir.)	Ch.	3	1844–1846	—
Johns. (John.; Johns (V.C.)	Johnson Ch. Rep.	V.C.	1	1859	70
Johns. & Hem.	Johnson & Hemming	V.C.	2	1860–1862	70
Jon. & Car	Jones & Cary (Ir.)	Ex.	1	1838–1839	—
Jon. Ex.	Jones (Ir.)	Ex.	2	1834–1838	—
Jones	Jones (Ir.)	Ex.	2	1834–1838	—
Jones	Jones' Upper Canada Common Pleas Reports	C.P.	32	1850–1882	—
Jones (1)	Jones, Sir Wm	K.B.	1	1620–1641	82
Jones (2)	Jones, Sir Thos	K.B.	1	1667–1685	84
Jones, T.	Jones, Sir Thos.	K.B.	1	1667–1685	84
Jones, W.	Jones, Sir Wm.	K.B.	1	1620–1641	82
Jud. & Sw.	Judah & Swan Reports, Jamaica	—		1839	—
Jur.	Jurist Reports	All Cts.	18	1837–1854	—
Jur. N.S.	Jurist Reports, New Series	All Cts.	12	1855–1866	—
Juta.	Juta's Reports Supreme Court, Cape of Good Hope	—	27	1880–1910	
K.	Kenyon	K.B.	3	1753–1759	96
K.	Kotze's High Court Reports, Transvaal	—		1877–1881	
K. & B.	Kotze's and Barber High Court Reports, Transvaal	—	2	1885–1888	

ABBR.	REPORTS	SERIES	VOLS.	PERIOD	E.R. [R.R.]
K. & G.	Keane & Grant's Appeals	Reg.	1	1854–1862	—
K. & J.	Kay & Johnson	V.C.	4	1854–1858	69–70
K. & O.	Knapp & Ombler	Elec.	1	1834–1835	—
K. & W. Dic.	Kames & Woodhouselee's folio dictionary (Sc.)	C.S.	5	1540–1796	—
K.B.	See "Law Reports."				
K.I.R.	Knight's Industrial Reports	—	—	1966–1975	—
K.L.R.	Kenya Law Reports	—		1919–date	
Kam. Rem.	Kame's Remarkable Decisions (Sc.)	C.S.	2	1716–1752	—
Kam. Sel	Kames' Select Decisions (Sc.)	C.S.	1	1752–1768	—
Kay	Kay	V.C.	1	1853–1854	69
Kay & J.	Kay & Johnson	V.C.	4	1854–1858	69–70
Ke.	Keen	R.C.	—	1836–1838	48
Keane & Gr.	Keane & Grant's Appeals	Reg.	1	1854–1862	—
Keb.	Keble	K.B.	3	1661–1679	83–4
Keil. (Keilw.)	Keilway	K.B.	1	1496–1578	72
Kel. (1)	Kelyng, Sir John	K.B.	1	1662–1669	84
Kel. (2)	Kelynge, W., temp. Hardwicke	Ch.	1	1730–1735	25
Kel J.	Kelyng, Sir John	K.B.	1	1662–1669	84
Kel. W.	Kelynge, W., temp. Hardwicke	Ch.	1	1730–1735	25
Keny.	Kenyon	K.B.	3	1753–1759	96
Kerr	Kerr's New Brunswick Reports	All	3	1840–1848	—
Keyl.	Keilway (Keylway)	K.B.	1	1496–1578	72
Kilk.	Kilkerran (Sc.)	C.S.	1	1738–1752	—
King	Select Cases, t. King, ed. Macnaghten	Ch.	1	1724–1733	25
Kn. (Kn. A.C.)	Knapp's Appeal Cases	P.C.	3	1829–1836	12
Kn. & O.	Knapp & Ombler	Elec.	1	1834–1835	—
Knox.	Knox's Reports New South Wales	All	1	1877	—
Konst. & W. Rat. App.	Konstam & Ward's Rating Appeals	—		1909–1912	
Konst.Rat.App.	Konstam's Rating Appeals	—		1904–1908	
Kotze	Kotze High Court Reports, Transvaal	—		1877–1881	
LAG Bull.	Legal Action Group Bulletin		★	1979–date	—
L. & C.	Leigh & Cave	C.C.	1	1861–1865	169
L. & G. t. Plunk	Lloyd & Goold, temp. Plunkett (Ir.)	Ch.	1	1834–1839	—
L. & G. t. Sug	Lloyd & Goold, temp. Sugden (Ir.)	Ch.	1	1835	—
L. & M.	Lowndes & Maxwell	Bail Ct.	1	1852–1854	—
L. & T.	Longfield & Townsend (Ir.)	Ex.	1	1841–1842	—
L. & W.	Lloyd and Welsby Commercial Cases	—	3	1829–1830	—
L.C.	Scottish Land Court Reps. (Sc.)	L.C.	★	1913–date	—
L.C.C. (N.S.W.)	Land Court Cases, New South Wales	—	31	1890–1921	—
L.C.J.	Lower Canada Jurist, Montreal	—	35	1848–1891	—
L.C.L.J.	Lower Canada Law Journal, Montreal	All	4	1865–1868	—
L.C.R.	Lower Canada Reports	All	17	1850–1867	—
L.G.R.	Local Government Reports	All	★	1903–date	—

ABBR.	REPORTS	SERIES	VOLS.	PERIOD	E.R. [R.R.]
L.G.R.	Local Government Law Reports, New South Wales	All	20	1911–1956	—
L.G.R.A.	Local Government Reports, Australia			1956–	
L.J.	Law Journal Reports, New Series (See "L.J.R.")	All	118	1831–1949	—
Adm.	Admiralty				
Bk.	Bankruptcy				
C.C.R.	Crown Cases Reserved				
C.P.	Common Pleas				
Ch.	Chancery				
Ecc.	Ecclesiastical				
H.L.	House of Lords				
K.B.	King's Bench				
M.C.	Magistrate's Cases				
P.	Probate, Divorce, and Admiralty				
P.C.	Privy Council				
P.D. & A.	Probate, Divorce, & Admiralty				
P. & M.	Probate and Matrimonial				
Q.B.	Queen's Bench				
L.J.C.C.A.	Law Journal Newspaper County Court Appeals	Co. Ct.	1	1935	—
L.J.N.C.C.R.	Law Journal Newspaper County Court Reports	Co. Ct.	14	1934–1947	—
L.J.O.S.	Law Journal Reports, Old Series	All	9	1822–1831	—
L.J.R.	Law Journal Reports (See "L.J.")	All	—	1947–1949	—
L.L.R.	Lagos Federal Territory Law Reports		★	1956–date	—
L.M. & P.	Lowndes, Maxwell & Pollock	Bail Ct.	2	1850–1851	[86]
L.O.	Legal Observer	All Cts.	52	1830–1856	—
L.Q.R.	Law Quarterly Review	—	★	1885–date	—
L.R.	Law Reports First Series	All	★	1865–date	—
L.R. A. & E.	Admiralty and Ecclesiastical Cases	—	4	1865–1875	—
L.R. C.C.R.	Crown Cases Reserved	—	2	1865–1875	—
L.R. C.P.	Common Pleas Cases	—	10	1865–1875	—
L.R. Ch. App.	Chancery Appeal Cases	—	10	1865–1875	—
L.R. Eq.	Equity Cases	—	20	1866–1875	—
L.R. Ex.	Exchequer Cases	—	10	1865–1875	—
L.R. H.L.	English and Irish Appeals	—	7	1866–1875	—
L.R. P. & D.	Probate and Divorce Cases	—	3	1865–1875	—
L.R. P.C.	Privy Councils Appeals	—	6	1865–1875	—
L.R. Q.B.	Queen's Bench	—	10	1865–1875	—
L.R. R.P.C.	Restrictive Practices Cases	—		1958–1972	—
L.R. Sc. & Div.	Scotch and Divorce Appeals	—	2	1866–1875	—
—	Statutes	—	10	1866–1875	—
	Second Series				
App.Cas	Appeal Cases	—	15	1875–1890	—
Ch D.	Chancery Division	—	45	1875–1890	—
C.P.D.	Common Pleas Division	—	5	1875–1880	—
Ex. D.	Exchequer Division	—	5	1875–1880	—
P.D.	Probate Division	—	15	1875–1890	—
Q.B.D.	Queen's Bench Division	—	25	1875–1890	—
—	Statutes	—	15	1876–1890	—

ABBR.	REPORTS	SERIES	VOLS.	PERIOD	E.R. [R.R.]
	Third Series				
A.C.	Appeal Cases	—	★	1891–date	—
Ch.	Chancery Division	—	★	1891–date	—
Fam.	Family Division	—	★	1971–date	
K.B. (Q.B.)	King's (Queen's) Bench	—	★	1891–date	—
P.	Probate Division	—	★	1891–1971	—
—	Statutes	—	★	1891–date	—
L.R.B.G.	Law Reports, British Guiana	—		1890–1955	
L.R. Burma	Law Reports, Burma	—	★	1948–date	
L.R.E.A.	Law Reports, East Africa	—	9	1897–1921	
L.R.Ind.App.	Law Reports, Indian Appeals	H.L.	77	1872–1950	—
L.R.Ir.	See "Irish Reports."				
L.R. (N.S.W.)	Law Reports, New South Wales	All	21	1880–1900	—
L.S.	Legal Studies	—	★	1981–date	—
L.S. Gaz.	Law Society Gazette	—	—	1903–date	—
L.S.R.	Locus Standi Reports	—	1	1936–1960	—
L.T.	Law Times Reports	All	177	1859–1947	—
L. (T.C.)	Tax Cases Leaflets			1938–date	
L.T. Jour.	Law Times Newspaper	All		1843	—
L.T.O.S.	Law Times, Old Series	All	34	1843–1859	—
L.T.R.A.	Lands Tribunal Rating Appeals	—	★	1950–date	—
L.V.R.	Land and Valuation Court Reports (New South Wales)	—		1922–	
La (Lane)	Lane	Ex	1	1605–1611	145
Lah.	Indian Law Reports, Lahore	—	28	1920–1947	
Lap. Dec.	Laperriere's Speaker's Decisions, Canada	—	1	1841–1872	—
Lat. (Latch)	Latch	K.B.	1	1625–1628	82
Law Rec., N.S.	Law Recorder, New Series	Prac. Cas.	6	1833–1838	—
Law Rec. (O.S.)	Law Recorder (Ir.)			1827–1831	
Lawr.	Lawrence High Court Reports, Griqualand				
Laws. Reg. Cas.	Lawson's Irish Registration Cases	—		1885–1914	
Ld. Ken	Kenyon	K.B.	3	1753–1759	96
Ld. Ray	Raymond, Lord	K.B.	3	1694–1732	91–2
Le. & Ca.	Leigh & Cave	C.C.	1	1861–1865	169
Leach	Leach	C.C.	2	1730–1815	168
Lee	Lee	Ecc.	2	1752–1758	161
Lee & H.	Cases, temp. Hardwicke	K.B.	1	1733–1738	95
Lee t. Hard.	Cases, temp. Hardwicke	K.B.	1	1733–1738	95
Lef. & Cass.	Lefroy and Cassel's Practice Cases, Ontario	—	1	1881–1883	—
Leg. News	Legal News, Montreal	All	20	1878–1897	—
Leg. Ob.	Legal Observer	All Cts.	52	1830–1856	—
Leg. Rep	Legal Reporter (Ir.)	—		1840–1843	
Legge	Legge's Supreme Court Cases, New South Wales	All	2	1825–1862	—
Leigh	Ley's Reports	K.B.	1	1608–1629	80
Leigh & C.	Leigh & Cave	C.C.	1	1861–1865	169
Leo.	Leonard	K.B.	4	1540–1615	74
Lev.	Levinz	K.B.	3	1660–1697	83
Lew.	Lewin	C.C.	2	1822–1838	168
Ley	Ley	K.B.	1	1608–1629	80
Lil.	Lilly, Assize	N.P.	1	1688–1693	170

					E.R. [R.R.]
ABBR.	REPORTS	SERIES	VOLS.	PERIOD	
Lit.	Litigation		★	1981–date	—
Lit. (Litt.)	Littleton	C.P.	1	1626–1632	124
Little Brooke	Brooke's New Cases	K.B.	1	1515–1558	73[1]
Ll. & G. t. P.	Lloyd & Goold, temp. Plunkett (Ir.)	Ch.	1	1834–1839	—
Ll. & G. t. S	Lloyd & Goold, temp. Sugden (Ir.)	Ch.	1	1835	—
Ll. & W.	Lloyd & Welsby Commercial Cases	—	3	1829–1830	—
Ll. L.R.	Lloyd's List Law Reports	All	84	1919–1950	—
Ll.M.C.L.Q.	Lloyd's Maritime and Commercial Law Quarterly		★	1974–date	—
Ll. Pr. Cas.	Lloyd's Reports of Prize Cases	Adm.	10	1914–1924	—
Ll. Pr. Cas. N.S.	Lloyd's Reports of Prize Cases, 2nd Series	Adm.	1	1939–1953	—
Lloyd's Rep.	Lloyd's List Law Reports	All	★	1951–date	—
Lofft	Lofft	K.B.	★	1772–1774	98
Longf. & T.	Longfield & Townsend (Ir.)	Ex.	1	1841–1842	—
Lorenz	Lorenz Reports, Ceylon	—	3	1856–1859	
Low. Can. Jur.	Lower Canada Jurist	—	35	1848–1891	
Low. Can. Rep.	Lower Canada Reports	—	17	1850–1867	
Lownd. & M.	Lowndes & Maxwell	Bail Ct.	1	1852–1854	—
Lownd. M. & P.	Lowndes Maxwell & Pollock	Bail Ct.	2	1850–1851	[86]
Luc.	Modern Cases, temp. Lucas (10 Modern Reports)	K.B.	1	1710–1725	88
Lud. El. Cas	Luder's Cases	Elec.	3	1784–1787	—
Lum. (P.L.C.)	Lumley's Poor Law Cases	Q.B.	2	1834–1842	—
Lush.	Lushington	Adm.	1	1859–1862	167
Lut. R.C.	Lutwyche	Reg.	2	1843–1853	—
Lutw.	Lutwyche	C.P.	2	1682–1704	125
Lyne (Wall.)	Wallis' Select Cases, ed. by Lyne (Ir.)	Ch.	1	1766–1791	—
M.	Session Cases, 3rd Series [Macpherson] (Sc.)	C.S.	11	1862–1873	—
M.	Morison's Dictionary of Decisions (Sc.)	C.S.	42	1540–1808	—
M.	Menzies Supreme Court Reports, Cape of Good Hope			1828–1849	
M. & A.	Montagu & Ayrton	Bky.	3	1833–1838	—
M. & B.	Montagu & Bligh	Bky.	1	1832–1833	—
M. & C.	Montagu & Chitty	Bky.	1	1838–1840	—
M. & C.	Mylne & Craig	Ch.	5	1835–1851	140–1
M. & G.	Macnaghten & Gordon	Ch.	3	1849–1851	41–2
M. & G.	Maddock & Geldart	V.C.	1	1815–1822	56
M. & G.	Manning & Granger	C.P.	7	1840–1844	133–5
M. & H.	Murphy & Hurlstone	Ex.	1	1836–1837	[51]
M. & K.	Mylne & Keen	Ch.	3	1832–1835	39–40
M. & M.	Moody & Malkin	N.P.	1	1826–1830	173
M. & M'A	Montagu & MacArthur	Bky.	1	1828–1829	—
M. & P.	Moore & Payne	C.P.	5	1827–1831	[29–33]
M. & R.	Maclean & Robinson (Sc.)	H.L.	1	1839	9
M. & R.	Manning & Ryland	K.B.	5	1827–1830	[31–4]
M. & R.	Moody & Robinson	N.P.	2	1830–1844	174
M. & R.M.C.	Manning & Ryland	M.C.	3	1827–1830	—
M. & S.	Manning & Scott	C.P.	19	1845–1856	135–9

[1] See note on p.353.

ABBR.	REPORTS	SERIES	VOLS.	PERIOD	E.R. [R.R.]
M. & S.	Maule & Selwyn	K.B.	6	1813–1817	105
M. & S.	Moore & Scott	C.P.	4	1831–1834	[34–8]
M. & W.	Meeson & Welsby	Ex.	16	1836–1847	150–3
M.A.R.	Municipal Association Reports New South Wales	—		1886–1911	—
M.C.	Magistrates Cases. See "Law Journal."				
M.C.C.	Moody	C.C.		1824–1844	168–9
M.C.R.	Magistrates Reports, New Zealand			1939–date	
M.D. & D. (M.D. & De G.)	Montague, Deacon & De Gex	Bky.	3	1840–1844	—
M.G. & S.	Common Bench (Manning Granger & Scott) Reports	C.P.	19	1845–1856	135–9
M.I.A.	Moore's Indian Appeals			1836–1871	18–20
M.L.J.	Madras Law Journal		★	1891–date	
M.L.J.	Malaya Law Journal		★	1932–date	
M.L.R.	Modern Law Review		★	1937–date	
M.P.C.	Moore, E. F.	P.C.	15	1836–1862	12–5
M.P.R.	Maritime Provinces Reports, Canada		★	1929–date	—
M.R.	Mauritius Decisions		★	1861–date	
M.W.N.	Madras Weekly Notes		★	1910–date	
Mac.	Macassey's Reports, New Zealand	—	1	1861–1872	—
Mac. & G.	Macnaghten & Gorden	Ch.	3	1849–1851	41–2
Mac. & H.	Macrae & Hertslet	Bky.	2	1847–1852	—
Mac. & H.	Cox, Macrae & Hertslet	C.C.	3	1847–1858	—
Mac. & R.	Maclean & Robinson (Sc.)	H.L.	1	1839	9
Mac. C.C.	Macgillivrays Copyright Cases	—	9	1901–1949	—
Mac. P.C.	Macrory	Pat. Cas.	1	1847–1860	—
MacCarthy	MacCarthy's Irish Land Cases			1887–1892	
Maccl.	Modern Cases, temp. Macclesfield (10 Modern Reports)	K.B.	1	1710–1724	88
MacDev.	MacDevitt's Irish Land Cases			1882–1884	
Macf.	Macfarlane	C.S.	1	1838–1839	—
Macl. Rem. Cas.	Maclaurin's Remarkable Cases (Scotland)			1670–1773	
Macph.	Session Cases, 3rd Series [Macpherson] (Sc.)	C.S.	11	1862–1873	—
Macq.	Macqueen (Sc.)	H.L.	4	1851–1865	—
Macr.	Macrory	Pat. Cas.	1	1847–1860	—
Macr. & H.	Macrae & Hertslet	Bky.	2	1847–1852	—
Macr. P. Cas.	Macrory	Pat. Cas.	1	1847–1860	—
Mad. & Gel.	Maddock & Geldart	V.C.	1	1821–1822	56
Madd.	Maddock	V.C.	6	1815–1822	56
Madd. & G.	Maddock & Geldart	V.C.	1	1821–1822	56
Mag. Cas.	Magistrates Cases. See "Law Journal."			1832–1835	
Man.	Manning's Revision Cases			1832–1835	
Man. & G.	Manning & Granger	C.P.	7	1840–1844	133–5
Man. & Ry.	Manning & Ryland	K.B.	5	1827–1830	[31–4]
Man. & Ry. M.C.	Manning & Ryland	M.C.	3	1827–1830	—
Man. & Sc.	Manning, Granger & Scott, Common Bench Reports	C.P.	19	1845–1856	135–9
Man. Gr. & S	Manning, Granger & Scott, Common Bench Reports	C.P.	19	1845–1856	135–9

ABBR.	REPORTS	SERIES	VOLS.	PERIOD	E.R. [R.R.]
Man. L.J.	Manitoba Law Journal		★	1962–date	—
Man. L.R.	Manitoba Law Reports	All	★	1884–date	—
Man. Law	Managerial Law	—	—	1975–date	—
Manson	Manson	Bky.	21	1894–1914	—
Mar.	March	K.B.	1	1639–1642	82
Mar. L.C. (Mar. L.R.)	Maritime Law Cases (Crockford)	Adm.	3	1860–1871	—
Mar. L.C., N.S.	See "Aspinall."				
March [N.C.]	March's Translation of Brooke's New Cases	K.B.	1	1515–1558	73[1]
March N.C.	March's New Cases	K.B.	1	1639–1642	82
Marr.	Marriott	Adm.	1	1776–1779	165
Marsh.	Marshall	C.P.	2	1813–1816	[15,17]
Marsh.	Marshall High Court Reports, Bengal: Marshall's Reports, Ceylon.				
Mau. & Sel.	Maule & Selwyn	K.B.	6	1813–1817	105
Mayn.	Maynard's Reports	—		1273–1326	
McCle (McCl.)	M'Cleland	Ex.	1	1824	148
McCle. & Yo.	M'Cleland & Younge	Ex.	1	1824–1825	148
Mees. & Wels.	Meeson & Welsby	Ex.	16	1836–1847	150–3
Megone	Megone's Company Cases	—	2	1888–1890	—
Melb. Univ. L.R.	Melbourne University Law Review			1957–	
Menz.	Menzies Reports, Cape of Good Hope		4	1828–1849	
Mer.	Merivale	Ch.	3	1815–1817	35–6
Milw. Ir. Ecc. Rep.	Irish Reports by Milward	Ecc.	1	1819–1843	—
Mo.	Modern Reports (ed. Leach)	K.B.	12	1669–1755	86–8
Mo.	Moore, E.F.	P.C.	15	1836–1862	12–5
Mo.	Moore, E. F., Indian Appeals	P.C.	14	1836–1872	18–20
Mo.	Moore, Sir Francis	K.B.	1	1512–1621	72
Mo.	Moore, J.B.	C.P.	12	1817–1827	[19–29]
Mo. & R.	Moody & Robinson	N.P.	2	1830–1844	174
Mo. & Sc.	Moore & Scott	C.P.	4	1831–1834	[34–38]
Mo. I.A.	Moore, E. F., Indian Appeals	P.C.	14	1836–1872	18–20
Mod.	Modern Reports	K.B.	12	1669–1755	86–8
Mod. Ca L. & Eq.	8 & 9 Modern Reports	K.B.	2	1721–1755	88
Mod. Ca. Per Far.	7 Modern Reports	K.B.	1	1702–1745	87
Mod. Ca. t. Holt	7 Modern Reports	K.B.	1	1702–1745	87
Mod. Cas.[1]	Modern Cases[1]	K.B.	12	1702–1745	87–8[2]
Mod. Rep.	Modern Reports	K.B.	12	1669–1755	86–8
Mol. (Moll.)	Molloy (Ir.)	Ch.	3	1827–1831	—
Mont.	Montagu	Bky.	1	1829–1832	—
Mont. & Ayr.	Montagu & Ayrton	Bky.	3	1833–1838	—
Mont. & Bl.	Montagu & Bligh	Bky.	1	1832–1833	—
Mont. & C.	Montagu & Chitty	Bky.	1	1838–1840	—
Mont. & MacA	Montagu & MacArthur	Bky.	1	1828–1829	—
Mont. Cond. Rep.	Montreal Condensed Reports	All	1	1853–1854	—
Mont. D. & De G.	Montagu, Deacon & De Gex	Bky.	3	1840–1844	—
Mont. L.R.	Montreal Law Reports	All	7	1885–1891	—
Moo.	Moody	C.C.	2	1824–1844	168–9
Moo.	More, E.F.	P.C.	15	1836–1862	12–5

[1] See note on p.353.
[2] Mod. Case. = 6. 7 Mod.; 2 Mod. Cas. sometimes = 7 Mod., sometimes 8 Mod.

ABBR.	REPORTS	SERIES	VOLS.	PERIOD	E.R. [R.R.]
Moo.	Moore, Sir Francis	K.B.	1	1512–1621	72
Moo.	Moore, J.B.	C.P.	12	1817–1827	[19–29]
Moo. & M.	Moody & Malkin	N.P.	1	1826–1830	173
Moo. & Pay.	Moore & Payne	C.P.	5	1827–1831	[29–33]
Moo. & Rob.	Moody & Robinson	N.P.	2	1831–1844	174
Moo. & Sc.	Moore & Scott	C.P.	4	1831–1834	[34–8]
Moo. A.	1 Bosanquet & Puller, 471 ff	C.P.	1	1796–1797	126
Moo. C.C.	Moody	C.C.	2	1824–1844	168–9
Moo. F.	Moore, Sir Francis	K.B.	1	1512–1621	72
Moo. Ind. App.	Moore, E. F., Indian Appeals	P.C.	14	1836–1872	18–20
Moo. K.B.	Moore, Sir Francis	K.B.	1	1512–1621	72
Moo. N.S.	Moore, E. F., New Series	P.C.	9	1862–1873	15–7
Moo. P.C.	Moore, E. F.	P.C.	15	1836–1862	12–5
Mor.	Morris's Reports, Jamaica		1	1836–1844	
Mor. Dic.	Morrison's Dictionary of Decisions (Sc.)	C.S.	42	1540–1808	—
Mor. Syn.	Morison's Synopsis (Sc.)	C.S.	2	1808–1816	—
Morr.	Morrell	Bky.	10	1884–1893	—
Mos.	Mosely	Ch.	1	1726–1730	25
Mumf.	Mumford's Reports, Jamaica			1838	
Mun.	Munitions Appeal Reports			1916–1920	
Mun. App. Sc.	Munitions of War Acts, Scottish Appeals			1916–1920	
Mundy	Mundy's Abstracts of Star Chamber			1550–1558	
Mur. (Murr.)	Murray (Sc.)	Jury Ct.	5	1815–1830	—
Mur. & Hurl.	Murphy & Hurlstone	Ex.	1	1836–1837	[51]
Myl. & Cr.	Mylne & Craig	Ch.	5	1835–1841	40–1
Myl. & K.	Mylne & Keen	Ch.	3	1832–1835	39–40
N. & M.	Neville & Manning	K.B.	6	1832–1836	[38–43]
N. & M.M.C.	Neville & Manning	M.C.	3	1832–1836	—
N. & McN.	Neville & McNamara	Rail. Ca.	19	1855–1928	—
N. & P.	Neville & Perry	K.B.	3	1836–1838	[44–5]
N. & P.M.C.	Neville & Perry	M.C.	1	1836–1837	—
N. & S.	Nicholls & Stops. Reports, Tasmania	—	2	1897–1904	—
N.A.C.	Native Appeal Cases, South Africa			1894–1929	—
N.B.Eq.R.	New Brunswick Equity Reports	Eq.	4	1894–1912	—
N.B.R.	New Brunswick Reports	All	34	1825–1929	—
N.Ben	Benloe	K.B.	1	1515–1628	73
N.C.	Bingham, New Cases	C.P.	6	1834–1840	131–3
N.C.	Notes of New Cases (ed. Thornton)	Ecc.	7	1841–1850	—
N.C.C.	Younge & Collyer	V.C.	2	1841–1844	62–3
N.C.Str.	Strange's Notes of Cases, Madras		2	1798–1816	—
N.F.	Newfoundland Law Reports		★	1817–date	—
N.H. & C.	Nicholl, Hare, & Carrow	Rail Ca.	7	1835–1854	—
N.I.	Northern Ireland Law Reports	All	★	1925–date	—
N.I.J.	New Irish Jurist (Ir.)		5	1900–1905	—
N.L.J.	New Law Journal	—	—	1965–date	—
N.L.R.	New Law Reports, Ceylon: Natal Laws Reports				
N.L.R.	Newfoundland Law Reports	All	★	1817–date	—

ABBR.	REPORTS	SERIES	VOLS.	PERIOD	E.R. [R.R.]
N.L.R.	Nigeria Law Reports		★	1881–date	
N.L.R.	Nyasaland Law Reports		★	1922–date	
N.P.C.	New Practice Cases	Bail Ct.	3	1844–1848	—
N.P.D.	Natal Province Divison, South African Law Reports.			1910–1946	—
N.R.	Bosanquet & Puller, New Reports	C.P.	2	1804–1807	127
N.R.	New Reports	All	6	1862–1865	—
N.R.L.R.	Northern Rhodesia Law Reports		★	1931–1955	
N.R.N.L.R.	Northern Region of Nigeria Law Reports		★	1956–date	
N.S.C.	New Sessions Cases by Carrow, Hamerton & Allen	M.C.	4	1844–1851	—
N.S. Dec.	Nova Scotia Decisions	All	3	1867–1874	—
N.S.L.R.	Nova Scotia Law Reports	All	1	1834–1852	—
N.S.W.A.R.	New South Wales Arbitration Reports			1902–date	
N.S.W.L.R.	New South Wales Law Reports	All	21	1880–1900	—
N.S.W.L.V.R.	New South Wales Land Valuation Reports		★	1922–date	
N.S.W.S.R.	New South Wales State Reports		★	1901–date	
N.S.W. W.C.R.:	New South Wales Workmen's Compensation Reports		★	1926–date	
N.S.W.W.N.	New South Wales Weekly Notes			1884–date	
N.W.T.R.	North West Territories Reports, Canada		7	1885–1907	
N.Z. Jur.	New Zealand Jurist	All	6	1873–1878	—
N.Z.L.R.	New Zealand Law Reports	All	★	1883–date	—
Nell	Nell's Reports, Ceylon			1845–1855	
Nels. (Nels. 8vo)	Nelson	Ch.	1	1625–1693	21
Nels. (Nels. Fol.)	Finch's Reports (ed. by Nelson)	Ch.	1	1673–1681	23
Nelson's Rep.	Nelson t. Finch	Ch.	1	1673–1681	23
Nev. & M.M.C.	Neville & Manning	M.C.	3	1832–1836	—
Nev. & Man	Neville & Manning	K.B.	6	1832–1836	[38–43]
Nev. & McN.	See "Traffic Cases."				
Nev. & McN.	See "Traffic Cases."				
Nev. & P.	Neville & Perry	K.B.	3	1836–1838	[44–5]
Nev. & P. Mag. Cas.	Neville & Perry	M.C.	1	1836–1837	—
New Benl.	Benloe	K.B.	1	1531–1628	73
New Cas. Eq.	Modern Cases (8 & 9 Modern Reports)	K.B.	2	1721–1755	88
New Mag. Cas.	New Magistrates Cases	M.C.	5	1844–1851	—
New Pr. Cas.	New Practice Cases	Bail Ct.	3	1844–1848	—
New Rep.	New Reports	All	6	1862–1865	—
New Sess. Cas.	New Sessions Cases by Carrow, Hamerton & Allen	M.C.	4	1844–1851	—
Newf. Sel. Cas	Newfoundland Select Cases	—	1	1817–1828	—
Nic. Ha. C.	Nicholl, Hare & Carrow	Rail Ca.	7	1835–1855	—
Nig. L.R.	Nigeria Law Reports				
Nolan	Nolan's Magistrates Cases			1791–1792	
Not. Cas.	Notes of Cases, ed, Thornton	Ecc.	7	1841–1850	—
Noy	Noy	K.B.	1	1559–1649	74
Ny. L.R.	Nyasaland Law Reports		★	1922–date	

ABBR.	REPORTS	SERIES	VOLS.	PERIOD	E.R. [R.R.]
O.A.R.	Ontario Appeal Reports		27	1876–1900	
O.B. & F.	Ollivier, Bell & Fitzgerald's Reports, New Zealand	All	1	1878–1880	—
O.B.S.P.	Old Bailey, Sessional Papers			1715–1834	
O. Benl.	Benloe & Dalison	C.P.	1	1486–1580	123[1]
O. Bridg.	Bridgman, O.	C.P.	1	1660–1667	124
O.F.S.	Orange Free State High Court Reports		5	1879–1883	
O.J.L.S.	Oxford Journal of Legal Studies		★	1981–date	—
O.L.R.	Ontario Law Reports		66	1901–1931	
O'M. & H.	O'Malley & Hardcastle	Elec.	7	1869–1929	—
O.P.D.	South Africa Law Reports, Orange Free State Province Division			1910–1946	
O.P.R.	Ontario Practice Reports			1850–1900	
O.R.	Ontario Reports			1882–1900, 1931–date	
O.W.N.	Ontario Weekly Notes			1909–1962	
O.W.R.	Ontario Weekly Reporter			1902–1914	
Old Benloe	Benloe & Dalison	C.P.	1	1486–1580	123[1]
Oldr.	Oldright's Reports, Nova Scotia			1860–1867	
Oll. B. & F.	As O.B. & F. (above)				
Ont.	Ontario Reports	All	32	1882–1900	—
Ont. App.	Ontario Appeal Reports	All	27	1876–1900	—
Ont. Elect.	Ontario Election Cases	—	—	1884–1900	—
Ont. L.R.	Ontario Law Reports	All	66	1901–1931	—
Ont. Pr. Rep.	Ontario Practice Reports	—	19	1850–1900	—
Ont. W.R.	Ontario Weekly Reporter	All	27	1902–1914	—
Ow.	Owen	K.B.	1	1556–1615	74
Oxley	Young's Vice-Admiralty Decisions, Nova Scotia, by Oxley	Am.	27	1865–1880	—
P	See "Law Reports."				
P. & C.R.	Property & Compensation Reports	All	★	1949–date—	
P. & D.	Perry & Davison	K.B.	4	1838–1841	[48–54]
P. & D.	See "Law Reports."				
P. & K.	Perry & Knapp	Elec.	1	1833	—
P. & R.	Pigott & Rodwell	Reg.	1	1843–1845	—
P. & T.	Pugsley and Trueman Reports, New Brunswick			1882–1883	
P.C.	See "Law Reports."				
P. Cas	British and Colonial Prize Cases (Trehern & Grant)	Adm.	3	1914–1922	—
P.D.	See "Law Reports."				
P.E.I. Rep.	Prince Edward Island Reports	—	—	1850–1872	—
P.L.	Public Law	—	★	1956–date	—
P.L. Mag.	Poor Law Magazine (Sc.)	All	72	1858–1930	—
P.N.P.	Peake	N.P.	2	1790–1794	170
P.O. Cas	Perry's Oriental Cases, Bombay			1843–1852	
P. R. & D.	Power, Rodwell & Dew	Elec.	2	1847–1856	—
P.R.U.C.	Practice Reports, Upper Canada	—	19	1850–1900	—
P. Shaw	Patrick Shaw (Sc.)	Just.	1	1819–1831	—

[1] See Wallace's "The Reporters," 4th ed., p. 118, n.2.

Law Reports

ABBR.	REPORTS	SERIES	VOLS.	PERIOD	E.R.[R.R.]
P. W. (P. Wms.)	Peere Williams	Ch.	3	1695–1735	24
Pal. (Palm.)	Palmer	K.B.	1	1619–1629	81
Park.	Parker	Ex.	1	1743–1767	145
Pat. & Mur.	Paterson and Murray's Reports, New South Wales			1870–1871	
Pat. Abr.	Paterson's Abstracts of Poor Law Cases			1857–1863	
Pat. App.	Paton's Appeals (Sc.)	H.L.	6	1726–1821	—
Paters. App.	Paterson Appeals (Sc.)	H.L.	2	1851–1873	—
Patr. Elect. Cas	Patrick's Election Cases, Upper Canada	Elect.	1	1824–1849	—
Pea. (2)	Peake's Additional Cases	N.P.	1	1795–1812	170
Pea. (Peake)	Peake	N.P.	2	1790–1794	170
Peck	Peckwell	Elec.	2	1802–1806	—
Peere Wms	Peere Williams	Ch.	3	1695–1735	24
Pelham	Pelham's Reports, South Australia	All	1	1865–1866	—
Per. & Dav.	Perry & Davison	K.B.	4	1838–1841	[48–54]
Per. Or. Cas.	Perry Oriental Cases, Bombay			1843–1852	
Perry Ins.	Perry's Insolvency Cases			1831	
Pet.	Peters' Prince Edward Island Reports	Ch.	1	1850–1872	—
Pet. Br.	Brooke's New Cases	K.B.	1	1515–1558	73[1]
Ph. (Phil.)	Phillimore's Reports	Ecc.	3	1809–1821	161
Ph. (Phil.)	Phillips	Ch.	2	1841–1849	41
Ph. (Phil.)	Phillips' Election Cases	Elec.	1	1780–1781	—
Phil. Ecc. Judg.	Phillimore's Judgments	Ecc.	1	1867–1875	—
Phil. Ecc. R.	Phillimore's Reports	Ecc.	3	1809–1821	161
Phil. El. Cas.	Phillips' Election Cases	Elec.	1	1780–1781	—
Phil. Judg.	Phillimore's Judgments	Ecc.	1	1867–1875	—
Pig. & R.	Pigott & Rodwell	Reg.	1	1843–1845	—
Pist.	Piston's Reports, Mauritius			1861–1862	
Pitc.	Pitcairn Criminal Trials (Scotland)			1488–1624	
Pl.	Plowden's Commentaries	K.B.	2	1550–1580	75
Pl. & Pr. Cas.	Pleading and Practice Cases			1837–1838	
Plac. Angl. Nor.	Placita Anglo-Normannica	—	1	1066–1195	—
Pol.	Pollexfen	K.B.	1	1669–1685	86
Pop. (Poph.)	Popham	K.B.	1	1592–1627	79
Pow. R. & D.	Power, Rodwell & Dew	Elec.	2	1847–1856	—
Pr.	Price	Ex.	13	1814–1824	145–7
Pr. Ch.	Precedents in Chancery (Finch)	Ch.	1	1689–1722	24
Pr. Exch.	Price	Ex.	13	1814–1824	145–7
Pratt	Pratt's Supplement to Bott's Poor Laws			1833	
Pres. Fal.	Falconer's Decisions (Sc.)	C.S.	1	1744–1751	—
Price, P.C.	Price Practice Cases	Ex.	1	1830–1831	—
Prid. & C.	Prideaux and Cole's Reports (New Sessions Cases), Volume 4			1850–1851	
Prop.L.Bull.	Property Law Bulletin		★	1980–date	
Pugs.	Puglsey's Reports, New Brunswick	All	3	1872–1877	—
Pugs. & Bur.	Puglsey & Burbridge's Reports, New Brunswick	All	4	1878–1882	—

[1] See note on p.353.

ABBR.	REPORTS	SERIES	VOLS.	PERIOD	E.R. [R.R.]
Pugs. & Tru.	Puglsey's and Trueman's Reports, New Brunswick			1882–1883	
Pyke	Pyke's Lower Canada King's Bench Reports	K.B.	1	1809–1810	—
Q.B.	See "Law Reports."				
Q.B. (Q.B.R.)	Queen's Bench Reports (Adolphus & Ellis, N.S.)	Q.B.	18	1841–1852	113–18
Q.B.U.C.	Queen's Bench Reports, Upper Canada	Q.B.	46	1844–1882	—
Q.C.L.L.R.	Crown Lands Law Reports (Queensland)	—	★	1859–date	—
Q.C.R.	Queensland Criminal Reports	Crim.	1	1860–1907	—
Q.J.P.R.	Queensland Justice of the Peace Reports	—	★	1907–date	—
Q.L.J.	Queensland Law Journal	All	11	1879–1901	—
Q.L.R.	Quebec Law Reports	All	17	1874–1891	—
Q.L.R.	Queensland Law Reports	All	1	1876–1878	—
Q.O.R.	Quebec Official Reports	K.B. & Q.B. All Cts.	★	1892–date	—
Q.P.R.	Quebec Practice Reports.	—	★	1897–date	—
Q.R.S.C.	Quebec Reports, Superior Court		★	1892–date	
Q.S.C.R.	Queensland Supreme Court Reports	All	5	1860–1881	—
Q.S.R.	State Reports (Queensland)	All	50	1902–1957	—
Q.U.L.J.	Queensland University Law Journal			1948–date	
Q.W.N.	Queensland Law Reporter & Weekly Notes	All	★	1908–date	—
Qd. R.	Queensland Reports			1958–date	
R.	The Reports	All	15	1893–1895	—
R.	Session Cases, 4th Series [Rettie] (Sc.)	C.S.	18	1873–1898	—
R. & C.	Russell & Chesley Reports, Nova Scotia		3	1875–1879	
R. & G.	Russell & Geldart Equity Reports, Nova Scotia		15	1879–1895	
R. & I.T.	Rating and Income Tax		53	1924–1960	
R. & M.	Russell & Mylne	Ch.	2	1829–1831	39
R. & M.	Ryan & Moody	N.P.	1	1823–1826	171
R. & McG.	Income Tax Decisions of Australiasia, Ratcliffe M'Grath	—	2	1891–1930	—
R. & McG. Ct. of Rev.	Court of Review Decisions, Ratcliffe and McGrath, N.S.W.	Tax.	1	1913–1927	—
R. & N.	Rhodesia and Nyasaland Law Reports		★	1956–date	
R. & R.C.C.	Russell & Ryan	C.C.	1	1799–1824	168
R. & V.R.	Rating and Valuation Reports	—	★	1960–date	—
R.A.C.	Ramsay's Appeal Cases, Canada			1873–1886	
R.C.	See "Nicholl, Hare & Carrow."				
R.C. & C.R.	Revenue Civil and Criminal Reporter, Calcutta			1866–1868	

ABBR.	REPORTS	SERIES	VOLS.	PERIOD	E.R. [R.R.]
R.E.D.	Reserved and Equity Decisions, New South Wales			1845	
R.H.C.	Road Haulage Cases	—	★	1950–date	—
R.J.	Judgments of the Supreme Court of N.S.W. for the district of Port Phillip. A'Beckett	—	1	1846–1851	—
R.J.O.	Rapports Judiciaires Officiels, Quebec	K.B.	★	1892–date	
R.L. & S.	Ridgway, Lapp & Schoales (Ir.)	K.B.	1	1793–1795	—
R.L., N.S.	Revue Legale, New Series Quebec		22	1869–1942	
R.L. & W.	Robert, Leaming and Wallis	Co. Ct.	5 pts.	1849–1851	—
R.P.C.	Reports of Patent Cases	Pat. Cas.	★	1884–date	—
R.R.	Revised Reports	All	152	1785–1866	—
R.R.C.	Ryde's Rating Cases			1956–date	
R.T.R.	Road Traffic Reports	—	—	1970–date	—
R.V.R.	Rating and Valuation Reporter	—	—	1965–date	—
Rams. App.	Ramsey's Appeal Cases, Quebec	All	1	1873–1886	—
Ray. Ti. Cas	Rayner's Tithe Cases	Ch.	3	1575–1782	—
Raym.	Raymond, Lord	K.B.	3	1694–1732	91–2
Raym.	Raymond, Sir. T.	K.B.	1	1660–1684	83
Rayn.	Rayner's Tithe Cases		3	1575–1782	
Real Prop. Cas.	Real Property Cases			1843–1847	
Rep.	Coke	K.B.	13	1572–1616	76–7
Rep. Cas. Eq.	Gilbert, Equity Reports	Ch.	1	1705–1727	25
Rep. Ch.	Reports in Chancery	Ch.	1	1615–1712	21
Rep. Eq.	Gilbert, Equity Reports	Ch.	1	1705–1727	25
Rep. in Ch.	Reports in Chancery	Ch.	1	1615–1712	21
Rep. in Cha.	Bittleston's Chamber Cases	K.B.	1	1883–1884	—
Rep. of Sel. Cas in Ch.	Kelynge, W., temp. Hardwicke	Ch.	1	1730–1736	125
Rep. Q.A.	Cases temp. Queen Anne (11 Modern Reports)	K.B.	1	1702–1710	88
Rep. t. F.	Reports, temp. Finch	Ch.	1	1673–1681	23
Rep. t. Hard.	Cases temp. Hardwicke (ed. Lee)	K.B.	1	1733–1738	95
Res. & Eq. J.	Reserved and Equity Judgments, New South Wales	—	1	1845	—
Reserv. Cas.	Reserved Cases (Irish)			1860–1864	
Rett.	Session Cases, 4th Series [Rettie] (Sc.)	C.S.	25	1873–1898	—
Rev. Lég.	La Revue Légale, Quebec	All	22	1869–1892	—
Rev. Lég. N.S.	La Revue Légale, New Series, Quebec	All	★	1892–date	
Rick. & M.	Rickards & Michael	L.S.	1	1885–1889	—
Rick. & S.	Rickards & Saunders	L.S.	1	1890–1894	—
Ridg. (Ridg. t. Hard.)	Ridgeway, temp. Hardwicke	K.B.	1	1733–1736	94
Ridg. (Ridg. t. Hard.)	Ridgeway, Temp. Hardwicke	Ch.	1	1744–1746	27
Ridg., L. & S.	Ridgeway, Lapp & Schoales (Ir.)	K.B.	1	1793–1795	—
Ridg. P.C.	Ridgeway's Parliamentary Reports (Ir.)	App.	3	1784–1796	—

ABBR.	REPORTS	SERIES	VOLS.	PERIOD	E.R. [R.R.]
Ritch.	Ritchie, Reports by Francis Bacon	Ch.	1	1617–1721	—
Ritch.	Ritchie's Equity Reports, Nova Scotia	—	1	1872–1882	—
Rob.	Robertson's Appeal (Sc.)	H.L.	1	1707–1727	—
Rob.	Robinson's Appeals (Sc.)	H.L.	2	1840–1841	—
Rob.	Robinson, Christopher	Adm.	6	1799–1808	165
Rob.	Robinson, William	Adm.	3	1838–1852	166
Rob. A.	Robinson, Christopher	Adm.	6	1799–1808	165
Rob. App.	Robinson's Appeals (Sc.)	H.L.	2	1840–1841	—
Rob. Cas.	Robertson's Appeals (Sc.)	H.L.	1	1707–1727	—
Rob. Chr.	Robinson, Christopher	Adm.	6	1799–1808	165
Rob. E.	Robertson	Ecc.	2	1844–1853	163
Rob. Jun.	Robinson, William	Adm.	3	1838–1852	166
Rob. Sc. App.	Robertson's Appeals (Sc.)	H.L.	1	1707–1727	—
Rob. U.C.	Robinson's Reports, Upper Canada	K.B.		1831–1844, 1844–1882	
Robin Sc. App.	Robinson's Appeals (Sc.)	H.L.	2	1840–1841	—
Robinson	Robinson, Christopher	Adm.	6	1799–1808	165
Robinson	Robinson, William	Adm.	3	1838–1852	166
Roche D. & K.	Roche, Dillon and Kehoe Irish Land Reports			1881–1882	
Roll. (Rolle)	Rolle	K.B.	2	1614–1625	81
Rom.	Romilly's Notes of Cases	Ch.		1767–1787	
Rose, P.C.	Roscoe's Prize Cases	Adm.	2	1745–1859	—
Rose	Rose	Bky.	2	1810–1816	—
Ross L.C.	Ross Leading Cases (Scotland)			1638–1849	
Rot. Cur. Regis	Rotuli Curiae Regis (by Palgrave)	K.B.	2	1194–1199	—
Rul. Cas.	Ruling Cases, edited Campbell			1894–1908	
Russ.	Russell	Ch.	5	1823–1829	38
Russ. & Ches.	Russell & Chesley's Reports, Nova Scotia	All	3	1875–1879	—
Russ. & Geld.	Russell & Geldert's Reports, Nova Scotia	All	15	1879–1895	—
Russ. & M.	Russell & Mylne	Ch.	2	1829–1831	39
Russ. & R.	Russell & Ryan	C.C.	1	1799–1824	168
Russ. Elect. Cas.	Russell's Election Cases, Nova Scotia	—	1	1874	—
Ry.&Can.Tr.Cas.	Railway, Canal and Road Traffic Cases	Rail Ca.	29	1885–1949	—
	For continuation *see* Traffic Cases				
Ry. & M.	Ryan & Moody	N.P.	1	1823–1826	171
Ry. Cas.	Railway Cases	Rail Ca.	7	1835–1854	—
Ryde	Ryde Rating Appeals			1871–1893	
Ryde & K.	Ryde and Konstam Rating Appeals			1894–1904	
S.	Session Cases, 1st Series [Shawl] (Sc.)	C.S.	16	1821–1838	—
S.	Shaw's Appeals (Sc.)	H.L.	2	1821–1824	—
S. & A.	Saunders & Austin	L.S.	2	1895–1904	—
S. & B.	Saunders & Bidder	L.S.	2	1905–1919	—
S. & B.	Smith & Batty (Ir.)	K.B.	1	1824–1825	—
S. & C.	Saunders & Cole	Bail Ct.	2	1846–1848	[82]
S. & D.	Session Cases, 1st Series (Shaw & Dunlop) Sc.)	C.S.	16	1821–1838	—
S. & G.	Smale & Giffard	V.C.	3	1852–1857	65
S. & L.	Schoales & Lefroy (Ir.	Ch.	2	1802–1806	—
S. & M.	Shaw & Maclean (Sc.)	H.L.	2	1835–1838	—

ABBR.	REPORTS	SERIES	VOLS.	PERIOD	E.R. [R.R.]
S. & S.	Sausse & Scully (Ir.)	Ch.	1	1837–1840	—
S. & S.	Simons & Stuart	V.C.	2	1822–1826	57
S. & Sm.	Searle & Smith	P. & D.	1	1859–1860	—
S. & T.	Swabey & Tristam	Ecc.	4	1858–1865	164
S.A.I.R.	South Australian Industrial Reports	—	24	1916–date	—
S.A.L.J.	South African Law Journal		★	1884–date	
S.A.L.R.	South Australian Law Reports	All	25	1865–1892	—
			20	1899–1920	—
S.A.L.R.	South African Law Reports	All	★	1948–date	—
S.A.R.	South Australian Industrial Court Reports		★	1916–date	
S.A.S.R.	South Australian State Reports	All	★	1921–date	—
S.Bell	Bell (Sc.)	H.L.	7	1842–1850	—
S.C.	Supreme Court Reports, Cape of Good Hope			1880–1910	
S.C.	Session Cases (Sc.)[And see "Sess. Cas."]	C.S.	★	1906–date—	
S.C.C.	Select Cases in Chancery, t. King, ed. Macnaghten	Ch.	1	1724–1733	25
S.C. (H.L.)	Sessions Cases (House of Lords)		★	1850–date	
S.C.(J.)	Session Cases (Justiciary Reports)			1907–1916	
S.C.R.	Supreme Court Reports, Canada	All	64	1876–1922	—
S.C.R. (N.S.W.)	Supreme Court Reports, New South Wales	All	14	1862–1876	—
S.C.R. (N.S.) (N.S.W.)	Supreme Court Reports, New South Wales, New Series	All	2	1878–1879	—
S.J.	Solicitors' Journal	All	★	1857–date	—
S.J.	Scottish Jurist	C.S.	46	1829–1873	—
S.L.C.	Stuart's Appeals, Lower Canada			1810–1853	
S.L.C.R.	Scottish Land Court Reports	L.C.	★	1913–date	—
S.L.R.	Scottish Law Reporter	C.S.	61	1865–1925	—
S.L.R.	Scottish Land Reports		★	1913–date	
S.L. Rev.	Scottish Law Review	Sh. Ct.	★	1885–date	—
S.L.T.	Scots Law Times	C.S.	★	1893–date	—
S.L.T. (Lyon Ct.)	Scot Law Times (Lyon Court)			1950–date	
S.L.T. (Notes)	Scots Law Times (Notes)			1846–date	
S.L.T. (Sh. Ct.)	Scots Law Times (Sheriff Court)			1893–date	
S.N.	Session Notes	C.S.	24	1925–1948	—
S.R., H.C.R.	Southern Rhodesia High Court Reports			1911–1955	
S.R. (N.S.W.)	State Reports, New South Wales	All	★	1901–date	
S.R.Q.	State Reports, Queensland		★	1905–date	
S.T.	State Trials			1163–1820	
S.T.C.	Simon's Tax Cases	—	—	1973–date	—
S.V.A.R.	Stuart's Vice Admiralty Reports, Quebec		2	1836–1874	
S.W.A.	South West Africa Reports			1920–1945	
Salk.	Salkeld	K.B.	3	1689–1712	91
Sask.	Saskatchewan Law Reports		25	1908–1931	

ABBR.	REPORTS	SERIES	VOLS.	PERIOD	E.R. [R.R.]
Saund.	Saunders (ed. Williams)	K.B.	2	1666–1673	85[1]
Saund. & C.	Saunders & Cole	Bail Ct.	2	1846–1848	[82]
Saund. B.C.	Saunders & Cole	Bail Ct.	2	1846–1848	[82]
Sausse & Sc.	Sausse & Scully (Ir.)	Ch.		1837–1840	—
Sav.	Savile	C.P.	1	1580–1594	123
Say.	Sayer	K.B.	1	1751–1756	96
Sc.	Scott	C.P.	8	1834–1840	[41–54]
Sc. & Div.	See "Law Reports."				
Sc. N.R.	Scott's New Reports	C.P.	8	1840–1845	[56–66]
Sch. & Lef.	Schoales & Lefroy (Ir.)	Ch.	2	1802–1806	—
Schalk.	Schalk's Reports, Jamaica			1855–1876	
Scot. Jur.	Scottish Jurist (Sc.)	C.S.	46	1829–1873	—
Searle	Searle's Supreme Court Reports, Cape Colony		5	1850–1867	
Searle & Sm.	Searle & Smith	P. & D.	1	1859–1860	—
Seign. Rep.	Seigniorial Reports, Lower Canada	—	2	1856	—
Sel. Cas. Ch.	Select Cases in Chancery t. King, ed. Macnaghten	Ch.	1	1724–1733	25
Sel. Cas. N.F.	Select Cases, Newfoundland	—	1	1817–1828	—
Sel. Cas. t. King	Select Cases in Chancery, t. King. ed. Macnaghten	Ch.	1	1724–1733	25
Sess. Ca. (Sess. Cas.)	Sessions Cases	K.B.	2	1710–1748	93
Sess. Cas.	Session Cases (Sc.)—				
S.	1st Series [Shaw]	C.S.	16	1821–1838	—
D.	2nd Series [Dunlop]	C.S.	24	1838–1862	—
M.	3rd Series [Macpherson]	C.S.	11	1862–1873	—
R.	4th Series [Rettie]	C.S.	25	1873–1898	—
F.	5th Series [Fraser]	C.S.	8	1898–1906	—
Sess. Cas. (6 Ser.)	6th Series (See "S.C.")	C.S.	★	1906–date	—
Sess. Pap. C.C.	Sessional Papers, Central Criminal Court			1834–1913	
Sett. & Rem.	Cases of Settlements and Removals	K.B.	1	1710–1742	—
Sh.	Shower (ed. Butt)	K.B.	2	1678–1695	89
Sh.	Shower's Parliamentary Cases	H.L.	1	1694–1699	1
Sh. & Macl.	Shaw & Maclean (Sc.)	H.L.	3	1835–1838	—
Sh. App.	Shaw's Appeals (Sc.)	H.L.	2	1821–1824	—
Sh. Ct. Rep.	Sheriff Court Reports (Sc.)	Sh. Ct.	★	1885–date	—
Sh. Teind. Ct.	Shaw's Teind Court Decisions (Scotland)			1821–1831	
Shaw, J.	John Shaw (Sc.)	Just.	1	1848–1852	—
Shaw, P.	Patrick Shaw (Sc.)	Just.	1	1819–1831	—
Shill W.C.	Irish Workmen's Compensation Cases			1934–1938	
Show.	Shower (ed. Butt)	K.B.	2	1678–1695	89
Show, K.B.	Shower (ed. Butt)	K.B.	2	1678–1695	89
Show. P.C.	Shower's Parliamentary Cases	H.L.	1	1694–1699	1
Sid.	Siderfin	K.B.	2	1657–1670	82
Sim.	Simons	V.C.	17	1826–1850	57–60
Sim. & St.	Simons & Stuart	V.C.	2	1822–1826	57
Sim. N.S.	Simons, New Series	V.C.	2	1850–1852	61
Six Circ.	Cases on the Six Circuits (Irish)			1841–1843	
Skin.	Skinner	K.B.	1	1681–1698	90

[1] The reprint in the E.R. is from the 6th edition (1845). The reader's reference may be to the 1871 edition, in which case the pagination is different.

ABBR.	REPORTS	SERIES	VOLS.	PERIOD	E.R. [R.R.]
Sm. (Smith)	Smith, J.P.	K.B.	3	1803–1806	[7–8]
Sm. & Bat.	Smith & Batty (Ir.)	K.B.	1	1824–1825	—
Sm. & G.	Smale & Giffard	V.C.	3	1852–1857	65
Smith L.C.	Smith Leading Cases				
Smith Reg. Cas.	Smith Registration Cases	—	3	1895–1914	—
Smy. (Smythe)	Smythe (Ir.)	C.P.	1	1839–40	—
Smy. & B.	Smythe and Bourke Irish Marriage Cases			1842	
Sol.	The Solicitor	All		1934–1961	—
Sol. J.	Solicitors' Journal	All	★	1857–date	—
Sp.	Spinks	Ecc.&Adm.	2	1853–1855	164
Sp.	Spink's Prize Cases	Adm.	1	1854–1856	164
Sp. & Sel. Cas.	Special and Selected Law Cases	C.P.&K.B.		1648	
St. Brown	Stewart–Brown Cases in the Court of the Star Chamber			1455–1547	
St. Tr.	State Trials (Cobbett & Howell)	—	34	1163–1820	—
St. Tr., N.S.	State Trials, New Series	—	8	1820–1858	—
Stair	Stair (Sc.)	C.S.	2	1661–1681	—
Star. (Stark.)	Starkie	N.P.	3	1814–1823	171
Stat.L.Rev.	Statute Law Review		★	1980–date	—
Stew. Adm.	Stewart's Vice-Admiralty Reports, Nova Scotia	Adm.	1	1803–1813	—
Stil.	Stillingfleet	Ecc.	2	1698–1704	—
Sto. & G.	Stone and Graham Private Bill Decisions			1865	
Stock	Stockton's Vice-Admiralty Reports, New Brunswick	Adm.	1	1879–1891	—
Str.	Strange, J. (ed. by Nolan)	K.B.	2	1716–1749	93
Str. Ev.	Strange Cases of Evidence			1698–1732	
Stu. Adm.	Stuart's Vice-Admiralty Reports, Lower Canada	Adm.	1	1836–1874	—
Stu. K.B.	Stuart's Lower Canada Reports	All	1	1810–1853	—
Stu. M. & P.	Stuart, Milne and Peddie's Reports (Scotland)	C.S.	2	1851–1853	—
Stuart, M. & P.	Stuart, Milne & Peddie (Sc.)	C.S.	2	1851–1853	—
Sty. (Style)	Style	K.B.	1	1646–1655	82
Suth. W.R.	Sutherlands Weekly Reporter		26	1864–1876	—
Sw.	Swabey	Adm.	1	1855–1859	166
Sw.	Swanston	Ch.	3	1818–1819	36
Sw. & Tr.	Swabey & Tristram	Ecc.	4	1858–1865	164
Swab.	Swabey	Adm.	1	1855–1859	166
Swan.	Swanston	Ch.	3	1818–1819	36
Swin.	Swinton (Sc.)	Just.	2	1835–1841	—
Sin. Reg. App.	Swinton Registration Appeals (Scotland)			1835–1841	
Syd. L.R.	Sydney Law Review	—	★	1953–date	—
Syme	Syme (Sc.)	Just.	1	1826–1830	—
T. & G.	Tyrwhitt & Granger	Ex.	1	1835–1836	[46]
T. & M.	Temple & Mew's Cases	C.C.	1	1848–1851	169
T. & R.	Turner & Russell	Ch.	1	1822–1824	37
T.C.	Tax Cases	All	★	1875–date	—
T. Jo.	Jones, Sir Thomas	K.B.	1	1667–1685	84
T.L.R.	Times Law Reports	All	71	1884–1952	
T.L.R.	Tasmanian Law Reports		35	1905–1940	
T.L.R.	Tanganyika Law Reports			1921–1952	

ABBR.	REPORTS	SERIES	VOLS.	PERIOD	E.R. [R.R.]
T.P.D.	Transvaal Province Division South Africa		37	1910–1946	
T.R.	Taxation Reports	All	★	1939–date	—
T.R.	Term Reports (By Durnford & East)	K.B.	8	1785–1800	99–101
T.R.N.S.	East	K.B.	16	1801–1812	102–4
T. Raym.	Raymond, Sir T.	K.B.	1	1660–1684	83
Tal. (Talb.)	Talbot, Cases In Equity, ed. Williams	Ch.	1	1733–1738	25
Tam.	Tamlyn	Rolls. Ct.	1	1829–1830	48
Tarl.	Tarleton Term Reports (New South Wales)			1881–1883	
Tas. L.R.	Tasmanian Law Reports	All	35	1905–1940	—
Tas. S.R.	Tasmanian State Reports			1941–date	
Tas. Univ. L. Rev.	Tasmanian University Law Review	—	★	1959–date	—
Taun. (Taunt.)	Taunton	C.P.	8	1807–1819	127–9
Tax Cas.	Tax Cases	All	★	1875–date	—
Tay.	Taylor's Reports, Ontario	K.B.	1	1823–1827	—
Temp. & M.	Temple & Mews' Cases	C.C.	1	1848–1851	169
Term.	Term Reports (By Dunford & East)	K.B.	8	1785–1800	99–101
Terr. L.R.	Territories Law Reports, Canada		7	1885–1907	
Thom. Dec.	Nova Scotia Reports	All	1	1834–1851	—
To. Jo.	Jones, Sir Thomas	K.B.	1	1667–1685	84
Toml. Supp Br.	Supplement to Brown's Parliamentary Cases by Tomlin			1689–1795	
Tot (Toth.)	Tothill	Ch.	1	1559–1646	21
Town. St. Tr.	Townsend Modern State Trials			1850	
Tr. Consist. J.	Tristram's Consistory Judgments	Ecc.	1	1872–1890	—
Tr. L.R.	Trinidad Law Reports		★	1893–date	
Traff. Cas.	Railway, Canal and Road Traffic Cases	Rail Ca.	29	1885–1949	—
	Traffic Cases, New Series (with Vol. 30)			1952–date	
Tru.	Trueman's Equity Cases, New Brunswick	—	1	1876–1893	—
Tuck.	Tucker's Select Cases, Newfoundland	—	1	1817–1828	—
Tupp.	Tupper Reports, Ontario			1876–1900	
Tur. & Rus.	Turner & Russell	Ch.	1	1822–1824	37
Tyr. (Tyrw.)	Tyrwhitt	Ex.	5	1830–1835	[35–40]
Tyr. & G.	Tyrwhitt & Granger	Ex.	1	1835–1836	[46]
U.C.C.P.	Upper Canada Common Pleas Reports	—	32	1850–1882	—
U.C. Ch.	Upper Canada Chancery Reports	Ch.	29	1849–1882	—
U.C. Chamb.	Upper Canada Chambers Reports	—	2	1846–1852	—
U.C.E. & A.	Upper Canada Error and Appeal Reports	—	3	1846–1866	—
U.C. Jur.	Upper Canada Jurist			1844–1848	—
U.C.K.B.	Upper Canada King's Bench Reports, Old Series	K.B.	6	1831–1844	—
U.C.L.J.	Upper Canada Law Journal	All	68	1855–1922	—

ABBR.	REPORTS	SERIES	VOLS.	PERIOD	E.R. [R.R.]
U.C.O.S.	Upper Canada King's Bench Reports (Old Series)		6	1831–1844	—
U.C. Pr. R.	Upper Canada Practice Reports	—	19	1850–1900	—
U.C.Q.B.	Upper Canada Queen's Bench Reports	Q.B.	46	1844–1881	—
U.L.R.	Uganda Law Reports		★	1904–date	—
Udal	Udal's Reports (Fiji) Vol. 1		1	1875–1897	—
Univ. Q.L.J.	University of Queensland Law Journal	—	★	1948–date	—
V. & B.	Vesey & Beames	Ch.	3	1812–1814	35
V. & S.	Vernon & Scriven (Ir.)	K.B.	1	1786–1788	—
V.A.T.T.R.	Value Added Tax Tribunal Reports	—	—	1973–date	—
V.C. Adm.	Victoria Reports, Admiralty				
V.C. Eq.	Victoria Reports, Equity.				
V.L.R.	Victorian Law Reports, Australia	All		1875–1956	—
V.L.T.	Victorian Law Times	All	2	1856–1857	—
V.R.	Victorian Reports, Webb, etc.	All	3	1870–1872	—
V.R.	Victorian Reports	All	★	1957–date	—
Van K.	Van Koughwet's Reports, Upper Canada		7	1864–1871	—
Vanderst.	Vanderstraaten's Reports Ceylon		1	1869–1871	—
Vaug. (Vaugh.)	Vaughan	C.P.	1	1665–1674	124
Vent.	Ventris	K.B.	2	1668–1688	86
Vern.	Vernon	Ch.	2	1681–1720	23
Vern. & Sc.	Vernon & Scriven (Ir.)	K.B.	1	1786–1788	—
Ves. & Bea.	Vesey & Beames	Ch.	3	1812–1814	35
Ves. Jr.	Vesey Junior	Ch.	19	1789–1817	30–34
Ves. Sen.	Vesey Senior (ed. by Belt)	Ch.	2	1747–1756	27–8
Ves. Sen. Sup.	Vesey Senior (Belt's Supplement)	Ch.	1	1747–1756	28
Ves. Supp.	Vesey Junior & Hovenden's Supplement	Ch.	2	1789–1817	34
Vict. L.R.	Victorian Law Reports			1875–1956	—
W.	Watermayer's Supreme Court Reports, Cape of Good Hope		1	1857	—
W. & B.	Wolferstan & Bristowe	Elec.	1	1859–1864	—
W. & D.	Wolferstan & Drew	Elec.	1	1856–1858	—
W. & S.	Wilson & Shaw (Sc.)	H.L.	7	1825–1835	—
W. & W.	Wyatt & Webb's Reports, Victoria		3	1861–1863	—
W.A.A.R.	Western Australian Arbitration Reports	—	14	1901–1920	—
W.A'B & W.	Webb, A'Beckett & Williams Reports, Victoria		3	1870–1872	—
W.A.C.A.	West Africa Court of Appeal Reports			1930–1955	
W.A.L.R.	Western Australian Law Reports	All	★	1898–date	—
W.A.U.L.R.	Western Australia University Law Review			1948–date	—
W. Bl.	Blackstone, W.	K.B.	2	1746–1780	96
W.C. & I.R.	Workmen's Compensation and Insurance Reports	—	22	1912–1933	—

ABBR.	REPORTS	SERIES	VOLS.	PERIOD	E.R. [R.R.]
W.C.C.	Workmen's Compensation Cases			1898–1907	—
W.C.R. (N.S.W.)	Worker's Compensation Reports (New South Wales)	—	★	1926–date	—
W.H.C.	Witwatersrand High Court Reports, South Africa		37	1910–1946	—
W.I.R.	West Indian Reports	—	★	1959–	—
W. Jones	Sir William Jones' Reports	K.B.	1	1620–1641	82
W.L.D.	Witwatersrand Local Division, South Africa Law Reports		37	1910–1946	—
W.L.R.	Weekly Law Reports	All	★	1953–date	—
W.L.R.	Western Law Reporter, Canada	All	34	1905–1916	—
W.L.T.	Western Law Times, Canada			1889–1895	—
W.N.	Weekly Notes (Reports)	All	87	1866–1952	—
W.N. (Calc.)	Weekly Notes (Calcutta)			1896–1941	—
W.N. Misc.	Weekly Notes (Miscellaneous)		87	1866–1952	—
W.N. (N.S.W.)	Weekly Notes, New South Wales	All	★	1884–date	—
W.R.	Weekly Reporter	All	54	1853–1906	—
W.R.	West's Reports, temp. Hardwicke	Ch.	1	1736–1739	25
W.R.N.L.R.	Western Region of Nigeria Law Reports		★	1955–date	—
W. Rob.	W. Robinson's Reports	Adm.	3	1838–1852	166
W.W.	Wyatt and Webb's Reports, (Victorian)	—	2	1861–1863	—
W.W. & A'B.	Wyatt, Webb & A'Beckett's Reports Victoria		6	1864–1869	—
W.W. & D.	Willmore, Wollaston & Davison	K.B.	1	1837	[52]
W.W. & H.	Willmore, Wollaston & Hodges	K.B.	2	1838–1839	[52]
W.W.R.	Western Weekly Reports	All	★	1911–date	—
Wall.	Wallis' Reports (Ir.)	Ch.	1	1766–1791	—
Wall. Lyn.	Wallis's Select Cases by Lyne (Ir.)	Ch.	1	1766–1791	—
Wat.	Watermayer's Supreme Court Reports, Cape of Good Hope		1	1857	—
Web. P.C.	Webster	Pat. Cas.	2	1601–1855	—
Welsb. H. & G.	Exchequer Reports (Welsby, Hurlstone & Gordon)	Ex.	11	1847–1856	154–6
Welsh	Welsh (Ir.)	Reg.	1	1832–1840	—
West	West	H.L.	1	1839–1841	9
West	West's Reports, temp. Hardwicke	Ch.	1	1736–1739	25
West. A.U.L.R.	West Australia University Law Review		★	1948–date	—
West. L.R.	Western Law Reporter, Canada	All	34	1905–1916	—
West. L.T.	Western Law Times, Canada	All	12	1889–1895	—
West. Ti. Cas.	Western's Tithe Cases	Tithe	1	1535–1822	—
Wh. & Tud. L.C.	White & Tudor Leading Cases in Equity				
White	White (Sc.)	Just.	3	1886–1893	—

ABBR.	REPORTS	SERIES	VOLS.	PERIOD	E.R. [R.R.]
Wight.	Wightwick	Ex.	1	1810–1811	145
Wilk. & Ow.	Wilkinson and Owen Reports, New South Wales		3	1862–1865	—
Will.	Willes (ed. Durnford)	C.P.	1	1737–1760	125
Will. Saund.	Notes to Saunders' Reports, by Williams	K.B.	2	1666–1673	85[1]
Will. Woll & D.	Willmore, Wollaston & Davison	K.B.	1	1837	[52]
Will. Woll. & H.	Willmore, Wollaston & Hodges	K.B.	2	1838–1839	[52]
Willes	Willes (ed. Durnford)	C.P.	1	1737–1760	125
Williams	Peere Williams' Reports	Ch.	3	1695–1735	24
Williams P.	Peere Williams' Reports	Ch.	3	1695–1735	24
Wilm.	Wilmot's Notes of Cases	K.B.	1	1757–1770	97
Wils.	Wilson	Ch.	2	1818–1819	37
Wils.	Wilson's King's Bench Reports	K.B.	3	1742–1774	95
Wils. & Sh.	Wilson & Shaw (Sc.)	H.L.	7	1825–1835	—
Wils. Exch.	Wilson's Reports	Ex.	1	1805–1817	159
Win. (Winch)	Winch	C.P.	1	1621–1625	124
Wm. Bl.	Sir William Blackstone	K.B.	2	1746–1780	96
Wm. Rob.	W. Robinson's Reports	Adm.	3	1838–1852	166
Wms. P.	Peere Williams' Reports	Ch.	3	1695–1735	24
Wms. Saund.	Saunders' Reports, annotated by Williams	K.B.	2	1666–1673	85[1]
Wol. (Woll.)	Wollaston	Bail Ct.	1	1840–1841	—
Wolf. & B.	Wolferstan & Bristow	Elec.	1	1859–1864	—
Wolf. & D.	Wolferstan & Dew	Elec.	1	1856–1858	—
Wood. Tit. Cas.	Wood's Tithe Cases	—	4	1650–1798	—
Wyatt, W. & A'B.	Wyatt, Webb & A'Beckett's Reports, Victoria		6	1864–1869	—
Y. & C. Ch.	Younge & Collyer, temp. Bruce	V.C.	2	1841–1843	62–3
Y. & C. Ex.	Younge & Collyer	Ex.	4	1834–1842	160
Y. & J.	Younge & Jervis	Ex.	3	1826–1830	148
Y.B.	Year Books (ed. Dieser)	—	1	1388–1389	—
Y.B.	Year Books (ed. Maynard)	K.B.	11	1367–1537	—
Y.B. (R.S.)	Year Books (ed. Horwood) (Roll Series)	K.B.	5	1292–1307	—
Y.B. (R.S.)	Year Books (ed. Horwood & Pike) (Rolls Series)	K.B.	15	1337–1346	—
Y.B. (S.S.)	Year Books (Selden Society)	K.B.	17	1307–1319	—
Y.B. Rich II.	Bellewe's Richard II	K.B.	1	1378–1400	72
Yel. (Yelv.)	Yelverton	K.B.	1	1602–1613	80
You. (Younge)	Younge	Ex.	1	1830–1832	159
Young Adm.	Young's Nova Scotia Admiralty Cases	Adm.	1	1865–1880	—
Z.L.R.	Zanzibar Law Reports		7	1919–1950	—

---

[1] The reprint in the E.R. is from the 6th edition (1845). The reader's reference may be to the 1871 edition, in which case the pagination is different.

THE REGNAL YEARS
OF
ENGLISH SOVEREIGNS

	FROM	TO	YEARS
William I	Oct. 14, 1066	Sept. 9, 1087	21
William II	Sept. 26, 1087	Aug. 2, 1100	13
Henry I	Aug. 5, 1100	Dec. 1, 1135	36
Stephen	Dec. 26, 1135	Oct. 25, 1154	19
Henry II	Dec. 19, 1154	July 6, 1189	35
Richard I	Sept. 3, 1189	Apr. 6, 1199	10
John	May 27, 1199	Oct. 19, 1216	18
Henry III	Oct. 28, 1216	Nov. 16, 1272	57
Edward I	Nov. 20, 1272	July 7, 1307	35
Edward II	July 8, 1307	Jan. 20, 1327	20
Edward III	Jan. 25, 1327	June 21, 1377	51
Richard II	June 22, 1377	Sept. 29, 1399	23
Henry IV	Sept. 30, 1399	Mar. 20, 1413	14
Henry V	Mar. 21, 1413	Aug. 31, 1422	10
Henry VI	Sept. 1, 1422	Mar. 4, 1461	39
Edward IV[1]	Mar. 4, 1461	Apr. 9, 1483	23
Edward V	Apr. 9, 1483	June 25, 1483	1
Richard III	June 26, 1483	Aug. 22, 1485	3
Henry VII	Aug. 22, 1485	Apr. 21, 1509	24
Henry VIII	Apr. 22, 1509	Jan. 28, 1547	38
Edward VI	Jan. 28, 1547	July 6, 1553	7
Mary[2]	July 6, 1553	Nov. 17, 1558	6
Elizabeth I	Nov. 17, 1558	Mar. 24, 1603	45
James I	Mar. 24, 1603	Mar. 27, 1625	23
Charles I	Mar. 27, 1625	Jan. 30, 1649	24
Charles II[3]	Jan. 30, 1649	Feb. 6, 1685	37
James II	Feb. 6, 1685	Dec. 11, 1688	4
William and Mary[4]	Feb. 13, 1689	Mar. 8, 1702	14
Anne	Mar. 8, 1702	Aug. 1, 1714	13
George I	Aug. 1, 1714	June 11, 1727	13
George II	June 11, 1727	Oct. 25, 1760	34
George III[5]	Oct. 25, 1760	Jan. 29, 1820	60
George IV	Jan. 29, 1820	June 26, 1830	11
William IV	June 26, 1830	June 20, 1837	7
Victoria	June 20, 1837	Jan. 22, 1901	64

[1] Henry VI (restored)–Oct. 9, 1470, to about Apr. 1471.
[2] Jane—July 6 to July 17, 1553. Mary married Philip, July 25, 1554.
[3] Not king *de facto* until May 29, 1660.
[4] Mary died Dec. 27, 1694.
[5] Regency from Feb. 5, 1811.

Regnal Years

	FROM	TO	YEARS
Edward VII	Jan. 22, 1901	May 6, 1910	10
George V	May 6, 1910	Jan. 20, 1936	26
Edward VIII[6]	Jan. 20, 1936	Dec. 11, 1936	1
George VI	Dec. 11, 1936	Feb. 6, 1952	17
Elizabeth II	Feb. 6, 1952		

[6] Executed an Instrument of Abdication on December 10, 1936 which took effect on December 11, 1936 (His Majesty's Declaration of Abdication Act, 1936; 1 Edw. 8, c. 3).